Psychological Dimensions of Organizational Behavior

THIRD EDITION

Barry M. Staw

Haas School of Business
University of California, Berkeley

PEARSON

Prentice
Hall

Upper Saddle River, New Jersey 07458

For Harold and Shirley Staw

Library of Congress Cataloging-in-Publication Data

Psychological dimensions of organizational behavior / edited by Barry M. Staw.—3rd ed.
   p. cm.
   Includes bibliographical references.
   ISBN 0-13-040654-6 (pbk.)
   1. Organizational behavior. 2. Psychology, Industrial. I. Staw, Barry M.

HD58.7.P758 2003
158.7—dc21

2002044565

Senior Editor: Jennifer Simon
Editor-in-Chief: Jeff Shelstad
Editorial Assistant: Jill Wasiowich
Media Project Manager: Jessica Sabloff
Executive Marketing Manager: Shannon Moore
Marketing Assistant: Patrick Danzuso
Managing Editor (Production): John Roberts
Production Editor: Maureen Wilson

Production Assistant: Joe DeProspero
Permissions Supervisor: Suzanne Grappi
Manufacturing Buyer: Michelle Klein
Art Director: Jayne Conte
Cover Illustration: Getty—Digital Vision
Composition: Rainbow Graphics
Full-Service Project Management: Linda Begley/Rainbow Graphics
Printer/Binder: Hamilton Printing Co.
Cover Printer: Lehigh Press

Credits and acknowledgments borrowed from other sources and reproduced, with permission, in this textbook appear on appropriate page within the text.

Pearson Education LTD.
Pearson Education Singapore, Pte. Ltd
Pearson Education, Canada, Ltd
Pearson Education–Japan

Pearson Education Australia PTY, Limited
Pearson Education North Asia Ltd
Pearson Educación de Mexico, S.A. de C.V.
Pearson Education Malaysia, Pte. Ltd

10 9 8 7 6 5 4 3 2 1
ISBN 0-13-040654-6

CONTENTS

Preface   vi

DIMENSION I: WHY AND HOW WE WORK   1

Part A   Foundations of Human Differences   3

   Reading 1. Individual Differences: Personality and Ability   3
   Jennifer M. George/Gareth R. Jones

Part B   Strategies for Increasing Individual Performance in Organizational Settings   25

   Reading 2. Motivation: A Diagnostic Approach   25
   David A. Nadler/Edward E. Lawler III

   Reading 3. Goal-Setting—A Motivational Technique That Works   37
   Gary P. Latham/Edwin A. Locke

   Reading 4. On the Folly of Rewarding A, While Hoping for B   49
   Steven Kerr

   Reading 5. A New Strategy for Job Enrichment   59
   J. Richard Hackman/Greg Oldham/Robert Janson/Kenneth Purdy

   Reading 6. Fighting the War for Talent Is Hazardous to Your Organization's Health   77
   Jeffrey Pfeffer

Part C   Satisfaction and Emotion in Organizational Life   89

   Reading 7. Organizational Psychology and the Pursuit of the Happy/Productive Worker   89
   Barry M. Staw

   Reading 8. The Subtle Significance of Job Satisfaction   100
   Dennis W. Organ

   Reading 9. Expression of Emotion as Part of the Work Role   106
   Anat Rafaeli/Robert I. Sutton

DIMENSION II: THINKING AND MAKING DECISIONS   121

Part A   Foundations of Social Cognition   123

   Reading 10. The Rationalizing Animal   123
   Elliot Aronson

   Reading 11. Escape from Reality: Illusions in Everyday Life   131
   Shelley E. Taylor

Part B   Perceiving Ourselves and the Work Situation   157

   Reading 12. The Self-Perception of Motivation   157
   Barry M. Staw

Reading 13. The Power of Social Information in the Workplace   172
Joe G. Thomas/Ricky W. Griffin

Part C Making Rational and Irrational Decisions   181

Reading 14. Common Biases   181
Max H. Bazerman

Reading 15. Understanding Behavior in Escalation Situations   206
Barry M. Staw/Jerry Ross

Reading 16. Napoleon's Tragic March Home from Moscow: Lessons
in Hubris   215
Mark J. Kroll/Leslie A. Toombs/Peter Wright

Part D Making Ethical and Unethical Decisions   229

Reading 17. Business Ethics: Four Spheres of Executive
Responsibility   229
Joseph L. Badaracco, Jr.

Reading 18. Ethical Leadership and the Psychology of Decision
Making   241
David M. Messick/Max H. Bazerman

DIMENSION III: INTERACTING WITH OTHERS: SOCIAL AND GROUP PROCESSES   259

Part A Foundations of Conformity, Obedience, and Persuasion   261

Reading 19. Opinions and Social Pressure   261
Solomon E. Asch

Reading 20. Behavioral Study of Obedience   268
Stanley Milgram

Reading 21. Harnessing the Science of Persuasion   279
Robert B. Cialdini

Part B Organizational Socialization and Commitment   287

Reading 22. Commitment and the Control of Organizational Behavior
and Belief   287
Gerald R. Salancik

Reading 23. The Smile Factory: Work at Disneyland   294
John Van Maanen

Part C Organizational Culture   307

Reading 24. Corporations, Culture, and Commitment: Motivation
and Social Control in Organizations   307
Charles O'Reilly

Reading 25. The Role of the Founder in Creating Organizational
Culture   320
Edgar H. Schein

Part D Managing Person–Organization Conflicts   335

Reading 26. Unexpected Connections: Considering Employees' Personal Lives Can
Revitalize Your Business   335
Lotte Bailyn/Joyce K. Fletcher/Deborah Kolb

Reading 27. Managing Attraction and Intimacy at Work   345
Marcy Crary

Reading 28. Executive Women and the Myth of Having It All   358
Sylvia Ann Hewlett

Part E   Power, Influence, and Interpersonal Attraction   369

Reading 29. Who Gets Power—And How They Hold On to It:
A Strategic-Contingency Model of Power   369
Gerald R. Salancik/Jeffrey Pfeffer

Reading 30. Influence Without Authority: The Use of Alliances, Reciprocity, and
Exchange to Accomplish Work   385
Allan R. Cohen/David L. Bradford

Reading 31. Who Tempered Radicals Are and What They Do   395
Debra Meyerson

Part F   Group Processes   407

Reading 32. Suppose We Took Groups Seriously . . .   407
Harold J. Leavitt

Reading 33. Groupthink   416
Irving L. Janis

Reading 34. The Design of Work Teams   424
J. Richard Hackman

DIMENSION IV: FACING THE FUTURE: CREATIVITY, INNOVATION, AND ORGANIZATIONAL LEADERSHIP   445

Part A   Foundations of Creativity   447

Reading 35. Within You, Without You: The Social Psychology
of Creativity, and Beyond   447
Teresa M. Amabile

Reading 36. Weirder Than Fiction: The Reality and Myths
of Creativity   468
Joseph V. Anderson

Reading 37. Why No One Really Wants Creativity   476
Barry M. Staw

Part B   Managing Creativity and Innovation in Organizations   481

Reading 38. The Weird Rules of Creativity   481
Robert I. Sutton

Reading 39. Managing Innovation: When Less Is More   490
Charlan Jeanne Nemeth

Reading 40. The Political Nature of Innovation   502
Peter J. Frost/Carolyn P. Egri

Part C   Leadership and Change   513

Reading 41. Pathfinding, Problem Solving, and Implementing:
The Management Mix   513
Harold J. Leavitt

Reading 42. Managing with Power   524
Jeffrey Pfeffer

Reading 43. Ambidextrous Organizations: Managing Evolutionary and
Revolutionary Change   529
Michael L. Tushman/Charles A. O'Reilly III

PREFACE

Welcome to the fascinating world of organizational behavior. Here you will learn about the nature of people and how their behavior is influenced by others in organizations. You will study some basics of individual motivation, attitudes, and decision making, and see how these human tendencies can be forged into productive and ethical actions. You will read about how people are influenced by the politics and culture of an organization, and also how people may themselves shape the environment in which they work. Finally, you will study what it takes to be creative in an organizational setting, with tips about how to lead organizations in new and innovative directions.

This book is organized into four major dimensions. In each, one or more "foundation" readings are presented in which basic knowledge from the organizational sciences is reviewed. Then "applications" are presented from the literature of organizational behavior. The readings cover most of the major topics in the organizational behavior field and reflect the current state of our knowledge. Some chapters are research summaries; some are think pieces. All have been selected by the combined criteria of writing style and content. Thus, if a piece appears a bit dry, bear with it; it should contain enough content to be worth the effort. If a piece is especially interesting, enjoy the experience. When you finish this anthology, you should not only understand more about how people think and behave, but have some new ideas about how such behavior can be combined to build a productive and healthy organization.

I would like to thank the following for their helpful reviews of the manuscript:

M. Kenneth Holt—Union University
Deborah J. Dwyer—The University of Toledo
Grace B. Dyrud—Augsburg College
K. Peter Kuchinke—University of Illinois

Dimension I

Why and How We Work

Part A

Foundations of Human Differences

1. Individual Differences: Personality and Ability

Jennifer M. George/Gareth R. Jones

OVERVIEW

In this chapter, we focus on **individual differences,** the ways in which people differ from each other. Managers need to understand individual differences because they have an impact on the feelings, thoughts, and behaviors of each member of an organization. Individual differences affect, for example, job satisfaction, job performance, job stress, and leadership. Organizational members interact with each other on a daily basis, and only if they understand each other are their interactions likely to result in high levels of satisfaction and performance.

Individual differences may be grouped into two categories: personality differences and differences in ability. We focus on the nature, meaning, and determinants of personality and on the ways that personality and situational factors combine to influence feelings, thoughts, and behavior in organizations. We discuss specific personality traits that are particularly relevant to organizational behavior. We then turn our attention to differences in ability. After describing various types of ability, we discuss the key issue for managers: how ability can be managed to ensure that workers can effectively perform their jobs.

THE NATURE OF PERSONALITY

People's personalities can be described in a variety of ways. Some people seem to be perfectionists; they can be critical, impatient, demanding, and intense. Other kinds of people are more relaxed and easygoing. You may have friends or co-workers who always seem to have something to smile about and are fun to be around. Or perhaps you have friends or co-workers who are shy and quiet; they are hard to get to know and may sometimes seem dull. In each of these examples, we are describing what people are generally like without referring to their specific feelings, thoughts, and behaviors in any specific situation. In formulating a general description of someone, we try to pinpoint something that is relatively enduring about the person, something that seems to explain the regularities or patterns we observe in the way the person thinks, feels, and behaves.

Personality is the pattern of relatively enduring ways in which a person feels, thinks, and behaves. Personality is an important factor in accounting for why workers act the way they do in organizations and why they have favorable or unfavorable attitudes toward their jobs and organizations. Personality has been shown to influence career choice, job satisfaction, stress, leadership, and some aspects of job performance.

Determinants of Personality: Nature and Nurture

Why are some workers happy and easygoing and others intense and critical? An answer to this question can be found by examining the determinants of personality: nature and nurture.

Personality is partially determined by **nature,** or biological heritage. The genes that you inherited from your parents influence how your personality has been unfolding. Although specific genes for personality have not yet been identified, psychologists have studied identical twins in an attempt to discover the extent to which personality is inherited.[1]

Because identical twins possess identical genes, they have the same genetic determinants of personality. Identical twins who grow up together in the same family have the same permissive or strict parents and similar life experiences. If the twins have similar personalities, it is impossible to identify the source of the similarity because they have not only the same genetic makeup but similar life experiences.

In contrast, identical twins who are separated at birth and raised in different settings (perhaps because they are adopted by different families) share the same genetic material but often have very different life experiences. Evidence from research on separated identical twins and other studies suggests that approximately 50 percent of the variation we observe in people's personalities can be attributed to nature—to genetic factors (see Figure 1.1).[2] Thus, about half of the variation we observe in workers' personalities in organizations reflects the distinctive ways of thinking, feeling, and behaving they inherited from their parents. The other 50 percent reflects the influence of **nurture,** or life experiences.

Personality develops over time, responding to the experiences people have as children and as adults. Factors such as the strictness or permissiveness of a child's parents, the number of other children in the family, the extent to which parents and teachers demand a lot from a child, success or lack of success at making friends or getting and keeping a job, and even the culture in which a person is raised and lives as an adult are shapers of personality.

Because about half of the variation in people's personalities is inherited from their

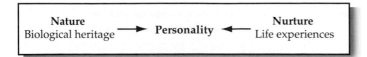

FIGURE 1.1
Nature and Nurture: The Determinants of Personality

parents and thus is basically fixed at birth, it comes as no surprise that personality is quite stable over periods of time ranging from 5 to 10 years. This does not mean that personality cannot change; it means that personality is likely to change only over many years. Thus, the impact of any specific work situation or crisis on a worker's personality is likely to be felt only if the situation continues for many years. An important outcome of this fact is that managers should not expect to change workers' personalities in the short run. In fact, for all practical purposes, managers should view workers' personalities as relatively fixed in the short run.

Personality, nevertheless, is an important individual difference that managers and other organizational members need to take into account in order to understand why people feel, think, and act as they do in organizations. For example, realizing that a worker complains a lot and often gets upset because of his or her personality will help a manager deal with this type of subordinate, especially if the person's job performance is acceptable.

Personality and the Situation

Because personality accounts for observable regularities in people's attitudes and behaviors, it would seem reasonable to assert that it would account for such regularities at work. A substantial body of literature in psychology and a growing set of studies in organizational behavior suggest that personality *is* useful for explaining and predicting how workers generally feel, think, and behave on the job.[3] Personality has been shown to influence several work-related attitudes and behaviors, including job satisfaction, the ability to handle work-related stress, the choice of a career, and leadership.[4] Because of personality, some people are very conscientious about most things they do and thus perform at a higher level than do those who are not so conscientious, as we discuss later in this chapter.[5]

However, in addition to personality, the organizational situation also affects work attitudes and behaviors. In some organizations, there are strong situational constraints and pressures (such as job requirements or strict rules and regulations) that force people to behave in a certain way, regardless of their personalities.[6] For example, a worker on an assembly line manufacturing bicycles must put handlebars on each bicycle that passes by. A bike passes by every 75 seconds, and the worker has to be sure that the handlebars are properly attached to each bicycle within that time frame. It doesn't matter whether the worker is shy or outgoing; regardless of his or her personality, the worker has a specific task to perform day in and day out in the same manner. Because the worker is not free to vary his or her behavior, personality is not useful for understanding or predicting job performance in this situation.

Consider another example. Workers at McDonald's and other fast-food restaurants follow clearly specified procedures for preparing large quantities of burgers, fries, and shakes and serving them to large numbers of customers. Because each worker knows exactly what the procedures are and how to carry them out (they are spelled out in a detailed manual), the food is always prepared in the same manner, regardless of the workers' personalities.

As those two examples show, in organizations in which situational pressures on workers' behavior are strong, personality may not be a good predictor of on-the-job behavior. When situational pressures are weak, however, and workers have more choice about how to perform a job, personality plays a more important role, and what a person can put into his or her job performance will sometimes depend on the kind of person he or she is. For instance, a statewide English curriculum requires English teachers to teach Shakespeare's *Macbeth* to high school seniors, but the curriculum does not specify exactly how the play is to be taught. A teacher who is outgoing and has a flair for the dramatic may bring the play and its themes to life by dressing up in period costumes and acting out scenes. A teacher who is less outgoing may simply ask students to take turns reading aloud from the play or ask them to write a paper on how Shakespeare reveals a certain theme through the play's dialogue and action.

By now it should be clear to you that both personality and situational factors affect organizational behavior.[7] It is the interaction of personality and situational factors that determines how people think, feel, and behave in general and, specifically, how they do so within an organization (see Figure 1.2). Robert Greene, for example, is an executive in an advertising agency who is responsible for coming up with advertising campaigns and presenting them to the agency's clients. Greene is a creative, achievement-oriented person who has good ideas and has developed the agency's most successful and lucrative campaigns. But Greene is also shy and quiet and cannot always effectively communicate his ideas to clients. Greene's personality and the situation combine or interact to determine his overall performance. He performs well when working on his own or with his team to develop advertising campaigns, but in interpersonal situations such as when he presents his campaigns to clients, he performs poorly. A manager who understands this interaction can capitalize on the personality strengths (creativity and achievement orientation) that propel Greene to develop successful advertising campaigns. The manager can also guard against the possibility of clients' having a negative reaction to Greene's shyness by teaming him up for presentations with a gregarious executive whose strong suit is pitching campaigns to clients. If Greene's manager did not understand how Greene's personality and the situation interacted to shape Greene's perfor-

mance, the advertising agency might lose clients because of Greene's inability to relate to them effectively and convince them of the merits of his campaigns.

Effective managers recognize the various ways that personality and situation interact to determine feelings, thoughts, attitudes, and behaviors at work. An understanding of workers' personalities and the situations in which they perform best enables a manager to help workers perform at a high level and feel good about the work they are doing. Furthermore, when workers at all levels in an organization understand how personality and situation interact, good working relationships and organizational effectiveness are promoted.

Personality: A Determinant of the Nature of Organizations

Ben Schneider, a prominent organizational researcher at the University of Maryland, has come up with an interesting view of the way in which personality determines the nature of whole organizations. He calls his schema the **attraction–selection–attrition (ASA) framework**.[8] Schneider proposes that the "personality" of a whole organization is largely a product of the personalities of its workers. He suggests that individuals with similar personalities tend to be attracted to an organization (*attraction*) and hired by it (*selection*), and individuals with other types of personalities tend to leave the organization (*attrition*). As a result of the interplay of attraction, selection, and attrition, there is some consistency or similarity of personalities within an organization, and this "typical" personality determines the nature of the organization itself.[9]

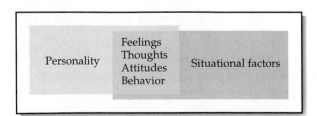

FIGURE 1.2
The Interaction of Personality and Situational Factors

ASA processes operate in numerous ways. When organizations hire new employees, they implicitly size up the extent to which prospective hires fit in with the organization—that is, the extent to which their personalities match the personalities of current members. This sizing up is especially likely to occur in small organizations. Larry Pliska, who heads up Planterra, a Michigan company that sells plants and trees, hires all new managers himself so that he can be sure they relate to and support his philosophy for the company. John Schaeffer, founder of the California company Real Goods Trading, conducts most of the final interviewing and does most of the hiring for his company in an attempt to find what he calls "even-tempered" workers.[10]

What are the implications of the ASA framework? We would expect, for example, that people who are creative and like to take risks would be attracted to entrepreneurial organizations and would be likely to be hired by such organizations. Individuals who do not have this orientation either would not seek jobs with these organizations or would be likely to leave them. Over time, ASA processes may result in these organizations' being composed of large numbers of creative risk takers who, in turn, give the organization its entrepreneurial nature. The entrepreneurial nature of the organization, in turn, influences employees' feelings, thoughts, and behavior and reinforces their own propensity for risk taking. It is important to realize that although ASA processes can strengthen an organization, they can also lead an organization to perform poorly or fail. This negative outcome occurs when most members of the organization view opportunities and problems in the same way and, as a result of their shared point of view, are resistant to making needed changes.

THE BIG FIVE MODEL OF PERSONALITY

When people describe other people, they often say things like "She's got a lot of personality," meaning that the person is fun loving, friendly, and outgoing, or "He's got no personality," meaning that the person is dull and boring. In fact, there is no such thing as a lot of personality or no personality; everyone has a specific type of personality.

Because personality is an important determinant of how a person thinks, feels, and behaves, it is helpful to distinguish between different types of personality. Researchers have spent considerable time and effort trying to identify personality types. One of the most important ways that researchers have found to describe personality is in terms of traits. A **trait** is a specific component of personality that describes particular tendencies a person has to feel, think, and act in certain ways, such as shy or outgoing, critical or accepting, compulsive or easygoing. Thus, when we speak of a person's personality, we are really referring to a collection of traits that describe how the person generally tends to feel, think, and behave.

Researchers have identified many personality traits, and most psychologists agree that the traits that make up a person's personality can be organized in a hierarchy.[11] The "Big Five" model of personality places five general personality traits at the top of the trait hierarchy: extraversion, neuroticism, agreeableness, conscientiousness, and openness to experience (see Figure 1.3).[12] Each of the Big Five traits is composed of various specific traits. Extraversion (the tendency to have a positive outlook on life), for example, consists of specific traits such as positive emotions, gregariousness, and warmth. The Big Five and the specific traits lower in the hierarchy are universal. They can be used to describe the personalities of people regardless of their age, gender, race, ethnicity, religion, socioeconomic background, or country of origin.

Each of the general and specific traits represents a continuum along which a certain aspect or dimension of personality can be placed. A person can be high, low, average, or anywhere in between on the continuum for each trait. Figure 1.4 shows a profile of a person who is low on extraversion, high on neuroticism, about average on agreeableness and conscientious-

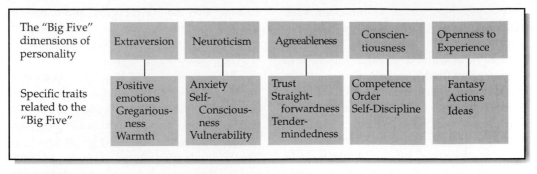

FIGURE 1.3
The Hierarchical Organization of Personality

Source: Adapted from R. R. McCrae and P. T. Costa, "Discriminant Validity of NEO-PIR Facet Scales." *Educational and Psychological Measurement* 52: 1992, pp. 229–37. Copyright © 1992 by Sage, Inc. Reprinted by permission of Sage Publications, Inc.

ness, and relatively high on openness to experience. To help you understand what a Big Five personality profile means, we describe the extremes of each trait below. Keep in mind that a person's standing on the trait could be anywhere along the continuum (as in Figure 1.4).

Extraversion

Extraversion, or positive affectivity, is a personality trait that predisposes individuals to experience positive emotional states and feel good about themselves and about the world around them. Extraverts—people high on the extraversion scale—tend to be sociable, affectionate, and friendly. Introverts—people low on

the extraversion scale—are less likely to experience positive emotional states and have fewer social interations with others. At work, extraverts are more likely than introverts to experience positive moods, be satisfied with their jobs, and generally feel good about the organization and those around them. Extraverts also are more likely to enjoy socializing with their co-workers. They may do particularly well in jobs requiring frequent social interaction, such as in sales and customer relations positions.

Neuroticism

In contrast to extraversion, **neuroticism,** or negative affectivity, reflects people's tendency

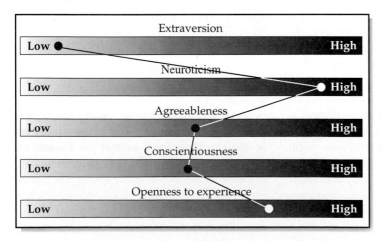

FIGURE 1.4
A Big Five Personality Profile

This is the profile of a person who is low on extraversion, high on neuroticism, about average on agreeableness and conscientiousness, and relatively high on openness to experience.

to experience negative emotional states, feel distressed, and generally view themselves and the world around them negatively. Individuals high on neuroticism are more likely than individuals low on neuroticism to experience negative emotions and stress over time and across situations. Individuals who are high on neuroticism are more likely to experience negative moods at work, feel stressed, and generally have a negative orientation toward the work situation.[13] Often, the term *neurotic* is used in the media and popular press to describe a person who has a psychological problem. Neuroticism, however, is a trait that all normal, psychologically healthy individuals possess to a certain degree.

Individuals high on neuroticism are sometimes more critical of themselves and their performance than are people low on neuroticism. That tendency may propel them to improve their performance, so they may be particularly proficient in situations, such as quality control, that require critical thinking and evaluation. Individuals high on neuroticism may also exert a needed sobering influence in group decision making by playing a devil's advocate and pointing out the negative aspects of a proposed decision. Individuals low on neuroticism do not tend to experience negative emotions and are not as critical and pessimistic as their high-neuroticism counterparts.

Agreeableness

Agreeableness is the trait that captures the distinction between individuals who get along well with other people and those who do not. Likability in general, and the ability to care for others and to be affectionate, characterize individuals who are high on agreeableness. Individuals low on agreeableness are antagonistic, mistrustful, unsympathetic, uncooperative, and rude. A low measure of agreeableness might be an advantage in jobs that require a person to be somewhat antagonistic, such as a bill collector or a drill sergeant. Agreeable individuals generally are easy to get along with and are "team players." Agreeableness can be an asset in jobs that hinge on developing good relationships with other people.

Conscientiousness

Conscientiousness is the extent to which an individual is careful, scrupulous, and persevering. Individuals high on conscientiousness are organized and have a lot of self-discipline. Individuals low on conscientiousness may lack direction and self-discipline. Conscientiousness is important in many organizational situations and has been found to be a good predictor of performance in many jobs in a wide variety of organizations.[14] Roger Salquist, entrepreneur and CEO of the successful Calgene Incorporated, is known for his attention to details. In trying to win U.S. Food and Drug Administration (FDA) approval for his genetically altered tomato, for instance, Salquist made over 25 trips to Washington, D.C., and was relentless in his efforts to provide the FDA and other agencies with all the scientific data he could in support of the safety of his tomato. Salquist's conscientiousness paid off because the FDA agreed that no special labeling or testing would be necessary for genetically engineered foods such as Calgene's new tomato.[15]

Openness to Experience

The last of the Big Five personality traits, **openness to experience**, captures the extent to which an individual is original, open to a wide variety of stimuli, has broad interests, and is willing to take risks as opposed to being narrow-minded and cautious. For jobs that change frequently, require innovation, or involve considerable risk, individuals who are open to experience may have an advantage. For openness to experience to be translated into creative and innovative behavior in organizations, however, the organization must remove obstacles to innovation. Moreover, jobs and tasks must not be too closely defined so that job holders are able to use their openness to experience to come up with new ideas.[16] Entrepreneurs, who are often characterized as risk takers,[17] frequently start their own businesses because the large organizations that employed them placed too many restrictions on them and gave them too little reward for innovation and risk taking.

Although openness to experience clearly is an advantage for entrepreneurs and in jobs that require innovation, organizations also need people to perform jobs that do not allow much opportunity for independent thinking. In addition, organizations are sometimes afraid to take the risks that workers high on openness to experience may thrive on.

Conclusions

Research suggests that the Big Five traits are important for understanding work-related attitudes and behaviors, and thus our understanding of organizational behavior. Researchers have found that individuals high on negative affectivity are more likely to indicate that there are significant stressors in the workplace and to experience stress at work.[18] Research has also shown that individuals high on positive affectivity are more likely to feel good at work and be satisfied with their jobs and are likely to perform well in jobs (such as management and sales) that require social interaction.[19]

As you have undoubtedly recognized from our discussion of the Big Five traits, there is no such thing as a good or bad personality profile. Each person is unique and has a different type of personality that may be suited to different kinds of organizational situations. Good man-

agers need to understand and learn to deal with people of all personality types.

OTHER ORGANIZATIONALLY RELEVANT PERSONALITY TRAITS

Several other personality traits are relevant to understanding and managing behavior in organizations (see Figure 1.5).

Locus of Control

People differ in how much control they believe they have over the situation they are in and over what happens to them. Some people think they have relatively little impact on their surroundings and little control over important things that happen in their lives. Others believe that they can have a considerable impact on the world around them and on the path their lives take. The locus of control trait captures this difference among individuals.[20]

Externals, individuals with an **external locus of control,** tend to believe that outside forces are largely responsible for their fate, and they see little connection between their own actions and what happens to them. Internals, individuals with an **internal locus of control,** think that their own actions and behaviors have an impact in determining what happens to them. When people with an internal locus of control perform well, they are likely to attribute their performance to qualities within themselves, such

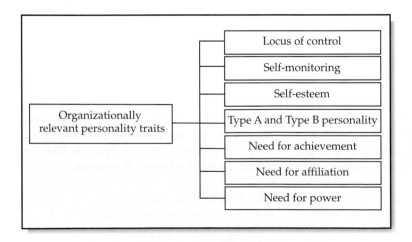

FIGURE 1.5
Personality Traits Specifically Relevant to Organizations

as their own ability or effort. When people with an external locus of control perform well, they are likely to attribute their performance to external forces such as luck, the effects of powerful people, or simply the fact that the task was easy. In organization, internals are more easily motivated than externals and do not need as much direct supervision because they are more likely to believe that their work behaviors influence important outcomes such as how well they perform their jobs and the pay increases, praise, job security, and promotions they receive.

Self-Monitoring

Self-monitoring is the extent to which people try to control the way they present themselves to others.[21] High self-monitors want their behavior to be socially acceptable and so are attuned to any social cues that signal appropriate behavior in a situation. High self-monitors strive to behave in a situationally appropriate manner. For example, they don't yell, stamp, and whistle at a symphony concert, as they would at a football game. They are also good at managing the impressions that others have of them. In contrast, low self-monitors are not particularly sensitive to cues indicating acceptable behavior, nor are they overly concerned about behaving in a situationally appropriate manner. For example, they may act bored in a meeting with a president of an organization, tell customers about the merits of a competing product, or voice their concerns about working long hours in a job interview. People who are low self-monitors are guided by their own attitudes, beliefs, feelings, and principles and are not too concerned about what others think of their behavior.

High self-monitors are more likely than low self-monitors to tailor their behavior to fit a given situation. Thus, high self-monitors may perform especially well in jobs such as sales or consulting, which require workers to interact with different types of people on a regular basis. In addition, because high self-monitors can modify their behavior to be appropriate for the individual or group they are interacting with, they may be particularly effective when an organization needs someone to communicate with an outside group

whose support is being sought, such as when nonprofit organizations and universities try to secure donations from wealthy individuals.

Low self-monitors are more likely than high self-monitors to say what they think is true or correct and are not overly concerned about how others will react to them. Thus, low self-monitors may be especially adept at providing organizational members with open, honest feedback (particulary when it's negative) and playing devil's advocate in decision-making groups. A scale that measures self-monitoring is provided in Table 1.1.

Self-Esteem

Self-esteem is the extent to which people have pride in themselves and their capabilities. Individuals with high self-esteem think they are generally capable and worthy people who can deal with most situations. Individuals with low self-esteem question their self-worth, doubt their capabilities, and are apprehensive about their ability to succeed in different endeavors.

Self-esteem has several implications for understanding behavior in organizations.[22] Self-esteem influences people's choices of activities and jobs. Individuals with high self-esteem are more likely than individuals with low self-esteem to choose challenging careers and jobs. Once they are on the job, individuals with high self-esteem may set higher goals for themselves and may be more likely to tackle difficult tasks. High self-esteem also has a positive impact on motivation and job satisfaction. It must be kept in mind however, that people with low self-esteem can be just as capable as those with high self-esteem in spite of their doubts about their abilities.

Type A and Type B Personalities

In the popular press, you will often hear someone referred to as a "Type A" or read that "Type A personalities" are prone to high blood pressure. Individuals who are **Type A** have an intense desire to achieve, are extremely competitive, have a sense of urgency, are impatient, and can be hostile.[23] Such individuals have a strong need to get a lot done in a short time period and can be difficult to get along with because they

TABLE 1.1

A Measure of Self-monitoring

Instructions: Please indicate the extent to which each of the following statements is true or false for you personally.

_____ 1. I find it hard to imitate the behavior of other people.

_____ 2. At parties and social gatherings, I do not attempt to do or say things that others will like.

_____ 3. I can only argue for ideas that I already believe.

_____ 4. I can make impromptu speeches even on topics about which I have almost no information.

_____ 5. I guess I put on a show to impress or entertain others.

_____ 6. I would probably make a good actor.

_____ 7. In a group of people, I am rarely the center of attention.

_____ 8. In different situations and with different people, I often act like very different persons.

_____ 9. I am not particularly good at making other people like me.

_____ 10. I'm not always the person I appear to be.

_____ 11. I would not change my opinions (or the way I do things) in order to please someone or win their favor.

_____ 12. I have considered being an entertainer.

_____ 13. I have never been good at games like charades or improvisational acting.

_____ 14. I have trouble changing my behavior to suit different people and different situations.

_____ 15. At a party I let others keep the jokes and stories going.

_____ 16. I feel a bit awkward in public and do not show up quite as well as I should.

_____ 17. I can look anyone in the eye and tell a lie with a straight face (if for a right end).

_____ 18. I may deceive people by being friendly when I really dislike them.

Scoring: Individuals high on self-monitoring tend to indicate that questions 4, 5, 6, 8, 10, 12, 17, and 18 are *true* and that questions 1, 2, 3, 7, 9, 11, 13, 14, 15, and 16 are *false.*

Source: S. Gangestad and M. Snyder, "'To Carve Nature at Its Joints': On the Existence of Discrete Classes in Personality," *Psychological Review* 92 (1985): 317–49. Copyright © 1985 by the American Psychological Association. Reprinted with permission.

are so driven. They often interrupt other people and sometimes finish their sentences for them because they are so impatient. More relaxed and easygoing individuals are labeled **Type B.**

Given the Type A drive to get so much done, Type A's would seem to be ideal workers for the organization's perspective, especially in situations in which a lot of work needs to be done in a short time. Because Type A's can be difficult to get along with, however, they may not be effective in situations that require a lot of interaction with others. Consistent with this observation, one study found that Type A managers were more likely to have conflicts with their subordinates and with co-workers than were Type B managers.[24] Type A workers are not particularly good team players and often work best alone. In addition, Type A's may get frustrated in long-term situations or projects because they like to see results.

Another important difference between Type A and Type B individuals has contributed to the attention this trait has received in the popular press. Type A individuals are sometimes more likely than Type B's to have coronary heart disease. In fact, two heart doctors identified this trait after they realized that many of their heart attack patients were very impatient, sometimes hostile, and always in a hurry and watching the clock. Some research suggests that a tendency toward hostility is particularly responsible for Type A's heart problems.

Needs for Achievement, Affiliation, and Power

David McClelland has done extensive research on three traits that are present in all people to varying degrees: the need for achievement, the need for affiliation, and the need for power.[25]

Individuals with a high **need for achievement** have a special desire to perform challenging tasks well and to meet their own personal standards for excellence. They like to be in situations in which they are personally responsible for what happens, like to set clear goals for themselves, are willing to take personal responsibility for outcomes, and like to receive performance feedback. Not surprisingly, such individuals are often found in jobs that help them to satisfy their strong desire to achieve. Indeed, McClelland has found that entrepreneurs and managers are especially likely to have a high need for achievement. In one study, for example, McClelland found that 10 years after graduation, undergraduates who had shown a high need for achievement were more likely to be found in entrepreneurial occupations than were those who had shown a low need for achievement.[26] In addition, effective managers often have a strong goal orientation and tend to take moderate risks—a finding that is consistent with the profile of an individual with a high need for achievement. It is not surprising, therefore, that a high need for achievement often goes hand in hand with career success.

Individuals with a high **need for affiliation** are especially concerned about establishing and maintaining good relations with other people. They not only want to be liked by others but also want everyone to get along with everyone else. As you might expect, they like working in groups, tend to be sensitive to other people's feelings, and avoid taking actions that would result in interpersonal conflict. In organizations, individuals with a high need for affiliation are especially likely to be found in jobs that require a lot of social interaction. Although they make good team players, a manager might not want a group to be composed primarily of individuals with a high need for affiliation because the group might be more concerned about maintaining good interpersonal relations than about actually accomplishing the group's tasks. Individuals with a high need for affiliation may also be less effective in situations in which they need to evaluate others because it may be hard for them to give negative feedback to a co-worker or a subordinate, a task that might disrupt interpersonal relations.

Individuals with a high **need for power** have a strong desire to exert emotional and behavioral control or influence over others.[27] These individuals are especially likely to be found in situations, such as in managerial jobs and leadership positions, that require one person to exert influence over others. Individuals with a high need for power may actually be more effective as leaders than those with a low need for power. In a study of the effectiveness of former presidents of the United States, for example, Robert House of the University of Pennsylvania and his colleagues found that a president's need for power predicted presidential performance or the president's effectiveness in office.[28] The levels of the presidents' need for power were assessed by analyzing their inaugural speeches for thoughts and ideas reflective of a high need for power.

What combination of the needs for achievement, affiliation, and power results in higher managerial motivation and performance? Although it might seem that high levels of all three are important for managerial effectiveness, research by Michael Stahl suggests that managers should have a high need for achievement and power.[29] A high need for affiliation might not necessarily be a good quality in managers because they may try too hard to be liked by their subordinates instead of trying to lead them to higher performance levels. Stahl's findings on managerial effectiveness primarily apply to lower- and middle-level managers.[30] For top executives and managers, the need for power appears to be the need that dominates all others in determining their success.[31]

How Personality Is Measured

We have been discussing the various traits that make up an individual's personality without much mention of how to determine an individual's standing on any of these traits. By far the most common and cost-effective means of assessing the personality traits of adults is through scales developed to measure personality. To complete these scales, individuals answer a series of questions about themselves. Figures 1.5, 1.6, and 1.8 provide examples of scales that measure positive affectivity, negative affectivity, and self-monitoring. Personality scales like these are often used for research purposes, for example, to determine how people who vary on these traits respond to different work situations. Although the use of such scales always run the risk of respondents' intentionally distorting their answers to portray themselves in a desirable fashion, research suggests that this is not a significant problem.[32]

THE NATURE OF ABILITY

While looking at individual differences and the way they affect the attitudes and behaviors of workers, we must look not only at each worker's personality but also at the *abilities, aptitudes,* and *skills* the worker possesses. Those terms are often used interchangeably. In our discussion, however, we focus on **ability,** which has been defined as "what a person is capable of doing."[33] Ability has important implications for understanding and managing organizational behavior. It determines the level of performance a worker can achieve, and, because the effectiveness of an organization as a whole depends on the performance levels of all individual workers—from janitors and clerks to upper managers and the CEO—ability is an important determinant of organizational performance. Two basic types of ability affect performance: cognitive or mental ability and physical ability.

Cognitive Ability

Psychologists have identified many types of cognitive ability and grouped them in a hierarchy. The most general dimension of cognitive ability is *general intelligence.*[34] Below general intelligence are specific types of cognitive ability that reflect competence in different areas of mental functioning (see Figure 1.6). Eight types of cognitive ability identified and described by psychologist Jum Nunnally, whose work was based in part on the pioneering work of L. L. and T. G. Thurstone in the 1940s are described in Table 1.2.[35]

Physical Ability

People differ not only in cognitive ability but also in physical ability. Two types of physical ability are motor skill and physical skill.[36] *Motor skill* is the ability to physically manipulate objects in an environment. *Physical skill* is a person's fitness and strength. E. A. Fleishman has

FIGURE 1.6
Types of Cognitive Ability

TABLE 1.2

Cognitive Abilities

Ability	Description	Examples of Jobs in Which the Ability Is Especially Important
Verbal ability	Ability to understand and use written and spoken language	Comedians, teachers, lawyers, writers
Numerical ability	Ability to solve arithmetic problems and deal with numbers	Waiters, investment bankers, engineers, accountants
Reasoning ability	Ability to come up with solutions for problems and understand the principles by which different problems can be solved	Therapists, interior designers, car mechanics, computer software designers
Deductive ability	Ability to reach appropriate conclusions from an array of observations or evaluate the implications of a series of facts	Medical researchers, detectives, scientists, investigative reporters
Ability to see relationships	The ability to see how two things are related to each other and then apply this knowledge to other relationships and solutions	Anthropologists, travel agents, consultants, wedding planners
Ability to remember	Ability to recall things ranging from simple associations to complex groups of statements or sentences	Translators, salespeople, managers, researchers
Spatial ability	Ability to determine the location or arrangement of objects in relation to one's own position and to imagine how an object would appear if its position in space were altered	Air traffic controllers, architects, clothing designers, astronauts
Perceptual	Ability to uncover visual patterns and see relationships within and across patterns	Professional photographers, airplane pilots, cruise ship captains, landscape designers

Source: Based, in part, on J. C. Nunnally, *Psychometric Theory,* 2nd ed. (New York: McGraw-Hill, 1978).

devoted considerable attention to identifying and studying physical ability and has concluded that there are 11 basic motor skills (such as reaction time, manual dexterity, and speed of arm movement) and nine physical skills (such as static strength, which includes the ability to lift weights and stamina).[37]

Where Do Abilities Come from and How Are They Measured?

Like personality, both cognitive ability and physical ability are determined by nature and nurture (see Figure 1.7). General intelligence is determined by the genes we inherit from our parents (nature)[38] and by situational factors (nurture). Standardized tests such as GMAT (General Management Aptitude Test) or the SAT (Scholastic Aptitude Test) are designed to measure certain basic aptitudes and abilities that people are probably born with, but we know that people's scores on these tests change over time and that situational changes such as repeated training on practice exams can improve performance on the tests. Moreover, an individual may be genetically endowed with superior intelligence, but if that person grows up in a severely impoverished environment (characterized by poor nutrition, parents who are drug abusers, or irregular attendance at school), his or her scores on standard intelligence tests will probably suffer.

Both nature and nurture also determine physical ability. Height, bone structure, limb length, and relative proportions are genetically determined and cannot be changed. Through practice and training such as weight lifting and aerobic exercise, however, people can enhance some of their physical and motor skills.

Researchers have developed many accurate paper-and-pencil measures of cognitive ability, so managers can often rely on the results of tests that have been shown to be useful indicators of the underlying ability they are measuring. These tests can be used to ensure that prospective employees have the types of ability necessary to perform a job, to place existing employees in different jobs in an organization, to identify individuals who might need additional training, and to evaluate how successful training programs are in raising ability levels (we discuss each of these issues in the next section). Before using any of these tests, however, managers have to make sure that the tests are ethical and do not unfairly discriminate against different kinds of employees. Some tests of cognitive ability have been criticized for being culturally biased. Critics say that they ask questions that, because of differences in the test takers' ethnic backgrounds, may be relatively easy for members of certain groups to answer and more difficult for members of other groups to answer.

Physical ability can be measured by having a person engage in the relevant activity. Managers who need to see whether a prospective employee is strong enough to deliver, unpack, and set up heavy appliances could ask the individual to lift progressively heavier weights to determine the level of his or her static strength. New York City evaluates the physical ability of prospective sanitation workers by having them pick up trash bags and toss them into garbage trucks.

While organizations spend considerable time and effort to ensure that the people they hire have the abilities needed to be effective in their jobs, sometimes people are not given the opportunity to use their abilities on the job. A recent study of over 600 managers and 700 hourly workers found that two thirds of the managers and workers surveyed thought that their companies used only about 50 percent of their employees' cognitive abilities.[39] Even some IT professionals believe that their abilities are not being effectively utilized. A recent study of over 200 IT professionals found that over 40 percent of them were so bored at work that they thought about quitting their current jobs.[40] Hence, in addition to ensuring that employees have the abilities needed to perform at a high level, organizations also should strive to provide employees with the opportunity to use their abilities on the job.

Cognitive and physical abilities can degenerate or become impaired because of disease, drug or alcohol abuse, excessive levels of stress, or fatigue. In many organizations, it is important to accurately assess ability level to know what a worker is capable of doing, and it is also necessary to know when and why ability may be impaired on the job. Organizations' traditional response to potential impairment on the job is to test workers for substance abuse by means of urine analysis and such testing has been found to reduce illegal drug use.[41]

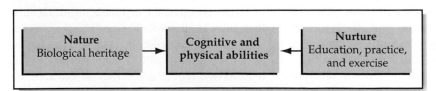

FIGURE 1.7
Nature and Nurture: The Determinants of Cognitive and Physical Abilities

Such testing may detect the presence of drugs and alcohol, but it does not tap into impairment due to other sources such as excessive fatigue. Another problem with urine tests is that it usually takes at least two to three days to get the results. In response to those problems, some firms have developed "fitness for duty" performance tests to determine whether workers can safely perform their jobs. Some of these tests involve the use of computer terminals and games that measure accuracy and reaction time against a worker's baseline score.[42]

Emotional Intelligence: A New Kind of Ability

A new kind of ability has been identified by psychologists that is not so much concerned with cognitive or physical capabilities but rather with emotional capabilites. *Emotional intelligence* is the ability to understand and manage one's own feelings and emotions and the feelings and emotions of others.[43] People differ in terms of the extent to which they know how they are feeling, they know why they are feeling that way, and they are able to manage their feelings. Similarly, people differ in terms of the extent to which they understand how other people are feeling and why, and are able to influence or manage other people's feelings. Emotional intelligence describes these individual differences.[44]

Research on emotional intelligence is in its early stages. However, it is plausible that emotional intelligence may facilitate job performance in a number of ways and a low level of emotional intelligence may actually impair performance. For example, psychologist Martin Seligman found that salespeople at Metropolitan Life who were high on optimism (an aspect of emotional intelligence), sold considerably more insurance policies than salespeople who were less able to manage their feelings and think positively.[45] Emotional intelligence is also likely to be important for managers and people in leadership positions who must understand how others feel and manage these feelings.[46] For Sir Rocco Forte, CEO of Forte Hotels, the ability to understand how customers feel and determine what they want is key to excellent customer service.[47] As a final example, consider the case of Jane, who was hired by George McCown of McCown Dee Leeuw, a buyout company in Menlo Park, California, to help determine which companies are good purchase opportunities. Jane was highly intelligent with excellent numerical skills and a top-notch educational background. McCown sent Jane to visit a company he was interested in purchasing. After visiting the company and performing various calculations, Jane advised McCown to buy the company because the numbers looked good. McCown, however, decided to visit the company himself and he was glad he did. As he puts it, "I could tell in the first two minutes of talking to the CEO that he was experiencing serious burnout. The guy was being overwhelmed by problems. On paper, things looked great. But he knew what was coming down the line. Jane had missed those cues completely.[48] Evidently, Jane's low level of emotional intelligence prevented her from understanding how the CEO of the targeted company was feeling and why—cues her boss was able to pick up on. Jane is no longer with McCown Dee Leeuw.[49]

THE MANAGEMENT OF ABILITY IN ORGANIZATIONS

Although we have mentioned the many types of ability that people possess, only a few abilities are likely to be relevant for the performance of any particular job. Managerial work, for example, requires cognitive ability, not very many physical abilities, and probably some degree of emotional intelligence, whereas being a grocery store shelf stocker or a car washer requires mainly physical ability. A brain surgeon, for instance, must rely on cognitive and physical abilities when performing highly complicated and delicate operations.

For managers, the key issue regarding ability is to make sure that workers have the abilities they need to perform their jobs effectively. There are three fundamental ways to manage ability in organizations to ensure that this matchup happens: selection, placement, and training.

Selection

Managers can control ability in organizations by selecting individuals who have the abilities the organization needs. Managers have to identify the tasks they want the worker to accomplish. Then managers need to identify which abilities are needed to accomplish these tasks. Once these abilities are identified, managers need to develop accurate measures of these abilities. The key question at this point is whether a person's score on the ability measure actually predicts performance on the task in question. If it does not, there is no point in using the ability measure as a selection device, and it would be unethical to do so. An organization that uses an inappropriate measure and rejects capable applicants leaves itself open to potential lawsuits for unfair hiring practices. But if the ability measure does predict task performance, then managers can use it as a selection tool to ensure that the organization has the mix of abilities needed to accomplish organizational goals.

Placement

Once individuals are selected and become part of an organization, managers must accurately match each worker to a job that will capitalize on his or her abilities. Again, managers need to identify the ability requirements of the jobs to be filled, and they need accurate measures of these abilities. Once these measures are available, the aim is to place workers in positions that match their abilities. Placement, however, involves more than just assigning new workers to appropriate positions. It is also an issue in horizontal moves or promotions within the organization. Obviously, an organization wants to promote only its most able workers to higher-level positions.

Training

Selection and placement, as ability management techniques, are concerned with *nature* aspects of ability. Training acknowledges that *nurture* also contributes to ability levels. Training can be an effective means of enhancing workers' abilities. We often think that the goal of training is to improve workers' ability beyond the minimum level required. Frequently, however, organizations use training to bring workers' skills up to some minimum required level.

To gain a competitive advantage, organizations often need to use new and advanced technology to lower costs and increase quality, efficiency, and performance. Companies that use advanced technology often find that their workers' abilities and skills are deficient in a number of ways. In the factories of the past, workers could get by with sheer physical strength and stamina; but those days are gone forever, and automation and computer technology require higher levels of skill. Many American workers lack even basic abilities in reading, writing, and arithmetic. The Work in America Institute estimates that about 30 million workers in the United States are illiterate. Ford Motor Company, General Motors, and Chrysler have invested millions of dollars in training initiatives, and the need for more training is one issue on which union officials and management agree.[50]

The need for training became obvious at Collins & Aikman, a carpet firm, when it computerized its factory to remain competitive.[51] Workers started to tell managers that they couldn't work with computers. Managers soon realized that they had significantly underestimated the number of workers needed to keep the factory running, because workers who could read and perform necessary calculations were covering for those who could not. A little probing indicated that about a third of the factory's workforce had not completed high school.

Rather than resorting to drastic measures such as abandoning the new technology or moving production overseas where labor costs are cheaper, Collins & Aikman decided to equip workers with the skills they needed to be competitive. An adult education instructor was hired to teach classes two days a week on every shift; the classes covered reading, writing, science, social studies, and math. Workers, some of them older, were at first apprehensive about taking classes, but the instructor's warmth and agreeableness soon overcame their misgivings and embarrassment over their own shortcomings.

So far, Collins & Aikman's investment seems to be paying off. Productivity is up, returns due to poor quality are down, and workers are feeling more confident about their new jobs. Worker morale and even health seem to have improved (judging by the number of sick days taken), and even workers' children may be benefiting because their parents are encouraging them to stay in school.[52]

Rapid advances in IT have increased training requirements for many organizations. Manpower, Inc. has instituted a 12-month training program for students in high school to help train IT workers.[53] At Trilogy Software, young college graduates receive unique training at Trilogy University to help them learn how to take risks and be creative and innovative. (see details below.)

Training for risk-taking and creativity at Trilogy Software

Trilogy Software, with over 1,000 employees in offices in Austin, Texas (headquarters), Boston, and Paris, was found by Joe Liemandt and four other Stanford University students in 1989. Trilogy now has served over 300 major corporate customers including such household names as Ford Motor Company, IBM Corporation, Whirlpool Corporation, Fidelity Brokerage Services, Inc., Motorola, and Nokia. Trilogy provides e-business solutions tailored to particular customers' needs, designs software, and provides technical training and consulting services to its global customers.[54]

Trilogy seems to hire only "the best" and then trains new employees to stretch their limits, take risks, and come up with creative solutions to business challenges. New hires attend Trilogy University during their first few months on the job; during the first month, classes start at 8:00 A.M. and continue until 12:00 midnight. During their second week of training, trainees are grouped into teams in which they have complete responsibility for a real project such as improving an existing product, creating a new one, or designing a recruitment strategy for new hires. Active learning is stressed while new hires build teamwork skills and develop creative solutions to business problems. Communications skills are also developed by making presentations to Joe Liemandt and other top managers early on in the program.[55]

In addition to pushing new hires to take responsibility for a project and develop a creative solution for it, Trilogy University also trains employees to be risk takers. In starting his own company, Joe Liemandt learned that to be truly creative and innovative, you must be able to take risks and accept the consequences (whether positive or negative). He goes to somewhat extreme lengths to train new hires to take risks as well. When Lauren Arbittier, a 21-year-old graduate of the University of Pennsylvania attended Trilogy University, Liemandt took 300 new hires to Las Vegas and challenged them to bet $2,000 of their own money at the roulette table. If they won, they could keep their winnings; if they lost, they had the $2,000 deducted from their subsequent paychecks over the next several months. Arbittier, always careful with her money and definitely not a gambler, surprised herself when she was one of 36 new hires to meet the challenge and bet $2,000. Although she lost the bet, she won the respect of her colleagues, Liemandt's recognition, and is a member of the "L2K" (lost $2,000) club at Trilogy.[56]

SUMMARY

The two main types of individual differences are personality differences and ability differences. Understanding the nature, determinants, and consequences of individual differences is essential for managing organizational behavior. Because people differ so much from each other, an appreciation of the nature of individual differences is necessary to understand why people act the way they do in organizations. In this chapter, we made the following major points:

1. Personality is the pattern of relatively enduring ways in which a person feels, thinks, and behaves. Personality is determined both by nature (biological heritage) and nurture (situational factors). Organizational outcomes that have been shown to be predicted by personality include job satisfaction, work stress, and leadership effectiveness. Personality is not a useful predictor of organizational outcomes when there are strong situational constraints. Because personality tends to be stable over time, managers should not expect to change personality in the short run. Managers should accept workers' personalities as they are and develop effective ways to deal with people.

2. Feelings, thoughts, attitudes, and behaviors in an organization are determined by the interaction of personality and situation.

3. The Big Five personality traits are extraversion (positive affectivity), neuroticism (negative affectivity), agreeableness, conscientiousness, and openness to experience. Other personality traits particularly relevant to organizational behavior include locus of control, self-monitoring, self-esteem, Type A and Type B personalities, and the needs for achievement, affiliation, and power.

4. In addition to possessing different personalities, workers also differ in their abilities, or what they are capable of doing. The two major types of ability are cognitive ability and physical ability.

5. Types of cognitive ability can be arranged in a hierarchy with general intelligence at the top. Specific types of cognitive ability are verbal ability, numerical ability, reasoning ability, deductive ability, ability to see relationships, ability to remember, spatial ability, and perceptual ability.

6. There are two types of physical ability: motor skills (the ability to manipulate objects) and physical skills (a person's fitness and strength).

7. Both nature and nurture contribute to determining physical ability and cognitive ability. A third, recently identified, ability is emotional intelligence.

8. In organizations, ability can be managed by selecting individuals who have the abilities needed to accomplish tasks, placing workers in jobs that capitalize on their abilities, and training workers to enhance their ability levels.

REFERENCES

1. A. Tellegen, D. T. Lykken, T. J. Bouchard, et al., "Personality Similarity in Twins Reared Apart and Together," *Journal of Personality and Social Psychology* 54 (1988): 1031–39.

2. Ibid.

3. J. M. George, "The Role of Personality in Organizational Life: Issues and Evidence," *Journal of Management* 18 (1992): 185–213.

4. R. D. Arvey, T. J. Bouchard, N. L. Segal, and L. M. Abraham, "Job Satisfaction: Environmental and Genetic Components," *Journal of Applied Psychology* 74 (1989): 187–92; A. P. Brief, M. J. Burke, J. M. George, B. Robinson, and J. Webster, "Should Negative Affectivity Remain an Unmeasured Variable in the Study of Job Stress?" *Journal of Applied*

Psychology 73 (1988): 193–98; J. L. Holland, *Making Vocational Choices: A Theory of Careers* (Upper Saddle River, NJ: Prentice Hall, 1973); R. J. House, W. D. Spangler, and J. Woycke, "Personality and Charisma in the U.S. Presidency: A Psychological Theory of Leader Effectiveness," *Administrative Science Quarterly* 36 (1991): 364–96.

5. M. R. Barrick, M. K. Mount, and J. P. Strauss, "Conscientiousness and Performance of Sales Representatives: Test of the Mediating Effects of Goal Setting," *Journal of Applied Psychology* 78 (1993): 715–22.

6. A. Davis-Blake and J. Pfeffer, "Just a Mirage: The Search for Dispositional Effects in Organizational Research," *Academy of Management Review* 14 (1989): 385–400.

7. R. C. Carson, "Personality," *Annual Review of Psychology* 40 (1989): 227–48; D. T. Kenrick and D. C. Funder, "Profiting from Controversy: Lessons from the Person–Situation Debate," *American Psychologist* 43 (1988): 23–34; D. C. Rowe, "Resolving the Person–Situation Debate: Invitation to an Interdisciplinary Dialogue," *American Psychologist* 42 (1987): 218–27.

8. B. Schneider, "The People Make the Place," *Personnel Psychology* 40 (1987): 437–53.

9. J. Schaubroeck, D. C. Ganster, and J. R. Jones, "Organization and Occupation Influences in the Attraction–Selection–Attrition Process," *Journal of Applied Psychology* 83 (1998): 869–91.

10. "Who Hires at Small Concerns? Often, It Is the Head Honcho," *Wall Street Journal*, November 17, 1992, p. A1.

11. J. M. Digman, "Personality Structure: Emergence of the Five Factor Model," *Annual Review of Psychology* 41 (1990): 417–40.

12. Ibid.; R. R. McCrae and P. T. Costa, "Validation of the Five Factor Model of Personality Across Instruments and Observers," *Journal of Personality and Social Psychology* 52 (1987): 81–90; R. R. McCrae and P. T. Costa, "Discriminant Validity of NEO-PIR Facet Scales," *Educational and Psychological Measurement* 52 (1992): 229–37.

13. J. M. George and A. P. Brief, "Personality and Work-Related Distress." In B. Schneider and B. Smith (Eds.), *Personality and Organization*, Mahwah, NJ: Erlbaum.

14. M. R. Barrick and M. K. Mount, "The Big Five Personality Dimensions and Job Performance: A Meta-Analysis," *Personnel Psychology* 44 (1991): 1–26; Barrick, Mount, and Strauss, "Conscientiousness and Performance of Sales Representatives."

15. J. O'C. Hamilton, "Roger Salquist," *Business Week, Reinventing America*, 1992, p. 186.

16. J. M. George and J. Zhou, "When Openness to Experience and Conscientiousness Are Related to Creative Behavior: An Interactional Approach," *Journal of Applied Psychology*, forthcoming.

17. "A Gallery of Risk Takers," *BusinessWeek, Reinventing America*, 1992, p. 183.

18. M. A. Burke, A. P. Brief, and J. M. George, "The Role of Negative Affectivity in Understanding Relationships Between Self-Reports of Stressors and Strains: A Comment on the Applied Psychology Literature," *Journal of Applied Psychology* 78 (1993): 402–12.

19. Barrick and Mount, "The Big Five Personality Dimensions and Job Performance"; J. M. George, "Mood and Absence," *Journal of Applied Psychology* 74 (1989): 317–24; J. M. George, "Time Structure and Purpose as a Mediator of Work-Life Linkages," *Journal of Applied Social Psychology* 21 (1991): 296–314.

20. J. B. Rotter, "Generalized Expectancies for Internal vs. External Control of Reinforcement," *Psychological Monographs* 80 (1966): 1–28; P. Spector, "Behavior in Organizations as a Function of Employees' Locus of Control," *Psychological Bulletin* 91 (1982): 482–97.

21. M. Snyder, "Self-Monitoring of Expressive Behavior," *Journal of Personality and Social Psychology* 30 (1974): 526–37; M. Snyder, "Self-Monitoring Processes." In L. Berkowitz (Ed.), *Advances in Experimental Social Psychology* 12 (1979): 85–128.

22. J. Brockner, *Self-Esteem at Work* (Lexington, MA: Lexington Books, 1988).

23. D. C. Ganster, J. Schaubroeck, W. E. Sime, and B. T. Mayes, "The Nomological Validity of Type A Personality Among Employed Adults," *Journal of Applied Psychology* 76 (1991): 143–68; R. H. Rosenman, "Current and Past History of Type A Behavior Pattern." In T. Schmidt, J. M. Dembrowski, and G. Blumchen (Eds.), *Biological and Psychological Factors in Cardiovascular Disease* (New York: Springer-Verlag, 1986).

24. R. A. Baron, "Personality and Organizational Conflict: Effects of the Type A Behavior Pattern and Self-Monitoring," *Organizational Behavior and Human Decision Processes* 44 (1989): 281–97.

25. D. C. McClelland, *Human Motivation* (Glenview, IL: Scott, Foresman, 1985); D. C. McClelland, "How Motives, Skills, and Values Determine What People Do," *American Psychologist* 40 (1985): 812–25; D. C. McClelland, "Managing Motivation to Expand Human Freedom," *American Psychologist* 33 (1978): 201–10.

26. D. C. McClelland, "Achievement and Entrepreneurship: A Longitudinal Study," *Journal of Personality and Organizational Behavior* 1 (1965): 389–92.

27. D. G. Winter, *The Power Motive* (New York: Free Press, 1973).

28. R. J. House, W. D. Spangler, and J. Woycke, "Personality and Charisma in the U.S. Presidency: A Psychological Theory of Leader Effectiveness," *Administrative Science Quarterly* 36 (1991): 364–96.

29. M. J. Stahl, "Achievement, Power, and Managerial Motivation: Selecting Managerial Talent with the Job Choice Exercise," *Personnel Psychology* 36 (1983): 775–89.

30. Ibid.

31. D. C. McClelland and D. H. Burnham, "Power Is the Great Motivator," *Harvard Business Review* 54 (1976): 100–110.

32. L. M. Hough, N. K. Eaton, M. D. Dunnette, J. D. Kamp, and R. A. McCloy, "Criterion-Related Validities of Personality Constructs and the Effect of Response Distortion on Those Validities," *Journal of Applied Psychology* 75 (1990): 581–95.

33. D. Lubinski and R. V. Dawis, "Aptitudes, Skills, and Proficiencies." In M. D. Dunnette and L. M. Hough (Eds.), *Handbook of Industrial and Organizational Psychology*, 2nd ed., vol. 3. (Palo Alto, CA: Consulting Psychologists Press, 1992), pp. 1–59.

34. Ibid.

35. J. C. Nunnally, *Psychometric Theory,* 2nd ed. (New York: McGraw-Hill, 1978); T. G. Thurstone, "Primary Mental Abilities & Children," *Educational and Psychological Measurement* 1 (1941): 105–16.

36. M. D. Dunnette, "Aptitudes, Abilities, and Skills." In M. D. Dunnette (Ed.), *Handbook of Industrial and Organizational Psychology* (Chicago: Rand McNally, 1976), pp. 473–520.

37. E. A. Fleishman, "The Description and Prediction of Perceptual-Motor Skill Learning." In R. Glaser (Ed.), *Training Research and Education* (Pittsburgh: University of Pittsburgh Press, 1962); E. A. Fleishman, "On the Relation Between Abilities, Learning, and Human Performance," *American Psychologist* 27 (1972): 1017–32.

38. H. M. Chipuer, M. Rovine, and R. Plomin, "LISREL Modeling: Genetic and Environmental Influences on IQ Revisited," *Intelligence* 14 (1990): 11–29; N. L. Pedersen, R. Plomin, J. R. Nesselroade, and G. E. McClearn, "A Quantitative Genetic Analysis of Cognitive Abilities During the Second Half of the Life Span," *Psychological Science* 3 (1992): 346–53.

39. "Think About It: Your Brainpower May Be Vastly Underused on the Job," *Wall Street Journal,* May 11, 1997, p. A1.

40. R. Merle, "Technology Workers See No Sizzle in What They Do," *Wall Street Journal,* April 26, 2000, p. T2.

41. "Drug Tests Keep Paying Off, But Continued Gains Are Tougher," *Wall Street Journal,* April 5, 1998, p. A1.

42. L. McGinley, "'Fitness' Exams Help to Measure Worker Acuity," *Wall Street Journal,* April 21, 1992, pp. B1, B6.

43. D. Goleman, *Emotional Intelligence* (New York: Bantam Books, 1994); J. D. Mayer and

P. Salovey, "The Intelligence of Emotional Intelligence," *Intelligence* 17 (1993): 433–42; J. D. Mayer and P. Salovey, "What Is Emotional Intelligence?" In P. Salovey and D. Sluyter (Eds.), *Emotional Development and Emotional Intelligence: Implications for Education* (New York: Basic Books, 1997); P. Salovey and J. D. Mayer, "Emotional Intelligence," *Imagination, Cognition, and Personality* 9 (1989–1990): 185–211.

44. Ibid.

45. A. Farnham, "Are You Smart Enough to Keep Your Job?," *Fortune* (January 15, 1996): 34–48; M. E. P. Seligman, *Learned Optimism* (New York, A. A. Knopf, 1990).

46. J. M. George, "Emotions and Leadership: The Role of Emotional Intelligence," *Human Relations,* 2000.

47. A. Farnham, "Are You Smart Enough To Keep Your Job?," *Fortune* (January 15, 1996): 34–48.

48. Ibid., p. 35.

49. Ibid.

50. K. Miller, "At GM, the Three R's Are the Big Three," *Wall Street Journal,* July 3, 1992, pp. B1, B6.

51. H. Cooper, "Carpet Firm Sets Up an In-House School to Stay Competitive," *Wall Street Journal,* October 5, 1992, pp. A1, A5.

52. Ibid.

53. "KIDPOWER: Staffing Agency Taps Teens as a New Pool of Contract Workers," *Wall Street Journal,* April 27, 1999, p. A1.

54. www.trilogy.com/.

55. www.trilogy.com/; E. Ramstad, "How Trilogy Software Trains Its Raw Recruits to Be Risk Takers," *Wall Street Journal,* September 21, 1998, pp. A1, A10.

56. E. Ramstad, "How Trilogy Software Trains Its Raw Recruits to Be Risk Takers," *Wall Street Journal,* September 21, 1998, pp. A1, A10.

Strategies for Increasing Individual Performance in Organizational Settings

2. Motivation: A Diagnostic Approach

David A. Nadler/Edward E. Lawler III

- What makes some people work hard while others do as little as possible?
- How can I, as a manager, influence the performance of people who work for me?
- Why do people turn over, show up late to work, and miss work entirely?

These important questions about employees' behavior can only be answered by managers who have a grasp of what motivates people. Specifically, a good understanding of motivation can serve as a valuable tool for *understanding* the causes of behavior in organizations, for *predicting* the effects of any managerial action, and for *directing* behavior so that organizational and individual goals can be achieved.

EXISTING APPROACHES

During the past twenty years, managers have been bombarded with a number of different approaches to motivation. The terms associated with these approaches are well known—"human relations," "scientific management," "job enrichment," "need hierarchy," "self-actualization," etc. Each of these approaches has something to offer. On the other hand, each of these different approaches also has its problems in both theory and practice. Running through almost all of the approaches with which managers are familiar are a series of implicit but clearly erroneous assumptions.

> *Assumption 1: All Employees Are Alike.* Different theories present different ways of looking at people, but each of them assumes that all employees are basically similar in their makeup: Employees all want economic gains, or all want a pleasant climate, or all aspire to be self-actualizing, etc.
>
> *Assumption 2: All Situations Are Alike.* Most theories assume that all managerial situations are alike, and that the managerial course of action for motivation (for example, participation, job enlargement, etc.) is applicable in all situations.
>
> *Assumption 3: One Best Way.* Out of the other two assumptions there emerges a basic principle that there is "one best way" to motivate employees.

When these "one best way" approaches are tried in the "correct" situation they will work. However, all of them are bound to fail in some situations. They are therefore not adequate managerial tools.

A NEW APPROACH

During the past ten years, a great deal of research has been done on a new approach to looking at motivation. This approach, frequently called "expectancy theory," still needs further testing, refining, and extending. However, enough is known that many behavioral scientists have concluded that it represents the most comprehensive, valid, and useful approach to understanding motivation. Further, it is apparent that it is a very useful tool for understanding motivation in organizations.

The theory is based on a number of specific assumptions about the causes of behavior in organizations.

> *Assumption 1: Behavior Is Determined by a Combination of Forces in the Individual and Forces in the Environment.* Neither the individual nor the environment alone determines behavior. Individuals come into organizations with certain "psychological baggage." They have past experiences and a developmental history which has given them unique sets of needs, ways of looking at the world, and expectations about how organizations will treat them. These all influence how individuals respond to their work environment. The work environment provides structures (such as a pay system or a supervisor) which influence the behavior of people. Different environments tend to produce different behavior in similar people just as dissimilar people tend to behave differently in similar environments.
>
> *Assumption 2: People Make Decisions About Their Own Behavior in Organizations.* While there are many constraints on the behavior of individuals in organizations, most of the behavior that is observed is the result of individuals' conscious decisions. These decisions usually fall into two categories. First, individuals make decisions about *membership behavior*—coming to work, staying at work, and in other ways being a member of the organization. Second, individuals make decisions about the amount of effort they will direct *towards performing their jobs*. This includes decisions about how

hard to work, how much to produce, at what quality, etc.

Assumption 3: Different People Have Different Types of Needs, Desires, and Goals. Individuals differ on what kinds of outcomes (or rewards) they desire. These differences are not random; they can be examined systematically by an understanding of the differences in the strength of individuals' needs.

Assumption 4: People Make Decisions Among Alternative Plans of Behavior Based on Their Perceptions (Expectancies) of the Degree to Which a Given Behavior Will Lead to Desired Outcomes. In simple terms, people tend to do those things which they see as leading to outcomes (which can also be called "rewards") they desire and avoid doing those things they see as leading to outcomes that are not desired.

In general, the approach used here views people as having their own needs and mental maps of what the world is like. They use these maps to make decisions about how they will behave, behaving in those ways which their mental maps indicate will lead to outcomes that will satisfy their needs. Therefore, they are inherently neither motivated nor unmotivated; motivation depends on the situation they are in, and how it fits their needs.

THE THEORY

Based on these general assumptions, expectancy theory states a number of propositions about the process by which people make decisions about their own behavior in organizational settings. While the theory is complex at first view, it is in fact made of a series of fairly straightforward observations about behavior. (The theory is presented in more technical terms in Appendix A.) Three concepts serve as the key building blocks of the theory.

Performance–Outcome Expectancy.
Every behavior has associated with it, in an individual's mind, certain outcomes (rewards

or punishments). In other words, the individual believes or expects that if he or she behaves in a certain way, he or she will get certain things.

Examples of expectancies can easily be described. An individual may have an expectancy that if he produces ten units he will receive his normal hourly rate while if he produces fifteen units he will receive his hourly pay rate plus a bonus. Similarly an individual may believe that certain levels of performance will lead to approval or disapproval from members of her work group or from her supervisor. Each performance can be seen as leading to a number of different kinds of outcomes and outcomes can differ in their types.

Valence.
Each outcome has a "valence" (value, worth, attractiveness) to a specific individual. Outcomes have different valences for different individuals. This comes about because valences result from individual needs and perceptions, which differ because they in turn reflect other factors in the individual's life.

For example, some individuals may value an opportunity for promotion or advancement because of their needs for achievement or power, while others may not want to be promoted and leave their current work group because of needs for affiliation with others. Similarly, a fringe benefit such as a pension plan may have great valence for an older worker but little valence for a young employee on his first job.

Effort–Performance Expectancy.
Each behavior also has associated with it in the individual's mind a certain expectancy or probability of success. This expectancy represents the individual's perception of how hard it will be to achieve such behavior and the probablity of his or her successful achievement of that behavior.

For example, you may have a strong expectancy that if you put forth effort, you can produce ten units an hour, but that you have only a fifty-fifty chance of producing fifteen units an hour if you try.

Putting these concepts together, it is possible to make a basic statement about motivation. In general, the motivation to attempt to behave in a certain way is greatest when:

a. The individual believes that the behavior will lead to outcomes (performance–outcome expectancy)
b. The individual believes that these outcomes have positive value for him or her (valence)
c. The individual believes that he or she is able to perform at the desired level (effort–performance expectancy)

Given a number of alternative levels of behavior (ten, fifteen, and twenty units of production per hour, for example) the individual will choose that level of performance which has the greatest motivational force associated with it, as indicated by the expectancies, outcomes, and valences.

In other words, when faced with choices about behavior, the individual goes through a process of considering questions such as, "Can I perform at that level if I try?" "If I perform at that level, what will happen?" "How do I feel about those things that will happen?" The individual then decides to behave in that way which seems to have the best chance of producing positive, desired outcomes.

A General Model

On the basis of these concepts, it is possible to construct a general model of behavior in organizational settings (see Figure 2.1). Working from left to right in the model, motivation is seen as the force on the individual to expend effort. Motivation leads to an observed level of effort by the individual. Effort, alone, however, is not enough. Performance results from a combination of the effort that an individual puts forth *and* the level of ability which he or she has (reflecting skills, training, information, etc.). Effort thus combines with ability to produce a given level of performance. As a result of performance, the individual attains certain outcomes. The model indicates this relationship in a dotted line, reflecting the fact that sometimes people perform but do not get desired outcomes. As this process of performance–reward occurs, time after time, the actual events serve to provide information which influences the individual's perceptions (particularly expectancies) and thus influences motivation in the future.

Outcomes, or rewards, fall into two major categories. First, the individual obtains outcomes from the environment. When an individual performs at a given level he or she can receive posi-

FIGURE 2.1
The Basic Motivation–Behavior Sequence

tive or negative outcomes from supervisors, coworkers, the organization's rewards systems, or other sources. These environmental rewards are thus one source of outcomes for the individual. A second source of outcomes is the individual. These include outcomes which occur purely from the performance of the task itself (feelings of accomplishment, personal worth, achievement, etc.). In a sense, the individual gives these rewards to himself or herself. The environment cannot give them or take them away directly; it can only make them possible.

Supporting Evidence

Over fifty studies have been done to test the validity of the expectancy-theory approach to predicting employee behavior.[1] Almost without exception, the studies have confirmed the predictions of the theory. As the theory predicts, the best performers in organizations tend to see a strong relationship between performing their jobs well and receiving rewards they value. In addition they have clear performance goals and feel they can perform well. Similarly, studies using the expectancy theory to predict how people choose jobs also show that individuals tend to interview for and actually take those jobs which they feel will provide the rewards they value. One study, for example, was able to correctly predict for 80 percent of the people studied which of several jobs they would take.[2] Finally, the theory correctly predicts that beliefs about the outcomes associated with performance (expectancies) will be better predictors of performance than will feelings of job satisfaction since expectancies are the critical causes of performance and satisfaction is not.

Questions About the Model

Although the results so far have been encouraging, they also indicate some problems with the model. These problems do not critically affect the managerial implications of the model, but they should be noted. The model is based on the assumption that individuals make very rational decisions after a thorough exploration of all the available alternatives and on weighing the possible outcomes of all these alternatives. When we talk to or observe individuals, however, we find that their decision processes are frequently less thorough. People often stop considering alternative behavior plans when they find one that is at least moderately satisfying, even though more rewarding plans remain to be examined.

People are also limited in the amount of information they can handle at one time, and therefore the model may indicate a process that is much more complex than the one that actually takes place. On the other hand, the model does provide enough information and is consistent enough with reality to present some clear implications for managers who are concerned with the question of how to motivate the people who work for them.

Implications for Managers

The first set of implications is directed toward the individual manager who has a group of people working for him or her and is concerned with how to motivate good performance. Since behavior is a result of forces both in the person and in the environment, you as a manager need to look at and diagnose both the person and the environment. Specifically, you need to do the following:

Figure Out What Outcomes Each Employee Values.

As a first step, it is important to determine what kinds of outcomes or rewards have valence for your employees. For each employee you need to determine "what turns him or her on." There are various ways of finding this out, including (a) finding out employees' desires through some structured method of data collection, such as a questionnaire, (b) observing the employees' reactions to different situations or rewards, or (c) the fairly simple act of asking them what kinds of rewards they want, what kind of career goals they have, or "what's in it for them." It is important to stress here that it is very difficult to change what people want, but fairly easy to find out what they want. Thus, the skillful manager emphasizes diagnosis of needs, not changing the individuals themselves.

Determine What Kinds of Behavior You Desire.

Managers frequently talk about "good performance" without really defining what good performance is. An important step in motivating is for you yourself to figure out what kinds of performance are required and what are adequate measures or indicators of performance (quantity, quality, etc.). There is also a need to be able to define those performances in fairly specific terms so that observable and measurable behavior can be defined and subordinates can understand what is desired of them (e.g., produce ten products of a certain quality standard—rather than only produce at a high rate).

Make Sure Desired Levels of Performance Are Reachable.

The model states that motivation is determined not only by the performance-to-outcome expectancy, but also by the effort-to-performance expectancy. The implication of this is that the levels of performance which are set as the points at which individuals receive desired outcomes must be reachable or attainable by these individuals. If the employees feel that the level of performance required to get a reward is higher than they can reasonably achieve, then their motivation to perform well will be relatively low.

Link Desired Outcomes to Desired Performances.

The next step is to directly, clearly, and explicitly link those outcomes desired by employees to the specific performances desired by you. If your employee values external rewards, then the emphasis should be on the rewards system concerned with promotion, pay, and approval. While the linking of these rewards can be initiated through your making statements to your employees, it is extremely important that employees see a clear example of the reward process working in a fairly short period of time if the motivating "expectancies" are to be created in the employees' minds. The linking must be done by some concrete public acts, in addition to statements of intent.

If your employee values internal rewards (e.g., achievement), then you should concentrate on changing the nature of the person's job, for he or she is likely to respond well to such things as increased autonomy, feedback, and challenge, because these things will lead to a situation where good job performance is inherently rewarding. The best way to check on the adequacy of the internal and external reward system is to ask people what their perceptions of the situation are. Remember it is the perceptions of people that determine their motivation, not reality. It doesn't matter for example whether you feel a subordinate's pay is related to his or her motivation. Motivation will be present only if the subordinate sees the relationship. Many managers are misled about the behavior of their subordinates because they rely on their own perceptions of the situation and forget to find out what their subordinates feel. There is only one way to do this: ask. Questionnaires can be used here, as can personal interviews.

Analyze the Total Situation for Conflicting Expectancies.

Having set up positive expectancies for employees, you then need to look at the entire situation to see if other factors (informal work groups, other managers, the organization's reward systems) have set up conflicting expectancies in the minds of the employees. Motivation will only be high when people see a number of rewards associated with good performance and few negative outcomes. Again, you can often gather this kind of information by asking your subordinates. If there are major conflicts, you need to make adjustments, either in your own performance and reward structure, or in the other sources of rewards or punishments in the environment.

Make Sure Changes in Outcomes Are Large Enough.

In examining the motivational system, it is important to make sure that changes in outcomes or rewards are large enough to motivate significant behavior. Trivial rewards will result in trivial amounts of effort and thus trivial improvements in performance. Rewards must be large enough to motivate individuals to put forth the effort required to bring about significant changes in performance.

Check the System for Its Equity. The model is based on the idea that individuals are different and therefore different rewards will need to be used to motivate different individuals. On the other hand, for a motivational system to work it must be a fair one—one that has equity (not equality). Good performers should see that they get more desired rewards than do poor performers, and others in the system should see that also. Equity should not be confused with a system of equality where all are rewarded equally, with no regard to their performance. A system of equality is guaranteed to produce low motivation.

Implications for Organizations

Expectancy theory has some clear messages for those who run large organizations. It suggests how organizational structures can be designed so that they increase rather than decrease levels of motivation of organization members. While there are many different implications, a few of the major ones are as follows:

Implication 1: The Design of Pay and Reward Systems. Organizations usually get what they reward, not what they want. This can be seen in many situations, and pay systems are a good example.[3] Frequently, organizations reward people for membership (through pay tied to seniority, for example) rather than for performance. Little wonder that what the organization gets is behavior oriented towards "safe," secure employment rather than effort directed at performing well. In addition, even where organizations do pay for performance as a motivational device, they frequently negate the motivational value of the system by keeping pay secret, therefore preventing people from observing the pay-to-performance relationship that would serve to create positive, clear, and

strong performance-to-reward expectancies. The implication is that organizations should put more effort into rewarding people (through pay, promotion, better job opportunities, etc.) for the performances which are desired, and that to keep these rewards secret is clearly self-defeating. In addition, it underscores the importance of the frequently ignored performance evaluation or appraisal process and the need to evaluate people based on how they perform clearly defined specific behaviors, rather than on how they score on ratings of general traits such as "honesty," "cleanliness," and other, similar terms which frequently appear as part of the performance appraisal form.

Implication 2: The Design of Tasks, Jobs, and Roles. One source of desired outcomes is the work itself. The expectancy-theory model supports much of the job enrichment literature, in saying that by designing jobs which enable people to get their needs fulfilled, organizations can bring about higher levels of motivation.[4] The major difference between the traditional approaches to job enlargement or enrichment and the expectancy-theory approach is the recognition by the expectancy theory that different people have different needs and, therefore, some people may not want enlarged or enriched jobs. Thus, while the design of tasks that have more autonomy, variety, feedback, meaningfulness, etc., will lead to higher motivation in some, the organization needs to build in the opportunity for individuals to make choices about the kind of work they will do so that not everyone is forced to experience job enrichment.

Implication 3: The Importance of Group Structures. Groups, both formal and informal, are powerful and potent sources of desired outcomes for individuals. Groups can provide or withhold acceptance, approval, affection, skill training, needed information, assistance, etc. They are a powerful force in the total motivational environment of individuals. Several implications emerge from the importance of groups. First, organizations should consider the structuring of at least a portion of rewards around group performance rather than individual performance. This is particularly important where group members have to cooperate with each other to produce a group product or service, and where the individual's contribution is often hard to determine. Second, the organization needs to train managers to be aware of how groups can influence individual behavior and to be sensitive to the kinds of expectancies which informal groups set up and their conflict or consistency with the expectancies that the organization attempts to create.

Implication 4: The Supervisor's Role.

The immediate supervisor has an important role in creating, monitoring, and maintaining the expectancies and reward structures which will lead to good performance. The supervisor's role in the motivation process becomes one of defining clear goals, setting clear reward expectancies, and providing the right rewards for different people (which could include both organizational rewards and personal rewards such as recognition, approval, or support from the supervisor). Thus, organizations need to provide supervisors with an awareness of the nature of motivation as well as the tools (control over organizational rewards, skill in administering those rewards) to create positive motivation.

Implication 5: Measuring Motivation.

If things like expectancies, the nature of the job, supervisor-controlled outcomes, satisfaction, etc., are important in understanding how well people are being motivated, then organizations need to monitor employee perceptions along these lines. One relatively cheap and reliable method of doing this is through standardized employee questionnaires. A number of organizations already use such techniques, surveying employees' perceptions and attitudes at regular intervals (ranging from once a month to once every year-and-a-half) using either standard-

ized surveys or surveys developed specifically for the organization. Such information is useful both to the individual manager and to top management in assessing the state of human resources and the effectiveness of the organization's motivation systems.[5]

Implication 6: Individualizing Organizations.

Expectancy theory leads to a final general implication about a possible future direction for the design of organizations. Because different people have different needs and therefore have different valences, effective motivation must come through the recognition that not all employees are alike and that organizations need to be flexible in order to accommodate individual differences. This implies the "building in" of choice for employees in many areas, such as reward systems, fringe benefits, job assignments, etc., where employees previously have had little say. A successful example of the building in of such choice can be seen in the experiments at TRW and the Educational Testing Service with "cafeteria fringe-benefits plans" which allow employees to choose the fringe benefits they want, rather than taking the expensive and often unwanted benefits which the company frequently provides to everyone.[6]

SUMMARY

Expectancy theory provides a more complex model of man for managers to work with. At the same time, it is a model which holds promise for the more effective motivation of individuals and the more effective design of organizational systems. It implies, however, the need for more exacting and thorough diagnosis by the manager to determine (a) the relevant forces in the individual, and (b) the relevant forces in the environment, both of which combine to motivate different kinds of behavior. Following diagnosis, the model implies a need to act—to develop a system of pay, promotion, job assignments, group structures, supervision, etc.—to bring about effective motivation by providing different outcomes for different individuals.

Performance of individuals is a critical issue in making organizations work effectively. If a manager is to influence work behavior and performance, he or she must have an understanding of motivation and the factors which influence an individual's motivation to come to work, to work hard, and to work well. While simple models offer easy answers, it is the more complex models which seem to offer more promise. Managers can use models (like expectancy theory) to understand the nature of behavior and build more effective organizations.

APPENDIX A: THE EXPECTANCY THEORY MODEL IN MORE TECHNICAL TERMS

A person's motivation to exert effort towards a specific level of performance is based on his or her perceptions of associations between actions and outcomes. The critical perceptions which contribute to motivation are graphically presented in Figure 2.2. These perceptions can be defined as follows:

a. The effort-to-performance expectancy ($E \rightarrow P$): This refers to the person's subjective probability about the likelihood that he or she can perform at a given level, or that effort on his or her part will lead to successful performance. This term can be thought of as varying from 0 to 1. In general, the less likely a person feels that he or she can perform at a given level, the less likely he or she will be to try to perform at that level. A person's $E \rightarrow P$ probabilities are also strongly influenced by each situation and by previous experience in that and similar situations.

b. The performance-to-outcomes expectancy ($P \rightarrow 0$) and valence (V): This refers to a com-

FIGURE 2.2
Major Terms in Expectancy Theory

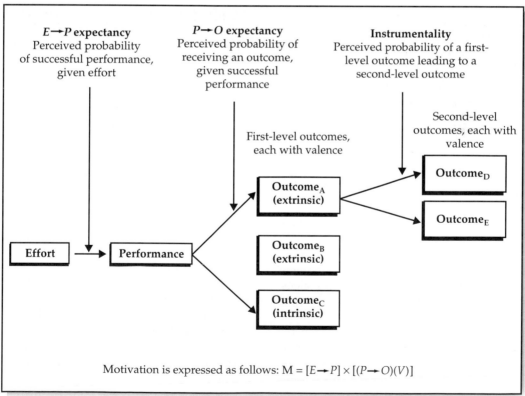

Motivation is expressed as follows: $M = [E \rightarrow P] \times [(P \rightarrow O)(V)]$

bination of a number of beliefs about what the outcomes of successful performance will be and the value or attractiveness of these outcomes to the individual. Valence is considered to vary from +1 (very desirable) to –1 (very undesirable) and the performance-to-outcomes probabilities vary from +1 (performance sure to lead to outcomes) to 0 (performance not related to outcome). In general, the more likely a person feels that performance will lead to valent outcomes, the more likely he or she will be to try to perform at the required level.

c. Instrumentality: As Figure 2.2 indicates, a single level of performance can be associated with a number of different outcomes, each having a certain degree of valence. Some outcomes are valent because they have direct value or attractiveness. Some outcomes, however, have valence because they are seen as leading to (or being "instrumental" for) the attainment of other "second level" outcomes which have direct value or attractiveness.

d. Intrinsic and extrinsic outcomes: Some outcomes are seen as occurring directly as a result of performing the task itself and are outcomes which the individual thus gives to himself (i.e., feelings of accomplishment, creativity, etc.). These are called "intrinsic" outcomes. Other outcomes that are associated with performance are provided or mediated by external factors (the organization, the supervisor, the work group, etc.). These outcomes are called "extrinsic" outcomes.

Along with the graphic representation of these terms presented in Figure 2.2, there is a simplified formula for combining these perceptions to arrive at a term expressing the relative level of motivation to exert effort towards performance at a given level. The formula expresses these relationships:

a. The person's motivation to perform is determined by the $P \rightarrow O$ expectancy multiplied by the valence (V) of the outcome. The valence of the first order outcome subsumes the instrumentalities and valences of second order outcomes. The relationship is multiplicative since there is no motivation to perform if either of the terms is zero.

b. Since a level of performance has multiple outcomes associated with it, the products of all probability-times-valence combinations are added together for all the outcomes that are seen as related to the specific performance.

c. This term (the summed $P \rightarrow O$ expectancies times valences) is then multiplied by the $E \rightarrow P$ expectancy. Again the multiplicative relationship indicates that if either term is zero, motivation is zero.

d. In summary, the strength of a person's motivation to perform effectively is influenced by (1) the person's belief that effort can be converted into performance, and (2) the net attractiveness of the events that are perceived to stem from good performance.

So far, all the terms have referred to the individual's perceptions which result in motivation and thus an intention to behave in a certain way. Figure 2.3 is a simplified representation of the total model, showing how these intentions get translated into actual behavior.[7] The model envisions the following sequence of events:

a. First, the strength of a person's motivation to perform correctly is most directly reflected in his or her effort—how hard he or she works. This effort expenditure may or may not result in good performance, since at least two factors must be right if effort is to be converted into performance. First, the person must possess the necessary abilities in order to perform the job well. Unless both ability and effort are high, there cannot be good performance. A second factor is the person's perception of how his or her effort can best be converted into performance. It is assumed that this perception is learned by the individual on the basis of previous experience in similar situations. This "how to do it" perception can obviously vary widely in accu-

FIGURE 2.3
Simplified Expectancy-Theory Model of Behavior

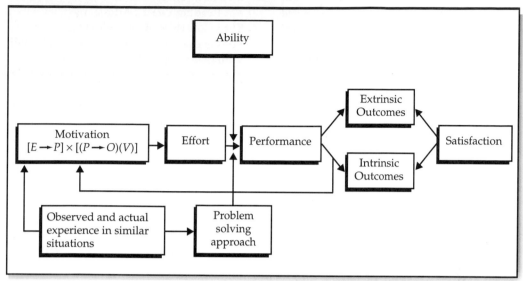

racy, and—where erroneous perceptions exist—performance is low even though effort or motivation may be high.

b. Second, when performance occurs, certain amounts of outcomes are obtained by the individual. Intrinsic outcomes, not being mediated by outside forces, tend to occur regularly as a result of performance, while extrinsic outcomes may or may not accrue to the individual (indicated by the wavy line of the model).

c. Third, as a result of the obtaining of outcomes and the perceptions of the relative value of the outcomes obtained, the individual has a positive or negative affective response (a level of satisfaction or dissatisfaction).

d. Fourth, the model indicates that events which occur influence future behavior by altering the $E \rightarrow P, P \rightarrow O,$ and V perceptions. This process is represented by the feedback loops running from actual behavior back to motivation.

REFERENCES

1. For reviews of the expectancy theory research see Mitchell, T. R. Expectancy models of job satisfaction, occupational preference and effort: A theoretical, methodological, and empirical appraisal. *Psychological Bulletin,* 1974, 81, 1053–1077. For a more general discussion of expectancy theory and other approaches to motivation see Lawler, E. E. *Motivation in work organizations.* Belmont, Calif.: Brooks/Cole, 1973.

2. Lawler, E. E., Kuleck, W. J., Rhode, J. G., & Sorenson, J. E. Job choice and post-decision dissonance. *Organizational Behavior and Human Performance,* 1975, 13, 133–145.

3. For a detailed discussion of the implications of expectancy theory for pay and reward systems, see Lawler, E. E. *Pay and organizational effectiveness: A psychological view.* New York: McGraw-Hill, 1971.

4. A good discussion of job design with an expectancy-theory perspective is in Hackman, J. R., Oldham, G. R., Janson, R., & Purdy, K. A new strategy for job enrichment. *California Management Review,* Summer, 1975, p. 57.

5. The use of questionnaires for understanding and changing organizational behavior is discussed in Nadler, D. A. *Feedback and organizational development: Using data-based methods.* Reading, Mass.: Addison-Wesley, 1977.

6. The whole issue of individualizing organizations is examined in Lawler, E. E. The individualized organization: Problems and promise. *California Management Review,* 1974, 17 (2), 31–39.

7. For a more detailed statement of the model see Lawler, E. E. Job attitudes and employee motivation: Theory, research and practice. *Personnel Psychology,* 1970, 23, 223–237.

3. Goal-Setting—A Motivational Technique That Works

Gary P. Latham/Edwin A. Locke

The problem of how to motivate employees has puzzled and frustrated managers for generations. One reason the problem has seemed difficult, if not mysterious, is that motivation ultimately comes from within the individual and therefore cannot be observed directly. Moreover, most managers are not in a position to change an employee's basic personality structure. The best they can do is try to use incentives to direct the energies of their employees toward organizational objectives.

Money is obviously the primary incentive, since without it few if any employees would come to work. But money alone is not always enough to motivate high performance. Other incentives, such as participation in decision making, job enrichment, behavior modification, and organizational development, have been tried with varying degrees of success. A large number of research studies have shown, however, that one very straightforward technique—goal setting—is probably not only more effective than alternative methods, but may be the major mechanism by which these other incentives affect motivation. For example, a recent experiment on job enrichment demonstrated that unless employees in enriched jobs set higher, more specific goals than do those with unenriched jobs, job enrichment has absolutely no effect on productivity. Even money has been found most effective as a motivator when the bonuses offered are made contingent on attaining specific objectives.

THE GOAL-SETTING CONCEPT

The idea of assigning employees a specific amount of work to be accomplished—a specific task, a quota, a performance standard, an objective, or a deadline—is not new. The task concept, along with time and motion study and incentive pay, was the cornerstone of scientific management, founded by Frederick W. Taylor more than 70 years ago. He used this system to increase the productivity of blue-collar workers. About 20 years ago the idea of goal setting reappeared under a new name, management by objectives, but this technique was designed for managers.

In a 14-year program of research, we have found that goal setting does not necessarily have to be part of a wider management system to motivate performance effectively. It can be used as a technique in its own right.

Laboratory and Field Research

Our research program began in the laboratory. In a series of experiments, individuals were assigned different types of goals on a variety of simple tasks—addition, brainstorming, assembling toys. Repeatedly it was found that those assigned hard goals performed better than did people assigned moderately difficult or easy goals. Furthermore, individuals who had specific, challenging goals outperformed those who were given such vague goals as to "do your best." Finally, we observed that pay and performance feedback led to improved performance only when these incentives led the individual to set higher goals.

While results were quite consistent in the laboratory, there was no proof that they could be applied to actual work settings. Fortunately, just as Locke published a summary of the laboratory studies in 1968, Latham began a separate series of experiments in the wood products industry that demonstrated the practical significance of these findings. The field studies did not start out as a validity test of a laboratory theory, but rather as a response to a practical problem.

In 1968, six sponsors of the American Pulpwood Association became concerned about increasing the productivity of independent loggers in the South. These loggers were entrepreneurs on whom the multimillion-dollar companies are largely dependent for their raw material. The problem was twofold. First, these entrepreneurs did not work for a single company; they worked for themselves. Thus they were free to (and often did) work two days one week, four days a second week, five half-days a third week, or whatever schedule they preferred. In short, these workers could be classified as marginal from the standpoint of their productivity and attendance, which were considered highly unsatisfactory by conventional company standards. Second, the major approach taken to alleviate this problem had been to develop equipment that would make the industry less dependent on this type of worker. A limitation of this approach was that many of the logging supervisors were unable to obtain the financing necessary to purchase a small tractor, let alone a rubber-tired skidder.

Consequently, we designed a survey that would help managers determine "what makes these people tick." The survey was conducted orally in the field with 292 logging supervisors. Complex statistical analyses of the data identified three basic types of supervisor. One type stayed on the job with their men, gave them instructions and explanations, provided them with training, read the trade magazines, and had little difficulty financing the equipment they needed. Still, the productivity of their units was at best mediocre.

The operation of the second group of supervisors was slightly less mechanized. These supervisors provided little training for their workforce. They simply drove their employees to the woods, gave them a specific production goal to attain for the day or week, left them alone in the woods unsupervised, and returned at night to take them home. Labor turnover was high and productivity was again average.

The operation of the third group of supervisors was relatively unmechanized. These leaders stayed on the job with their men, provided training, gave instructions and explanations, and in addition, set a specific production goal for the day or week. Not only was the crew's productivity high, but their injury rate was well below average.

Two conclusions were discussed with the managers of the companies sponsoring this study. First, mechanization alone will not increase the productivity of logging crews. Just as the average tax payer would probably commit more mathematical errors if he were to try to use a computer to complete his income tax return, the average logger misuses, and frequently abuses, the equipment he purchases (for example, drives a skidder with two flat tires, doesn't change the oil filter). This increases not only the logger's downtime, but also his costs which, in turn, can force him out of business. The second conclusion of the survey was that setting a specific production goal combined with supervisory presence to ensure goal commitment will bring about a significant increase in productivity.

These conclusions were greeted with the standard, but valid, cliché, "Statistics don't prove causation." And our comments regarding the value of machinery were especially irritating to these managers, many of whom had received degrees in engineering. So one of the companies decided to replicate the survey in order to check our findings.

The company's study placed each of 892 independent logging supervisors who sold wood to the company into one of three categories of supervisory styles our survey had identified—namely, (1) stays on the job but does not set specific production goals; (2) sets specific production goals but does not stay on the job; and (3) stays on the job and sets specific production goals. Once again, goal setting, in combination with the on-site presence of a supervisor, was shown to be the key to improved productivity.

TESTING FOR THE HAWTHORNE EFFECT

Management may have been unfamiliar with different theories of motivation, but it was fully aware of one label—the Hawthorne effect. Managers in these wood products companies remained unconvinced that anything so simple as staying on the job with the men and setting a specific production goal could have an appreciable effect on productivity. They pointed out that the results simply reflected the positive effects any supervisor would have on the work unit after giving his crew attention. And they were unimpressed by the laboratory experiments we cited—experiments showing that individuals who have a specific goal solve more arithmetic problems or assemble more tinker toys than do people who are told to "do your best." Skepticism prevailed.

But the country's economic picture made it critical to continue the study of inexpensive techniques to improve employee motivation and productivity. We were granted permission to run one more project to test the effectiveness of goal setting.

Twenty independent logging crews who were all but identical in size, mechanization level, terrain on which they worked, productivity, and attendance were located. The logging supervisors of these crews were in the habit of staying on the job with their men, but they did not set production goals. Half the crews were randomly selected to receive training in goal setting; the remaining crews served as a control group.

The logging supervisors who were to set goals were told that we had found a way to increase productivity at no financial expense to anyone. We gave the ten supervisors in the training group production tables developed through time-and-motion studies by the company's engineers. These tables made it possible to determine how much wood should be harvested in a given number of man hours. They were asked to use these tables as a guide in determining a specific production goal to assign their employees. In addition, each sawhand was given a tallymeter (counter) that he could wear on his belt. The sawhand was asked to punch the counter each time he felled a tree. Finally, permission was requested to measure the crew's performance on a weekly basis.

The ten supervisors in the control group—those who were not asked to set production goals—were told that the researchers were interested in learning the extent to which productivity is affected by absenteeism and injuries. They were urged to "do your best" to maximize the crew's productivity and attendance and to minimize injuries. It was explained that the data might be useful in finding ways to increase productivity at little or no cost to the wood harvester.

To control for the Hawthorne effect, we made an equal number of visits to the control group and the training group. Performance was measured for 12 weeks. During this time, the productivity of the goal-setting group was significantly higher than that of the control group. Moreover, absenteeism was significantly lower in the groups that set goals than in the groups who were simply urged to do their best. Injury and turnover rates were low in both groups.

Why should anything so simple and inexpensive as goal setting influence the work of these employees so significantly? Anecdotal evidence from conversations with both the loggers and the company foresters who visited them suggested several reasons.

Harvesting timber can be a monotonous, tiring job with little or no meaning for most workers. Introducing a goal that is difficult, but attainable, increases the challenge of the job. In addition, a specific goal makes it clear to the worker what it is he is expected to do. Goal feedback via the tallymeter and weekly recordkeeping provide the worker with a sense of achievement, recognition, and accomplishment. He can see how well he is doing now as against his past performance and, in some cases, how well he is doing in comparison with others. Thus the worker not only may expend greater effort, but may also devise better or more creative tactics for attaining the goal than those he previously used.

NEW APPLICATIONS

Management was finally convinced that goal setting was an effective motivational technique for increasing the productivity of the independent woods worker in the South. The issue now raised by the management of another wood products company was whether the procedure could be used in the West with company logging operations in which the employees were unionized and paid by the hour. The previous study had involved employees on a piece-rate system, which was the practice in the South.

The immediate problem confronting this company involved the loading of logging trucks. If the trucks were underloaded, the company lost money. If the trucks were overloaded, however, the driver could be fined by the Highway Department and could ultimately lose his job. The drivers opted for underloading the trucks.

For three months management tried to solve this problem by urging the drivers to try harder to fill the truck to its legal net weight, and by developing weighing scales that could be attached to the truck. But this approach did not prove cost effective, because the scales continually broke down when subjected to the rough terrain on which the trucks traveled. Consequently, the drivers reverted to their former practice of underloading. For the three months in which the problem was under study the trucks were seldom loaded in excess of 58 to 63 percent of capacity.

At the end of the three-month period, the results of the previous goal-setting experiments were explained to the union. They were told three things—that the company would like to set a specific net weight goal for the drivers, that no monetary reward or fringe benefits other than verbal praise could be expected for improved performance, and that no one would be criticized for failing to attain the goal. Once again, the idea that simply setting a specific goal would solve a production problem seemed too incredible to be taken seriously by the union. However, they reached an agreement that a difficult, but attainable, goal of 94 percent of the truck's legal net weight would be assigned to the drivers, provided that no one could be reprimanded for failing to attain the goal. This latter point was emphasized to the company foremen in particular.

Within the first month, performance increased to 80 percent of the truck's net weight. After the second month, however, performance decreased to 70 percent. Interviews with the drivers indicated that they were testing management's statement that no punitive steps would be taken against them if their performance suddenly dropped. Fortunately for all concerned, no such steps were taken by the foremen, and performance exceeded 90 percent of the truck's capacity after the third month. Their performance has remained at this level to this day, seven years later.

The results over the nine-month period during which this study was conducted saved the company $250,000. This figure, determined by the company's accountants, is based on the cost of additional trucks that would have been required to deliver the same quantity of logs to the mill if goal setting had not been implemented. The dollars-saved figure is even higher when you factor in the cost of the additional diesel fuel that would have been consumed and the expenses incurred in recruiting and hiring the additional truck drivers.

Why could this procedure work without the union's demanding an increase in hourly wages? First, the drivers did not feel that they were really doing anything differently. This, of course, was not true. As a result of goal setting, the men began to record their truck weight in a pocket notebook, and they found themselves bragging about their accomplishments to their peers. Second, they viewed goal setting as a challenging game: "It was great to beat the other guy."

Competition was a crucial factor in bringing about goal acceptance and commitment in this study. However, we can reject the hypothesis that improved performance resulted solely from competition, because no special prizes or formal recognition programs were provided for those who came closest to, or exceeded, the goal. No effort was made by the company to single out one "winner." More important, the opportunity for competition among drivers had existed before goal setting was instituted; after all, each driver knew his own truck's weight, and the truck weight of each of the 36 other drivers every time he hauled wood into the yard. In short, competition affected productivity only in the sense that it led to the acceptance of, and commitment to, the goal. It was the setting of the goal itself and the working toward it that brought about increased performance and decreased costs.

PARTICIPATIVE GOAL SETTING

The inevitable question always raised by management was raised here: "We know goal setting works. How can we make it work better?" Was there one best method for setting goals? Evidence for a "one best way" approach was cited by several managers, but it was finally concluded that different approaches would work best under different circumstances.

It was hypothesized that the woods workers in the South, who had little or no education, would work better with assigned goals, while the educated workers in the West would achieve higher productivity if they were allowed to help set the goals themselves. Why the focus on education? Many of the uneducated workers in the South could be classified as culturally disadvantaged. Such persons often lack self-confidence, have a poor sense of time, and are not very competitive. The cycle of skill mastery, which in turn guarantees skill levels high enough to prevent discouragement, doesn't apply to these employees. If, for example, these people were allowed to participate in goal setting, the goals might be too difficult or they might be too easy. On the other hand, participation of the

educated worker was considered critical in effecting maximum goal acceptance. Since these conclusions appeared logical, management initially decided that no research was necessary. This decision led to hours of further discussion.

The same questions were raised again and again by the researchers. What if the logic were wrong? Can we afford to implement these decisions without evaluating them systematically? Would we implement decisions regarding a new approach to tree planting without first testing it? Do we care more about trees than we do about people? Finally, permission was granted to conduct an experiment.

Logging crews were randomly appointed to either participative goal setting, assigned (non-participative) goal setting, or a do-your-best condition. The results were startling. The uneducated crews, consisting primarily of black employees who participated in goal setting, set significantly higher goals and attained them more often than did those whose goals were assigned by their supervisor. Not surprisingly, their performance was higher. Crews with assigned goals performed no better than did those who were urged to do their best to improve their productivity. The performance of white, educationally advantaged workers was higher with assigned rather than participatively set goals, although the difference was not statistically significant. These results were precisely the opposite of what had been predicted.

Another study comparing participative and assigned goals was conducted with typists. The results supported findings obtained by researchers at General Electric years before. It did not matter so much *how* the goal was set. What mattered was *that* a goal was set. The study demonstrated that both assigned and participatively set goals led to substantial improvements in typing speed. The process by which these gains occurred, however, differed in the two groups.

In the participative group, employees insisted on setting very high goals regardless of whether they had attained their goal the previous week. Nevertheless, their productivity improved—an outcome consistent with the theory that high goals lead to high performance.

In the assigned-goal group, supervisors were highly supportive of employees. No criticism was given for failure to attain the goals. Instead, the supervisor lowered the goal after failure so that the employee would be certain to attain it. The goal was then raised gradually each week until the supervisor felt the employee was achieving his or her potential. The result? Feelings of accomplishment and achievement on the part of the worker and improved productivity for the company.

These basic findings were replicated in a subsequent study of engineers and scientists. Participative goal setting was superior to assigned goal setting only to the degree that it led to the setting of higher goals. Both participative and assigned-goal groups outperformed groups that were simply told to "do your best."

An additional experiment was conducted to validate the conclusion that participation in goal setting may be important only to the extent that it leads to the setting of difficult goals. It was performed in a laboratory setting in which the task was to brainstorm uses of wood. One group was asked to "do your best" to think of as many ideas as possible. A second group took part in deciding, with the experimenter, the specific number of ideas each person would generate. These goals were, in turn, assigned to individuals in a third group. In this way, goal difficulty was held constant between the assigned-goal and participative groups. Again, it was found that specific, difficult goals—whether assigned or set through participation—led to higher performance than did an abstract or generalized goal such as "do your best." And, when goal difficulty was held constant, there was no significant difference in the performance of those with assigned as compared with participatively set goals.

These results demonstrate that goal setting in industry works just as it does in the laboratory. Specific, challenging goals lead to better performance than do easy or vague goals, and feedback motivates higher performance only when it leads to the setting of higher goals.

It is important to note that participation is not only a motivational tool. When a manager has competent subordinates, participation is also a useful device for increasing the manager's knowledge and thereby improving decision quality. It can lead to better decisions through input from subordinates.

A representative sample of the results of field studies of goal setting conducted by Latham and others is shown in Table 3.1. Each of these ten studies compared the performance of employees given specific challenging goals with those given "do best" or no goals. Note that goal setting has been successful across a wide variety of jobs and industries. The effects of goal setting have been recorded for as long as seven years after the onset of the program, although the results of most studies have been followed for only a few weeks or months. The median improvement in performance in the ten studies shown in Table 3.1 was 17 percent.

A CRITICAL INCIDENTS SURVEY

To explore further the importance of goal setting in the work setting, Dr. Frank White conducted another study in two plants of a high-technology, multinational corporation on the East Coast. Seventy-one engineers, 50 managers, and 31 clerks were asked to describe a specific instance when they were especially productive and a specific instance when they were especially unproductive on their present jobs. Responses were classified according to a reliable coding scheme. Of primary interest here are the external events perceived by employees as being responsible for the high-productivity and low-productivity incidents. The results are shown in Table 3.2.

The first set of events—pursuing a specific goal, having a large amount of work, working under a deadline, or having an uninterrupted routine—accounted for more than half the high-productivity events. Similarly, the converse of these—goal blockage, having a small amount of

TABLE 3.1
Representative Field Studies of Goal Setting

Researcher(s)	Task	Duration of Study or of Significant Effects	Percent of Change in Performance*
Blumenfeld and Leidy	Servicing soft drink coolers	Unspecified	+27
Dockstader	Keypunching	3 mos.	+27
Ivancevich	Skilled technical jobs	9 mos.	+15
Ivancevich	Sales	9 mos.	+24
Kim and Hammer	Five telephone service jobs	3 mos.	+13
Latham and Baldes	Loading trucks	9 mos.†	+26
Latham and Yukl	Logging	2 mos.	+18
Latham and Yukl	Typing	5 weeks	+11
Migliore	Mass production	2 years	+16
Umstot, Bell, and Mitchell	Coding land parcels	1–2 days‡	+16

*Percentage of changes were obtained by subtracting pre-goal-setting performance from post-goal-setting performance and dividing by pre-goal-setting performance. Different experimental groups were combined where appropriate. If a control group was available, the percentage figure represents the difference of the percentage changes between the experimental and control groups. If multiple performance measures were used, the median improvement on all measures was used. The authors would like to thank Kena Feren and Vicki McCaleb for performing these calculations.
†Performance remained high for seven years.
‡Simulated organization.

work, lacking a deadline, and suffering work interruptions—accounted for nearly 60 percent of the low-productivity events. Note that the first set of four categories are all relevant to goal setting and the second set to a lack of goals or goal blockage. The goal category itself—that of pursuing an attainable goal or goal blockage—was the one most frequently used to describe high- and low-productivity incidents.

The next four categories, which are more pertinent to Frederick Herzberg's motivator–hygiene theory—task interest, responsibility, promotion, and recognition—are less important, accounting for 36.8 percent of the high-productivity incidents (the opposite of these four categories accounted for 19.1 percent of the lows). The remaining categories were even less important.

Employees were also asked to identify the responsible agent behind the events that had led to high and low productivity. In both cases, the employees themselves, their immediate supervisors, and the organization were the agents most frequently mentioned.

The concept of goal setting is a very simple one. Interestingly, however, we have gotten two contradictory types of reaction when the idea was introduced to managers. Some claimed it was so simple and self-evident that everyone, including themselves, already used it. This, we have found, is not true. Time after time we have gotten the following response from subordinates after goal setting was introduced: "This is the first time I knew what my supervisor expected of me on this job." Conversely, other managers have argued that the idea would not work, precisely *because* it is so simple (implying that something more radical and complex was needed). Again, results proved them wrong.

But these successes should not mislead managers into thinking that goal setting can be

TABLE 3.2

Events Perceived as Causing High and Low Productivity*

EVENT	PERCENTAGE OF TIMES EVENT CAUSED	
	HIGH PRODUCTIVITY	LOW PRODUCTIVITY
Goal pursuit/Goal blockage	17.1	23.0
Large amount of work/Small amount of work	12.5	19.0
Deadline or schedule/No deadline	15.1	3.3
Smooth work routine/Interrupted routine	5.9	14.5
Intrinsic/Extrinsic factors	50.6	59.8
Interesting task/Uninteresting task	17.1	11.2
Increased responsibility/Decreased responsibility	13.8	4.6
Anticipated promotion/Promotion denied	1.3	0.7
Verbal recognition/Criticism	4.6	2.6
People/Company conditions	36.8	19.1
Pleasant personal relationships/Unpleasant personal relationships	10.5	9.9
Anticipated pay increase/Pay increase denied	1.3	1.3
Pleasant working conditions/Unpleasant working conditions	0.7	0.7
Other (miscellaneous)	—	9.3

*$N = 152$ in this study by Frank White.

used without careful planning and forethought. Research and experience suggest that the best results are obtained when the following steps are followed:

Setting the Goal.

The goal set should have two main characteristics. First, it should be specific rather than vague: "Increase sales by 10 percent" rather than "Try to improve sales." Whenever possible, there should be a time limit for goal accomplishment: "Cut costs by 3 percent in the next six months."

Second, the goal should be challenging yet reachable. If accepted, difficult goals lead to better performance than do easy goals. In contrast, if the goals are perceived as unreachable, employees will not accept them. Nor will employees get a sense of achievement from pursuing goals that are never attained. Employees with low self-confidence or ability should be given more easily attainable goals than those with high self-confidence and ability.

There are at least five possible sources of input, aside from the individual's self-confidence and ability, that can be used to determine the particular goal to set for a given individual.

The scientific management approach pioneered by Frederick W. Taylor uses time and motion study to determine a fair day's work. This is probably the most objective technique available, but it can be used only where the task is reasonably repetitive and standardized. Another drawback is that this method often leads to employee resistance, especially in cases where the new standard is substantially higher than previous performance and where rate changes are made frequently.

More readily accepted, although less scientific than time and motion study, are standards based on the average past performance of employees. This method was used successfully in some of our field studies. Most employees consider this approach fair but, naturally, in cases where past performance is far below capacity, beating that standard will be extremely easy.

Since goal setting is sometimes simply a matter of judgment, another technique we have used is to allow the goal to be set jointly by supervisor and subordinate. The participative approach may be less scientific than time and motion study, but it does lead to ready acceptance by both employee and immediate supervisor in addition to promoting role clarity.

External constraints often affect goal setting, especially among managers. For example, the goal to produce an item at a certain price may be dictated by the actions of competitors, and deadlines may be imposed externally in line with contract agreements. Legal regulations, such as attaining a certain reduction in pollution levels by a certain date, may affect goal setting as well. In these cases, setting the goal is not so much the problem as is figuring out a method of reaching it.

Finally, organizational goals set by the board of directors or upper management will influence the goals set by employees at lower levels. This is the essence of the MBO process.

Another issue that needs to be considered when setting goals is whether they should be designed for individuals or for groups. Rensis Likert and a number of other human relations experts argue for group goal setting on grounds that it promotes cooperation and team spirit. But one could argue that individual goals better promote individual responsibility and make it easier to appraise individual performance. The degree of task interdependence involved would also be a factor to consider.

Obtaining Goal Commitment.

If goal setting is to work, then the manager must ensure that subordinates will accept and remain committed to the goals. Simple instruction backed by positive support and an absence of threats or intimidation were enough to ensure goal acceptance in most of our studies. Subordinates must perceive the goals as fair and reasonable and they must trust management, for if they perceive the goals as no more than a means of exploitation, they will be likely to reject the goals.

It may seem surprising that goal acceptance was achieved so readily in the field studies. Remember, however, that in all cases the employees were receiving wages or a salary (although these were not necessarily directly contingent on goal attainment). Pay in combination with the supervisor's benevolent authority and supportiveness were sufficient to bring about goal acceptance. Recent research indicates that whether goals are assigned or set participatively, supportiveness on the part of the immediate superior is critical. A supportive manager or supervisor does not use goals to threaten subordinates, but rather to clarify what is expected of them. His or her role is that of a helper and goal facilitator.

As noted earlier, the employee gets a feeling of pride and satisfaction from the experience of reaching a challenging but fair performance goal. Success in reaching a goal also tends to reinforce acceptance of future goals. Once goal setting is introduced, informal competition frequently arises among the employees. This further reinforces commitment and may lead employees to raise the goals spontaneously. A word of caution here, however: We do not recommend setting up formal competition, as this may lead employees to place individual goals ahead of company goals. This emphasis should be on accomplishing the task, getting the job done, not "beating" the other person.

When employees resist assigned goals, they generally do so for one of two reasons. First, they may think they are incapable of reaching the goal because they lack confidence, ability, knowledge, and the like. Second, they may not see any personal benefit—either in terms of personal pride or in terms of external rewards like money, promotion, recognition—in reaching assigned goals.

There are various methods of overcoming employee resistance to goals. One possibility is more training designed to raise the employee's level of skill and self-confidence. Allowing the subordinate to participate in setting the goal—deciding on the goal level—is another method. This was found most effective among uneducated and minority group employees, perhaps because it gave them a feeling of control over their fate. Offering monetary bonuses or other rewards (recognition, time off) for reaching goals may also help.

The last two methods may be especially useful where there is a history of labor-management conflict and where employees have become accustomed to a lower level of effort than currently considered acceptable. Group incentives may also encourage goal acceptance, especially where there is a group goal, or when considerable cooperation is required.

Providing Support Elements. A third step to take when introducing goal setting is to ensure the availability of necessary support ele-

ments. That is, the employee must be given adequate resources—money, equipment, time, help—as well as the freedom to utilize them in attaining goals, and company policies must not work to block goal attainment.

Before turning an employee loose with these resources, however, it's wise to do a quick check on whether conditions are optimum for reaching the goal set. First, the supervisor must make sure that the employee has sufficient ability and knowledge to be able to reach the goal. Motivation without knowledge is useless. This, of course, puts a premium on proper selection and training that requires that the supervisor know the capabilities of subordinates when goals are assigned. Asking an employee to formulate an action plan for reaching the goal, as

FIGURE 3.1
Goal-Setting Model

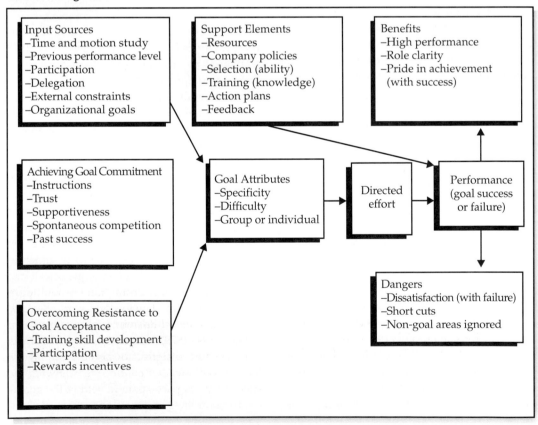

in MBO, is very useful, as it will indicate any knowledge deficiencies.

Second, the supervisor must ensure that the employee is provided with precise feedback so that he will know to what degree he's reaching or falling short of his goal and can thereupon adjust his level of effort or strategy accordingly. Recent research indicates that, while feedback is not a sufficient condition for improved performance, it is a necessary condition. A useful way to present periodic feedback is through the use of charts or graphs that plot performance over time.

Elements involved in taking the three steps described are shown in Figure 3.1, which illustrates in outline form our model of goal setting.

CONCLUSION

We believe that goal setting is a simple, straightforward, and highly effective technique for motivating employee performance. It is a basic technique, a method on which most other methods depend for their motivational effectiveness. The currently popular technique of behavior modification, for example, is mainly goal setting plus feedback, dressed up in academic terminology.

However, goal setting is no panacea. It will not compensate for underpayment of employees or for poor management. Used incorrectly, goal setting may cause rather than solve problems. If, for example, the goals set are unfair, arbitrary, or unreachable, dissatisfaction and poor performance may result. If difficult goals are set without proper quality controls, quantity may be achieved at the expense of quality. If pressure for immediate results is exerted without regard to how they are attained, short-term improvement may occur at the expense of long-run profits. That is, such pressure often triggers the use of expedient and ultimately costly methods—such as dishonesty, high-pressure tactics, postponing of maintenance expenses, and so on—to attain immediate results. Furthermore, performance goals are more easily set in some areas than in others. It's all too easy, for example, to concentrate on setting readily measured production goals and ignore employee development goals. Like any other management tool, goal setting works only when combined with good managerial judgment.

SELECTED BIBLIOGRAPHY

A summary of the early (mainly laboratory) research on goal setting may be found in E. A. Locke's "Toward a Theory of Task Motivation and Incentives" (*Organization Behavior and Human Performance*, May 1968). More recent reviews that include some of the early field studies are reported by G. P. Latham and G. A. Yukl's "Review of Research on the Application of Goal Setting in Organizations" (*Academy of Management Journal*, December 1975) and in R. M. Steers and L. W. Porter's "The Role of Task-Goal Attributes in Employee Performance" (*Psychological Bulletin*, July 1974).

An excellent historical discussion of management by objectives, including its relationship to goal-setting research, can be found in G. S. Odiorne's "MBO: A Backward Glance" (*Business Horizons,* October 1978).

A thorough review of the literature on participation, including the relationship of participation and goal setting, can be found in a chapter by E. A. Locke and D. M. Schweiger, "Participation in Decision-Making: One More Look," in B. M. Staw's edited work, *Research in Organizational Behavior* (Vol. 1, Greenwich, JAI Press, 1979). General Electric's famous research on the effect of participation in the appraisal interview is summarized in H. H. Meyer, E. Kay, and J. R. P. French, Jr.'s "Split Roles in Performance Appraisal" (*Harvard Business Review,* January–February 1965).

The relationship of goal setting to knowledge of results is discussed in E. A. Locke, N. Cartledge, and J. Koeppel's "Motivational Effects of Knowledge of Results: A Goal Setting Phenomenon?" (*Psychological Bulletin,* December 1968) and L. J. Becker's "Joint Effect of Feedback and Goal Setting on Performance: A Field Study of Residential Energy Conservation" (*Journal of Applied Psychology,* August 1978). Finally, the role of goal setting in virtually all theories of work motivation is documented in E. A. Locke's "The Ubiquity of the Technique of Goal Setting in Theories of and Approaches to Employee Motivation" (*Academy of Management Review,* July 1978).

4. On the Folly of Rewarding A, While Hoping for B

Steven Kerr

Whether dealing with monkeys, rats, or human beings, it is hardly controversial to state that most organisms seek information concerning what activities are rewarded and then seek to do (or at least pretend to do) those things, often to the virtual exclusion of activities not rewarded. The extent to which this occurs of course will depend on the perceived attractiveness of the rewards offered, but neither operant nor expectancy theorists would quarrel with the essence of this notion.

Nevertheless, numerous examples exist of reward systems that are fouled up in that behaviors which are rewarded are those which the rewarder is trying to discourage, while the behavior he desires is not being rewarded at all.

In an effort to understand and explain this phenomenon, this paper presents examples from society, from organizations in general, and from profit-making firms in particular. Data from a manufacturing company and information from an insurance firm are examined to demonstrate the consequences of such reward systems for the organizations involved, and possible reasons why such reward systems continue to exist are considered.

SOCIETAL EXAMPLES

Politics

Official goals are "purposely vague and general and do not indicate . . . the host of decisions that must be made among alternative ways of achieving official goals and the priority of multiple goals . . ." (8, p. 66). They usually may be relied on to offend absolutely no one, and in this sense can be considered high-acceptance, low-quality goals. An example might be "build better schools." Operative goals are higher in quality but lower in acceptance, since they specify where the money will come from, what alternative goals will be ignored, etc.

The American citizenry supposedly wants its candidates for public office to set forth operative goals, making their proposed programs "perfectly clear," specifying sources and uses of funds, etc. However, since operative goals are lower in acceptance, and since aspirants to public office need acceptance (from at least 50.1 percent of the people), most politicians prefer to speak only of official goals, at least until after the election. They of course would agree to speak at the operative level if "punished" for not doing so. The electorate could do this by refusing to support candidates who do not speak at the operative level.

Instead, however, the American voter typically punishes (withholds support from) candidates who frankly discuss where the money will come from, rewards politicians who speak only of official goals, but hopes that candidates (despite the reward system) will discuss the issues operatively. It is academic whether it was moral for Nixon, for example, to refuse to discuss his 1968 "secret plan" to end the Vietnam war, his 1972 operative goals concerning the lifting of price controls, the reshuffling of his cabinet, etc. The point is that the reward system made such refusal rational.

It seems worth mentioning that no manuscript can adequately define what is "moral" and what is not. However, examination of costs and benefits, combined with knowledge of what motivates a particular individual, often will suffice to determine what for him is "rational."[1] If the reward system is so designed that it is irrational to be moral, this does not necessarily mean that immorality will result. But is this not asking for trouble?

War

If some oversimplification may be permitted, let it be assumed that the primary goal of the organization (Pentagon, Luftwaffe, or whatever) is to win. Let it be assumed further that the primary goal of most individuals on the front lines is to get home alive. Then there appears to be an important conflict in goals— personally rational behavior by those at the bottom will endanger goal attainment by those at the top.

But not necessarily! It depends on how the reward system is set up. The Vietnam war was indeed a study of disobedience and rebellion, with terms such as "fragging" (killing one's own commanding officer) and "search and evade" becoming part of the military vocabulary. The difference in subordinates' acceptance of authority between World War II and Vietnam is reported to be considerable, and veterans of the Second World War often have been quoted as being outraged at the mutinous actions of many American soldiers in Vietnam.

Consider, however, some critical differences in the reward system in use during the two conflicts. What did the GI in World War II want? To go home. And when did he get to go home? When the war was won! If he disobeyed the orders to clean out the trenches and take the hills, the war would not be won and he would not go home. Furthermore, what were his chances of attaining his goal (getting home alive) if he obeyed the orders compared to his chances if he did not? What is being suggested is that the rational soldier in World War II, *whether patriotic or not*, probably found it expedient to obey.

Consider the reward system in use in Vietnam. What did the man at the bottom want? To go home. And when did he get to go home? When his tour of duty was over! This

was the case *whether or not* the war was won. Furthermore, concerning the relative chance of getting home alive by obeying orders compared to the chance if they were disobeyed, it is worth noting that a mutineer in Vietnam was far more likely to be assigned rest and rehabilitation (on the assumption that fatigue was the cause) than he was to suffer any negative consequence.

In his description of the "zone of indifference," Barnard stated that "a person can and will accept a communication as authoritative only when . . . at the time of his decision, he believes it to be compatible with his personal interests as a whole" (1, p. 165). In light of the reward system used in Vietnam, would it not have been personally irrational for some orders to have been obeyed? Was not the military implementing a system which *rewarded* disobedience, while *hoping* that soldiers (despite the reward system) would obey orders?

Medicine

Theoretically, a physician can make either of two types of errors, and intuitively one seems as bad as the other. A doctor can pronounce a patient sick when he is actually well, thus causing him needless anxiety and expense, curtailment of enjoyable foods and activities, and even physical danger by subjecting him to needless medication and surgery. Alternatively, a doctor can label a sick person well and thus avoid treating what may be a serious, even fatal ailment. It might be natural to conclude that physicians seek to minimize both types of error.

Such a conclusion would be wrong.[2] It is estimated that numerous Americans are presently afflicted with iatrogenic (physician *caused*) illnesses (9). This occurs when the doctor is approached by someone complaining of a few stray symptoms. The doctor classifies and organizes these symptoms, gives them a name, and obligingly tells the patient what further symptoms may be expected. This information often acts as a self-fulfilling prophecy, with the result that from that day on the patient for all practical purposes is sick.

Why does this happen? Why are physicians so reluctant to sustain a type 2 error (pronouncing a sick person well) that they will tolerate many type 1 errors? Again, a look at the reward system is needed. The punishments for a type 2 error are real: guilt, embarrassment, and the threat of lawsuit and scandal. On the other hand, a type 1 error (labeling a well person sick) "is sometimes seen as sound clinical practice, indicating a healthy conservative approach to medicine" (9, p. 69). Type 1 errors also are likely to generate increased income and a stream of steady customers who, being well in a limited physiological sense, will not embarrass the doctor by dying abruptly.

Fellow physicians and the general public therefore are really *rewarding* type 1 errors and at the same time *hoping* fervently that doctors will try not to make them.

GENERAL ORGANIZATIONAL EXAMPLES

Rehabilitation Centers and Orphanages

In terms of the prime beneficiary classification (2, p. 42) organizations such as these are supposed to exist for the "public-in-contact," that is, clients. The orphanage therefore theoretically is interested in placing as many children as possible in good homes. However, often orphanages surround themselves with so many rules concerning adoption that it is nearly impossible to pry a child out of the place. Orphanages may deny adoption unless the applicants are a married couple, both of the same religion as the child, without history of emotional or vocational instability, with a specified minimum income and a private room for the child, etc.

If the primary goal is to place children in good homes, then the rules ought to constitute means toward that goal. Goal displacement results when these "means become ends-in-themselves that displace the original goals" (2, p. 229).

To some extent these rules are required by law. But the influence of the reward system on the orphanage's management should not be ignored. Consider, for example, that the:

1. Number of children enrolled often is the most important determinant of the size of the allocated budget.
2. Number of children under the director's care also will affect the size of his staff.
3. Total organizational size will determine largely the director's prestige at the annual convention, in the community, etc.

Therefore, to the extent that staff size, total budget, and personal prestige are valued by the orphanage's executive personnel, it becomes rational for them to make it difficult for children to be adopted. After all, who wants to be the director of the smallest orphanage in the state?

If the reward system errs in the opposite direction, paying off only for placements, extensive goal displacement again is likely to result. A common example of vocational rehabilitation in many states, for example, consists of placing someone in a job for which he has little interest and few qualifications, for two months or so, and then "rehabilitating" him again in another position. Such behavior is quite consistent with the prevailing reward system, which pays off for the number of individuals placed in any position for 60 days or more. Rehabilitation counselors also confess to competing with one another to place relatively skilled clients, sometimes ignoring persons with few skills who would be harder to place. Extensively disabled clients find that counselors often prefer to work with those whose disabilities are less severe.[3]

Universities

Society *hopes* that teachers will not neglect their teaching responsibilities but *rewards* them almost entirely for research and publications. This is most true at the large and prestigious universities. Clichés such as "good research and good teaching go together" notwithstanding, professors often find that they must choose between teaching and research oriented activities when allocating their time. Rewards for good teaching usually are limited to outstanding teacher awards, which are given to only a small percentage of good teachers and which usually bestow little money and fleeting prestige. Punishments for poor teaching also are rare.

Rewards for research and publications, on the other hand, and punishments for failure to accomplish these, are commonly administered by universities at which teachers are employed. Furthermore, publication oriented resumés usually will be well received at other universities, whereas teaching credentials, harder to document and quantify, are much less transferable. Consequently, it is rational for university teachers to concentrate on research, even if to the detriment of teaching and at the expense of their students.

By the same token, it is rational for students to act based upon the goal displacement which has occurred within universities concerning what they are rewarded for. If it is assumed that a primary goal of a university is to transfer knowledge from teacher to student, then grades become identifiable as a means toward that goal, serving as motivational, control, and feedback devices to expedite the knowledge transfer. Instead, however, the grades themselves have become much more important for entrance to graduate school, successful employment, tuition refunds, parental respect, etc., than the knowledge or lack of knowledge they are supposed to signify.

It therefore should come as no surprise that information has surfaced in recent years concerning fraternity files for examinations, term paper writing services, organized cheating at the service academies, and the like. Such activities constitute a personally rational response to a reward system which pays off for grades rather than knowledge.

BUSINESS RELATED EXAMPLES
Ecology
Assume that the president of XYZ Corporation is confronted with the following alternatives:

1. Spend $11 million for antipollution equipment to keep from poisoning fish in the river adjacent to the plant; or

2. Do nothing, in violation of the law, and assume a one-in-ten chance of being caught, with a resultant $1 million fine plus the necessity of buying the equipment.

Under this not unrealistic set of choices it requires no linear program to determine that XYZ Corporation can minimize its probabilities by flouting the law. Add the fact that XYZ's president is probably being rewarded (by creditors, stockholders, and other salient parts of his task environment) according to criteria totally unrelated to the number of fish poisoned, and his probable course of action becomes clear.

Evaluation of Training
It is axiomatic that those who care about a firm's well-being should insist that the organization get fair value for its expenditures. Yet it is commonly known that firms seldom bother to evaluate a new GRID, MBO, job enrichment program, or whatever, to see if the company is getting its money's worth. Why? Certainly it is not because people have not pointed out that this situation exists; numerous practitioner oriented articles are written each year to just this point.

The individuals (whether in personnel, manpower planning, or wherever) who normally would be responsible for conducting such evaluations are the same ones often charged with introducing the change effort in the first place. Having convinced top management to spend the money, they usually are quite animated afterwards in collecting arigorous vignettes and anecdotes about how successful the program was. The last thing many desire is a formal, systematic, and revealing evaluation. Although members of top management may actually *hope* for such systematic evaluation, their reward systems continue to *reward* ignorance in this area. And if the personnel department abdicates its responsibility, who is to step into the breach? The change agent himself? Hardly! He is likely to be too busy collecting anecdotal "evidence" of his own, for use with his next client.

Miscellaneous

Many additional examples could be cited of systems which in fact are rewarding behaviors other than those supposedly desired by the rewarder. A few of these are described briefly below.

Most coaches disdain to discuss individual accomplishments, preferring to speak of teamwork, proper attitude, and a one-for-all spirit. Usually, however, rewards are distributed according to individual performance. The college basketball player who feeds his teammates instead of shooting will not compile impressive scoring statistics and is less likely to be drafted by the pros. The ballplayer who hits to right field to advance the runners will win neither the batting nor home run titles and will be offered smaller raises. It therefore is rational for players to think of themselves first and the team second.

In business organizations where rewards are dispensed for unit performance or for individual goals achieved without regard for overall effectiveness, similar attitudes often are observed. Under most Management by Objectives (MBO) systems, goals in areas where quantification is difficult often go unspecified. The organization therefore often is in a position where it *hopes* for employee effort in the areas of team building, interpersonal relations, creativity, etc., but it formally *rewards* none of these. In cases where promotions and raises are formally tied to MBO, the system itself contains a paradox in that it "asks employees to set challenging, risky goals, only to face smaller paychecks and possibly damaged careers if these goals are not accomplished" (5, p. 40).

It is *hoped* that administrators will pay attention to long-run costs and opportunities and will institute programs which will bear fruit later on. However, many organizational reward systems pay off for short-run sales and earnings only. Under such circumstances it is personally rational for officials to sacrifice long-term growth and profit (by selling off equipment and property, or by stifling research and development) for short-term advantages. This probably is most pertinent in the public sector, with the

result that many public officials are unwilling to implement programs which will not show benefits by election time.

As a final, clear-cut example of a fouled-up reward system, consider the cost-plus contract or its next of kin, the allocation of next year's budget as a direct function of this year's expenditures. It probably is conceivable that those who award such budgets and contracts really hope for economy and prudence in spending. It is obvious, however, that adopting the proverb "to him who spends shall more be given," rewards not economy, but spending itself.

TWO COMPANIES' EXPERIENCES
A Manufacturing Organization

A Midwestern manufacturer of industrial goods had been troubled for some time by aspects of its organizational climate it believed dysfunctional. For research purposes, interviews were conducted with many employees, and a questionnaire was administered on a company-wide basis, including plants and offices in several American and Canadian locations. The company strongly encouraged employee participation in the survey and made available time and space during the workday for completion of the instrument. All employees in attendance during the day of the survey completed the questionnaire. All instruments were collected directly by the researcher, who personally administered each session. Since no one employed by the firm handled the questionnaires, and since respondent names were not asked for, it seems likely that the pledge of anonymity given was believed.

A modified version of the Expect Approval scale (7) was included as part of the questionnaire. The instrument asked respondents to indicate the degree of approval or disapproval they could expect if they performed each of the described actions. A seven point Likert scale was used, with one indicating that the action would probably bring strong disapproval and seven signifying likely strong approval.

Although normative data for this scale from studies of other organizations are unavailable, it is possible to examine fruitfully the data obtained from this survey in several ways. First, it may be worth noting that the questionnaire data corresponded closely to information gathered through interviews. Furthermore, as can be seen from the results summarized in Table 4.1,

TABLE 4.1
Summary of Two Divisions' Data Relevant to Conforming to Risk-Avoidance Behaviors (extent to which subjects expect approval)

			PERCENTAGE OF WORKERS RESPONDING			
DIMENSION	ITEM	DIVISION AND SAMPLE	TOTAL RESPONSES	1, 2, OR 3 DISAPPROVAL	4	5, 6, OR 7 APPROVAL
Risk avoidance	Making a risky decision based on the best information available at the time, but which turns out wrong	A, levels 1–4 (lowest)	127	61	25	14
		A, levels 5–8	172	46	31	23
		A, levels 9, and above	17	41	30	30
		B, levels 1–4 (lowest)	31	58	26	16
		B, levels 5–8	19	42	42	16
		B, levels 9 and above	10	50	20	30
	Setting extremely high and challenging standards and goals and then narrowly failing to make them	A, levels 1–4	122	47	28	25
		A, levels 5–8	168	33	26	41
		A, levels 9+	17	24	6	70
		B, levels 1–4	31	48	23	29
		B, levels 5–8	18	17	33	50
		B, levels 9+	10	30	0	70
	Setting goals which are extremely easy to make and then making them	A, levels 1–4	124	35	30	35
		A, levels 5–8	171	47	27	26
		A, levels 9+	17	70	24	6
		B, levels 1–4	31	58	26	16
		B, levels 5–8	19	63	16	21
		B, levels 9+	10	80	0	20
Conformity	Being a "yes man" and always agreeing with the boss	A, levels 1–4	126	46	17	37
		A, levels 5–8	180	54	14	31
		A, levels 9+	17	88	12	0
		B, levels 1–4	32	53	28	19
		B, levels 5–8	19	68	21	11
		B, levels 9+	10	80	10	10
	Always going along with the majority	A, levels 1–4	125	40	25	35
		A, levels 5–8	173	47	21	32
		A, levels 9+	17	70	12	18
		B, levels 1–4	31	61	23	16
		B, levels 5–8	19	68	11	21
		B, levels 9+	10	80	10	10
	Being careful to stay on the good side of everyone, so that everyone agrees that you are a great guy	A, levels 1–4	124	40	18	37
		A, levels 5–8	173	47	22	33
		A, levels 9+	17	70	6	30
		B, levels 1–4	31	61	23	23
		B, levels 5–8	19	68	11	16
		B, levels 9+	10	80	10	10

sizable differences between various work units, and between employees at different job levels within the same work unit, were obtained. This suggests that response bias effects (social desirability in particular loomed as a potential concern) are not likely to be severe.

Most importantly, comparisons between scores obtained on the Expect Approval scale and a statement of problems which were the reason for the survey revealed that the same behaviors which managers in each division thought dysfunctional were those which lower-level employees claimed were rewarded. As compared to job levels 1 to 8 in Division B (see Table 4.1), those in Division A claimed a much higher acceptance by management of "conforming" activities. Between 31 and 37 percent of Division A employees at levels 1–8 stated that going along with the majority, agreeing with the boss, and staying on everyone's good side brought approval; only once (level 5–8 responses to one of the three items) did a majority suggest that such actions would generate disapproval.

Furthermore, responses from Division A workers at levels 1–4 indicate that behaviors geared toward risk avoidance were as likely to be rewarded as to be punished. Only at job levels 9 and above was it apparent that the reward system was positively reinforcing behaviors desired by top management. Overall, the same "tendencies toward conservatism and apple-polishing at the lower levels" which divisional management had complained about during the interviews were those claimed by subordinates to be the most rational course of action in light of the existing reward system. Management apparently was not getting the behaviors it was *hoping* for, but it certainly was getting the behaviors it was perceived by subordinates to be *rewarding*.

An Insurance Firm

The Group Health Claims Division of a large eastern insurance company provides another rich illustration of a reward system which reinforces behaviors not desired by top management.

Attempting to measure and reward accuracy in paying surgical claims, the firm systematically keeps track of the number of returned checks and letters of complaint received from policyholders. However, underpayments are likely to provoke cries of outrage from the insured, while overpayments often are accepted in courteous silence. Since it often is impossible to tell from the physician's statement which of two surgical procedures, with different allowable benefits, was performed, and since writing for clarifications will interfere with other standards used by the firm concerning "percentage of claims paid within two days of receipt," the new hire in more than one claims section is soon acquainted with the informal norm: "When in doubt, pay it out!"

The situation would be even worse were it not for the fact that other features of the firm's reward system tend to neutralize those described. For example, annual "merit" increases are given to all employees, in one of the following three amounts:

1. If the worker is "outstanding" (a select category, into which no more than two employees per section may be placed): 5 percent.
2. If the worker is "above average" (normally all workers not "outstanding" are so rated); 4 percent.
3. If the worker commits gross acts of negligence and irresponsibility for which he might be discharged in many other companies: 3 percent.

Now, since (a) the difference between the 5 percent theoretically attainable through hard work and the 4 percent attainable merely by living until the review date is small and (b) since insurance firms seldom dispense much of a salary increase in cash (rather, the worker's insurance benefits increase, causing him to be further overinsured), many employees are rather indifferent to the possibility of obtaining the extra one percent reward and therefore tend to ignore the norm concerning indiscriminate payments.

However, most employees are not indifferent to the rule which states that, should absences or latenesses total three or more in any six-month period, the entire 4 or 5 percent due at the next "merit" review must be forfeited. In this sense the firm may be described as *hoping* for performance, while *rewarding* attendance. What it gets, of course, is attendance. (If the absence–lateness rule appears to the reader to be stringent, it really is not. The company counts "times" rather than "days" absent, and a ten-day absence therefore counts the same as one lasting two days. A worker in danger of accumulating a third absence within six months merely has to remain ill (away from work) during his second absence until his first absence is more than six months old. The limiting factor is that at some point his salary ceases, and his sickness benefits take over. This usually is sufficient to get the young workers to return, but for those with 20 or more years' service, the company provides sickness benefits of 90 percent of normal salary, tax-free! Therefore. . . .)

CAUSES

Extremely diverse instances of systems which reward behavior A although the rewarder apparently hopes for behavior B have been given. These are useful to illustrate the breadth and magnitude of the phenomenon, but the diversity increases the difficulty of determining commonalities and establishing causes. However, four general factors may be pertinent to an explanation of why fouled up reward systems seem to be so prevalent.

Fascination with an "Objective" Criterion

It has been mentioned elsewhere that:

Most "objective" measures of productivity are objective only in that their subjective elements are (a) determined in advance, rather than coming into play at the time of the formal evaluation, and (b) well concealed on the rating instrument itself. Thus industrial firms seeking to devise objective rating systems first decide, in an arbitrary manner, what dimensions are to be rated, . . . usually including some items having little to do with organizational effectiveness while excluding others that do. Only then does

Personnel Division churn out official-looking documents on which all dimensions chosen to be rated are assigned point values, categories, or whatever (6, p. 92).

Nonetheless, many individuals seek to establish simple, quantifiable standards against which to measure and reward performance. Such efforts may be successful in highly predictable areas within an organization but are likely to cause goal displacement when applied anywhere else. Overconcern with attendance and lateness in the insurance firm and with the number of people placed in the vocational rehabilitation division may have been largely responsible for the problems described in those organizations.

Overemphasis on Highly Visible Behaviors

Difficulties often stem from the fact that some parts of the task are highly visible while other parts are not. For example, publications are easier to demonstrate than teaching, and scoring baskets and hitting home runs are more readily observable than feeding teammates and advancing base runners. Similarly, the adverse consequences of pronouncing a sick person well are more visible than those sustained by labeling a well person sick. Team-building and creativity are other examples of behaviors which may not be rewarded simply because they are hard to observe.

Hypocrisy

In some of the instances described the rewarder may have been getting the desired behavior, notwithstanding claims that the behavior was not desired. This may be true, for example, of management's attitude toward apple-polishing in the manufacturing firm (a behavior which subordinates felt was rewarded, despite management's avowed dislike of the practice). This also may explain politician's unwillingness to revise the penalties for disobedience of ecology laws, and the failure of top management to devise reward systems which would cause systematic evaluation of training and development programs.

Emphasis on Morality or Equity Rather than Efficiency

Sometimes consideration of other factors prevents the establishment of a system which rewards behaviors desired by the rewarder. The felt obligation of many Americans to vote for one candidate or another, for example, may impair their ability to withhold support from politicians who refuse to discuss the issues. Similarly, the concern for spreading the risks and costs of wartime military service may outweigh the advantage to be obtained by committing personnel to combat until the war is over.

It should be noted that only with respect to the first two causes are reward systems really paying off for other than desired behaviors. In the case of the third and fourth causes the system *is* rewarding behaviors desired by the rewarder, and the systems are fouled up only from the standpoints of those who believe the rewarder's public statements (cause 3), or those who seek to maximize efficiency rather than other outcomes (cause 4).

CONCLUSIONS

Modern organization theory requires a recognition that the members of organizations and society possess divergent goals and motives. It therefore is unlikely that managers and their subordinates will seek the same outcomes. Three possible remedies for this potential problem are suggested.

Selection

It is theoretically possible for organizations to employ only those individuals whose goals and motives are wholly consonant with those of management. In such cases the same behaviors judged by subordinates to be rational would be perceived by management as desirable. State-of-the-art reviews of selection techniques, however, provide scant grounds for hope that such an approach would be successful (for example, see 12).

Training

Another theoretical alternative is for the organization to admit those employees whose goals are not consonant with those of management and

then, through training, socialization, or whatever, alter employee goals to make them consonant. However, research on the effectiveness of such training programs, though limited, provides further grounds for pessimism (for example, see 3).

Altering the Reward System

What would have been the result if:

1. Nixon had been assured by his advisors that he could not win reelection except by discussing the issues in detail?
2. Physicians' conduct was subjected to regular examination by review boards for type 1 errors (calling healthy people ill) and to penalties (fines, censure, etc.) for errors of either type?
3. The President of XYZ Corporation had to choose between (*a*) spending $11 million dollars for antipollution equipment, and (*b*) incurring a 50-50 chance of going to jail for five years?

Managers who complain that their workers are not motivated might do well to consider the possibility that they have installed reward systems which are paying off for behaviors other than those they are seeking. This, in part, is what happened in Vietnam, and this is what regularly frustrates societal efforts to bring about honest politicians, civic-minded managers, etc. This certainly is what happened in both the manufacturing and the insurance companies.

A first step for such managers might be to find out what behaviors currently are being rewarded. Perhaps an instrument similar to that used in the manufacturing firm could be useful for this purpose. Chances are excellent that these managers will be surprised by what they find—that their firms are not rewarding what they assume they are. In fact, such undesirable behavior by organizational members as they have observed may be explained largely by the reward systems in use.

This is not to say that all organizational behavior is determined by formal rewards and punishments. Certainly it is true that in the absence of formal reinforcement some soldiers will be patriotic, some presidents will be ecology minded, and some orphanage directors will care about children. The point, however, is that in such cases the rewarder is not *causing* the behaviors desired but is only a fortunate bystander. For an organization to *act* upon its members, the formal reward system should positively reinforce desired behaviors, not constitute an obstacle to be overcome.

It might be wise to underscore the obvious fact that there is nothing really new in what has been said. In both theory and practice these matters have been mentioned before. Thus in many states Good Samaritan laws have been installed to protect doctors who stop to assist a stricken motorist. In states without such laws it is commonplace for doctors to refuse to stop, for fear of involvement in a subsequent lawsuit.

In college basketball additional penalties have been instituted against players who foul their opponents deliberately. It has long been argued by Milton Friedman and others that penalties should be altered so as to make it irrational to disobey the ecology laws, and so on.

By altering the reward system the organization escapes the necessity of selecting only desirable people or of trying to alter undesirable ones. In Skinnerian terms (as described in 11, p. 704), "As for responsibility and goodness—as commonly defined—no one . . . would want or need them. They refer to a man's behaving well despite the absence of positive reinforcement that is obviously sufficient to explain it. Where such reinforcement exists, 'no one needs goodness.' "

REFERENCES

1. Barnard, Chester I. *The functions of the executive.* Cambridge, Mass.: Harvard University Press, 1964.
2. Blau, Peter M., and Scott, W. Richard. *Formal organizations.* San Francisco: Chandler, 1962.
3. Fiedler, Fred E. Predicting the effects of leadership training and experience from the contingency model, *Journal of Applied Psychology,* 1972, 56:114–19.
4. Garland, L. H. Studies of the accuracy of diagnostic procedures, *American Journal Roentgenological, Radium Therapy Nuclear Medicine,* 1959, 82:25–38.
5. Kerr, Steven. Some modifications in MBO as an OD strategy, *Academy of Management Proceedings,* 1973:39–42.
6. Kerr, Steven. What price objectivity? *American Sociologist,* 1973, 8:92–93.
7. Litwin, G. H., and Stringer, R. A., Jr. *Motivation and organizational climate.* Boston: Harvard University Press, 1968.
8. Perrow, Charles. The analysis of goals in complex organizations, in A. Etzioni (ed.), *Readings on modern organizations.* Englewood Cliffs, N.J.: Prentice Hall, 1969.
9. Scheff, Thomas J. Decision rules, types of error, and their consequences in medical diagnosis, in F. Massarik and P. Ratoosh (eds.), *Mathematical explorations in behavioral science.* Homewood, Ill.: Richard D. Irwin, Inc., 1965.
10. Simon, Herbert A. *Administrative behavior.* New York: Free Press, 1957.
11. Swanson, G. E. Review symposium: Beyond freedom and dignity, *American Journal of Sociology,* 1972, 78:702–705.
12. Webster, E. *Decision making in the employment interview.* Montreal Industrial Relations Center, McGill University, 1964.

NOTES

1. In Simon's (10, pp. 76–77) terms, a decision is "subjectively rational" if it maximizes an individual's valued outcomes so far as his knowledge permits. A decision is "personally rational" if it is oriented toward the individual's goals.

2. In one study (4) of 14,867 films for signs of tuberculosis, 1,216 positive readings turned out to be clinically negative; only 24 negative readings proved clinically active, a ratio of 50 to 1.

3. Personal interviews conducted during 1972–1973.

5. A New Strategy for Job Enrichment

J. Richard Hackman/Greg Oldham/Robert Janson/Kenneth Purdy

Practitioners of job enrichment have been living through a time of excitement, even euphoria. Their craft has moved from the psychology and management journals to the front page and the Sunday supplement. Job enrichment, which began with the pioneering work of Herzberg and his associates, originally was intended as a means to increase the motivation and satisfaction of people at work—and to improve productivity in the bargain.[1-5] Now it is being acclaimed in the popular press as a cure for problems ranging from inflation to drug abuse.

Much current writing about job enrichment is enthusiastic, sometimes even messianic, about what it can accomplish. But the hard questions of exactly what should be done to improve jobs, and how, tend to be glossed over. Lately, because the harder questions have not been dealt with adequately, critical winds have begun to blow. Job enrichment has been described as yet another "management fad," as "nothing new," even as a fraud. And reports of job-enrichment failures are beginning to appear in management and psychology journals.

This article attempts to redress the excesses that have characterized some of the recent writings about job enrichment. As the technique increases in popularity as a management tool, top managers inevitably will find themselves making decisions about its use. The intent of this paper is to help both managers and behavioral scientists become better able to make those decisions on a solid basis of fact and data.

Succinctly stated, we present here a new strategy for going about the redesign of work. The strategy is based on three years of collaborative work and cross-fertilization among the authors—two of whom are academic researchers and two of whom are active practitioners in job enrichment. Our approach is new, but it has been tested in many organizations. It draws on the contributions of both management practice and psychological theory, but it is firmly in the middle ground between them. It builds on and complements previous work by Herzberg and others, but provides for the first time a set of tools for *diagnosing* existing jobs—and a map for translating the diagnostic results into specific action steps for change.

What we have, then, is the following:

1. A theory that specifies when people will get personally "turned on" to their work. The theory shows what kinds of jobs are most likely to generate excitement and commitment about work, and what kinds of employees it works best for.
2. A set of action steps for job enrichment based on the theory, which prescribe in concrete terms what to do to make jobs more motivating for the people who do them.
3. Evidence that the theory holds water and that it can be used to bring about measurable—and sometimes dramatic—improvements in employee work behavior, in job satisfaction and in the financial performance of the organizational unit involved.

THE THEORY BEHIND THE STRATEGY
What Makes People Get Turned on to Their Work?

For workers who are really prospering in their jobs, work is likely to be a lot like play. Consider, for example, a golfer at a driving range, practicing to get rid of a hook. His activity is *meaningful* to him; he has chosen to do it because he gets a "kick" from testing his skills by playing the game. He knows that he alone is *responsible* for what happens when he hits the ball. And he has *knowledge of the results* within a few seconds.

Behavioral scientists have found that the three "psychological states" experienced by the golfer in the above example also are critical in determining a person's motivation and satisfaction on the job.

1. *Experienced meaningfulness:* The individual must perceive his work as worthwhile or important by some system of values he accepts.
2. *Experienced responsibility:* He must believe that he personally is accountable for the outcomes of his efforts.
3. *Knowledge of results:* He must be able to determine, on some fairly regular basis, whether or not the outcomes of his work are satisfactory.

When these three conditions are present, a person tends to feel very good about himself when he performs well. And those good feelings will prompt him to try to continue to do well—so he can continue to earn the positive feelings in the future. That is what is meant by "internal motivation"—being turned on to one's work because of the positive internal feelings that are generated by doing well, rather than being dependent on external factors (such as incentive pay or compliments from the boss) for the motivation to work effectively.

What if one of the three psychological states is missing? Motivation drops markedly. Suppose, for example, that our golfer has settled in at the driving range to practice for a couple of hours. Suddenly a fog drifts in over the range. He can no longer see if the ball starts to tail off to the left a hundred yards out. The satisfaction he got from hitting straight down the middle— and the motivation to try to correct something whenever he didn't—are both gone. If the fog stays, it's likely that he soon will be packing up his clubs.

The relationship between the three psychological states and on-the-job outcomes is illus-trated in Figure 5.1. When all three are high, then internal work motivation, job satisfaction, and work quality are high, and absenteeism and turnover are low.

What Job Characteristics Make It Happen?

Recent research has identified five "core" characteristics of jobs that elicit the psychological states described above.[6–8] These five core job dimensions provide the key to objectively measuring jobs and to changing them so that they have high potential for motivating people who do them.

Toward Meaningful Work. Three of the five core dimensions contribute to a job's meaningfulness for the worker:

1. Skill variety—the degree to which a job requires the worker to perform activities that challenge his skills and abilities. When even a single skill is involved, there is at least a seed of potential meaningfulness. When several are involved, the job has the potential of appealing to more of the whole person, and also of avoiding the monotony of performing the same task repeatedly, no matter how much skill it may require.
2. Task identity—the degree to which the job requires completion of a "whole" and identifiable piece of work—doing a job from beginning to end with a visible outcome. For example, it is clearly more meaningful to an employee to build complete toasters than to attach electrical cord after electrical cord, especially if he never sees a completed toaster. (Note that the whole job, in this example, probably would involve greater skill variety as well as task identity.)
3. Task significance—the degree to which the job has a substantial and perceivable impact on the lives of other people, whether in the immediate organization or the world at large. The worker who tightens nuts on aircraft brake assemblies is more likely to perceive his work as significant than the worker who fills small boxes with paper clips—even though the skill levels involved may be comparable.

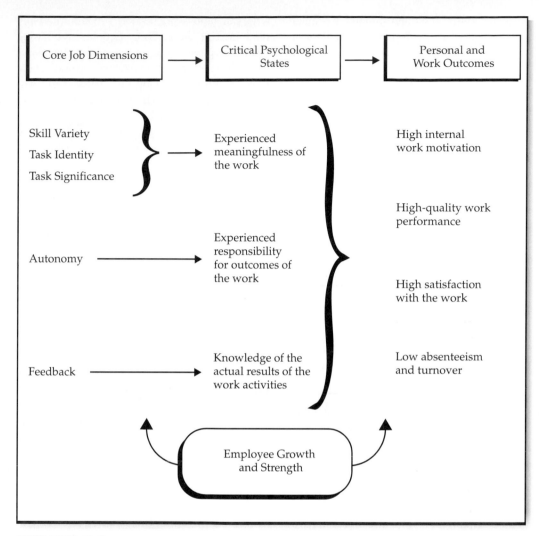

FIGURE 5.1
Relationships Among Core Job Dimensions, Critical Psychological States, and On-the-Job Outcomes

Each of these three job dimensions represents an important route to experienced meaningfulness. If the job is high in all three, the worker is quite likely to experience his job as very meaningful. It is not necessary, however, for a job to be very high in all three dimensions. If the job is low in any one of them, there will be a drop in overall experienced meaningfulness. But even when two dimensions are low the worker may find the job meaningful if the third is high enough.

Toward Personal Responsibility. A fourth core dimension leads a worker to experience increased responsibility in his job. This is *autonomy,* the degree to which the job gives the worker freedom, independence, and discretion in scheduling work and determining how he will carry it out. People in highly autonomous jobs know that they are personally responsible for successes and failures. To the extent that their autonomy is high, then, how the work goes will be felt to depend more on the individual's own efforts and initiatives—rather than on detailed instructions from the boss or from a manual of job procedures.

Toward Knowledge of Results.
The fifth and last core dimension is *feedback*. This is the degree to which a worker, in carrying out the work activities required by the job, gets information about the effectiveness of his efforts. Feedback is most powerful when it comes directly from the work itself—for example, when a worker has the responsibility for gauging and otherwise checking a component he has just finished, and learns in the process that he has lowered his reject rate by meeting specifications more consistently.

The Overall "Motivating Potential" of a Job.
Figure 5.1 shows how the five core dimensions combine to affect the psychological states that are critical in determining whether or not an employee will be internally motivated to work effectively. Indeed, when using an instrument to be described later, it is possible to compute a "motivating potential score" (MPS) for any job. The MPS provides a single summary index of the degree to which the objective characteristics of the job will prompt high internal work motivation. Following the theory outlined above, a job high in motivating potential must be high in at least one (and hopefully more) of the three dimensions that lead to experienced meaningfulness and high in both autonomy and feedback as well. The MPS provides a quantitative index of the degree to which this is in fact the case (see Appendix for detailed formula). As will be seen later, the MPS can be very useful in diagnosing jobs and in assessing the effectiveness of job-enrichment activities.

Does the Theory Work for Everybody?
Unfortunately not. Not everyone is able to become internally motivated in his work, even when the motivating potential of a job is very high indeed.

Research has shown that the *psychological needs* of people are very important in determining who can (and who cannot) become internally motivated at work. Some people have strong needs for personal accomplishment, for learning and developing themselves beyond where they are now, for being stimulated and challenged, and so on. These people are high in "growth-need strength."

Figure 5.2 shows diagrammatically the proposition that individual growth needs have the power to moderate the relationship between the characteristics of jobs and work outcomes. Many workers with high growth needs will turn on eagerly when they have jobs that are high in the core dimensions. Workers whose growth needs are not so strong may respond less eagerly—or, at first, even balk at being "pushed" or stretched too far.

Psychologists who emphasize human potential argue that everyone has within him at least a spark of the need to grow and develop personally. Steadily accumulating evidence shows, however, that unless that spark is pretty strong, chances are it will get snuffed out by one's experiences in typical organizations. So, a person who has worked for twenty years in stultifying jobs may find it difficult or impossible to become internally motivated overnight when given the opportunity.

We should be cautious, however, about creating rigid categories of people based on their measured growth-need strength at any particular time. It is true that we can predict from these measures who is likely to become internally motivated on a job and who will be less willing or able to do so. But what we do not know yet is whether or not the growth-need "spark" can be rekindled for those individuals who have had their growth needs dampened by years of growth-depressing experience in their organizations.

Since it is often the organization that is responsible for currently low levels of growth desires, we believe that the organization also should provide the individual with the chance to reverse that trend whenever possible, even if that means putting a person in a job where he may be "stretched" more than he wants to be. He can always move back later to the old job—and in the

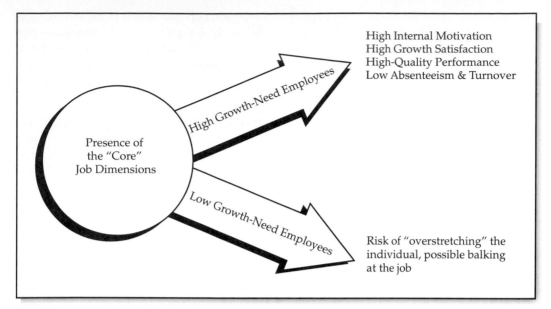

FIGURE 5.2
The Moderating Effect of Employee Growth-Need Strength

meantime the embers of his growth needs just might burst back into flame, to his surprise and pleasure, and for the good of the organization.

FROM THEORY TO PRACTICE: A TECHNOLOGY FOR JOB ENRICHMENT

When job enrichment fails, it often fails because of inadequate *diagnosis* of the target job and employees' reactions to it. Often, for example, job enrichment is assumed by management to be a solution to "people problems" on the job and is implemented even though there has been no diagnostic activity to indicate that the root of the problem is in fact how the work is designed. At other times, some diagnosis is made—but it provides no concrete guidance about what specific aspects of the job require change. In either case, the success of job enrichment may wind up depending more on the quality of the intuition of the change agent—or his luck—than on a solid base of data about the people and the work.

In the paragraphs to follow, we outline a new technology for use in job enrichment which explicitly addresses the diagnostic as well as the action components of the change process. The technology has two parts: (1) a set of diagnostic tools that are useful in evaluating jobs and people's reactions to them prior to change—and in pinpointing exactly what aspects of specific jobs are most critical to a successful change attempt; and (2) a set of "implementing concepts" that provide concrete guidance for action steps in job enrichment. The implementing concepts are tied directly to the diagnostic tools; the output of the diagnostic activity specifies which action steps are likely to have the most impact in a particular situation.

The Diagnostic Tools

Central to the diagnostic procedure we propose is a package of instruments to be used by employees, supervisors, and outside observers in assessing the target job and employees' reactions to it.[9] These instruments gauge the following:

1. The objective characteristics of the jobs themselves, including both an overall indication of the "motivating potential" of the job as it exists (that is, the MPS score) and the score

of the job on each of the five core dimensions described previously. Because knowing the strengths and weaknesses of the job is critical to any work-redesign effort, assessments of the job are made by supervisors and outside observers as well as the employees themselves—and the final assessment of a job uses data from all three sources.

2. The current levels of motivation, satisfaction, and work performance of employees on the job. In addition to satisfaction with the work itself, measures are taken of how people feel about other aspects of the work setting, such as pay, supervision, and relationships with coworkers.

3. The level of growth-need strength of the employees. As indicated earlier, employees who have strong growth needs are more likely to be more responsive to job enrichment than employees with weak growth needs. Therefore, it is important to know at the outset just what kinds of satisfactions the people who do the job are (and are not) motivated to obtain from their work. This will make it possible to identify which persons are best to start changes with and which may need help in adapting to the newly enriched job.

What then, might be the actual steps one would take in carrying out a job diagnosis using these tools? Although the approach to any particular diagnosis depends upon the specifics of the particular work situation involved, the sequence of questions listed below is fairly typical.

Step 1. Are Motivation and Satisfaction Central to the Problem?
Sometimes organizations undertake job enrichment to improve the work motivation and satisfaction of employees when in fact the real problem with work performance lies elsewhere—for example, in a poorly designed production system, in an error-prone computer, and so on. The first step is to examine the scores of employees on the motivation and satisfaction portions of the diagnostic instrument. (The questionnaire taken by the employees is called the Job

Diagnostic Survey and will be referred to hereafter as the JDS.) If motivation and satisfaction are problematic, the change agent would continue to Step 2; if not, he would look to other aspects of the work situation to identify the real problem.

Step 2. Is the Job Low in Motivating Potential?
To answer this question, one would examine the motivating potential score of the target job and compare it to the MPS's of other jobs to determine whether or not *the job itself* is a probable cause of the motivational problems documented in Step 1. If the job turns out to be low on the MPS, one would continue to Step 3; if it scores high, attention should be given to other possible reasons for the motivational difficulties (such as the pay system, the nature of supervision, and so on).

Step 3. What Specific Aspects of the Job Are Causing the Difficulty?
This step involves examining the job on each of the five core dimensions to pinpoint the specific strengths and weaknesses of the job as it is currently structured. It is useful at this stage to construct a "profile" of the target job, to make visually apparent where improvements need to be made. An illustrative profile for two jobs (one "good" job and one job needing improvement) is shown in Figure 5.3.

Job A is an engineering maintenance job and is high on all of the core dimensions; the MPS of this job is a very high 260. (MPS scores can range from 1 to about 350; an "average" score would be about 125.) Job enrichment would not be recommended for this job; if employees working on the job were unproductive and unhappy, the reasons are likely to have little to do with the nature or design of the work itself.

Job B, on the other hand, has many problems. This job involves the routine and repetitive processing of checks in the "back room" of a bank. The MPS is 30, which is quite low—and indeed, would be even lower if it were not for the moderately high task significance of the job. (Task significance is moderately high because the people are handling large amounts of other

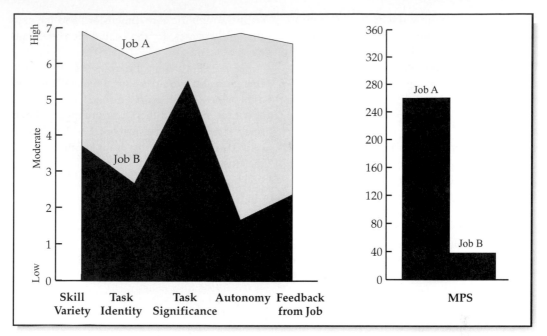

FIGURE 5.3
The JDS Diagnostic Profile for a "Good" and a "Bad" Job

people's money, and therefore the quality of their efforts potentially has important consequences for their unseen clients.) The job provides the individuals with very little direct feedback about how effectively they are doing it; the employees have little autonomy in how they go about doing the job; and the job is moderately low in both skill variety and task identity.

For Job B, then, there is plenty of room for improvement—and many avenues to examine in planning job changes. For still other jobs, the avenues for change often turn out to be considerably more specific: for example, feedback and autonomy may be reasonably high, but one or more of the core dimensions that contribute to the experienced meaningfulness of the job (skill variety, task identity, and task significance) may be low. In such a case, attention would turn to ways to increase the standing of the job on these latter three dimensions.

Step 4. How "Ready" Are the Employees for Change? Once it has been documented that there is need for

improvement in the job—and the particularly troublesome aspects of the job have been identified—then it is time to begin to think about the specific action steps which will be taken to enrich the job. An important factor in such planning is the level of growth needs of the employees, since employees high on growth needs usually respond more readily to job enrichment than do employees with little need for growth. The JDS provides a direct measure of the growth-need strength of the employees. This measure can be very helpful in planning how to introduce the changes to the people (for instance, cautiously versus dramatically), and in deciding who should be among the first group of employees to have their jobs changed.

In actual use of the diagnostic package, additional information is generated which supplements and expands the basic diagnostic questions outlined above. The point of the above discussion is merely to indicate the kinds of questions which we believe to be most important in diagnosing a job prior to changing it. We now turn to how the diagnostic conclusions are translated into specific job changes.

The Implementing Concepts

Five "implementing concepts" for job enrichment are identified and discussed below.[10] Each one is a specific action step aimed at improving both the quality of the working experience for the individual and his work productivity. They are (1) forming natural work units; (2) combining tasks; (3) establishing client relationships; (4) vertical loading; (5) opening feedback channels.

The links between the implementing concepts and the core dimensions are shown in Figure 5.4—which illustrates our theory of job enrichment, ranging from the concrete action steps through the core dimensions and the psychological states to the actual personal and work outcomes.

After completing the diagnosis of a job, a change agent would know which of the core dimensions were most in need of remedial attention. He could then turn to Figure 5.4 and select those implementing concepts that specifically deal with the most troublesome parts of the existing job. How this would take place in practice will be seen below.

Forming Natural Work Units. The notion of distributing work in some logical way may seem to be an obvious part of the design of any job. In many cases, however, the logic is one

FIGURE 5.4
The Full Model: How Use of the Implementing Concepts Can Lead to Positive Outcomes

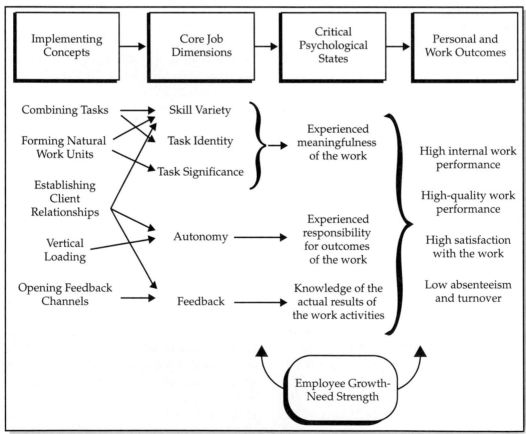

imposed by just about any consideration except job-holder satisfaction and motivation. Such considerations include technological dictates, level of worker training or experience, "efficiency" as defined by industrial engineering, and current workload. In many cases the cluster of tasks a worker faces during a typical day or week is natural to anyone *but* the worker.

For example, suppose that a typing pool (consisting of one supervisor and ten typists) handles all work for one division of a company. Jobs are delivered in rough draft or dictated form to the supervisor, who distributes them as evenly as possible among the typists. In such circumstances the individual letters, reports, and other tasks performed by a given typist in one day or week are randomly assigned. There is no basis for identifying with the work or the person or department for whom it is performed, or for placing any personal value upon it.

The principle underlying natural units of work, by contrast, is "ownership"—a worker's sense of continuing responsibility for an identifiable body of work. Two steps are involved in creating natural work units. The first is to identify the basic work items. In the typing pool, for example, the items might be "pages to be typed." The second step is to group the items in natural categories. For example, each typist might be assigned continuing responsibility for all jobs requested by one or several specific departments. The assignments should be made, of course, in such a way that workloads are about equal in the long run. (For example, one typist might end up with all the work from one busy department, while another handles jobs from several smaller units.)

At this point we can begin to see specifically how the job-design principles relate to the core dimensions (cf. Figure 5.4). The ownership fostered by natural units of work can make the difference between a feeling that work is meaningful and rewarding and the feeling that it is irrelevant and boring. As the diagram shows, natural units of work are directly related to two of the core dimensions: task identity and task significance.

A typist whose work is assigned naturally rather than randomly—say, by department—has a much greater chance of performing a whole job to completion. Instead of typing one section of a large report, the individual is likely to type the whole thing, with knowledge of exactly what the product of the work is (task identity). Furthermore, over time the typist will develop a growing sense of how the work affects coworkers in the department serviced (task significance).

Combining Tasks. The very existence of a pool made up entirely of persons whose sole function is typing reflects a fractionalization of jobs that has been a basic precept of "scientific management." Most obvious in assembly-line work, fractionalization has been applied to nonmanufacturing jobs as well. It is typically justified by efficiency, which is usually defined in terms of either low costs or some time-and-motion type of criteria.

It is hard to find fault with measuring efficiency ultimately in terms of cost-effectiveness. In doing so, however, a manager should be sure to consider *all* the costs involved. It is possible, for example, for highly fractionalized jobs to meet all the time-and-motion criteria of efficiency, but if the resulting job is so unrewarding that performing it day after day leads to high turnover, absenteeism, drugs and alcohol, and strikes, then productivity is really lower (and costs higher) than data on efficiency might indicate.

The principle of combining tasks, then, suggests that whenever possible existing and fractionalized tasks should be put together to form new and larger modules of work. At the Medfield, Massachusetts, plant of Corning Glass Works the assembly of a laboratory hot plate has been redesigned along the lines suggested here. Each hot plate now is assembled from start to finish by one operator, instead of going through several operations that are performed by different people.

Some tasks, if combined into a meaningfully large module of work, would be more than an individual could do by himself. In such cases, it is often useful to consider assigning the new, larger task to a small *team* of workers—who are given great autonomy for its completion. At the Racine, Wisconsin, plant of Emerson Electric, the assembly process for trash disposal appliances was restructured this way. Instead of a sequence of moving the appliance from station to station, the assembly now is done from start to finish by one team. Such teams include both men and women to permit switching off the heavier and more delicate aspects of the work. The team responsible is identified on the appliance. In case of customer complaint, the team often drafts the reply.

As a job-design principle, task combination, like natural units of work, expands the task identity of the job. For example, the hot-plate assembler can see and identify with a finished product ready for shipment, rather than a nearly invisible junction of solder. Moreover, the more tasks that are combined into a single worker's job, the greater the variety of skills he must call on in performing the job. So task combination also leads directly to greater skill variety—the third core dimension that contributes to the overall experienced meaningfulness of the work.

Establishing Client Relationships.

One consequence of fractionalization is that the typical worker has little or no contact with (or even awareness of) the ultimate user of his product or service. By encouraging and enabling employees to establish direct relationships with the clients of their work, improvement often can be realized simultaneously on three of the core dimensions. Feedback increases because of additional opportunities for the individual to receive praise or criticism of his work outputs directly. Skill variety often increases because of the necessity to develop and exercise one's interpersonal skills in maintaining the client relationship. And autonomy can increase because the individual often is given personal responsibility for deciding how to manage his relationships with the clients of his work.

Creating client relationships is a three-step process. First, the client must be identified. Second, the most direct contact possible between the worker and the client must be established. Third, criteria must be set up by which the client can judge the quality of the product or service he receives. And whenever possible, the client should have a means of relaying his judgments directly back to the worker.

The contact between worker and client should be as great as possible and as frequent as necessary. Face-to-face contact is highly desirable, at least occasionally. Where that is impossible or impractical, telephone and mail can suffice. In any case, it is important that the performance criteria by which the worker will be rated by the client must be mutually understood and agreed upon.

Vertical Loading.

Typically the split between the "doing" of a job and the "planning" and "controlling" of the work has evolved along with horizontal fractionalization. Its rationale, once again, has been "efficiency through specialization." And once again, the excess of specialization that has emerged has resulted in unexpected but significant costs in motivation, morale, and work quality. In vertical loading, the intent is to partially close the gap between the doing and the controlling parts of the job—and thereby reap some important motivational advantages.

Of all the job-design principles, vertical loading may be the single most crucial one. In some cases, where it has been impossible to implement any other changes, vertical loading alone has had significant motivational effects.

When a job is vertically loaded, responsibilities and controls that formerly were reserved for higher levels of management are added to the job. There are many ways to accomplish this:

1. Return to the job holder greater discretion in setting schedules, deciding on work methods, checking on quality, and advising or helping to train less experienced workers.

2. Grant additional authority. The objective should be to advance workers from a position of no authority or highly restricted authority to positions of reviewed, and eventually, near-total authority for their own work.
3. Time management. The job holder should have the greatest possible freedom to decide when to start and stop work, when to break, and how to assign priorities.
4. Troubleshooting and crisis decisions. Workers should be encouraged to seek problem solutions on their own, rather than calling immediately for the supervisor.
5. Financial controls. Some degree of knowledge and control over budgets and other financial aspects of a job can often be highly motivating. However, access to this information frequently tends to be restricted. Workers can benefit from knowing something about the costs of their jobs, the potential effect upon profit, and various financial and budgetary alternatives.

When a job is vertically loaded it will inevitably increase in *autonomy*. And as shown in Figure 5.4, this increase in objective personal control over the work will also lead to an increased feeling of personal responsibility for the work, and ultimately to higher internal work motivation.

Opening Feedback Channels.

In virtually all jobs there are ways to open channels of feedback to individuals or teams to help them learn whether their performance is improving, deteriorating, or remaining at a constant level. While there are numerous channels through which information about performance can be provided, it generally is better for a worker to learn about his performance directly as he does his job—rather than from management on an occasional basis.

Job-provided feedback usually is more immediate and private than supervisor-supplied feedback, and it increases the worker's feelings of personal control over his work in the bargain. Moreover, it avoids many of the potentially disruptive interpersonal problems that can develop when the only way a worker has to find out how he is doing is through direct messages or subtle cues from the boss.

Exactly what should be done to open channels for job-provided feedback will vary from job to job and organization to organization. Yet in many cases the changes involve simply removing existing blocks that isolate the worker from naturally occurring data about performance—rather than generating entirely new feedback mechanisms. For example:

1. Establishing direct client relationships often removes blocks between the worker and natural external sources of data about his work.
2. Quality-control efforts in many organizations often eliminate a natural source of feedback. The quality check on a product or service is done by persons other than those responsible for the work. Feedback to the workers—if there is any—is belated and diluted. It often fosters a tendency to think of quality as "someone else's concern." By placing quality control close to the worker (perhaps even in his own hands), the quantity and quality of data about performance available to him can dramatically increase.
3. Tradition and established procedure in many organizations dictate that records about performance be kept by a supervisor and transmitted up (not down) in the organization hierarchy. Sometimes supervisors even check the work and correct any errors themselves. The worker who made the error never knows it occurred—and is denied the very information that could enhance both his internal work motivation and the technical adequacy of his performance. In many cases it is possible to provide standard summaries of performance records directly to the worker (as well as to his superior), thereby giving him personally and regularly the data he needs to improve his performance.
4. Computers and other automated operations sometimes can be used to provide the individual with data now blocked from him.

Part B Strategies for Increasing Individual Performance   69

Many clerical operations, for example, are now performed on computer consoles. These consoles often can be programmed to provide the clerk with immediate feedback in the form of a CRT display or a printout indicating that an error has been made. Some systems even have been programmed to provide the operator with a positive feedback message when a period of error-free performance has been sustained.

Many organizations simply have not recognized the importance of feedback as a motivator. Data on quality and other aspects of performance are viewed as being of interest only to management. Worse still, the *standards* for acceptable performance often are kept from workers as well. As a result, workers who would be interested in following the daily or weekly ups and downs of their performance, and in trying accordingly to improve, are deprived of the very guidelines they need to do so. They are like the golfer we mentioned earlier, whose efforts to correct his hook are stopped dead by fog over the driving range.

THE STRATEGY IN ACTION: HOW WELL DOES IT WORK?

So far we have examined a basic theory of how people get turned on to their work; a set of core dimensions of jobs that create the conditions for such internal work motivation to develop on the job; and a set of five implementing concepts that are the action steps recommended to boost a job on the core dimensions and thereby increase employee motivation, satisfaction, and productivity.

The remaining question is straightforward and important: *Does it work?* In reality, that question is twofold. First, does the theory itself hold water, or are we barking up the wrong conceptual tree? And second, does the change strategy really lead to measurable differences when it is applied in an actual organizational setting?

This section summarizes the findings we have generated to date on these questions.

Is the Job-Enrichment Theory Correct?

In general, the answer seems to be yes. The JDS instrument has been taken by more than 1,000 employees working on about 100 diverse jobs in more than a dozen organizations over the last two years. These data have been analyzed to test the basic motivational theory—and especially the impact of the core job dimensions on worker motivation, satisfaction, and behavior on the job. An illustrative overview of some of the findings is given below.[11]

1. People who work on jobs high on the core dimensions are more motivated and satisfied than are people who work on jobs that score low on the dimensions. Employees with jobs high on the core dimensions (MPS scores greater than 240) were compared to those who held unmotivating jobs (MPS scores less than 40). As shown in Figure 5.5, employees with high MPS jobs were higher on (a) the three psychological states, (b) internal work motivation, (c) general satisfaction, and (d) "growth" satisfaction.

2. Figure 5.6 shows that the same is true for measures of actual behavior at work—absenteeism and performance effectiveness—although less strongly so for the performance measure.

3. Responses to jobs high in motivating potential are more positive for people with weak needs for growth. In Figure 5.7 the linear relationship between the motivating potential of a job and employees' level of internal work motivation is shown, separately for people with high versus low growth needs as measured by the JDS. While both groups of employees show increases in internal motivation as MPS increases, the *rate* of increase is significantly greater for the group of employees who have strong needs for growth.

How Does the Change Strategy Work in Practice?

The results summarized above suggest that both the theory and the diagnostic instrument

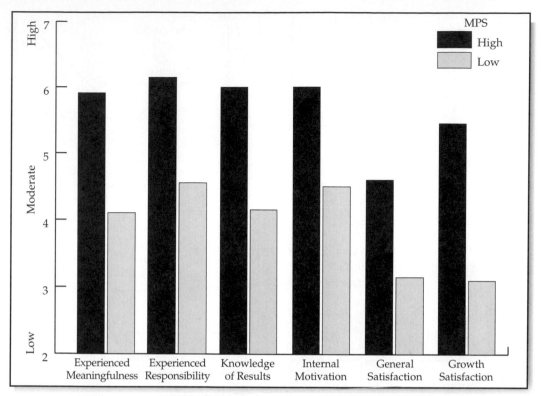

FIGURE 5.5
Employee Reactions to Jobs High and Low in Motivating Potential for Two Banks and a Steel Firm

work when used with real people in real organizations. In this section, we summarize a job-enrichment project conducted at The Travelers Insurance Companies, which illustrates how the change procedures themselves work in practice.

The Travelers project was designed with two purposes in mind. One was to achieve improvements in morale, productivity, and other indicators of employee well-being. The other was to test the general effectiveness of the strategy for job enrichment we have summarized in this article.

The work group chosen was a keypunching operation. The group's function was to transfer information from printed or written documents onto punched cards for computer input. The work group consisted of ninety-eight keypunch operators and verifiers (both in the same job

classification), plus seven assignment clerks. All reported to a supervisor who, in turn, reported to the assistant manager and manager of the data-input division.

The size of individual punching orders varied considerably, from a few cards to as many as 2,500. Some work came to the work group with a specified delivery date, while other orders were to be given routine service on a predetermined schedule.

Assignment clerks received the jobs from the user departments. After reviewing the work for obvious errors, omissions, and legibility problems, the assignment clerk parceled out the work in batches expected to take about one hour. If the clerk found the work not suitable for punching it went to the supervisor, who either returned the work to the user department or

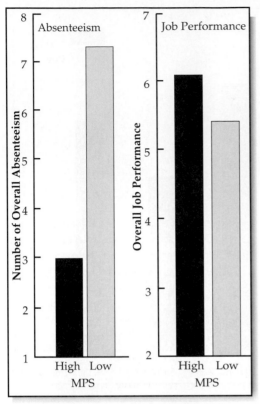

FIGURE 5.6
Absenteeism and Job Performance
for Employees with Jobs High
and Low in Motivating Potential

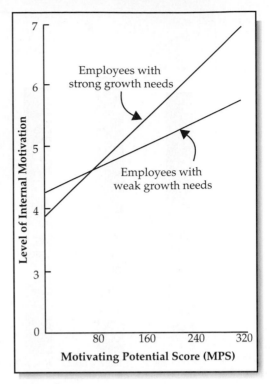

FIGURE 5.7
Relationship Between the Motivating
Potential of a Job and the Internal Work
Motivation of Employees (Shown
Separately for Employees with Strong
versus Weak Growth-Need Strength)

cleared up problems by phone. When work went to operators for punching, it was with the instruction, "Punch only what you see. Don't correct errors, no matter how obvious they look."

Because of the high cost of computer time, keypunched work was 100 percent verified—a task that consumed nearly as many man-hours as the punching itself. Then the cards went to the supervisor, who screened the jobs for due dates before sending them to the computer. Errors detected in verification were assigned to various operators at random to be corrected.

The computer output from the cards was sent to the originating department, accompanied by a printout of errors. Eventually the

printout went back to the supervisor for final correction.

A great many phenomena indicated that the problems being experienced in the work group might be the result of poor motivation. As the only person performing supervisory functions of any kind, the supervisor spent most of his time responding to crisis situations, which recurred continually. He also had to deal almost daily with employees' salary grievances or other complaints. Employees frequently showed apathy or outright hostility toward their jobs.

Rates of work output, by accepted work-measurement standard, were inadequate. Error rates were high. Due dates and schedules frequently were missed. Absenteeism was higher than average, especially before and after weekends and holidays.

The single, rather unusual exception was turnover. It was lower than the companywide average for similar jobs. The company has attributed this fact to poor job market in the base period just before the product began, and to an older, relatively more settled workforce—made up, incidentally, entirely of women.

The Diagnosis. Using some of the tools and techniques we have outlined, a consulting team from the Management Services Department and from Roy W. Walters & Associates concluded that the keypunch-operator's job exhibited the following serious weaknesses in terms of the core dimensions.

1. Skill variety: there was none. Only a single skill was involved—the ability to punch adequately the data on the batch of documents.
2. Task identity: virtually nonexistent. Batches were assembled to provide an even workload, but not whole identifiable jobs.
3. Task significance: not apparent. The keypunching operation was a necessary step in providing service to the company's customers. The individual operator was isolated by an assignment clerk and a supervisor from any knowledge of what the operation meant to the using department, let alone its meaning to the ultimate customer.
4. Autonomy: none. The operators had no freedom to arrange their daily tasks to meet schedules, to resolve problems with the using department, or even to correct, in punching, information that was obviously wrong.
5. Feedback: none. Once a batch was out of the operator's hands, she had no assured chance of seeing evidence of its quality or inadequacy.

Design of Experimental Trial. Since the diagnosis indicated that the motivating potential of the job was extremely low, it was decided to attempt to improve the motivation and productivity of the work group through job enrichment. Moreover, it was possible to design an experimental test of the effects of the changes to be introduced: the results of the changes made in the target work group were to be compared with trends in a control work group of similar size and demographic makeup. Since the control group was located more than a mile away, there appeared to be little risk of communication between members of the two groups.

A base period was defined before the start of the experimental trial period, and appropriate data were gathered on the productivity, absenteeism, and work attitudes of members of both groups. Data also were available on turnover; but since turnover was already below average in the target group, prospective changes in this measure were deemed insignificant.

An educational session was conducted with supervisors, at which they were given the theory and implementing concepts and actually helped to design the job changes themselves. Out of this session came an active plan consisting of about twenty-five change items that would significantly affect the design of the target jobs.

The Implementing Concepts and the Changes. Because the job as it existed was rather uniformly low on the core job dimensions, all five of the implementing concepts were used in enriching it.

1. Natural units of work. The random batch assignment of work was replaced by assigning to each operator continuing responsibility for certain accounts—either particular departments or particular recurring jobs. Any work for those accounts now always goes to the same operator.
2. Task combination. Some planning and controlling functions were combined with the central task of keypunching. In this case, however, these additions can be more suitably discussed under the remaining three implementing concepts.
3. Client relationships. Each operator was given several channels for direct contact with

clients. The operators, not their assignment clerks, now inspect their documents for correctness and legibility. When problems arise, the operator, not the supervisor, takes them up with the client.

4. Feedback. In addition to feedback from client contact, the operators were provided with a number of additional sources of data about their performance. The computer department now returns incorrect cards to the operators who punched them, and operators correct their own errors. Each operator also keeps her own file of copies of her errors. These can be reviewed to determine trends in error frequency and types of errors. Each operator receives weekly a computer printout of her errors and productivity, which is sent to her directly, rather than given to her by the supervisor.

5. Vertical loading. Besides consulting directly with clients about work questions, operators now have the authority to correct obvious coding errors on their own. Operators may set their own schedules and plan their daily work, as long as they meet schedules. Some competent operators have been given the option of not verifying their work and making their own program changes.

Results of the Trial.
The results were dramatic. The number of operators declined from ninety-eight to sixty. This occurred partly through attrition and partly through transfer to other departments. Some of the operators were promoted to higher-paying jobs in departments whose cards they had been handling—something that had never occurred before. Some details of the results are given below.

1. Quantity of work. The control group, with no job changes made, showed an increase in productivity of 8.1 percent during the trial period. The experimental group showed an increase of 39.6 percent.

2. Error rates. To assess work quality, error rates were recorded for about forty operators in the experimental group. All were experienced, and all had been in their jobs before the job-enrichment program began. For two months before the study, these operators had a collective error rate of 1.53 percent. For two months toward the end of the study, the collective error rate was 0.99 percent. By the end of the study the number of operators with poor performance had dropped from 11.1 percent to 5.5 percent.

3. Absenteeism. The experimental group registered a 24.1 percent decline in absences. The control group, by contrast, showed a 29 percent increase.

4. Attitudes toward the job. An attitude survey given at the start of the project showed that the two groups scored about average, and nearly identical, in nine different areas of work satisfaction. At the end of the project the survey was repeated. The control group showed an insignificant 0.5 percent improvement, while the experimental group's overall satisfaction score rose 16.5 percent.

5. Selective elimination of controls. Demonstrated improvements in operator proficiency permitted them to work with fewer controls. Travelers estimates that the reduction of controls had the same effect as adding seven operators—a saving even beyond the effects of improved productivity and lowered absenteeism.

6. Role of the supervisor. One of the most significant findings in the Travelers experiment was the effect of the changes on the supervisor's job, and thus on the rest of the organization. The operators took on many responsibilities that had been reserved at least to the unit leaders and sometimes to the supervisor. The unit leaders, in turn, assumed some of the day-to-day supervisory functions that had plagued the supervisor. Instead of spending his days supervising the behavior of subordinates and dealing with crises, he was able to devote time to developing feedback systems, setting up work modules and spearheading the enrichment effort—in other words, managing. It should

be noted, however, that helping supervisors change their own work activities when their subordinates' jobs have been enriched is itself a challenging task. And if appropriate attention and help are not given to such supervisors in such cases, they rapidly can become disaffected—and a job-enrichment "backlash" can result.[12]

Summary. By applying work-measurement standards to the changes wrought by job enrichment—attitude and quality, absenteeism, and selective administration of controls—Travelers was able to estimate the total dollar impact of the project. Actual savings in salaries and machine rental charges during the first year totaled $64,305. Potential savings by further application of the changes were put at $91,937 annually. Thus, by almost any measure used—from the work attitudes of individual employees to dollar savings for the company as a whole—the Travelers test of the job-enrichment strategy proved a success.

CONCLUSIONS

In this article we have presented a new strategy for the redesign of work in general and for job enrichment in particular. The approach has four main characteristics:

1. It is grounded in a basic psychological theory of what motivates people in their work.
2. It emphasizes that planning for job changes should be done on the basis of *data* about the jobs and the people who do them—and a set of diagnostic instruments is provided to collect such data.
3. It provides a set of specific implementing concepts to guide actual job changes, as well as a set of theory-based rules for selecting *which* action steps are likely to be most beneficial in a given situation.
4. The strategy is buttressed by a set of findings showing that the theory holds water, that the diagnostic procedures are practical and informative, and that the implementing concepts can lead to changes that are beneficial

both to organizations and to the people who work in them.

We believe that job enrichment is moving beyond the stage where it can be considered "yet another management fad." Instead, it represents a potentially powerful strategy for change that can help organizations achieve their goals for higher quality work—and at the same time further the equally legitimate needs of contemporary employees for a more meaningful work experience. Yet there are pressing questions about job enrichment and its use that remain to be answered.

Prominent among these is the question of employee participation in planning and implementing work redesign. The diagnostic tools and implementing concepts we have presented are neither designed nor intended for use only by management. Rather, our belief is that the effectiveness of job enrichment is likely to be enhanced when the tasks of diagnosing and changing jobs are undertaken *collaboratively* by management and by the employees whose work will be affected.

Moreover, the effects of work redesign on the broader organization remain generally uncharted. Evidence now is accumulating that when jobs are changed, turbulence can appear in the surrounding organization—for example, in supervisory–subordinate relationships, in pay and benefit plans, and so on. Such turbulence can be viewed by management either as a problem with job enrichment, or as an opportunity for further and broader organizational development by teams of managers and employees. To the degree that management takes the latter view, we believe, the oft-espoused goal of achieving basic organizational change through the redesign of work may come increasingly within reach.

The diagnostic tools and implementing concepts we have presented are useful in deciding on and designing basic changes in the jobs themselves. They do not address the broader issues of who plans the changes, how they are carried out, and how they are followed up. The way these broader questions are dealt with, we believe, may determine whether job enrichment will grow up—or whether it will die an early and unfortunate death, like so many other fledging behavioral-science approaches to organizational change.

APPENDIX

For the algebraically inclined, the motivating Potential Score is computed as follows:

$$MPS = \frac{\dfrac{Skill}{Variety} + \dfrac{Task}{Identity} + \dfrac{Task}{Significance}}{3} \times Autonomy \times Feedback$$

It should be noted that in some cases the MPS score can be *too* high for positive job satisfaction and effective performance—in effect overstimulating the person who holds the job. This paper focuses on jobs which are toward the low end of the scale—and which potentially can be improved through job enrichment.

Acknowledgments

The authors acknowledge with great appreciation the editorial assistance of John Hickey in the preparation of this paper, and the help of Kenneth Brousseau, Daniel Feldman, and Linda Frank in collecting the data that are summarized in part by the Organizational Effectiveness Research Program of the Office of Naval Research, and the Manpower Administration of the U.S. Department of Labor, both through contracts to Yale University.

NOTES

1. F. Herzberg, B. Mausner, and B. Snyderman, *The Motivation to Work* (New York: John Wiley & Sons, 1959).
2. F. Herzberg, *Work and the Nature of Man* (Cleveland: World, 1966).
3. F. Herzberg, "One More Time: How Do You Motivate Employees?" *Harvard Business Review* (1968): 53–62.
4. W. J. Paul, Jr., K. B. Robertson, and F. Herzberg, "Job Enrichment Pays Off," *Harvard Business Review* (1969): 61–78.
5. R. N. Ford, *Motivation Through the Work Itself* (New York: American Management Association, 1969).
6. A. N. Turner and P. R. Lawrence, *Industrial Jobs and the Worker* (Cambridge, Mass.: Harvard Graduate School of Business Administration, 1965).
7. J. R. Hackman and E. E. Lawler, "Employee Reactions to Job Characteristics," *Journal of Applied Psychology Monograph* (1971): 259–86.
8. J. R. Hackman and G. R. Oldham, *Motivation Through the Design of Work: Test of a Theory,* Technical Report No. 6, Department of Administrative Services, Yale University, 1974.
9. J. R. Hackman and G. R. Oldham, "Development of the Job Diagnostic Survey," *Journal of Applied Psychology* (1975): 159–70.
10. R. W. Walters and Associates, *Job Enrichment for Results* (Cambridge, Mass.: Addison-Wesley, 1975).
11. Hackman and Oldham, "Development of the Job Diagnostic Survey."
12. E. E. Lawler III, J. R. Hackman, and S. Kaufman, "Effects of Job Redesign: A Field Experiment," *Journal of Applied Social Psychology* (1973): 49–62.

6. Fighting the War for Talent Is Hazardous to Your Organization's Health

Jeffrey Pfeffer

There is this widespread idea, made popular by McKinsey & Co., *Fast Company,* and others, that we are in a "war for talent." In an intellectual capital world, talent is what matters, and we are told that the companies that will win in the competitive arena are those that are the best at locating, assessing, recruiting, and keeping the most talented people. A typical statement of this position is this opening sentence from an article entitled "The Great Talent Caper" in the September, 2000, issue of *Fast Company,* the enormously successful business magazine for the new economy: "It's hard to argue with the idea that the company with the best talent wins."

Actually, it's quite easy to argue with that seemingly common-sense statement, while still granting the importance of intellectual capital and knowledge work in today's economy. As John Chambers, CEO of Cisco Systems, has noted, great teams outperform collections of individuals—even when the individuals are more talented. Even in professional sports, the teams with the best talent, often nicely proxied by the highest salaries, don't always (or even usually) have the best records or invariably win championships. In business and nonprofit organizations, characterized by interdependence among individuals so that productivity is affected not only by one individual's skills and abilities but also by the capabilities and actions of others, individual talent matters even less in determining organizational success.

As W. Edwards Deming and the quality movement pointed out a long time ago—a lesson that we clearly need to relearn—what is important is not so much *individual* motivation or ability but the attributes of the *system* in which the person works. Some organizations have systems that bring out the best in their people, while others, filled with talented, motivated, hard-working people, have practices and policies that interfere with the ability of these individuals to do their best and to make a difference. For example, does anyone really think that United Airlines has less capable or talented people than Southwest Airlines, even though United has much poorer service as assessed by on-time performance, lost bags, and customer complaints? To take another case, would the long-standing and pervasive business problems of Xerox Corp., a company that has been the source of business world–changing inventions such as the first personal computer, word processing software, and local area networks, be solved if Xerox somehow got more talented, brighter people?

It's bad enough that fighting the "war for talent" has companies fighting the wrong war, often using the wrong methods. But there is an even worse problem, namely the consequences that are unleashed by even waging the talent war in the first place. In this article, I describe the various organizational processes and dynamics that are frequently unleashed when companies adopt the "war for talent" mind-set. Considering these social psychological processes helps make the argument that not only should your company not necessarily try to win the war for talent, even adopting this image as a management metaphor

Reprinted from Organizational Dynamics, Vol. 29, No. 4, pp. 248–259. Copyright © 2001, with permission from Organizational Dynamics.

can be quite hazardous to your organization's health.

What happens in a war for talent? There is:

- An invariable emphasis on individual performance (rewarding the individual stars), thereby diminishing teamwork, creating destructive internal competition, and retarding learning and the spread of best practices inside the company;
- A tendency to glorify the talents of those *outside* the company and downplay the skills and abilities of insiders, leading to a loss of motivation on the part of those inside the firm and to their turnover (thereby ensuring that the recruiting challenge will be even greater as the company tries to replace those it has inadvertently sent packing);
- The creation of a self-fulfilling prophecy where those labeled as less able *become* less able because they are asked to do less, given fewer resources, training, and mentoring, and become discouraged—in the process ensuring that the organization has way too many people who are in the process of dropping out of the competitive fray;
- A de-emphasis on fixing the systematic, cultural, and business process issues that are invariably much more important for enhancing performance, as the company seeks success solely through getting the right people in the door;
- And finally, the development of an elitist, arrogant attitude—once you have successfully competed in the war for talent, you have the best people—an attitude that makes building a wise organization almost impossible. In wise organizations, people know what they know and they know what they don't know. Companies that think they are winning the war for talent think they are so full of smart people that they know everything!

Let's consider each of these processes and their consequences for the company.

OVEREMPHASIS ON THE INDIVIDUAL, UNDEREMPHASIS ON THE TEAM

One of the assumptions of the "talent" language is that there are individual stars. It only makes sense, then, to provide these stars differentiated rewards that recognize their stardom. Indeed, pay for performance is a common recommendation found in the literature on attracting and retaining talent. The assumption is that if you don't pay your stars inordinately well, someone else will and you'll lose them. Seems logical, but like much conventional wisdom, it ignores some important dynamics and facts.

Let's begin with one fact on which virtually everyone agrees—sharing best practices and knowledge inside organizations is difficult and frequently not very successfully done. For instance, a study of oil refineries by the consulting firm Solomon Associates found that in a statistical analysis predicting refinery performance (uptime and maintenance costs), there was *no* effect of company on the results. What this means is that there was as much variation in performance across refineries *within* a single oil company as there was across refineries owned by different companies. The absence of a company effect on refinery performance is prima facie evidence for the absence of intraorganizational learning.

Nor is this case unique. A study of 42 food manufacturing plants in a single company doing essentially the same task found a difference in performance of 300% between the best and worst performing plant. Another study of a multinational food producer operating in seven countries and producing the same products using the same machines found a performance difference of 112% between the best and worst performing plant. An intensive study of an effort to make a Hewlett–Packard Co. manufacturing unit more effective also reported that opportunities to share innovative process technologies or other sources of competitive advantage were overlooked. Indeed, Carla O'Dell and Jackson Grayson have written a book detailing the problems of spreading better practices and knowledge inside companies.

Why is it so hard to share best practices and knowledge? One of the answers must surely be the internal competition set up by the zero-sum reward systems that are part and parcel of the war for talent. Differentiated pay means that we want to pay the best more and the worst less. So what are the behavioral implications of this? If you are a plant manager having problems in your performance, are you going to ask others for help? Not likely, because when you do, you signal publicly to everyone in the company that you are not doing as well as they are. And why would you do that in a competition for salary and status—in a competition to see who has the most "talent?" Moreover, even if someone has the audacity to ask for help, why would anyone else offer such help? Why would I help a competitor? We are competing for the zero-sum rewards of promotions, recognition as a winner, and raises parceled out only to those who excel. Self-interest dictates not being very helpful or forthcoming to those with whom someone competes for those rewards. Tom Lasorda, in charge of diffusing lean manufacturing when he worked for General Motors Corp., was quite articulate about how the internal competition inside GM hindered plant managers' learning from each other, in the process costing the company billions of dollars. Ironically, even as companies spend hundreds of millions of dollars on technologies to collect and distribute knowledge, they do things to create a culture in which knowledge sharing is unlikely to occur.

Logically, if internal competition retards the spread of best practices across a company, leaders who are concerned with improving internal knowledge transfer and subsequent organizational performance should try and stamp out excessive internal competition. And that's just what our research has found. Shortly after taking over IBM Corp., Lou Gerstner issued a number of edicts designed to ensure cooperation and stop internal competition that was hindering the performance of the company. Chris Galvin at Motorola Inc. has recently done

the same thing, as did John Pizzey at Alcoa Inc.'s smelters. Guidant Cardiovascular some time ago began providing everyone the same percentage bonus, based on the division's achieving revenue, profit, and technological development goals. According to Peter McInnes, a vice president at Guidant, the company does this to encourage teamwork and to encourage people to focus on business results instead of maneuvering to be on the right project or work on the right team. Willamette Industries, by any measure the most successful integrated forest products company, does not pay short-term performance bonuses to anyone in the company. It certainly does not pay annual bonuses to division managers who need to cooperate rather than fight over transfer prices in this integrated wood products company. There are many other examples of companies that have decided excessive internal competition is getting in the way of achieving business results and have implemented management practices designed to curtail, rather than exacerbate, internal rivalry.

The point is that the emphasis on the individual rather than the team or the company is almost an inevitable outcome of a war for talent mind set. Not only are such individual, zero-sum reward practices encouraged by virtually all those who have written about talent wars, but even if they weren't, rewarding the individual is what logically follows from the belief that it is *individuals* who make the difference.

Even though the talent-war mentality has led to an emphasis on rewarding "the best" to attract and retain those people, there is little evidence that simply paying people more is the most critical factor in recruiting or particularly in retaining employees. Most surveys show that money is not the most important reason why people take or leave jobs. In fact, in some surveys money is not even in the top ten. And money is the most available of all rewards—any organization can offer it. That is why years ago Tandem Computers didn't even tell people while they were being recruited what their precise salaries would be. If the person asked, the statement that Tandem paid good, competitive salaries would be offered in return. If the person insisted on knowing the precise salary and negotiating over it, they would not be offered the job. Tandem understood something quite simple but profound: people who come for money leave for money. Why play that game? SAS Institute, the largest privately owned software company in the world—with turnover less than four percent—doesn't win the retention game by paying the best, but by treating its people the best. There is a lesson there for us all.

THE GLORIFICATION OF OUTSIDERS

In the search to find the best people, there is a tendency to see those people as existing primarily, although not exclusively, outside of the organization. Although theories of in-group favoritism suggest that people tend to like and identify more with those with whom they share a social identity, such as an organization affiliation, outsiders have the advantages of mystery and scarcity value. In other words, there is more than a little truth to the adage that familiarity breeds contempt.

Why? First of all, there is the effect of behavioral commitment. Insiders are already there, coming to work and immediately available. Recruiting or even looking for someone from outside requires more effort. Initially, there is the effort of searching, hiring a search firm, running advertisements, tapping social networks, posting jobs online, and reviewing resumes. One way to justify and make sense of that extra effort is to convince oneself that the people uncovered through this effortful activity are, in fact, worth the effort—that they are really better than those immediately at hand.

Once an outside candidate has been found, then comes the effort of interviewing and recruiting that person. Again, the expenditure of effort elicits a commitment response, in which there is tendency to justify the effort by thinking the person hired is better than those inside, for whom no such comparable effort has been recently expended.

Second and somewhat related, there is the effect of scarcity. As the play Romeo and Juliet illustrates, we always want what we can't or don't have. Research has shown, for instance, that cookies are rated as tasting better if there are fewer of them on the plate. Outsiders are scarcer and less available than the insiders working for the firm. Attracting them is invariably an uncertain process—will they come, or won't they? The relative scarcity of outsiders means that they will probably be valued more highly simply because of their comparative unavailability.

Finally, there is the mystery and allure of the outsider. Someone who is not known as well, but who has a reputation for being an outstanding performer, looks larger than life. We don't see the inevitable mistakes, the efforts required to achieve that performance, the hard work, and the fact that the person is a person pretty much like everyone else. Once inside the organization, the individual's foibles and faults are more readily apparent. Moreover, once inside the organization the person becomes a competitor for status, and a tendency to derogate the individual's abilities in this status competition can emerge.

There are many examples of the process just described. In the 1980s, Japanese management practices were venerated by many American companies, and Japanese competitors were seen as larger than life. Ironically, one of those management practices that received so much acclaim and attention was total quality management, a management technique largely developed by an American, W. Edwards Deming, who was ignored until the practices he advocated were adopted by others outside the U.S. Or as another example, consider the many mergers that don't fulfill their expectations. Some of the reason for this is the postmerger integration process, but another part of the story is that the aquired firm was probably not very realistically appraised in the first place. Moreover, once inside the firm, those from the acquired organization are seen as less competent than they really are.

We saw this process in full force when Fresh Choice Inc., a publicly traded salad buffet restaurant chain headquartered in California, purchased Zoopa, a four-unit subsidiary of Restaurants Unlimited, located in Seattle. While they were competitors, Fresh Choice admired and even tried to copy Zoopa's recipes, look and feel, and service orientation. Once the merger was completed, Fresh Choice leaders told us that the Zoopa store managers weren't actually that great and that the acquisition had been mostly done for real estate, not organizational learning. The turnover in the Zoopa units increased after the merger, and much of the knowledge acquired walked out the door. Once inside Fresh Choice, Zoopa people looked neither so special nor so valuable as they did when they were outsiders.

THE SELF-FULFILLING PROPHECY, WORKING IN REVERSE

The war-for-talent imagery has consistently emphasized identifying the top ten percent, not just for hiring but for retaining and cultivating once inside the company. Indeed, one of the suggestions coming out of some of the war-for-talent consulting goes like this: identify the top ten and the bottom ten percent. The top ten percent of your people should be lavished with rewards, interesting job assignments, fast-track opportunities, and special training and mentoring. The bottom ten percent should be either removed from the organization or helped to improve. Implicitly, such recommendations suggest ignoring everyone else.

There are two problems with this course of action. First, there is the question of whether or not there really are two (or three) kinds of people in your company—the stars, the dogs, and everyone else. To presume that some people are better than others presumes that there are some reasonably stable attributes, such as talent and drive, which differentiate among people, and that such traits are largely not amenable to being changed. That's why the war for talent has such an emphasis on selection and retention—there

are better and worse people, and you'd better get more of the first kind and less of the second. But is this true?

Some American readers will recognize the name of Steve Young, the now-retired quarterback of the San Francisco 49ers, considered to be one of the better quarterbacks in professional football history. Fewer people may also remember that Young's career began outside of the National Football League, because he was deemed not good enough. A similar story holds for Kurt Warner, the quarterback who led the St. Louis Rams to the Super Bowl victory in 2000. More systematically, a study of professional baseball players in the early 1990s revealed that better managers were able to not only get their teams to perform better, but that players under those managers performed better than might have been expected given their lifetime records. And this is for a sport, baseball, in which there is relatively little interdependence, and where natural ability would appear to play an important role. The point is that although there are certainly differences across people, such differences are not invariably related to their performance, because people can perform above or below their natural level depending on a myriad of factors.

One of the most important of these factors affecting performance is the expectation for performance. And that's the second problem— the very labeling of people will affect their performance. Labeling only a few as stars will cause the majority to perform way below their potential.

The self-fulfilling prophecy is one of the oldest and most established principles for understanding organizational behavior. Simply put, the self-fulfilling prophecy holds that high expectations increase performance, and low expectations will decrease performance. This effect has been found in early studies of intelligence and performance in the classroom, where measurable changes in intelligence quotient (IQ) were observed depending on the expectations for children's performance. It has been found in studies of performance in the Israeli defense forces, and in studies of sales force performance. There is, in fact, a vast literature on the effects of expectations on behavior.

Why might such effects be observed? For some fairly straightforward reasons. If a person confronts low expectations, one rational (and observed) response is something called "defensive effort"—fancy ways of saying that people don't try very hard. If you aren't going to succeed anyway, why expend effort that will just wind up being wasted? Other things being equal, if you don't expend as much effort, you probably won't do as well. Conversely, if you think you will have a good chance at success, you are quite likely to try harder and, as a consequence of this increased effort, probably do better. Another reason is anxiety. Most people don't find the prospect of failing very comforting, and indeed, failure or the prospect of failure can produce anxiety. As anyone who has ever taken a test can attest, beyond some level anxiety itself interferes with performance. To the extent that expectations of failure produce anxiety, that stress can itself induce poorer performance.

A third factor is that the resources you get depend on what people expect from you. Students labeled as not as bright tend to get less guidance and help from teachers. Bosses are less likely to spend time with people who aren't too good, saving their precious time for coaching and mentoring those who have a real chance of benefitting. Who is going to get sent to training and given more challenging job assignments, those that are labeled as stars or the others? These resource allocation choices have real consequences for performance. People who receive less coaching, mentoring, training, and fewer challenging job assignments will—other things being equal—learn less and be less able to perform at a higher level. In this way, labeling people produces an allocation of resources, including time and attention, that almost guarantees the initial labels will come to be true.

In a company obsessed with fighting the war for talent, such labeling will go on with a vengeance, as the company will be consumed with figuring out who is the best and who are the rest. But that very labeling process will produce many discouraged people—those not accorded the most favorable labels. Two consequences can result. Either those labeled as less than star-like will leave, in which case the company will have to recruit even more people to replace them, or else they will simply give up and retire in place, depriving the company of their effort and ideas.

What happens when you don't fight the war for talent, thereby giving up on most of your people (only 10% of the people can be in the top 10%)? Consider the case of The Men's Wearhouse. The company operates in the difficult industry of selling tailored men's clothing, an industry that is not only competitive, but one that is declining. Nonetheless, the compound annual growth rate achieved by The Men's Wearhouse over the past five years has been almost 30% in sales and more than 25% in earnings per share. The Men's Wearhouse Inc. has an interesting operating philosophy. Its founder and chairman, George Zimmer, has stated that the company is in the people business, not the suit business. Charlie Bresler, in charge of human resources, has the interesting title of executive vice president for human development. The company aspires to help people become better than they (or probably anyone else) ever thought they could be—a difficult challenge in retailing, a low-wage industry that has typically not attracted the best people. But the company has succeeded to an astonishing degree by giving people second, and even third chances, even when they have put a deposit in their pockets for a few days or ripped off a pair of socks. The company's success comes in large measure from its emphasis on training. Training not only imparts knowledge of clothing and sales techniques. Training enhances people's self-esteem, by signaling that the organization values them and is interested in investing in them. By helping people unleash their full potential, The Men's Wearhouse has lowered its turnover, has among the lowest losses because of theft in the retail industry even without electronic security, and has developed wardrobe consultants who provide a service experience that permits the company to achieve outstanding profit margins. If the company had adopted the talent-war mentality, it would have been finished before it even began.

IGNORING THE SYSTEMIC, CULTURAL PROBLEMS THAT AFFECT PERFORMANCE

The scarcest resource in most organizations is not money; it is time and attention. There are too many problems and issues competing for managers' time and too many things to think about. It is obvious that time spent on one set of issues or initiatives is time (and effort) that cannot be devoted to other things. Fighting the war for talent focuses the company on first grading or ranking and then seeking to select and retain the best people. It focuses the company, in other words, on individuals—no groups, teams, or the entire company—and it focuses on these individuals with the presumption that there are better and worse ones, and there's not much to be done to change anyone. It causes companies to ignore or downplay the importance of intervening to build cultures and systems that bring out the best in everyone.

The American automobile industry illustrates this problem quite nicely. In the 1980s, General Motors concluded that the problem with its automobile plants was its people. Many of them had worked in the industry for years and were, in the opinion of the company, old, tired, and burnt out. Most were unionized, which, the company thought, put them in an adversarial relationship. Many were not highly educated, therefore lacking the skills to help GM compete in an increasingly quality-conscious, technologically complex industry. GM's response was to invest in factory automation to eliminate as many of these autoworkers as possible. The outcome of that process was, as described by a number of observers, to leave the company with the highest fixed costs in the industry and with machines that didn't really work the way they were supposed to.

By contrast, Toyota Motor Corp. and a number of the other Japanese automobile manufacturers took a different approach, nicely illustrated by what happened in the Toyota–GM joint venture in Fremont, California, New United Motors Manufacturing, Inc. (NUMMI). At that plant, formerly operated by General Motors, Toyota neither tried to replace the people (85% of those who worked at NUMMI when it started production in 1985 had worked for the former GM plant, well known for absenteeism, poor quality, and drug abuse and alcoholism), nor did it substitute machines for employees. Rather, the company did those things that are well known as being associated with high performance or high commitment management practices:

- Established a policy of mutual commitment and employment security. NUMMI employees were promised that they would be laid off only under extreme conditions—the viability of the enterprise was at stake. Instead, when demand was slack, employees used the time to rehabilitate and upgrade the plant and to take courses that enhanced their skills in quality, statistical process control, working in teams, and so forth. As Lincoln Electric Co. and its executives recognized a long time ago, no one will voluntarily contribute ideas for enhancing productivity if the result is that they or their colleagues will lose their jobs. In return for working cooperatively to enhance productivity, people in the NUMMI plant were promised security and were treated as real partners in the enterprise.
- Selective hiring. Although under the terms of the UAW contract people formerly employed at the GM plant that had been closed were promised recall rights, these individuals nonetheless went through interviews and screening. Even though few were actually culled during this process, the selectivity provided an opportunity for some who didn't like or agree with the new culture to self-select out. More important, it gave those who came back to the plant a feeling that the company cared about who they were, and

a feeling of pride for having gone through the selection process.

- High pay. NUMMI offered the highest wage in the industry at that time. The deal was high pay and security in return for a new spirit of cooperation.
- Information sharing. At the NUMMI plant (and subsequently at Saturn, which learned a lot from the experience of NUMMI), information on production, quality, and productivity was widely shared and readily available. People who were expected to take some responsibility for the operation of the plant were given the information necessary to do so.
- Decentralization of decision making. NUMMI really excelled at giving front-line people, who had years of experience and the wisdom and insight that comes from that experience, responsibilities for improving performance. Virtually all industrial engineers were removed from the plant. Front-line people were trained in analyzing work methods and processes and were given the time and the freedom to implement productivity and quality-enhancing changes in the production process. Layers of management were eliminated, one reason why NUMMI was able to cut its costs. The idea of self-managing teams was one of the organizing principles that governed the operations of the plant.
- An egalitarian culture. When Toyota assumed control of the management of NUMMI, it abolished the executive dining room and reserved parking spaces. Everyone, including the president of NUMMI wore the same smock, ate in the same place, and socialized with each other. The idea, conveyed symbolically, was that all employees shared the responsibility and the obligation to make the organization successful.
- An emphasis on training and skill development. As already noted, NUMMI expected its front-line people to contribute their ideas to making things better. They were given

training in how to analyze jobs and work processes and when there was a downturn in demand, the slack permitted even more extensive training to occur.

The Toyota production system has been remarkably effective because it is a *system* that permits regular people to achieve world-class results on a consistent basis over long periods of time. It is a system of organizing that recognizes the connection between the social and the technical aspects of organization and that puts in place a culture that helps to ensure the motivation and performance of the employees. Why don't other automobile companies copy this system, acknowledged to be superior? One reason is that although other companies would like to implement flexible manufacturing, time and attention is diverted to other activities such as fighting with the union, implementing complicated robotics, engaging in internal politics and competing with each other. Time is indeed a scarce resource, and time spent fighting a war for talent is time diverted from building a culture and set of management practices that permits everyone to perform as if he or she were in the top 10%.

WINNING THE WAR FOR TALENT BATTLE BUT LOSING THE WAR FOR WISDOM

A corollary of the war for talent imagery is that what companies want is "smart" people. However, companies may be much better served by having "wise" people. As originally defined by Plato, wisdom is the attitude of knowing what you know and knowing also what you don't know. The attitude of wisdom, as characterized by a number of scholars, represents a midpoint between arrogance and insecurity. Having an attitude of wisdom permits an organization to take action even as it doubts what it knows, so that it continues to learn even as it acts.

IDEO Product Development, an award-winning product design firm headquartered in Palo Alto, nicely exemplifies a wise organization. When David Kelley, the CEO, announced a reorganization a while ago, he stated that all he knew was that the new structure was the best the company could come up with at the time, and that it was wrong. Not only does that statement illustrate that it is all right to make mistakes at the company, it shows that it is all right to act without having the complete right answer. Another motto at IDEO is that enlightened trial and error outperforms the planning of flawless intellects. This cultural norm means that people learn from doing, so the only mistake is not to take action based on what is known at the time. It is a norm that facilitates rapid prototyping, important not only for product design but for organizational learning more generally. A third aphorism is that the company believes in failing early and failing often—which is better than failing once, failing at the end, and failing big.

In each of these statements, you see the attitude of wisdom. Each reflects having enough confidence to try something, be it a new structure or a prototype, while keeping open the idea that no one in the company or the company itself knows everything, so it needs to continue learning even as it does things.

We are surrounded by examples of companies that have gotten into trouble by being too arrogant. The recent books on the Microsoft Corp. antitrust trial show that Microsoft could have reached a settlement in the trial, but it was so sure of itself it delayed entering into serious negotiations. The company's arrogance during the trial offended the trial judge. Arrogance, however, may be a natural by-product of operating in the software industry—an industry that makes a practice of announcing "vaporware" and selling prototypes into the marketplace, letting customers find the bugs, and then selling upgrades that fix the problems the company shipped in the first place (this is called versions of the product).

To listen to your customers, you need to think you don't know everything. James Goodnight, a cofounder and CEO of SAS Institute, the largest privately owned software company in the world, is fond of saying that he is not a technological visionary and that he can't predict the future. Therefore, what SAS Institute must do is to listen to its customers, give them the software that they want and need, and be ready and able to change as market demands and conditions change. It is a formula that has produced more than 23 consecutive years of double-digit growth and a 98% license renewal rate. John Chambers of Cisco Systems is another person in another company that shows an attitude of wisdom. Cisco has no technology religion. The company is fond of saying it is agnostic with respect to specific technologies. Rather, it listens to the market and provides the technology that the market demands. It is not a company too proud to go out and purchase the technology it needs. Indeed, Cisco's ability to not only acquire companies but retain their people is one of its important sources of success. Chambers and other senior managers spend most of their time with customers and employees, listening. Watch John Chambers at a conference. In the world of high technology, typically populated by people with a surfeit of ego and self-confidence, he spends most of his time listening and asking questions. If you think about it, that is the best way to learn, and learning is important in a rapidly changing market environment.

What does this have to do with the "war for talent?" Just this—if you hire the best people who think (or even know) they are the best, how likely are they to be willing to listen and learn? How likely are they to treat others as "smart" as they are with respect, as opposed to the contempt more often seen? One of the geniuses of Toyota was recognizing that the people on the assembly line actually knew something about automobile assembly, regardless of formal degrees and the ability to talk smoothly. One of the marks of the wisdom of Jeff Hawkins, cofounder of Handspring, is his interest in watching people who use paper instead of personal digital assistants so he can see what they do, how they do it, and why. It would be easy for a technological guru (and billionaire) to think that those that don't use the latest technology are not only uncool but are not too smart. Hawkins wants to learn from them. The ability to learn from others depends importantly on not thinking yourself or your organization so superior to them that you have nothing to learn. Maybe that means not thinking that you have the smartest people, just the best listeners.

CONCLUSION

Is it possible to wage the war for talent and not fall into these problems and pitfalls? Of course. But it is not likely, nor is it easy. Any theory, implicit or explicit, causes us to see some things in specific ways and to ignore other things. The war for talent has embedded within it a theory that holds: 1) that organizational performance is essentially the aggregation of a bunch of individual performances (which is why if you get people who do well individually you can win the competitive battle); and 2) people are essentially unchanged, at least by the time they are adults in the workforce, in terms of their abilities and capabilities, which is why selecting (and keeping) the right people is so crucial.

Once explained in this way, we can see that neither assumption can be accepted uncritically.

There is a lot of evidence that suggests teams can outperform groups of more talented individuals, and that people can perform above or below their natural abilities depending on the situation, including the leadership they receive and the help they get from others in their immediate environment.

But the problem is not just that the war-for-talent imagery may be wrong. It is an image that almost naturally produces a set of management actions that cause problems. Fighting the war for talent can readily create self-fulfilling prophecies that leave a large portion of the workforce demotivated or ready to quit, and produce an arrogant attitude that makes it hard to learn or listen. It can cause the company to focus always on getting better people, mostly from outside, instead of fixing the culture and system of management practices that research has shown are consequential for performance. It is for these reasons that fighting the war for talent can indeed be hazardous to an organization's health, and why great companies get the best out of their people instead of always searching for different people.

SELECTED BIBLIOGRAPHY

The war for talent has been described in Charles Fishman, "The War for Talent," *Fast Company* (August, 1998); Elizabeth G. Chambers, Mark Foulon, Helen Hanfield-Jones, Steven M. Hankin and Edward G. Michaels III, "The War for Talent," *McKinsey Quarterly* (1998); and in a forthcoming book by Michaels and his McKinsey colleagues. Many of these examples of the importance of teamwork and of building great cultures found in this article come from Charles A. O'Reilly and Jeffrey Pfeffer, *Hidden Value: How Great Companies Achieve Extraordinary Results with Ordinary People* (Boston, MA: Harvard Business School Press, 2000).

Research evidence on the importance of how companies manage people for organizational success is summarized in several places,

including Pfeffer, *The Human Equation: Building Profits by Putting People First* (Boston, MA: Harvard Business School Press, 1998) and Brian E. Becker and Mark S. Huselid, "High Performance Work Systems and Firm Performance: A Synthesis of Research and Managerial Implications," in *Research in Personnel and Human Resources Management,* Vol. 16 (Greenwich, CT: JAI Press, 1998), 53–101. Our discussion of the Toyota production system and flexible production is based on material from James Womack, Daniel Jones, and Daniel Ross, *The Machine That Changed the World: The Story of Lean Production* (New York: Harper Perennial, 1990) and from John Paul MacDuffie's research, including "Human Resource Bundles and Manufacturing Performance: Organizational Logic and

Flexible Production Systems in the World Auto Industry," *Industrial and Labor Relations Review* (1995).

The discussion of the elements of high performance or high commitment work systems comes from *The Human Equation*. Discussions of organizational culture and its importance can be found in Michael L. Tushman and Charles A. O'Reilly III, *Winning Through Innovation* (Boston: Harvard Business School Press, 1997). Also see Carla O'Dell and C. Jackson Grayson, Jr., *If Only We Knew What We Know* (New York: Free Press, 1998).

The self-fulfilling prophecy, or the effects of expectations on behavior, is a powerful and important theory often overlooked in the current emphasis on rewards and incentives. Some good, classic articles on the phenomenon include, W. Peter Archibald, "Alternative Explanations for Self-Fulfilling Prophecy," *Psychological Bulletin* (1974): 74–84; Dov Eden, "Self-Fulfilling Prophecy as a Management Tool: Harnessing Pygmalion," *Academy of Management Review* (1984): 64–67; and J. Sterling Livingston, "Pygmalion in Management," *Harvard Business Review* (July–August, 1969): 81–89.

Part C

Satisfaction and Emotion in Organizational Life

7. Organizational Psychology and the Pursuit of the Happy/Productive Worker

Barry M. Staw

What I am going to talk about in this article is an old and overworked topic, but one that remains very much a source of confusion and controversy. It is also a topic that continues to attract the attention of managers and academic researchers alike, frequently being the focus of both popular books and scholarly articles. The issue is how to manage an organization so that employees can be both happy and productive—a situation where workers and managers are both satisfied with the outcomes.

The pursuit of the happy/productive worker could be viewed as an impossible dream from the Marxist perspective of inevitable worker–management conflict. Such a goal could also be seen as too simple or naive from the traditional industrial relations view of outcomes being a product of necessary bargaining and compromise. Yet, from the psychological perspective, the pursuit of the happy/productive worker has seemed a worthwhile though difficult endeavor, one that might be achieved if we greatly increase our knowledge of work attitudes and behavior. In this article, I will examine this psychological perspective and try to provide a realistic appraisal of where we now stand in the search for satisfaction and productivity in work settings.

APPROACHES TO THE HAPPY/PRODUCTIVE WORKER

One of the earliest pursuits of the happy/productive worker involved the search for a relationship between satisfaction and productivity. The idea was that the world might be neatly divided into situations where workers are either happy and productive or unhappy and unproductive. If this were true, then it would be a simple matter to specify the differences between management styles present in the two sets of organizations and to come up with a list of prescriptions for improvement. Unfortunately, research has never supported such a clear relationship between individual satisfaction and productivity. For over thirty years, starting with Brayfield and Crockett's classic review of the job satisfaction–performance literature,[1] and again with Vroom's dicussion of satisfaction–performance research,[2] organizational psychologists have had to contend with the fact that happiness and productivity may not necessarily go together. As a result, most organizational psychologists have come to accept the argument that satisfaction and performance may relate to two entirely different individual decisions—decisions to participate and to produce.[3]

Though psychologists have acknowledged the fact that satisfaction and performance are not tightly linked, this has not stopped them from pursuing the happy/productive worker. In fact, over the last thirty years, an enormous variety of theories have attempted to show how managers can reach the promised land of high satisfaction and productivity. The theories shown in Table 7.1 constitute only an abbreviated list of recent attempts to reach this positive state.

None of the theories in Table 7.1 have inherited the happy/productive worker hypothesis in the simple sense of believing that job satisfaction and performance generally co-vary in the world *as it now exists.* But, these models all make either indirect or direct assumptions that *it is possible* to achieve a world where both satisfaction and performance will be present. Some of the theories focus on ways to increase job satisfaction, with the implicit assumption that performance will necessarily follow; some strive to directly increase performance, with the assumption that satisfaction will result; and some note that satisfaction and performance will be a joint product of implementing certain changes in the organization.

Without going into the specifics of each of these routes to the happy/productive worker, I think it is fair to say that most of the theories in Table 7.1 have been oversold. Historically, they each burst on the scene with glowing and almost messianic predictions, with proponents tending to simplify the process of change, making it seem like a few easy tricks will guarantee benefits to workers and management alike. The problem, of course, is that as results have come in from both academic research and from wider

TABLE 7.1
Paths to the Happy/Productive Worker

Worker Participation	The Pursuit of Excellence
Supportive Leadership	Socio-Technical Systems
9–9 Systems	Organizational Commitment
Job Enrichment	High Performing Systems
Behavior Modification	Theory Z
Goal Setting	Strong Culture

Dimension I   Why and How We Work

practical application, the benefits no longer have appeared so strong nor widespread. Typically, the broader the application and the more well-documented the study (with experimental controls and measures of expected costs and benefits), the weaker have been the empirical results. Thus, in the end, both managers and researchers have often been left disillusioned, sceptical that any part of these theories are worth a damn and that behavioral science will ever make a contribution to management.

My goal with this article is to *lower our expectations*—to show why it is so difficult to make changes in both satisfaction and performance. My intention is not to paint such a pessimistic picture as to justify not making any changes at all, but to innoculate us against the frustrations of slow progress. My hope is to move us toward a reasoned but sustainable pursuit of the happy/productive worker—away from the alternating practice of fanfare and despair.

CHANGING JOB ATTITUDES

Although organizational psychologists have accepted the notion that job satisfaction and performance do not necessarily co-vary, they have still considered job attitudes as something quite permeable or subject to change. This "blank slate" approach to job attitudes comes from prevailing psychological views of the individual, where the person is seen as a creature who constantly appraises the work situation, evaluates the merits of the context, and formulates an attitude based on these conditions. As the work situation changes, individuals are thought to be sensitive to the shifts adjusting their attitudes in a positive or negative direction. With such an approach to attitudes, it is easy to see why job satisfaction has been a common target of organizational change, and why attempts to redesign work have evolved as a principal mechanism for improving job satisfaction.

Currently, the major debate in the job design area concerns whether individuals are more sensitive to objective job conditions or social cues. In one camp are proponents of job redesign who propose that individuals are highly receptive to concrete efforts to improve working conditions. Hackman and Oldham, for example, argue that satisfaction can be increased by improving a job in terms of its variety (doing a wider number of things), identity (seeing how one's various tasks make a meaningful whole), responsibility (being in charge of one's own work and its quality), feedback (knowing when one has done a good job), and significance (the meaning or relative importance of one's contribution to the organization or society in general).[4] In the opposing camp are advocates of social information processing. These researchers argue that jobs are often ambiguous entities subject to multiple interpretations and perceptions.[5] Advocates of social information processing have noted that the positive or negative labeling of a task can greatly determine one's attitude toward the job, and that important determinants of this labeling are the opinions of co-workers who voice positive or negative views of the work. These researchers have shown that it may be as easy to persuade workers that their jobs are interesting by influencing the *perception* of a job as it is to make objective changes in the work role.

The debate between job design and social information processing has produced two recent shifts in the way we think about job attitudes. First, organizational psychology now places greater emphasis on the role of cognition and subjective evaluation in the way people respond to jobs. This is probably helpful, because even though we have generally measured job conditions with perceptual scales, we have tended to confuse these perceptions with objective job conditions. We need to be reminded that perceptions of job characteristics do not necessarily reflect reality, yet they can determine how we respond to that reality.

The second shift in thinking about job attitudes is a movement toward situationalism, stressing how even slight alterations in job context can influence one's perception of a job. It is now believed that people's job attitudes may be influenced not only by the objective properties of the work, but also by subtle cues given off by co-workers or supervisors that the job is dull or interesting. I think this new view is a mistake since it overstates the role of external influence in the determination of job attitudes. The reality may be that individuals are quite resistant to change efforts, with their attitudes coming more as a function of personal disposition than situational influence.

THE CONSISTENCY OF JOB ATTITUDES

Robert Kahn recently observed that, although our standard of living and working conditions have improved dramatically since World War II, reports of satisfaction on national surveys have not changed dramatically.[6] This implies that job satisfaction might be something of a "sticky variable," one that is not easily changed by outside influence. Some research on the consistency of job attitudes leads to the same conclusion. Schneider and Dachler, for example, found very strong consistency in satisfaction scores over a 16-month longitudinal study (averaging .56 for managers and .58 for non-managers).[7] Pulakos and Schmitt also found that high school students' pre-employment expectations of satisfaction correlated significantly with ratings of their jobs several years later.[8] These findings, along with the fact that job satisfaction is generally intertwined with both life satisfaction and mental health, imply that there is some ongoing consistency in job attitudes, and that job satisfaction may be determined as much by dispositional properties of the individual as any changes in the situation.

A Berkeley colleague, Joseph Garbarino, has long captured this notion of a dispositional source of job attitudes with a humorous remark, "I always told my children at a young age that their most important decision in life would be whether they wanted to be happy or not; everything else is malleable enough to fit the answer to this question." What Garbarino implies is that job attitudes are fairly constant, and when reality changes for either the better or worse, we can easily distort that reality to fit our underlying

disposition. Thus, individuals may think a great deal about the nature of their jobs, but satisfaction can result as much from the unique way a person views the world around him as from any social influence or objective job characteristics. That is, individuals predisposed to be happy may interpret their jobs in a much different way than those with more negative predispositions.

The Attitudinal Consistency Study

Recently, I have been involved with two studies attempting to test for dispositional sources of job attitudes. In the first study, Jerry Ross and I reanalyzed data from the National Longitudinal Survey, a study conducted by labor economists at Ohio State.[9] We used this survey to look at the stability of job attitudes over time and job situations. The survey's measures of attitudes were not very extensive but did prove one of the few available sources of data on objective job changes.

The National Longitudinal Survey data revealed an interesting pattern of results. We found that job satisfaction was fairly consistent over time, with significant relationships among job attitudes over three- and five-year time intervals. We also found that job satisfaction showed consistency *even when people changed jobs*. This later finding is especially important, since it directly contradicts the prevailing assumptions of job attitude research.

Most job design experiments and organizational interventions that strive to improve job attitudes change a small aspect of work, but look for major changes in job satisfaction. However, the National Longitudinal Survey data showed that when people changed their place of work (which would naturally include one's supervisor, working conditions, and procedures), there was still significant consistency in attitudes. One could, of course, argue that people leave one terrible job for another, and this is why such consistency in job attitude arises. Therefore, we checked for consistency across occupational changes. The National Longitudinal Survey showed consistency not only across occupational changes, but also when people changed *both* their employers and their occupations. This evidence of consistency tells us that people may not be as malleable as we would like to think they are, and that there may be some underlying tendency toward equilibrium in job attitudes. If you are dissatisfied in one job context, you are also likely to be dissatisfied in another (perhaps better) environment.

The Dispositional Study

The consistency data from the National Longitudinal Survey, while interesting, do not tell us what it is that may underlie a tendency to be satisfied or dissatisfied on the job. Therefore, Nancy Bell (a doctoral student at the Berkeley Business School), John Clausen (a developmental sociologist at Berkeley), and I undertook a study to find some of the dispositional sources of job satisfaction.[10] We sought to relate early personality characteristics to job attitudes later in life, using a very unusual longitudinal data source.

There are three longitudinal personality projects that have been running for over fifty years at Berkeley (the Berkeley Growth Study, the Oakland Growth Study, and the Guidance Study), and they have since been combined into what is now called the Intergenerational Study. Usually when psychologists speak of longitudinal studies, they mean data collected from one- or two-year intervals. These data span over 50 years. Usually, when psychologists refer to personality ratings, they mean self-reports derived from the administration of various questionnaires. Much of the Intergenerational Study data are clinical ratings derived from questionnaires, observation, and interview materials evaluated by a different set of raters for each period of the individual's life. Thus, these data are of unusual quality for psychological research.

Basically what we did with data from the Intergenerational Study was to construct an affective disposition scale that measured a very general positive–negative orientation of people. We then related this scale to measures of job attitudes at different periods in people's lives. The ratings used for our affective disposition scale included items such as "cheerful," "satisfied with self," and "irritable" (reverse coded), and we correlated this scale with measures of job and career satisfaction. The results were very provocative. We found that affective dispositions, from as early as the junior-high-school years, significantly predicted job attitudes during middle and late adulthood (ages 40–60). The magnitude of correlations was not enormous (in the .3 to .4 range). But, these results are about as strong as we usually see between the two attitudes measured on the same questionnaire by the same person at the same time—yet, these data cut across different raters and over fifty years in time.

What are we to conclude from this personality research as well as our reanalyses of the National Longitudinal Survey? I think we can safely conclude that there is a fair amount of consistency in job attitudes and that there may be dispositional as well as situational sources of job satisfaction. Thus, it is possible that social information processing theorists have been on the right track in viewing jobs as ambiguous entities that necessitate interpretation by individuals. But, it is also likely that the interpretation of jobs (whether they are perceived as positive or negative) can come as much from internal, dispositional causes (e.g., happiness or depression) as external sources. Consequently, efforts to improve job satisfaction via changes in job conditions will need to contend with stable personal dispositions toward work—forces that may favor consistency or equilibrium in the way people view the world around them.

THE INTRANSIGENCE OF JOB PERFORMANCE

Although we have not conducted research on the consistency of performance or its resistance to change, I think there are some parallels between the problems of changing attitudes and performance. Just as job attitudes may be constrained by individual dispositions, there are many elements of both the individual and work situation that can make improvements in job performance difficult.[11]

Most of the prevailing theories of work performance are concerned with individual motivation. They prescribe various techniques intended to stimulate, reinforce, or lure people into working harder. Most of these theories have little to say about the individual's limits of task ability, predisposition for working hard, or the general energy or activity level of the person. Somewhat naively, our theories have maintained that performance is under the complete control of the individual. Even though there are major individual differences affecting the quantity or quality of work produced, we have assumed that *if the employee really wants to perform better, his or her performance will naturally go up.*

There already exist some rather strong data that refer these implicit assumptions about performance. A number of studies[12] have shown that mental and physical abilities can be reliable predictors of job performance, and it is likely that other dispositions (e.g., personality characteristics) will eventually be found to be associated with effective performance of certain work roles. Thus, influencing work effort may not be enough to cause wide swings in performance, unless job performance is somewhat independent of ability (e.g., in a low skill job). Many work roles may be so dependent on ability (such as those of a professional athlete, musician, inventor) that increases in effort may simply not cause large changes in the end product.

In addition to ability, there may also be other individual factors that contribute to the consistency of performance. People who work hard in one situation are likely to be the ones who exert high effort in a second situation. If, for example, the person's energy level (including need for sleep) is relatively constant over time, we should not expect wide changes in available effort. And, if personality dimensions such as dependability and self-confidence can predict one's achievement level over the life-course,[13] then a similar set of personal attributes may well constitute limitations to possible improvements in performance. Already, assessment centers have capitalized on this notion by using personality measures to predict performance in many corporate settings.

Performance may not be restricted just because of the individual's level of ability and effort, however. Jobs may *themselves* be designed so that performance is not under the control of the individual, regardless of ability or effort. Certainly we are aware of the fact that an assembly line worker's output is more a product of the speed of the line than any personal preference. In administrative jobs too, what one does may be constrained by the work cycle or technical procedures. There may be many people with interlocking tasks so that an increase in the performance of one employee doesn't mean much if several tasks must be completed sequentially or simultaneously in order to improve productivity. Problems also arise in situations where doing one's job better may not be predicted upon a burst of energy or desire, but upon increases in materials, financial support, power, and resources. As noted by Kanter, the administrator must often negotiate, hoard, and form coalitions to get anything done on the job, since there are lots of actors vying for the attention and resources of the organization.[14] Thus, the nature of the organization, combined with the abilities and efforts of individuals to maneuver in the organization, may serve to constrain changes in individual performance.

ASSESSING THE DAMAGE

So far I have taken a somewhat dark or pessimistic view of the search of the happy/productive worker. I have noted that in terms of satisfaction and performance, it may not be easy to create perfect systems because both happiness and performance are constrained variables, affected by forces not easily altered by our most popular interventions and prescriptions for change. Should organizational psychologists therefore close up shop and go home? Should we move to a more descriptive study of behavior as opposed to searching for improvements in work attitudes and performance?

I think such conclusions are overly pessimistic. We need to interpret the stickiness of job attitudes and performance not as an invitation to complacency or defeat, but as a realistic assessment that it will take very strong treatments to move these entrenched variables. Guzzo, Jackson, and Katzell have recently made a similar point after a statistical examination (called meta-analysis) of organizational interventions designed to improve productivity.[15] They noted that the most effective changes are often *multiple treatments,* where several things are changed at once in a given organization. Thus, instead of idealistic and optimistic promises, we may literally need to throw the kitchen sink at the problem.

The problem of course is that we have more than one kitchen sink! As noted earlier, nearly every theory of organizational behavior has been devoted to predicting and potentially improving job attitudes and performance. And, simply aggregating these treatments is not likely to have the desired result, since many of these recommendations consist of conflicting prescriptions for change. Therefore, it would be wiser to look for compatible *systems* of variables that can possibly be manipulated in concert. Let us briefly consider three systems commonly used in organizational change efforts and then draw some conclusions about their alternative uses.

THREE SYSTEMS OF ORGANIZATIONAL CHANGE

The Individually Oriented System

The first alternative is to build a strong individually oriented system, based on the kind of traditional good management that organizational psychologists have been advocating for years. This system would emphasize a number of venerable features of Western business organizations such as:

- Tying extrinsic rewards (such as pay) to performance.
- Setting realistic and challenging goals.
- Evaluating employee performance accurately and providing feedback on performance.
- Promoting on the basis of skill and performance rather than personal characteristics, power, or connections.

- Building the skill level of the workforce through training and development.
- Enlarging and enriching jobs through increases in responsibility, variety, and significance.

All of the above techniques associated with the individually oriented system are designed to promote both satisfaction and productivity. The major principle underlying each of these features is to structure the work and/or reward system so that high performance is either intrinsically or extrinsically rewarding to the individual, thus creating a situation where high performance contributes to job satisfaction.

In practice, there can be numerous bugs in using an individually oriented system to achieve satisfaction and performance. For example, just saying that rewards should be based on performance is easier than knowing what the proper relationship should be or whether there should be discontinuities at the high or low end of that relationship. Should we, for instance, lavish rewards on the few highest performers, deprive the lowest performers, or establish a constant linkage between pay and performance? In terms of goal setting, should goals be set by management, workers, or joint decision making, and what should be proper baseline for measuring improvements? In terms of job design, what is the proper combination of positive social cues and actual job enrichment that will improve motivation and satisfaction?

These questions are important and need to be answered in order to "fine-tune" or fully understand an individually oriented system. Yet, even without answers to these questions, we already know that a well-run organization using an individually oriented system *can* be effective. The problem is we usually don't implement such a system, either completely or very well, in most organizations. Instead, we often compare poorly managed corporations using individually oriented systems (e.g., those with rigid bureaucratic structures) with more effectively run firms using another motivational system (e.g., Japanese organizations), concluding that the individual model is wrong. The truth may be that the individual model may be just as correct as other approaches, but we simply don't implement it as well.

The Group-Oriented System

Individually oriented systems are obviously not the only way to go. We can also have a group-oriented system, where satisfaction and performance are derived from group participation. In fact, much of organizational life could be designed around groups, if we wanted to capitalize fully on the power of groups to influence work attitudes and behavior.[16] The basic idea would be to make group participation so important that groups would be capable of controlling both satisfaction and performance. Some of the most common techniques would be:

- Organizing work around intact groups.
- Having groups charged with selection, training, and rewarding of members.
- Using groups to enforce strong norms for behavior, with group involvement in off-the-job as well as on-the-job behavior.
- Distributing resources on a group rather than individual basis.
- Allowing and perhaps even promoting inter-group rivalry so as to build within-group solidarity.

Group-oriented systems may be difficult for people at the top to control, but they can be very powerful and involving. We know from military research that soldiers can fight long and hard, not out of special patriotism, but from devotion and loyalty to their units. We know that participation in various high-tech project groups can be immensely involving, both in terms of one's attitudes and performance. We also know that people will serve long and hard hours to help build or preserve organizational divisions or departments, perhaps more out of loyalty and altruism than self-interest. Thus, because individuals will work to achieve group praise and adoration, a group-oriented system, effectively managed, can potentially contribute to high job performance and satisfaction.

The Organizationally Oriented System

A third way of organizing work might be an organizationally oriented system, using the principles of Ouchi's Theory Z and Lawler's recommendations for developing high-performing systems.[17] The basic goal would be to arrange working conditions so that individuals gain satisfaction from contributing to the entire organization's welfare. If individuals were to identify closely with the organization as a whole, then organizational performance would be intrinsically rewarding to the individual. On a less altruistic basis, individuals might also gain extrinsic rewards from association with a high-performing organization, since successful organizations may provide greater personal opportunities in terms of salary and promotion. Common features of an organizationally oriented system would be:

- Socialization into the organization as a whole to foster identification with the entire business and not just a particular subunit.
- Job rotation around the company so that loyalty is not limited to one subunit.
- Long training period with the development of skills that are specific to the company and not transferable to other firms in the industry or profession, thus committing people to the employing organization.
- Long-term or protected employment to gain organizational loyalty, with concern for survival and welfare of the firm.
- Decentralized operations, with few departments or subunits to compete for the allegiance of members.
- Few status distinctions between employees so that dissention and separatism are not fostered.
- Economic education and sharing of organizational information about products, financial condition, and strategies of the firm.
- Tying individual rewards (at all levels of the firm) to organizational performance through various forms of profit sharing, stock options, and bonuses.

The Japanese have obviously been the major proponents of organizationally oriented systems, although some of the features listed here (such as profit sharing) are very American in origin. The odd thing is that Americans have consistently followed an organizationally oriented system for middle and upper management and for members of professional organizations such as law and accounting firms. For these high-level employees, loyalty may be as valued as immediate performance, with the firm expecting the individual to defend the organization, even if there does not seem to be any obvious self-interest involved. Such loyalty is rarely demanded or expected from the lower levels of traditional Western organizations.

EVALUATING THE THREE SYSTEMS

I started this article by noting that it may be very difficult to change job performance and satisfaction. Then I noted that recognition of this difficulty should not resign us to the present situation, but spur us to stronger and more systematic actions—in a sense, throwing more variables at the problem. As a result, I have tried to characterize three syndromes of actions that might be effective routes toward the happy/productive worker.

One could build a logical case for the use of any of the three motivational systems. Each has the potential for arousing individuals, steering their behavior in desired ways, and building satisfaction as a consequence of high performance. Individually oriented systems work by tapping the desires and goals of individuals and by taking advantage of our cultural affinity for independence. Group-oriented systems work by taking advantage of our more social selves, using group pressures and loyalty as the means of enforcing desired behavior and dispensing praise for accomplishments. Finally, organizationally oriented systems function by building intense attraction to the goals of an institution, where individual pleasure is desired from serving the collective welfare.

If we have three logical and defensible routes toward achieving the happy/productive worker, which is the best path? The answer to this question will obviously depend on how the question is phrased. If "best" means appropriate from a cultural point of view, we will get one answer. As Americans, although we respect organizational loyalty, we often become suspicious of near total institutions where behavior is closely monitored and strongly policed—places like the company town and religious cult. If we define "best" as meaning the highest level of current performance, we might get a different answer, since many of the Japanese-run plants are now outperforming the American variety. Still, if we phrase the question in terms of *potential* effectiveness, we may get a third answer. Cross-cultural comparisons, as I mentioned, often pit poorly managed individually oriented systems (especially those with non-contingent rewards and a bureaucratic promotion system) against more smoothly running group- or organizationally oriented systems. Thus, we really do not know which system, managed to its potential, will lead to the greatest performance.

Mixing the Systems

If we accept the fact that individual-, group-, and organizationally oriented systems may each do *something* right, would it be possible to take advantage of all three? That is, can we either combine all three systems into some suprasystem or attempt to build a hybrid system by using the best features of each?

I have trepidations about combining the three approaches. Instead of a stronger treatment, we may end up with either a conflicted or confused environment. Because the individually oriented system tends to foster competition among individual employees, it would not, for example, be easily merged with group-oriented systems that promote intragroup solidarity. Likewise, organizationally oriented systems that emphasize how people can serve a common goal may not blend well with group-oriented systems that foster intergroup rivalry. Finally, the use of either a group- or organizationally oriented reward system may diminish individual motivation, since it becomes more difficult for the person to associate his behavior with collective accomplishments and outcomes. Thus, by mixing the motivational approaches, we may end up with a watered-down treatment that does not fulfill the potential of *any* of the three systems.

In deciding which system to use, we need to face squarely the costs as well as benefits of the three approaches. For example, firms considering an individually oriented system should assess not only the gains associated with increases in individual motivation, but also potential losses in collaboration that might result from interpersonal competition. Similarly, companies thinking of using a group-oriented system need to study the trade-offs of intergroup competition that can be a byproduct of increased intragroup solidarity. And, before thinking that an organizationally oriented system will solve all the firm's problems, one needs to know whether motivation to achieve collective goals can be heightened to the point where it outweighs potential losses in motivation toward personal and group interests. These trade-offs are not trivial, they trigger considerations of human resource policy as well as more general philosophical issues of what the organization wants to be. They also involve technical problems for which current organizational research has few solutions, since scholars have tended to study treatments in isolation rather than the effect of larger systems of variables.

So far, all we can be sure of is that task structure plays a key role in formulating the proper motivational strategy. As an example, consider the following cases: a sales organization can be divided into discrete territories (where total performance is largely the sum of individual efforts), a research organization

where several product groups are charged with making new developments (where aggregate performance is close to the sum of group efforts), and a high-technology company where success and failure is due to total collaboration and collective effort. In each of these three cases, the choice of the proper motivational system will be determined by whether one views individual, group, or collective effort as the most important element. Such a choice is also determined by the degree to which one is willing to sacrifice (or trade-off) a degree of performance from other elements of the system, be they the behavior of individuals, groups, or the collective whole. Thus, the major point is that each motivational system has its relative strengths and weaknesses—that despite the claims of many of our theories of management, there is no simple or conflict-free road to the happy/productive worker.

CONCLUSION

Although this article started by noting that the search for the happy/productive worker has been a rather quixotic venture, I have tried to end the discussion with some guarded optimism. By using individual, group, and organizational systems, I have shown how it is *at least possible* to create changes that can overwhelm the forces for stability in both job attitudes and performance. None of these three approaches are a panacea that will solve all of an organization's problems, and no doubt some very hard choices must be made between them. Yet, caution need not preclude action. Therefore, rather than the usual academic's plea for further research or the consultant's claim for bountiful results, we need actions that are flexible enough to allow for mistakes and adjustments along the way.

REFERENCES

1. A. H. Brayfield and W. H. Crockett, "Employee Attitudes and Employee Performance," *Psychological Bulletin*, 51 (1955): 396–424.

2. Victor H. Vroom, *Work and Motivation* (New York, NY: Wiley, 1969).

3. James G. March and Herbert A. Simon, *Organizations* (New York, NY: Wiley, 1958).

4. Richard J. Hackman and Greg R. Oldham, *Work Redesign* (Reading, MA: Addison-Wesley, 1980).

5. E.g., Gerald R. Salancik and Jeffrey Pfeffer, "A Social Information Processing Approach to Job Attitudes and Task Design" *Administrative Science Quarterly,* 23 (1978):224–253.

6. Robert Kahn (1985).

7. Benjamin Schneider and Peter Dachler, "A Note on the Stability of the Job Description Index," *Journal of Applied Psychology,* 63 (1978):650–653.

8. Elaine D. Pulakos and Neil Schmitt, "A Longitudinal Study of a Valence Model Approach for the Prediction of Job Satisfaction of New Employees," *Journal of Applied Psychology,* 68 (1983):307–312.

9. Barry M. Staw and Jerry Ross, "Stability in the Midst of Change: A Dispositional Approach to Job Attitudes," *Journal of Applied Psychology,* 70 (1985):469–480.

10. Barry M. Staw, Nancy E. Bell, and John A. Clausen, "The Dispositional Approach to Job Attitudes: A Lifetime Longitudinal Test," *Administrative Science Quarterly* (March 1986).

11. See Lawrence H. Peters, Edward J. O'Connor, and Joe R. Eulberg, "Situational Constraints: Sources, Consequences, and Future Considerations," in Kendreth M. Rowland and Gerald R. Ferris, eds., *Research in Personnel and Human Resources Management,* Vol. 3 (Greenwich, CT: JAI Press, 1985).

12. For a review, see Marvin D. Dunnette, "Aptitudes, Abilities, and Skills" in Marvin D. Dunnette, ed., *Handbook of Industrial and Organizational Psychology* (Chicago, IL: Rand McNally, 1976).

13. As found by John Clausen, personal communications, 1986.

14. Rosabeth M. Kanter, *The Change Masters* (New York, NY: Simon & Schuster, 1983).

15. Richard A. Guzzo, Susan E. Jackson, and Raymond A. Katzell, "Meta-analysis Analysis," in Barry M. Staw and Larry L. Cummings, eds., *Research in Organizational Behavior,* Volume 9 (Greenwich, CT: JAI Press, 1987).

16. See Harold J. Leavitt, "Suppose We Took Groups Seriously," in E. L. Cass and F. G. Zimmer, eds., *Man and Work in Society* (New York, NY: Van Nostrand, 1975).

17. William Ouchi, *Theory Z: How American Business Can Meet the Japanese Challenge* (Reading, MA: Addison-Wesley, 1981); Edward E. Lawler, III, "Increasing Worker Involvement to Enhance Organizational Effectiveness," in Paul Goodman, ed., *Change in Organizations* (San Francisco, CA: Jossey-Bass, 1982).

8. The Subtle Significance of Job Satisfaction

Dennis W. Organ

Imagine that Michael Jordan were to become dissatisfied with the Chicago Bulls organization. Suppose, for example, Jordan felt that the team's management had reneged on some promise, or violated some understanding, or sullied his reputation. How would Jordan act out his dissatisfaction? Would he deliberately turn over the ball, let an opposing player score an easy uncontested basket, commit silly fouls to exit the game early?

I submit that it is virtually unthinkable that Jordan or any other professional athlete would respond this way, for two reasons. First, to do so would severely compromise the player's own interests—the "stats" would suffer, and, with that, the bargaining wedge for future contracts. Second, and more important, true professionals cannot bear the intrinsic pain of deliberately botching their individual performance. Whatever grievance Jordan might have against the Bulls, he would inflict unbearable grief on himself as he mentally replayed episodes of shoddy workmanship.

So, given the prohibitive personal and psychic costs of betraying one's craft, how does a professional act out dissatisfaction—aside from merely voicing it? Perhaps voicing dissatisfaction is as far as some would go. But athletes, like other professionals—including those in the clinical laboratory—have some other options. They can choose to define their obligations and their roles narrowly; they will do what they contractually must do. They will do what rebounds directly to their self-interests, but contribute only grudgingly (if at all) in other ways. They can choose not to help teammates improve their skills, not to sacrifice leisure hours to "rubber chicken" banquets for community groups, not to take part in (or not

to attend) informal discussions off the playing arena, not to make suggestions for improving the organization, not to sign autographs. They can tie up valuable management time by pressing every imaginable petty grievance, sour the whole atmosphere for players and staff, and undermine confidence in the organization.

Research now indicates that precisely these effects on Organizational Citizenship Behavior, rather than in-role performance or productivity as traditionally defined, are the casualty of dissatisfaction.

SATISFACTION CAUSES PRODUCTIVITY—AN APPEALING BUT DISCREDITED PREMISE

The notion that "a happy employee is a productive employee" lay for a long time at the center of one popular school of management thought. This concept of worker motivation, probably traceable to some distorted accounts of the legendary Hawthorne research of the 1920s and 1930s, certainly has its appeal. Most managers want productivity, and they prefer a satisfied workforce over one that is dissatisfied. So practitioners espouse that whatever makes people happy is justifiable as "an investment in higher productivity." Not surprisingly, surveys have shown a strong tendency by human resource and line managers and union leaders to agree than an individual's job satisfaction translates into a corresponding level of productivity.[1,2]

Unfortunately, researchers began to discredit this theory almost from the start. Nearly 35 years ago, Brayfield and Crockett[3] reviewed an already large body of empirical study of the relationship between job attitudes and productivity. They concluded that no

From *Clinical Laboratory Management Review* (Jan/Feb 1990) 4, no. 1, 94–98. Copyright © 1990 by Clinical Laboratory Management Association, Inc. Reprinted with permission.

"appreciable" relationships existed. Periodic updates have found no reason to modify this general assessment.

THE PENDULUM TURNS

Interestingly, the findings of "rigorous research" have not disturbed practicing managers. Well into the 1970s, possibly into the early 1980s, most managers—either because they did not know about the results of behavioral research, or perhaps because they chose to believe evidence from their own experience— held to the premise that satisfaction does significantly affect productivity. In retrospect, it is doubtful if management science research alone would have ever seriously undermined that premise.

A much more powerful stimulus to revising management opinion was the combined form of double-digit inflation in the late 1970s and the recession of the early 1980s. Malaise about the state of the "body economic" saturated the financial tabloids and the after-dinner speeches of corporate CEOs. We must wake up, it was argued, to the dawning of a new era—one of global competition, deregulation, and accountability. "Country-club-style" management led to creeping costs—costs that only beget more costs rather than increasing ouput. The ethos of the day was for organizations to hack away the dead wood, downsize to a lean and mean profile, and get more bang for the buck. That meant *every* buck, including the one spent on amenities to make people happy or put into their pay checks.

Tough-minded management came to the fore. Its rationale was the rigorous research showing no consistent or "appreciable" effect of satisfaction on productivity. The old model that a happy worker is a productive worker was rejected as simplistic, if not soft-headed. The new model emphasized performance; let satisfaction fall where it may. The important consideration was not *how many* people were happy but *which* people. The underlying logic was to obtain results from those able and willing to supply them and to ensure that those people, and only those, had any reason for satisfaction.

The new, tough-minded management doctrine was evident in a variety of reforms in human resource practices. For example, many firms took steps to ensure that performance appraisals differentiated among people to a much greater extent. Supervisors could no longer rate a few people as, for example, a 5 on a 5-point scale and everyone else a 4. They had to use the 1s and 2s on the scale. Some programs required every manager to rank people from top to bottom. By definition every department had 50 percent of its people "below average." Moreover, performance measurement was not based on the subjective impressions of supervisors. Feverish activity went into the design of quantitative indicators of specific accomplishments. The message was clear and emphatic: "Let's see your stats as they relate to the bottom line." Merit-pay plans, although nominally in effect in most organizations for many years, acquired new and sharp teeth. Those in the top quartile of ratings and statistical categories received substantial raises; those in the bottom quartile were "zeroed out."

How did such reforms affect job satisfaction? For some, the effect was positive. Overall, as some research suggests,[4,5] the effect was reduced satisfaction. But so what? Job satisfaction doesn't affect a person's productivity, so it doesn't matter. Or does it?

SATISFACTION AND ORGANIZATIONAL CITIZENSHIP BEHAVIOR

Research currently distinguishes between *in-role* performance and productivity and *extra-role* contributions in the form of Organizational Citizenship Behavior (OCB). Individual in-role performance consists of well-specified job requirements—what the person must do according to the job description—and accomplishments (such as meeting certain quotas or statistical norms) that contractually qualify the individual for incremental rewards, such as bonus pay or prizes. Such performance is to some degree a function of attitude, but also of aptitude, expertise, work flow, dependence on others, and resources (such as equipment, budget, staff). Positive attitudes can add little to a person's in-role performance once the limits of those other constraints are reached.

Negative attitudes that might otherwise cause reduced effort for this kind of performance often will not have this effect—people can be disciplined (even terminated) for unsatisfactory in-role performance. And, negative attitudes toward management notwithstanding, someone who needs bonus pay and qualifies for it will perform accordingly.

But for the professional—not only the Michael Jordans but also the highly skilled specialists in the laboratory—there is an even more compelling reason why in-role performance will not suffer because of dissatisfaction. The reason is ego-involvement. For the ego-involved professional, poor or even mediocre performance is intrinsically painful. It arouses feelings of guilt, embarrassment, and self-reproach.

So neither satisfaction nor dissatisfaction will necessarily manifest itself by effects on individual in-role performance.

The problem is that in-role performance is never enough. As Daniel Katz noted:

> An organization which depends solely upon its blueprints of prescribed behavior is a very fragile system. . . . The patterned activity which makes up an organization is so intrinsically a cooperative set of interrelationships, that we are not aware of the cooperative nexus any more than we are of any habitual behavior like walking. Within every work group in a factory, within every division in a government bureau, or within any department of a university are countless acts of cooperation without which the system would break down. We take these everyday acts for granted. . . .[6]

An effective organization depends on many forms of discretionary, voluntary contributions for which people seldom get direct credit. These contributions make up OCB. Satisfied people do more of these things (because OCB is primarily a function of attitude and not very dependent on ability or resources); dissatisfied people can choose to do less of them without incurring the risk of sanctions or lost benefits. Because OCB includes many humble and mundane gestures, cutting back on OCB does not hurt the ego as would inferior task performance.

Characteristics of OCB

The concept of OCB becomes less abstract, and much more intuitively familiar to the practicing manager, by understanding some of its characteristics.

Altruism consists of those voluntary actions that help another person with a work problem—instructing a new hire on how to use equipment, helping a co-worker catch up with a backlog of work, fetching materials that a colleague needs and cannot procure on his own.

Courtesy subsumes all of those foresightful gestures that help someone else prevent a problem—touching base with people before committing to action that will affect them, providing advance notice to someone who needs to know to schedule work.

Sportsmanship is a citizen-like posture of tolerating the inevitable inconveniences and impositions of work without whining and grievances—for example, the forbearance shown by a technician whose vacation schedule must yield to unexpected contingencies, or by the programmer who must temporarily endure cramped work quarters.

Conscientiousness is a pattern of going well beyond minimally required levels of attendance, punctuality, housekeeping, conserving resources, and related matters of internal maintenance.

Civic virtue is responsible, constructive involvement in the political process of the organization, including not just expressing opinions but reading one's mail, attending meetings, and keeping abreast of larger issues involving the organization.

At Indiana University, we have developed reliable research instruments for rating people's contributions in these forms. Two other categories for which we do not presently have measures, but which logically relate to OCB, are

Peacemaking—actions that help to prevent, resolve, or mitigate unconstructive interpersonal conflict—and *Cheerleading*—the words and gestures of encouragement and reinforcement of co-workers' accomplishments and professional development.

A key point is that the person who shows these characteristics of OCB seldom sees it register in his or her individual productivity or "stats" (an exception, perhaps, would be an outstanding attendance record). More often, OCB contributes either to a colleague's performance or to improving the efficiency of the system. A manager, for example, has more time and stamina for important business when not mediating protracted grievances by a staff lacking in sportsmanship. The operator who ignores matters of courtesy generally does not sacrifice his or her individual productivity but creates snafus farther down the line, eventually hurting other's work.

The experienced administrator may, as Katz suggested, take OCB for granted. But if, for whatever reasons, OCB diminishes, the perceptive manager either sees or foresees the eventual effects. As Max Depree, chairman of Herman Miller, Inc., observed,[7] one of the warning signs of a company in decline is a "general loss of grace and civility."

Research at Indiana University[8] and elsewhere confirms that OCB is where we must look for the effects of dissatisfaction. The effects are indirect and not generally visible in lower in-role performance. The loss is in those discretionary forms of citizenship on which effective systems depend.

Interdependence and OCB

Management theorists have always noted the essential condition of interdependence created by organization. Much of their creative energies have involved formulating principles, rules, and design structures that address this condition.

James D. Thompson[9] pointed out that formal structure suffices for only certain types of interdependence as they arise from the basic technology of organization. *Mediating technologies*—common to banks, telephone exchanges, libraries, and retail establishments—link clients or customers who wish to be interdependent. This technology creates what Thompson termed "pooled interdependence," which can be managed by standardized rules and procedures. *Long-linked technologies*, of which the archetype is the assembly line, give rise to serial or "linear interdependence." Detailed plans and forecasts are needed to cope with long-linked technologies.

Thompson's third form, *intensive technology*, perhaps best describes the clinical laboratory. Thompson defines this form to "signify that a variety of techniques is drawn upon in order to achieve a change in some specific object; but the selection, combination, and order of application are determined by feedback from the object itself."[9] This type of technology breeds complex, often unforeseeable, reciprocal interdependence. Thompson argued that formal structure, standardized procedures, and elaborate plans are not sufficient to manage this dependence. It requires "mutual adjustment," spontaneous give-and-take, informal helping, teamwork, and cooperation—in other words, OCB. OCB always matters, but especially when intensive technologies breed complex reciprocal interdependence among people, managers, and departments.

SATISFACTION: FAIRNESS, NOT HAPPINESS

So job satisfaction is important after all. Does this mean reverting to country-club-style management, with all its attendant concern for making people happy? The answer is "no" because recent research[10] suggests that happiness has little to do with job satisfaction. When people answer questions about their satisfaction—with work, pay, supervision, promotion—they think about fairness. They compare what they might reasonably have expected and what they actually experience.

Fairness certainly is an inherently subjective and complex issue. People have different ideas about what makes an arrangement fair or unfair. One person will think in terms of visible accomplishments; another will think in terms of loyalty and commitment (e.g., seniority). Still others think of ability, effort, external markets (such as supply and demand for specific expertise), precedent (the fact that certain groups "have always rated a premium"), or education. Seldom is there consensus about the relative weights of these criteria. Fortunately, most people have a reasonably high threshold for perceiving inequity. A system need not match any one person's preferred formula so long as the rank and file understand that an array of relevant criteria have been considered. Most employees expect the technically excellent performer to command a differential in pay or status; they just don't want other criteria of worthiness to be totally ignored. When differentials become marked, and when they are determined by unduly narrow conceptions or measures of contribution, the threshold of unfairness is breached. Dissatisfaction mounts, OCB suffers, and eventually, so does the organization.

Any discussion of fairness at work must reckon with procedural and distributive justice. The process in which decisions are made and benefits determined can affect satisfaction just as much as the decisions and benefits themselves. Studies of employee personnel systems and managerial leadership point to four critical factors in perceptions of fairness:

- *Feedback*—ample and prompt.
- *Recourse*—the option of appeal.
- *Fundamental respect for human dignity*— Even the most incompetent and incorrigible subordinate has the right to be addressed civilly.
- *Some form of input*—We do not mean pure democracy, but simply the opportunity to be heard. As one CEO put it, "having a voice does not mean having a vote."

CONCLUSION

Management research and theory have taken a long time and a torturous path in catching up with the insights of Chester Barnard. More than half a century ago, Barnard[11] noted the essential condition of the *"willingness* of persons to contribute efforts to the cooperative system." This quality of willingness "is something different from effectiveness, ability, or value of personal contributions. . . . [it] means self-abnegation." Willingness is characterized by "[an] indefinitely large range of variation in its intensity among individuals" and, within individuals, "it cannot be constant in degree." Finally, this "willingness to cooperate, positive or negative, is the expression of the net satisfactions and dissatisfactions experienced or anticipated."

Barnard underscored the very nature of organizations as cooperative systems. Rules, structures, policies, job descriptions, sanctions, incentives—they all play necessary roles in collaborative endeavors, but as derivatives of, not as substitues for, the underlying disposition to cooperate. Such a disposition can be sustained only by a sense of the organization as a microcosm of a just world. Occasional inequities can be tolerated if there is faith that the system works fairly over the long run, with self-correcting tendencies. When faith yields to a narrowly defined, *quid pro quo* contractual relationship, the disposition to cooperate ebbs. Surveys show that most of the nation's labor force begins work with a fairly high degree of job satisfaction and that most of the people, most of the time, will describe themselves as "all in all, satisfied." There is a generally prevalent inclination to give the employer the benefit of the doubt—"I'll assume you're treating me fairly until you persuade me otherwise." So the disposition is generally present to render a substantial contribution via OCB. A good-faith effort by managers to provide a "square deal" will do much to ensure the quality of OCB.

REFERENCES

1. Gannon, M. J., and J. P. Noon. "Management's critical deficiency." *Business Horizons* (1971) *14,* 49–56.

2. Katzell, R. A., and D. Yankelovich. *Work, productivity, and job satisfaction.* New York: The Psychological Corporation, 1975.

3. Brayfield, A. H., and W. H. Crockett. "Employee attitudes and employee performance." *Psychological Bulletin* (1955) *52,* 396–424.

4. Baird, L. S., and W. C. Hammer. "Individual versus system rewards: Who's dissatisfied, why and what is their likely response?" *Academy of Management Journal* (1979) *22,* 783–92.

5. Pearce, J. L., and L. W. Porter. "Employee responses to formal performance appraisal feedback." *Journal of Applied Psychology* (1986) *71,* 211–18.

6. Katz, D. "The motivational basis of organizational behavior." *Behavioral Science* (1964) *9,* 131–46.

7. Labich, K. "Hot company, warm culture." *Fortune* (February 27, 1989), 74–78.

8. Organ, D. W. *Organizational citizenship behavior.* Lexington, Mass.: Lexington Books, 1988.

9. Thompson, J. D. *Organizations in action.* New York: McGraw-Hill, 1967.

10. Organ, D. W., and J. P. Near. "Cognition vs. affect in measures of job satisfaction." *International Journal of Psychology* (1985) *20,* 241–53.

11. Barnard, C. I. *The functions of the executive.* Cambridge, Mass.: Harvard University Press, 1938.

9. Expression of Emotion as Part of the Work Role

Anat Rafaeli/Robert I. Sutton

Research on feelings experienced and expressed by organizational members emphasizes emotions as indicators of well-being and happiness. Writings on job stress, for example, view affective responses primarily as dependent variables that change in response to objective or subjective threats to well-being (Kahn, 1981). Related writings convey that "burnout" is a syndrome of emotional exhaustion among workers in the helping professions (Maslach, 1978a). Perhaps the greatest attention to emotion as a dependent variable is found in the job satisfaction literature. Locke's (1976) widely cited review defines job satisfaction as "a pleasurable or positive emotional state resulting from the appraisal of one's job or job experiences" (p. 1300).

Yet viewing emotion only as an intrapsychic outcome masks the complex role it plays in organizational life. In service organizations, for example, effectiveness is thought to hinge partly on the emotions expressed by employees (Czepiel, Solomon, & Surprenant, 1985). To illustrate, check-out clerks working at one chain of supermarkets are issued a handbook that commands:

YOU are the company's most effective representative. Your customers judge the entire company by your actions. A cheerful "Good Morning" and "Good Evening" followed by courteous, attentive treatment, and a sincere "Thank you, please come again," will send them away with a friendly feeling and a desire to return. A friendly smile is a must.

The feelings offered by this employee to customers are not indicators of well-being.

Rather, smiling and acting "friendly" are part of the work role.

The display of friendliness and good cheer are expected in an array of service occupations including flight attendants, servants, and sales clerks. In contrast, bill collectors and bouncers are paid to convey hostility. Funeral directors express sadness. Other roles call for the suppression of emotion: "good" academic deans display neutrality, especially around budget time. Many roles call for variation in expressed emotions. For example, a case study of a team of surgical nurses (Denison & Sutton, in press) revealed that members were expected to present an emotionally flat demeanor in the operating room, to be warm when talking with patients and their families, and to encourage one another to express "true feelings" such as rage and disgust during breaks and informal meetings with other nurses.

Yet expectations about emotional expression have been largely ignored by organizational theorists who have adopted role theory. The widely cited work by Kahn and his colleagues (Kahn, Wolfe, Quinn, Snoek, & Rosenthal, 1964; Katz & Kahn, 1978) focused on sent and received role expectations that are excessive, ambiguous, or in conflict. The sources of expectations about emotional expressions and the effects of displayed feelings are not addressed explicitly in Kahn's work, or in the more general writings on role theory (Biddle, 1979). Goffman's (1969) work, however, addressed the causes and consequences of expressed emotions. His writings on strategic interaction focus on how people manipulate emotional expression to promote their own interests. But employees also display feelings to promote the interest of other role senders including clients and co-workers. This paper follows the spirit of Goffman's writings and considers work settings in which employees display emotions in order to fulfill role expectations.

CONCEPTUAL FRAMEWORK

The conceptual territory covered by the framework proposed here includes the sources of role expectations about emotional expression, the range of such emotional expressions, and the influence expressed feelings have on the organization and on the role occupant (see Figure 9.1). The underlying assumption is that many of the emotions conveyed by employees can be thought of as "control moves" (Goffman, 1969), which refer to "the intentional effort of an informant to produce expressions that he thinks will improve his situation if they are gleaned by the observer" (p. 12). It is further proposed that emotions expressed without the intention of influencing others can serve as control moves.

The attributes of expressed emotions are central to our framework. Developing a complete theory of emotion is a task that has intrigued and puzzled writers from a variety of disciplines. Such theories are sometimes the subject of entire books (Darwin, 1965; DeRivera, 1977; Hillman, 1961); identifying the full range of human emotion is beyond the scope of this paper. Nonetheless, a pair of imperfect dimensions is useful for developing theory about emotions conveyed as part of the job. First, emotions can be arrayed on a continuum ranging from positive, through neutral, to negative. Expression of positive affect includes smiling and enthusiasm. Negative affect includes frowning and disgust.

One limitation of this continuum is that some emotions are difficult to classify. Is the sadness expressed by a funeral director positive or negative? Further, depending on which perspective is adopted, the same expressed emotion can be positive or negative. The friendly smile of, say a waitress, may be positive from the customer's point of view, but may

FIGURE 9.1
Expression of Emotion as Part of the Work Role: A Conceptual Framework

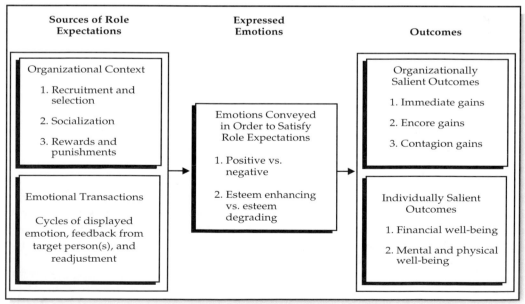

be construed as artificial and thus negative by the waitress.

The second continuum is the extent that expressed emotions reinforce the target person's self-esteem. Some occupations require employees to support co-workers or clients (social workers, physicians, receptionists); others require employees to remain neutral (judges and referees); and some jobs require the role occupant to degrade the self-esteem of others (drill sergeants, poker players).

This second continuum is also imperfect; because of differences in cultural backgrounds and personality, it is difficult to predict the influence an expressed emotion will have on a person's self-esteem. Taken together, however, these continua indicate that for expressed emotions (or any other human communication) to convey meaning, the message must be encoded by a source and decoded by a receiver (Osgood, Suci, & Tannenbaum, 1957). The positive–negative continuum highlights feelings encoded by the role occupant; the esteem enhancing–degrading continuum accentuates expressed emotions decoded by the audience.

SOURCES OF ROLE EXPECTATIONS

Two sources of role expectations are proposed that create, influence, and maintain the emotions expressed in organizational life: the *organizational context* and *emotional transactions*. The organizational context comprises formal and informal practices used by a larger organization to influence emotions displayed by members. Following Trist's (1977) distinction between contextual and transactional environments, the organizational context can be distinguished from emotional transactions. The organizational context includes selection, socialization, and reward systems; emotional transactions comprise the sequence of communication that occurs when an employee displays emotion, notes the reaction of a "target" person, and adjusts or maintains expressed feelings.

Organizational Context

The present authors propose that three dimensions of the organizational context create and maintain expectations about emotional expression: recruitment and selection, socialization, and rewards and punishments. For the sake of simplicity, most of this discussion considers incumbents who are influenced by the context of a single organization. Nevertheless, in practice, a person may be affected by the selection, socialization, and reward systems of more than one organization. Some people are members of more than one organization. Boundary-spanners are influenced by the norms of outside organizations encountered in their work. Moreover, contexts encountered in prior organizational memberships (schools attended, previous jobs) may influence emotions that are expressed in current roles.

Recruitment and Selection. Organizations seek to employ people who can convey emotions deemed to be appropriate for the role. For example, a manual produced by McDonald's "Hamburger University" urges store managers "Your window-men and outside order-takers must impress customers as being 'All American' boys. They must display desirable traits such as sincerity, enthusiasm, confidence, and a sense of humor" (Boas & Chain, 1976, p. 84). Newspaper ads solicit sales people who are "young-minded with a positive attitude," "personable," "aggressive," and "convincing." Also, Playboy bunnies were required to be charming as well as sexy (Steinem, 1983).

Although emotional expression is not discussed explicitly in the literature on job analysis, some job analysis techniques imply that displayed feelings are job requirements (McCormick, 1979). For example, the traits required to deal with other people such as diverting, serving, and persuading are included in the rating scales used by the United States Employment Service (U.S. Department of Labor, 1972).

Hypothesis testing studies on the recruitment and selection of incumbents on the basis of emotional skills are rare, but some research suggests that job prospects are brighter for interviewees who convey positive emotions and hide negative feelings. Forbes and Jackson (1980) reported that interviewees who smiled, maintained eye contact, and nodded their heads were most likely to be offered jobs. In contrast, rejected candidates in this study "were characterized by more avoidance gaze; eye wandering, more neutral facial expression, and less smiling" (p. 70). Similar findings were reported by Imada and Hakel (1977), as well as McGovern and Tinsley (1978).

Research is needed, however, on whether such decisions are intentional. Moreover, these studies do not distinguish between the emotions required to get a job and the emotions needed to do the job.

Socialization. Organizational socialization often includes learning norms, or "feeling rules" (Hochschild, 1979), about which emotions ought to be displayed and which ought to be hidden. Feeling rules can be learned in an organization other than the one in which a member practices his or her occupation. The "University of Santa Claus," for example, teaches Santas who will work in department stores to smile and be jolly "even when a kid who isn't quite potty trained has an accident" ("Rules for Santas," 1984). Similarly, law schools and medical schools teach professional norms, including norms about emotional expression.

Many organizations provide internal training about feeling rules. Walt Disney World uses classes, handbooks, and billboards to teach newcomers that they must convey positive and esteem-enhancing emotions to customers. A handbook advises:

First, we practice a friendly smile at all times with our guests and among ourselves. Second, we use friendly, courteous phrases. "May I help you." . . . "Thank you." . . . "Have a nice day." . . . "Enjoy the rest of your stay." and many others are all part of our daily working vocabulary (Walt Disney Productions, 1982, p. 6, emphasis in the original).

In the Disney tradition, newcomers learn the sharp distinction between being "onstage" (where Disney patrons can go) and being "off-stage" (where only employees are allowed). When onstage, employees must follow concise guidelines about which emotions can, and cannot, be expressed (Peters & Waterman, 1982; Tyler & Nathan, 1985). Newcomers hear in lectures at Disney University and read in handbooks (Walt Disney Productions, 1982, p. 2): "You were cast for a role, not hired for a job" and "Our audience is composed of *guests* not customers . . . and we as cast members are *hosts* and *hostesss*" (emphasis in original). Such metaphors teach and maintain an organizational culture that emphasizes the display of good cheer and the skilled utterance of social amenities, perhaps above all else.

Disney's approach may seem extreme, but socialization practices used by other service organizations place similar emphasis on the display of appropriate feelings. Examples include Mrs. Fields' Cookies (Richman, 1984), Delta Airlines (Hochschild, 1983), and McDonald's Hamburgers (Boas & Chain, 1976).

Some organizations even use operant conditioning to teach employees how to express appropriate emotions. Behavioral modification was used by Komaki, Blood, and Holder (1980) to teach employees in a fast food restaurant how to be friendly. Friendliness was operationalized as smiling at customers and exchanging polite remarks such as "Is this your first visit?"

Perhaps more powerful than formal socialization practices are lessons about emotional display learned through the informal organization. The stories told and actions taken by role models provide opportunities for social learning (Bandura, 1977). Bandura's work suggests that newcomers learn norms about emotional expression through both vicarious processes and imitation. The expression and control of emotions is frequently mentioned in the "war stories" that experienced street cops tell to rookie officers (Van Maanen, 1973, 1978). Storytelling provides an opportunity for vicarious learning about feeling rules; as role models tell stories, rookies imagine how *they* would have acted.

Social learning theory also suggests that newcomers learn about the display of emotion by observing and then imitating more experienced co-workers. By watching experienced physicians, for example, medical interns learn that mild compassion is the expected emotional posture and that there is a permissive attitude about physicians who express indifference toward patients (Daniels, 1960).

Explicit feedback from insiders and other newcomers is another means through which feeling rules are learned. A medical intern writes in the *Journal of the American Medical Association*:

> In my first months as a medical student, I was called a "softie" when I cried about patients; being a woman made it only worse. Classmates and physicians told me "You get too emotionally involved with patients. You will never be a 'good' doctor." (Bell, 1984, p. 2684).

Employees not only learn which feelings should be expressed to clients or other outsiders; they also learn which feelings should be displayed in the presence of co-workers. The medical intern in the above example learned that fellow interns and teaching physicians did not want to see her cry.

The treatment of socialization presented here emphasizes the expression of emotion. Yet socialization in some roles entails learning how to suppress or disguise feelings—examples include judges, academic deans, and referees. Margaret Mead (1951) described a technique used by a communist party member to suppress his emotions:

> By smoking a heavy pipe, you are sure of yourself. Through the heaviness of the pipe, the lips become deformed and cannot react spontaneously (pp. 65–66).

Rewards and Punishments.
Reward and solicitation processes overlap since learning a role includes encounters with the reward system. Yet it is useful to discuss these processes separately: Socialization teaches newcomers which emotions are expected, while rewards and punishments maintain (or alter) such behaviors.

As with socialization, rewards and punishments are supplied by both the formal and informal organization. Many organizations monitor employees to assure that displayed feelings are "correct." To illustrate, The University of Michigan's Survey Research Center monitors telephone interviewers (see Groves & Kahn, 1979; Survey Research Center, 1976). Feedback to interviewers includes comments about the quality of their emotion work. Interviewers are encouraged to say kind things when respondent's answers are "acceptable" (e.g., "Thanks" or "That's helpful"), and to withhold positive affect when the respondent's actions are unacceptable. Moreover, interviewers are forbidden to express certain emotions such as anger. Data gatherers who convey a "professional attitude of neutrality and acceptance" (Survey Research Center, 1976, p. 130) are more likely to receive pay increases; those who do not express required emotions are reprimanded.

Similarly, conversations with executives from a national chain of grocery stores reveal that "employee courtesy" is monitored by "mystery shoppers." Ratings provided by such shoppers are entered into the employee's personnel file. A recent study by another chain of stores indicated that, in over 2000 interactions between "mystery shoppers" and clerks, only 21 percent of the clerks smiled and only 25 percent greeted customers. These findings disappointed top executives. As a result, employee courtesy contests are being held in some regions. Clerks who are "caught" smiling, greeting customers, and expressing thanks may receive prizes including a new car.

Emotional Transactions
An organization may use selection, socialization, and rewards to encourage the display of certain emotions. But the verbal and nonverbal cues sent by target persons also may influence the feelings conveyed by an employee. Thus, the organizational context can be distinguished from

emotional transactions. Emotional transactions are a sequence of communication between sender and receiver. The organizational context has the strongest influence over feelings conveyed at the outset of an emotional transaction. Yet the emotions sent by an employee may be modified as the sequence of communication unfolds; the reactions of "receivers" or "targets" serve as feedback that can influence and constrain subsequent sent emotions.

Emotional transactions can be viewed as "double interacts" (Weick, 1979). According to Weick (1979, p. 115), the initial emotions sent by a focal employee (an "act") stimulate the target person to respond with implicit or explicit feedback about the continuation of the displayed emotion (an "interact"). The sender of emotion reacts to such feedback by readjustments including abandoning, revising, or maintaining the displayed emotion (completing a "double interact"). The sender and receiver of displayed emotion use one or more double interacts to reach agreement, or reduce equivocality (Weick, 1979), about which feelings should be conveyed and which should be hidden.

Clark and LaBeef (1982), for example, studied the tactics used by physicians, nurses, police officers, and clergy in delivering the news of a person's death. Their qualitative research suggests that "death tellers" first deliver the news of death to the friend or relative in a somber manner (an initial emotional "act"). Next, the reactions of people who receive the bad news can influence the "death tellers" subsequent emotion work (an "interact"). Finally, the death teller continues, modifies, or abandons displayed emotions in response to such cues (a "double interact"). Reactions by friends or relatives to the sad news range from crying, to silence, to expressing anger and blame toward the death teller. The professionals studied by Clark and LaBeef made a similarly wide range of adjustments in the emotions they expressed. They sometimes hugged crying relatives and friends, or even cried along with them. In contrast, when family or fiends became angry, death tellers tended to withdraw.

The cycles of displayed emotion, reaction, and readjustment may reinforce or weaken the effects of feeling rules as an emotional transaction unfolds. For example, Hochschild (1983) described a double interact in which a somewhat insulting customer encourages an unsmiling flight attendant to conform to organizational rules.

On a 15-hour flight from Hong Kong to New York, a young businessman puts his drink down, leans back, and takes in a flight attendant. . . . "Hey honey," he calls out, "give me a smile" (p. 35).

Reactions by the targets of emotion also can encourage employees to abandon required emotional displays. Consider the advice offered by two restaurant reviewers (Unterman & Sesser, 1984) who are appalled by food servers who offer organizationally specified emotions:

Nothing can put a damper on a meal quicker than having a waiter bug you with "Hi, my name's Bruce" and continuing with "Is everything satisfactory?" about twenty times. When you see that sort of behavior going on at other tables, bring out a good put-down line. We've found one that works: as soon as the waiter walks up, stick out your hand and say in as cheerful a voice as you can manage, "Hi, my name's Dave and I'm your customer tonight." That's guaranteed to stop them speechless (p. vi).

OUTCOMES OF EXPRESSED EMOTIONS
Organizationally Salient Outcomes

The expression of emotions by organizational members may, in the aggregate, have a positive or a negative influence on organizational performance. The present authors propose that emotions work can bring about immediate, encore, and contagion gains (or losses) for the organization (see Figure 9.1).

Immediate Gains. Emotions can have an immediate impact on organizationally salient outcomes. Such effects are obvious in sales jobs.

Rosci (1981) urged vendors to "Grin and Sell It" because "salespeople profit by combining the principles of body language with professional selling skills" (p. 106). Rosci described a training course that teaches salespeople to employ nonverbal signals such as "friendly, smiling, enthusiastic face, arms and hands that are relaxed and open" (p. 107) to enhance sales. The consultants who offer the course claim that 2,400 salespeople have taken the course and average sales for these people have increased by 41 percent.

Arthur and Caputo (1959) also illustrated how employees can use emotional expressions to garner immediate gains. Their book *Interrogation for Investigators* provides guidance for police officers who seek to gain confessions from criminals. They suggest using the "Silent Approach" on "The Cool Customer":

Using this approach, you enter the interrogation room with a slight smile on your face, sit comfortably down in your chair, look him straight in the eye, and say absolutely nothing. . . . The senior author once sat for some 25 minutes without moving or taking his gaze from the suspect's face. The suspect, who was very loud before the interrogation, suddenly broke down and began to cry. Within 3 minutes he gave a full confession (pp. 75–76).

To use Goffman's (1969) terminology, such police interrogation techniques are a rich example of "control moves" that influence the actions of others.

In contrast, Driscoll, Meyer, and Schanie (1973) described how other police officers used positive and esteem-enhancing emotions to garner immediate gains. They used presentations, films, roleplays, and feedback sessions to train six teams in the skills required for family crisis investigations. Much of the training focused on emotion work. The program was evaluated with telephone interviews and questionnaires completed by complaining citizens. The study compared 129 "domestic trouble" calls answered by trained officers to 292 calls answered by untrained officers. The trained officers were perceived to be more supportive of citizens and to have greater overall effectiveness at crisis intervention.

The link between emotion work and immediate gains does not always depend on formal training. Consider the following example:

Bradshaw (1980) noticed that nuns who regularly solicit alms in Grand Central Terminal in New York customarily look rather glum. One day, however, Bradshaw saw one nun smiling brightly and "the activity at her basket seemed unusually brisk." Bradshaw subsequently disguised herself as a nun and positioned herself in the terminal. She spent the first day with a suitable glum visage and collected $143 . . . and the second day with a smile which resulted in a total contribution of $186 (described in Webb, Campbell, Schwartz, Sechrest, & Grove, 1981, p. 154).

Encore Gains. The emotions conveyed by role occupants also have long-term effects on the organization. Emotion work may lead to further gains either by repeat encounters with the same 'other' (i.e., encore gains), or through the comments that are passed by him or her to a third party (i.e., contagion gains).

Skilled emotion work can bring encore gains even when the organization's product is of quesitonable quality:

This is hard for some restaurant reviewers to stomach, but there are some restaurants where it just doesn't seem to matter whether the food is good or not. While we may be sitting at a table with plates of barely tasted food everyone in the place seems to be having a great time. The North Beach Restaurant, almost a San Francisco insitution, is a prime example. . . . The waiters, probably the best group we've ever seen in a large restaurant, don't hurt any. No matter how pressed they are, they're resolutely cheerful and always willing to explain and offer suggestions. However, this book is about food and not about atmosphere, and here the North Beach Restaurant strikes out (Unterman & Sesser, 1984, p. 118).

Quantitative evidence for the influence of emotion work on encore gains was found in the police training intervention mentioned earlier (Driscoll, Meyer, & Schanie, 1973). The evaluation indicated that, in addition to greater immediate success at crisis intervention, families treated by trained police were more likely to ask for assistance the next time that they faced a crisis.

Contagion Gains.

The long-term effects of emotion work also transcend the reactions of the target person. The reputation of a sales clerk or a university administrator may spread through word of mouth. Advertising research suggests that word of mouth is among the most potent of communication sources. In a study of the effectiveness of a bank advertising campaign, for example, Anderson and Golden (1984) found that word of mouth communication (in comparison to other sources) was associated with the highest believability and increased likelihood of bank patronage.

Individually Salient Outcomes

Expressed emotions also influence outcomes that are salient to the role occupant (see Figure 9.1). Here, the influence of emotion work on individual financial well-being and on mental and physical well-being are explored.

Financial Well-Being.

The link between emotion work and financial well-being is explicit when employees depend on tips from customers. We have all noticed how friendly even the most incompetent food server can become as "tip time" approaches. And empirical research suggests that such friendliness is rewarded. Tidd and Lockard (1978), for example, described the "Monetary Significance of the Affiliative Smile." They examined the influence of a "maximal" versus a "minimal" smile on the tips received by a cocktail waitress who served 48 men and 48 women. The waitress:

approached each individual with either a minimal smile (mouth corners noticably turned up but no teeth showing) or a maximal smile (mouth corners turned up to extensively expose

the closed front on a "natural" appearing broad smile) (p. 344).

Tidd and Lockard (1978) reported that the degree of smiling had no effect on the number of drinks ordered. But broad smiles yielded bigger tips. In the aggregate, the maximal smile brought $23.20, while the 48 victims of the minimal smile tipped a total of $9.40.

Emotion work also includes physical contact. Crusco and Wetzel (1984) described "The Midas Touch"—the positive effect of touching (by 2 waitresses) on tipping (by 114 diners). Customers who were not touched tipped an average of 12.2 percent. Customers who received a fleeting touch on the palm tipped an average of 16.7 percent, while the diners given longer touches on a shoulder tipped an average tip of 14.4 percent.

Professional poker players use an array of emotion work techniques to influence opponents (Goffman, 1967). Hayano's (1982) participant-observation research on *poker faces* indicates that successful players are skilled at "stifling emotions when defeated, tired, or angry" (p. 89). Further, while the exchange of ritualistic insults may ease tension, Hayano contended:

Insults may also have the intended or unintended effect of changing, destroying, or weakening opponents thereby making them more likely to commit errors or begin "steaming." ["Steaming" is the expression used by poker players to describe what happens when a poker player loses his or her temper.] Raking in the chips the winner tells the loser to "get a job" or threatens to send him and the other "poker bums" back to the freeway forever. These gabby methods of intimidation are highly effective in many instances, especially against players who are easily flustered (p. 56).

Hayano also reported that insults are used to convince "tight" players or "rocks" (i.e., financially conservative players) to bet their money more freely.

The influence of displayed emotions on financial well-being is sometimes more subtle.

A pediatrician who does not express warmth and empathy may lose clients and a lawyer who is cold and abrupt may alienate juries, hence losing his or her share of the damages awarded.

Mental and Physical Well-Being.

Hochschild (1983) is perhaps most adamant about the negative impact of emotion work on psychological well-being. She compares the physical exploitation of a child laborer in the 19th century to the emotional exploitation of a female flight attendant in the 20th century. Hochschild argued that, while the hours of work and physical conditions for the flight attendant are superior to those of the child laborer, the flight attendant gives even more of herself to the organization than did the child laborer; the employer controls not only her physical activities, but also her feelings.

Hochschild's qualitative evidence from flight attendants at Delta Airlines leads her to argue that, in the short-term, the strain of emotional labor can cause a loss of emotional control:

> A young businessman said to a flight attendant, "Why aren't you smiling?" She put her tray back on the food cart, looked him in the eye, and said, "I'll tell you what. You smile first, then I'll smile." The businessman smiled at her. "Good," she replied. "Now freeze and hold that smile for fifteen hours." (Hochschild, 1983, p. 127).

In the long-term, Hochschild contended, the constant pressure of emotional labor may lead to drug use, excessive drinking, headaches, absenteeism, and sexual dysfunction.

The display of expected emotion is not always detrimental to well-being. The financial gains described above for food servers and poker players likely evolve feelings of satisfaction and security. Moreover, despite Hochschild's emphasis on the damage caused by emotion work, flight attendants whom the present authors have spoken with take pride in their ability to cope with airborne emergencies by hiding their own fears and offering calm faces to passengers.

The display of normative emotions may also protect incumbents from ill-being. The professional socialization of physicians, for example, entails learning how to appear concerned, but not so concerned that it causes severe psychological distress (Daniels, 1960). Thus, the physician's ability to distinguish between the emotions they feel and those they convey to others helps them to continue performing effectively.

Further, Zajonc (1985) argued that smiling brings about physiological changes that cause the experience of subjective well-being. In other words, smiling makes us feel happy. Zajonc reclaimed a theory first proposed by Wynbaum in 1906. In brief, Wynbaum pointed out that the face has over 80 muscles and that all changes in facial expression influence the flow of blood to the brain. Smiling and laughing entail contraction of the zygomatic muscle, which increases blood flow to the brain. Zajonc contended that "It is like taking an oxygen bath. The cells and tissues receive an increased supply of oxygen, causing a feeling of exuberance" (p. 10). This creative argument suggests that employees who are expected to smile may benefit from feelings of elation and exuberance. We must learn more about this interesting hypothesis, but implications for the link between emotional labor and subjective well-being are intriguing.

EXPERIENCED EMOTIONS, FEELING RULES, AND INTERNALIZED FEELING RULES

The framework presented here emphasizes emotional expression, not emotions as intrapsychic states. But the discussion of well-being suggests that the match between felt emotions and expectations about emotional display is a promising area for future research. Specifically, expressed feelings may match well or poorly with: (a) experienced feelings, especially "true" feelings about the target of emotional expression; (b) external feeling rules; and (c) internalized feeling rules. Building on Hochschild (1979, 1983) and Thoits (1985), the match between feelings expressed in the role and these three demands on expression can lead to: *emotional harmony, emotional dissonance,* or *emotional deviance.*

Emotional harmony occurs when expressed feelings are congruent with experienced emotions, feeling rules, and expectations the incumbent holds for himself or herself about emotional expression. To illustrate, Mary Kay Ash, the founder of Mary Kay Cosmetics, insists that her salespeople exude enthusiasm (Ash, 1984). They are expected to take a "Vow of Enthusiasm" and sing the lyrics to "I've Got the Mary Kay Enthusiasm." Emotional harmony is experienced by a salesperson who expresses normative enthusiasm, feels enthusiastic, and expects himself or herself to act enthusiastic.

Emotional harmony is an indicator of good fit between person and environment. More specifically, according to person–environment fit theory (Caplan, 1983), an employee will be free from occupational stress to the extent there is congruence among the behavior expected by role senders, the behavior that an employee expects of himself or herself, and the employee's personal characteristics. Thoits (1985) made a stronger argument: she contended that freedom from mental illness depends, in part, on the belief that one is acting in concert with feeling norms. Both perspectives lead to the hypothesis that emotional harmony is associated with well-being.

Emotional dissonance, according to Hochschild (1983), occurs when expressed emotions satisfy feeling rules, but clash with inner feelings. The effects of emotional dissonance depend on the internalization of feeling rules. Some people display "fake" emotions, yet believe that such acting should *not* be part of the job; this is *faking in bad faith.* To illustrate, a check-out clerk who was interviewed resented acting friendly to customers because "pasting on a smile should not be part of the job." The present authors are unable to find quantitative research on such emotional dissonance. But this is an example of person–role conflict, or a clash between personal values and role requirements. Research indicates that person–role conflict is a clear threat

to employee well-being (Caplan, Cobb, French, Harrison, & Pinneau, 1975; Kahn et al., 1964). Moreover, since people who fake in bad faith have not internalized feeling rules, they are likely to be poor employees because they may comply with feeling rules only when monitored closely.

In contrast, the effects of suppressing true feelings are less clear when feeling rules are internalized. Some people display "fake" normative emotions and believe that such expressions should be part of the job; this is *faking in good faith.* Hochschild (1983) argued that faking in good faith is a threat to well-being because it causes estrangement between felt and expressed emotions. She contended, for example, that poor mental health may be suffered by outwardly cheerful flight attendants who have internalized norms about acting friendly, and who hide their contempt for passengers.

Yet writings on the burnout syndrome (e.g., Maslach, 1978a, 1978b, 1982) identify settings in which faking in good faith can enhance well-being. Mashlach (1978a) argued that members of helping professions can cope with burnout by acting concerned about clients, but allowing themselves to feel emotionally detached. Perhaps these are competing hypotheses. Or perhaps faking in good faith decreases stress only when it helps an employee cope with emotions that are felt too deeply.

Emotional deviance occurs when expressed emotions clash with local norms. Emotional deviance is the opposite of emotional dissonance because the organization member expresses inner feelings and disregards feeling rules. Again, however, internalization of feeling rules may influence the effects of incongruence between felt and expressed emotions.

Employees who express inner feelings and who reject local feeling rules may be punished. A rude flight attendant is likely to be fired, as is a funeral director who displays good cheer. Or such employees may quit. One student quit working as a Mary Kay Cosmetics salesperson because she thought that the norms were silly and "I couldn't bring myself to act happy and enthusiastic enough."

However, more serious consequences may haunt employees who express inner feelings that clash with role expectations, but have internalized those expectations. One sign of the burnout syndrome is that a person is unable to express empathy and concern, even though he or she believes that expressing such feelings is part of the job (Maslach, 1978a, 1978b). Similarly, Thoits (1985) maintained that people who perceive themselves as consistently expressing deviant emotions may label themselves as mentally ill. Essential to Thoits' argument is that the emotional deviant has internalized feeling rules. Both perspectives suggest that such emotional deviants risk poor mental health because they want to control the expression of inner feelings, but are unable to do so. Research is needed on emotional deviance in organizations. Is it as damaging as Thoits implies? Or are there unrecognized advantages?

Emotional harmony, dissonance, and deviance are thought to influence behavior in all work roles. Nevertheless, the most valuable occupations for research are those in which the demands on emotional expression or experience are strongest. Occupations with strong external demands for emotional display discussed here include flight attendants, "performers" at Disney World, and bill collectors. Perhaps the most revealing occupations, however, are those in which the internal feelings evoked by the job clash with feeling rules. Examples include poker players, judges, and referees; performing these jobs requires tolerating, and even enjoying, emotional dissonance.

TOWARD FUTURE RESEARCH

The perspective outlined here is intended to encourage and guide further research on emotions displayed as part of the job. Future research on the match between experienced and expressed emotions has been discussed. Subsequent work in this area may also benefit from consideration of three additional questions: How should expressed emotions be measured? How powerful are the effects of displayed emotions? How should emotion work be managed?

How Should Expressed Emotions Be Measured?

The study of displayed feelings is fraught with methodological hazards. Distinguishing between varieties of expressed emotions will be essential for future research. But this task may prove impossible because scholars do not agree about how long the list of emotions should be, nor do they agree about the boundaries between types of emotions (Kemper, 1981).

Studies also may be hampered because questionnaires, interviews, and records data—the staples of organizational research—will be of limited use. Employee self-reports about displayed emotions are suspect and few organizations keep records about such behaviors. Structured observation, the most promising method, could be difficult because emotions are displayed through a complex combination of facial expression, body language, spoken words, and tone of voice. Thus, a comprehensive method would require elaborate coding schemes for all four of these modes of emotional expression.

Some evidence suggests that initial efforts at structured observation may benefit from focusing on facial expressions. Leathers and Emigh (1980) reported that laboratory subjects who examined photographs could reliably associate emotion labels with facial expressions. For example, happiness, sadness, and surprise were decoded with over 95 percent accuracy. These results imply that structured observation could be used to reliably decode the facial expressions of organizational members. But field research poses the additional problem of rating the variable behavior of live subjects rather than the constant stimuli provided by photographs. Perhaps this hazard could be overcome by using multiple raters and video tape.

How Powerful Are the Effects of Displayed Emotions?

A causal link between emotional display and outcomes for organizations and individuals has been proposed. These links require further empirical support. Managers of retail stores, for example, assume that "friendly" employees produce profits. Is this a valid assumption? Or are sales only influenced by variables such as store location or prices? A field study could be conducted to test the hypothesis that organizational gains are greater in stores where employees act friendlier.

That emotional transactions between members of the same organization may influence organizational performance also was suggested. For example, members of the team that designed Apple's Macintosh computer only selected newcomers who displayed wild enthusiasm about the machine (Tyler & Nathan, 1985). They claimed that shared enthusiasm about the machine and each other was essential to the team's success. Research could be conducted to discover if effort and creativity is higher among product design teams in which members act more enthusiastic. Or perhaps a curvilinear relationship between enthusiasm and creativity should be hypothesized—teams in which members feel compelled to express constant enthusiasm may suffer from groupthink (Janis, 1982).

The relationship between expressed emotion and organizational outcomes may be influenced by a host of contingencies; two are offered as a start for future research. The first contingency is the extent to which attributes other than expressed emotions do not vary. For example, the prices of airline tickets were strictly controlled by the Civil Aeronautics Board before the Airline Deregulation Act was passed in 1978. Before deregulation, advertisements focused heavily on the quality of service because all airlines were required to charge identical prices. The 1978 Act enabled airlines to compete on the basis of ticket prices. It is hypothesized that the strength of relationship between employee courtesy and ticket sales has been weakened by deregulation since the prices of tickets are no longer held constant.

The second contingency is the extent to which employees experience role overload, particularly when employees have too many customers or clients. Customers of uncrowded stores and patrons of empty restaurants expect employees to act friendly and relaxed. In contrast, customers who have been waiting for a clerk in a store or a seat in a restaurant may care only about the speed of the service, and may become irritated by employees who take time for polite conversation with each customer.

How Should Emotion Work Be Managed?

There is a dearth of literature about how management can best influence the emotions conveyed in organizational settings. The emerging literature on interactions between employees and customers addresses a range of issues including the structure of verbal exchanges (Stiles, 1985), control over employee behavior (Mills, 1985), and the psychology of waiting in lines (Maister, 1985). The management of emotional display is addressed indirectly in this literature, but little research explores this subject explicitly. Hypotheses testing is rare, and to what extent emotion work can be managed is not even known.

If organizations seek to hire employees who can convey certain emotions, then more questions arise. Can the ability to display such emotions be predicted? If so, how? Previous research suggests that behavior in the employment interview does not generalize well to the work role (Arvey & Campion, 1982). Thus, emotions displayed in the interview may not be expressed on the job. Moreover, as argued earlier, the emotions that enable an interviewee to *get* a job may be different than the emotions needed to *do* the job. Can interviewers be trained to overcome these weaknesses of the selection interview? Or perhaps other tools can be developed to identify a candidate's emotional skills.

A related question is how to teach emotion work skills, or perhaps such skills cannot be taught. Classroom programs often are used to teach employees to display expected emotions (Hochschild, 1983; Tyler & Nathan, 1985). Transfer of such behaviors from the classroom to the job is unlikely (Goldstein, 1974), but the present authors are not aware of any evaluation reports. Komaki, Blood, and Holder (1980) reported that behavior modification techniques can be used to enhance emotion work, but additional evidence is needed.

CONCLUSION

The proposed framework is best viewed as a point of departure for both theory testing and theory building. The discussion suggests testable hypotheses. But it also suggests that more inductive work is needed so that our theories can capture the complexities of emotional expression in organizational life. And such inductive work ought to include field research. As Sherlock Holmes put it, "The temptation to form premature theories upon insufficient data is the bane of our profession" (Barring-Gould, 1967; cited in Van Maanen, 1979, p. 539).

REFERENCES

Anderson, W. T., & Golden, L. (1984) Bank promotion strategy. *Journal of Advertising Research*, 24(2), 53–65.

Arther, R. O., & Caputo, R. R. (1959) *Interrogation for investigators*. New York: William C. Copp and Associates.

Arvey, R. P., & Campion, J. E. (1982) The employment interview: A summary and review of recent research. *Personnel Psychology*, 35, 281–322.

Ash, M. K. (1984) *Mary Kay on people management*. New York: Warner Books.

Bandura, A. (1977) *Social learning theory*. Englewood Cliffs, NJ: Prentice Hall.

Bell, M. (1984) Teaching of the heart. *The Journal of the American Medical Association*, 252, 2684.

Biddle, B. J. (1979) *Role theory: Expectations, identities, and behaviors*. San Francisco: Academic Press.

Boas, M., & Chain, S. (1976) *Big Mac: The unauthorized story of McDonald's*. New York: Dutton.

Caplan, R. D. (1983) Person-environment fit: Past, present and future. In C. L. Cooper (Ed.), *Stress research: Issues for the eighties* (pp. 35–77). Ann Arbor, MI: Institute for Social Research.

Caplan, R. D., Cobb, S., French, J. R. P., Harrison, R. V., & Pinneau, S. R. (1975) *Job demands and worker health* (Report No. 75–160). Washington, DC: U.S. Department of Health, Education, & Welfare.

Clark, R. E., & LaBeef, E. E. (1982) Death telling: Managing the delivery of bad news. *Journal of Health and Social Behavior*, 23, 366–380.

Crusco, A. H., & Wetzel, C. G. (1984) The Midas touch: The effects of interpersonal touch on restaurant tipping. *Personality and Social Psychology Bulletin*, 10(4), 512–517.

Czepiel, J. A., Solomon, M. E., & Surprenant, C. F. (1985) *The service encounter*. Lexington, MA: Lexington Books.

Daniels, M. J. (1960) Affect and its control in the medical intern. *American Journal of Sociology*, 66, 259–267.

Darwin, C. (1965) *The expression of emotions in man and animals*. Chicago: University of Chicago Press.

Denison, D. R., & Sutton, R. I. (in press) Surgical nurses: Issues in the design of a loosely-bounded team. In J. R. Hackman (Ed.), *Groups that work*.

De Rivera, J. (1977) *A structural theory of emotions*. New York: International Universities Press.

Driscoll, J. M., Meyer, R. G., & Schanie, C. F. (1973) Training police in family crisis intervention. *Journal of Applied Behavioral Science*, 9, 62–82.

Forbes, R. J., & Jackson, P. R. (1980) Non-verbal behavior and the outcome of selection interviews. *Journal of Occupational Psychology,* 53, 65–72.

Goffman, E. (1959) *The presentation of self in everyday life.* New York: Doubleday Anchor.

Goffman, E. (1967) *Interaction ritual.* New York: Doubleday Anchor.

Goffman, E. (1969) *Strategic interaction.* Philadelphia: University of Pennsylvania Press.

Goldstein, I. I. (1974) *Training: Program development and evaluation.* Monterey, CA: Brooks/Cole.

Groves, R., & Kahn, R. L. (1979) *Surveys by telephone: A national comparison with personal interviews.* New York: Academic Press.

Hayano, D. M. (1982) *Poker faces.* Berkeley: University of California Press.

Hillman, J. (1961) *Emotion.* Evanston, IL: Northwestern University Press.

Hochschild, A. (1979) Emotion work, feeling rules and social structure. *American Journal of Sociology,* 85, 551–575.

Hochschild, A. R. (1983) *The managed heart.* Berkeley: University of California Press.

Imada, A. S., & Hakel, M. D. (1977) Influence of nonverbal communication and rater proximity on impressions and decisions in simulated employment interviews. *Journal of Applied Psychology,* 62, 295–300.

Janis, I. L. (1982) *Groupthink.* Boston: Houghton Mifflin.

Kahn, R. L. (1981) *Work and health.* New York: Wiley.

Kahn, R. L., Wolfe, D. M., Quinn, R. P., Snoek, J. D., & Rosenthal, R. A. (1964) *Organizational stress: Studies in role conflict and ambiguity.* New York: Wiley.

Katz, D., & Kahn, R. L. (1978) *Social psychology of organizations* (2nd ed.). New York: Wiley.

Kemper, T. D. (1981) Social constructionist and positivist approaches to the sociology of emotions. *American Journal of Sociology,* 87, 336–362.

Komaki, J., Blood, M. R., & Holder, D. (1980) Fostering friendliness in a fast food franchise. *Journal of Organizational Behavior Management,* 2, 151–164.

Leathers, D. G., & Emigh, T. H. (1980) Decoding facial expressions: A new test with decoding norms. *Quarterly Journal of Speech,* 66, 418–436.

Locke, E. A. (1976) The nature and causes of job satisfaction. In M. D. Dunnette (Ed.), *Handbook of industrial and organizational psychology* (pp. 1297–1350). Chicago: Rand McNally.

Maister, D. H. (1985) The psychology of waiting in lines. In J. A. Czepiel, M. R. Solomon, & C. F. Surprenant (Eds.), *The service encounter* (pp. 113–123). Lexington, MA: Lexington Books.

Maslach, C. (1978a, Spring) How people cope. *Public Welfare,* 36, 56–58.

Maslach, C. (1978b) The client role in staff burnout. *Journal of Social Issues,* 34, 4.

Maslach, C. (1982) Understanding burnout: Definitional issues in analyzing a complex phenomenon. In W. S. Paine (Ed.), *Job stress and burnout* (pp. 111–124). Beverly Hills, CA: Sage.

McCormick, E. J. (1979) *Job analysis: Methods and applications.* New York: American Management Association.

McGovern, T. V., & Tinsley, H. E. (1978) Interviewer evaluations of interviewee nonverbal behavior. *Journal of Vocational Behavior,* 13, 163–171.

Mead, M. (1951) *Soviet attitudes toward authority.* New York: McGraw-Hill.

Mills, P. K. (1985) The control mechanisms of employees at the encounter of service organizations. In J. A. Czepiel, M. R. Solomon, & C. F. Surprenant (Eds.), *The service encounter* (pp. 163–178). Lexington, MA: Lexington Books.

Osgood, C. E., Suci, G. J., & Tannenbaum, P. H. (1957) *The measurement of meaning.* Urbana: University of Illinois Press.

Peters, T. J., & Waterman, R. H., Jr. (1982) *In search of excellence.* New York: Harper & Row.

Richman, T. (1984, July) A tale of two companies. *Inc.,* pp. 38–43.

Rosci, F. (1981, June) Grin and sell it. *Successful Meetings,* 106–107.

Rules for Santas—Don't say "ho, ho, ho." (1984, November 15) *San Francisco Chronicle,* p. 3.

Steinem, G. (1983) *Outrageous acts and everyday rebellions.* New York: Holt, Rinehart and Winston.

Stiles, W. B. (1985) Measuring roles in service encounters: The verbal exchange structure. In J. A. Czepiel, M. R. Solomon, & C. F. Surprenant (Eds.), *The service encounter* (pp. 213–224). Lexington, MA: Lexington Books.

Survey Research Center (1976) *Interviewer's manual* (rev. ed.). Ann Arbor, MI: Institute for Social Research.

Thoits, P. A. (1985) Self-labeling processes in mental illness: The role of emotional deviance. *American Journal of Sociology, 91,* 221–247.

Tidd, K. L., & Lockard, J. S. (1978) Monetary significance of the affiliative smile. *Bulletin of the Psychonomic Society, 11,* 344–346.

Trist, E. (1977) Collaboration in work settings: A personal perspective. *Journal of Applied Behavioral Science, 13,* 268–278.

Tyler, S. (Producer), & Nathan, J. (Producer) (1985) *In search of excellence* [Film]. New York: Public Broadcast System.

Unterman, P., & Sesser, S. (1984) *Restaurants of San Francisco.* San Francisco: Chronicle Books.

U.S. Department of Labor, Manpower Administration (1972) *Handbook for analyzing jobs* (Stock No. 2900–0131). Washington, DC: U.S. Government Printing Office.

Van Maanen, J. (1973) Observations on the making of policemen. *Human Organizations, 32,* 407–417.

Van Maanen, J. (1978) The asshole. In P. K. Manning & J. Van Maanen (Eds.), *Policing: A view from the streets* (pp. 231–238). Santa Monica, CA: Goodyear.

Van Maanen, J. (1979) The fact of fiction in organizational ethnography. *Administrative Science Quarterly, 24,* 539–550.

Walt Disney Productions (1982) *Your role in the Walt Disney World show.* Orlando, FL: Walt Disney Productions.

Webb, E. J., Campbell, D. T., Schwartz, D. S., Sechrest, L., & Grove, J. B. (1981) *Nonreactive measures in the social sciences.* Boston: Houghton Mifflin.

Weick, K. (1979) *The social psychology of organizing* (2nd ed.). Reading, MA: Addison-Wesley.

Zajonc, R. B. (1985, April 5) Emotion and facial efference: An ignored theory reclaimed. *Science,* pp. 15–21.

Dimension II

Thinking and Making Decisions

Foundations of Social Cognition

Two conflicting beliefs in a single mind don't cohabit comfortably.
To defend his ego, man becomes

10. The Rationalizing Animal

Elliot Aronson

Man likes to think of himself as a rational animal. However, it is more true that man is a *rationalizing* animal, that he attempts to appear reasonable to himself and to others. Albert Camus even said that man is a creature who spends his entire life in an attempt to convince himself that he is not absurd.

Some years ago a woman reported that she was receiving messages from outer space. Word came to her from the planet Clarion that her city would be destroyed by a great flood on December 21. Soon a considerable number of believers shared her deep commitment to the prophecy. Some of them quit their jobs and spent their savings freely in anticipation of the end.

On the evening of December 20, the prophet and her followers met to prepare for the event. They believed that flying saucers would pick them up, thereby sparing them from disaster. Midnight arrived, but no flying saucers. December 21 dawned, but no flood.

What happens when prophecy fails? Social psychologists Leon Festinger, Henry Riecken, and Stanley Schacther infiltrated the little band of believers to see how they would react. They predicted that persons who had expected the disaster, but awaited it alone in their homes, would simply lose faith in the prophecy. But those who awaited the outcome in a group, who had thus admitted their belief publicly, would come to believe even more strongly in the prophecy and turn into active proselytizers.

This is exactly what happened. At first the faithful felt despair and shame because all their predictions had been for nought. Then, after waiting nearly five hours for the saucers, the prophet had a new vision. The city had been spared, she said, because of the trust and faith of her devoted group. This revelation was elegant in its simplicity, and the believers accepted it enthusiastically. They now sought the press that they had previously avoided. They turned from believers into zealots.

LIVING ON THE FAULT

In 1957 Leon Festinger proposed his theory of *cognitive dissonance,* which describes and predicts man's rationalizing behavior. Dissonance occurs whenever a person simultaneously holds two inconsistent cognitions (ideas, beliefs, opinions). For example, the belief that the world will end on a certain day is dissonant with the awareness, when the day breaks, that the world has not ended. Festinger maintained that this state of inconsistency is so uncomfortable that people strive to reduce the conflict in the easiest way possible. They will change one or both cognitions so that they will "fit together" better.

Consider what happens when a smoker is confronted with evidence that smoking causes cancer. He will become motivated to change either his attitudes about smoking or his behavior. And as anyone who has tried to quit knows, the former alternative is easier.

The smoker may decide that the studies are lousy. He may point to friends ("If Sam, Jack, and Harry smoke, cigarettes can't be all that dangerous"). He may conclude that filters trap all the cancer-producing materials. Or he may argue that he would rather live a short and happy life with cigarettes than a long and miserable life without them.

The more a person is committed to a course of action, the more resistant he will be to information that threatens that course. Psychologists have reported that the couple who are least likely to believe the dangers of smoking are those who tried to quit—and failed. They have become more committed to smoking. Similarly,

a person who builds a $100,000 house astride the San Andreas Fault will be less receptive to arguments about imminent earthquakes than would a person who is renting the house for a few months. The new homeowner is committed; he doesn't want to believe that he did an absurd thing.

When a person reduces his dissonance, he defends his ego, and keeps a positive self-image. But self-justification can reach startling extremes; people will ignore danger in order to avoid dissonance, even when that ignorance can cause their deaths. I mean that literally.

Suppose you are Jewish in a country occupied by Hitler's forces. What should you do? You could try to leave the country; you could try to pass as "Aryan"; you could do nothing and hope for the best. The first two choices are dangerous: if you are caught you will be executed. If you decide to sit tight, you will try to convince yourself that you made the best decision. You may reason that while Jews are indeed being treated unfairly, they are not being killed unless they break the law.

Now suppose that a respected man from your town announces that he has seen Jews being butchered mercilessly, including everyone who had recently been deported from your village. If you believe him, you might have a chance to escape. If you don't believe him, you and your family will be slaughtered.

Dissonance theory would predict that you will not listen to the witness, because to do so would be to admit that your judgment and decisions were wrong. You will dismiss his information as untrue, and decide that he was lying or hallucinating. Indeed, Eli Wiesel reported that this happened to the Jews in Sighet, a small town in Hungary, in 1944. Thus people are not passive receptacles for the deposit of information. The manner in which they view and distort the objective world in order to avoid and reduce dissonance is entirely predictable. But one cannot divide the world into rational people on one side and dissonance reducers on the other. While people vary in their ability to tolerate dissonance, we are all capable of rational or irrational behavior, depending on the circumstances—some of which follow.

DISSONANCE BECAUSE OF EFFORT

Judson Mills and I found that if people go through a lot of trouble to gain admission to a group, and the group turns out to be dull and dreary, they will experience dissonance. It is a rare person who will accept this situation with an "Oh, pshaw. I worked hard for nothing. Too bad." One way to resolve the dissonance is to decide that the group is worth the effort it took to get admitted.

We told a number of college women that they would have to undergo an initiation to join a group that would discuss the psychology of sex. One third of them had severe initiation: they had to recite a list of obscene words and read some lurid sexual passages from novels in the presence of a male experimenter (in 1959, this really was a "severe" and embarrassing task). One third went through a mild initiation in which they read words that were sexual but not obscene (such as "virgin" and "petting"); and the last third had no initiation at all. Then all of the women listened to an extremely boring taped discussion of the group they had presumably joined. The women in the severe initiation group rated the discussion and its drab participants much more favorably than those in the other groups.

I am not asserting that people enjoy painful experiences, or that they enjoy things that are associated with painful experiences. If you got hit on the head by a brick on the way to a fraternity initiation, you would not like that group any better. But if you volunteered to get hit with a brick *in order to join* the fraternity, you definitely would like the group more than if you had been admitted without a fuss.

After a decision—especially a difficult one that involves much time, money, or effort—people almost always experience dissonance. Awareness of defects in the preferred object is dissonant with having chosen it; awareness of positive aspects of the unchosen object is dissonant with having rejected it.

Accordingly, researchers have found that *before* making a decision, people seek as much information as possible about the alternatives. Afterwards, however, they seek reassurance that they did the right thing, and do so by seeking information in support of their choice or by simply changing the information that is already in their heads. In one of the earliest experiments on dissonance theory, Jack Brehm gave a group of women their choice between two appliances, such as a toaster or a blender, that they had previously rated for desirability. When the subjects reevaluated the appliances after choosing one of them, they increased their liking for the one they had chosen and downgraded their evaluation of the rejected appliance. Similarly, Danuta Ehrlich and her associates found that a person about to buy a new car does so carefully, reading all ads and accepting facts openly on advertisements more selectively, and he will tend to avoid ads for Volkswagens, Chevrolets, and so on.

THE DECISION TO BEHAVE IMMORALLY

Your conscience, let us suppose, tells you that it is wrong to cheat, lie, steal, seduce your neighbor's husband or wife, or whatever. Let us suppose further that you are in a situation in which you are sorely tempted to ignore your conscience. If you give in to temptation, the cognition "I am a decent moral person" will be dissonant with the cognition "I have committed an immoral act." If you resist, the cognition "I want to get a good grade (have that money, seduce that person)" is dissonant with the cognition "I could have acted so as to get that grade, but I chose not to."

The easiest way to reduce dissonance in either case is to minimize the negative aspects of the action one has chosen, and to change one's attitude about its immorality. If Mr. C. decides to cheat, he will probably decide that cheating isn't really so bad. It hurts no one; everyone does it; it's part of human nature. If Mr. D. decides not to cheat, he will no doubt come to believe that cheating is a sin, and deserves severe punishment.

The point here is that the initial attitudes of these men is virtually the same. Moreover, their decisions could be a hair's breadth apart. But once the action is taken, their attitudes diverge sharply.

Judson Mills confirmed these speculations in an experiment with sixth-grade children. First he measured their attitudes toward cheating, and then put them in a competitive situation. He arranged the test so that it was impossible to win without cheating, and so it was easy for the children to cheat, thinking they would be unwatched. The next day, he asked the children again how they felt about cheating. Those who had cheated on the test had become more lenient in their attitudes; those who had resisted the temptation adopted harsher attitudes.

These data are provocative. They suggest that the most zealous crusaders are not those who are removed from the problem they oppose. I would hazard to say that the people who are most angry about "the sexual promiscuity of the young" are *not* those who have never dreamed of being promiscuous. On the contrary, they would be persons who had been seriously tempted by illicit sex, who came very close to giving in to their desires, but who finally resisted. People who almost live in glass houses are the ones who are most likely to throw stones.

INSUFFICIENT JUSTIFICATION

If I offer George $20 to do a boring task, and offer Richard $1 to do the same thing, which one will decide that the assignment was mildly interesting? If I threaten one child with harsh punishment if he does something forbidden, and threaten another child with mild punishment, which one will transgress?

Dissonance theory predicts that when people find themselves doing something and they have neither been rewarded adequately for doing it nor threatened with dire consequences for not doing it, they will find *internal* reasons for their behavior.

Suppose you dislike Woodrow Wilson, and I want you to make a speech in his favor. The most efficient thing I can do is to pay you a lot of money for making the speech, or threaten to kill you if you don't. In either case, you will probably comply with my wish, but you won't change your attitude toward Wilson. If that were my goal, I would have to give you a *minimal* reward or threat. Then, in order not to appear absurd, you would have to seek additional reasons for your speech—this could lead you to find good things about Wilson and hence, to conclude that you really do like Wilson after all. Lying produces great attitude change only when the liar is undercompensated.

Festinger and J. Merrill Carlsmith asked college students to work on boring and repetitive tasks. Then the experimenters persuaded the students to lie about the work, to tell a fellow student that the task would be interesting and enjoyable. They offered half of their subjects $20 for telling the lie, and they offered the others only $1. Later they asked all subjects how much they had really liked the tasks.

The students who earned $20 for their lies rated the work as deadly dull, which it was. They experienced no dissonance: they lied, but they were well paid for that behavior. By contrast, students who got $1 decided that the tasks were rather enjoyable. The dollar was apparently enough to get them to tell the lie, but not enough to keep them from feeling that lying for so paltry a sum was foolish. To reduce dissonance, they decided that they hadn't lied after all; the task was fun.

Similarly, Carlsmith and I found that mild threats are more effective than harsh threats in changing a child's attitude about a forbidden object, in this case a delightful toy. In the severe-threat condition, children refrained from playing with the toys and had a good reason for refraining—the very severity of the threat provided ample justification for not playing with the toy. In the mild-threat condition, however, the children refrained from playing with the toy but when they asked themselves, "How come I'm not playing with the toy?" they did not have a superabundant justification (because the threat was not terribly severe). Accordingly, they provided additional justification in the form of convincing themselves that the attractive toy was really not very attractive and that they didn't really want to play with it very much in the first place. Jonathan Freedman extended our findings and showed that severe threats do not have a lasting effect on a child's behavior. Mild threats, by contrast, can change behavior for many months.

Perhaps the most extraordinary example of insufficient justification occurred in India, where Jamuna Prasad analyzed the rumors that were circulated after a terrible earthquake in 1950. Prasad found that people in towns that were *not* in immediate danger were spreading rumors of impending doom from floods, cyclones, or unforeseeable calamities. Certainly the rumors could not help people feel more secure; why then perpetrate them? I believe that dissonance helps explain this phenomenon. The people were terribly frightened—after all, the neighboring villages had been destroyed—but they did not have ample excuse for their fear, since the earthquake had missed them. So they invented their own excuse; if a cyclone is on the way, it is reasonable to be afraid. Later, Durganand Sinha studied rumors in a town that had actually been destroyed. The people were scared, but they had good reason to be; they didn't need to seek additional justification for their terror. And their rumors showed no predictions of impending disaster and no serious exaggerations.

THE DECISION TO BE CRUEL

The need for people to believe that they are kind and decent can lead them to say and do unkind and indecent things. After the National Guard killed four students at Kent State, several rumors quickly spread: the slain girls were pregnant, so their deaths spared their families from shame; the students were filthy and had lice on them. These rumors were totally untrue, but the townspeople were eager to believe them. Why? The local people were conservative, and infuriated at the radical behavior of some of the students. Many had hoped that the students would get their comeuppance. But death is an awfully severe penalty. The severity of this penalty outweighs and is dissonant with the "crimes" of the students. In these circumstances, any information that put the victims in a bad light reduces dissonance by implying, in effect, that it was good that the young people died. One high-school teacher even avowed that anyone with "long hair, dirty clothes, or [who goes] barefooted deserves to be shot."

Keith Davis and Edward Jones demonstrated the need to justify cruelty. They persuaded students to help them with an experiment, in the course of which the volunteers had to tell another student that he was a shallow, untrustworthy, and dull person. Volunteers managed to convince themselves that they didn't like the victim of their cruel analysis. They found him less attractive than they did before they had to criticize him.

Similarly, David Glass persuaded a group of subjects to deliver electric shocks to others. The subjects, again, decided that the victim must deserve the cruelty; they rated him as stupid, mean, etc. Then Glass went a step further. He found that a subject with high self-esteem was most likely to derogate the victim. This led Glass to conclude, ironically, that it is precisely because a person thinks he is nice that he decides that the person he has hurt is a rat. "Since nice guys like me don't go around hurting innocent people," Glass's subjects seemed to say, "you must have deserved it." But individuals who have *low* self-esteem do not feel the need to justify their behavior and derogate their victims; it is *consonant* for such persons to believe they have behaved badly. "Worthless people like me do unkind things."

Ellen Berscheid and her colleagues found another factor that limits the need to derogate one's victim: the victim's capacity to retaliate. If the person doing harm feels that the situation is balanced, that his victim will pay him back in coin, he has no need to justify his behavior. In Berscheid's experiment, which involved electric shocks, college students did not derogate or dislike the persons they shocked if they believed the victims could retaliate. Students who were led to believe that the victims would not be able to retaliate *did* derogate them. Her work suggests that soldiers may have a greater need to disparage civilian victims (because they can't retaliate) than military victims. Lt. William L. Calley, who considered the "gooks" at My Lai to be something less than human, would be a case in point.

DISSONANCE AND THE SELF-CONCEPT

On the basis of recent experiments, I have reformulated Festinger's original theory in terms of the self-concept. That is, dissonance is most powerful when self-esteem is threatened. Thus the important aspect of dissonance is not "I said one thing and I believe another," but "I have misled people—and I am a truthful, nice person." Conversely, the cognitions, "I believe the task is dull," and "I told someone the task was interesting," are not dissonant for a psychopathic liar.

David Mettee and I predicted in a recent experiment that persons who had low opinions of themselves would be more likely to cheat than persons with high self-esteem. We assumed that if an average person gets a temporary blow to his self-esteem (by being jilted, say, or not getting a promotion), he will temporarily feel stupid and worthless, and hence do any number of stupid and worthless things—cheat at cards, bungle an assignment, break a valuable vase.

Mettee and I temporarily changed 45 female students' self-esteem. We gave one third of them positive feedback about a personality test they had taken (we said that they were interesting, mature, deep, etc.); we gave one third negative feedback (we said that they were relatively immature, shallow, etc.); and one third of the students got no information at all. Then all the students went on to participate in what they thought was an unrelated experiment, in which they gambled in a competitive game of cards. We arranged the situation so that the students could cheat and thereby win a considerable

sum of money, or not cheat, in which case they were sure to lose.

The results showed that the students who had received blows to their self-esteem cheated far more than those who had gotten positive feedback about themselves. It may well be that low self-esteem is a critical antecedent of criminal or cruel behavior.

The theory of cognitive dissonance has proved useful in generating research; it has uncovered a wide range of data. In formal terms, however, it is a very sloppy theory. Its very simplicity provides both its greatest strength and its most serious weakness. That is, while the theory has generated a great deal of data, it has not been easy to define the limits of the theoretical statements, to determine the specific predictions that can be made. All too often researchers have had to resort to the very unscientific rule of thumb, "If you want to be sure, ask Leon."

LOGIC AND PSYCHOLOGIC

Part of the problem is that the theory does not deal with *logical* inconsistency, but *psychological* inconsistency. Festinger maintains that two cognitions are inconsistent if the opposite of one follows from the other. Strictly speaking, the information that smoking causes cancer does not make it illogical to smoke. But these cognitions produce dissonance because they do not make sense psychologically, assuming that the smoker does not want cancer.

One cannot always predict dissonance with accuracy. A man may admire Franklin Roosevelt enormously and discover that throughout his marriage FDR carried out a clandestine affair. If he places a high value on fidelity and he believes that great men are not exempt from this value, then he will experience dissonance. Then I can predict that he will either change his attitudes about Roosevelt or soften his attitudes about fidelity. But, he may believe that marital infidelity and political greatness are totally unrelated; if this were the case, he might simply shrug off these data without modifying his opinions either about Roosevelt or about fidelity.

Because of the sloppiness in the theory several commentators have criticized a great many of the findings first uncovered by dissonance theory. These criticisms have served a useful purpose. Often, they have goaded us to perform more precise research, which in turn has led to a clarification of some of the findings which, ironically enough, has eliminated the alternative explanations proposed by the critics themselves.

For example, Alphonse and Natalia Chapanis argued that the "severe initiation" experiment could have completely different causes. It might be that the young women were not embarrased at having to read sexual words, but rather were aroused, and their arousal in turn led them to rate the dull discussion group as interesting. Or, to the contrary, the women in the severe-intitiation condition could have felt much sexual anxiety, followed by relief that the discussion was so banal. They associated relief with the group, and so rated it favorably.

So Harold Gerard and Grover Mathewson replicated our experiment, using electric shocks in the initiation procedure. Our findings were supported—subjects who underwent severe shocks in order to join a discussion group rated that group more favorably than subjects who had undergone mild shocks. Moreover, Gerard and Mathewson went on to show that merely linking an electric shock with the group discussion (as in a simple conditioning experiment) did not produce greater liking for the group. The increase in liking for the group occurred only when subjects volunteered for the shock *in order to* gain membership in the group—just as dissonance theory would predict.

ROUTES TO CONSONANCE

In the real world there is usually more than one way to squirm out of inconsistency. Laboratory experiments carefully control a person's alternatives, and the conclusions drawn may be misleading if applied to everyday situations. For example, suppose a prestigious university rejects a young Ph.D. for its one available teaching position. If she feels that she is a good scholar, she will experience dissonance. She can then decide that members of that department are narrow-minded and senile, sexist, and wouldn't recognize talent if it sat on their laps. Or she could decide that if they could reject someone as fine and intelligent as she, they must be extraordinarily brilliant. Both techniques will reduce dissonance, but not that they leave this woman with totally opposite opinions about professors at the university.

This is a serious conceptual problem. One solution is to specify the conditions under which a person will take one route to consonance over another. For example, if a person struggles to reach a goal and fails, he may decide that the goal wasn't worth it (as Aesop's fox did) or that the effort was justified anyway (the fox got a lot of exercise in jumping for the grapes). My own research suggests that a person will take the first means when he has expended relatively little effort. But when he has put in a great deal of effort, dissonance will take the form of justifying the energy.

This line of work is encouraging. I do not think that it is very fruitful to demand to know what *the* mode of dissonance reduction is; it is more instructive to isolate the various modes that occur, and determine the optimum conditions for each.

IGNORANCE OF ABSURDITY

No dissonance theorist takes issue with the fact that people frequently work to get rewards. In our experiments, however, small rewards tend to be associated with greater attraction and greater attitude change. Is the reverse ever true?

Jonathan Freedman told college students to work on a dull task after first telling them (*a*) their results would be of no use to him, since his experiment was basically over, or (*b*) their results would be of great value to him. Subjects in the first condition were in a state of dissonance, for they had unknowingly agreed to work on a boring chore that apparently had no purpose. They reduced their dissonance by deciding that the task was enjoyable.

Then Freedman ran the same experiment with one change. He waited until the subjects finished the task to tell them whether their work would be important. In this study he found incentive effects: students told that the task was valuable enjoyed it more than those who were told that their work was useless. In short, dissonance theory does not apply when an individual performs an action in good faith without having any way of knowing it was absurd. When we agree to participate in an experiment we naturally assume that it is for a purpose. If we are informed afterward that it *had* no purpose, how were we to have known? In this instance we like the task better if it had an important purpose. But if we agreed to perform it *knowing* it had no purpose, we try to convince ourselves that it is an attractive task in order to avoid looking absurd.

MAN CANNOT LIVE BY CONSONANCE ALONE

Dissonance reduction is only one of several motives, and other powerful drives can counteract it. If human beings had a pervasive, all-encompassing need to reduce all forms of dissonance, we would not grow, mature, or admit to our mistakes. We would sweep mistakes under the rug, or worse, turn the mistakes into virtues; in neither case would we profit from error.

But obviously people do learn from experience. They often do tolerate dissonance because the dissonant information has great utility. A person cannot ignore forever a leaky roof, even if that flaw is inconsistent with having spent a fortune in the house. As utility increases, individuals will come to prefer dissonance-arousing but useful information. But as dissonance increases, or when commitment is high, future utility and information tend to be ignored.

It is clear that people will go to extraordinary lengths to justify their actions. They will lie, cheat, live on the San Andreas Fault, accuse innocent bystanders of being vicious provocateurs, ignore information that might save their lives, and generally engage in all manner of absurd postures. Before we write off such behavior as bizarre, crazy, or evil, we would be wise to examine the situations that set up the need to reduce dissonance. Perhaps our awareness of the mechanism that makes us so often irrational will help turn Camus' observation on absurdity into a philosophic curiosity.

11. Escape from Reality: Illusions in Everyday Life

Shelley E. Taylor

INTRODUCTION

One of the first things an infant learns is that the self is a separate person. Upon seeing his reflection, the very young baby will pat his image and pat himself in return, knowing that what he is seeing is himself. Much of early knowledge involves distinguishing what is the self from other important people in the environment, especially the mother and father. As a consequence the self helps to organize thinking around its attributes and its relationships to the social world.[1] Mental health experts suggest that the process by which this differentiation of self occurs should involve the capacity to perceive the self realistically, that is, to acknowledge faithfully both one's strengths and one's weaknesses. This is not, in fact, how the process evolves.

Before the exigencies of the world impinge upon the child's self-concept, the child is his or her own hero. With few exceptions, most children think very well of themselves. They believe they are capable at many tasks and abilities, including those they have never tried. They see themselves as popular. Most kindergartners and first-graders say they are at or near the top of the class. They have great expectations for their future success. Moreover, these grandiose assessments are quite unresponsive to negative feedback, at least until approximately age seven. Children see themselves as successful on most tasks, even ones on which they failed. They seem quite cheerfully oblivious to feedback from others that they have not performed as well as they think they have.[2] An architect friend recounts the time he took his five-year-old daughter to work with him. As he finalized some building plans at his drafting table, the child scrupulously mimicked the behavior at a nearby desk. Amused passersby came over to see what the child had accomplished, and one kindly friend remarked, "Someday you'll be an even better architect than your daddy." The child looked up in surprise and responded, "But I already am," and went back to work.

Why do children have such unrealistically positive assessments of their abilities that, moreover, appear to be so unresponsive to feedback? Psychologist Deborah Stipek argues, in part, that children do not necessarily view failure as failure. To a child, the fact that a goal has not been attained does not mean that something bad has occurred or that the experience has any implications for the future. Eventually children learn to judge their performance as a success or failure, but in very young children these concepts have little meaning. Children have fairly short memories and may actually forget how they have done. Children also see ability and effort as very much the same thing, and so they see any activity in pursuit of a goal, whether successful or unsuccessful, as progress. As one child noted, "If you study, it helps the brain and you get smarter."[3] Young children do not differentiate very well between what they wish could be true and what they think is true, and thus they show wishful thinking in their estimations of their abilities.[4]

The view of oneself as a hero who possesses all the qualities necessary to succeed in a world filled with opportunities fades somewhat in late childhood, but it is nonetheless present in adults as well as children. Although mental health experts regard the well-adjusted person as being aware and accepting of negative as well as positive aspects of the self, in fact, most adults hold very positive views of themselves. When asked to describe themselves, most people mention many positive qualities and few, if any, negative ones.[5] Even when people acknowledge that they have faults, they tend to downplay those weaknesses as unimportant or dismiss them as inconsequential.[6]

For those who are mathematically inclined, the world is awash with arithmetic problems waiting to be solved. For those with little talent in that direction, the tasks are best left undone or delegated to a spouse or an accountant. People regard activities that do not hold their interest as less important than things that interest them. To a football fan, football is an important part of life. To those uninterested in football, it is a slow-moving, bizarre contest between surreal giants who could surely think of better ways to spend their time. When people recognize their lack of talent in a particular area, they are likely to see it as a common fault shared by others. Favored abilities, in contrast, are typically regarded as rare and distinctive signs of unusual talent.[7] The child who can hop on one foot is convinced no one else can do it quite as well, while this same child would insistently argue that all her friends eat cereal with their fingers, too. Thus, far from being balanced between positive and negative conceptions, the image that most people hold of themselves is heavily weighted in a positive direction.[8]

But are those self-perceptions actually unrealistic? Is the positive self-image an illusion or a reality? An imbalance in self-perceptions does not in and of itself mean that people's self-perceptions are biased. Most people commit positive actions most of the time, and consequently people's favorable attributes and actions considerably outweigh their negative ones. There is, however, some evidence that adult's positive self-perceptions are unrealistic. Most people, for example, see themselves as better than others and as above average on most of their qualities. When asked to describe themselves and other people, most people provide more positive descriptions of themselves than

they do of friends. This tendency to see the self as better than others occurs across a wide variety of tasks and abilities.[9] Because it is logically impossible for most people to be better than everyone else, the positive view that most people have of themselves appears to be, at least to some degree, illusory in nature. Most people even believe that they drive better than others. For example, in one survey, 90 percent of automobile drivers considered themselves better than average drivers. Indeed, these beliefs sometimes show an unresponsiveness to feedback that reminds one of the very young child. When people whose driving had involved them in accidents serious enough to involve hospitalization were interviewed about their driving skills and compared with drivers who had not had accident histories, the two groups gave almost identical descriptions of their driving abilities. Irrespective of their accident records, people judged themselves to be more skillful than average, and this was true even when the drivers involved in accidents had been responsible for them.[10]

The evaluations people offer of themselves are also typically more favorable than judgments made by others about them.[11] For example, when people's descriptions are contrasted with the descriptions of them offered by their friends or acquaintances, the self-descriptions tend to be more positive. Typically, we see ourselves in more flattering terms than we are seen by others. The perception of self that most people hold, then, is not as well balanced as traditional theories of mental health suggest. Rather than being attentive to both the favorable and unfavorable aspects of the self, most people appear to be very cognizant of their strengths and assets and considerably less aware of their weaknesses and faults. Our self-aggrandizing perceptions may result in part from biases in how we remember ourselves and our past actions.

The Self as Personal Historian
Our minds are constructed not only to sift through and digest the information available to

us in the present, but to store and make sense of all the information that has been part of the past. In a sense each person acts as a personal historian, recording the events of which he or she has been a part. Rather than acting as a dispassionate recorder of events as they transpire, the self appears to actively fabricate and revise personal history. Moreover, this task is accomplished in a way that makes the self an important, central, and positive figure in that history.

In his landmark essay, "The Totalitarian Ego," psychologist Anthony Greenwald argues that "the past is remembered as if it were a drama in which the self is the leading player."[12] In some ways, this fact is a necessity of memory. One can remember only events in which one participated because, by definition, events from which one was absent cannot be remembered, only heard about. Moreover, memory must be limited by our own perceptions of what transpired. We cannot remember other people's interpretations of situations, only our own. We can experience only our own sensations and emotional reactions to situations and not other people's. Since memory is often enriched by the recall of particular feelings or sensations, these details will, of necessity, be egocentric, that is, centered around the self. In recalling a dinner party of the night before, I may remember that I had slightly too much to drink, told an off-color story about a colleague that might best have been censored, and was otherwise fairly outgoing and a little funnier than usual. Were I to share these perceptions with another who had been a guest at the party, they would no doubt bear little resemblance to his recollections. He might dimly remember my off-color story, have no awareness that I had slightly too much to drink, nor be particularly cognizant of the fact that I was entertaining. Rather, his own recollection of the party might involve wondering whether people noticed that he was feeling low and whether they would properly attribute this to problems in his marriage. He might remember several of the stories told, but not necessarily who told which one. He might recall

wondering at ten o'clock if the party would ever end, and the relief he felt when at eleven fifteen people finally pushed their chairs away from the table to say good night. The comparison of these experiences suggests that we were at different dinner parties, which indeed is exactly what happened in certain respects. In the absence of any active reconstruction or distortion, memory is egocentric, organized entirely around the experiences of the person constructing the memory.

But memory is egocentric in more important ways as well. Our memories of situations not only bear the traces of egocentric sensations and perspectives, but are also actively organized around our own interests and concerns. Each of us has qualities that we consider to be characteristic of ourselves. One person may think of himself as witty, musical, and hopelessly lacking in athletic ability. Another person may regard herself as kind, overweight, and intelligent. Psychologists call these enduring beliefs that people have about themselves *self-schemas*.[13] Self-schemas are important because they guide the selection and interpretation of information in social situations. The man who thinks of himself as musical will almost certainly remember that a Mozart clarinet concerto played in the background during the dinner party, whereas someone who does not consider himself to be musical might not even be aware that music was playing. The person who thinks of himself as witty is likely to interpret his barbed remark toward another dinner guest as humorous, whereas a person for whom kindness is an important dimension may interpret the same behavior as rude and unkind. The woman who thinks of herself as overweight will almost certainly remember the entire menu, what she ate and what she didn't eat, and the approximate caloric value of each food item.

Self-schemas, then, impose an additional selectivity on the information that people construe from situations and later remember about them. In recalling information that fits self-schemas, those self-schemas are inadvertently reinforced by memory. For example, each situation that a witty person interprets as an example of his own witty banter provides him with additional evidence that he is witty. If he construes three to four remarks that he made as examples of his wit, then his self-perception as a witty person is strengthened by each of these events. Other guests at the party, however, may remember only one or two of the remarks, considering neither especially funny. Self-schemas, then, enable us to take in the information that fits our prior conceptions of what we are like and what interests us and simultaneously helps cement those self-impressions.

Psychologists generally interpret the effects of self-schemas on memory to mean that memory is organized efficiently in a limited number of categories. That is, given that no one can take in all of the available information in a situation, self-schemas provide guidelines for which information should be noticed, thought about, and put away in memory. The fact that these organizing categories are related to the self is in some respects an accident of the fact that the self is taking in the information. If one takes a functional perspective for a moment, however, it is clear that the egocentric organization of information can be very useful. People make a rough cut on information as "relevant to me" or "not relevant to me." Next they interpret exactly how the information is relevant. When that information is later stored egocentrically in memory, it can be applied in extremely useful ways. For example, a woman for whom kindness is important not only uses kindness as a way of sorting people into the categories of kind and unkind, she may also use the information as a basis for her own future social interactions. Having determined that the witty man is unkind, she would be very likely to avoid him in future situations, a highly adaptive maneuver from her standpoint. Clearly, the egocentric organization of memory is useful from an economic standpoint, that is, in reducing information to a manageable load.[14] But beyond this, it may be very adaptive in helping people to construct their future activities.[15]

Most of us think well of ourselves on most attributes, so self-schemas are more likely to be positive than negative. This recognition leads to the realization that memory for past events will likely be recalled in a positive manner, one that reflects well on the self. This logical inference yields a third way in which memory is biased, namely toward positive construals of one's own attributes and roles in events gone by.[16] Indeed, the capacity of memory to recast events in a positive light almost immediately after they have transpired is almost astonishing. People who have just performed poorly on a task such as doing mathematics problems can be asked to recall their performance a scant twenty minutes later, and even in the short interval they misremember their performance as better than it actually was. Within a few days or weeks, the event may be forgotten altogether. If I rush a student in and out of my office in a few minutes, knowing that he has not had a chance to discuss his research with me fully, I may feel guilty shortly thereafter, but will likely have put the event totally out of mind within days. If I later learn that he has told other students that I am too busy to provide useful advice, I might be hurt and amazed by this betrayal, totally forgetting that I once believed it to hold a kernel of truth.

When people are asked to recall their personal qualities, they typically come up with more positive than negative information. Positive information about one's own personality is easily recalled and efficiently processed, whereas negative information about one's personality is poorly processed and difficult to recall.[17] There are, of course, qualifications to this general rule. Most of us know that in making our qualities known to another person, to brag endlessly of our talents without any assessment of our weaknesses would make us appear conceited. In order to achieve the positive picture we wish to construct for others, sometimes we may admit to certain faults. However, even the faults or weaknesses may be carefully chosen to round out a warm, human portrait, rather than one that is balanced between the positive and negative.[18] A woman may be more likely to admit to others that she is hopeless at math than to confess that she sometimes cheats on her husband. Thus, while our characterizations of ourselves to others may incorporate a certain socially desirable modesty, the portraits that we actually believe, when we are given freedom to voice them, are dramatically more positive than reality can sustain. As writer Carlos Fuentes so acutely noted, "Desire will send you back into memory . . . for memory is desire satisfied."[19]

Greenwald's characterization of these memory processes as totalitarian is apt. Unlike the academic historian, who is expected to adhere closely to the facts and insert a personal evaluation only in the interpretation, the personal historian takes unbridled license with the facts themselves, rearranging and distorting them and omitting aspects of history altogether in an effort to create and maintain a positive image of the self. We control the present by using our own interests and attributes as ways of selecting and organizing available information, and then we store it in memory in ways that are both highly positive and consistent with our existing impressions of ourselves. We use the present to construct a benign portrait of the past with ourselves as central actors. In so doing, we pave the way for a similar future.

The Self as Causal Actor

Taking in and recalling information are not the only cognitive tasks that people must perform. Active interpretation of the present is also required. Perceptions of what caused events to happen are among the most important beliefs that people hold about social situations. Here, too, the self is self-serving. A consistent and ubiquitous research finding is that people take credit for good things that happen and deny responsibility for the bad things that happen.[20] This self-serving bias, as it has been called, shows up in a broad array of situations. For example, on the tennis court, after you have soundly beaten an opponent, rarely do you hear the gratifying, "Gee, you're much better than I am, aren't you?" Usually you hear that it was a bad day, your opponent's serve was off, he is still working on

his backhand, or the light was in his eyes. On the other hand, when you have just been badly beaten, the smug look and condescending "bad luck" from the opponent are particularly grating because you know that he does not believe it was bad luck for a moment; he simply thinks he is better. Positive outcomes or actions tend to be attributed to one's own personal qualities, whereas negative outcomes are regarded as the result of bad luck or factors beyond one's control.

The following examples from the *San Francisco Chronicle* of drivers' explanations of their accidents to the police reveal how reluctantly people assume blame for negative events.

> As I approached an intersection, a sign suddenly appeared in a place where a stop sign had never appeared before. I was unable to stop in time to avoid an accident.
> The telephone pole was approaching. I was attempting to swerve out of its way when it struck my front end.[21]

And commenting on students' evaluations of final exams, Greenwald notes:

> I have repeatedly found a strong correlation between obtained grade and the belief that the exam was a proper measure. Students who do well are willing to accept credit for success; those who do poorly, however, are unwilling to accept responsibility for failure, instead seeing the exam (or the instructor) as being insensitive to their abilities.[22]

How do people maintain the perception that they cause good things to happen but bear less responsibility for bad outcomes? Is this simply some sleight of mind analogous to the magician's sleight of hand? Or can it be understood as an adaptive cognitive process? Perhaps when people try to understand why an event occurred, they confuse their intentions with their actions.[23] Usually we intend to cause good things and not bad things. When those good things do occur, the tendency to see ourselves as having brought them about may be quite justifiable, given that we did indeed mean to bring the outcome about. However, when our actions produce bad outcomes, we may look for circumstantial explanations precisely because no adverse outcomes were intended. The man who backs out of his driveway and hits a small child may blame the automobile manufacturers for having rear-view mirrors that fail to pick up low objects. Alternatively, he may blame the child's parents for not having trained the child to stay out of the street. He is unlikely to blame himself, because he never intended to hit the child. Whether the confusion of intention and causality underlies the tendency to attribute good outcomes to oneself to a greater degree than bad outcomes remains to be seen. The interpretational bias itself, however, is well established and constitutes yet another way in which the mind actively fosters a positive view of the self.

Self-serving biases in the perception of the causes of events are strengthened by the fact that people typically exaggerate how much of a role they have in any task, particularly one with a good outcome.[24] To take a simple example, when two people have written a book together and are asked to estimate how much of the book they are personally responsible for, the estimates added together will typically exceed 100 percent. The same feature characterizes more mundane tasks. Asked to estimate how much of a contribution they make to housework, adding together husbands' and wives' estimates of their own efforts produces a total that greatly exceeds 100 percent.[25] Even the lore surrounding Nobel Prize winners is filled with such accounts.

In 1923, two Canadians, Banting and Macleod, were awarded the Nobel Prize for their discovery of insulin. Upon receiving the prize, Banting contended that Macleod, who was head of the laboratory, had been more of a hindrance than a help. On the other hand, Macleod managed to omit Banting's name in speeches describing the research leading up to discovery of insulin.[26]

What leads people to overestimate their role in jointly undertaken ventures? Egocentric memory appears once again to be the culprit. We notice our own contributions to a joint task

because we are mentally and physically present when making our own contributions. When the other person is contributing his or her share to the joint task, we may not be physically present to observe it or we may be distracted from noticing the other person's effort. When asked to recall who contributed what to the task, it will subsequently be easier to recall one's own contributions, having attended to them better in the first place, than to recall the other person's.[27]

There will also likely be interpretational biases in what constitutes a contribution.[28] A recent tiff between two authors of a book centered on the fact that while one wrote his share of the chapters rather quickly, the other put a great deal more time into preparing his chapters. Because the first writer was more experienced, his chapters needed few revisions; but the second author's chapters required several drafts and received comments from the first author. The first author perceived that he had borne the lion's share of the effort, by both being responsible for his own chapters and critiquing those of his collaborator. The collaborator, in contrast, felt that he had done the most, because his work had taken three times as long as the first author's. Who is right? Clearly it depends on one's perspective, and one can make a case for either position.

The tendency to take more than one's share of credit for a joint outcome would appear to be a maladaptive bias, inasmuch as it creates so many opportunities for misunderstandings. However, the bias may have benefits as well as potential liabilities. By perceiving one's share of a joint product to be larger than it is, people may feel more responsible for the outcome and work harder to make it a positive one. Moreover, the process of contributing to the activity may instill a sense of commitment to the project and to one's collaborators that may undermine, at least temporarily, any feelings of having done more than one's share. The bias, too, may be more one of memory than of active construction during the time that the tasks are being performed. Often, when two people have jointly achieved greatness, the falling out over who was most responsible for the product occurs after the outcome has been achieved, not while the task is going on. Commitment and a sense of responsibility may carry the joint product through completion, but egocentric memory may distort later reconstructions of what actually took place.[29]

At this point, it is useful to take stock and reassess whether normal human self-perception is characterized by realism or not. The evidence from numerous research investigations with both children and adults clearly indicates that people's assessments of their own capabilities are ego-enhancing rather than realistic. The fact that this bias is so clearly prevalent in the normal human mind is surprising. Psychologists have typically interpreted blatant ego enhancement as the resort of weak and insecure people attempting to bolster fragile self-esteem. Weak egos are thought to need narcissism to survive.[30] Alternatively, ego defensiveness has been viewed as a handy refuge for all of us during weak or threatening moments.[31] In this view, we may need the occasional self-serving interpretation to recover from a blow to self-esteem, but not otherwise. The picture furnished by the evidence, however, is quite different and suggests that ego enhancement characterizes most perception most of the time. This fact, in itself, does not make self-enhancement adaptive, but it does make it normal. As such, this picture is in opposition to the portrait of normal functioning painted by many theories of mental health.

THE NEED FOR CONTROL

In 1971, psychologist B. F. Skinner published a book, *Beyond Freedom and Dignity,* that sparked heated debate. Among other points, Skinner argued that freedom and individual will are illusions because behavior is under the control of positive and negative reinforcements provided by the environment. The uproar created by this argument is testimony to the attachment people have to their perceptions of freedom, personal choice, and control. Indeed, Skinner may have gone too far. While there is certainly a basis for contending that freedom, control, and personal will are constructions that people impose on events rather than factors inherent in events themselves, what people construe about their behavior is of great importance. Interpretations enable people to make sense of their experience; moreover, they can have important personal consequences. As psychologist Herbert Lefcourt notes:

> To believe that one's freedom is a false myth and that one should submit to wiser or better controls contains the assumption that beliefs or illusions have no immediate consequences. . . . This assumption is specious. Illusions have consequences and . . . the loss of the illusion of freedom may have untoward consequences for the way men live.[32]

Since the days of Aristotle and Plato, philosophers have argued that a sense of personal control is vital to human functioning. Psychologists from many theoretical viewpoints, including social psychologist Fritz Heider, developmental psychologist Robert White, learning theorist Albert Bandura, and psychoanalytic theorists Alfred Adler and Sandor Fenichel, have maintained that the self-concept cannot mature without a sense of personal control.

The Child's Need for Control

The desire to control and manipulate the world is evident from a remarkably early age. Within weeks after birth, an infant actively explores the environment, responding to a new stimulus, such as a brightly colored rattle, with rapt attention and babbling. Soon, however, when the rattle has been fully explored, the infant shows little response when the rattle is again dangled before her, but may react with the same excitement to a new checkerboard that she has not previously seen. The infant, then, is primed to master new experiences.[33] At first, psychologists observing this behavior tried to identify what reinforcements it might bring for the child. Were the parents more likely to feed or comfort the child when he or she explored and manipulated the environment? What rewards did curiosity evoke that maintained this behavior? Soon it became evident that the child pursued these exploratory activities for their own sake. Exploration and the ability to bring about change in the environment are their own rewards.[34]

As a result of these observations, psychologists believe that even newborn infants have an intrinsic need to understand and manage the environment.[35] Even the youngest children seem to do what is good for them to bring about their own effective learning. They seek out tasks and sources of stimulation that lead to the development of new skills. Children seem to derive pleasure from engaging in this mastery-oriented behavior, and when a child has accomplished some task—that is, when mastery is attained—he or she seems to experience joy and satisfactions. Both pleasure in the activity itself and enjoyment of the sense of mastery promote similar activities in the future.

So evident is this drive toward mastery that psychologists believe the need to master the environment, or at least its basic elements, is wired in via a mastery-motivation system that instigates, maintains, and reinforces activities that lead to the development of new skills. White refers to this as competence motivation, arguing that the process of learning about the environment and gaining mastery over it is actually intrinsic to the child's development and will occur of its own accord unless disrupted by a biological malfunction or an impoverished environment.[36] Daniel Berlyne refers to a curiosity motivation by which the child constantly seeks more and varied objects to manipulate and explore.[37]

Some of the child's exploratory activities involve stretching already evident skills to try something new. For example, the infant who is able to reach and grasp a stationary toy may be stimulated more by a new toy that is moving than by another stationary toy. The moving toy forces her to extend her abilities to track the toy with her eyes and grasp it as it comes into reach. Children seek and produce novel activity and stimulus variability. Moderately new environments that include objects the child has not seen before are far more interesting and stimulating than either radically different environments or environments full of familiar objects.

The child's mastery needs, then, have a certain orderly progression to them that is responsive both to the demands of tasks and to the limits of existing skills.[38] Any parent attempting unrealistically to throw a birthday party for a one-year-old will stumble upon this fact. As each gift is unwrapped, the child reacts not to the contents but to the wrappings, balling up the paper to make a wonderful crumpling noise and waving the brightly colored ribbons overhead. The empty box makes a perfect hat and is far more valued a toy than the train that came in it, which may not be admired and played with for another six or eight months. Children learn and perform new tasks that are just beyond their range of competence. The young child does not try to drive a car. He depresses the accelerator repeatedly. The adolescent, ready for such a challenge, rolls the car down the driveway at night and practices driving while his parents sleep. The very young child's early cooking efforts extend to baking cookies by stirring in the flour and eating too many chocolate bits. The adolescent can cook an entire meal, assuming she can be induced to do so. Mastery skills are used in a discriminating fashion, moving a step or two ahead of the child's current abilities.

By learning to master their own environments, children alter their parents' behaviors dramatically. Parents quickly learn that if they want the infant to reward them with enthusiastic sounds, the best way to achieve this goal is to gradually introduce more and varied novel experiences. Even infants are able to enlist the cooperation of the social environment to their own mastery needs.[39]

The desire to master the environment, then, appears to be a basic drive, perhaps even a fundamental need of the human organism. By learning that he or she can have an impact on the environment, the child acquires the valuable skills, crucial for adult functioning, that enable him or her to actively intervene in the world so as to bring about desired outcomes. The implicit assumption that underlies a functional interpretation of the need to master is that such early experiences provide the child with a realistic sense of self-efficacy, that is, a realization of those things that can be actively changed and controlled in order to realize personal goals. In fact, however, the sense of control that young children develop appears to be exaggerated rather than tempered by realism.

As young children are learning *how* to control the environment, so too are they learning *that* they can control it. Early in development, children gain the sense that they can make things happen.[40] This, too, may be intrinsic to the child's nature, for it can easily be observed in extreme and dramatic form in the young child. In his conversations with children, the esteemed developmental psychologist Jean Piaget discovered that children believe not only that they can master what goes on in the immediate environment but that they control the movements of the sun, moon, and stars as well.[41] The child's sense of omnipotence is so strong that when family crises arise, such as a sibling's illness or parents' divorce, young children may react very strongly, in part because they believe they brought the tragic events about.[42]

The child's sense of omnipotence extends to schoolwork and other learning tasks. When asked to guess how well they will do on tasks, young children usually substantially overestimate their performance because they believe they can master the tasks easily. Psychologist Carol Dweck and her associates argue that a mastery orientation toward tasks develops and coheres quite early in life.[43] Mastery-oriented children approach new tasks with the question, "How can this best be accomplished and what should I do to solve it correctly?" When they run into trouble on a difficult task, these mastery-oriented children talk to themselves, trying to figure out what is wrong with their performance and developing strategies to change it so they will be more effective. Often they encourage themselves, letting themselves know that they can do the task correctly.

The competence drive that one sees in the infant and young child is remarkably simple, but extraordinary in its effects. On the one hand, it requires no plan or intention. Yet it enables the child to fashion his or her environment in an increasingly complex way, enlisting the cooperation and talents of several powerful adults in the process, and to derive great pleasure and satisfaction from the results, while simultaneously building essential intellectual skills.

Over time, the child's sense of personal control diminishes somewhat, becoming responsive to realistic limits on talents and the limitations inherent in difficult tasks.[44] Despite this movement toward realism, adults not only continue to have a need and desire to control the environment, but also maintain an exaggerated faith in their ability to do so.

The Adult's Need for Control

Most adults believe the world to be inherently controllable. They have faith that a combination of personal effort and advanced technology can solve most of the world's problems. To the extent that we have been unsuccessful in controlling natural forces or, for that matter, the economic, social, and political dilemmas we have ourselves created, we perceive it to be through lack of effort, not ability, that the problems have remained unsolved. We believe that people succeed through their own efforts, and this leads us to impute effort to those who are highly successful and laziness to those who are not.[45] Even if evidence is all around us suggesting that events are less orderly and systematic than we think they are, rarely do we develop a full appreciation of this fact. The failure to recognize the role of random, unsystematic forces in many aspects of life may come, in part, from our need to see the world as a systematic and orderly place. As Ernest Becker noted in his Pulitzer Prize–winning book, *The Denial of Death,* through the imposition of logic and order on the world we spare ourselves the constant realization of the random terror of death.

One source of faith in personal control is that the environment often cooperates in maintaining it. People are typically quite cognizant of the effects of their own actions on the environment, but are considerably less so regarding the effects of the environment on their own actions. We underestimate the degree to which our behavior is determined by social and physical forces that not only are uncontrollable but often escape awareness altogether.[46] One of my colleagues believes, only half in jest, that he can will a parking place in any lot in which he needs to find one. The reason he holds this belief is that apparently most lots into which he drives have one or two spaces left. Until recently, it had escaped his attention that building projects must create an appropriate number of parking spaces. Thus, while he no doubt overestimates the number of times he gets the last spot, it is also the case that getting one of the last spots is a highly probably event, given the small miracle of city planning.

Another source of the belief in control is that people confuse what they want to have happen with what they can actually bring about, and if the desired event occurs, they conclude that they controlled it.[47] I once observed this in a young boy who had been hospitalized for diabetes. Although not confined to bed, he remained in the hospital for observation because his blood sugar level changed erratically and required monitoring. The hospital environment was dull for this youngster, and he soon took to riding the elevators to provide himself with some semblance of stimulation. Deciding that he would become the elevator operator, he positioned himself in front of the control panel, making it impossible for others to press any but the floor numbers. At each floor, the boy would push the "Door Open" button; when the passenger had departed, the boy would push the "Door Close" button. The door obediently opened and shut. The regular passengers tolerated this unusual behavior because they could see that the boy needed to believe that something, however small, was under his personal control. No one had the heart to tell him, and he never figured out on his own, that the elevator was controlled

entirely automatically, and that his button presses had no effect whatsoever on its operation. Because the door repeatedly opened and shut when he wanted it to, he mistakenly assumed that his behavior was actually bringing it about.

The process of evaluating whether or not an event is controllable is an example of a broader fallacy of reasoning, namely the search for examples that confirm prior beliefs.[48] To see how this logical fallacy operates, consider the popular belief that people can cure themselves of serious illnesses through positive thinking. Many people believe that illness results primarily from stressful events and that those who are able to maintain a positive attitude can exert control over their bodily processes and drive illness away. What kind of evidence leads people to hold such a belief? Examples of the mental control of illness are readily available. Norman Cousin's book, *Anatomy of an Illness,* describes in warm and humorous detail the methods the author used to treat himself for a disease that is usually fatal. Magazines contain stories of people who have apparently healed themselves of advanced malignancies through positive thinking. Cultural mythology abounds with examples of shamans who cured their sick neighbors through a variety of useless but dramatic ceremonies. These positive examples make compelling reading, but the logical error lies in precisely this point: they are all positive instances.

Suppose one wanted to determine scientifically whether people are able to cure their diseases through positive attitudes. What would one need to know? Most people immediately recognize the need to find examples of people who tried to cure their diseases through positive thinking and were successful. If pushed, one might come up with the observation that it would be useful to find out how many people tried to cure their diseases through positive thinking and failed. What most people miss is that an accurate sense of whether people can cure their illnesses depends on at least two more types of information: the number of people who did not try to cure their incurable illnesses and survived nonetheless, and the number of people who did not make an effort to cure their illnesses and died. In other words, to establish that people can survive a serious illness if they have effectively tried to control it, one needs all four types of information.

Unfortunately, the world of disease is full of people who have tried valiantly to cure themselves of their illnesses and have ultimately failed. Those who have worked extensively with the chronically ill also know that many people survive years longer than expected without having made any effort in their own behalf at all. These people are often just as bewildered as their physicians, family, and friends to find themselves alive some five or ten years after their initial diagnosis, when everyone expected them to die within months.

In short, it is logically incorrect to conclude that people can control their illnesses simply because one can readily find apparent examples. When one is forced to survey all of the evidence—instead of just the positive cases that are so compelling—judgments of control are considerably more muted, and enthusiasm for the initial belief is somewhat diminished.

This is not to say that people are unable to improve their health by maintaining a positive attitude. The jury is still out on this issue. Rather, the point is that people "see" their beliefs confirmed in incomplete evidence that leads them prematurely to desired conclusions. They fail to see that evidence they have ignored is also relevant. Decision theorists despair of ever getting people to avoid this error. Moreover, on this bias, the average person is in good company. The error is virtually irresistible, not only to the general public but to high-level decision makers in government and industry as well. The analysis of numerous policy decisions, such as the disastrous Bay of Pigs invasion in 1961, has implicated as the basis of the failure the tendency to incorporate primarily positive information and to ignore negative information.[49]

The Illusion of Control

As the previous analysis suggests, people not only believe that the world is inherently controllable, they believe that their own ability to personally control events around them is exceptional. Psychologist Ellen Langer argues that most people succumb to an illusion of control, in which they believe they can affect events more than is actually the case. To demonstrate this point, Langer chose gambling.[50]

Gambling is a clear case in which the relative importance of personal control and chance are often confused. Sociologist Erving Goffman, who once took a job as a croupier in Las Vegas, noted that dealers who experienced runs of bad luck, leading the house to lose heavily, ran the risk of losing their jobs, even though the reason for the run of bad luck was ostensibly chance.[51] Experienced dice players engaged in a variety of behaviors suggesting a belief that they could control what numbers the dice turned up. They threw the dice softly if they wanted low numbers to come up and hard if they were trying to get high numbers. Moreover, they believed that effort and concentration were important and often would not roll the dice unless there was silence and they had a few seconds to concentrate on the number they wanted to get.[52] These kinds of behaviors make perfect sense if a game involves skill. They do not make much sense when the outcome is controlled by chance.

Most of us are not heavy gamblers. In an intriguing set of studies, however, Langer was able to demonstrate that virtually all people are subject to the same illusions of control as veteran gamblers. Beginning with the recognition that people often fail to distinguish between controllable and uncontrollable events, she argued that one reason for this fact is that the cues people use to differentiate situations of luck and skill are often confused. In skill situations, there is a causal link between one's own behavior and likely outcomes. By choosing materials appropriate for a problem, deciding what responses to make, familiarizing oneself with those materials and responses, spending time thinking about the tasks, coming up with strategies that might be used, and exerting effort, people increase their likelihood of succeeding on a skill-based task.[53] On tasks determined by chance, such behaviors have no effect at all.

Langer showed that by introducing skill-related cues into a chance situation, people came to behave as if the situations were under their personal control and not a result of luck at all. Among her observations were the following: If a person had to bet against a suave, confident opponent, he bet less money than if the opponent appeared to be meek and ineffective. When people were able to choose their own lottery card, as opposed to having it chosen for them, they were less likely to turn it in for a new lottery card that offered them a better chance of winning, simply because they felt it was now *their* card and they wanted to hold onto it. The longer a person held on to a lottery card and presumably had time to think about the likelihood of winning and what he would do with all the money, the less likely he was to turn the lottery card in for a ticket in a drawing with better odds. Langer was able to show that perfectly normal people engaged in a wide variety of superstitious and nonsensical behaviors in chance situations, when cues suggesting skill had been subtly introduced.[54]

The significance of Langer's research extends far beyond its curious but rather minor implications regarding gambling. Any situation in which a person confronts options, develops strategies, and devotes thought to a problem is vulnerable to an illusion of control. For several months, I have been plagued with a problem that until recently proved to be intractable, namely the fact that my dogs eat the pansies growing in the backyard. A variety of disciplinary actions as well as the application of foul-smelling but harmless chemicals to the flower beds have proven unsuccessful in keeping them from these meals. Now, however, I have mastered the situation, by planning to plant pansies only in the beds around the front door. In the backyard I will plant marigolds, which are not nearly as appealing to dogs. The successful solution to this problem bolsters my confidence that I am able to handle stressful events. One can legitimately ask, of course, who actually has control in this situation, me or the dogs? While in my weaker moments I acknowledge that one can probably make the stronger case for the dogs, most of the time this does not dampen my self-congratulations at having successfully mastered the problem by choosing an effective solution. The fact that this "choice" was fully constrained by the situation and was the only option remaining, other than eliminating the dogs, is conveniently forgotten.

The illusion of control has powerful effects on the human psyche. Psychologists have demonstrated that people can tolerate extreme distress if they believe they have the ability to control the source of that distress.[55] The following study conducted with college students makes this point. The students were brought into the laboratory for a study of reactions to electric shock. Half of the students were told that once the shock began, they could terminate it simply by pressing a button in front of them. The other half of the students were not given a button to press to terminate the shock. All the students were then exposed to a series of uncomfortable but harmless electric shocks. The shocks were rigged so that both groups of students received exactly the same amount of shock. Despite this fact, those able to terminate the event by pressing the button themselves experienced less psychological distress, fewer symptoms of physiological arousal, and less physical discomfort.[56] This study and ones like it have been carried out many times with different stressful events and, in every known case, those who can exert control over the stressful event experience less distress and arousal than those who cannot. In fact, those able to control the event often show no more psychological distress or physiological arousal than people receiving no aversive experience at all.[57] Clearly it is not the adverse event itself that leads people to feel physically aroused and psychologically distressed, but rather the perception that it cannot be controlled.

Why do we perceive as controllable things that either are not controllable or are much less so than we think they are? We understand control. We know what it means to seek a goal, to develop methods for obtaining it, and then to employ those methods until the goal is obtained. There is an order, logic, and process to control. There is no order or logic to randomness. Perhaps as well we need to see events as controllable and this is why our minds are predisposed to focus in selectivity on instances that support our preconceptions. Perhaps it is the false belief in control that makes people persist in pursuing their goals. Would a novelist undertaking her first work want to contemplate other writers who were catapulted into success by their first works, or would she want to focus instead on the far larger group of writers whose first novels never even attracted a publisher? Clearly, the answer is the former. Our need to see things as inherently controllable may well be adaptive, and our tendency to focus on positive cases of the relationships we expect and so badly wish to see may have value, even as it distorts perceptions.

UNREALISTIC OPTIMISM ABOUT THE FUTURE

Most people are oriented toward the future. When asked to describe what occupies their thoughts, people typically mention issues of immediate or future concern.[58] Moreover, optimism pervades thinking about the future. We seem to be optimistic by nature, some of us more than others, but most more than reality can support.[59] Each year, survey researchers query the American public about their current lives and what they think their lives will be like in five years. Most surveys find people reporting that the present is better than the past and that the future will be even better. More than 95 percent of people questioned in these surveys typically believe that the economic picture will be good for everyone and that their personal economic future will be even better than that of others. People are characteristically hopeful and confident that things will improve.[60] Although this warm and generous vision is extended to all people, it is most clearly evident in visions of one's own future. Students asked to envision what their future lives would be like said they were more likely to graduate at the top of the class, get a good job, have a high starting salary, like their first job, receive an award for work, get written up in the paper, and give birth to a gifted child than their classmates. Moreover, they considered themselves far less likely than their classmates to have a drinking problem, to be fired from a job, to get divorced after a few years of marriage, to become depressed, or to have a heart attack or contract cancer.[61]

Unrealistic optimism is not confined to the idealistic young. Older adults also underestimate the likelihood that they will encounter a large number of negative, but unhappily common, events such as having an automobile accident, being a crime victim, having job problems, contracting major diseases, or becoming depressed. Unrealistic optimism appears to be unaffected by age, education, sex, or occupational prestige. The old and young, the well- and the poorly educated, men and women, and people in all areas of life show unrealistic optimism in their assessments of the future.[62]

When asked to predict the future, most people predict what they would like to see happen, rather than what is objectively likely. Whether it be in a volleyball game, on a driving test, or on a report prepared for one's boss, most people believe that they will do well in the future. People expect to improve their performance over time, and moreover, this optimism typically increases with the importance of the task.[63] People are more unrealistically optimistic about the prospects of their future jobs than about their gardens, for example. People are even unrealistically optimistic about events that are completely determined by chance, such as whether they will win the lottery and whether the weather will be good for a picnic. People seem to be saying, in effect, "The future will be great, especially for me."

One of the more charming optimistic biases that people share is the belief that they can accomplish more in a given period of time than is humanly possible. This bias persists in the face of innumerable contradictions. Perhaps the most poignant example of this unrealistic optimism is the daily to-do list. Each day, the well-organized person makes a list of the tasks to be accomplished and then sets out to get them done. Then the exigencies of the day begin to intrude: phone calls, minor setbacks, a miscalculation of how long a task will take, or a small emergency. The list that began the day crisp and white is now in tatters, with additions, cross-outs and, most significantly, half its items left undone. Yet at the end of the day, the list maker cheerfully makes up another overly optimistic list for the next day, or if much was left undone, simply crosses out the day at the top of the list and writes in the next day. This all-too-familiar pattern is remarkable not only because a to-do list typically includes far more than any person could reasonably expect to accomplish in a given time period, but also because the pattern persists day after day, completely unresponsive to the repeated feedback that it is unrealistic.[64]

Like the overly positive view of the self and the illusion of control, unrealistic optimism develops very early in life. When children are asked how well they will do on a future task, their expectations are typically very high, higher than is realistic. Moreover, unrealistically optimistic assessments of future performance are not very responsive to feedback, such as actual performance, grades in class, comments from teachers, or reactions of parents. By about age seven or eight, children begin to be aware of the meaning of negative feedback. They become more responsive to what their teachers and parents tell them. They also know what objective tests are, and so they are able to use both objective information and feedback from others to evaluate whether or not they have done a good job.[65] In some respects, this intruding realism is a sad aspect of growing older. Stipek notes:

It is perhaps unfortunate that children's naive optimism declines so soon after they enter school. To some degree the development of more realistic expectations is unavoidable and even desirable. However . . . if children were only

given tasks on which they could succeed with some effort, continually high expectations for success and the adaptive behaviors that are associated with high expectations might be maintained throughout the school years. Rather than lamenting children's unrealistic judgments about their competencies, perhaps we should try harder to design educational environments that maintain their optimism and eagerness.[66]

But is unrealistic optimism adaptive? Just as ego-enhancing biases have been regarded as defenses against threats to self-esteem, unrealistic optimism has been thought of as a defensive reaction, a distortion of reality designed to reduce anxiety.[67] Consider the following opinions:

Optimism . . . is a mania for maintaining that all is going well when things are going badly. (Voltaire)

Optimism, not religion, is the opiate of the people. (Lionel Tiger)

The place where optimism most flourishes is in the lunatic asylum. (Havelock Ellis)

Two arguments have been made against unrealistic optimism. The first is that optimism about the future is an irrational defense against reality that enables people to ward off the anxiety of threatening events without successfully coming to terms with it. The second is related to the first in maintaining that unrealistic optimism keeps people from perceiving the objective risks of external threats and preparing for them.[68] Several points argue against the appropriateness of these concerns. If unrealistic optimism were merely a defense against anxiety, one would expect that more serious and threatening events would elicit more unrealistic optimism than minor risks. In fact, the evidence does not support this position. The degree of threat posed by a risk is unrelated to the amount of unrealistic optimism people have about their lack of susceptibility to the problem.[69]

Moreover, unrealistic optimism about the future is highly and appropriately responsive to objective qualities of events, including their frequency and whether or not a person has any past experience with that event. People are less unrealistically optimistic about their chances of experiencing common events like divorce or chronic illness than they are about less frequent events, such as being the victim of a flood or fire. Past experience with a threatening event can eliminate unrealistic optimism altogether. Children of divorced parents, for example, regard their own chances of getting divorced as higher than people whose parents were not divorced. People are also more unrealistically optimistic about future events over which they have some control than they are about those that are uncontrollable. For example, although people estimate their chances of winning a lottery to be higher than is objectively likely, they recognize that winning a large amount of money in a lottery is far less likely than having a satisfying job, an event over which they presumably have more direct control. And finally, unrealistic optimism is responsive to information. When people receive objective evidence about the likelihood of risks, they change their estimates accordingly.[70] These qualities most clearly distinguish illusion from delusion. Delusions are false beliefs that persist despite the facts. Illusions accommodate them, though perhaps reluctantly.

Unrealistic optimism, then, is not a Panglossian whitewash that paints all positive events as equally and commonly likely and all negative events as equally and uncommonly unlikely. Rather, unrealistic optimism shows a patterning that corresponds quite well to the objective likelihood of events, to relevant personal experiences with events, and to the degree to which one can actively contribute to bringing events about. Positive events are simply regarded as somewhat more likely and negative events as somewhat less likely to occur than is actually the case.

What accounts for unrealistic optimism? Optimism seems to be intimately bound up with other illusions of life, especially the belief in personal control.[71] Most people think they can control future events more than is actually the case, and consequently they may underestimate their vulnerability to random events. A driver may perceive the chance of an automobile accident to be low because she belives she is a better than average driver who can avoid such problems. She may conveniently forget the joy-riding teenager or the drunk driver who may cause an accident. People think they can avoid health problems by getting enough sleep or eating well, forgetting that hereditary factors, chance encounters with viruses, or environmental threats of which they may be ignorant can override even the most careful program of health habits. An active homosexual man in the 1970s might have given some thought to the possibility of contracting gonorrhea, but could he possibly have anticipated the horror of AIDS? Could the people attending the American Legion convention in Philadelphia in 1976 have guessed that the air in their hotel held a deadly contaminant, producing what we now call Legionnaires' disease? When people think of the future, they think of events they would like to see happen and the ones they believe they can bring about, rather than the chance events that may disrupt goals and plans.

Reflection suggests that the failure to consider the role of chance is not as surprising as first might appear. What exactly would constitute an effective recognition of chance? Should one begin driving each day with the image of a truck out of control bearing down on one's car? Should one regard every social situation as a potential opportunity for viruses to spread? Should every walk along city streets be considered a potential encounter with a mugger or rapist? While people certainly need to incorporate a certain amount of caution and defensiveness into their daily behavior, to do so by envisioning these potentially tragic but random events is hardly appropriate. Because chance and random factors are precisely that, their importance cannot be assessed in any reasonable way for any given situation. Therefore, people quite properly do not have chance at the forefront of consciousness when they assess their risks.

The belief in personal control may also account for why people see their personal likelihood of experiencing positive events as higher and negative events as lower than those of other people. When people focus on their own behaviors that might enable them to achieve desirable outcomes or avoid bad ones, they may forget that other people have just as many resources in their own lives.[72] People misjudge their risk that negative events can befall them because they have clear-cut stereotypes of the kinds of people who typically succumb to these events.[73] People who foolishly wander down dark streets at night are people who get mugged. Passive, repressed people who do not express their feelings get cancer. With these stereotypes in mind, we are able to comfort ourselves that adverse events will not befall us. The fact that each of us is engaging in this process—that is, imagining how he or she can avoid negative events—appears to escape attention altogether.

Unrealistic optimism may result from more than simple stereotypes about the kinds of people on whom bad outcomes descend. Psychologist Ziva Kunda suggests that people actively construct theories of why positive and negative events occur; in so doing they draw on their own attributes in order to defend against the possibility that the negative events might befall them and to enhance the perceived likelihood that the positive events will happen to them. For example, upon learning that the divorce rate for first marriages is 50 percent, most people predict that they will not be in that 50 percent, but rather will remain married to their spouse throughout their lifetime. They convince themselves that this is the case, Kunda has shown, by highlighting their personal attributes that might be associated with a stable marriage and downplaying the significance of or actively refuting information that might suggest a vulnerability to divorce. Thus, for example, one might point to one's parents' fifty-year marriage, the close family life that existed in one's early childhood, and the fact that one's high school relationship lasted a full four years as evidence to predict a stable marriage. The fact that one's husband has already been divorced once—a factor that predicts a second

divorce—might be reinterpreted not only as not leading to divorce in one's own case, but as a protective factor ("He knows he does not want this marriage to fail like the last one, and so he's working especially hard to keep our relationship strong"). The ability to draw seemingly rational relationships between our own assets and good events and to argue away associations between our own attributes and negative events helps to maintain unrealistic optimism.[74]

The Illusion of Progress

The ability to sustain an optimistic view of the future may also come in part from the ability to misconstrue events as progress. There is a well-established bias indicating that people see themselves as having improved even when no actual progress has been made.[75] We all know that people seek out the company of others who are likely to give them positive feedback. It is only reasonable that we should want as friends people who like and value us. There is a corresponding, less obvious tendency to like others whose evaluations of us improve over time. The initially hard to get girlfriend or boyfriend may, for example, be more highly valued than an old faithful partner who was responsive all along. When people's impressions improve over time, rather than staying at a positive level, it simultaneously enhances several other positive beliefs: it encourages a feeling of personal impact, the idea that one can positively affect other people's evaluations. In so doing, it encourages feelings of interpersonal control, the belief that one can bring out in people the kinds of evaluations and judgments of the self that one would like to achieve. And it creates a future as optimistic as the one mentally constructed because just as one fantasizes that progress will occur, progress appears to be made.[76]

This tendency to construct the future so that it will be better than the past is not limited to social interaction. In an intriguing study, Michael Conway and Michael Ross invited college students who were having difficulty studying to enroll in a program designed to show them how to improve their study skills and achieve higher grades.[77] Half of the students who applied to the program were accepted immediately and the other half were put on a waiting list. The first group of students then went through a three-week study skills program. As it happens, most study skills programs are actually quite ineffective in imparting new skills and raising grades,[78] and such was the case with the study skills program initiated by Conway and Ross. The students who took the program did not differ in final grades or study skills from students who had not participated in the program.

Nonetheless, students in the program perceived that they had improved dramatically. They reported better study skills, and they expected better final exam grades. They also distorted retrospectively how bad their study skills had been before going into the program. Moreover, even after final grades had been calculated, the students overestimated their grades for the term. Thus, by revising what they had initially had, the students were able to achieve, at least mentally, what they wanted, namely improvement in their study skills and grades. Failure ("I failed the test") can be reinterpreted as progress ("but I got practice that will help on this kind of test next time"). Through such distortions, several positive biases may be enhanced. One sees oneself in a positive light and as efficacious, and one simultaneously reconstructs the past and future so as to achieve an illusion of progress.

The Effects of Outcomes on Optimism

People are optimistic about the future most of the time, but when something good happens to them, they become even more so.[79] Doing well at work, for example, leads a person to believe that his children will improve their grades in school and that he will win the weekend tennis tournament. Moreover, a good event acts as a generalized opportunity signal, increasing the belief in the likelihood of all kinds of positive events. Happy events are seen as portents of yet more happy things to come. Similarly, when a

bad event happens, it increases the perception that other bad events may lie ahead.[80] Getting sick, being burglarized, or failing a test all move beliefs in the direction of pessimism. Even a transitory mood can yield these same effects.[81] On a day when a person feels good for no particular reason, optimism is higher. Likewise, on a day when a person is low for no particular reason, pessimism may set in. The negative event or mood seems to act as a danger signal. Moreover, this danger signal appears to be a general one, in that it sometimes increases the perception that any bad event may follow, even ones having little or nothing to do with the negative event that has already transpired. If a person fails her driving test, she might logically fear that she may do so again, but why should her fear of developing cancer increase? Why should a burglary increase a sense of vulnerability to diabetes? Similarly, why should receiving a raise at work lead to the belief that one can improve one's marriage?

Perhaps when something good happens, it reinforces a person's belief that he or she is an effective, competent person who can make things happen. Since people exaggerate their ability to control events, even those that are determined by chance, any positive outcome may make people think that they can produce other positive outcomes. Similarly, a negative event, such as getting sick, may undermine a person's sense of control and competence by pointing out that one can get in harm's way without much effort. As the person attempts to make sense of the negative event, he or she may become aware of vulnerability in general, increasing the sense that he or she can fall victim to other negative events. Sociologist Kai Erikson describes this feeling from the standpoint of natural disasters:

One of the bargains men make with one another in order to maintain their sanity is to share an illusion that they are safe, even when the physical evidence in the world around them does not seem to warrant that conclusion. The survivors of a disaster, of course, are prone to overestimate the perils of their situation, if only to compensate for the fact that they underestimated those perils once before; but what is worse, far worse, is that they sometimes live in a state of almost constant apprehension because they have lost the human capacity to screen out the signs of danger out of their line of vision.[82]

The generalized danger signal created by negative events lasts only as long as the negative event or bad mood exists. Once these unpleasant experiences pass, unrealistic optimism returns. An obvious and therefore tempting interpretation is that the generalized danger signal has a certain survival value. When the organism is in a weakened state, physically or psychologically, the generalized perception of danger may keep it appropriately timid, modest, and relatively inactive in order that it not overextend its reduced resources. Once the problem passes and physical and psychological resources are replenished, the organism is once again able to assert itself in the world. At this point, unrealistic optimism may return to diminish the sense of threat. Similarly, the generalized opportunity signal created by optimism may lead people to investigate opportunities that they might not otherwise pursue and to pay little heed to information that would suggest more caution. Optimism may, then, be a significant factor in personal progress.[83]

Illusions of the Mind

What we see in the normal human mind does not correspond very well to the predominant view of mental health. Instead of an awareness and acceptance of both the positive and the negative elements of their personalities, most people show a keen awareness of their positive qualities and attributes, an extreme estimation of their ability to master the environment, and a positive assessment of the future. Not only are these assessments positive, they appear to be unrealistically so. It is not just that people believe they are good, but that they think they are better than reality can sustain. Judgments of mastery greatly exceed the actual ability to control many events. Views of the future are so rosy that they would make Pollyanna blush.

Should we say simply that most people are optimists at heart? Are these so-called illusions of everyday life merely a reflection of some underlying optimistic stance, a tendency to look on the good side of things? While there is surely an optimistic core to self-aggrandizing beliefs about the self, the world, and the future, these illusions also differ in important ways from optimism. One difference is that illusions critically concern the self. While most people are optimistic, the illusions they demonstrate habitually in their thought patterns concern their own attributes, their beliefs in personal mastery, and concerns about their own futures, rather than a positive view of the world more generally. Another difference is that as a general term, *optimism* refers simply to the expectation that things will turn out well, without any consideration of how those beneficial outcomes will be achieved. The illusion of control, a vital part of people's beliefs about their own attributes, is a personal statement about how positive outcomes will be achieved, not merely by wishing and hoping that they will happen, but by making them happen through one's own capabilities. Finally, . . . it is the specific content of illusions, namely beliefs about the self, one's mastery, and the future, that promote psychological adjustment, not simply the underlying optimism reflected in those illusions.

I have repeatedly referred to these beliefs as illusions, and a word must be said about the selection of this term. In some respects, *illusion* is an unfortunate choice, for it evokes images of a conjuror flirting with the border between reality and fantasy. Moreover, when applied to human thought, it suggests a naive blind spot or weakness. Yet *illusion* is appropriate. The terms *error* and *bias,* which one might employ instead, suggest short-term accidental mistakes and distortions, respectively, that might be caused by some careless oversight or other temporary negligence. The term *illusion,* in contrast, reflects a broader and more enduring pattern of beliefs.

Illusion is a perception that represents what is perceived in a way different from the way it is in reality. An illusion is a false mental image or conception which may be a misinterpretation of a real appearance or may be something imagined. It may be pleasing, harmless or even useful.[84]

In this sense, then, illusion captures the essence of these phenomena. People hold mild and benignly positive illusions about themselves, the world, and the future. Moreover, they are linked in mutually reinforcing and thematically consistent ways. While illusion does not characterize everyone's thinking about all issues regarding the self, the world, and the future, these illusions are common, widespread, and easily documented.

The fact that positive illusions are so dramatic in early childhood and lessen over time is especially intriguing. It suggests that they are natural, intrinsic to the cognitive system, and become worn down and tamed through the feedback that life provides. What we see in adults is not a carefully cultivated and crafted positive glow that is provided by years of experience with the adaptiveness of viewing things in a positive light. Rather, we see instead the residual inflated view of oneself and the future that exists in extreme and almost magical form in very young children.

The illusions that adults hold about their attributes, their capacity for control, and the beneficent future are, in fact, quite mild, nowhere near the dillusional distortions that one frequently observes in mental patients, for example. As a consequence, it is tempting to dismiss them as ultimately inconsequential, amusing peccadillos that put a pleasant twist on incoming information without many consequences for important matters. Indeed, one argument for the adaptiveness of positive illusions maintains that these biases are evident primarily when information is inconsequential and not when the stakes are higher. According to this argument, people may hold falsely positive judgments about themselves on unimportant matters that may buffer them in more serious and consequential circumstances when they are forced to become more realistic. In fact, the evidence tends to suggest the opposite conclusion: people's positive distortions often increase, not decrease, as matters become more important and consequential.[85] The more ego-enhancing a situation is, the more likely it is to evoke positive, self-serving interpretations. When outcomes are important, self-enhancing causal attributions are more likely. Positive illusions, then, are pervasive and not confined to the unimportant matters of life.

The fact that positive illusions exist in normal thought raises the larger question of why they exist and whether they serve any useful purpose. Are they simply a surprising and rather charming aspect of human thought, or are they actually adaptive? Trying to understand their prevalence leads one prematurely to suggest why they might be functional, the implicit assumption being that, like other organs, the mind does not evolve in ways that are inherently injurious to its own functioning. Yet these suggestions of adaptiveness have been speculative only, and the next task is to determine whether this is indeed the case.

NOTES

1. Stipek, 1984; Harter, 1981; Greenwald, 1980.
2. See Stipek, 1984; Stipek and MacIver, in press; Harter, 1981, for reviews.
3. Harari and Covington, 1981, p. 25.
4. Stipek, 1984.
5. Alicke, 1985; Brown, 1986; Campbell, 1986; Larwood and Whittaker, 1977; see also Shrauger and Kelly, in press.
6. Campbell, 1986; Marks, 1984; Harackiewicz, Sansone, and Manderlink, 1985; Lewicki, 1984.
7. Campbell, 1986; Marks, 1984.
8. See Greenwald, 1980; Taylor and Brown, 1988, for reviews. One might argue that overly positive self-descriptions reflect public posturing rather than privately held

beliefs. Several factors, however, argue against the plausibility of a strict self-presentational interpretation of this phenomenon. For example, Greenwald and Breckler (1985) reviewed evidence indicating that (a) self-evaluations are at least as favorable under private conditions as they are under public conditions; (b) favorable self-evaluations occur even when strong constraints to be honest are present; (c) favorable self-referent judgments are made very rapidly, suggesting that people are not engaging in deliberate (time-consuming) fabrication; and (d) self-enhancing judgments are acted on. For these as well as other reasons, a consensus is emerging at the theoretical level that individuals offer flattering self-evaluations not merely as a means of managing a public impression of competency but also as a means of managing impressions of themselves for themselves (see Schlenker, 1980; Tesser and Moore, 1986; Tetlock and Manstead, 1985).

9. Brown, 1986; Lewinsohn, Mischel, Chaplin, and Barton, 1980; Forsyth and Schlenker, 1977; Green and Gross, 1979; Mirels, 1980; Schlenker and Miller, 1977; Brown, 1985; Campbell, 1986; Rosenberg, 1979; Sachs, 1982.
10. Svenson, 1981.
11. E.g., Lewinsohn et al., 1980; see Shrauger 1975, 1982, for a review.
12. Greenwald, 1980, p. 64.
13. Markus, 1977.
14. Greenwald, 1980.
15. Markus, 1977.
16. Greenwald, 1980.
17. Kuiper and Derry, 1982; Kuiper and MacDonald, 1982; Kuiper, Olinger, MacDonald, and Shaw, 1985.
18. Schlenker, 1980; Snyder and Wicklund, 1981.
19. Fuentes, 1964, p. 58.
20. See Bradley, 1978; Miller and Ross, 1975; Ross and Fletcher, 1985; Zuckerman, 1979, for reviews.
21. *San Francisco Sunday Examiner and Chronicle.* April 22, 1979, cited in Greenwald, 1980.
22. Greenwald, 1980, p. 605.
23. Miller and Ross, 1975.
24. Ross, 1981; Ross and Sicoly, 1979.
25. Thompson and Kelley, 1981.
26. Harris, 1946, recounted in Ross, 1981.
27. Ross, 1981; Thompson and Kelley, 1981; Ross and Sicoly, 1979.
28. Thompson and Kelley, 1981.
29. See Ross, 1981.
30. Erikson, 1950; Alper, 1952; Sherif and Cantril, 1947.
31. Miller and Ross, 1975; Snyder, Stephan, and Rosenfield, 1978.
32. Lefcourt, 1973, p. 417.
33. White, 1959.
34. Berlyne, 1960; Fowler, 1965; White, 1959.
35. Donaldson, 1978; Harter, 1981; White, 1959.
36. White, 1959.
37. Berlyne, 1960.
38. Piaget, 1954; White, 1959.
39. White, 1959.
40. Diener and Dweck, 1978, 1980; Weisz, 1986.
41. Piaget, 1954.
42. E.g., Lindsay and McCarthy, 1974.
43. Diener and Dweck, 1978, 1980.
44. Stipek, 1984.
45. Ryan, 1971.
46. Jones and Davis, 1965; Jones and Harris, 1967.
47. Miller and Ross, 1975.
48. Crocker, 1981; Smedslund, 1963; Ward and Jenkins, 1965; Arkes and Harkness, 1980; Bower, Black, and Turner, 1979; Franks and Bransford, 1971; Owens, Bower, and Black, 1979; Harris, Teske, and Ginns, 1975; Jennings, Amabile, and Ross, 1982.
49. Janis, 1982.
50. Langer, 1975; Langer and Roth, 1975.
51. Goffman, 1967.
52. Henslin, 1967.
53. Langer, 1975; Langer and Roth, 1975; see also Gilovich, 1983.
54. Langer, 1975.
55. See Thompson, 1981; Averill, 1973; Miller, 1979, for reviews.
56. Geer, Davison, and Gatchel, 1970; Geer and Maisel, 1972.
57. Laudenslager, Ryan, Drugan, Hyson, and Maier, 1983; Hanson, Larson, and Snowden, 1976.
58. Gonzales and Zimbardo, 1985. In this study, 57 percent of the people interviewed said that they thought primarily about the

present and the future, and another 33 percent were oriented primarily toward the future. Only 1 percent spent most of the time thinking about the past.
59. Tiger, 1979.
60. Free and Cantril, 1968; Brickman, Coates, and Janoff-Bulman, 1978.
61. Markus and Nurius, 1986; Weinstein, 1980, 1982, 1984; see Perloff, 1983, for a review.
62. Crandall, Solomon, and Kelleway, 1955; Irwin, 1944, 1953; Marks, 1951; Robertson, 1977; Perloff and Fetzer, 1986; Weinstein, 1980; Kuiper, MacDonald, and Derry, 1983.
63. Frank, 1953; Pruitt and Hoge, 1965.
64. Hayes-Roth and Hayes-Roth, 1979.
65. Stipek, 1984; Marks, 1951; Irwin, 1953.
66. Stipek, 1984, p. 53.
67. Kirscht, Haefner, Kegeles, and Rosenstock, 1966; Lund, 1975.
68. Weinstein, 1980, 1982.
69. Weinstein, 1980, 1982.
70. Weinstein, 1980, 1982, 1984.
71. Seligman, 1975; Tiger, 1979.
72. Weinstein and Lachendro, 1982.
73. Kunda, 1987.
74. Kunda, 1987.
75. Conway and Ross, 1984.
76. Aronson and Linder, 1965.
77. Conway and Ross, 1984.
78. Gibbs, 1981.
79. Johnson and Tversky, 1983.
80. Kulik and Mahler, 1987.
81. See Clark and Isen, 1982.
82. Erikson, 1976, p. 234.
83. See Tiger, 1979, for a discussion of these issues.
84. *Random House Dictionary, the English Language*, ed. J. Stein, New York: Random House, p. 662.
85. E.g., Nicholls, 1975; Miller, 1976; Snyder et al., 1978; see Greenwald, 1980, for a review and discussion of this issue.

REFERENCES

Alicke, M. D. (1985). Global self-evaluation as determined by the desirability and uncontrollability of trait adjectives. *Journal of Personality and Social Psychology, 49*, 1621–1630.

Alper, T. G. (1952). The interrupted task method in studies of selective recall: A re-evaluation of some recent experiments. *Psychological Review, 59*, 71–88.

Arkes, R. M., & Harkness, A. R. (1980). Effect of making a diagnosis on subsequent recognition of symptoms. *Journal of Experimental Psychology: Human Learning and Memory, 6*, 568–575.

Aronson, E., & Linder, D. (1965). Gain and loss of esteem as determinants of interpersonal attractiveness. *Journal of Experimental Social Psychology, 1*, 156–172.

Averill, J. R. (1973). Personal control over aversive stimuli and its relationship to stress. *Psychological Bulletin, 80*, 286–303.

Berlyne, D. C. (1960). *Conflict, arousal, and curiosity.* New York: McGraw-Hill.

Bower, G. H., Black, J. B., & Turner, T. J. (1979). Scripts in memory for text. *Cognitive Psychology, 11*, 177–220.

Bradley, G. W. (1978). Self-serving biases in the attribution process: A reexamination of the fact or fiction question. *Journal of Personality and Social Psychology, 36*, 56–71.

Brickman, P., Coates, D., & Janoff-Bulman, R. (1978). Lottery winners and accident victims: Is happiness relative? *Journal of Personality and Social Psychology, 35*, 917–927.

Brown, J. D. (1985). *Self-esteem and unrealistic optimism about the future.* Unpublished data, University of California, Los Angeles.

Brown, J. D. (1986). Evaluations of self and others: Self-enhancement biases in social judgments. *Social Cognition, 4*, 353–376.

Campbell, J. D. (1986). Similarity and uniqueness: The effects of attribute type, relevance, and individual differences in self-esteem and depression. *Journal of Personality and Social Psychology, 50*, 281–294.

Clark, M. S., & Isen, A. M. (1982). Toward understanding the relationship between feeling states and social behavior. In A. H. Hastorf & A. M. Isen (Eds.), *Cognitive social psychology* (pp. 73–108). New York: Elsevier.

Conway, M., & Ross, M. (1984). Getting what you want by revising what you had. *Journal of Personality and Social Psychology, 47,* 738–748.

Crandall, V. J., Solomon, D., & Kelleway, R. (1955). Expectancy statements and decision times as functions of objective probabilities and reinforcement values. *Journal of Personality, 24,* 192–203.

Crocker, J. (1981). Judgment of covariation by social perceivers. *Psychological Bulletin, 90,* 272–292.

Diener, C. I., & Dweck, C. S. (1978). An analysis of learned helplessness: Continuous changes in performance, strategy, and achievement cognitions following failure. *Journal of Personality and Social Psychology, 36,* 451–462.

Diener, C. I., & Dweck, C. S. (1980). An analysis of learned helplessness: 2. The processing of success. *Journal of Personality and Social Psychology, 39,* 940–952.

Donaldson, M. (1978). *Children's minds.* New York: Norton.

Erikson, E. H. (1950). *Childhood and society* (2nd ed.). New York: Norton.

Erikson, K. T. (1976). *Everything in its path: Destruction of community in the Buffalo Creek flood.* New York: Simon & Schuster.

Forsyth, D. R., & Schlenker, B. R. (1977). Attributing the causes of group performance: Effects of performance quality, task importance, and future testing. *Journal of Personality, 45,* 220–236.

Fowler, H. (1965). *Curiosity and exploratory behavior.* New York: Macmillan.

Frank, J. D. (1953). Some psychological determinants of the level of aspiration. *American Journal of Psychology, 47,* 285–293.

Franks, J. J., & Bransford, J. D. (1971). Abstraction of visual patterns. *Journal of Experimental Social Psychology, 90,* 65–74.

Free, L. A., & Cantril, H. (1968). *The political beliefs of Americans: A study of public opinion.* New York: Clarion.

Fuentes, C. (1964). *The death of Artemio Cruz.* New York: Farrar Straus Giroux.

Geer, J. H., Davison, G. C., & Gatchel, R. I. (1970). Reduction of stress in humans through nonveridical perceived control of aversive stimulation. *Journal of Personality and Social Psychology, 16,* 731–738.

Geer, J. H., & Maisel, E. (1972). Evaluating the effects of the prediction-control confound. *Journal of Personality and Social Psychology, 23,* 314–319.

Gibbs, G. (1981). *Teaching students to learn.* Milton Keynes, England: Open University Press.

Gilovich, T. (1983). Biased evaluation and persistence in gambling. *Journal of Personality and Social Psychology, 44,* 1110–1126.

Goffman, E. (1967). *Interaction ritual.* Newport Beach, CA: Westcliff.

Gonzales, A., & Zimbardo, P. G. (1985, March). Time in perspective. *Psychology Today,* pp. 21–26.

Green, S. K., & Gross, A. E. (1979). Self-serving biases in implicit evaluations. *Personality and Social Psychology Bulletin, 5,* 214–217.

Greenwald, A. G. (1980). The totalitarian ego: Fabrication and revision of personal history. *American Psychologist, 35,* 603–618.

Greenwald, A. G., & Breckler, S. J. (1985). To whom is the self presented? In B. Schlenker (Ed.), *The self and social life* (pp. 126–145). New York: McGraw-Hill.

Hanson, J. D., Larson, M. C., & Snowden, C. T. (1976). The effects of control over high intensity noise on plasma control in rhesus monkeys. *Behavioral Biology, 16,* 333–334.

Harackiewicz, J. M., Sansone, C., & Manderlink, G. (1985). Competence, achievement orientation, and intrinsic motivation: A process analysis. *Journal of Personality and Social Psychology, 48,* 493–508.

Harari, O., & Covington, M. (1981). Reactions to achievement from a teacher and student perspective: A developmental analysis. *American Educational Research Journal, 18,* 15–28.

Harris, R. J., Teske, R. R., & Ginns, M. J. (1975). Memory for pragmatic implications from courtroom testimony. *Bulletin of the Psychonomic Society, 6,* 494–496.

Harris, S. (1946). *Banting's miracle: The story of the discovery of insulin.* Toronto: J. M. Dent & Sons.

Harter, S. (1981). A model of intrinsic mastery motivation in children: Intrinsic differences and developmental change. In W. A. Collins (Ed.), *Minnesota Symposium on Child Psychology* (Vol. 14, pp. 215–255). Hillsdale, NJ: Erlbaum.

Hayes-Roth, B., & Hayes-Roth, F. (1979). A cognitive model of planning. *Cognitive Science, 3,* 275–310.

Henslin, J. M. (1967). Craps and magic. *American Journal of Sociology, 73,* 316–330.

Irwin, F. W. (1944). The realism of expectations. *Psychological Review, 51,* 120–126.

Irwin, F. W. (1953). Stated expectations as functions of probability and desirability of outcomes. *Journal of Personality, 21,* 329–335.

Janis, I. L. (1982). *Groupthink: Psychological studies of policy decisions and fiascoes* (2nd ed.). Boston: Houghton Mifflin.

Jennings, D., Amabile, T. M., & Ross, L. (1982). Informal covariation assessment: Data-based versus theory-based judgments. In A. Tversky, D. Kahneman, & P. Slovic (Eds.), *Judgment under uncertainty: Heuristics and biases* (pp. 211–230). New York: Cambridge University Press.

Johnson, J. E., & Tversky, A. (1983). Affect generalization and the perception of risk. *Journal of Personality and Social Psychology, 45,* 20–31.

Jones, E. E., & Davis, K. E. (1965). From acts to dispositions: The attribution process in person perception. In L. Berkowitz (Ed.), *Advances in experimental social psychology* (Vol. 2, pp. 219–266). New York: Academic Press.

Jones, E. E., & Harris, V. A. (1967). The attribution of attitudes. *Journal of Experimental Social Psychology, 3,* 1–24.

Kirscht, J. P., Haefner, D. P., Kegeles, F. S., & Rosenstock, I. M. (1966). A national study of health beliefs. *Journal of Health and Human Behavior, 7,* 248–254.

Kuiper, N. A., & Derry, P. A. (1982). Depressed and nondepressed content self-reference in mild depression. *Journal of Personality, 50,* 67–79.

Kuiper, N. A., & MacDonald, M. R. (1982). Self and other perception in mild depressives. *Social Cognition, 1,* 233–239.

Kuiper, N. A., MacDonald, M. R., & Derry, P. A. (1983). Parameters of a depressive self-schema. In J. Suls & A. G. Greenwald (Eds.), *Psychological perspectives on the self* (Vol. 2, pp. 191–217). Hillsdale, NJ: Erlbaum.

Kuiper, N. A., Olinger, L. J., MacDonald, M. R., & Shaw, B. F. (1985). Self-schema processing of depressed and nondepressed content: The effects of vulnerability on depression. *Social Cognition, 3,* 77–93.

Kulik, J. A., & Mahler, I. M. (1987). Health status, perceptions of risk, and prevention interest for health and nonhealth problems. *Health Psychology, 6,* 15–28.

Kunda, Z. (1987). Motivated inference: Self-serving generation and evaluation of causal theories. *Journal of Personality and Social Psychology, 53,* 636–647.

Langer, E. J. (1975). The illusion of control. *Journal of Personality and Social Psychology, 32,* 311–328.

Langer, E. J., & Roth, J. (1975). Heads I win, tails it's chance: The illusion of control as a function of the sequence of outcomes in a purely chance task. *Journal of Personality and Social Psychology, 32,* 951–955.

Larwood, L., & Whittaker, W. (1977). Managerial myopia: Self-serving biases in organizational planning. *Journal of Applied Psychology, 62,* 194–198.

Laudenslager, M. C., Ryan, S. M., Drugan, R. C., Hyson, R. L., & Maier, S. F. (1983). Coping and immunosuppression: Inescapable but not escapable shock suppresses lymphocyte proliferation. *Science, 231,* 568–570.

Lefcourt, H. M. (1973, May). The function of the illusions of control and freedom. *American Psychologist,* pp. 417–425.

Lewicki, P. (1984). Self-schema and social information processing. *Journal of Personality and Social Psychology, 48,* 463–574.

Lewinsohn, P. M., Mischel, W., Chaplin, W., & Barton, R. (1980). Social competence and depression: The role of illusory self-perceptions. *Journal of Abnormal Psychology, 89,* 203–212.

Lindsay, M., & McCarthy, D. (1974). Caring for the brothers and sisters of a dying child. In T. Burton (Ed.), *Care of the child facing death* (pp. 189–206). Boston, MA: Routledge & Kegan Paul.

Lund, F. H. (1975). The psychology of belief: A study of its emotional and volitional determinants. *Journal of Abnormal and Social Psychology, 20,* 63–81.

Marks, G. (1984). Thinking one's abilities are unique and one's opinions are common. *Personality and Social Psychological Bulletin, 10,* 203–208.

Marks, R. W. (1951). The effect of probability, desirability, and "privilege" on the stated expectations of children. *Journal of Personality, 19,* 332–351.

Markus, H. (1977). Self-schemata and processing information about the self. *Journal of Personality and Social Psychology, 35,* 63–78.

Markus, H., & Nurius, P. (1986). Possible selves. *American Psychologist, 41,* 954–969.

Miller, D. T. (1976). Ego involvement and attributions for success and failure. *Journal of Personality and Social Psychology, 34,* 901–906.

Miller, D. T., & Ross, M. (1975). Self-serving biases in attribution of causality: Fact or fiction? *Psychological Bulletin, 82,* 213–225.

Miller, S. M. (1979). Controllability and human stress: Method, evidence and theory. *Behaviour Research and Therapy, 17,* 287–304.

Mirels, H. L. (1980). The avowal of responsibility for good and bad outcomes: The effects of generalized self-serving biases. *Personality and Social Psychology Bulletin, 6,* 299–306.

Nicholls, J. G. (1975). Causal attributions and other achievement-related cognitions: Effects of task outcome, attainment value, and sex. *Journal of Personality and Social Psychology, 31,* 379–389.

Owens, J., Bower, G. H., & Black, J. B. (1979). The "soap-opera" effect in story recall. *Memory and Cognition, 7,* 185–191.

Perloff, L. S. (1983). Perceptions of vulnerability to victimization. *Journal of Social Issues, 39,* 41–61.

Perloff, L. S., & Fetzer, B. K. (1986). Self-other judgments and perceived vulnerability and victimization. *Journal of Personality and Social Psychology, 50,* 502–510.

Piaget, J. (1954). *The construction of reality in the child.* New York: Basic Books.

Pruitt, D. G., & Hoge, R. D. (1965). Strength of the relationship between the value of an event and its subjective probability as a function of method of measurement. *Journal of Experimental Psychology, 5,* 483–489.

Robertson, L. S. (1977). Car crashes: Perceived vulnerability and willingness to pay for crash protection. *Journal of Community Health, 3,* 136–141.

Rosenberg, M. (1979). *Conceiving the self.* New York: Basic Books.

Ross, L. (1981). The "intuitive scientist" formulation and its developmental implications. In J. H. Flavell & L. Ross (Eds.), *Social cognitive development: Frontiers and possible futures* (pp. 1–42). Cambridge: Cambridge University Press.

Ross, M., & Fletcher, G. J. O. (1985). Attribution and social perception. In G. Lindzey & A. Aronson (Eds.), *The handbook of social psychology* (3rd ed., pp. 73–122). Reading, MA: Addison-Wesley.

Ross, M., & Sicoly, F. (1979). Egocentric biases in availability and attribution. *Journal of Personality and Social Psychology, 37,* 322–337.

Ryan, W. (1971). *Blaming the victim.* New York: Vintage Books.

Sachs, P. R. (1982). Avoidance of diagnostic information in self-evaluation of ability. *Personality and Social Psychology Bulletin, 8,* 242–246.

Schlenker, B. R. (1980). *Impression management.* Monterey, CA: Brooks/Cole.

Schlenker, B. R., & Miller, R. S. (1977). Egocentrism in groups: Self-serving biases or logical information processing? *Journal of Personality and Social Psychology, 35,* 755–764.

Seligman, M. E. P. (1975). *Helplessness: On depression, development and death.* San Francisco: Freeman.

Sherif, M., & Cantril, H. (1947). *The psychology of ego-involvements.* New York: Wiley.

Shrauger, J. S. (1975). Responses in evaluation as a function of initial self-perception. *Psychological Bulletin, 82,* 581–596.

Shrauger, J. S. (1982). Selection and processing of self-evaluative information: Experimental evidence and clinical implications. In G. Weary & H. L. Mirels (Eds.), *Integrations of clinical and social psychology* (pp. 128–153). New York: Oxford University Press.

Shrauger, J. S., & Kelly, R. J. (in press). Global self-evaluation and changes in self description as a function of information. *Journal of Personality.*

Smedslund, J. (1963). The concept of correlation in adults. *Scandinavian Journal of Psychology, 4,* 165–173.

Snyder, M. L., Stephan, W. G., & Rosenfield, C. (1978). Attributional egotism. In J. H. Harvey, W. J. Ickes, & R. F. Kidd (Eds.), *New directions in attribution research* (Vol. 2, pp. 91–117). Hillsdale, NJ: Erlbaum.

Snyder, M. L., & Wicklund, R. A. (1981). Attributive ambiguity. In J. H. Harvey, W. Ickes, & R. F. Kidd (Eds.), *New directions in attribution research* (Vol. 3, pp. 197–221). Hillsdale, NJ: Erlbaum.

Stipek, D. J. (1984). Young children's performance expectations: Logical analysis or wishful thinking? In I. Nicholls (Ed.), *Advances in motivation and achievement* (Vol. 3, pp. 33–56). Greenwich, CT: JAI Press.

Stipek, D., & MacIver, D. (in press). Developmental changes in children's assessment of intellectual competence. *Child Development.*

Svenson, O. (1981). Are we all less risky and more skillful than our fellow drivers? *Acta Psychologica, 47,* 143–148.

Taylor, S. E., & Brown, J. (1988). Illusion and well-being: A social psychological perspective on mental health. *Psychological Bulletin, 103,* 193–210.

Tesser, A., & Moore, J. (1986). On the convergence of public and private aspects of self. In R. F. Baumeister (Ed.), *Public self and private life* (pp. 99–116). New York: Springer.

Tetlock, P. E., & Manstead, A. S. R. (1985). Impression management versus intrapsychic explanations in social psychology: A useful dichotomy? *Psychological Review, 92,* 59–77.

Thompson, S. C. (1981). Will it hurt less if I can control it? A complex answer to a simple question. *Psychological Bulletin, 90,* 89–101.

Thompson, S. C., & Kelley, J. J. (1981). Judgments of responsibility for activities in close relationships. *Journal of Personality and Social Psychology, 41,* 469–477.

Tiger, L. (1979). *Optimism: The biology of hope.* New York: Simon & Schuster.

Ward, W. D., & Jenkins, H. M. (1965). The display of information and the judgment of contingency. *Canadian Journal of Psychology, 19,* 231–241.

Weinstein, N. D. (1980). Unrealistic optimism about future life events. *Journal of Personality and Social Psychology, 39,* 806–820.

Weinstein, N. D. (1982). Unrealistic optimism about susceptibility to health problems. *Journal of Behavioral Medicine, 5,* 441–460.

Weinstein, N. D. (1984). Why it won't happen to me: Perceptions of risk factors and susceptibility. *Health Psychology, 3,* 431–457.

Weinstein, N. D., & Lachendro, E. (1982). Egocentrism as a source of unrealistic optimism. *Personality and Social Psychology Bulletin, 8,* 195–200.

Weisz, J. R. (1986). Understanding the developing understanding of control. In M. Perlmutter (Ed.), *Minnesota symposia on child psychology: Vol. 18. Cognitive perspectives on children's social and behavioral development* (pp. 219–285). Hillsdale, NJ: Erlbaum.

White, R. W. (1959). Motivation reconsidered: The concept of competence. *Psychological Review, 66,* 297–335.

Zuckerman, M. (1979). Attribution of success and failure revisited, or: The motivational bias is alive and well in attribution theory. *Journal of Personality, 47,* 245–287.

B

Perceiving Ourselves and the Work Situation

12. The Self-Perception of Motivation[1]

Barry M. Staw

Within the area of interpersonal perception, it has been noted (Heider, 1958) that an individual may infer the causes of another's actions to be a function of personal and environmental force:

$$Action = f \text{ (personal force + environmental force)}$$

This is quite close to saying that individuals attempt to determine whether another person is intrinsically motivated to perform an activity (action due to personal force), or extrinsically motivated (action due to environmental force), or both. The extent to which an individual will infer intrinsic motivation on the part of another is predicted to be affected by the clarity and strength of external forces within the situation (Jones & Davis, 1965; Jones & Nisbett, 1971; Kelley, 1967). When there are strong forces bearing on the individual to perform an activity, there is little reason to assume that a behavior is self-determined, whereas a high level of intrinsic motivation might be inferred if environmental force is minimal. Several studies dealing with interpersonal perception have supported this general conclusion (Jones, Davis, & Gergen, 1961; Jones & Harris, 1967; Strickland, 1958; Thibaut & Riecken, 1955).

Bem (1967a, b) extrapolated this interpersonal theory of causal attribution to the study of self-perception or how one views his *own* behavior within a social context. Bem hypothesized that the extent to which external pressures are sufficiently strong to account for one's behavior will determine the likelihood that a person will attribute his own actions to internal causes. Thus if a person acts under strong external rewards or punishments, he is likely to assume that his behavior is under external control. However, if extrinsic contingencies are not strong

---

or salient, the individual is likely to assume that his behavior is due to his own interest in the activity or that his behavior is intrinsically motivated. De Charms has made a similar point in his discussion of an individual's perception of personal causation (1968, p. 328):

> As a first approximation, we propose that whenever a person experiences himself to be the locus of causality for his own behavior (to be an Origin), he will consider himself to be intrinsically motivated. Conversely, when a person perceives the locus of causality for his behavior to be external to himself (that he is a Pawn), he will consider himself to be extrinsically motivated.

De Charms emphasized that the individual may attempt psychologically to label his actions on the basis of whether or not he has been instrumental in affecting his own behavior; that is, whether his behavior has been intrinsically or extrinsically motivated.

THE CASE FOR A NEGATIVE RELATIONSHIP BETWEEN INTRINSIC AND EXTRINSIC MOTIVATION

The self-perception approach to intrinsic and extrinsic motivation leads to the conclusion that there may be a negative interrelationship between these two motivational factors. The basis for this prediction stems from the assumption that individuals may work backward from their own actions in inferring sources of causation (Bem 1967a, b; 1972). For example, if external pressures on an individual are so high that they would ordinarily cause him to perform a given task regardless of the internal characteristics of the activity, then the individual might logically infer that he is extrinsically motivated. In contrast, if external reward contingencies are extremely low or nonsalient, the individual might then infer that his behavior is intrinsically motivated. What is important is the fact that a person, in performing an activity, may *seek out* the probable cause of his own actions. Since behavior has no doubt been caused by something, it makes pragmatic, if not scientific, sense

for the person to conclude that the cause is personal (intrinsic) rather than extrinsic if he can find no external reasons for his actions.

Two particular situations provide robust tests of the self-perception prediction. One is a situation in which there is insufficient justification for a person's actions, a situation in which the intrinsic rewards for an activity are very low (e.g., a dull task) and there are no compensating extrinsic rewards (e.g., monetary payment, verbal praise). Although rationally, one ordinarily tries to avoid these situations, there are occasions when one is faced with the difficult question of "why did I do that?". The self-perception theory predicts that in situations of insufficient justification, the individual may cognitively reevaluate the intrinsic characteristics of an activity in order to justify or explain his own behavior. For example, if the individual performed a dull task for no external reward, he may "explain" his behavior by thinking that the task was not really so bad after all.

Sometimes a person may also be fortunate enough to be in a situation in which his behavior is oversufficiently justified. For example, a person may be asked to perform an interesting task and at the same time be lavishly paid for his efforts. In such situations, the self-perception theory predicts that the individual may actually reevaluate the activity in a downward direction. Since the external reward would be sufficient to motivate behavior by itself, the individual may mistakenly infer that he was extrinsically motivated to perform the activity. He may conclude that since he was forced to perform the task by an external reward, the task probably was not terribly satisfying in and of itself.

Figure 12.1 graphically depicts the situations of insufficient and overly sufficient justification. From the figure, we can see that the conceptual framework supporting self-perception theory raises several interesting issues. First, it appears from this analysis that there are only two fully stable attributions of behavior: (1) the perception of extrinsically motivated behavior in which the internal rewards associated with performing an activity

| | Level of Extrinsic Rewards | |
	Low	High
Low **Level of Intrinsic Rewards** **High**	Insufficient Justification (unstable perception)	Perception of Extrinsically Motivated Behavior
	Perception of Intrinsically Motivated Behavior	Overly Sufficient Justification (unstable perception)

FIGURE 12.1
A Conceptual of Self-Perception Theory

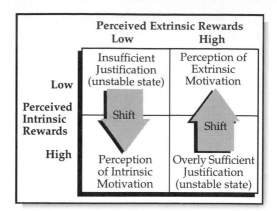

FIGURE 12.2
A Schematic Analysis of the Self-Perception of Intrinsic and Extrinsic Motivation

are low while external rewards are high; and (2) the perception of intrinsically motivated behavior in which the task is inherently rewarding but external rewards are low. Furthermore, it appears that situations of insufficient justification (where intrinsic and extrinsic rewards are both low) and oversufficient justification (where intrinsic and extrinsic rewards are both high) involve unstable attribution states. As shown in Figure 12.2, individuals apparently resolve this attributional instability by altering their perceptions of intrinsic rewards associated with the task.

An interesting question posed by the self-perception analysis is why individuals are predicted to resolve an unstable attribution state by cognitively reevaluating a task in terms of its intrinsic rewards rather than changing their perceptions of extrinsic factors. The answer to this question may lie in the relative clarity of extrinsic as compared with intrinsic rewards, and the individual's relative ability to distort the two aspects of the situation. Within many settings (and especially within laboratory experiments) extrinsic rewards are generally quite salient and specific, whereas an individual must judge the intrinsic nature of a task for himself. Any shifts in the perception of intrinsic and extrinsic rewards may therefore be more likely to occur in the intrinsic factor. As shown in Figure 12.2 it is these predicted shifts in

perceived intrinsic rewards that may theoretically underlie a negative relationship between intrinsic and extrinsic motivation.

Empirical Evidence: Insufficient Justification

Several studies have shown that when an individual is induced to commit an unpleasant act for little or no external justification, he may subsequently conclude that the act was not so unpleasant after all. Actually, the first scientific attempt to account for this phenomenon was the theory of cognitive dissonance (Festinger, 1957). It was predicted by dissonance theorists (Aronson, 1966; Festinger, 1957) that, since performing an unpleasant act for little or no reward would be an inconsistent (and seemingly irrational) thing to do, an individual might subsequently change his attitude toward the action in order to reduce the inconsistency or to appear rational. Bem's self-perception theory yields the same predictions but does not require one to posit that there is a motivating state such as dissonance reduction or self-rationalization. To Bem, since the individual examines his own behavior in light of the forces around him, he is simply more likely to come to the conclusion that his actions were intrinsically satisfying if they were performed under minimal external force.

In general, two types of experiments have been designed to assess the consequences of insufficient justification. One type of design has involved the performance of a dull task with varied levels of reward (Brehm & Cohen, 1962; Freedman, 1963; Weick, 1964; Weick & Penner, 1965). A second and more popular design has involved some form of counterattitudinal advocacy, either in terms of lying to a fellow subject about the nature of an experiment or writing an essay against one's position on an important issue (Carlsmith, Collins, & Helmreich, 1966; Festinger & Carlsmith, 1959; Linder, Cooper, & Jones, 1967). Fundamentally, the two types of designs are not vastly different. Both require subjects to perform an intrinsically dissatisfying act under varied levels of external inducement, and both predict that, in the low payment condition, the subject will change his attitude toward the activity (i.e., think more favorably of the task or begin to believe the position advocated).

The most well-known experiment designed to test the insufficient justification paradigm was conducted by Festinger and Carlsmith (1959). Subjects participated in a repetitive and dull task (putting spools on trays and turning pegs) and were asked to tell other waiting subjects that the experiment was enjoyable, interesting, and exciting. Half the experimental subjects were paid $1, and half were paid $20 for the counterattitudinal advocacy (and to be "on call" in the future), while control subjects were not paid and did not perform the counterattitudinal act. As predicted, the smaller the reward used to induce subjects to perform the counterattitudinal act, the greater the positive change in their attitudes toward the task. Although the interpretation of the results of this study have been actively debated (e.g., between dissonance and self-perception theorists) the basic findings have been replicated by a number of different researchers. It should be noted, however, that several mediating variables have also been isolated as being necessary for the attainment of this dissonance or self-perception effect: free choice (Linder, Cooper, & Jones, 1967), commitment or

irrevocability of behavior (Brehm & Cohen, 1962), and substantial adverse consequences (Calder, Ross, & Insko, 1973; Collins & Hoyt, 1972).

Recently, a strong test of the insufficient justification paradigm was also conducted outside the laboratory (Staw, 1974a). A natural field experiment was made possible by the fact that many young men had joined an organization (Army ROTC) in order to avoid being drafted, *and* these same young men subsequently received information (a draft lottery number) that changed the value of this organizational reward. Of particular relevance was the fact that those who joined ROTC did so not because of their intrinsic interest in the activities involved (e.g., drills, classes, and summer camp), but because they anticipated a substantial extrinsic reward (draft avoidance). As a result, those who received draft numbers that exempted them from military service subsequently faced a situation of low extrinsic as well as intrinsic rewards, a situation of insufficient justification. In contrast, persons who received draft numbers that made them vulnerable to military call-up found their participation in ROTC perfectly justified—they were still successfully avoiding the draft by remaining in the organization. To test the insufficient justification effect, both the attitudes and the performance of ROTC cadets were analyzed by draft number before and after the national draft lottery. The results showed that those in the insufficient justification situation enhanced their perception of ROTC and even performed somewhat better in ROTC courses after the lottery. It should be recognized, however, that this task enhancement occurred only under circumstances very similar to those previously found necessary for the dissonance or self-perception effect (i.e., high commitment, free choice, and adverse consequences).

Empirical Evidence: Overly Sufficient Justification

There have been several empirical studies designed to test the self-perception prediction within the context of overly sufficient justification. Generally, a situation in which an extrinsic reward is added to an intrinsically rewarding task has been experimentally contrived for this purpose. Following self-perception theory, it is predicted that an increase in external justification will cause indivduals to lose confidence in their intrinsic interest in the experimental task. Since dissonance theory cannot make this prediction (it is neither irrational nor inconsistent to perform an activity for too many rewards), the literature on overly sufficient justification provides the most important data on the self-perception prediction. For this reason, we will examine the experimental evidence in some detail.

In an experiment specifically designed to test the effect of overly sufficient justification on intrinsic motivation, Deci (1971) enlisted a number of college students to participate in a problem-solving study. All the students were asked to work on a series of intrinsically interesting puzzles for three experimental sessions. After the first session, however, half of the students (the experimental group) were told that they would also be given an extrinsic reward (money) for correctly solving the second set of puzzles, while the other students (the control group) were not told anything about the reward. In the third session, neither the experimental nor the control subjects were rewarded. This design is schematically outlined in Table 12.1.

Deci had hypothesized that the payment of money in the second experimental session might decrease subjects' intrinsic motivation to perform the task. That is, the introduction of an external force (money) might cause participants to alter their self-perception about why they are working on the puzzles. Instead of being intrinsically motivated to solve the interesting puzzles, they might find themselves working primarily to get the money provided by the experimenter. Thus Deci's goal in conducting the study was to compare the changes in subjects' intrinsic motivation from the first to third sessions for both the experimental and control groups. If the self-perception hypothesis was correct, the intrinsic motivation of the previously paid experimental subjects would decrease in the third session, whereas the intrinsic motivation of the unpaid controls should remain unchanged.

As a measure of intrinsic motivation, Deci used the amount of free time participants spent on the puzzle task. To obtain this measure, the experimenter left the room during each session, supposedly to feed some data into the computer. As the experimenter left the room, he told the subjects they could do anything they wanted with their free time. In addition to the puzzles, current issues of *Time, The New Yorker,* and *Playboy* were placed near the subjects. However, while the first experimenter was out of the laboratory, a second experimenter, unknown to the subjects, observed their behavior through a one-way mirror. It was reasoned that if the subject worked on the puzzles during this free time period, he must be intrinsically motivated to perform the task. As shown in Table 12.2, the amount of free time spent on the task decreased for those who were previously paid to perform the activity, while there was a slight increase for the unpaid controls. Although the difference between the experimental and control groups was only marginally significant, the results are suggestive of the fact that an overly sufficient extrinsic reward may decrease one's intrinsic motivation to perform a task.

TABLE 12.1
Basic Design of Deci (1971) Study

	Time 1	Time 2	Time 3
Experimental group	No payment	No payment	No payment
Control group	No payment	No payment	No payment

TABLE 12.2

Mean Number of Seconds Spent Working on the Puzzles during the Free Time Periods

Group	Time 1	Time 2	Time 3	Time 3 Time 1
Experimental ($n = 12$)	248.2	313.9	198.5	−49.7
Control ($n = 12$)	213.9	202.7	241.8	27.9

Source: E. L. Deci, "The Effects of Externally Mediated Rewards as Intrinsic Motivation," *Journal of Personality and Social Psychology* 18 (1971) 105–15. Copyright © 1971 by the American Psychological Association. Reprinted by permission.

Lepper, Greene, and Nisbett (1973) also conducted a study that tested the self-perception prediction in a situation of overly sufficient justification. Their study involved having nursery school children perform an interesting activity (playing with Magic Markers) with and without the expectation of an additional extrinsic reward. Some children were induced to draw pictures with the markers by promising them a Good Player Award consisting of a big gold star, a bright red ribbon, and a place to print their name. Other children either performed the activity without any reward or were told about the reward only after completing the activity. Children who participated in these three experimental conditions (expected reward, no reward, unexpected reward) were then covertly observed during the following week in a free-play period. As in the Deci (1971) study, the amount of time children spent on the activity when they could do other interesting things (i.e., playing with other toys) was taken to be an indicator of intrinsic motivation.

The findings of the Lepper, Greene, and Nisbett study showed that the introduction of an extrinsic reward for performing an already interesting activity caused a significant decrease in intrinsic motivation. Children who played with Magic Markers with the expectations of receiving the external reward did not spend as much subsequent free time on the activity as did the children who were not given a reward or those who were unexpectedly offered the reward. Moreover, the rated quality of drawings made by children with the markers was significantly poorer in the expected-reward group than either the no-reward or unexpected-reward groups.

The results of the Lepper et al. study help to increase our confidence in the findings of the earlier Deci experiment. Not only are the earlier findings replicated with a different task and subject population, but an important methodological problem is minimized. By reexamining Table 12.1, we can see that the second time period in the Deci experiment was the period in which payment was expected by subjects for solving the puzzles. However, we can also see that in time 2 there was a whopping increase in the free time subjects spent on the puzzles. Deci explained this increase as an attempt by subjects to practice puzzle solving to increase their chances of earning money. However, what Deci did not discuss is the possibility that the subsequent decrease in time 3 was due not to the prior administration of rewards but to the effect of satiation or fatigue. One contribution of the Lepper et al. study is that its results are not easily explained by this alternative. In the Lepper et al. experiment, there was over one week's time between the session in which an extrinsic reward was administered and the final observation period.

Although both the Deci and Lepper et al. studies support the notion that the expectation of an extrinsic reward may decrease intrinsic interest in an activity, there is still one important source of ambiguity in both these studies. You may have noticed that the decrease in intrinsic motivation follows not only the prior administration of an extrinsic reward, but also the withdrawal of this reward. For example, in the Deci study, subjects were not paid in the third experimental session in which the decrease in intrinsic motivation was reported. Likewise, subjects were not rewarded when the final observation of intrinsic motivation was taken by Lepper, Greene, and Nisbett. It is therefore difficult to determine whether the decrease in intrinsic interest is due to a change in the self-perception of motivation following the application of an extrinsic reward or merely to frustration following the removal of the reward. An experiment by Kruglanski, Freedman, and Zeevi (1971) helps to resolve this ambiguity.

Kruglanski et al. induced a number of teenagers to volunteer for some creativity and memory tasks. To manipulate extrinsic rewards, the experimenters told half the participants that because they had volunteered for the study, they would be taken on an interesting tour of the psychology laboratory; the other participants were not offered this extrinsic reward. The results showed that teenagers offered the reward were less satisfied with the experimental tasks and were less likely to volunteer for future experiments of a similar nature than were teenagers who were not offered the extrinsic reward. In addition, the extrinsically rewarded group did not perform as well on the experimental task (in terms of recall, creativity, and the Zeigarnik effect) as the nonrewarded group. These findings are similar to those of Deci (1971) and Lepper et al. (1973), but they cannot be as easily explained by a frustration effect. Since in the Kruglanski et al. study the reward was never withdrawn for the experimental group, the differences between the experimental (reward) and control (no reward) conditions are better explained by a change in self-perception than by a frustration effect.

The designs of the three overly sufficient justification studies described above have varying strengths and weaknesses (Calder & Staw, 1975a), but taken together, their results can be interpreted as supporting the notion that extrinsic rewards added to an already interesting task can decrease intrinsic motivation. This effect, if true, has important ramifications for educational, industrial, and other work settings. There are many situations in which people are offered extrinsic rewards (grades, money, special privileges) for accomplishing a task which may already be intrinsically interesting. The self-perception effect means that, by offering external rewards, we may sometimes be sacrificing an important source of task motivation and not necessarily increasing either the satisfaction or the performance of the participant. Obviously, because the practical implications of the self-perception effect are large, we should proceed with caution. Thus, in addition to scrutinizing the validity of the findings themselves (as we have done above), we should also attempt to determine the exact conditions under which they might be expected to hold.

Earlier, Deci (1971, 1972) had hypothesized that only rewards contingent on a high level of task performance are likely to have an adverse effect on intrinsic motivation. He had reasoned that a reward contingent upon specific behavioral demands is most likely to cause an individual to infer that his behavior is extrinsically rather than intrinsically motivated and that a decrease in intrinsic motivation may result from this change in self-perception. Although this assumption seems reasonable, there is not a great deal of empirical support for it. Certainly in the Kruglanski et al. and Lepper et al. studies all that was necessary to cause a decrease in intrinsic motivation was for rewards to be contingent upon the completion of an activity. In each of these studies what seemed to be important was the cognition that one was performing an activity in order to get an extrinsic reward rather than a prescribed goal for a particular level of output. Thus as long as it is salient, a reward contingency based upon the completion of an activity may decrease intrinsic motivation just like a reward contingency based on the quality or quantity of performance.

Ross (1975) recently conducted two experiments that dealt specifically with the effect of the salience of rewards on changes in intrinsic motivation. In one study, children were asked to play a musical instrument (drums) for either no reward, a nonsalient reward, or a salient reward. The results showed that intrinsic motivation, as measured by the amount of time spent on the drums versus other activities in a free-play situation, was lowest for the salient reward condition. Similar results were found in a second study in which some children were asked to think either of the reward (marshmallows) while playing a musical instrument, think of an extraneous object (snow), or not think of anything in particular. The data for this second study showed that intrinsic motivation was lowest when children consciously thought about the reward while performing the task.

In addition to the salience of an external reward, there has been empirical research on one other factor mediating the self-perception effect, the existing norms of the task situation. In examining the prior research using situations of overly sufficient justification, Staw, Calder, and Hess (1976) reasoned that there is one common element which stands out. Always, the extrinsic reward appears to be administered in a situation in which persons are not normally paid or otherwise reimbursed for their actions. For example, students are not normally paid for laboratory participation, but the Deci (1971) and Kruglanski et al. (1971) subjects were. Likewise, nursery school children are not normally enticed by special recognition or rewards to play with an interesting new toy, but both the Lepper et al. (1973) and Ross (1975) subjects were. Thus Staw, Calder, and Hess (1976) manipulated norms for payment as well as the actual payment of money for performing an interesting task. They found an interaction of norms and payment such that the introduction of an extrinsic reward decreased intrinsic interest in a task only when there existed a situational norm for no payment. From these data and the findings of the Ross study, it thus appears that an extrinsic reward must be both salient and situationally inappropriate for there to be a reduction in intrinsic interest.

Reassessing the Self-Perception Effect

At present there is growing empirical support for the notion that intrinsic and extrinsic motivation *can* be negatively interrelated. The effect of extrinsic rewards on intrinsic motivation has been replicated by several researchers using different classes of subjects (males, females, children, college students) and different activities (puzzles, toys), and the basic results appear to be internally valid. As we have seen, however, the effect of extrinsic rewards is predicated on certain necessary conditions (e.g., situational norms and reward salience), as is often the case with psychological findings subjected to close examination.

To date, the primary data supporting the self-perception prediction have come from situations of insufficient and overly sufficient justification. Empirical findings have shown that individuals may cognitively reevaluate intrinsic rewards in an upward direction when their behavior is insufficiently justified and in a downward direction when there is overly sufficient justification. In general, it can be said that the data of these two situations are consistent with the self-perception hypothesis. Still, theoretically, it is not immediately clear why previous research has been restricted to these two particular contexts. No doubt it is easier to show an increase in intrinsic motivation when intrinsic interest is initially low (as under insufficient justification) or a decrease when intrinsic interest is initially high (as under overly sufficient justification). Nevertheless, the theory should support a negative interrelationship of intrinsic and extrinsic factors at *all levels,* since it makes the rather general prediction that the greater the extrinsic rewards, the less likely is the individual to infer that he is intrinsically motivated.

One recent empirical study has tested the self-perception hypothesis by manipulating *both* intrinsic and extrinsic motivation. Calder and Staw (1975b) experimentally manipulated both the intrinsic characteristics of a task as well as extrinsic rewards in an attempt to examine the interrelationship of these two factors at more than one level. In the study male college students were asked to solve one of two sets of puzzles identical in all respects except the potential for intrinsic interest. One set of puzzles contained an assortment of pictures highly rated by students (chiefly from *Life* magazine but including several *Playboy* centerfolds); another set of puzzles was blank and rated more neutrally. To manipulate extrinsic rewards, half the subjects were promised $1 for their 20 minutes of labor (and the dollar was placed prominently in view), while for half of the subjects, money was neither mentioned nor displayed. After completing the task, subjects were asked to fill out a questionnaire on their reactions to the puzzle-solving activity. The two primary dependent variables included in the questionnaire were a measure of task satisfaction and a measure of subjects' willingness to volunteer for additional puzzle-solving exercises. The latter consisted of a sign-up sheet on which subjects could indicate the amount of time they would be willing to spend (without pay or additional course credit) in future experiments of a similar nature.

The results of the Calder and Staw experiment showed a significant interaction between task and payment on subjects' satisfaction with the activity and a marginally significant interaction on subjects' willingness to volunteer for additional work without extrinsic reward. These data provided empirical support for the self-perception effect in a situation of overly sufficient justification, but not under other conditions. Specifically, when the task was initially interesting (i.e., using the picture puzzle activity), the introduction of money caused a reduction of task satisfaction and volunteering. However, when the task was initially more neutral (i.e., using the blank puzzle activity), the introduction of money increased satisfaction and subjects' intentions to volunteer for additional work. Thus if we consider Calder and Staw's dependent measures as indicators of intrinsic interest, the first finding is in accord with the self-perception

hypothesis, while the latter result is similar to what one might predict from a reinforcement theory. The implications of these data, together with previous findings, are graphically depicted in Figure 12.3.

As shown in the figure, self-perception effects have been found *only* at the extremes of insufficient and overly sufficient justification. Thus it may be prudent to withhold judgment on the general hypothesis that there is a uniformly negative relationship between intrinsic and extrinsic motivation. Perhaps we should no longer broadly posit that the greater external rewards and pressures, the weaker the perception of intrinsic interest in an activity; and the lower external pressures, the stronger intrinsic interest. Certainly, under conditions other than insufficient and overly sufficient justification, reinforcement effects of extrinsic rewards on intrinsic task satisfaction have readily been found (Cherrington, 1973; Cherrington, Reitz, & Scott, 1971; Greene, 1974).

At present it appears that only in situations of insufficient or overly sufficient reward will there be attributional instability of such magnitude that shifts will occur in the perception of intrinsic rewards. We might therefore speculate that either no attributional instability is evoked in other situations or it is just not strong enough to overcome a countervailing force. This writer

FIGURE 12.3
The Relative Potency of Self-Perception and Reinforcement Mechanisms

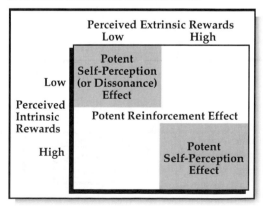

would place his confidence in the latter theoretical position. It seems likely that both self-perception *and* reinforcement mechanisms hold true, but that their relative influence over an individual's task attitudes and behavior varies according to the situational context. For example, only in situations with insufficient or overly sufficient justification will the need to resolve attributional instability probably be strong enough for external rewards to produce a decrease in intrinsic motivation. In other situations we might reasonably expect a more positive relationship between intrinsic and extrinsic factors, as predicted by reinforcement theory.

Although this new view of the interrelationship between intrinsic and extrinsic motivation remains speculative, it does seem reasonable in light of recent theoretical and empirical work. Figure 12.4 graphically elaborates this model and shows how the level of intrinsic and extrinsic

motivation may depend on the characteristics of the situation. In the figure, secondary reinforcement is depicted to be a general force for producing a positive relationship between intrinsic and extrinsic motivation. However, under situations of insufficient and overly sufficient justification, self-perception (and dissonance) effects are shown to provide a second but still potentially effective determinant of a negative interrelationship between intrinsic and extrinsic motivation. Figure 12.4 shows the joint operation of these two theoretical mechanisms and illustrates their ultimate effect on individuals' satisfaction, persistence, and performance on a task.

IMPLICATIONS OF INTRINSIC AND EXTRINSIC MOTIVATION

In this discussion we have noted that the administration of both intrinsic and extrinsic

FIGURE 12.4
The Interrelationship of Intrinsic and Extrinsic Motivation as a Function of Situational Characteristics

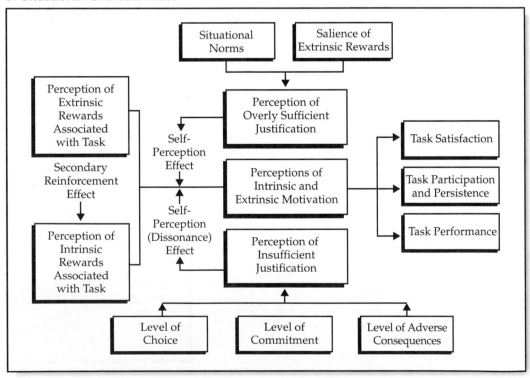

rewards can have important effects on a person's task attitudes and behavior. Individually, extrinsic rewards may direct and control a person's activity on a task and provide an important source of satisfaction. By themselves, intrinsic rewards can also motivate task-related behavior and bring gratification to the individual. As we have seen, however, the joint effect of intrinsic and extrinsic rewards may be quite complex. Not only may intrinsic and extrinsic factors not be additive in their overall effect on motivation and satisfaction, but the interaction of intrinsic and extrinsic factors may under some conditions be positive and under other conditions negative. As illustrated in Figures 12.3 and 12.4, a potent reinforcement effect will often cause intrinsic and extrinsic motivation to be positively interrelated, although on occasion a self-perception mechanism may be so powerful as to create a negative relationship between these two factors.

The reinforcement predictions of Figures 12.3 and 12.4 are consistent with our common sense. In practice, extrinsic rewards are relied upon heavily to induce desired behaviors, and most allocators of rewards (administrators, teachers, parents) operate on the theory that extrinsic rewards will positively affect an individual's intrinsic interest in a task. We should therefore concentrate on those situations in which our common sense may be in error— those situations in which there may in fact be a negative relationship between intrinsic and extrinsic motivation.

Motivation in Educational Organizations

One of the situations in which intrinsic and extrinsic motivation may be negatively interrelated is our schools. As Lepper and Greene (1975) have noted, many educational tasks are inherently interesting to students and would probably be performed without any external force. However, when grades and other extrinsic inducements are added to the activity, we may, via overly sufficient justification, be converting an interesting activity into work. That is,

by inducing students to perform educational tasks with strong extrinsic rewards or by applying external force, we may be converting learning activities into behaviors that will not be performed in the future without some additional outside pressure or extrinsic force.

Within the educational context, a negative relationship between intrinsic and extrinsic motivation poses a serious dilemma for teachers who allocate external rewards. For example, there is no doubt that grades, gold stars, and other such incentives can alter the direction and vigor of specific "in school" behaviors (e.g., getting students to complete assigned exercises by a particular date). But because of their effect on intrinsic motivation, extrinsic rewards may also weaken a student's general interest in learning tasks and decrease voluntary learning behavior that extends beyond the school setting. In essence, then, the extrinsic forces that work so well at motivating and controlling specific task behaviors may actually cause the extinction of these same behaviors within situations devoid of external reinforcers. This is an important consideration for educational organizations, since most of an individual's learning activity will no doubt occur outside the highly regulated and reinforced setting of the classroom.[2]

In order to maintain students' intrinsic motivation in learning activities it is recommended that the use of extrinsic rewards be carefully controlled. As a practical measure, it is recommended that when a learning task is inherently interesting (and would probably be performed without any external force) all external pressures on the individual be minimized. Only when a task is so uninteresting that individuals would not ordinarily perform it should extrinsic rewards be applied. In addition, it is suggested that the student role be both enlarged and enriched to increase rather directly the level of intrinsic motivation. The significance of learning tasks, responsibility for results, feedback, and variety in student activities are all areas of possible improvement.

Motivation in Work Organizations

Voluntary work organizations are very much like educational organizations; their members are often intrinsically motivated to perform certain tasks and extrinsic rewards are generally not necessary to induce the performance of many desired behaviors. Moreover, if for some reason extrinsic rewards were to be offered to voluntary workers for performing their services we would expect to find, as in the educational setting, a decrease in intrinsic motivation. As in the educational context, we would expect an external reward to decrease self-motivated (or voluntary) behavior in settings free from external reinforcement, although the specific behaviors which are reinforced might be increased. As a concrete example, let us imagine a political candidate who decides to "motivate" his volunteer campaign workers by paying them for distributing flyers to prospective voters. In this situation, we might expect that the administration of an extrinsic reward will increase the number of flyers distributed. However, the political workers' subsequent interest in performing other campaign activities *without pay* may subsequently be diminished. Similarly, the volunteer hospital worker who becomes salaried may no longer have the same intrinsic interest in his work. Although the newly professionalized worker may exert a good deal of effort on the job and be relatively satisfied with it, his satisfaction may stem from extrinsic rather than intrinsic sources of reward.

Let us now turn to the implications of intrinsic and extrinsic motivation for nonvoluntary work organizations. Deci (1972), in reviewing his research on intrinsic motivation, cautioned strongly against the use of contingent monetary rewards within industrial organizations. He maintained that paying people contingently upon the performance of specific tasks may reduce intrinsic motivation for these activities, and he recommended noncontingent reinforces in their stead. As we have seen, however, a decrease in intrinsic motivation does not always occur following the administration of extrinsic rewards; certain necessary conditions must be present before there is a negative relationship between intrinsic and extrinsic motivation. Generally, industrial work settings do not meet these necessary conditions.

First, within industrial organizations, a large number of jobs are not inherently interesting enough to foster high intrinsic motivation. Persons would not ordinarily perform many of the tasks of the industrial world (e.g., assembly line work) without extrinsic inducements, and this initial lack of intrinsic interest will probably preclude the effect of overly sufficient justification. Second, even when an industrial job is inherently interesting, there exists a powerful norm for extrinsic payment. Not only do workers specifically join and contribute their labor in exchange for particular inducements, but the instrumental relationship between task behavior and extrinsic rewards is supported by both social and legal standards. Thus the industrial work situation is quite unlike that of either a voluntary organization or an educational system. In the latter cases, participants may be initially interested in performing certain tasks without external force, and the addition of overly sufficient rewards may convey information that the task is not intrinsically interesting. Within industrial organizations, on the other hand, extrinsic reinforcement is the norm, and tasks may often be perceived to be even more interesting when they lead to greater extrinsic rewards.

The very basic distinction between nonvoluntary work situations and other task settings (e.g., schools and voluntary organizations) is that, without extrinsic rewards, nonvoluntary organizations would be largely without participants. The important question for industrial work settings is therefore not one of payment versus nonpayment, but of the recommended degree of contingency between reward and performance. On the basis of current evidence, it would seem prudent to suggest that, within industrial organizations, rewards continue to be made contingent upon behavior. This could be accomplished through performance evaluation, profit sharing, or piece-rate incentive schemes.

In addition, intrinsic motivation should be increased directly via the planned alteration of specific job characteristics (e.g., by increasing task variety, complexity, social interaction, task identity, significance, responsibility for results, and knowledge of results).

A FINAL COMMENT

Although the study of the interaction of intrinsic and extrinsic motivation is a relatively young era within psychology, it has been the intent of this paper to outline a theoretical model and provide some practical suggestions based upon the research evidence available to date. As we have seen, the effects of intrinsic and extrinsic motivation are not always simple, and several moderating variables must often be taken into account before specific predictions can be made. Thus in addition to providing "answers" to theoretical and practical problems, this paper may illustrate the complexities involved in drawing conclusions from a limited body of research data. The main caution for the reader is to regard these theoretical propositions and practical recommendations as working statements subject to the influence of future empirical evidence.

NOTES

1. The author wishes to express his gratitude to Bobby J. Calder and Greg R. Oldham for their critical reading of the manuscript, and to the Center for Advanced Study at the University of Illinois for the resources and facilities necessary to complete this work.
2. It is interesting to note that Kazdin and Bootzen (1972) have made a quite similar point in their recent review of research on token economies. They noted that while operant conditioning procedures have been quite effective in altering focal behaviors within a controlled setting, seldom have changes been found to generalize to natural, nonreinforcing environments.

REFERENCES

Aronson, E. "The Psychology of Insufficient Justification: An Analysis of Some Conflicting Data." In *Cognitive Consistency: Motivational Antecedents and Behavior Consequences,* edited by S. Feldman. Academic Press, 1966.

Bem, D. J. "Self-perception: An Alternative Interpretation of Cognitive Dissonance Phenomena." *Psychological Review* 74 (1967a): 183–200.

_____. "Self-perception: The Dependent Variable of Human Performance." *Organizational Behavior and Human Performance* 2 (1967b): 105–21.

_____. "Self-perception Theory." In *Advances in Experimental Social Psychology,* Vol. 6, edited by L. Berkowitz. New York: Academic Press, 1972.

Brehm, J. W., and Cohen, A. R. *Explorations in Cognitive Dissonance.* New York: Wiley, 1962.

Calder, B. J., Ross, M., and Insko, C. A. "Attitude Change and Attitude Attribution: Effects of Incentive, Choice, and Consequences." *Journal of Personality and Social Psychology* 25 (1973): 84–100.

_____, and Staw, B. M. "The Interaction of Intrinsic and Extrinsic Motivation: Some Methodological Notes." *Journal of Personality and Social Psychology* 31 (1975a): 76–80.

_____, and Staw, B. M. "Self-perception of Intrinsic and Extrinsic Motivation." *Journal of Personality and Social Psychology* 31 (1975b): 599–605.

Carlsmith, J. M., Collins, B. E., and Helmreich, R. L. "Studies in Forced Compliance: The Effect of Pressure of Compliance on Attitude Change Produced by Face-to-Face Role Playing and Anonymous Essay Writing." *Journal of Personality and Social Psychology* 4 (1966): 1–13.

Cherrington, D. J. "The Effects of a Central Incentive—Motivational State on Measures of Job Satisfaction." *Organizational Behavior and Human Performance* 10 (1973): 27–89.

_____, Reitz, H. J., and Scott, W. E. "Effects of Reward and Contingent Reinforcement on Satisfaction and Task Performance." *Journal of Applied Psychology* 55 (1971): 531–36.

Collins, B. E., and Hoyt, M. F. "Personal Responsibility-for-Consequences: An Integration and Extension of the Forced Compliance Literature." *Journal of Experimental Social Psychology* 8 (1972): 558–94.

de Charms, R. *Personal Causation: The Internal Affective Determinants of Behavior.* New York: Academic Press, 1968.

Deci, E. L. "The Effects of Externally Mediated Rewards on Intrinsic Motivation." *Journal of Personality and Social Psychology* 18 (1971): 105–15.

_____. "The Effects of Contingent and Noncontingent Rewards and Controls on Intrinsic Motivation." *Organizational Behavior and Human Performance* 8 (1972): 217–29.

Festinger, L. *A Theory of Cognitive Dissonance.* Palo Alto: Stanford University Press, 1957.

_____, and Carlsmith, J. M. "Cognitive Consequences of Forced Compliance." *Journal of Abnormal and Social Psychology* 58 (1959): 203–10.

Freedman, J. L. "Attitudinal Effects of Inadequate Justification." *Journal of Personality* 31 (1963): 371–85.

Greene, C. N. "Causal Connections Among Manager's Merit Pay, Job Satisfaction, and Performance." *Journal of Applied Psychology* 58 (1974): 95–100.

Heider, F. *The Psychology of Interpersonal Relations.* New York: Wiley, 1958.

Jones, E. E., and Davis, K. E. "From Acts to Dispositions: The Attribution Process in Person Perception." In *Advances in Experimental Psychology,* Vol. 2, edited by L. Berkowitz. New York: Academic Press, 1965.

_____, Davis, K. E., and Gergen, K. E. "Role Playing Variations and Their Informational Value for Person Perception." *Journal of Abnormal and Social Psychology* 63 (1961): 302–10.

_____, and Harris, V. A. "The Attribution of Attitudes." *Journal of Experimental Social Psychology* 3 (1967): 1–24.

_____, and Nisbett, R. E. *The Actor and the Observer: Divergent Perceptions of the Causes of Behavior.* New York: General Learning Press, 1971.

Kazdin, A. E., and Bootzen, R. R. "The Token Economy: An Evaluative Review." *Journal of Applied Behavior Analysis* 5 (1972): 343–72.

Kelley, H. H. "Attribution Theory in Social Psychology." In *Nebraska Symposium on Motivation,* Vol. 15, edited by D. Levine. University of Nebraska Press, 1967.

Kruglanski, A. W., Freedman, I., and Zeevi, G. "The Effects of Extrinsic Incentives on Some Qualitative Aspects of Task Performance." *Journal of Personality* 39 (1971): 606–17.

Lepper, M. R., and Greene, D. "Turning Play into Work: Effects of Adult Surveillance and Extrinsic Rewards on Children's Intrinsic Motivation." *Journal of Personality and Social Psychology,* in press.

_____, Greene, D., and Nisbett, R. E. "Undermining Children's Intrinsic Interest with Extrinsic Rewards: A Test of the 'Overjustification' Hypothesis." *Journal of Personality and Social Psychology* 28 (1973): 129–37.

Linder, D. E., Cooper, J., and Jones, E. E. "Decision Freedom as a Determinant of the Role of Incentive Magnitude in Attitude Change." *Journal of Personality and Social Psychology* 6 (1967): 245–54.

Ross, M. "Salience of Reward and Intrinsic Motivation." *Journal of Personality and Social Psychology* 32 (1975): 245–54.

Staw, B. M. "Attitudinal and Behavioral Consequences of Changing a Major Organizational Reward: A Natural Field Experiment." *Journal of Personality and Social Psychology* 6 (1974a): 742–51.

_____. "Notes Toward a Theory of Intrinsic and Extrinsic Motivation." Paper presented at Eastern Psychological Association, 1974b.

_____, Calder, B. J., and Hess, R. "Intrinsic Motivation and Norms About Payment."

Working paper, Northwestern University, 1975.

Strickland, L. H. "Surveillance and Trust." *Journal of Personality* 26 (1958): 200–15.

Thibaut, J. W., and Riecken, H. W. "Some Determinants and Consequences of the Perception of Social Causality." *Journal of Personality* 24 (1955): 113–33.

Weick, K. E. "Reduction of Cognitive Dissonance Through Task Enhancement and Effort Expenditure." *Journal of Abnormal and Social Psychology* 68 (1964): 533–39.

_____, and Penner, D. D. "Justification and Productivity." Unpublished manuscript, University of Minnesota, 1965.

13. The Power of Social Information in the Workplace

Joe G. Thomas/Ricky W. Griffin

After meeting with his district sales managers for the first time, John Rogers, the newly hired vice-president of marketing, reflected on the particularly puzzling conversations he had with two of them—Bill Adams and Dick Woods. Both men had very similar backgrounds and experiences: They had been classmates at a prestigious eastern university and had started employment with the company immediately after college. They had been successful sales representatives and had been promoted to regional sales manager positions after approximately four years with the company. Although they managed different sales areas, both areas appeared equally attractive.

The puzzling part of the conversations with Adams and Woods was their inconsistent views of the organization and their future roles in it. Woods had been particularly positive about the work environment, describing the company as "fair" and the work as "challenging, exciting, and worthwhile." He had praised the company for its excellent reputation with its employees and customers, saying "It's really nice to have a job where you are helping people, where what you do really makes a difference!" Adams, on the other hand, had complained that the company was "ripping off" everybody and that the work was "a real bore." "The customers do not appreciate the quality of service they receive. The employees constantly complain about hours and working conditions. You just cannot keep them happy," he had said. Since both managers were working for the same company and in the same capacity—and had so much in common—how could they see things so differently?

Most people have been in situations similar to the one experienced by John Rogers—situations in which, from an objective viewpoint, everything seems the same yet the people involved see things quite differently. Even though managers recognize that people's perceptions differ, they tend to assume that all employees evaluate and react to their jobs similarly. That kind of attitude is reflected in the following comment, made by a client in an executive development program: "The job is the same for everybody. There are job descriptions for each job. The employees do exactly what is stated in the job description. We are careful to stick to the job descriptions and not let anyone do more for fear of having problems with the union and EEOC."

The common thread between the experiences of John Rogers and the client in the executive development program is the assumption that employees respond only to the "objective" job. In reality, employees respond to their jobs as they perceive them. Moreover, their perceptions are influenced, at least to some degree, by information they receive from others. Yet much of management research and practice is based on the assumption that managers and employees respond strictly to an objective job.

In their article "A Social Information Processing Approach to Job Attitudes and Task Design" (*Administrative Science Quarterly*, June 1978), Gerald Salancik and Jeffrey Pfeffer reopened the question as to the extent of objectivity in evaluating work settings. Their theoretical framework, depicted in a simplified form in Figure 13.1, has served as a springboard for

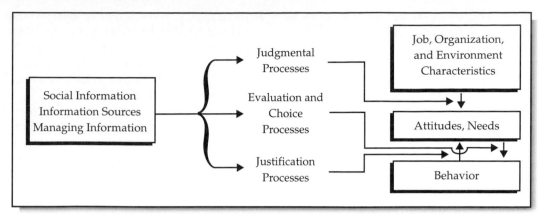

FIGURE 13.1
Strategic Influence Processes

various research studies examining employees' reactions to social information. This line of research, commonly referred to as "social information processing," argues that people adopt attitudes, behaviors, and beliefs in light of social information provided by others.

In his book *Organizations and Organization Theory* (Pitman, 1982), Pfeffer notes that "whether one characterizes jobs using dimensions such as variety, autonomy, feedback, and skill required or dimensions such as pay, effort required, and physical surroundings is in part under the control of a social environment in which some dimensions become talked about and other dimensions are ignored and thus are not salient." In one early experiment examining the influence of information from the social environment ("Informational Influence as a Determinant of Perceived Task Characteristics and Job Satisfaction," *Journal of Applied Psychology,* February 1979), Charles O'Reilly and David Caldwell showed that informational cues have a greater impact on reported task characteristics than do the objective task dimensions. In a later study of public health nurses in which objective jobs were identical ("Perceptual Measures of Task Characteristics: The Biasing Effects of Differing Frames of Reference and Job Attitudes," *Academy of Management Journal,* March 1980), Charles O'Reilly, G. N. Parlette, and J. R. Bloom reported that the perception of task characteristics is influenced by family and professional orientations. In a more recent study of nurses ("Sources of Social Information: A Longitudinal Analysis," *Human Relations,* September 1986), Joe G. Thomas found that information sources perceived as most relevant varied for different aspects of jobs. For example, family members were perceived as important in helping nurses see the significance of their work, but co-workers were perceived as most important in helping nurses develop new job skills.

Social information refers to comments, observations, and similar cues provided by people whose view of the job an employee considers relevant. It may be provided by people directly associated with the job, such as co-workers, supervisors, and customers, or it may be provided by people not employed by the company, such as family members and friends. Although not all aspects of a job are likely to be influenced by cues from others (a hot work environment will be hot despite what anyone tells a worker), it seems realistic to assume that most of an employee's perceptions of job characteristics are subject to influence from information provided by others with whom the employee has contact.

IMPACT OF SOCIAL INFORMATION

Social information can influence an employee's view of the job in several different ways, as shown in Figure 13.1. Social information causes some characteristics of the job to be judged important, and attitudes about these salient characteristics are formed. Once attitudes are formed, social cues offer suggestions in evaluating and choosing appropriate behaviors. Finally, social cues influence the explanations or rationales offered for behavior. To understand and use social information, a manager must first recognize the probable impact of such information on employees and identify sources of information considered relevant.

IDENTIFICATION OF ORGANIZATION AND JOB CHARACTERISTICS

Jobs have many different facets. They allow varying degrees of autonomy, feedback, and job significance. They aid (or inhibit) employees in developing new skills and preparing for advancement. They are performed in a variety of settings, differing in terms of work conditions (such as temperature and noise level), work schedules (such as starting times, break schedules, and time clocks), rewards, and quality of supervision. Organizations differ in terms of attitudes, policies, and treatment of workers. All of these characteristics may influence an employee's feelings about his or her job. However, not all of them are viewed as equally important in each organization.

IMPORTANCE OF CHARACTERISTICS

Social information helps employees identify which characteristics of the job and the organization are considered important by other people. If the temperature in a work area or the requirement of clocking in and out is frequently discussed, those characteristics of the job setting receive increased attention from workers. Frequent discussion of such characteristics increases their perceived importance, and they become more salient.

Rarely discussed job characteristics are less likely to be considered important by job incumbents, although the same job characteristics may be considered essential in another organization.

Relatively high noise levels or bureaucratic travel-reimbursement policies, for example, may be major sources of employee concern in one organization, while employees of another organization may dismiss those job characteristics as just a fact of organizational life.

Mining accidents provide an example of job characteristics that may be perceived quite differently by people, depending on their situation. Someone outside the industry may be astonished at a miner's ability to go to work with little apparent fear shortly after a disastrous mining accident at a neighboring mine. Miners *want to believe* information provided by the company and co-workers that there is little probability of an accident happening to them. They perceive occasional industrial accidents as an undesirable but largely unavoidable part of the job. To people outside the industry, however, the danger seems unbelievably high. The different assessments of the danger are at least partly the result of different evaluations of the information provided about the risks of an accident.

EVALUATION OF JOB CHARACTERISTICS

Other people's information about a job reveals their perceptions of the job to employees. All organizations develop cultures that are transmitted to workers. Organizations differ, for example, in terms of the importance attached to customer satisfaction and quality versus quantity of output, employee and subunit autonomy, administrative structures, and attitudes toward risk and diversification. Rituals, stories, symbols, and language are all used to inform employees about the organization and individual jobs.

Military training provides recruits the information they need to evaluate military jobs. That information, much like the information provided to miners, may initially be perceived as inconsistent with the information held by the general public. However, as boot camp continues, the recruits generally become more accepting of authority, place greater importance on military values, and become willing to sacrifice their lives for the good of others. Rituals (such as basic training and mock battles), stories of both successful and unsuccessful missions, symbols (such as the U.S. flag and military heroes), as well as language (such as code words and slang) are used to influence the recruits' perceptions of the organization and their place in it. In effect, social information leads to a reevaluation of the basic meaning of life and its importance to the individual. Orientation programs for new employees are designed to accomplish similar ends, although the change in attitudes may be less marked.

People outside the organization also provide information that is used to evaluate job and organization characteristics. Statements such as "You guys sure have to work some odd hours" or "Isn't that work boring!" provide information about what the speaker considers important as well as the speaker's evaluation of the work situation. A family member who constantly reminds a miner about the dangers of the job will likely increase the attention the miner gives to safety and may force the miner to reassess the risks of the occupation.

JUSTIFICATION OF WORKERS' PERCEPTIONS

Employees who have perceptions of their jobs or behavior that is inconsistent with the social information they receive may attempt to convince the information source of the inaccuracy of the information. Alternately, employees may justify (or rationalize) away the differences, or they may decide to adjust their perceptions to be consistent with the information they receive.

Employees frequently change their perception of a situation to conform with the perception of information sources. In what has become known as the "Asch light experiment," subjects were asked to judge the lengths of lines of light. Less than 1% of the subjects misjudged line length when working individually. However, when co-workers (actually confederates in the experiment) provided incorrect judgments, more than one-third of the subjects gave an incorrect answer consistent with the incorrect answer provided by their co-workers. (See "Studies of Independence and Conformity: A Minority of One Against a Unanimous Majority" by Solomon E. Asch in *Psychological Monographs,* No. 9, 1956.) If people are willing to change their perceptions of objective phenomena such as the length of a line, they probably are even more likely to change their views of the less objective elements of jobs.

SOURCES OF INFORMATION

Employees can receive information from a wide variety of sources, ranging from bathroom graffiti to the evening news. However, the most likely sources of social information are the people employees come into contact with regularly—co-workers, supervisors, friends, family members and, in some cases, customers or clients.

Co-workers

Generally, co-workers are important sources of information for an employee. They not only spend several hours per day with the employee but also are most likely to be familiar with the employee's work. Co-workers' knowledge of a job makes their views of job characteristics, the importance of specific characteristics, and the evaluation of those characteristics particularly credible. Furthermore, the day-to-day contact with co-workers allows frequent discussion of workplace phenomena and thereby reinforces the perceptions co-workers have of a particular job.

To illustrate the latter point, let's return to the story of John Rogers. As John became better acquainted with his new employer and with Adams and Woods, he began to agree with Adams that the work environment was less than ideal. Adams had complained that his job was boring and that he felt unappreciated—relatively mild criticisms compared with the news held by most of the salesforce. Adams and many other employees perceived the company as a place to obtain work experience and a "livable" salary until something better came along. His co-workers explained to John that other companies in the industry offered better benefits, more autonomy, and greater opportunities for advancement. As most employees agreed, promotion out of their adequately paid but dead-end jobs should be a primary career goal.

Supervisors

In many instances, supervisors are also a source of information. They can have a dual impact on worker's job perceptions. Obviously, a supervisor is a representative of higher levels of management and as such has an opportunity to present the organization's view of the job and the characteristics of the job considered important by the organization. For employees seeking rapid upward mobility and other "company" employees, the organization's view of the workplace as presented by the supervisor may be accepted with minimal questioning.

In addition to being "management's representative," a supervisor may function in the capacity of a friend or co-worker. Employees and their supervisors may work as peers to solve particular problems. Similarly, they may interact on an informal basis during breaks, lunch, social functions, and so forth. The supervisor is in a position to comment on various elements of an employee's job during these informal times and may indirectly influence the employee's job perception.

Woods, who had given John a positive view of the job during their conversation, was not particularly influenced by the information provided by his co-workers. Woods had been a personal friend of his division manager before being hired. The division manager continually provided Woods with information from upper management that advancement was almost automatic for employees who remained loyal to the company. Loyalty, seniority, and good performance were the keys to advancement. The division manager had convinced Woods that, although promotions were not as rapid as at other organizations, job pressures were less and job security was better. Woods did not consider

himself to be a fast-track employee and preferred the relative safety and low pressure he associated with his current employer.

Friends and Family

Friends and family members provide a perspective on an employee's work situation that is often quite different from the perspective provided by supervisors and co-workers. Friends and family members who are not employed by the company are less subject to its influence and the influence of its employees. Thus they often are in a position to provide a different, and probably more objective, assessment of what a worker should experience on a job. New employees may attach greater validity to information provided by someone from outside the organization, believing that person to be less biased than a co-worker, especially if the person has the added credibility of being a trusted friend or family member. Alternately, some people may discount evaluations made by family members as being uninformed or naive.

Family members and friends also are in a position to provide an external reference point. For example, they can inform a worker about jobs at other organizations. Discussing such jobs allows the employee to compare his or her job with situations elsewhere to determine the relative importance of various job characteristics and the relative merit of the company.

Further, family members and friends often are an especially powerful source of support for new employees and employees who are having problems at work. Discussions with people outside the company allow employees to vent their feelings about their jobs. Family members and friends also provide support for the employee's self-image. They help an employee understand the rationale for particular characteristics of the job. Particularly for new employees, this kind of rationalizing is part of the process whereby a person's perception of what is important is modified to more closely parallel the information provided by others.

In the original example, Wood's family members provided additional information, causing him to be satisfied with the company's slow rate of promotion. John learned that Woods was from a family of blue-collar workers. Woods had been the first family member to earn a college degree and to advance to a management position. Relative to other members of the family, Woods was doing quite well and was earning more than any of them. Besides, a quick promotion would almost certainly mean a transfer from the area, an alternative he did not really want to consider. Therefore, Woods was content to remain in his position and wait for a promotion that did not require a move.

Customers or Clients

In some cases, customers or clients provide workers with job-related information. Especially for employees of service companies, customers provide an evaluation of the company and its products. Such evaluations may not pertain to a specific job, but customers' assessments of the organization become part of its culture. Companies whose products are poorly received by customers are likely to have different expectations for their employees. Pressures to reduce costs, improve product quality, and/or increase quantity of output are usually greater at companies that are performing poorly. On the other hand, contacts with customers and customer treatment may be important considerations for an organization. These customers contacts, for example, often distinguish a self-service discount store from a store providing full service.

Employees may perceive the importance of their work differently if the product is well accepted. Extremely poor customer relations may threaten the survival of the company and increase the attention employees focus on job security. Employees are more likely to feel that their job is secure and that they have career opportunities when a company has good customer relations.

In organizations that encourage full service and personal contact with customers, the customer is likely considered an important source of job-related information. Both the employee and the employer are encouraged to be atten-

tive to the needs and reactions of customers. Organizations with cultures attaching less significance to customer contact and satisfaction would likewise be expected to attribute less validity to information provided by customers. At those organizations, the line "This would not be a bad place to work if it were not for the customers" is too often said with sincerity by employees.

GUIDELINES FOR USING AND MANAGING SOCIAL INFORMATION

Managers often discuss the influence that groups have on the behavior of workers. Yet in planning interactions with employees, managers tend to overlook the social influence on employee behavior. Employee experience is an important factor affecting the ability of social information to influence behavior. Managers should also be sensitive to the impact of different information sources on employee behavior and attitudes. Moreover, they should use caution in attributing the results of various job measures to the "true, objective" job rather than to cues provided by others about the job.

Employee Experience

The length of time an employee has been in a particular position will likely influence the employee's susceptibility to information about the job. Employees who are new to the job, either newly hired workers or those transferred or promoted into a new position, are likely to be more receptive to social information than are employees who have greater seniority in the position. Especially when an employee is new to the job and the organization, a considerable amount of time is spent listening to many employees' views about the company's operations.

The variety of information sources used by an employee decreases with his or her experience in the job, although reliance on a few selected sources may increase. The number of sources used decreases since much of the information provided from some sources is learned quickly. Thus those sources no longer contribute information of significant value to the employee. Other people, however, evolve as credible sources of worthwhile information. The latter will exert increased influence as employees gain work experience.

INFORMATION SOURCE USAGE

There are a vast number of potential sources of job-related information. As discussed above, family members, friends, customers, co-workers, and supervisors often are highly valued sources of information.

During crisis periods of employment, family members and friends can be especially useful sources of information for an employee by helping the employee retain self-confidence. Family members and friends can encourage a new employee to keep trying and promise support if the new job does not work out.

Although there is very little that managers can do to control information obtained from family members and friends, they need to be aware that information from such sources restricts the range of strategies available for responding to employees. Managers also must realize that employees are aware of the things other companies are doing. Depending on their information sources, some employees may know more about other organizations than their supervisors know.

Customers and clients provide information about the value of a company's products relative to a competitor's products. Their evaluations may give employees insight into the probable success (or failure) of the company's product line. Frequent negative criticism of a company's product, for example, tells an employee that the product is inferior in some respect. Continued criticism may cause the employee to question the quality of the product, the quality of the company, and the probability of stable long-term employment. Ultimately, such negative information may provide the incentive for an employee to leave the organization.

As with feedback from the family members and friends, companies have little opportunity to insulate employees from feedback from cus-tomers. Instead, they must be sensitive to the feedback employees are receiving. Discussing with employees the information they receive enables management to explain steps the company is taking to correct problems and to assure employees of the company's integrity and stability. It also gives management the opportunity to learn about major developments at other organizations.

Managers may be able to influence the initial image new employees have of the organization by selecting the co-workers to whom they are exposed. Assigning a new employee to a work group supportive of management will likely produce a more favorable initial attitude toward the company than assigning the worker to a more negative work group. However, assignment of co-workers is obviously a temporary control measure. Eventually, the new employee will be exposed to negative views of the company. If the criticisms seem more credible than the positive information provided by the first co-workers, management may be perceived as manipulative. Thus control of co-worker information must be used with discretion.

The social information over which management has the greatest control is information provided by supervisors. Managers often overlook the influence supervisors have on their employees. For many employees, the immediate supervisor *is* the organization. A supervisor's negative attitude about the company or its management can be transmitted to employees, who in turn develop a negative attitude. Employees often know little about top management. Frequent critical remarks by a supervisor, even if the remarks are made in jest, may support negative information from other sources and cause employees to develop critical views of top management as well as the organization.

In his article "Objective and Social Sources of Information in Task Redesign: A Field Experiment" (*Administrative Quarterly,* June 1983), Ricky W. Griffin reported that managers could change employees' perceptions of the job and organization *without* changing the job. One group of managers was trained to provide positive social or informational cues to employees. The employees' perceptions of task characteristics such as task variety, autonomy, feedback, and friendship opportunities differed significantly from the perceptions of the control group whose managers had no training in providing positive social or informational cues.

Objective Job Versus Social Information

Managers must be cautious when interpreting data gathered from employees through surveys and interviews. In taking steps to change jobs in response to data collected from employees, managers must be careful to distinguish between responses stemming from the "objective" job and from social information. If the responses are the result of the objective job, changing the objective job likely will change employees' perceptions and attitudes. However, if the responses are the result of information from the social context in which the job is being performed, changing the job will likely have minimal impact on employees' perceptions of and attitudes about the job as long as the social information provided about the job remains unchanged.

SUMMARY

Jobs and the characteristics associated with them rarely are totally objective. Employees' reactions to their jobs are influenced by information provided by co-workers, supervisors, family members, friends, and perhaps customers or clients. New employees are especially likely to use information from external sources to shape their perceptions of the job and the company. Long-term employees also respond to information provided by others. However, they tend to be more selective about their information sources than are new employees.

Recent research suggests that for some aspects of work, social information about the job may be more important to understanding how employees view the job than is the actual "objective" job. Managers frequently overlook the impact that information from various sources may have on employees' perceptions. In fact, changing the job may have little effect on employees' feelings about the job if information provided by others remains unchanged.

SELECTED BIBLIOGRAPHY

The sources of citations in this article are, in order: Gerald R. Salancik and Jeffrey Pfeffer's "A Social Information Processing Approach to Job Attitudes and Task Design" (*Administrative Science Quarterly,* June 1978); Jeffrey Pfeffer's *Organizations and Organization Theory* (Pitman, 1982); Charles O'Reilly and David Caldwell's "Informational Influence as a Determinant of Perceived Task Characteristics and Job Satisfaction" (*Journal of Applied Psychology,* February 1979); Charles O'Reilly, G. N. Parlette, and J. R. Bloom's "Perceptual Measures of Task Characteristics: The Biasing Effects of Differing Frames of Reference and Job Attitudes" (*Academy of Management Journal,* March 1980); Joe G. Thomas' "Sources of Social Information: A Longitudinal Analysis" (*Human Relations,* September 1986); Solomon E. Asch's "Studies of Independence

and Conformity: A Minority of One Against a Unanimous Majority" (*Psychological Monographs,* No. 9, 1956); Ricky W. Griffin's "Objective and Social Sources of Information in Task Redesign: A Field Experiment" (*Administrative Science Quarterly,* June 1983).

The previous citations are intended to provide some insight into the social information processing literature. More extensive reviews of the literature can be found in Gary J. Blau and Ralph Katerburg's "Toward Enhancing Research with the Social Information Processing Approach to Job Design," (*Academy of Management Review,* October 1982); Joe G. Thomas and Ricky W. Griffin's "The Social Information Processing Model of Task Design: A Review of the Literature" (*Academy of Management Review,* October 1983); and Ricky W. Griffin, Thomas

S. Bateman, Sandy J. Wayne, and Thomas C. Head's "Objective and Social Factors as Determinants of Task Perceptions and Responses: An Integrated Perspective and Empirical Investigation" (*Academy of Management Journal,* September 1987).

As shown in Figure 13.1, the environment in which an employee and organization operate is also subject to social influence. Questions of whether organizations respond to "real" or "constructed" environments is gaining acceptance in the literature on strategic planning. Insight into the social influence processes at a macro-level can be found in Gregory G. Dess and Nancy Origer's "Environment, Structure, and Consensus in Strategy Formulation: A Conceptual Integration" (*Academy of Management Review,* April 1987); Jane Dutton and Susan Jackson's "Categorizing Strategic Issues: Links to Organizational Action" (*Academy of Management Review,* January 1987); Don Hambrick and Phyllis Mason's "Upper Echelons: The Organization as a Reflection of Its Top Managers" (*Academy of Management Review,* April 1984).

The importance attached to developing a clear mission and the ability to focus an organization's energies on the external, on service, on quality, on people, on informality, and on wanting to be "the best" at something has been effectively presented by Tom Peters and Robert H. Waterman in their book *In Search of Excellence: Lessons from America's Best-Run Companies* (Harper & Row, 1982). According to Peters and Waterman, part of the function of top management is to clarify to employees what the company views as important. The argument, as developed by Linda Smircich and Charles Stubbart in "Strategic Management in an Enacted World" (*Academy of Management Review,* October 1985), is essentially that a company's strategy becomes a reflection of the concerns of top management; it is a reflection of the issues management considers important.

The position that the receptiveness of employees to social cues varies with work experience draws from research on socialization. Two of the most cited books on socialization, John Wanous' *Organizational Entry* (Addison-Wesley, 1980) and Edgar Schein's *Career Dynamics* (Addison-Wesley, 1978), support the view that information source usage becomes more selective and limited as employees become more oriented to their jobs. This view is also supported in Joe G. Thomas's "Sources of Social Information: A Longitudinal Analysis" (*Human Relations,* September 1986).

Part C

Making Rational and Irrational Decisions

14. Common Biases

Max H. Bazerman

*P*eople make mistakes. More interestingly, people make a variety of systematic and predictable mistakes. The predictability of these mistakes means that once we identify them, we can learn to avoid them. Individuals develop rules of thumb, or heuristics, to reduce the information-processing demands of decision making. By providing managers with efficient ways of dealing with complex problems, heuristics produce good decisions a significant proportion of the time. However, heuristics also can lead managers to make systematically biased mistakes. Cognitive bias occurs in situations in which an individual inappropriately applies a heuristic when making a decision.

By highlighting a number of mistakes that even very smart people make on a regular basis, this chapter offers you the opportunity to audit your own decision-making process and identify the biases that affect you. Throughout the chapter, quiz items allow you to examine your problem-solving abilities and discover how your judgments compare to those of others. The quiz items illustrate 13 predictable biases that frequently lead managers to judgments that systematically deviate from rationality.

To begin, answer the following two problems:

Problem 1. The following 10 corporations were ranked by *Fortune* magazine to be among the largest 500 United States-based firms according to sales revenues for 1999:

Group A: Avis Rent a Car, TWA, Hershey Foods, Barnes and Noble, Hasbro
Group B: SBC Communications, McKesson, Ingram Micro, United Technologies, Utilicorp United

Which group of five organizations listed (A or B) had the larger total sales revenues?

Problem 2 (Adapted from Kahneman and Tversky, 1973). The best student in my introductory MBA class this past semester writes poetry and is rather shy and small in stature. What was the student's undergraduate major:

(A) Chinese studies or (B) Psychology?

If you answered A for each of the two problems, you may gain comfort in knowing that the majority of respondents choose A. If you answered B, you are in the minority. In this case, however, the minority represents the correct response. All corporations in group B were ranked in the *Fortune* 100, while none of the corporations in group A had sales as large. In fact, the total sales for group B was more than eight times the total sales for group A. In the second problem, the student described was actually a psychology major, but more important, selecting psychology as the student's major represents a more rational response given the limited information.

Problem 1 illustrates the availability heuristic. In this problem, group A consists of consumer firms, while group B consists of firms less well known to consumers. Because most of us are more familiar with consumer firms than conglomerates, we can more easily generate information in our minds about their size. If we were aware of our bias resulting from the availability heuristic, we would recognize our differential exposure to this information and adjust our judgments accordingly, or at least question them.

Problem 2 illustrates the representativeness heuristic. The reader who responds "Chinese studies" has probably overlooked relevant base-rate information—namely, the likely ratio of Chinese studies majors to psychology majors within the MBA student population. When asked to reconsider the problem in this context, most people acknowledge the relative scarcity of Chinese studies majors seeking MBAs, and change their response to "psychology." This example emphasizes that logical base-rate reasoning is often overwhelmed by qualitative judgments drawn from available descriptive information.

Problems 1 and 2 demonstrate how easy it is to draw faulty conclusions when we over-rely on cognitive heuristics. Throughout this chapter, additional quiz items are presented to further increase your awareness of the impact of heuristics on your decisions and to help you develop an appreciation for the systematic errors that emanate from overdependence on them. The 13 biases examined in this chapter are relevant to virtually all individuals. Each bias is related to at least one of the three judgmental heuristics introduced in Chapter 1, and an effort has been made to categorize them accordingly. However, the way our minds develop and use heuristics is not straightforward. Often, when we approach cognitive tasks, we use heuristics in tandem.

The goal of the chapter is to help you "unfreeze" your decision-making patterns by showing you how easily heuristics become biases when improperly applied. By working on numerous problems that demonstrate the failures of these heuristics, you will become more aware of the biases in your decision making. Once you are able to spot these biases, you will be able to improve the quality of your decisions.

Before reading further, please take a few minutes to respond to the problems presented in Table 14.1.

TABLE 14.1
Chapter Problems

Respond to the following problems before reading the chapter.
Problem 3: Which of the following lists was the cause of more premature deaths in the United States in 1999?
a. Tobacco use, obesity/inactivity, and alcohol   **b.** Cancer, heart disease, and auto accidents

(continued)

TABLE 14.1
Chapter Problems *(continued)*

Problem 4a: In four pages of a novel (about 2,000 words), how many words would you expect to find that have the form _ _ _ _ ing (seven-letter words that end with "ing")? Indicate your best estimate by circling one of the following values:

0   1–2   3–4   5–7   8–10   11–15   16+

Problem 4b: In four pages of a novel (about 2,000 words), how many words would you expect to find that have the form _ _ _ _ _ n _ (seven-letter words that have the letter "n" in the sixth position)? Indicate your best estimate by circling one of the following values:

0   1–2   3–4   5–7   8–10   11–15   16+

Problem 5: Mark is finishing his MBA at a prestigious university. He is very interested in the arts and at one time considered a career as a musician. Is he more likely to take a job:

(A) in arts management, or **(B)** with an Internet start-up?

Problem 6 (from Tversky and Kahneman, 1974): A certain town is served by two hospitals. In the larger hospital about 45 babies are born each day and in the smaller hospital about 15 babies are born each day. As you know, about 50 percent of all babies are boys. However, the exact percentage varies from day to day. Sometimes it may be higher than 50 percent, sometimes lower.

For a period of one year, each hospital recorded the days in which more than 60 percent of the babies born were boys. Which hospital do you think recorded more such days?

(A) The larger hospital.   **(B)** The smaller hospital.

(C) About the same (that is, within 5 percent of each other).

Problem 7: You have started buying stocks on the Internet, beginning with five different stocks. Each stock goes down soon after your purchase. As you prepare to make a sixth purchase, you reason that it should be more successful, since the last five were "lemons." After all, the odds favor making at least one successful pick in six decisions. This thinking is:

(A) correct   **(B)** incorrect.

Problem 8: You are the sales forecaster for a department store chain with nine locations. The chain depends on you for quality projections of future sales in order to make decisions on staffing, advertising, information system developments, purchasing, renovation, and the like. All stores are similar in size and merchandise selection. The main difference in their sales occurs because of location and random fluctuations. Sales for 2000 were as follows:

Store	2000	2002
1	$12,000,000	
2	11,500,000	
3	11,000,000	
4	10,500,000	
5	10,000,000	
6	9,500,000	
7	9,000,000	
8	8,500,000	
9	8,000,000	
TOTAL	$90,000,000	$99,000,000

Your economic forecasting service has convinced you that the best estimate of total sales increases between 2000 and 2002 is 10 percent (to $99,000,000). Your task is to predict 2002 sales for each store. Since your manager believes strongly in the economic forecasting service, it is imperative that your total sales equal $99,000,000.

(continued)

Part C Making Rational and Irrational Decisions

TABLE 14.1
Chapter Problems *(continued)*

Problem 9: Linda is 31 years old, single, outspoken, and very bright. She majored in philosophy. As a student, she was deeply concerned with issues of discrimination and social justice, and she participated in antinuclear demonstrations.

Rank order the following eight descriptions in terms of the probability (likelihood) that they describe Linda:

__ a. Linda is a teacher in an elementary school.

__ b. Linda works in a bookstore and takes yoga classes.

__ c. Linda is active in the feminist movement.

__ d. Linda is a psychiatric social worker.

__ e. Linda is a member of the League of Women Voters.

__ f. Linda is a bank teller.

__ g. Linda is an insurance salesperson.

__ h. Linda is a bank teller who is active in the feminist movement.

Problem 10: A new Internet company recently made its initial public offering, becoming publicly traded. At its opening, the stock sold for $20/share. The company's closest competitor went public one year ago, also at a price of $20/share. The competitor's stock is now priced at $100/share. What will the new firm be worth one year from now?

$_____/share

Problem 11: Which of the following appears most likely? Which appears second most likely?

a. Drawing a red marble from a bag containing 50 percent red marbles and 50 percent white marbles.

b. Drawing a red marble seven times in succession, with replacement (a selected marble is put back into the bag before the next marble is selected), from a bag containing 90 percent red marbles and 10 percent white marbles.

c. Drawing at least one red marble in seven tries, with replacement, from a bag containing 10 percent red marbles and 90 percent white marbles.

Problem 12: Listed below are 10 uncertain quantities. Do not look up any information on these items. For each, write down your best estimate of the quantity. Next, put a lower and upper bound around your estimate, so that you are 98 percent confident that your range surrounds the actual quantity.

Estimate	Lower	Upper	
____	____	____	a. Wal-Mart's 1999 revenue
____	____	____	b. Kmart's 1999 revenue
____	____	____	c. Market value of General Motors as of March 14, 2000
____	____	____	d. Market value of Microsoft as of March 14, 2000
____	____	____	e. Market value of Cisco Systems as of March 14, 2000
____	____	____	f. Rank of Supervalu in the 1999 *Fortune* 500
____	____	____	g. Rank of Qualcomm in the 1999 *Fortune* 500
____	____	____	h. Total households in the United States, according to a 1994 Bureau of the Census poll
____	____	____	i. Number of species and subspecies of North American mammals extinct since 1600
____	____	____	j. Plastic waste generated in the United States in 1993 in tons

BIASES EMANATING FROM THE AVAILABILITY HEURISTIC

Bias 1—Ease of Recall (based on vividness and recency)

Problem 3. Which of the following lists was the cause of more premature deaths in the United States in 1999?

(A) Tobacco use, obesity/inactivity, and alcohol
(B) Cancer, heart disease, and auto accidents

Most people are highly influenced by the vividness of the diseases listed in group B, and choose this list as a result. In fact, list A provides the three leading causes of premature death in the United States (*BusinessWeek*, 4/17/2000, p. 8). By contrast, auto accidents are only eighth on the list of premature killers, and cancer and heart disease are even farther down the list. The availability of vivid stories in the media biases our perception of the frequency of events. As a result, we may tend to underestimate the likelihood of premature death due to tobacco, alcohol, or overeating, causing us to miss opportunities to reduce these hazards through preventative measures such as school and workplace health programs.

Many life decisions are affected by the vividness of information. Although most people recognize that AIDS is a devastating disease, many individuals ignore clear data about how to avoid contracting AIDS. In the fall of 1991, however, sexual behavior in Dallas was dramatically affected by one vivid piece of data that may or may not have been true. In a chilling interview, a Dallas woman calling herself C. J. claimed she had AIDS and was trying to spread the disease out of revenge against the man who had infected her. After this vivid interview made the local news, attendance at Dallas AIDS seminars increased dramatically, AIDS became the main topic of Dallas talk shows, and requests for HIV tests surged citywide. Although C. J.'s possible actions were a legitimate cause for concern, it is clear that most of the health risks related to AIDS are not a result of one woman's actions. There are many more important reasons to be concerned about AIDS. However, C. J.'s vivid report had a more substantial effect on many people's behavior than the mountains of data available.

Tversky and Kahneman (1974) argue that when an individual judges the frequency with which an event occurs by the availability of its instances, an event whose instances are more easily recalled will appear to be more frequent than an event of equal frequency whose instances are less easily recalled. They cite evidence of this bias in a lab study in which individuals were read lists of names of well-known personalities of both genders. Different lists were presented to two groups. One group was read a list in which the women listed were relatively more famous than the listed men, but the list included more men's names overall. The other group was read a list in which the men listed were relatively more famous than the listed women, but the list included more women's names overall. After hearing their group's list, participants in both groups were asked if the list contained the names of more women or men. In both groups, participants incorrectly guessed that the gender that included the relatively more famous personalities was the more numerous. Participants apparently paid more attention to vivid household names than to less well-known figures, leading to inaccurate judgments.

While this example of vividness may seem fairly benign, it is not difficult to see how the availability bias could lead managers to make potentially destructive workplace decisions. The following came from the experience of one of my MBA students: As a purchasing agent, he had to select one of several possible suppliers. He chose the firm whose name was the most familiar to him. He later found out that the salience of the name resulted from recent adverse publicity concerning the firm's extortion of funds from client companies!

Managers conducting performance appraisals often fall victim to the availability heuristic. Working from memory, vivid instances of an employee's behavior (either positive or negative) will be most easily recalled from memory, will appear more numerous than commonplace incidents, and will therefore be weighted more heavily in the performance appraisal. The recency of events is also a factor: Managers give more weight to performance during the three months prior to the evaluation than to the previous nine months of the evaluation period.

Because of our susceptibility to vividness and recency, Kahneman and Tversky suggest that we are particularly prone to overestimating unlikely events. For instance, if we actually witness a burning house, our assessment of the probability of such accidents is likely to be greater than if we had merely read about the fire in the local newspaper; our direct observation of the event makes it more salient to us. Similarly, Slovic and Fischhoff (1977) discuss the implications of the misuse of the availability heuristic in debates about the perceived risks of nuclear power. They point out that any discussion of potential hazards, regardless of their likelihood, will increase the salience of these hazards and increase their perceived risks.

Bias 2—Retrievability (based on memory structures)

Problem 4a. In four pages of a novel (about 2,000 words), how many words would you expect to find that have the form _ _ _ _ ing (seven-letter words that end with "ing")? Indicate your best estimate by circling one of the following values:

0   1–2   3–4   5–7   8–10   11–15   16+

Problem 4b. In four pages of a novel (about 2,000 words), how many words would you expect to find that have the form _ _ _ _ _ n _ (seven-letter words that have the letter "n" in the sixth position)? Indicate your best estimate by circling one of the following values:

0   1–2   3–4   5–7   8–10   11–15   16+

Tversky and Kahneman (1983) found that most people respond with a higher number for Problem 4a than for Problem 4b. However, this response pattern must be incorrect. Since all words with seven letters that end in "ing" also have an "n" as their sixth letter, the frequency of words that end in "ing" cannot be larger than the number of words with "n" as the sixth letter. Tversky and Kahneman (1983) argue that "ing" words are more retrievable from memory because of the commonality of the "ing" suffix, whereas the search for words that have an "n" as the sixth letter does not easily generate this group of words.

Just as retrievability affects our vocabulary-search behavior, organizational modes affect information-search behavior within our work lives. We structure organizations to provide order, but this same structure can lead to confusion if the presumed order is not exactly as suggested. For example, many organizations have an information systems division that has generalized expertise in computer applications. Assume that you are a manager in a product division and need computer expertise. If that expertise exists within the information systems group, the organizational hierarchy will lead you to the correct resource. If, however, the information systems group lacks expertise in a specific application, but this expertise exists elsewhere in the organization, the hierarchy is likely to bias the effectiveness of your search. I am not arguing for the overthrow of organizational hierarchies; I am merely identifying the dysfunctional role of hierarchies in potentially biasing search behavior. If we are aware of the potential bias, we need not be affected by this limitation.

Retail store location is influenced by the way in which consumers search their minds when seeking a particular commodity. Why are multiple gas stations at the same intersection? Why do "upscale" retailers want to be in the same mall? Why are the biggest bookstores in a city often located within a few blocks of each other? An important reason for this pattern is that consumers learn the "location" for a particular type of product or store and organize their minds accordingly. To maximize traffic, the retailer needs to be in the location that consumers associate with this type of product or store.

Bias 3—Presumed Associations

People frequently fall victim to the availability bias in their assessment of the likelihood of two events occurring together. For example, consider your response to the following two questions: Is marijuana use related to delinquency? Are couples who get married under age 25 more likely to have bigger families? In assessing the marijuana question, most people typically try to remember several delinquent marijuana users and either assume or do not assume a correlation based on the availability of this mental data. However, a proper analysis would require you to recall *four* groups of people: marijuana users who are delinquents, marijuana users who are not delinquents, delinquents who do not use marijuana, and nondelinquents who do not use marijuana. The same analysis applies to the marriage question. Proper analysis would include four groups: couples who married young and have large families, couples who married young and have small families, couples who married older and have large families, and couples who married older and have small families.

Indeed, there are always at least four separate situations to consider when assessing the association between two dichotomous events. However, our everyday decision making commonly ignores this scientifically valid fact. Chapman and Chapman (1967) have noted that when the probability of two events co-occurring is judged by the availability of perceived co-occurring instances in our minds, we usually assign an inappropriately high probability that the two events will co-occur again. Thus, if we know a lot of marijuana users who are delinquents, we assume that marijuana use is related to delinquency. Similarly, if we know of a lot of couples who married young and have had large families, we assume that this trend is more prevalent than it may actually be. In testing for this bias, Chapman and Chapman provided participants with information about hypothetical psychiatric patients. The information included a written clinical diagnosis of a "patient" and a drawing of a person made by

the "patient." The participants were asked to estimate the frequency with which each diagnosis (for example, suspiciousness or paranoia) was accompanied by various facial and body features in the drawings (for example, peculiar eyes). Throughout the study, participants markedly overestimated the frequency of pairs commonly associated together by social lore. For example, diagnoses of suspiciousness were overwhelmingly associated with peculiar eyes.

Summary. A lifetime of experience has led us to believe that, in general, we recall frequent events more easily than infrequent events, and recall likely events more easily than unlikely events. In response to this learning, we have adopted the availability heuristic to help us estimate the likelihood of events. This simplifying heuristic often leads us to accurate, efficient judgments. However, as these first three biases (ease of recall, retrievability, and presumed associations) indicate, the misuse of the availability heuristic can lead to systematic errors in managerial judgment. We too easily assume that our available recollections are truly representative of the larger pool of events that exists outside our range of experience.

BIASES EMANATING FROM THE REPRESENTATIVENESS HEURISTIC

Bias 4—Insensitivity to Base Rates

> *Problem 5.* Mark is finishing his MBA at a prestigious university. He is very interested in the arts and at one time considered a career as a musician. Is he more likely to take a job:
>
> (A) in arts management, or (B) with an Internet start-up?

How did you decide on your answer? Odds are, you responded like most people. Using the representativeness heuristic, most people approach this problem by analyzing the degree to which Mark is representative of their image of individuals who take jobs in each of the two areas. Consequently, they usually conclude that

Mark took the arts management job. However, as we discussed in our analysis of Problem 2 earlier in this chapter, this response overlooks relevant base-rate information. Reconsider the problem in light of the fact that a much larger number of MBAs take jobs with Internet start-ups than in arts management—relevant information that should enter into any reasonable prediction of Mark's career path. With this base-rate data, it is only reasonable to predict that he will be more likely to work for an Internet start-up.

Judgmental biases of this type frequently occur when individuals cognitively ask the wrong question. If you answered "arts management," you probably wondered, "How likely is it that a person working in the management of the arts would fit Mark's description?" In fact, the problem requires you to ask the question, "How likely is it that someone fitting Mark's description will choose arts management?" By itself, the representativeness heuristic incorrectly results in a similar answer to both questions, since this heuristic leads individuals to compare the resemblance of the personal description and the career path. However, when base-rate data are considered, they are irrelevant to the first question listed, but crucial to a reasonable prediction based on the second question. While a large percentage of individuals in arts management may fit Mark's description, there are undoubtedly a larger absolute number of management consultants fitting Mark's description because of the relative preponderance of MBAs in Internet start-ups.

Participants do use base-rate data correctly when no other information is provided (Kahneman and Tversky, 1972). In the absence of a personal description of Mark in Problem 5, people will choose "Internet start-up" based on the past frequency of this career path for MBAs. Thus, people understand the relevance of base-rate information, but tend to disregard such data when descriptive data are also available. Ignoring base rates has many unfortunate implications. Prospective entrepreneurs typically spend far too much time imagining their success and far too little time considering the base rate for business failures. Entrepreneurs think that the base rate for failure is not relevant to their situation, and many individuals lose their life savings as a result. Similarly, unnecessary emotional distress is caused in the divorce process because of the failure of couples to create prenuptial agreements that facilitate the peaceful resolution of a marriage. The suggestion of a prenuptial agreement is often viewed as a sign of bad faith. However, in far too many cases, the failure to create prenuptial agreements occurs when individuals approach marriage with the false belief that the very high base rate for divorce does not apply to them.

Bias 5—Insensitivity to Sample Size

Problem 6 (from Tversky and Kahneman, 1974). A certain town is served by two hospitals. In the larger hospital about 45 babies are born each day and in the smaller hospital about 15 babies are born each day. As you know, about 50 percent of all babies are boys. However, the exact percentage varies from day to day. Sometimes it may be higher than 50 percent, sometimes lower.

For a period of one year, each hospital recorded the days in which more than 60 percent of the babies born were boys. Which hospital do you think recorded more such days?

(A) The larger hospital.

(B) The smaller hospital.

(C) About the same (that is, within 5 percent of each other).

Most individuals choose C, expecting the two hospitals to record a similar number of days in which 60 percent or more of the babies born are boys. People seem to have some basic idea of how unusual it is to have 60 percent of a random event occurring in a specific direction. By contrast, simple statistics tell us that it is much more likely to observe 60 percent of male babies in a smaller sample than in a larger sample. The interested reader can verify this fact with an introductory statistics book. However, anecdotally, this effect is easy to understand. Think about which is more likely: getting 6 heads in 10 flips of a coin or getting 6,000 heads in 10,000 flips of a coin. Our intuition correctly tells us that 6 out of 10 is not that unusual, but 6,000 in 10,000 is very unusual. Sampling theory tells us that the expected number of days in which more than 60 percent of the babies are boys is three times greater in the small hospital, since a large sample is less likely to deviate from the mean. However, most people judge the probability to be the same in each hospital, effectively ignoring sample size.

Although the importance of sample size is fundamental in statistics, Tversky and Kahneman (1974) argue that sample size is rarely a part of our intuition. Why not? When responding to problems dealing with sampling, people often use the representativeness heuristic. For instance, they think about how representative it would be for 60 percent of babies born to be boys in a random event. As a result, people ignore the issue of sample size, which is critical to an accurate assessment of the problem.

Consider the implications of this bias for advertising strategies. Market research experts understand that a sizable sample will be more accurate than a small one, but use consumers' bias to the advantage of their clients: "Four out of five dentists surveyed recommend sugarless gum for their patients who chew gum." Without mention of the exact number of dentists surveyed, the results are meaningless. If only 5 or 10 dentists were surveyed, the size of the sample would not be generalizable to the overall population of dentists.

Bias 6—Misconceptions of Chance

Problem 7. You have started buying stocks on the Internet, beginning with five different stocks. Each stock goes down soon after your purchase. As you prepare to make a sixth purchase, you reason that it should be more successful, since the last five were "lemons." After all, the odds favor making at least one successful pick in six decisions. This thinking is:

(A) correct.
(B) incorrect.

Most people are comfortable with the preceding logic, or at least have used similar logic in the past. However, the logic in Problem 7 is incorrect. In fact, the performance of the first five stocks will not directly affect the performance of the sixth stock. Relying on their intuition and the representativeness heuristic, most individuals incorrectly conclude that a sixth poor performance is unlikely because the probability of getting six "lemons" in a row is extremely low. Unfortunately, this logic ignores the fact that we have already witnessed five "lemons" (in itself an unlikely occurrence), and the performance of the sixth stock is independent of the performance of the first five.

This question parallels research by Kahneman and Tversky (1972) showing that people expect a sequence of random events to "look" random. Specifically, participants routinely judged the sequence of coin flips H–T–H–T–T–H to be more likely than H–H–H–T–T–T, which does not "appear" random, and more likely than the sequence H–H–H–H–T–H, which does not represent the equal likelihood of heads and tails. Simple statistics, of course, tell us that each of these sequences is equally likely because of the independence of multiple random events.

Problem 7 moves beyond dealing with random events in recognizing our inappropriate tendency to assume that random and nonrandom events will balance out. Will the sixth stock perform well? Maybe! But your earlier failures are completely irrelevant to its potential for success.

The logic concerning misconceptions of chance provides a process explanation of the gambler's fallacy. After holding bad cards on ten hands of poker, the poker player believes he is "due" for a good hand. After winning $1,000 in the Pennsylvania State Lottery, a woman changes her regular number—after all, how likely is it that the same number will come up twice? Tversky and Kahneman (1974) note: "Chance is commonly viewed as a self-correcting process in which a deviation in one direction induces a deviation in the opposite direction to restore the equilibrium. In fact, deviations are not corrected as a chance process unfolds, they are merely diluted."

In the preceding examples, individuals expected probabilities to even out. In some situations, our minds misconstrue chance in exactly the opposite way. In sports such as basketball, we often think of a particular player as having a "hot hand" or "being on a good streak." If your favorite player has made his last four shots, is the probability of his making his next shot higher, lower, or the same as the probability of his making a shot without the preceding four hits? Most sports fans, sports commentators, and players believe that the answer is "higher." In fact, there are many biological, emotional, and physical reasons that this answer could be correct. However, it is wrong! In an extensive analysis of the shooting of the Philadelphia 76ers and the Boston Celtics, Gilovich, Vallone, and Tversky (1985) found that immediately prior shot performance did not change the likelihood of success on the upcoming shot. Out of all of the findings in this book, this is the effect that my managerial students have the hardest time accepting. We can all remember sequences of five hits in a row; streaks are part of our conception of chance in athletic competition. However, our minds do not think of a string of "four in a row" shots as a situation in which "he missed his fifth shot." As a result, we have a misconception of connectedness when, in fact, chance (or the player's normal probability of success) is really in effect.

The belief in the hot hand has interesting implications for how players compete. Passing the ball to the player who is "hot" is commonly endorsed as a good strategy. Similarly, the opposing team often will concentrate on guarding the "hot" player. Another player, who is less hot but is equally skilled, may have a better chance of scoring. Thus, the belief in the "hot hand" is not just erroneous, but could also be costly if you make decisions under this illusion.

The mythical perception of a hot hand is not limited to basketball. Imagine that you receive a free copy of an investor newsletter that advises you to sell stock because the market will fall during the next six months. You ignore this newsletter, and then it happens to be correct. At the end of the six months, another free copy of this newsletter tells you the market will rise during the next six months. Again, you ignore the advice, and again the newsletter is correct. A third free copy of the newsletter advises you to buy stocks for the next six-month period. Once again, you ignore the newsletter, and once again it is correct. After these 18 months, you receive a direct-mail solicitation for this newsletter, pointing out that they have been giving you great free advice for the past 18 months. If you want this excellent advice in the future, you must pay a small subscription fee. Are you tempted to subscribe to this publication? Many people would be impressed by its consistent past performance and would sign up, expecting more sound advice.

Now consider what this advice may look like from the other side. Suppose a publisher creates eight financial newsletters, each managed by a different expert. In their first issues, each of the eight makes a six-month recommendation about the general direction of the market; four predict a rise in the market, and four predict a fall in the market. The four who predicted a fall in the market were correct, and the four who predicted a rise go out of business. Of the remaining four newsletters, two predict a rise for the second six-month period and two predict a fall. The market rises, and the two that predicted a fall in the second six-month period go out of business. Of the two remaining in business after 12 months, one predicts a rise in the market for the third six-month period, and the other predicts a fall. The market rises, and the newsletter that was correct all three times advertises this fact. It seems they have some important insight into financial markets. Yet, we can see that if there are many "experts" making predictions, some will be consistently correct simply by chance, though we will be biased to give credit to the one that got lucky.

Tversky and Kahneman's (1971) work also shows that misconceptions of chance are not limited to gamblers, sports fans, or laypersons. Research psychologists also fall victim to the "law of small numbers." They believe that sample events should be far more representative of the population from which they were drawn than simple statistics would dictate. Putting too much faith in the results of initial samples, scientists often grossly overestimate the replicability of empirical findings. The representativeness heuristic may be so well institutionalized in our decision processes that even scientific training and its emphasis on the proper use of statistics may not eliminate its biasing influence.

Bias 7—Regression to the Mean

Problem 8. You are the sales forecaster for a department store chain with nine locations. The chain depends on you for quality projections of future sales in order to make decisions on staffing, advertising, information system developments, purchasing, renovation, and the like. All stores are similar in size and merchandise selection. The main difference in their sales occurs because of location and random fluctuations. Sales for 2000 were as follows:

Store	2000	2002
1	$12,000,000	
2	11,500,000	
3	11,000,000	
4	10,500,000	
5	10,000,000	
6	9,500,000	
7	9,000,000	
8	8,500,000	
9	8,000,000	
TOTAL	$90,000,000	$99,000,000

Your economic forecasting service has convinced you that the best estimate of total sales increases between 2000 and 2002 is 10 percent (to $99,000,000). Your task is to predict 2002 sales for each store. Since your manager believes strongly in the economic forecasting service, it is imperative that your total sales equal $99,000,000.

Think about the processes you might use to answer this problem. Consider the following logical pattern of thought: "The overall increase in sales is predicted to be 10 percent ([$99, 000,000 – $90,000,000]/$90,000,000). Lacking any other specific information on the stores, it makes sense simply to add 10 percent to each 2000 sales figure to predict 2002 sales. This means that I predict sales of $13,200,000 for store 1, sales of $12,650,000 for store 2, and so on." This logic, in fact, is the most common approach people use in response to this item.

Unfortunately, this logic is faulty. Why? Statistical analysis would dictate that we first assess the predicted relationship between 2000 and 2002 sales. This relationship, formally known as a correlation, can vary from total independence (that is, 2000 sales do not predict 2002 sales) to perfect correlation (2000 sales are a perfect predictor of 2002 sales). In the former case, the lack of a relationship between 2000 and 2002 sales would mean that 2000 sales would provide absolutely no information about 2002 sales, and your best estimates of 2002 sales would be equal to total sales divided by the number of stores ($99,000,000 ÷ 9 = $11,000,000). However, in the latter case of perfect predictability between 2000 and 2002 sales, our initial logic of simply extrapolating from 2000 performance by adding 10 percent to each store's performance would be completely accurate. Obviously, 2000 sales are likely to be partially predictive of 2002 sales—falling somewhere between independence and perfect correlation. Thus, the best prediction for store 1 should lie between $11,000,000 and $13,200,000, depending on how predictive you think 2000 sales will be of 2002 sales. The key point is that in virtually all such predictions, you should expect the naive $13,200,000 estimate to regress toward the overall mean ($11,000,000).

In a study of sales forecasting, Cox and Summers (1987) examined the judgments of professional retail buyers. They examined sales data, during a two-week period, from two department stores for six different apparel styles for a total of 12 different sales forecasts. The task was for professional buyers to forecast the sales in week 2 based on week 1 data. The sales from week 1, in fact, regressed to the mean in week 2. However, the forecasts of 31 professional buyers failed to reflect the tendency for regression to the mean.

Many effects regress to the mean. Brilliant students frequently have less successful siblings. Short parents tend to have taller children. Great rookies have mediocre second years (the "sophomore jinx"). Firms that achieve outstanding profits one year tend to perform less well the next year. In each case, individuals are often surprised when made aware of these predictable patterns of regression to the mean.

Why is the regression-to-the-mean concept, while statistically valid, counterintuitive? Kahneman and Tversky (1973) suggest that the representativeness heuristic accounts for this systematic bias in judgment. They argue that individuals typically assume that future outcomes (for example, 2002 sales) will be directly predictable from past outcomes (2000 sales). Thus, we tend to naively develop predictions based on the assumption of perfect correlation with past data.

In some unusual situations, individuals do intuitively expect a regression-to-the-mean effect. In 1998, when Mark McGwire hit 70 home runs, few expected him to repeat this performance the following year. When Wilt Chamberlain scored 100 points in a single game, most people did not expect him to score 100 points in his next game. When a historically 3.0 student got a 4.0 one semester, her parents did not expect a repeat performance the following semester. When a real estate agent sold five houses in one month (an abnormally high performance), his co-agents did not expect equally high sales from him the following month. Why is regression to the mean more intuitive in these cases? Because, when a performance is extreme, we know it cannot last. Thus, under very unusual circumstances, we expect performance to regress. However, we generally do not recognize the regression effect in less extreme cases.

Consider Kahneman and Tversky's (1973) classic example in which misconceptions about regression led to overestimation of the effectiveness of punishment and the underestimation of the power of reward. In a discussion about flight training, experienced instructors noted that praise for an exceptionally smooth landing was typically followed by a poorer landing on the next try, while harsh criticism after a rough landing was usually followed by an improvement on the next try. The instructors concluded that verbal rewards were detrimental to learning, while verbal punishments were beneficial. Obviously, the tendency of performance to regress to the mean can account for the results; verbal feedback may have had absolutely no effect. However, to the extent that the instructors were prone to biased decision making, they were liable to reach the false conclusion that punishment is more effective than positive reinforcement in shaping behavior.

What happens when managers fail to acknowledge the regression principle? Consider an employee who performs extremely well during one evaluation period. He (and his boss) may inappropriately expect similar performance in the next period. What happens when the employee's performance regresses toward the mean? He (and his boss) will begin to make excuses for not meeting expectations. Managers who fail to recognize the tendency of events to regress to the mean are likely to develop false assumptions about future results and, as a result, make inappropriate plans.

Bias 8—The Conjunction Fallacy

Problem 9. Linda is 31 years old, single, outspoken, and very bright. She majored in philosophy. As a student, she was deeply concerned with issues of discrimination and social justice, and she participated in antinuclear demonstrations.

Rank order the following eight descriptions in terms of the probability (likelihood) that they describe Linda:

a. Linda is a teacher in an elementary school.
b. Linda works in a bookstore and takes yoga classes.
c. Linda is active in the feminist movement.
d. Linda is a psychiatric social worker.
e. Linda is a member of the League of Women Voters.
f. Linda is a bank teller.
g. Linda is an insurance salesperson.
h. Linda is a bank teller who is active in the feminist movement.

Examine your rank orderings of descriptions C, F, and H. Most people rank order C as more likely than H and H as more likely than F. Their rationale for this ordering is that C–H–F reflects the degree to which the descriptions represent the short profile of Linda. Tversky and Kahneman constructed Linda's profile to be representative of an active feminist and unrepresentative of a bank teller. Recall from the representativeness heuristic that people make judgments according to the degree to which a specific description corresponds to a broader category within their minds. Linda's profile is more representative of a feminist than of a feminist bank teller, and is more representative of a feminist bank teller than of a bank teller. Thus, the representativeness heuristic accurately predicts that most individuals will rank order the items C–H–F.

Although the representativeness heuristic accurately predicts how individuals will respond, it also leads to another common, systematic distortion of human judgment—the conjunction fallacy (Tversky and Kahneman, 1983). This is illustrated by a reexamination of the potential descriptions of Linda. One of the simplest and most fundamental qualitative laws of probability is that a subset (for example, being a bank teller and a feminist) cannot be more likely than a larger set that completely includes the subset (for example, being a bank teller). Statistically speaking, the broad set "Linda is a bank teller" must be rated at least as likely, if not more so, than the subset "Linda is a bank teller who is active in the feminist movement." After all, there is some chance (although it may be small) that Linda is a bank teller but not a feminist. Based on this logic, a rational assessment of the eight descriptions will result in F being ranked more likely than H.

Simple statistics demonstrate that a conjunction (a combination of two or more descriptors) cannot be more probable than any one of its descriptors. By contrast, the conjunction fallacy predicts that a conjunction will be judged more probable than a single component descriptor when the conjunction appears more representative than the component descriptor. Intuitively, thinking of Linda as a feminist bank teller "feels" more correct than thinking of her as only a bank teller.

The conjunction fallacy can also be triggered by a greater availability of the conjunction than of one of its unique descriptors (Yates and Carlson, 1986). That is, if the conjunction creates more intuitive matches with vivid events, acts, or people than a component of the conjunction, the conjunction is likely to be perceived falsely as more probable than the component. Participants in a study by Tversky and Kahneman (1983) judged the chances of a massive flood somewhere in North America, in 1989, in which 1,000 people drown, to be less likely than the chances of an earthquake in California, sometime in 1989, causing a flood in which more than 1,000 people drown. Yet, the latter possibility (California earthquake leading to flood) is a subset of the former; many other events could cause a flood in North America. Tversky and Kahneman (1983) have shown that the conjunction fallacy is likely to lead to deviations from rationality in judgments of sporting events, criminal behavior, international relations, and medical decisions. The obvious concern arising from the conjunction fallacy is that it leads us to poor predictions of future outcomes, causing us to be ill-prepared to cope with unanticipated events.

Finally, one might hope that groups would be less prone to representativeness errors than individuals. Unfortunately, this is not the case. Argote, Seabright, and Dyer (1986) found that groups not only exhibit the representativeness heuristic in the same directional pattern as individuals, but the biasing effect is even greater in groups than in individuals. Thus, the biases covered in this section may affect group decision making to an even greater degree than they affect individual decision making.

Summary. We have examined five biases that emanate from the use of the representativeness heuristic: insensitivity to base rates, insensitivity to sample size, misconceptions of chance, regression to the mean, and the conjunction fallacy. Experience has taught us that the likelihood of a specific occurrence is related to the likelihood of a group of occurrences which that specific occurrence represents. Unfortunately, we tend to overuse this information in making decisions. The five biases we have just explored illustrate the systematic irrationalities that can occur in our judgments when we are unaware of this tendency.

BIASES EMANATING FROM ANCHORING AND ADJUSTMENT
Bias 9—Insufficient Anchor Adjustment

> ***Problem 10.*** A new Internet company recently made its initial public offering, becoming publicly traded. At its opening, the stock sold for $20/share. The company's closest competitor went public one year ago, also at a price of $20/share. The competitor's stock is now priced at $100/share. What will the new firm be worth one year from now?

Was your answer affected by the other firm's appreciation? Most people are influenced by this fairly irrelevant information. Reconsider how you would have responded if the other firm was now worth only $10/share. On average, individuals give higher estimates of the new firm's future value when the other firm is currently worth $100/share, rather than $10/share. Why? Studies have found that people develop estimates by starting from an initial anchor, based on whatever information is provided, and adjusting from there to yield a final answer. Slovic and Lichtenstein (1971) have provided conclusive evidence that individuals' adjustments away from anchors are usually not sufficient to negate the effects of the anchor. In all cases, answers are biased toward the initial anchor, even if it is irrelevant. Different starting points yield different answers.

Tversky and Kahneman (1974) have provided systematic, empirical evidence of the anchoring effect. In one study, participants were asked to estimate the percentage of African countries in the United Nations. For each participant, a random number (obtained by a spin of a roulette wheel, observed by the participant) was given as a starting point. From there, participants were asked to state whether the actual quantity was higher or lower than this random value and then develop their best estimate. It was found that the arbitrary values from the roulette wheel had a substantial impact on estimates. For example, for those who received 10 countries and 65 countries as starting points, median estimates were 25 and 45, respectively. Thus, even though the participants were aware that the anchor was random and unrelated to the judgment task, the anchor had a dramatic effect on their judgment. Interestingly, paying participants according to their accuracy did not reduce the magnitude of the anchoring effect.

Salary negotiations represent a very common context for observing anchoring in the managerial world. For example, pay increases often come in the form of a percentage increase. A firm may have an average increase of 8 percent, with increases for specific employees varying from 3 percent to 13 percent. While society has led us to accept such systems as equitable, I believe that such a system falls victim to anchoring and leads to substantial inequities. What happens if an employee has been substantially underpaid? The raise system described does not rectify past inequities, since a pay increase of 11 percent may leave that employee still underpaid. Conversely, the system would work in the employee's favor had she been overpaid. Employers often ask job applicants to reveal their current salaries. Why? Employers are searching for a value from which they can anchor an adjustment. If the employee is worth far more than his current salary, the anchoring and adjustment hypothesis predicts that the firm will make an offer below the employee's true value. Does an employee's current salary provide fully accurate information about his or her true worth? I think not. Thus, the use of such compensation systems accepts past inequities as an anchor and makes inadequate adjustments from that point. Furthermore, these findings suggest that when an employer is deciding what offer to make to a potential employee, any anchor that creeps into the discussion is likely to have an inappropriate effect on the eventual offer, even if the anchor is "ignored" as being ridiculous.

There are numerous examples of the anchoring-and-adjustment phenomenon in everyday life. For example:

- In education, children are tracked by a school system that may categorize them into a certain level of performance at an early age. For example, a child who is anchored in the C group may be expected to achieve a mediocre level of performance. Conversely, a child of similar abilities who is anchored in the A group may be perceived as being a better student than the student in group C merely because assignment to the A group confers high-performer status.
- We have all fallen victim to the first-impression syndrome when meeting someone for the first time. We often place so much emphasis on first impressions that we fail to adjust our opinion appropriately at a later date.

Joyce and Biddle (1981) have provided empirical support for the presence of the anchoring-and-adjustment effect among practicing auditors of Big Five accounting firms. Auditors participating in one condition were asked the following:

It is well known that many cases of management fraud go undetected even when competent annual audits are performed. The reason, of course, is that Generally Accepted Auditing Standards are not designed specifically to detect executive-level management fraud. We are interested in obtaining an estimate from practicing auditors of the prevalence of executive-level management fraud as a first step in ascertaining the scope of the problem.

1. Based on your audit experience, is the incidence of significant executive-level management fraud more than 10 in each 1,000 firms (that is, 1 percent) audited by Big Five accounting firms?
   a. Yes, more than 10 in each 1,000 Big Five clients have significant executive-level management fraud.
   b. No, fewer than 10 in each 1,000 Big Five clients have significant executive-level management fraud.
2. What is your estimate of the number of Big Five clients per 1,000 that have significant executive-level management fraud? (Fill in the blank below with the appropriate number.)

   _____ in each 1,000 Big Five clients have significant executive-level management fraud.

The second condition differed only in that participants were asked whether the fraud incidence was more or less than 200 in each 1,000 firms audited, rather than 10 in 1,000. Participants in the first condition estimated a fraud incidence of 16.52 per 1,000 on average, compared with an estimated fraud incidence of 43.11 per 1,000 in the second condition! Here, even professional auditors fell victim to anchoring and adjustment.

The tendency to make insufficient adjustments is a direct result of the anchoring-and-adjustment heuristic described in the first chapter. Interestingly, Nisbett and Ross (1980) present an argument that suggests that the anchoring-and-adjustment bias itself dictates that it will be very difficult to get you to change your decision-making strategies as a result of reading this book. They argue that the heuristics we identify are currently serving as your cognitive anchors and are central to your judgment processes. Thus, any cognitive strategy that I suggest must be presented and understood in a manner that will force you to break your existing cognitive anchors. Based on the evidence in this section, this should be a difficult challenge—but one that is important enough to be worth the effort!

Bias 10—Conjunctive and Disjunctive Events Bias

Problem 11. Which of the following appears most likely? Which appears second most likely?

a. Drawing a red marble from a bag containing 50 percent red marbles and 50 percent white marbles.

b. Drawing a red marble seven times in succession, with replacement (a selected marble is put back into the bag before the next marble is selected), from a bag containing 90 percent red marbles and 10 percent white marbles.

c. Drawing at least one red marble in seven tries, with replacement, from a bag containing 10 percent red marbles and 90 percent white marbles.

The most common ordering of preferences is B–A–C. Interestingly, the correct order of likelihood is C (52 percent), A (50 percent), B (48 percent)—the exact opposite of the most common intuitive pattern! This result illustrates a general bias to overestimate the probability of conjunctive events, or events that must occur in conjunction with one another (Bar–Hillel, 1973), and to underestimate the probability of disjunctive events, or events that occur independently (Tversky and Kahneman, 1974). Thus, when multiple events all need to occur (Problem B), we overestimate the true likelihood, while if only one of many events needs to occur (Problem C), we underestimate the true likelihood.

Tversky and Kahneman (1974) explain these effects in terms of the anchoring-and-adjustment heuristic. They argue that the probability of any one event occurring (for example, drawing one red marble) provides a natural anchor for the judgment of the total probability. Since adjustment from an anchor is typically insufficient, the perceived likelihood of choice B stays inappropriately close to 90 percent, while the perceived probability of choice C stays inappropriately close to 10 percent.

How is each of these biases manifested in an applied context? The overestimation of conjunctive events is a powerful explanation of the timing problems that typically occur with projects that require multistage planning. Individuals, businesses, and governments frequently fall victim to the conjunctive-events bias in terms of timing and budgets. Home remodeling, new product ventures, and public works projects seldom finish on time or on budget. Consider the following real-life scenarios:

- After three years of study, doctoral students typically dramatically overestimate the likelihood of completing their dissertations within a year. This occurs even when they plan how long each component of the project will take. Why do they not finish in one year?

- A partner managed a consulting project in which five teams were each analyzing a different strategy for a client. The alternatives could not be compared until all teams completed their analysis. As the client's deadline approached, three of the five teams were behind schedule, but the partner assured the client that all five would be ready on time. In the end, the manager only presented three of the five alternatives to the client (two were still missing). Unimpressed, the client dropped the consulting firm. Whose fault was it that the project failed?

- The City of Boston undertook a massive construction project to move Interstate Highway 93 below ground as it passes through the city (The Big Dig). City officials developed a very clear budget based on each subcontractor's estimate. Nevertheless, as of mid-2000, the

Big Dig was $1.9 billion over budget. What went wrong?

Why are we so optimistic in our assessments of a project's cost and time frame? Why are we so surprised when a seemingly unlikely setback occurs? Because of the human tendency to underestimate disjunctive events. "A complex system, such as a nuclear reactor or the human body, will malfunction if any of its essential components fails," argue Tversky and Kahneman. "Even when the likelihood of failure in each component is slight, the probability of an overall failure can be high if many components are involved." For this reason, complex projects from dissertations to highway digs often run into unexpected glitches. In his book "Normal Accidents," Perrow (1984) argues against the safety of advanced technologies such as nuclear reactors and DNA research. He fears that society significantly underestimates the potential for disaster because of our judgmental failure to recognize the multitude of things that can go wrong in these incredibly complex and interactive systems. This failure explains why, when an oil company like Exxon has a major spill off the Alaskan coast, it is perceived by the public as an unlikely, surprising event. However, when a company fails to double-line its tankers, or to monitor the alcohol intake of its captain, and so on, perhaps the likelihood of a "surprise" is higher than it appears.

An awareness of our underestimation of disjunctive events also has its positive side. Consider the following:

It's Monday evening (10:00 P.M.). Your boss calls to tell you that you must be at the Chicago office by 9:30 the next morning. You call all five airlines that have flights that get into Chicago by 9:00 A.M. Each has one flight, and all the flights are booked. When you ask the probability of getting on each of the flights if you show up at the airport in the morning, you are disappointed to hear probabilities of 30 percent, 25 percent, 15 percent, 20 percent, and 25 percent. Consequently, you do not expect to get to Chicago in time.

In this case, the disjunctive bias leads you to expect the worst. In fact, if the probabilities given by the airlines are unbiased and independent, you have a 73 percent chance of getting on one of the flights (assuming you can arrange to be at the right ticket counter at the right time)!

Bias 11—Overconfidence

Problem 12. Listed below are 10 uncertain quantities. Do not look up any information on these items. For each, write down your best estimate of the quantity. Next, put a lower and upper bound around your estimate, so that you are 98 percent confident that your range surrounds the actual quantity.

Estimate Lower Upper

____ ____ ____ a. Wal-Mart's 1999 revenue

____ ____ ____ b. Kmart's 1999 revenue

____ ____ ____ c. Market value of General Motors as of March 14, 2000

____ ____ ____ d. Market value of Microsoft as of March 14, 2000

____ ____ ____ e. Market value of Cisco Systems as of March 14, 2000

____ ____ ____ f. Rank of Supervalu in the 1999 *Fortune* 500

____ ____ ____ g. Rank of Qualcomm in the 1999 *Fortune* 500

____ ____ ____ h. Total households in the United States, according to a 1994 Bureau of the Census poll

____ ____ ____ i. Number of species and subspecies of North American mammals extinct since 1600

____ ____ ____ j. Plastic waste generated in the United States in 1993 in tons

How many of your 10 ranges will actually surround the true quantities? If you set your ranges so that you were 98 percent confident, you should expect to correctly bound approximately 9.8, or 9 to 10, of the quantities. Let's look at the correct answers: (a) $166,809,000,000, (b) $35,935,000,000, (c) $63,838,500,000, (d) $492,462,100,000, (e) $453,878,800,000, (f) 99, (g) 409, (h) 97,000,000, (i) 22, (j) 19,300,000.

How many of your ranges actually surrounded the true quantities? If you surround 9–10, we can conclude that you were appropriately confident in your estimation ability. Most people only surround between 3 (30 percent) and 7 (70 percent), despite claiming a 98 percent confidence that each range will surround the true value. Why? Most of us are overconfident in our estimation abilities and do not acknowledge our true uncertainty.

In Alpert and Raiffa's (1969) initial demonstration of overconfidence based on 1,000 observations (100 participants on 10 items), 42.6 percent of quantities fell outside 90 percent confidence ranges. Since then, overconfidence has been identified as a common judgmental pattern and demonstrated in a wide variety of settings. For example, Fischhoff, Slovic, and Lichtenstein (1977) found that participants who assigned odds of 1,000:1 of being correct were correct only 81 to 88 percent of the time. For odds of 1,000,000:1, their answers were correct only 90 to 96 percent of the time! Hazard and Peterson (1973) identified overconfidence among members of the armed forces, while Cambridge and Shreckengost (1980) found extreme overconfidence among CIA agents.

The most well-established finding in the overconfidence literature is the tendency of people to be most overconfident of the correctness of their answers when asked to respond to questions of moderate to extreme difficulty (Fischhoff, Slovic, and Lichtenstein, 1977). That is, as participants' knowledge of a question decreases, they do not correspondingly decrease their level of confidence. However, participants typically demonstrate no overconfidence, and often some underconfidence, when

asked questions with which they are familiar. Thus, we should be most alert to the potential for overconfidence when considering areas outside of our expertise.

Are groups as overconfident as individuals? Sniezek and Henry (1989) investigated the accuracy and confidence of group decisions about unknown situations. They found that, in general, groups make more accurate judgments than individuals about uncertain events. This is particularly true in groups in which there is a broad variance in individual judgments and a relatively high level of disagreement. However, groups are just as susceptible as individuals to unreasonably high levels of confidence in their judgments. Some 98 percent of participants believed that their group's judgments were in the top half of all group judgments with respect to accuracy. This finding suggests that overconfidence is a significant pitfall for groups as well as for individuals.

Theories about overconfidence have met with a great deal of controversy (see Lichtenstein, Fischhoff, and Phillips [1982] for an extensive discussion). Tversky and Kahneman (1974) explain overconfidence in terms of anchoring. Specifically, they argue that when individuals are asked to set a confidence range around an answer, their initial estimate serves as an anchor which biases their estimation of confidence intervals in both directions. As explained earlier, adjustments from an anchor are usually insufficient, resulting in an overly narrow confidence band. In their review of the literature, Lichtenstein, Fischhoff, and Phillips (1982) suggest two viable strategies for eliminating overconfidence. First, they have found that giving people feedback about their overconfident judgments has been moderately successful at reducing this bias. Second, Koriat, Lichtenstein, and Fischhoff (1980) found that asking people to explain why their answers might be wrong (or far off the mark) can decrease overconfidence by enabling them to recognize contradictions in their judgment.

Why should you be concerned about overconfidence? After all, it has probably given you the courage to attempt endeavors that have stretched your abilities. Unwarranted confidence can indeed be beneficial in some situations. However, consider the potential adverse effects of excess confidence in the following situations:

- You are a surgeon and are trying to persuade a patient's family to agree to a difficult operation. When the family asks you to estimate the likelihood that the patient will survive the operation, you respond, "95 percent." If the patient dies on the operating table, was he one of the unlucky 5 percent, or are you guilty of malpractice for an overconfident projection?
- You are the chief legal counsel for a firm that has been threatened with a multimillion dollar lawsuit. You are 98 percent confident that the firm will not lose in court. Is this degree of certainty sufficient for you to recommend rejecting an out-of-court settlement? Suppose you learn that if you lose the case, your firm will go bankrupt. Based on what you know now, are you still comfortable with your 98 percent estimate?
- You have developed a marketing plan for a new product. You are so confident in your plan that you have not developed any contingencies for early market failure. When the first stage of your plan falters, will you expedite changes in the marketing strategy, or will your overconfidence blind you to its flaws?

These examples demonstrate the serious problems that can result from the tendency to be overconfident. While confidence in your abilities is necessary for achievement in life, and can inspire respect and confidence in others, overconfidence can be a barrier to effective professional decision making.

Summary. Whenever we try to estimate likelihoods (such as the probability of on-time project completion) or establish values (such as what salary to offer), we tend to seek out an initial anchor, which often weighs strongly in our decision-making processes. Our experience determining such figures has taught us that starting from somewhere is easier than starting from nowhere. However, as the last three biases (insufficient anchor adjustment, conjunctive and disjunctive events bias, and overconfidence) show, we frequently over-rely on these anchors and seldom question their validity or appropriateness in a particular situation. As with the other heuristics, we frequently fail even to realize that this heuristic has an impact on our judgment.

TWO MORE GENERAL BIASES
Bias 12—The Confirmation Trap

Imagine that the sequence of three numbers below follows a rule, and your task is to diagnose that rule (Wason, 1960). When you write down other sequences of three numbers, an instructor will tell you whether or not your sequence follows the rule.

$$2\text{--}4\text{--}6$$

What sequences would you write down? How would you know when you had enough evidence to guess the rule? Wason's study participants tended to offer fairly few sequences, and the sequences tended to be consistent with the rule that they eventually guessed. Common rules included, "numbers that go up by two," or "the difference between the first two numbers equals the difference between the last two numbers." In fact, Wason's rule was much broader: "any three ascending numbers." This solution requires participants to accumulate disconfirming, rather than confirming, evidence. For example, if you think the rule is "numbers that go up by two," you must try sequences that do not conform to this rule to find the actual rule. Trying the sequences 1–3–5, 10–12–14, 122–124–126, and so on, will only lead you into the confirmation trap. Similarly, if you think the rule is "the difference between the first two numbers equals the difference between the last two numbers," you must try sequences that do not conform to this rule to find the actual rule.

Trying the sequences 1–2–3, 10–15–20, 122–126–130 again would only bring you feedback that strengthens your hypothesis. Only 6 out of 29 of Wason's participants found the correct rule on their first guess of the rule. Wason concluded that obtaining the correct solution necessitates "a willingness to attempt to falsify hypotheses, and thus to test those intuitive ideas that so often carry the feeling of certitude" (p. 139).

I have used this task hundreds of times in classes. My first volunteer typically guesses "numbers going up by two" and is quickly eliminated. My second volunteer is often just as quick with a wrong answer. Interestingly, at this stage, it is rare that I will have answered "no" to a sequence proposed by either volunteer. Why? Because people tend to seek confirmatory information, even when disconfirming information is more powerful and important.

Once you become aware of the confirmation trap, you are likely to find that it pervades your decision-making processes. When you make a tentative decision (to buy a new car, to hire a particular employee, to start research and development on a new product line), do you search for data that support your decision before making the final commitment? Most of us do. However, the existence of the confirmation trap implies that the search for challenging, or disconfirming, evidence will provide the most useful insights. For example, when you are seeking to confirm your decision to hire a particular employee, you will probably have no trouble finding positive information on the individual, such as recommendations from past employers. In fact, it may be more important for you to determine whether negative information on this individual, such as a criminal record, as well as positive information on another potential applicant, also exists. Now consider the last car you purchased. Imagine that, the day after you drove your new car home, your local newspaper printed two lists ranking cars by performance— one by fuel efficiency and one by crash test results. Which list would you pay more attention to? Most of us would pay more attention to whichever list confirms that we made a good purchase.

I recently watched my friend Dick Thaler engage a group of financial executives in the 2–4–6 task. After the basic demonstration, Thaler told the audience that he was forming two new consulting firms. One of them, called "Yes Person," would respond to any client's request for advice by telling them that all their ideas are great. In fact, to speed service and ensure satisfaction, Yes Person would allow the client to write the consulting report themselves if they liked. The other consulting firm, called "Devil's Advocate," would disapprove of any plans currently being considered by a client. Reports by Devil's Advocate would consist of a list of the top ten reasons a plan should not be undertaken.

Which consulting style would be more useful to the client? Thaler insisted to his audience that Devil's Advocate would provide a much more important service than Yes Person, and I agree. However, real-world consulting engagements often bear a closer resemblance to the Yes Person format than to that of Devil's Advocate, in part because consulting firms know that clients like to hear that their ideas are good. Our desire to confirm our initial ideas is so strong that we will pay people to back us up! When pressed, Thaler conceded that his two firms don't really exist, and could never succeed. After all, he pointed out, no firm would ever hire Devil's Advocate, and Yes Person already had too much competition from established consulting firms.

Bias 13—Hindsight and the Curse of Knowledge

Imagine yourself in the following scenarios:

- You are an avid football fan, and you are watching a critical game in which your team is behind 35–31. With three seconds left and the ball on the opponent's three-yard line, the quarterback calls a pass play into the corner of the endzone. When the play fails, you shout, "I *knew* that was a bad play."
- You are traveling by car in an unfamiliar area, and your spouse is driving. When you

approach an unmarked fork in the road, your spouse decides to go to the right. Four miles and fifteen minutes later, it is clear that you are lost. You blurt out, "I knew you should have turned left at the fork."

- A manager who works for you hired a new supervisor last year. You were well aware of the choices he had at the time and allowed him to choose the new employee on his own. You have just received production data on every supervisor. The data on the new supervisor are terrible. You call in the manager and claim, "There was plenty of evidence that he was the wrong man for the job."

- As director of marketing in a consumer-goods organization, you have just presented the results of an extensive six-month study on current consumer preferences for the products manufactured by your company. At the conclusion of your presentation, a senior vice president responds, "I don't know why we spent so much time and money collecting these data. I could have told you what the results were going to be."

Do you recognize any of your own behaviors in these scenarios? Do you recognize someone else's remarks? Each scenario exemplifies "the hindsight bias" (Fischhoff, 1975). People typically are not very good at recalling or reconstructing the way an uncertain situation appeared to them before finding out the results of the decision. What play would *you* have called? Did you really know that your spouse should have turned left? Was there really evidence that the selected supervisor was a bad choice? Could the senior vice president really have predicted your study's results? While our intuition is occasionally accurate, we tend to overestimate what we knew beforehand based upon what we later learned. The hindsight bias occurs when people look back on their own judgments, as well as those of others.

Fischhoff (1975) examined the differences between hindsight and foresight in the context of judging the outcome of historical events. In one study, participants were divided into five groups

and asked to read a passage about the war between the British and Gurka forces in 1814. One group was not told the result of the war. The remaining four groups of participants were told either that: (1) the British won, (2) the Gurkas won, (3) a military stalemate was reached with no peace settlement, or (4) a military stalemate was reached with a peace settlement. Obviously, only one group was told the truthful outcome— (1) in this case. Each participant was then asked what his or her subjective assessments of the probability of each outcome would have been without the benefit of knowing the reported outcome. Participants tended to believe that they would have judged the outcome that they were told happened as being most likely, even if they had not been told the outcome. Based on this and other varied examples, it becomes clear that knowledge of an outcome increases an individual's belief about the degree to which he or she would have predicted that outcome without the benefit of that knowledge.

Anchoring is often used to explain the hindsight bias. According to this view, knowledge of an event's outcome becomes an anchor by which individuals interpret their prior judgments of the event's likelihood. Since adjustments to anchors are known to be inadequate, hindsight knowledge can be expected to bias perceptions of what one thinks one knew in foresight. Furthermore, to the extent that various pieces of data about the event vary in support of the actual outcome, evidence that is consistent with the known outcome may become cognitively more salient and thus more available in memory (Slovic and Fischhoff, 1977). This tendency will lead an individual to justify a claimed foresight in view of "the facts provided." Finally, the relevance of a particular piece of data may later be judged important to the extent to which it is representative of the final observed outcome.

In the short run, hindsight has a number of advantages. For instance, it is flattering to believe that your judgment is far better than it actually is! In addition, hindsight allows us to criticize other people's apparent lack of foresight.

However, the hindsight bias reduces our ability to learn from the past and to evaluate decisions objectively. In general, individuals should be judged by the process and logic of their decisions, not on their results. A decision maker who makes a high-quality decision that does not work out should be rewarded, not punished. Why? Because results are affected by a variety of factors outside the direct control of the decision maker. When we rely on hindsight offered by results, we will inappropriately evaluate the decision maker's logic, judging their outcomes rather than their methods.

Closely related to the hindsight bias is the "curse of knowledge," which argues that when assessing others' knowledge, people are unable to ignore knowledge that they have that others do not have (Camerer, Loewenstein, and Weber, 1989). Knowledge that is psychologically available is hard to forget when a person is imagining how much others know; sophistication stands in the way of a fair assessment. This "curse" explains the difficulty teachers often have adjusting their lessons according to what students already know, and the tendency of product designers to overestimate the average person's ability to master high-tech devices. Similarly, Hoch (1988) found that marketing experts (who are also consumers) are generally worse at predicting the beliefs, values, and tastes of other consumers than nonexpert consumers are. This results from the marketing experts acting as if the nonexpert consumer understood as much about the products as they did.

Have you ever given someone what you believed were very clear directions to your home, only to find that they got lost? Keysar (1992) argues that an individual often assumes that when she sends an ambiguous message (which is clear to her) to another individual, based on information that the receiver does not possess, her intent will be magically understood by the other party. Keysar had people read scenarios that provided them with privileged information about "David." They read that David had dinner at a particular restaurant based on a friend's recommendation. Half of the participants in the experiment learned that he really enjoyed his meal, and the other half learned that he disliked it very much. All of the participants read that David wrote his friend the following note: "About the restaurant, it was marvelous, just marvelous." The participants who knew that David enjoyed the restaurant had a strong tendency to believe that the friend would take the comment as sincere. In contrast, participants who knew that David disliked the restaurant had a strong tendency to believe that the friend would take the comment as sarcastic. This result occurred despite the fact that both groups of participants knew that the friend had access to the same note and no additional information about David's dining experience. A great deal of disappointment occurs as a result of the failure to communicate clearly in organizations. Part of this disappointment results from our false belief that people understand our ambiguous messages.

INTEGRATION AND COMMENTARY

Heuristics, or rules of thumb, are the cognitive tools we use to simplify decision making. The preceding pages have described 13 of the most common biases that result when we over-rely on these judgmental heuristics. These biases, along with their associated heuristics, are summarized in Table 14.2. Again, I must emphasize that more than one heuristic can operate on our decision-making processes at any given time. Overall, the use of heuristic "shortcuts" results far more often in adequate decisions than inadequate ones. The logic of heuristics is that, on average, any loss in decision quality will be outweighed by time saved. However, as I have demonstrated in this chapter, a blanket acceptance of heuristics is unwise. First, as illustrated by the quiz items, there are many instances in which the loss in decision quality far outweighs the time saved by heuristics. Second, the foregoing logic suggests that we have voluntarily accepted the quality tradeoffs associated with heuristics. In reality, we have not: Most of us are

TABLE 14.2
Summary of the 13 Biases

BIAS	DESCRIPTION
Biases Emanating from the Availability Heuristic	
1. Ease of recall	Individuals judge events that are more easily recalled from memory, based on vividness or recency, to be more numerous than events of equal frequency whose instances are less easily recalled.
2. Retrievability	Individuals are biased in their assessments of the frequency of events based on how their memory structures affect the search process.
3. Presumed associations	Individuals tend to overestimate the probability of two events co-occurring based on the number of similar associations they can easily recall, whether from experience or social influence.
Biases Emanating from the Representativeness Heuristic	
4. Insensitivity to base rates	When assessing the likelihood of events, individuals tend to ignore base rates if any other descriptive information is provided—even if it is irrelevant.
5. Insensitivity to sample size	When assessing the reliability of sample information, individuals frequently fail to appreciate the role of sample size.
6. Misconceptions of chance	Individuals expect that a sequence of data generated by a random process will look "random," even when the sequence is too short for those expectations to be statistically valid.
7. Regression to the mean	Individuals tend to ignore the fact that extreme events tend to regress to the mean on subsequent trials.
8. The conjunction fallacy	Individuals falsely judge that conjunctions (two events co-occurring) are more probable than a more global set of occurrences of which the conjunction is a subset.
Biases Emanating from Anchoring and Adjustment	
9. Insufficient anchor adjustment	Individuals make estimates for values based upon an initial value (derived from past events, random assignment, or whatever information is available) and typically make insufficient adjustments from that anchor when establishing a final value.
10. Conjunctive and disjunctive events bias	Individuals exhibit a bias toward overestimating the probability of conjunctive events and underestimating the probability of disjunctive events.
11. Overconfidence	Individuals tend to be overconfident of the infallibility of their judgments when answering moderately to extremely difficult questions.
Two More General Biases	
12. The confirmation trap	Individuals tend to seek confirmatory information for what they think is true and fail to search for disconfirmatory evidence.
13. Hindsight and the curse of knowledge	After finding out whether or not an event occurred, individuals tend to overestimate the degree to which they would have predicted the correct outcome. Furthermore, individuals fail to ignore information they possess that others do not when predicting others' behavior.

unaware of their existence and their ongoing impact upon our decision making. Consequently, we fail to distinguish between situations in which they are beneficial and situations in which they are potentially harmful.

To emphasize the distinction between legitimate and illegitimate uses of heuristics, let's reconsider Problem 5. Participants tended to predict that Mark would be more likely to take a job in arts management, despite the fact that the contextual data overwhelmingly favored his choice of a position with an Internet start-up. In this case, the representativeness heuristic prevents us from appropriately incorporating relevant base-rate data. However, if the choice

of "Internet start-up" were replaced with a less common career path for an MBA from a prestigious university (such as steel industry management), then the representativeness heuristic is likely to lead to an accurate prediction. In other words, when base-rate data are unavailable or irrelevant (that is, when the choices have the same base rate), the representativeness heuristic provides a reasonably good cognitive tool for matching Mark to his most likely career path. The key to improved judgment, therefore, lies in learning to distinguish between appropriate and inappropriate uses of heuristics. This chapter gives you the foundation you need to learn to make this distinction.

REFERENCES

Alpert, M., and Raiffa, H. (1969). A progress report on the training of probability assessors. Later published in D. Kahneman, P. Slovic, and A. Tversky (Eds.), *Judgment under uncertainty: Heuristics and biases*. Cambridge: Cambridge University Press, 1982.

Argote, L., Seabright, M. A., and Dyer, L. (1986). Individual versus group: Use of base-rate and individuating information. *Organizational Behavior and Human Decision Processes* 38, 65–75.

Bar-Hillel, M. (1973). On the subjective probability of compound events. *Organizational Behavior and Human Performance* 9, 396–406.

Cambridge, R. M., and Shreckengost, R. C. (1980). Are you sure? The subjective probability assessment test. Unpublished manuscript. Langley, VA.: Office of Training, Central Intelligence Agency.

Camerer, C. F., Loewenstein, G. F., and Weber, M. (1989). The curse of knowledge in economic settings: An experimental analysis. *Journal of Political Economy* 97, 1232–1254.

Chapman, L. J., and Chapman, J. P. (1967). Genesis of popular but erroneous diagnostic observations. *Journal of Abnormal Psychology* 72, 193–204.

Cox, A. D., and Summers, J. O. (1987). Heuristics and biases in the intuitive projection of retail sales. *Journal of Marketing Research* 24, 290–297.

Fischhoff, B. (1975). Hindsight = foresight: The effect of outcome knowledge on judgment under uncertainty. *Journal of Experimental Psychology: Human Perception and Performance* 1, 288–299.

Fischhoff, B., Slovic, P., and Lichtenstein, S. (1977). Knowing with certainty: The appropriateness of extreme confidence. *Journal of Experimental Psychology: Human Perception and Performance* 3, 552–564.

Gilovich, T., Vallone, R., and Tversky, A. (1985). The hot hand in basketball: On the misperception of random sequences. *Cognitive Psychology* 17, 295–314.

Hazard, T. H., and Peterson, C. R. (1973). *Odds versus probabilities for categorical events* (Technical report, 73–2). McLean, Va.: Decisions and Designs.

Hoch, S. J. (1988). Who do we know: Predicting the interests and opinions of the American consumer. *Journal of Consumer Research* 5, 315–324.

Joyce, E. J., and Biddle, G. C. (1981). Anchoring and adjustment in probabilistic inference in auditing. *Journal of Accounting Research* 19, 120–145.

Kahneman, D., and Tversky, A. (1972). Subjective probability: A judgment of representativeness. *Cognitive Psychology* 3, 430–454.

Kahneman, D., and Tversky, A. (1973). On the psychology of prediction. *Psychological Review* 80, 237–251.

Keysar, B. (1992). The illusory transparency of intention: Linguistic perspective taking in text. University of Chicago. Working paper.

Koriat, A., Lichtenstein, S., and Fischhoff, B. (1980). Reasons for confidence. *Journal of Experimental Psychology: Human Learning and Memory* 6, 107–118.

Lichtenstein, S., Fischhoff, B., and Phillips, L. D. (1982). Calibration of probabilities: State of the art to 1980. In D. Kahneman, P. Slovic, and A. Tversky (Eds.), *Judgment under uncertainty: Heuristics and biases*. New York: Cambridge University Press.

Nisbett, R. E., and Ross, L. (1980). *Human inference: Strategies and shortcomings of social judgment*. Englewood Cliffs, N.J.: Prentice Hall.

Perrow, C. (1984). *Normal accidents*. New York: Basic Books.

Slovic, P., and Fischhoff, B. (1977). On the psychology of experimental surprises. *Journal of Experimental Psychology: Human Perception and Performance* 3, 544–551.

Slovic, P., and Lichtenstein, S. (1971). Comparison of Bayesian and regression approaches in the study of information processing in judgment. *Organizational Behavior and Human Performance* 6, 649–744.

Sniezek, J. A., and Henry, R. A. (1989). Accuracy and confidence in group judgment. *Organizational Behavior and Human Decision Processes* 4(3), 1–28.

Tversky, A., and Kahneman, D. (1971). The belief in the 'law of numbers.' *Psychological Bulletin* 76, 105–110.

Tversky, A., and Kahneman, D. (1974). Judgment under uncertainty: Heuristics and biases. *Science* 185, 1124–1131.

Tversky, A., and Kahneman, D. (1983). Extensional versus intuitive reasoning: The conjunction fallacy in probability judgment. *Psychological Review* 90, 293–315.

Wason, P. C. (1960). On the failure to eliminate hypotheses in a conceptual task. *Quarterly Journal of Experimental Psychology* 12, 129–140.

Yates, J. F., and Carlson, B. W. (1986). Conjunction errors: Evidence for multiple judgment procedures, including 'signed summation' *Organizational Behavior and Human Decision Processes* 37, 230–253.

15. Understanding Behavior in Escalation Situations

Barry M. Staw/Jerry Ross

At an early stage of the Vietnam War, George Ball, then Undersecretary of State, wrote the following memo to Lyndon Johnson, warning him about the likely consequences of making further commitments of men and material:

> The decision you face now is crucial. Once large numbers of U.S. troops are committed to direct combat, they will begin to take heavy casualties in a war they are ill-equipped to fight in a non-cooperative if not downright hostile countryside. Once we suffer large casualties, we will have started a well-nigh irreversible process. Our involvement will be so great that we cannot—without national humiliation—stop short of achieving our complete objectives. Of the two possibilities I think humiliation will be more likely than the achievement of our objectives—even after we have paid terrible costs [1 July 1965,[1] p. 450].

George Ball's remarks were not only prophetic about the U.S. experience in Vietnam, they also pointed to the more general problem of coping with what are now called "escalation situations." These are situations in which losses have resulted from an original course of action, but where there is the possibility of turning the situation around by investing further time, money, or effort.

The frequency of escalation situations can be depicted by everyday examples. When an individual has a declining investment, a faltering career, or even a troubled marriage, there is often the difficult choice between putting greater effort into the present line of behavior versus seeking a new alternative. At the organizational level, similar dilemmas occur. Laboratories must make difficult decisions about whether to continue with or withdraw from disappointing research and development (R&D) projects; banks must decide how to manage their involvement in nonperforming loans; and industrial firms often need to determine whether to abandon a questionable venture versus investing further resources. In each of these situations it is frequently observed that individuals as well as organizations can become locked in to the existing course of action, throwing good money or effort after bad. This "decision pathology" has been variously labeled the escalation of commitment,[2] the psychology of entrapment,[3] the sunk cost effect,[4] and the too-much-invested-to-quit syndrome.[5] We will review the state of research on this problem and then provide a summary theoretical model along with some guidelines for future research.

CLASSES OF ESCALATION DETERMINANTS

Much of the early work on the escalation problem focused on psychological factors that lead decision-makers to engage in seemingly irrational acts—that is, behavior not explained by either objective circumstances or standard economic decision-making.[5-7] In response, some researchers have stressed that escalation does involve rational decision-making, because individuals do attend to the economic realities of escalation situations once they are made salient or clear to the person.[8] Alternatively, others have found[9] that escalation behavior can

Reprinted from "Understanding Behavior in Escalation Situations" with permission from *Science*, Vol. 246, October 1986, pp. 216–220. Copyright © 1986 American Association for the Advancement of Science.

be depicted as a rational calculus, but this requires going beyond the narrow economics of the situation to include many psychological and social costs of withdrawal, such as the personal and public embarrassment of admitting failure.

Debates over the rationality of behavior in escalation or any other situation are not likely to be settled soon. In fact, these arguments may detract attention away from the central phenomenon of interest, which is the tendency of individuals and organizations to persist in failing courses of action. To understand this tendency, one must account for a variety of forces, both behavioral and economic. We will therefore summarize research on four classes of determinants: those associated with objective characteristics of the project as well as psychological, social, and organizational variables.

PROJECT DETERMINANTS

Project variables are the most obvious determinants of persistence in a course of action. Research has shown, for example, that commitment is affected by whether a setback is judged to be due to a permanent or temporary problem,[10] by whether further investment is likely to be efficacious;[11] by how large a goal or payoff may result from continued investment;[7] by future expenditures or costs necessary to achieve a project's payoff;[12] and by the number of times previous commitments have failed to yield returns.[13]

A few project variables are less obvious causes of persistence. Endeavors such as R&D and construction projects often foster commitment because there is a long delay between expenditures and economic benefits. In these cases, shortfalls in revenue or outcomes may not be monitored closely or cause alarm, since losses are (at least initially) expected to occur. In other cases, projects may continue, in part, because they have little salvage value and involve substantial closing costs if terminated in midstream.[8] For example, the World's Fair Expo 86 reached the point late in its construction in which continuation was expected to produce large losses, but even larger losses would have

been sustained if the project had been aborted before its formal opening.[14] In a few cases, projects can become so large that they literally trap the sponsoring organization into continuing the course of action. The Long Island Lighting Company's construction of the Shoreham Nuclear Power Plant is an example of such a no-win situation, in which persistence was seen as costly, yet withdrawal was (until very recently) veiwed as bringing even worse economic consequences to the organization.[15]

PSYCHOLOGICAL DETERMINANTS

In addition to the objective properties of a project, several psychological variables can also influence persistence in losing courses of action. Probably the simplest of these determinants are information processing errors on the part of decision-makers.

Although accounting and economics texts routinely state that investments should only be made when marginal (future) revenues exceed marginal costs,[16] people may not actually behave this way. Consider the responses of college students to the following two questions posed by Arkes and Blumer:[4]

Question 3A. As the president of an airline company, you have invested 10 million dollars of the company's money into a research project. The purpose was to build a plane that would not be detected by conventional radar, in other words, a radar-blank plane. When the project is 90% completed, another firm begins marketing a plane that cannot be detected by radar. Also, it is apparent that their plane is much faster and far more economical than the plane your company is building. The question is: should you invest the last 10% of the research funds to finish your radar-blank plane? Yes, 41; No, 7.

Question 3B. As president of an airline company, you have received a suggestion from one of your employees. The suggestion is to use the last 1 million dollars of your research funds to develop a plane that would not be detected by conventional radar, in other words, a radar-blank plane. However, another firm has just begun marketing a plane that cannot be detected by radar. Also, it is apparent that their plane is much faster and far more economical than the plane your company could build. The question is: should you invest the last million dollars of your research funds to build the radar-blank plane proposed by your employee? Yes, 10; No, 50.

These data clearly indicate that sunk costs (those previously expended but not supposed to affect investment decisions) are not sunk psychologically. They continue to influence subsequent investment decisions.

Not only do escalation situations involve sunk costs in terms of money, time, and effort; they also are framed as losing situations in which new investments hold the promise of turning one's fortunes around. Unfortunately, this is exactly the context in which Kahneman and Tversky[17] and others [18] found individuals to be risk-seeking. People take more risks on investment decisions framed in a negative manner (for example, to recover losses or prevent injuries) than when the same decision is positively framed (to achieve gains).

The miscalculation of sunk costs and negative framing can be characterized as rather "cool" information processing errors, as heuristics (however faulty) called on by individuals to solve escalation problems. Escalation situations can also involve "warmer," more motivated cognitions, however. Self-justification biases[19] have been singled out as a major motivational cause of persistence.

In one of the earliest escalation experiments, Staw[6] hypothesized that people may commit more resources to a losing cause so as to justify or rationalize their previous behavior. He suggested that being personally responsible for losses is an important factor in becoming locked in to a course of action. This hypothesis was first tested in an experimental simulation with business school students. All subjects played the role of a corporate financial officer in allocating R&D funds to the operating divisions of a hypothetical company. Half the subjects allocated R&D funds to one of the divisions, were given

feedback on their decisions, and then were asked to make a second allocation of R&D funds. The other half of the subjects did not make the initial investment decision themselves, but were told that it was made by another financial officer of the firm. Feedback was manipulated so that half the subjects received positive results on their initial decisions, while half received negative results.

Data from Staw's study showed that subjects allocated significantly more money to failing than to successful divisions. It was also found that more money was invested in the chosen division when the participants, rather than another financial officer, were responsible for the earlier funding decision. These results suggest that individuals responsible for previous losses may try to justify (or save) their earlier decisions by committing additional resources to them. Also, because both high- and low-responsibility subjects faced a negative financial scenario (one with previous losses), it can be argued that justification motives may affect commitment above and beyond any sunk cost or framing effects. Several experiments have replicated this self-justification finding with similar responsibility manipulations.[20]

Closely related to the self-justification explanation of persistence are the findings of other motivated biases. Cognitive studies show that people slant data in the direction of their preexisting beliefs and discredit information that conflicts with their opinions.[21] Parallel effects in the escalation area have demonstrated that decision-makers responsible for a failing course of action tend to make greatest use of positive and exonerating information.[22] Thus, it appears that justification motives may not only affect decisions to save a risky course of action, but may also affect the accuracy of data on which such decisions are made.

In addition to efforts to justify behavior, some passive self-inference processes may also affect individuals in escalation situations. Salancik[23] and Kiesler[24] have posited that individuals are likely to become especially bound or committed to a prior behavior when (i) the individual's acts are explicit or unambiguous, (ii) the behavior is irrevocable or not easily undone, (iii) the behavior has been entered into freely or has involved a high degree of volition, (iv) the act has importance for the individual, (v) the act is public or is visible to others, and (vi) the act has been performed a number of times. These six self-inference conditions assume that individuals draw inferences about their own behavior and the context in which it occurs. Though self-inference theories are less motivational than those that use self-justification concepts (no needs for rationalization are implied), the two approaches overlap almost entirely in their empirical predictions.[25]

SOCIAL DETERMINANTS

Although most of the research on escalation has dealt with psychological or project variables, escalation situations are often more complicated social phenomena. For example, administrators may persist in a course of action, not just because they do not want to admit a mistake to themselves, but because they hesitate to expose their errors to others. Fox and Staw[26] tested this notion of external justification in a role-playing experiment. They found that subjects holding administrative roles with low job security and lack of support by management allocated the greatest resources to a losing course of action. Conceptually similar results were reported by Brockner, Rubin, and Lang.[12] They found persistence to be highest under a large audience, high social-anxiety condition and interpreted these results as a face-saving effect. Additional evidence of face-saving can also be found in the bargaining literature,[27] in which it is common to find an escalation of hostilities as both parties refuse to back down from earlier positions. For example, using Shubik's[28] dollar auction game, Tegar[5] found that competitive bidding was influenced first by a simple desire to make money, then as a way to recoup prior losses, and finally, as a means to defeat the other party.

The external binding of people to behavior may also be important in escalation situations. Just as it is possible for individuals to form personal beliefs through a self-inference process,[23,24] observers tend to infer motivation and personal characteristics to actors after observing their behavior.[29] Thus, people's social identity may become externally bound by their actions with respect to a project. Though no research has specifically tested this idea, one would expect decision-makers to be most closely identified with a project when their advocacy of it has been public, explicit, perceived to be high in volition, and repeated. At the extreme, a project may start to carry the name of its sponsor (for example, "Reaganomics" or "Thatcherism"), increasing the binding of the person to the behavior, thus making withdrawal from the course of action much more difficult.

Although face-saving and external binding can both be viewed as social factors that increase decision-makers' costs of withdrawal, research has also isolated some social rewards for persistence. Staw and Ross[30] had business students study the behavior of managers in a failing situation. Managers were described as either persisting in a losing course of action or switching to another alternative. The descriptions read by subjects also noted that managers' persistence or experimentation led either to further negative results or ultimate success. As predicted, managers were rated highest when they were persistent and successful. Most interestingly, the data also showed a significant interaction of persistence and outcome. This interaction can be interpreted as a "hero effect"—special praise and adoration for managers who "stick to their guns" in the face of opposition and seemingly bleak odds.[31]

ORGANIZATIONAL DETERMINANTS

Since many of the most costly escalation situations involve the persistence of an entire organization (rather than an isolated individual) to a losing course of action, it is important to consider some organizational determinants of persistence. Unfortunately, few organization-level studies have yet been conducted. Therefore, we are forced to rely more on relevant theory than concrete data in outlining likely organizational determinants of escalation.

Probably the simplest organizational determinant is institutional inertia. Just as there is less than full consistency between individual attitudes and behavior,[32] there is also a very loose coupling between organizational goals and action.[33] Organizations have imperfect sensory systems, making them relatively impervious to changes in their environments. And, because of breakdowns in internal communication and difficulties in mobilizing their constituents, organizations are slow to respond. Thus, even when the need for change is recognized, it may not occur. Moreover, if actions require altering long-standing policies, violating rules, or discarding accepted procedures, movement is not likely to happen at all, even though (to an outsider) it may seem obviously useful.

Organizations attempting to withdraw from a losing course of action must also contend with political forces. Not only those who are directly involved with a project will resist its dismantling, but so too will units interdependent or politically aligned with the venture. This can become a special problem when projects are important or central enough to have political support on governing bodies and budget committees charged with their fate. As Pfeffer and Salancik[34] have shown in their research on organizational decision-making, organizational actions may turn as much on politics as on any objective economic criteria.

At times, a project's support can go beyond politics. The project may be tied so integrally to the values and purposes of an organization that it becomes institutionalized,[35] making withdrawal almost an "unthinkable" proposition. Two examples illustrate the problem. The first is Lockheed's L1011 Tri-Star Jet program. Although most outside analysts found the plane unlikely to earn a profit, Lockheed persisted in the venture for more than a decade, accumulating enormous losses.[36] The issue was not ending the project, per se, but in having to reinterpret the company's role in commercial aviation. For Lockheed to drop the L1011 meant having to change its identity from a pioneer in commercial aircraft to that of simply a defense contractor. Pan American Airlines recently faced a similar institutional issue. More than most airlines, Pan Am suffered major losses after deregulation of the industry. However, as losses accumulated, it successively sold off most of its nonairlines assets. First, the Pan Am building was sold to meet debt obligations. Then, as losses continued to mount, the Intercontinental Hotel chain was sold. Finally, Pan Am was forced to sell its valuable Pacific routes to United Airlines. Withdrawing from the real estate and hotel business was probably an easier decision for this organization than ending the more institutionalized airline operations, irrespective of the economics involved.

THE DYNAMICS OF ESCALATION

This review of escalation research has been more illustrative than exhaustive. Yet, it is evident from even this brief summary that studies of escalation behavior have focused primarily on psychological determinants, with social and organizational variables only recently receiving attention. Unfortunately, this difference in research emphasis has had less to do with the relevance of particular determinants of escalation than with the difficulty of operationalizing concepts and conducting empirical studies at more macroscopic levels. Because many of the most disastrous escalation situations involve larger social entities such as governmental and business organizations, further macro-level studies of escalation are therefore needed.

As we have noted, escalation situations are also a forum for a variety of forces, both behavioral and economic. Consequently, an important question for future research is how these various forces combine to affect behavior in escalation contexts. Already some research suggests that escalation behavior may not only be multi-determined, but also temporally dependent. That is, escalation situations may change character over time, such that different determinants of persistence and withdrawal become dominant at separate stages in an escalation cycle. A preliminary model of how the influence of several key variables may unfold over time, based on two field studies of naturally occurring escalation situations,[14,15] is shown in Figure 15.1.

The first phase of escalation is dominated by the economics of a project, with the decision to begin a course of action made largely on the basis of the anticipation of economic benefits. However, when questionable or negative results are received (at Phase 2), the decision to persist is based not just on project economics, but also on psychological and social determinants. Assuming that psychological and social forces are strong enough to outweigh (or bias) any negative economic forecasts, further investment or persistence in the project is likely. If this additional investment does not turn the situation around and further negative results are received (at Stage 3), withdrawal tendencies may be heightened. Unfortunately, at this

advanced stage in the escalation cycle any withdrawal tendencies (due to negative project economics) may be counterbalanced and biased by organizational forces for persistence. Thus, as economic outcomes worsen over time, it is possible for projects to be maintained by the accumulation of psychological, social, and organizational forces, each adding some weight to the decision to persist in a course of action.

At this time, the idea of distinct stages of escalation remains more of a heuristic for understanding the process of persistence than an empirically tested theory. Yet, two in-depth field studies—an analysis of British Columbia's decision to hold Expo 86[14] and an examination of Long Island Lighting's commitment to the Shoreham nuclear power plant[15]—have provided support for a temporally based model. In each situation, economic variables were salient early on and psychological and social variables became important after negative consequences started to accumulate, whereas organizational

FIGURE 15.1
A Three-Stage Model of the Escalation Process. The +, –, and 0 Show Positive, Negative, and Neutral Influences, Respectively

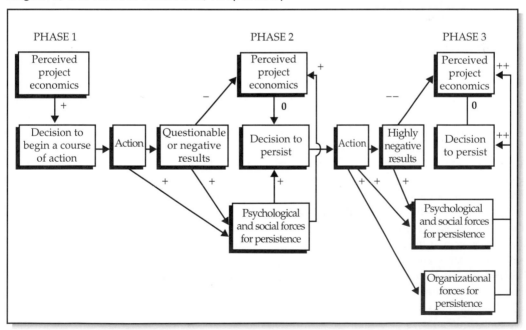

determinants were manifested rather late in the escalation cycle. Of course, whether these time dependencies are always abrupt enough to constitute distinct stages, or whether in other contexts a more gradual shifting of influence occurs, is still an open question.

No doubt an important step in validating a temporal model of escalation will be the isolation of critical incidents setting off or preconditioning particular determinants of persistence. If these preconditions are found to follow a predictable sequence (that is, arising early or late in the escalation cycle) across a variety of contexts, then a strong case can be made for a temporal model.

In searching for the preconditions of escalation, we would argue that escalation situations typically involve the following sequence of events. First, in launching a new product or project, individual "project champions" will not only work hard to promote the venture but in so doing will probably sow the seeds for subsequent commitment (for example, via self-inference effects). Once questionable or adverse results are received, a negative perceptual frame and sunk costs may then become associated with the project. At this time, those who have had an active hand in developing the project will likely suffer personal embarrassment (or even loss of employment) with the failing situation, leading to self-justification and face-saving effects. And, once the losses associated with the project are fully recognized throughout the organization, external binding of the proponents to the project (for example, "that's Jim's baby") is likely to make withdrawal even more costly to the individuals involved. Finally, assuming that the project does survive several rounds of negative feedback, then more global, organizational processes may start to manifest themselves. Political support may arise as individual careers and whole departments become dependent on the project. And, if the project lasts long enough, withdrawal can become extremely costly not only in terms of the economics involved, but also in terms of the identity of the firm itself.

As elaborated here, the sequence of critical incidents in escalation situations may tend to move from the individual, to the interpersonal environment, and then to the larger organization. We believe this is a natural evolution as project originators (or champions) try to defend a losing course of action, first by themselves (via risk-taking and information biasing) and then by the mobilization of resources involving the larger organization. Additional research on the development of escalation situations is obviously needed to verify these temporal dynamics.

ESCALATION AS A MULTIDETERMINED EVENT

Since several sources of commitment can be triggered by losing courses of action, one might conclude that persistence is an overdetermined variable, an almost inevitable consequence of escalation situations. A contrary view is that escalation is created by a series of small-impact variables, each insufficient by itself to cause one to remain in a losing situation. For example, if economic losses are large and they occur early in a project's life cycle, withdrawal may well be the dominant response. However, if losses do not appear until later in the process (after several behavior effects have been initiated), then persistence could be the typical response. Thus, the speed and severity of negative economic data could be a crucial element in how relative forces unfold in escalation situations. Though not an explicit test of this hypothesis, an experiment by Golz[37] has shown how sensitive investment decisions are to the pattern of negative consequences. A slow and irregular decline may not only make a line of behavior difficult to extinguish (in the reinforcement theory sense), but may also allow the forces for persistence to grow over time. Adding support to this "unfolding argument" is a study by Brockner and Rubin,[3] in which they found that negative economic data prompted withdrawal when it was introduced early in an escalation situation, but had little influence when introduced after the decision to commit resources had already been made.

CONCLUSION

As shown by our temporal model, escalation situations contain a confluence of forces—some pulling toward withdrawal and others pushing toward persistence—with their relative strengths varying over time. This dynamic view of escalation is consistent with the contextualist perspective[38] in which social reality is seen as dependent on the situation in which it occurs. Contextualist reasoning supports the continued pursuit of case studies on the dynamics of escalation situations and supports efforts to add realism to experimental tests. Greater efforts are needed to capture experimentally the life-span of escalation episodes so that the relative influence of contributing variables can be tracked over time. Only with such temporally based studies, from both the laboratory and the field, are the dynamics of escalation situations likely to be fully understood.

REFERENCES AND NOTES

1. The New York Times (based on the investigative reporting of Neil Sheehan), *The Pentagon Papers* (Bantam Books, New York, 1971).
2. B. M. Staw, *Acad. Manage. Rev. 6*, **577** (1981).
3. J. Brockner and J. Z. Rubin, *Entrapment in Escalating Conflicts* (Springer-Verlag, New York, 1985).
4. H. R. Arkes and C. Blumer, *Organ. Behav. Hum. Decis. Processes* **35**, 124 (1985).
5. A. Tegar, *Too Much Invested to Quit* (Pergamon Press, New York, 1980).
6. For example, B. M. Staw, *Organ. Behav. Hum. Performance* **16**, 27 (1976).
7. J. Z. Rubin and J. Brockner, *J. Pers. Soc. Psychol.* **31**, 1054 (1975).
8. For example, G. B. Northcraft and G. Wolf, *Acad. Manage. Rev.* **9**, 225 (1984).
9. B. M. Staw and J. Ross, in *Research in Organizational Behavior*, L. L. Cummings and B. M. Staw, Eds. (JAI Press, Greenwich, CT, 1987), Vol. 9, pp. 39–78.
10. L. Leatherwood and E. Conlon, "The impact of prospectively relevant information and setbacks in persistence in a project following setback" (working paper 85-1, College of Business Administration, University of Iowa, 1985).
11. B. M. Staw and F. V. Fox, *Hum. Relat.* **30**, 431 (1977); T. Bateman, "Resource allocation after success and failure: The roles of attributions of powerful others and probabilities of future success" (Department of Management, Texas A&M, College Station, TX 91983).
12. J. Brockner, J. Z. Rubin, E. Lang, *J. Exp. Soc. Psychol.* **17**, 68 (1981).
13. B. E. McCain, *J. Appl. Psychol.* **71**, 280 (1986).
14. J. Ross and B. Staw, *Adm. Sci. Q.* **31**, 224 (1986).
15. _____, "Escalation and the Long Island Lighting Company: The case of the Shoreham Nuclear Power Plant" (Working paper, Institute Européen d'Administration des Affaires, Fontainebleau, France, 1989).
16. P. A. Samuelson, *Economics* (McGraw-Hill, New York, 1988); C. T. Horngren, *Cost Accounting: A Managerial Emphasis* (Prentice Hall, Englewood Cliffs, NJ, 1982).
17. D. Kahneman and A. Tversky, *Econometrica* **47**, 263 (1979); D. Kahneman and A. Tversky, *Science* **211**, 453 (1981).
18. M. A. Davis and P. Bobko, *Organ. Behav. Hum. Decis. Processes* **37**, 121 (1986).
19. E. Aronson, *The Social Animal* (Freeman, San Francisco, 1984); L. Festinger, *Theory of Cognitive Dissonance* (Stanford Univ. Press, Stanford, CA, 1970).
20. M. H. Bazerman, R. I. Beekum, F. D. Schoorman, *J. Appl. Psychol.* **67**, 873 (1982); M. H. Bazerman *et al., Organ. Behav. Hum. Performance* **33**, 141 (1984); D. F. Caldwell and C. A. O'Reilly, *Acad. Manage. J.* **25**, 121 (1982).
21. T. Gilovich, *J. Pers. Soc. Psychol.* **44**, 1110 (1983); C. Lord, L. Ross, M. R. Lepper, *ibid.* **37**, 2098 (1979).
22. E. J. Conlon and J. M. Parks, *J. Appl. Psychol.* **72**, 344 (1987).

23. G. R. Salancik, in *New Directions in Organizational Behavior,* B. M. Staw and G. R. Salancik, Eds. (Krieger, Malabar, FL, 1977).

24. C. A. Kiesler, *The Psychology of Commitment* (Academic Press, New York, 1971).

25. P. E. Tetlock and A. Levi, *J. Exp. Soc. Psychol.* **18,** 68 (1982).

26. F. V. Fox and B. M. Staw, *Adm. Sci. Q.* **24,** 449 (1979).

27. H. Raiffa, *The Art and Science of Negotiation* (Harvard Univ. Press, Cambridge, MA, 1982).

28. M. Shubik, *J. Conflict Resolut.* **15,** 109 (1971).

29. E. E. Jones and K. E. Davis, in *Advances in Experimental Social Psychology,* L. Berkowitz, Ed. (Academic Press, New York, 1965), Vol. 2.

30. B. M. Staw and J. Ross, *J. Appl. Psychol.* **65,** 249 (1980).

31. M. G. Evans and J. W. Medcof, *Can. J. Adm. Sci.* **1,** 383 (1984).

32. M. P. Zanna and R. H. Fazio, in *Consistency in Social Behavior,* M. P. Zanna, E. T. Higgins, C. P. Herman, Eds. (Erlbaum, Hillsdale, NJ, 1982).

33. J. G. March and J. P. Olson, *Ambiguity and Choice in Organizations* (Universitetsforlaget, Bergen, Norway, 1976).

34. J. Pfeffer and G. R. Salancik, *Adm. Sci. Q.* **19,** 135 (1974); G. R. Salancik and J. Pfeffer, *ibid.,* p. 453.

35. P. S. Goodman, M. Bazerman, E. Conlon, in *Research in Organizational Behavior,* B. M. Staw and L. L. Cummings, Eds. (JAI Press, Greenwich, CT, 1980), Vol. 2, pp. 215–246; L. G. Zucker in *Research in the Sociology of Organizations,* S. Bacharach, Ed. (JAI Press, Greenwich, CT, 1983).

36. U. E. Reinhardt, *J. Finance* **28,** 821 (1973).

37. S. M. Golz, "A learning-based analysis of escalation of commitment, sunk cost, and entrapment," paper presented at American Psychological Association meeting, Atlanta, GA, August 1988.

38. W. J. McGuire, in *Advances in Experimental Social Psychology,* L. Berkowitz, Ed. (Academic Press, New York, 1984).

39. Supported by the Institute of Industrial Relations, University of California, Berkeley.

16. Napoleon's Tragic March Home from Moscow: Lessons in Hubris

Mark J. Kroll/Leslie A. Toombs/Peter Wright

> *Napoleon, supreme egoist that he was, ignored the significance of the omens until he and his host were completely and irrevocably committed to an undertaking that was doomed. Never did the gods punish hubris more severely.*
>
> —M. de Fezensac
> *The Russian Campaign, 1812*[1]

In June of 1812, Napoleon Bonaparte was ruler of the Empire of France, King of Italy, and master of the European continent. At the head of The Grand Army, numbering over 500,000 men, the largest force ever assembled at that point in history, he set out to conquer the one nation in Europe he had not yet subjugated—Imperial Russia. In December of the same year, less than 20,000 of those men would make it home alive, and as a practical matter, all that Emperor Napoleon had accomplished in his meteoric career would soon be lost. The tragedy of the Russian campaign, the loss of life, and the horrible suffering of those on the march back from Moscow have been a source of fascination for historians ever since. Explanations for the disaster include poor planning, unusually bad weather, insightful leadership on the opposing side, and plain bad luck. But, as indicated by our epigraph, almost all accounts of the campaign include a recognition of the role played by hubris.[2]

Hubris has been defined as exaggerated pride, self-confidence, or arrogance, frequently resulting in retribution.[3] Hubris may be blamed for the resounding failure of Napoleon's campaign because Napoleon possessed all its symptoms: unbounded confidence given his past successes and the accompanying narcissism, the adulation that fed that narcissism, and his callous indifference toward the rules that governed 19th century geopolitics.

As a result, Napoleon was able to convince himself that, despite all of the obvious obstacles, he could, through forces of will, succeed in bringing Russia and especially Emperor Alexander I, the sole power on the Continent that refused to pay him homage, to their knees. His campaign was much less about the need to thwart the hostile intentions of a rival power, and more about the need to satisfy a hubris-infected personality with an arrogant confidence about what great feats could be accomplished.

One frequently cited explanation for hubris is that leaders often hunger for reassurance and applause from others. This hunger may first arise when a child's narcissistic displays are fondly received by parents.[4] As such leaders grow and become a part of groups or organizations, however, they may seek the same adulation from organization members in response to their displays of skill. Those who excel in select skills may receive positive feedback from others as they produce beneficial results. Napoleon clearly excelled in the skills of warfare, as he planned and implemented winning campaigns.

Before the Russian attack, Napoleon had amassed a record of 35 wins versus only 3 losses. The losses were either early in his career, and then forgotten, or were only very temporary setbacks from which he quickly recovered. Through these warfare experiences, he developed a distinctive approach to command, along with considerable confidence in that approach. By the time of the Russian Campaign, however, this confidence had turned into arrogance and a sense of invincibility. Worse, given his record, he appears to have believed that unique problems of a war with Russia were minor details that the force of will could surmount.

In the contemporary corporate arena, actions such as takeovers, corporate expansion programs, and blatant disregard of the rules of the game may reflect the presence of hubris. These actions sometimes suggest that the firm's management believes that the world, and the major forces in it, including financial markets, government regulators, and competitors, are wrong, and that they are right, and are not governed by the same forces. As with Napoleon's Grand Army, corporate hubris is often punished severely. We will take a look at three circumstances in which hubris may set businesses and their leaders down a perilous path—corporate acquisitions, unbridled growth for its own sake, and disregard for the rules. Parallels are drawn with Napoleon's circumstances.

CORPORATE ACQUISITIONS

Well before the invasion of Russia, Napoleon's top lieutenants argued that the chances of failure, and the cost in lives and material were high. Napoleon rejected their warnings, pointing out that his plans called for a quick, decisive, and therefore low-cost campaign. He had conducted such campaigns before, and saw no difference this time.[5] Richard Roll has suggested that all too frequently takeover attempts results from an executive's belief that he or she can greatly improve the target firm's efficiency. The executive rejects feedback from others and, in particular, the wisdom of the financial markets,[6] even

though it is generally recognized that the securities markets provide accurate feedback by doing a fairly effective job of valuing publicly-traded firms.[7] The premiums executives sometimes pay over target firms' prevailing market prices often reflect a Napoleonic logic: "I will be able to overcome all the obstacles and make the acquired business far more successful than its incumbent management; I can turn a profit on the deal in spite of the high prices I am paying."

However, compelling research evidence shows that corporate acquisitions driven by managerial hubris are often financially harmful for the shareholders of acquiring firms.[8] It also appears that as the level of managerial hubris rises, so does the likelihood that a firm will grossly overpay for an acquisition.[9] Compounding the problem of overpayment is the possibility that managerial hubris will undermine the process of integrating the acquired and acquiring firms. There is the very real threat that the acquiring firm's management, imbued with a sense of conquest, will treat the acquired firm's management and employees as conquered supplicants. This is especially likely if the acquiring firm is perceived as having a better track record than the acquired firm.[10] The inevitable results are a failure to achieve potential synergies and a loss of talent from the acquired firm. Both outcomes will exacerbate the initial overpayment problem.

An example of potential corporate hubris in an acquisition is the buyout of WordPerfect by Novell in March 1994. Novell's CEO, Raymond Noorda, offered $1.4 billion for WordPerfect, in what industry observers suggested was an attempt to build a software empire comparable to Microsoft's. Following the acquisition, Novell reportedly ran roughshod over WordPerfect's management and culture, leading to a hemorrhage of managerial and technical talent and a significant deterioration in the performance of WordPerfect. In early 1996, Novell was forced to sell WordPerfect for about $124 million, or less than 10 percent of what it paid for the firm in 1994.[11]

UNBRIDLED GROWTH FOR ITS OWN SAKE

Hubris can also manifest itself in a drive to dominate others and engage in empire building for its own sake. Napoleon's determination to invade Russia was driven not only by a desire to take over that country, but also by a burning ambition to dominate Czar Alexander. The Czar was the only European monarch Napoleon had not subjugated, and by doing so Napoleon would have become the sole master of Europe. The same need for domination and empire building may surface in the corporate world. It is generally recognized that individual executives infected with hubris have narcissistic requirements that demand they control fiefdoms of such large scale as to justify their own importance.[12] An executive infected with hubris will likely see growth as a means of building a bureaucracy of sufficient size to reflect his or her prominence. For instance, the rise and fall of the Saatchi & Saatchi advertising empire in the 1990s reflected the ambition of a pair of brothers who no longer concerned themselves with building a profitable advertising business.[13] Instead, they aspired for dominance by building an advertising empire that was the very biggest, only to be forced out of the business they had built. Similarly, Barclay's Bank under CEO Sir John Quinton went on a quest to become Britain's largest bank in the early 1990s. This attempt also failed and Sir John was forced to abdicate.[14]

BLATANT DISREGARD OF THE RULES

Napoleon rose to power during the French Revolution, having been an officer in the army of the First Republic.[15] After establishing a winning record at the head of the Grand Army, he decided that he merited the title of first council or dictator, and later named himself emperor. These blatant power grabs were undertaken in spite of his earlier pledges of fidelity to the republic and its democratic ideals. He evidently concluded that obligations to the French people and living up to oaths were for others to fulfill.[16]

Managers afflicted with hubris can also create a climate in which they and the organizations they govern do not play by the same rules as everyone else.[17] For example, observers have remarked on the indifference of the managers of Archer Daniels Midland Company to the laws they broke and how the long-time CEO, Dwayne O. Andreas, allowed an anything-goes culture to develop.[18] Such hubris-prone personalities are likely to perceive themselves as having made great sacrifices and contributions that entitle them to special dispensation.[19]

SOURCES OF HUBRIS

As illustrated in Figure 16.1, hubris has four sources: a personality prone to narcissism; a string of successes that feed the narcissism; blindly believing the accolades of others, particularly the media; and a history of getting away with breaking the rules. All these conditions can lead executives to believe that they are above the rules.[20]

Narcissism

Hubris derives from an overbearing sense of grandiosity, need for admiration, and self-absorption—in a word, narcissism. Narcissism is commonly found in many successful people, and it often compels them to seek leadership positions, with their accompanying power, status, and self-affirmation.[21] However, narcissism can drive executives to use their leadership roles to create a reality that further reinforces their narcissism.[22] Even very charismatic leaders may use their leadership talents to gain position and status in order to satisfy their narcissism at the expense of others.[23] In *War and Peace*, Tolstoy comments on Napoleon's narcissism: "He alone—with his ideal of glory and grandeur developed in Italy and Egypt, his insane self-adulation, could justify what had to be done."[24]

A number of business analysts have attributed Quaker Oats's disastrous acquisitions of Snapple Beverages in part to the hubris of Quaker's management. Quaker's then CEO, William Smithburg, had made some very successful moves earlier in his tenure, often

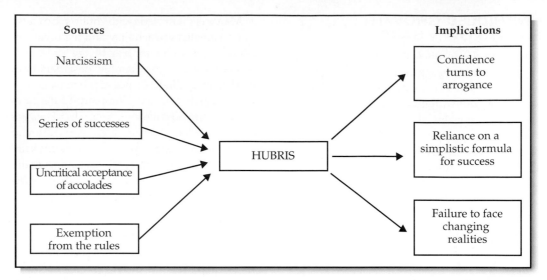

FIGURE 16.1
Sources and Implications of Hubris

proving the pundits wrong. The company's Gatorade purchase won Smithburg praise in the business press. Observers believe he saw in Snapple an opportunity to surpass past triumphs and establish Quaker as a force to be reckoned with in the beverage industry. In spite of the consensus view of Wall Street analysts that Quaker was paying at least double what Snapple was worth, Quaker paid $1.7 billion for the firm. Even worse, perhaps owing to their extreme confidence in their ability to turn things around, Quaker's management went ahead with the purchase in spite of strong indications that Snapple was in the process of imploding. On the day the deal was announced, Quaker's stock dropped $7.38, or over 10 percent.[25]

It is possible that the need to create a reality that fits an executive's narcissistic vision, even though it materially departs from actual facts, may often lead to organizational underperformance. Narcissism may be reinforced by subordinates who, having little sense of control over the world around them, look to and idolize a leader they believe can deal with the helplessness they feel.[26] The leader's apparent confidence and pride fulfill the needs of followers for someone to bring order and stability to their lives.[27] They in turn feed the leader's narcissism,

which transforms his or her self-confidence into arrogance.[28] Napoleon arrived on the French political stage in the midst of the confusion of post-revolutionary France. The population, exhausted by 10 years of violence and uncertainty, undoubtedly saw in Bonaparte the firm hand that could at last take the helm. Napoleon fed on that need. Having taken great pains to rid themselves of a royal monarchy in 1789, many French people embraced Napoleon as another type of monarch, consul for life, further contributing to his narcissism and hubris.

Series of Successes

Narcissism and hubris feed on further successes. As an executive accumulates a record of accomplishment, his or her susceptibility to hubris tends to grow.[29] Indeed, a consistent theme that runs through the various accounts of Napoleon's career is the inclination for his narcissism and hubris to grow with each successful campaign.[30] Following his successes in Italy, for instance, he remarked to one of his officers:

They haven't seen anything yet, and the future holds successes for us far beyond what we have so far accomplished. Fortune is a woman, and the more she does for me, the more I will demand from her. In our day no one has con-

ceived anything great; it is for me to give an example.[31]

In the context of contemporary business, the relationship between hubris and prior success and subsequent egoism makes particular sense when one recognizes that the executives of most organizations take disproportionate credit for high firm performance.[32] The valuable stock options and the lofty salaries American executives receive (mean executive total compensation in 1998 for the top 800 chief executives in the U.S. was $6.5 million) tend to reinforce the credit executives take for corporate performance.[33] Napoleon similarly took full credit for all the victories of the Grand Army. When Napoleon set off for Moscow at the head of an army of half a million soldiers, he had compiled an extraordinary win–loss record. In one 16-month period, beginning in November 1805, he had won the battles of Ulm, Austerlitz, Auerstadt, Eylau, and Freidland against the Austrians, Russians, and Prussians, making him the toast of Paris. This inclination on the part of most leaders to attribute successes primarily to their own actions[34] may be a natural one. Leaders may visualize how their own behavior brought about success and they may see a clear and linear connection between the two. If they had not initiated certain actions, accordingly, the desirable outcomes attained would probably not have occurred.

Uncritical Acceptance of Accolades

The third source of hubris is a natural outgrowth of the first—leaders come to believe the exaggerated accolades they receive from others. Praise from others, particularly the press, is likely to intensify hubris because it confirms and legitimizes an executive's narcissism and reinforces the executive's own feelings of grandiosity. As his or her fame spreads, especially in the media, the executive's hubris is in effect ratified.[35] Napoleon was widely heralded as a military genius of the first order. If he did not think of himself as the master of Europe early in his career, the newspapers of the day certainly helped him perpetuate this image.

For instance, the *Journal de Paris* reported in 1807 that "He [Napoleon] was invincible, grateful to God, forceful, modest, clever, magnanimous . . . and he combined the qualities of all the great men of history."[36]

Contemporary leaders may become more susceptible to hubris as the press increasingly focuses on them. The press, however, may not present a balanced view of leaders.[37] An excellent example of someone who recognized the extremes in which the press can portray individuals is James Carville, a key strategist in President Clinton's 1992 campaign. Shortly after the 1992 election, Carville was heralded as a political strategy genius. He acknowledged the accolades, but also pointed out that he had managed failing campaigns, and had received a heavy dose of criticism in the press. He said he knew he was not as good as the press made him out to be following Clinton's election, just as he knew he was not as bad as the press had portrayed him in his defeats.[38]

Exemption from the Rules

Finally, those possessed by hubris tend to be part of a group that Freud referred to as "the exceptions" to the rules, people with a history of breaking the rules, inflicting sacrifice on others, and getting away with it.[39] Narcissistic personalities are predisposed to break the rules because they tend to possess a sense of independence from the norms that govern others. This sense of independence from norms not only may be accompanied by a willingness to exploit others, but also to lack of empathy for them.[40]

Napoleon's behavior dramatically illustrates these inclinations. He consistently broke all of the 18th century rules limiting the scope of destructiveness of warfare. He encouraged his troops to loot the countries through which they passed rather than rely on provisions from France. During the 1796 Italian campaign, he invaded the neutral Duchy of Parma in order to escape a trap laid by the Austrians. Having overrun the Duchy for convenience, he also took hostage the governor of the capital city of Piacenze to make it easier to loot the city.[41] Following the Russian campaign, with loss of life in the hundreds of thousands, he issued his famous *29th Bulletin,* blaming the massive losses on the weather, but adding that "His Majesty's health has never been better."[42] On returning to Paris, Napoleon ordered lavish receptions and balls. An officer who attended one gala later commented: "I felt I was dancing on tombs."[43]

Breaking the rules has its counterpart in contemporary business. For instance, in August 1991, Salomon Brothers, a major bond trading house, admitted to a host of Treasury Department rule violations. These revelations caused the Treasury Department to suspend the firm's trading privileges and forced the resignation of the top three officers. From the accounts of both insiders and outsiders familiar with the firm, the violations were a direct result of what acting Salomon chairman Warren Buffett referred to as the firm's "macho and cavalier culture." Salomon's bond traders regularly flouted Treasury Department regulations designed specifically to rein in Salomon's excesses. Salomon's traders simply did not agree with the rules. This cultural deficiency appears to have been tolerated by Salomon's former CEO, John Gutfreund, who once told the *Economist* he was out for "the money, the power and the glory."[44]

Implications of Hubris

When senior managers succumb to hubris, they are likely to engage in behavior that reflects that hubris—confidence to the point of arrogance, relying on simplistic formulas for success, and failing to face changing realities.[45] All of these can be very costly to the firm in various ways.

Confidence Turns to Arrogance

Individuals possessed with hubris have an overbearing confidence in their abilities to make events conform to their will in spite of contrary external evidence. They believe that whatever external problems might arise will be easily and willfully overcome.[46] For example, Napoleon was advised by several of his senior officers that an attack on Russia was foolhardy. In fact, Napoleon's close friend and one-time ambassador to the Russian Court, General Armand

Louis de Caulaincourt, recounted to Napoleon Czar Alexander's explanation of how Russia would defeat him:

> *It will not be a one day war. Your [Emperor] will be obliged to return to Paris to manage his affairs [after a long absence], and every advantage will be with the Russians. Then the winter, the cruel climate, and most important of all, my determination and avowed intention to prolong the struggle, and not, like so many monarchs, have the weakness to sign a peace treaty in my own capital. All these will take their toll.[47]*

To this prophetic report, Napoleon responded with complete indifference, dismissing Czar Alexander's observations with the comment, "One good battle will knock the bottoms out of my friend Alexander's fine resolutions. He is fickle and feeble."[48]

This pattern of behavior is also evident in modern corporate takeovers. As mentioned earlier, the acquisition of Snapple by Quaker Oats appears to have been largely the result of management's assumption that it possessed unique talents that could breathe new life into Snapple. This high level of confidence appears to have been so strong that even a rapidly deteriorating situation at Snapple and an exorbitant price tag could not disuade the Quaker Oats managers. The net result was Quaker's later having to divest Snapple and write off a $1.4 billion loss.[49]

Relying on a Simplistic Formula for Success

Another ramification of hubris is the tendency for leaders to develop what they perceive as their own unique and ingenious formulas for success. Such formulas, having served well in the past, are reapplied in many situations. In effect, leaders may reduce their strategy formulation and implementation to predictable action plans.[50] Napoleon's Russian campaign clearly reflected a reliance on what had worked well in the past, to the point that former innovations became standard operating procedure. This predictability served the Russians well, as General Michael Barclay de Tolly and Major General

Prince Golenishchev-Kutuzov both consistently refused to play by Napoleon's established rules of warfare.

In an attempt to repeat past successes, Napoleon had sought to quickly engage the Russians early in the campaign in order to divide and destroy their army with overwhelming, decisive force. Quick and decisive engagements had worked well for Napoleon in Austria, Italy, and Prussia. Knowing this, both Russian commanders, and especially Kutuzov, baited the enemy with rear-guard attacks, followed by further retreats into Russia. These compelled Napoleon to follow the Russians, in the hope that perhaps at the next major city the sought-after engagement would occur. These pursuits progressively stretched his lines of supply and communication thinner.

Reliance on a simple formula has its counterpart in the world of business. A famous example is the strategy of General Motors in the 1970s. Company executives were committed to their big car, rear-wheel-drive formula for success despite the industry's changing around them. Well into the 1970s, and even after several oil shocks, GM's managers still clung to the belief that the land yacht products of the 1950s and 1960s would again prevail.[51] The commitment to this formula resulted in GM's market share dropping from 49 percent to 28 percent over two decades.[52]

Failure to Face Changing Realities

Another ramification of hubris is the tendency to create a simplified scanning process, selectively screening for external environmental cues that were previously relevant in implementing a time-tested formula for success. This screening process tends to exclude those environmental factors that have previously not been critical to implementing the formula for success. One of Napoleon's previous experiences has been that local populations often viewed him as a liberator. This reaction allowed him to provision his army and avoid attacks by partisans. Because Russia was a feudal society, he anticipated the same reaction from local peasants. Instead, he

was subject to incessant attacks by roving bands of Cossack partisans.

Senior executives of General Motors similarly exercised an external scanning process so simple that they did not even consider it necessary to establish a consumer market research department until 1985.[53] In fact, GM's competitive analysis in the early 1970s consisted largely of assessing the threats that its own Pontiac and Buick divisions posed for each other. Rarely did the analysis scrutinize the threats posed by Ford and Chrysler, much less by the Japanese auto makers.[54]

Given the obvious dangers hubris represents to a successful firm's future success, we will look at remedies both for the individual executive and the board of directors.

WHAT EXECUTIVES CAN DO TO GUARD AGAINST HUBRIS

A sincere self-examination of an executive's leadership behaviors may be the best place to start. Asking questions such as, "Am I willing to take the counsel of others when those ideas are counter to my own views of circumstances?" and "What do I need to do to improve my abilities to help the organization move forward?" will be helpful in this self-examination process.

Reflect on One's Own Performance

Managers sometimes exhibit the natural human tendency to attribute successes to their own actions, while blaming failures on external forces.[55] Those managers who have the capacity to recognize their own culpability in poor firm performance, however, tend to be more successful in the long-term.[56] Thus, to combat the tendency to blame externalities, managers need to confront their own failures. For instance, Daimler-Benz was an organization that by the 1980s had experienced enough success to infuse its managers with hubris. By the 1990s, according to industry observers, the firm had fallen victim to its managers' arrogance, as demonstrated by its deteriorating performance. Jürgen Schrempp had presided over the unbridled growth of

Daimler's aerospace division before becoming the CEO. However, Schrempp was reflective enough to realize that the decline in Daimler-Benz's fortunes was due as much to internal problems as to the downturn in Europe's economy. Schrempp began reinventing Daimler-Benz, including taking such personally painful steps as owning up to his failure with the aerospace division and his allowing it to go into bankruptcy. The result was a 45-percent appreciation in Daimler's share price over a 12-month period.[57]

Listen to Naysayers

Executives exhibiting hubris tend to fall into the trap of listening only to people whose opinions are compatible with their own. Indeed, such executives tend to build teams with members whose conception of the desirable closely resembles their own. Such behavior tends to promote "groupthink" that normally leads to inferior alternatives and decision making.[58] Alternatively, such managers may surround themselves with sycophants who echo what they believe the leader likes to hear, even if they inherently consider the leader's choices to be flawed. In 16th century Italy, Machiavelli observed: "Courts are always full of flatterers; men take such pleasure in their own concerns, and are so easily deceived, that this plague of flattery is hard to escape."[59]

To combat the limitations of groupthink and sycophants, senior executives need to make sure that their team is composed of members with diverse backgrounds as well as functional areas. Just as important, the members chosen must have the integrity and courage to argue for alternatives that may differ from those preferred by the senior executives. In fact, superior alternatives and strategizing are often the outcomes of groups whose members have dissimilar opinions and who are allowed to openly discuss their views without retribution.[60] Senior executives, however, must not only allow but also should encourage open discussions. Otherwise, even people of integrity and courage may be thwarted from fully contributing to discussions. Unfortunately, leaders often discourage open discourse. Napoleon's first wife,

Josephine, for example, recorded in her memoirs: ". . . in his presence, no one had the right to hazard the slightest [contrary] observation."[61]

Appoint an Alter Ego

Senior executives may also benefit from an alter ego who can tell them when they are wrong.[62] This is especially important in organizations where personnel are inclined to normally go along with the leader. The person who plays the role of alter ego should also serve as a mediator and a sounding board. Preferably, such a person should be nonthreatening to the senior executive, having developed a relationship of mutual trust. This alter ego must be respected by the top leader and not criticized for expressing different opinions.

Not only Napoleon's confidant Caulaincourt, but most of his lieutenants, offered a host of reasons why Napoleon should not invade Russia. Napoleon invariably accused them of being timid, weak, and incapable of seeing what could be accomplished. However, following Napoleon's departure from Russia, Caulaincourt found him far more willing to listen to what he had to say about the Russian campaign. Caulaincourt was in fact amazed by how frankly he could talk to the Emperor compared with the period before the campaign. Unfortunately, this willingness to listen came only after an estimated 570,000 casualties.[63]

Model Behavior That is in the Organization's Best Interest

Senior managers serve as role models for others employed by the company. Consequently, they should display behavior that contributes to firm performance. Herb Kelleher, CEO of Southwest Airlines, is a maverick who, by example, has created a culture in which employees can do things differently. In 1971, Southwest had three planes serving three Texas cities. Today the company has over 240 aircraft serving 50 cities. This growth is largely the result of Kelleher's leadership style, which values creativity and efficiency. As Kelleher puts it: "We've always [encouraged that] work be done differently. You know, we don't assign seats. Used to be we only had about four people on the whole plane, so the idea of assigned seats just made people laugh. Now the reason is you can turn airplanes quicker at the gate. And if you can turn an airplane quicker, you can have it fly more routes each day. That generates more revenue, so you can offer lower fares."[64]

WHAT CAN BOARD MEMBERS DO TO CONTROL HUBRIS?

Monitor Executives for Signs of Hubris

We are hearing increasing calls for boards of directors, and especially outside board members, to take on a greater monitoring role in confronting the potential hubris of senior executives.[65] The departure of Ronald Allen as CEO of Delta Airlines resulted when outside board members took such action. Allen had led Delta through a series of acquisitions and painful cost-cutting programs that made him look decisive but were costly to employees and customers. Allen had plans to buy Continental Airlines and to continue cost cutting. However, the board became disheartened by declining employee morale, which was detracting from customer service. The board also saw a need for Delta to revert to its strategy of disciplined internal growth rather than acquisitions. Allen was replaced by Leo Mullin, who promised that customers and employees would not take a back seat to the company's stockholders.[66]

Promote a Heterogeneous Corporate Culture

Boards should ensure that views that run counter to conventional wisdom are tolerated or encouraged, and should promote the use of a more decentralized organizational structure.[67] Board members may also recommend that corporate codes of ethics and values be developed. Such codes should emphasize that firm decisions will promote the benefits of all stakeholders.

Develop a Strong Organizational Knowledge Base

As the world's economy continues to prove both turbulent and extremely competitive, the information needs of firms will continue to change rapidly. Prevailing systems have done well in gathering information within organizations.[68] But if internal reports are positive, managers may be prone to staying with simplistic formulas for success even if external conditions are changing, threatening the viability of the firm.

A CALL TO ACTION

In ancient Greece, hubris was considered a crime under Athenian law, and in Greek tragedy it was considered the greatest of sins, reflecting an arrogance growing out of a misplaced sense of one's own abilities rather than the generosity of the gods.[69] As we have seen, many historians have concluded that Napoleon fell victim to his own over-inflated sense of what he could accomplish, losing an army and an empire.

Financial and managerial markets also exact their own form of retribution for corporate hubris. People afflicted with corporate hubris often find it necessary to build an organization that reflects their narcissistic requirements through such conquests as acquisitions, even though acquisitions have not uniformly proven the path to quick riches for shareholders. The pursuit of narcissistic gratification can also inspire growth and investment decisions that may lead to a larger, but not necessarily more profitable, organization. Finally, hubris can lead to arrogance that justifies breaking rules.

Hubris tends to appear most frequently in people already prone to narcissism. A string of successes, some good press, and subordinates willing to feed that narcissism, can exacerbate hubris. As did Napoleon in a military context, corporate executives infected with hubris may come to believe they possess abilities and insights others do not have, and may trivialize the wisdom and contributions of others. Predictably, such executives come to believe that their formula for success is infallible and that additional information is largely irrelevant. The results of this process are especially

TABLE 16.1

Examples of the Sources of Hubris

Sources	Napoleon	Executives
Narcissism	Napoleon's need for position and self-aggrandization to satisfy his narcissism.	Executives with hubris will seek out positions of power to satisfy their narcissism.
Recent successes	Napoleon's hubris grew as his record of battlefield victories lengthened.	A record of outstanding performance permits an executive to rationalize his or her hubris.
Exaggerated accolades of others	Napoleon's hubris fed on the adulation showered on him by the French people and press.	As executives receive praise from others and the media, their hubris is reinforced.
Exemption from the rules	Napoleon regularly broke the rules that governed 19th century Europe, and his hubris grew as he got away with more and more.	A sense of entitlement accompanies hubris in executives as they break the rules and get away with it.

unfortunate in competitive arenas such as war or commerce, as behavior becomes predictable and thus susceptible to attack in ways that are not part of the executive's model of reality. Tables 16.1 and 16.2 compare examples of the sources and implications of hubris.

The most practical way for an individual to combat hubris is to be introspective enough to realize one will never have all the answers and that the counsel of others is vital. One must also realize that success in an organizational context results from a complex interplay of the organization's various resources with the environment. While the leader may be a significant component in that success, it is dangerous to assume that the leader's role is the only factor. Executives should

TABLE 16.2

Examples of the Implications of Hubris

Implications	Napoleon	Executives
Confidence turns to arrogance	When Napoleon's officers pointed out the perils of the Russian campaign, he called them timid and weak.	Executives with hubris appear to undertake mergers that are overpriced out of a sense that they know better than others what is best.
Relying on a simplistic formula	Napoleon assumed the quick, hard-hitting attacks that had worked before would subdue Russia.	Once executives believe they alone know the formula for success, they repeatedly trot out the same strategy regardless of circumstances.
Unwillingness to see the obvious	Napoleon systematically refused to recognize the differences between the Russian campaign and earlier campaigns.	Once absorbed with hubris, and convinced of infallibility, executives may become blind to signals of environmental change.

also work to insure that they have at least one confidante who is in a position to speak the truth.

The most practical way to combat hubris in an organizational setting is to ensure that top executives are monitored by a vigilant board with a reasonable number of outside directors. In addition, organizations should work to establish cultural norms that encourage the membership to disagree without being disagreeable. Organizations should also encourage the kind of continuous environmental surveillance necessary to avoid assuming that the future will conform to the predictable patterns that allowed for past glories.

Hubris does not affect every organization, but it is important to monitor for hubris because it can lead to devastating consequences. Boards must learn to distinguish between the confidence of an executive who, in the face of opposition, pursues an entrepreneurial vision, and the blind disregard of an executive suffering from hubris. Confidence and arrogance may be intertwined, as in the case of Napoleon, who was both a military genius and a slave to his own narcissism. However, the lesson of history is clear: All too often, successful leaders with many positive qualities become their own worst enemies by succumbing to their narcissistic inclinations and allowing hubris to cloud their vision. When an organization and its leader have achieved their ambitions, they must not allow hubris to erode their hard-earned accomplishments.

ACKNOWLEDGMENT

The authors wish to thank Charles Pringle for his helpful comments.

NOTES

1. De Fezensac, M., translated by Lee Kennett. 1970. *The Russian campaign, 1812.* Athens, GA: The University of Georgia Press: viii.
2. Our discussion of the 1812 Russian campaign, and the geopolitical situation at the time of the campaign, is based on numerous sources. To avoid the bias of any single historian or account of the events, we have avoided taking any positions that are not reflected in at least two of the works listed below: Aldington, R. 1943. *The Duke: Being an account of the life and achievements of Arthur Wellesley, First Duke of Wellington.* New York: Viking; Aubry, O. 1938. *Napoleon: Soldier and emperor.* New York: Lippincott; Ballard, C. R. 1971. *Napoleon, an outline.* New York: Books for Libraries; Barnett, C. 1978. *Bonaparte.* New York: Hill and Wang; Carr, A. 1941. *Napoleon speaks.* New York: Viking; Cate, C. 1985. *The war of the two emperors.* New York: Random House; Duffy, C. 1973. *Borodino and the War of 1812.* New York: Charles Scribner's Sons; De Fezensac, op. cit.; Fournier, A. 1913. *Napoleon I.* New York: Henry Holt; Nicolson, N. 1985. *Napoleon 1812.* New York: Harper & Row; Tarle, E. 1942. *Napoleon's invasion of Russia, 1812.* New York: Oxford University Press; Tolstoy, L. N., translated by Louise & Aylmer Maude. 1970. *War and Peace.* London: Oxford University Press.
3. Hayward, M. L. A. & Hambrick, D. C. 1997. Explaining the premiums paid for large acquisitions: Evidence of CEO hubris. *Administrative Science Quarterly,* 42:103–127. Kets de Vries, M. F. R. 1990. The organizational fool: Balancing a leader's hubris. *Human Relations,* 43:751–770. Wilson, A. The Classics Pages, at http://www.globalnet.co.uk/~loxias.
4. Kohut, H. 1978. *Creativeness, charisma, group psychology.* In P. Ornstein (Ed.), *The search for the self,* Volume 2. New York: International Universities Press.
5. Cate, op. cit.: 9–11.
6. Roll, R. 1986. The hubris hypothesis of corporate takeovers. *Journal of Business,* 59:197–216.
7. Fischer, D. E. & Jordan, R. J. 1995. *Security analysis and portfolio management.* Upper Saddle River, New Jersey: Prentice Hall, sixth edition: 556.
8. Berkovitch, E. & Narayanan, M. P. 1993. Motives for takeovers: An empirical investigation. *Journal of Financial and Quantitative*

Analysis, 28:347–362. Bradley, M., Desai, A., & Kim, E. H. 1988. Synergistic gains from corporate acquisitions and their division between the stockholders of target and acquiring firms. *Journal of Financial Economics,* 21:3–40. Jarrell, G. A. & Poulsen, A. B. 1989. The returns to acquiring firms in tender offers: Evidence from three decades. *Financial Management,* Autumn: 12–19. Limmack, R. J. 1993. Bidder companies and defended bids: A test of Roll's hubris hypothesis. *Managerial Finance,* 19:25–36.

9. Hayward, M. L. & Hambrick, D. C., op. cit.: 103–127. Hitt, M., Harrison, J., Ireland, R. D. & Best, A. 1998. Attributes of successful and unsuccessful acquisitions of U.S. firms. *British Journal of Management,* 9:91–114.

10. Hambrick, D. C. & Cannella, A. A. Jr. 1993. Relative standing: A framework for understanding departures of acquired executives. *Academy of Management Journal,* 36:733–762.

11. *BusinessWeek.* 1994. How sweet a deal for Novell? April 4:38. *Wall Street Journal.* 1996. Software firm fights to remake business after ill-fated merger. January 12:A1, A8.

12. Kets de Vries, M. F. R. & Miller, D. 1985. Narcissism and leadership: An object relations perspective. *Human Relations,* 38:583–601.

13. Goldman, K. 1997. *Conflicting accounts: The creation and crash of the Saatchi & Saatchi advertising empire.* New York: Simon and Schuster. *Forbes.* 1997. Hubris redeemed. January 13:42–44.

14. *Economist.* 1992. The shake-up in the Barclay's boardroom. April 25, 83–84.

15. Barnett, op. cit.: 36–53.

16. Lefebvre, G. 1969. *Napoleon 1799–1807.* New York: Routledge and Kegan Paul: 141.

17. Kets de Vries, M. F. R. 1991. Whatever happened to the philosopher-king? The leader's addiction to power. *Journal of Management Studies,* 28:339–351.

18. *BusinessWeek.* 1996. Archer Daniel's cleanup: Don't stop now. January 29:37.

19. Frances, A. (Task Force Chair). 1994. *Diagnostic and statistical manual of mental disorders.* Fourth Edition. Washington, D.C.: American Psychiatric Association: 658–661. Miller, A. 1981. *Prisoners of childhood.* New York: Basic Books: 33–34.

20. The four sources of hubris we identify are derived from several works (which are listed below). As Hayward and Hambrick observe, there is no definitive set of factors that must always be present in significant amounts in order to engender hubris. However, there are clearly common threads that run through much of the hubris-related literature. We have distilled from that literature the four sources we have discussed. It would of course be unrealistic to assume that hubris can exist only in an intense presence of all four of the sources we discuss. However, it seems reasonable to conclude that greater degrees of the four sources of hubris will lead to elevated levels of hubris. Also see: Brockner, J. 1988. *Self-esteem at work: Research, theory and practice.* Lexington, MA: Lexington Books. Hayward & Hambrick, op. cit.: 103–127. Kets de Vries, The organizational fool, op. cit.: 751–770. Kets de Vries & Miller, op. cit.: 583–601. Salancik, G. R. & Meindl, J. R. 1984. Corporate attributions as strategic illusions of management control. *Administrative Science Quarterly,* 29:238–254.

21. Kets de Vries. The organizational fool, op. cit.: 764. Frances, op. cit.: 658–661.

22. Sankowsky, D. 1995. The charismatic leader as narcissist: Understanding the abuse of power. *Organizational Dynamics,* Spring: 57–71.

23. O'Connor, J., Mumford, M. D., Clifton, T. C., & Gessner, T. L. 1995. Charismatic leaders and destructiveness: An historiometric study. *Leadership Quarterly,* 6:529–555.

24. Tolstoy, op. cit.: 427.

25. *BusinessWeek.* 1996. Crunch time at Quaker Oats. September 23:71. *BusinessWeek.* 1996. Putting the snap back in Snapple. July 22:40. *Advertising Age.* 1995. Snapple is now up to Smithburg. October 30:8. *Wall Street Journal.* 1994. Quaker Oats to buy Snapple for $1.7 Billion. November 3:A3. *Forbes.* 1996. He who laughs last. January 1:42–43. *Beverage World.* 1997. Snapped up. April 15:92. *Fortune,* European Ed. 1997. Quaker acts— At last. May 26:30.

26. Kets de Vries. The organizational fool, op. cit.: 765.

27. Kets de Vries & Miller, op. cit.: 583–601.

28. Ibid., 589.
29. Brockner, op. cit.
30. Barnett, op. cit.: 45.
31. De Raguse, D. 1857. *Memoires I Paris:* 297.
32. Meindl, J. R. & Ehrlich, S. B. 1987. The romance of leadership and the evaluation of organizational performance. *Academy of Management Journal,* 30:91–109. Also see: Staw, B. M., McKechnie, P. & Puffer, S. M. 1983. The justification of organizational performance. *Administrative Science Quarterly,* 28:582–600. Bettman, J. R. & Weitz, B. A. 1983. Attributes in the board room: Causal reasoning in corporate annual reports. *Administrative Science Quarterly,* 28:165–183.
33. *Forbes.* 1999. The scorecard. May 17:216–286.
34. Clapham, S. E. & Schewenk, C. R. 1991. Self-serving attributions, managerial cognition, and company performance. *Strategic Management Journal,* 12:219–229.
35. Chen, C. C. & Meindl, J. R. 1991. The construction of leadership images in the popular press: The case of Donald Burr and People Express. *Administrative Science Quarterly,* 36:521–551. Hayward, & Hambrick, op. cit.: 109. Meindl, J. R., Ehrlich, S. B. & Dukerich, J. M. 1985. The romance of leadership. *Administrative Science Quarterly,* 30:78–102.
36. Holtman, R. 1969. *Napoleonic propaganda.* New York: Greenwood Press: 33.
37. Chen & Meindl, op. cit.: 521–551. Meindl, Ehrlich & Dukerich, op. cit.: 78–102.
38. James Carville, speech given before the student body and faculty of Louisiana State University, broadcast by CSPAN, November, 1992.
39. Freud, S. 1957. Some character-types met within psychoanalytic work. In J. Starchey (Ed.), *The Standard Edition of the Complete Psychological Works of Sigmund Freud:* Volume 14. London: Hogarth Press and Institute of Psychoanalysis.
40. Kets de Vries. Philosopher-king, op. cit.: 342.
41. Barnett, op. cit.: 45.
42. Ibid., 182.
43. Nicolson, op. cit.: 180.
44. *Economist.* 1991. Salomon brothers: Life after Gutfreund. August 24:67–68. *Institutional Investor.* 1991. Who should run Salomon Brothers? September: 11–14.
45. While the three behaviors we discuss here are not the only ones manifested by a hubris-infected executive, for the sake of brevity we address these three as they likely have the greatest strategic consequences for the firm. Another behavior not discussed that may manifest itself in someone imbued with hubris is abuse of authority that leads to the alienation and departure of valued employees. A charismatic leader who is also consumed with hubris may use his or her talents to achieve a position of leadership and trust, only to betray that trust when it becomes expedient to do so in order to satisfy his or her personal needs. Throughout his career, Napoleon betrayed those to whom he had made commitments when it became expedient to do so, including his first wife Empress Josephine. Please see: Sankowsky, op. cit.: 57–71.
46. Kets de Vries & Miller, op. cit. Kets de Vries, The organizational fool, op. cit.
47. Nicholson, op. cit.: 17.
48. Ibid., 18.
49. *Beverage World,* op. cit.: 92.
50. Miller, D. 1993. The architecture of simplicity. *Academy of Management Review,* 18: 116–138.
51. Keller, M. 1989. *Rude awakening.* New York: Harper Pernnial.
52. *BusinessWeek.* 1998. Slip slidin' away at General Motors. March 23:38.
53. Keller, op. cit.: 21.
54. Ibid., 51.
55. Clapham & Schwenk, op. cit.: 227.
56. Ibid., 227.
57. *Forbes.* 1996. A tough decline. April 22:165–174. *Forbes.* 1997. Mercedes-Benz's bold niche strategy. September 8:68–76. *Economist.* 1996. Neutron Jürgen?. March 16:72. Schrempp, J. E. 1997. Thriving on global economic changes, address delivered to the Economic Club of Detroit, Detroit, Michigan, January 6. *Fortune.* 1997. Neutron Jürgen ignites a revolution at Daimler-Benz. November 10:144–152. *BusinessWeek.* 1997. The bulldozer at Daimler-Benz. February 10:52.
58. Filley, A. C., House, R. J. & Kerr, S. 1976. *Managerial process and organizational behavior.* Glenview, IL: Scott, Foresman & Co.: 57–62.

Janis, I. L. 1972. *Victims of groupthink.* Boston: Houghton Mifflin: 13–15.

59. Kets de Vries. The organizational fool, op. cit.: 757.

60. Filley, et al., op. cit.: 353. Janis, op. cit.

61. Le Normand, M. A. 1895. *The historical and secret memoirs of the Empress Josephine.* London: 229.

62. Kets de Vries. The organizational fool, op. cit.: 757.

63. Nicolson, op. cit.: 162. The attentive reader may wonder at the 570,000 casualty figure, given that Napoleon entered Russia with an army of 500,000 and about 20,000 recrossed the Neiman River and escaped alive. However, several supplemental regiments of reinforcements joined the army at various points during the retreat, thus increasing the absolute number of men involved in the campaign. In addition to the 570,000 official casualties, there were many thousands of noncombatant casualties. Many of the officers brought with them wives, children, and personal servants who were not officially part of the army, but suffered the same fates as their husbands, fathers, and masters. In addition, early 19th century armies were often accompanied by merchants who sold various items to the troops along the way, as well as by women camp followers, many of whom faired poorly, ibid., 172.

64. Kelleher, Herb. http://www.iflyswa.com/herb/herbie.html.

65. It is worth noting some scholars have argued that subordinate insiders will check the behavior of the CEO as they are natural competitors for control of the firm and their fortunes are tied to the firm's. For these reasons, they will act to cause the replacement of the CEO by influencing outside board members when the CEO's behavior is truly harmful to the firm. See Fama, E. F. 1980. Agency problems and the theory of the firm. *Journal of Political Economy,* 88:288–307.

66. *BusinessWeek.* 1997. Bailing out of Delta. May 26:62. *Wall Street Journal.* 1997. Delta Air's Allen to quit three top posts. May 13.

67. As organizations become more decentralized and more toward the use of self-directed work teams, decision making occurs at lower levels in the organization. This is especially true in organizations where empowerment exists. In such organizations, hubris at the corporate level may be less of an issue in that control of decision making is reduced.

68. Drucker, P. F., Dyson, E., Handy, C., Saffo, P. & Senge, P. M. 1997. Looking ahead: Implications of the present. *Harvard Business Review,* September–October: 22.

69. Wilson, op. cit.

Part D

Making Ethical and Unethical Decisions

17. Business Ethics: Four Spheres of Executive Responsibility

Joseph L. Badaracco, Jr.

*I*n *The Functions of the Executive*, his landmark book on managers and organizations, Chester Barnard wrote: "It seems to me inevitable that the struggle to maintain cooperation among men should as surely destroy some men morally as battle destroys some physically."[1] This is a grim observation. It flies in the face of our widespread celebration of business leadership, entrepreneurial achievement, and the triumphal march of capitalism into Asia and now Eastern Europe. Barnard's view also seems unrealistic. Management life is surely not, after all, a series of anguishing moral dilemmas. And when ethical issues do arise, the right answer, morally and legally, is often clear. The typical challenge is finding practical ways to do the right thing, not discerning what is right. The investment bankers who met in dark garages to exchange inside information for suitcases of cash were not struggling on the horn of moral dilemmas but were breaking the law and violating their clients' trust.

Yet in other cases, the central challenge is deciding what is right. In 1988, for example, the executives of Roussel UCLAF, a French pharmaceutical company, had to decide whether to market a new drug called RU 486. Early tests had shown that the drug was 90 to 95% effective in causing a miscarriage during the first five weeks of a pregnancy. A scientific and medical breakthrough, RU 486 was an alternative to surgical abortions, and its creators believed it could ultimately help hundreds of thousands of women avoid injury and death from botched abortions. As researchers and business managers, many Roussel UCLAF executives had been personally committed to developing RU 486. They faced the question, however, of whether to introduce the drug and how to do so. Protests against Roussel and debates within the company were already diverting a great deal of management time and sapping employee morale. Some of the countries that faced severe population problems and wanted access to RU 486—such as China—did not have the medical infrastructure to use the drug safely. Anti-abortion groups were threatening an international boycott of the products made by Roussel UCLAF and Hoechst, the German chemical giant that was Roussel UCLAF's largest shareholder. Indeed, the costs of the boycott seemed likely to outstrip the profits from selling RU 486. Moreover, Hoechst's corporate credo emphasized support for life, a reaction to its collaboration with the Nazi death camps during the 1940s.

What were the moral responsibilities of Roussel's executives? How should they have balanced their ethical obligations to the company's shareholders, to their employees, to the women who might use RU 486, and to the medical, and scientific, governmental, and political groups their decisions would effect? What did they owe to their own consciences? In such situations, executives face morally treacherous problems. These are not issues of right versus wrong; they involve conflicts of right versus right, of responsibility versus responsibility. In such cases, managers cannot avoid getting their hands dirty: in meeting some responsibilities, they will fail to meet others, and so they face the anguishing struggle that Barnard described.

The problem of dirty hands is the lot of men and women with power and complex responsibilities. In a play by Jean-Paul Sartre, a young idealist accuses a veteran Communist leader of having sold out to the Nazi occupation. The older man replies:

> How you cling to your purity, young man! How afraid you are to soil your hands! All right, stay pure! What good will it do? Why did you join us? Purity is an idea for a yogi or a monk. . . . To do nothing, to remain motionless, arms at your sides, wearing kid gloves. Well I have dirty hands. Right up to the elbows. I've plunged them in filth and blood. But what do you hope? Do you think you can govern innocently?[2]

Yet hard moral choices are at times the inescapable lot of men and women in positions of power. How do you fire a friend, someone you have worked with for years? When is it right to violate an employee's privacy—someone with a drinking problem, for example—to get him help he badly needs? Can you have a clear conscience when your company's product will be misused by some customers and hurt innocent people? When can an executive wreak havoc on a workforce and a local community by moving an operation to a low-cost, overseas site? Is it sometimes right to pay a bribe to win a contract and protect jobs?

Some people believe there are fundamentally simple approaches to such situations: let the market decide, search one's heart and be true to one's values, do what is best for the shareholders, take care of the people in the company "family," do what is right for all of a company's stakeholders. These ways of resolving the moral dilemmas of management are beguilingly clear, simple, praiseworthy—and misleading. The search for a grand, unifying principle of management morality leads to frustration and often cynicism. The moral dilemmas of management are, at bottom, clashes among different, conflicting moralities, among very different spheres of responsibility. Each sphere is, in many ways, a nearly complete moral universe—its own world of commitments, human relationships, strong duties, norms of behavior, personal aspirations, and choices that bring happiness and suffering to others.[3] When the claims of these different spheres of commitment pull in different directions, managers face the hazards of which Chester Barnard warned.

FOUR SPHERES OF MORALITY
The Commitments of Private Life

The first of these moral worlds is the sphere of private life. In part, this realm consists of duties and obligations which are usually stated as abstract, universal principles: tell the truth, keep promises, and avoid injuring others. Individuals disagree about the origins of these duties and the priorities among them, but most people believe that certain fairly clear obligations are binding on everyone. Such principles, however, offer only an abstract, attenuated view—a philosopher's x-ray—of the complex morality of individuals' commitments, ideals, and aspirations.

Consider, for example, the case of a young woman who worked as an associate at a New York investment banking firm. She had contributed significantly to a successful assignment, and the client invited the project team to a celebratory luncheon. The young woman was eager to attend, but the luncheon would be held at a small men's club that required women to enter through a side door. As she struggled with this issue, the young woman did not find herself consulting a universal, prioritized list of abstract, ethical duties. She did spend a great deal of time thinking about her family, her experiences in college, her grandmother's decision not to pursue a career with an established law firm because she would have to learn typing and shorthand to get the job, the experiences of other women at her investment bank, and about her hopes for her career.

In short, her "analysis" was refracted through the personal realities of her life and past experience. Moreover, her decision was not simply a choice but an act of self-definition or self-creation: it would partially define the person she would become, someone who had gone through the side door or someone who had done something else. The poet Adrienne Rich observed that "the story of our life becomes our life," and this young woman was about to write—or live out—an important chapter of her personal narrative.

There was no single, universal, "right" decision in this case. The morality of private life differs from person to person, reflecting factors that are individual and often highly particular. Some people are deeply committed to their families, others to their work, or political reform, or strong friendships. For many, the sphere of private morality is suffused with religious belief, while others find ideals and aspirations elsewhere—in their parents' example, in philosophy, literature, the lives of people they admire, or convictions born of their own lives and reflection. Personal morality is usually embedded in the unexamined norms and assumptions, the slowly evolving commitments and responsibilities, and the enveloping ways of life of families, friends, and communities.

Much of the morality of private life is implicit and intuitive, and it appears clearest in retrospect, in the patterns underlying one's past actions. Few people have the skills and the inclinations—so highly prized in academia—to state their implicit morality in clear, precise, systematic terms. For some people, rational articulation is a betrayal, a denial of Pascal's observation that the heart has its reasons that reason does not know. Individuals often do not fully understand how or why they made a particular decision. After long reflection, something simply seems right.

Integrity and character play important roles in the morality of private life. From time to time, most people wonder about questions that ancient philosophers first articulated: What distinguishes a good person from a bad one? What ways of living, what guidelines, what virtues make for a good person and a good life? What do I want my life to add up to? What abiding aspirations and commitments will give my life purpose and a sense of wholeness, coherence, and integrity? In the Western world, such questions have defined the morality of private life ever since Socrates, Plato, and Aristotle asked them 2500 years ago.

This sphere of morality seems to be primary, to be morality in its truest and deepest sense. It seems clear, after all, that people are first and foremost individual moral agents and only later take on social roles as executives, attorneys, or physicians. But this is not the whole story. The men and women who become business executives, like others who hold positions of power in society, shoulder the weight of other moral responsibilities. The British historian R. H. Tawney wrote: "To argue, in the manner of Machiavelli, that there is one rule for business and another for private life, is to open the door to an orgy of unscrupulousness before which the mind recoils. To argue that there is no difference at all is to lay down a principle which few men who have faced the difficulty in practice will be prepared to endorse."[4] Like Chester Barnard, Tawney acknowledges a struggle: between the "rule for business" and the moral claims of private life. But what is this "rule for business?"

The answer, in short, is that certain moral responsibilities come with certain social roles. The job of being a military officer, a nurse, or an attorney brings particular obligations, as does the job of running a business. The chairman of Roussel UCLAF, Edouard Sakiz, decided at one point to overrule his strong, personal convictions and oppose the marketing of RU 486. Sakiz feared that protests and boycotts by anti-abortion groups would do too much damage to Roussel and Hoechst, saying "We have a responsibility in managing a company. But if I were a lone scientist, I would have acted differently."

Why couldn't Sakiz act on the basis of his personal values and commitments in life? The reason is that, as a business executive, Sakiz had to take account of other compelling responsibilities.

The Commitments of Economic Agents

Some of these responsibilities arose from a second sphere of moral claims, which derived from Sakiz's role as an economic agent. These obligations are familiar territory for American managers. Their job, as economists, corporate attorneys, and their superiors often remind them, is to serve the interests of shareholders. What is realized less often is that this is not just a legal and practical obligation but also the most visible and familiar element in a sphere of responsibilities that are deeply moral in character.

The ties between the owners of a company and the managers who act as their agents are inescapably moral. Shareholders entrust their assets to managers, and managers promise, implicitly or explicitly, to work for the shareholders' interests. Like any promise, this relationship of trust carries strong moral weight. Moreover, this obligation is reenforced by the duty that all citizens have to obey the law. In an overview of executives' legal obligations, Robert Clark, the Dean of the Harvard Law School, wrote: "Case law on managers' fiduciary duty of care can fairly be read to say that the manager has an affirmative, open-ended duty to maximize the beneficiaries' wealth, regardless of whether this is specified in any actual contract."[5] Of course, this obligation does not always trump all other moral claims, and difficulties arises when fiduciary obligations clash with other moral interests. Nevertheless, the laws obligating managers to serve shareholders' interests are woven deeply into the legal fabric of commercial life in the United States and many other countries. These laws reflect the preferences and considered judgments of societies; they have been enacted by legitimate government bodies; hence, they create strong moral claims on business executives.

The economic responsibilities of executives do not arise solely from duties to keep promises and obey the law. Consequences also matter. Society benefits when managers and companies compete vigorously to serve owners' interests. Much of the wealth flowing from the capitalist cornucopia directly alleviates human suffering and provides pleasure, security, health, and prosperity for many members of society. These consequences are a moral achievement, not simply a material or economic one. The British philosopher John Stuart Mill concluded that good actions—that is, *morally* good actions—are those that bring the greatest happiness to the greatest number. Indeed, Mill asked what else morality could be about, if it were not fundamentally a matter of promoting happiness and alleviating suffering. Does capitalism accomplish this? The economist Joseph Schumpeter gave this answer: "Verification is easy. There are no doubt some things available to the modern workman that Louis XIV himself would have been delighted to have—modern dentistry for instance . . . the capitalist process, not by coincidence but by virtue of its mechanism, progressively raises the standard of life of the masses."[6] Capitalism, in short, provides the material base for the lives, happiness, and welfare of many people.

Market systems, moreover, achieve these moral ends in moral ways. Individuals choose the work they wish to do, the products and services they wish to buy, and the ways they invest their savings. Vigorous competition expands the range of choices in the markets for labor, capital, and goods. When people make these choices, they are exercising their rights as autonomous individuals. Market transactions are, in Robert Nozick's phrase, "capitalist acts between consenting adults."[7] Of course, actual capitalist systems fall far short of these ideals— because of class interests, power politics, disparities in income and wealth, and the political influence of corporations and other groups. Nevertheless, market systems rest upon bedrock moral beliefs about the autonomy of individuals, the value of freedom and consent, and the centuries-long struggle to free individuals from the power of the state and the church. The Boston Tea Party was at once a commercial and a political act, and it is no accident that the nations of Eastern Europe are simultaneously embracing capitalism and democracy. To be sure, serious problems co-exist with market systems and are often exacerbated by them, and the failures and limits of capitalist economies have been well chronicled. But to acknowledge that markets fail is not to deny their basic moral traits: providing the material base for the happiness of many people and widening the range of ways of choices open to them.

It would be natural to think that the moral dilemmas of management arise when economic duties conflict with executives' personal values and convictions. But two other spheres of responsibility also make strong claims on managers and make these dilemmas even more complex. Both of these other spheres share the same origin: the fact that modern economies do not fit the Adam Smith picture of tiny economic units banging against each other like billiard balls in competitive markets. This view presupposes that firms and their managers have little power, a condition that holds mainly in theory. Under conditions of pure competition, firms are price-takers, and when a company innovates and earns exceptional profits, competitors rush in, drive prices down, and take from the innovator the market power that its breakthrough gave it. In actuality, however, firms and their managers often wield enormous economic, political, and social power. With this power, come other responsibilities.

Commitments as Company Leaders

Another sphere of responsibility exists because employees and managers are members of semi-permanent human communities, conventionally called companies. This new form of social organization emerged roughly a hundred years ago, when the entrepreneurial capitalism of small-scale business gave way in many industries to managerial capitalism. This was a development that the classical economists had not thought about or perhaps even imagined. In the 600 pages of *The Wealth of Nations*, Adam Smith treats firms only in a few passing references to tiny operations like apothecaries, collieries, and farms. However, within a century of Smith's death, giant firms, exploiting economies of scale and scope, came to dominate much of the economic landscape. They employed thousands or tens of thousands of people, as workers and managers, on a long-term basis. Some were larger than countries. In the mid-1960s, for example, General Motors' sales exceeded the gross national products of all but four countries, and despite its recent woes, General Motors has now survived longer than the Soviet Union.

A Japanese scholar has described firms in his own country as "capsules." Such firms are semi-closed societies, communal groups that enlist the loyalty and trust of employees and envelop much of their lives.[8] Indeed, the word "employee" is misleading. People become *members* of these business organizations, they devote much of their life's energy to their work, and their lives and livelihoods are deeply bound up in the firms' activities. This phenomenon, of course, is hardly unique to Japan. Consider an episode at Levi Strauss, a leading apparel maker, just a few years ago. The company had made substantial efforts to protect the rights of people with HIV and AIDS and help them continue working when they were ill. One man with AIDS said, "It was so important for me to come to work and get away from all the pain—the company was the environment that helped me keep my self-respect." Later, when this man died, one of his co-workers said "I shed tears for him and for the great friend I had lost."

What does this vignette suggest? First, that work is a powerful source of meaning and value—in this case, self-respect—in individuals' lives. Many people realize some of their deepest aspirations—for security, for a sense of belonging, contribution, and achievement—on the job. The co-worker's comment also reminds us how workplaces can nurture deep loyalties, strong friendships, and abiding ties among individuals. People live much of their lives at work, rather than in neighborhoods, religious and political groups, or even at home with families. Finally, the episode reveals managers' power: as business executives lead, guide, and shape these large, semi-permanent social and economic communities, they exert enormous power over the lives and welfare of many other human beings.

The power that executives exercise over the lives of others leads to two strong moral claims. The first is the obligation not to abuse this power. Consider, for a moment, how great the force of authority can be. In the early 1960s, a psychologist at Yale University performed a famous experiment in which volunteers from all walks of life were asked to help a researcher learn about the effects of punishment on memory. The learner, who was actually an accomplice of the experimenter, was strapped into a chair. The volunteers were told to give electrical shocks to the learner, depending on

whether or not his answers were correct. (In actuality, no shocks were given—the subject was just acting.) Approximately 60% of the volunteers were extraordinarily obedient to authority: when the learner erred, the volunteers followed the directions of the experimenter and administered the highest levels of shock, even though the learner shouted, screamed, pleaded, and eventually fell silent.[9]

In some respects, situations in companies differ from this experiment. People often have time to reflect before acting, and they can talk about hard choices with friends, peers, and family members. Yet the "tools of management"—measurement and reward systems, culture, and the examples of peers and bosses—exert enormous, cumulative pressures on employees and managers. People often give in to organizational pressure to act unethically, or they stand on the sidelines while others do so. Responsibilities in organizations are often shared so no one feels personally and directly accountable. People say to themselves "It's not part of my job," or "It's the CEO's call and he runs the place," or "I have to pick my battles and this isn't the right one." The great twentieth century theologian Reinhold Niebuhr believed that individuals tended to behave less morally in groups than in their own private lives. Niebuhr wrote: "In every human group, there is less reason to guide and check impulses, less capacity for self-transcendence, less ability to comprehend the needs of others and therefore more unrestrained egoism than the individuals, who compose the group, reveal in their personal relationships."[10]

Power begets responsibility. Hence, business executives must exercise their stewardship over company communities in ways that meet a basic threshold of decency and respect for the rights and dignity of employees and managers. But this duty merely sets a base level of responsibility: it says only "do no harm" and ignores the enduring commitments that motivate executives' work. For these men and women, work is the stage upon which they live out many of their hopes and fears, seek identity and purpose, and gain the sense of achievement and self-worth that undergirds their lives. Their ideals and aspirations take different forms but nearly all are variations on the same themes: many executives want to build companies that are independent, strong, growing, and vital; that attract and keep top-quality talent; that are challenging and rewarding places to work; that provide opportunities for employees to grow and develop; that will survive hostile, uncertain competitive environments, and will endure and prosper for decades. Some executives have even broader aspirations. Steve Job's mission for Apple Computer was "to make a contribution to this world by making tools for the mind that advance humankind." Merck's corporate purpose is "preserving and improving human life."

Many men and women commit much of their lives and energy to creating such companies. And while companies must serve shareholders' interests, neither their executives nor their employees leap from bed in the morning in order to maximize the risk-adjusted present value of streams of future cash flows. The animating, creative forces of great human institutions originate elsewhere. The men and women who build and guide enduring, productive, and challenging human communities are engaged in efforts which are not simply financial and administrative, but social, political, and moral. The political scientist James MacGregor Burns concluded that moral leadership arises when leaders and followers share needs, aspirations, and values. This is an aspect of successful companies that the widely touted notions of "family" and "team" try to capture. Not all companies and managers think in these terms; many, indeed, seem to subscribe to Woody Allen's observation that most of getting ahead in life is just showing up. But the many managers who are committed to higher aims are working within a distinctive, compelling sphere of moral responsibility.

Responsibilities Beyond Firm's Boundaries

It is natural to think that executives' responsibilities stop at their firms' boundaries. This supposes that companies are, in the words of one economist, islands of managerial coordination in a sea of market relations.[11] But this picture of the world is inaccurate and misleading. Many companies have complex relationships with government agencies, labor unions, or—through strategic alliances—with customers, suppliers, and even competitors. These firms resemble global networks and their boundaries are blurred.

This organizational reality creates a new and enormously complex sphere of responsibilities for managers. Again, the central issue is power. Just as business executives have enormous influence over the people "inside" their companies, they also have power over people and organizations that are "outside," but with which their operations and sometimes their destinies are intertwined. In Japan, West Germany, and other countries, groups of large and small firms are clustered in the form of cartels, keiretsu, and other confederations. America, despite its ideological preference for the Adam Smith model of small-firm competition, is home to many of the largest firms in the world, and they, too, are surrounded by vast cadres of suppliers and customers and often have close relationships with many government agencies.

Even when it is not part of a network of alliances, a firm's power extends beyond its boundaries. Through its products, the jobs it provides, the taxes it pays, and the business a firm gives its suppliers, a company influences, sometimes profoundly, the lives of many people. RU 486 provides a dramatic example. Its developers believed the drug could ultimately save tens of thousands of lives by providing another alternative to "coat hanger" abortions. Critics of RU 486 argued it would make abortion much easier, leading to more deaths of unborn children. RU 486 also seemed likely to change the politics of abortion: fewer abortions would take place in clinics, which were ready targets for protest, and abortions at the very start of a pregnancy seemed less likely to arouse political passions. In many other cases—less dramatic, but more commonplace

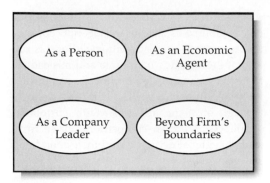

FIGURE 17.1
Four Spheres of Commitments

than RU 486—a company's power and influence, and hence the responsibilities of its managers, also extend beyond the traditional boundaries of the firm. Pollution, unsafe products, and unfair competitive practices all injure other parties. And, when a company fails and shutters its factories, employees, their families, schools, local governments, and sometimes entire communities pay a price.

Obviously, managers cannot be held responsible for everything. Other groups in society—government bodies, labor unions, and consumers—have significant responsibilities as well. In the case of RU 486, for example, government bodies were responsible for decisions on whether abortions were legal and whether particular drugs were safe and effective while physicians and women made choices among medical procedures. Sometimes, the law or widely accepted practices provide answers that are clear and morally sound, but in many cases the situation is more complex. Roussel UCLAF, for example, had to decide whether to make RU 486 available to the Chinese government. China wanted the drug for its population control program. The country's population was already 1.1 billion, and demographers had described the early 1990s as "the Himalayas of population growth" because 150 million Chinese women would soon reach their prime child-bearing years, and the government's decade-old "one couple, one child" policy seemed to have failed.

RU 486 might have helped China manage its population growth, but Roussel UCLAF had to consider how the drug might be used. In particular, would it be given to women under the strict medical supervision planned for France? Might women be forced to take RU 486, violating the "right to choose" that many company officials believed in? Given these uncertainties, how far did the company's responsibility extend? One could argue that they stopped at the "point of sale," that Chinese physicians and public officials then became accountable for the use or misuse of the drug. This viewpoint avoids the taint of cultural imperialism by respecting the rights and competence of the Chinese government. But suppose RU 486 was given improperly (too late in a pregnancy, for example) at several rural clinics in China and some women died, others were permanently injured, and some gave birth to handicapped children. Would the "point of sale" argument enable company executives to wash their hands of responsibility? Would this way of thinking allay the guilt they might feel? And would the publicity and fear resulting from these tragedies impede the use of the drug in other countries, even under careful medical supervision? Company responsibilities do not cease at the point when a customer exchanges cash for goods. But where does the buck stop in a web of interdependent actors and shared responsibility?

FOUR ENDURING QUESTIONS

Moral claims arising from different spheres of responsibility often collide with each other, creating difficult, sometimes anguishing dilemmas for business executives. There is, unfortunately, no final, supreme principle for resolving conflicts of responsibility—not in the Bible or the Koran, nor in philosophy or theology books, not in the law, nor deep in the human heart, nor anywhere else. There is instead a long tradition of serious thought about power and responsibility that can help executives deal with conflicts among commitments and mitigate the problem of dirty hands. This tradition of thought is not a progression of ideas, culminating in some final conclusion, but a long, reflective conversation—spanning many generations, varied cultures, different social, political, and economic conditions, and the experiences and insights of many individuals.

Four questions represent important voices in this long conversation. Each encapsulates a fundamental idea about the responsibilities of men and women in positions of power. Moreover, each is closely associated with a handful of thinkers who used the question to crystallize the moral issues that confronted their societies at crucial moments in human history. Used together, the four questions provide a basic framework for assessing possible ways of resolving a difficult dilemma. The four questions are:

- Which course of action will do the most good and the least harm?
- Which alternative best serves others' rights, including shareholders' rights?
- What plan can I live with, which is consistent with the basic values and commitments of my company?
- Which course of action is feasible in the world as it is?

The first question—what will do the most good and the least harm—focuses on the morality of consequences. It is, in rough terms, John Stuart Mill's question. His basic view, called utilitarianism, is that morally good actions bring the best consequences for everyone they affect and do so with the least cost, risk, and harm. In the case of RU 486, the consequences were enormous: the survival of the Roussel UCLAF, the health and safety of millions of women who might use RU 486, the health of people with diseases the drug could treat, and the morality, politics, and regulation of abortion around the world.

Mill's question asks managers to examine the full range of consequences that will result from different ways of resolving a dilemma. The basic question must be broken into subquestions: Which groups and individuals will benefit from different ways of resolving a dilemma? How greatly? Who will be put at risk or suffer? How severe will the suffering be? Can the risk and harm be alleviated? These questions, inevitably, serve as starting points of a process of fact-gathering and analysis; they are not a formula for reaching conclusions. There are no universal definitions of good or harm, nor are there any hard and fast ways of measuring and trading off harms and benefits against each other. Much depends upon particular circumstances, institutions, and legal and social arrangements. But the basic guiding question remains: Which course of action is likely to do the most good and the least harm?

The second question focuses on the morality of rights, an idea that crystallized in the seventeenth and eighteenth centuries. For Americans, the question is Thomas Jefferson's. His draft of the *Declaration of Independence* stated bluntly that human beings had inalienable rights to life, liberty, and the pursuit of happiness. We accept similar ideas in everyday life, believing that we and others have rights to be treated with respect, to have promises kept, to be told the truth, and to be spared unnecessary injury. Others have duties to respect these rights, particularly powerful individuals such as business executives. Hence, when executives consider various ways of resolving some dilemma, they must ask what rights are at stake. In the case of RU 486, this meant asking about the rights of women to have access to safer methods of abortion, about rights to safe medical procedures in countries with less developed medical infrastructures, and about the rights of the unborn.

Like the question of consequences, the question of rights does not draw sharp boundaries around companies or around managers' responsibilities. The question asks about the rights of everyone affected by a decision. Both questions are the ethical counterparts of what many management analysts now call the borderless world: they look beyond the familiar boundaries of firm and nations, acknowledging

Dr. Martin Luther King's insight that all people are bound together in a "seamless web of mutuality."

The third great force in moral thinking is captured in the third question. It asks: What course of action can I live with? What best serves my commitments and aspirations in life? And, for a business executive, this perspective asks: What course of action is most consistent with the kind of human community we are seeking to create? The roots of these questions lie in Aristotle's philosophy and in many religions. They ask executives who face difficult decisions to search their consciences, to regard their lives and aspirations as a whole, to ask, in effect, what they want to appear in their obituaries. This perspective also asks managers to think hard about what kind of human community their company is, and about the values that guide it and the purposes it solves. Inevitably, executives in wrenching situations, like that faced by the executives at Roussel UCLAF, will ask themselves—as they should—what course of action they can live with, as individuals and as leaders of a particular company.

The fourth question is Machiavelli's. It asks, purely pragmatically, what will work in the world as it is? In any situation, there may be several options that could, in theory, reconcile the competing claims. The crucial question then becomes: What is actually feasible—in view of a manager's actual power in an organization, a company's competitive, financial, and political strength, the likely costs and risks of various plans of action, and the time available for action?

For some people, this question is amoral or worse. It focuses on the means, not the ends, and it fails to examine the morality of the means. Moreover, Nicolo Machiavelli, the fifteenth-century Italian statesman and political philosopher, is widely considered an apologist for unscrupulous opportunism. But Machiavelli would not be remembered today for simply having argued the obvious: that unscrupulous people often get ahead. Machiavelli was a realist, preoccupied with "the necessities of power," with what leaders must do so their organizations can at least survive and perhaps prosper in the world that one finds, not the world one hopes for. Hence, morality must be practical. For people with real responsibility, meaning well is not good enough. A plan of action, however high-minded it may be, usually accomplishes little if it does not work. Moreover, Machiavelli's question was not a request for the cautious, satisficing action plans of the "organization man." He asked what will work if a leader is resourceful, persistent, imaginative, bold, and does not shun risk.

The four questions must be asked and answered together because, in crucial ways, they balance and correct each other. Enshrining any of them as "the answer" is dangerous. Machiavelli's question is a strong pull towards practicality, but as a sole perspective on difficult decisions it risks sleazy opportunism and needs to be balanced by the explicitly ethical concerns of the other three questions. Aristotle's question tries to root decisions in the abiding values of particular individuals and institutions; but this approach, by itself, can open the door to prejudiced, self-interested judgments.

In short, the moral dilemmas of management must be resolved through balancing acts—through decisions and actions that meet, as best they can, the conflicting claims of different spheres of responsibility. Edouard Sakiz's decision on RU 486 provides an instructive example. As mentioned earlier, Sakiz voted to suspend distribution of the drug. Five days later, Roussel UCLAF announced to the public that "pressure from anti-abortion groups" had led to this decision. The result was a firestorm of criticism—from women's groups, family planning organizations, and physicians in Europe and the United States. A few days later, the French Minister of Health told Roussel UCLAF that he would use his legal authority to transfer the RU 486 patent to another firm unless the company changed its decision. Roussel UCLAF quickly agreed to market the drug in France. After the Minister's decision, the company's vice-chairman said: "We are now

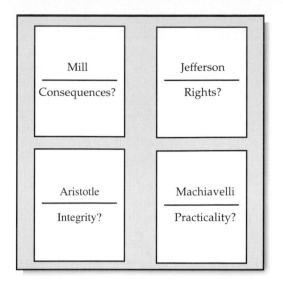

| Mill
Consequences? | Jefferson
Rights? |
| Aristotle
Integrity? | Machiavelli
Practicality? |

FIGURE 17.2
Four Questions

relieved of the moral burden weighing on our company."

How successfully did Roussel and its managers meet their conflicting responsibilities? Sakiz and his fellow executives met their personal aspirations, as scientists and medical researchers, to introduce an alternative to surgical abortions, one that might someday reduce the number of women who would suffer and die from abortions, especially in poor countries. Their decision respected the rights of women, guaranteed by French law, to decide whether to seek an abortion, and it also acknowledged the right of the French government to play a role in a decision with potentially vast moral, social, and medical consequences. The rights of shareholders were served because a promising new product was brought to market, but in a fashion that might have diverted protests and boycotts away from Roussel UCLAF and its parent since the French government made the final decision on marketing RU 486. Finally, the company sought to achieve important consequences—principally reducing suffering and death—while seeking to minimize the negative repercussions for the firm, its executives, and Roussel UCLAF employees.

Yet this decision was an anguishing one for Sakiz and had the marks of a "dirty hands" dilemma. Roussel UCLAF would not be spared protests and boycotts; threats of violence would continue. Its executives were accused of shirking their responsibilities by letting the government make the final decision: a prominent scientist who contributed greatly to the development of RU 486 called the company's initial decision against distribution a "moral scandal." Some people even accused Sakiz of Machiavellian maneuvering, alleging that he and the Minister of Health had orchestrated the whole series of decisions about RU 486. Opponents of abortions, in Europe and the United States, continued to criticize Roussel UCLAF and its executives for killing unborn children.

In some situations, there is no win–win solution. Life does not come with a guarantee that good intentions, hard work, imagination, and far-sightedness will turn all moral dilemmas into happy outcomes that satisfy the moral claims of all parties. The "best" way of resolving a dilemma may inevitably involve some violation of people's rights, it may bring harmful consequences, or it may severely test an executive's sense of integrity. Responsible, thoughtful, practical-minded people will often disagree on what is right in a particular situation. The four enduring questions posed above are not a formula for replacing judgment and are no guarantee against "dirty hands." They are, at best, an aid to judgment and a way to keep one's hands as clean as possible in the world as it is.

REFERENCES

1. Chester Barnard, *The Functions of the Executive* (Cambridge, MA: Harvard University Press, 1982), p. 278.

2. Jean-Paul Sartre, *Dirty Hands*, in *No Exit and Three Other Plays*, translated by Lionel Abel (New York, NY: Vintage International, 1989), p. 218. The specific problem Sartre poses, the problem of "dirty hands" in public life, is analyzed in Michael Walzer, "Political Action: The Problem of Dirty Hands," *Philosophy and Public Affairs* (Winter 1973), pp. 160–180.

3. I am using the notion of spheres in a way that is roughly analogous to that developed by the political philosopher Michael Walzer. His analysis of distributive justice is based upon a division of social life into different spheres of activities—each centered upon different goods—such as health or education. Walzer argues that the moral standards governing the distribution of each of these goods derive not from some grand, over-arching theory of justice but rather from the particular meanings associated with a good in a particular community with a particular history. See Michael Walzer, *Spheres of Justice* (New York, NY: Basic Books, 1983), pp. 3–30.

4. Richard H. Tawney, *Religion and the Rise of Capitalism* (New York, NY: Harcourt, Brace and Company, 1926), p. 184.

5. Robert C. Clark, "Agency Costs Versus Fiduciary Duties," in John W. Pratt and Richard J. Zeckhauser, eds., *Principals and Agents: The Structure of Business* (Boston, MA: Harvard Business School, 1985), pp. 71–79.

6. Joseph Schumpeter, *Capitalism, Socialism, and Democracy*, 3rd edition (New York, NY: Harper Colophon/Harper & Row, 1975), pp. 67–68, 83.

7. Robert Nozick, *Anarchy, State and Utopia* (New York, NY: Basic Books, Inc., 1974), p. 163.

8. See Moriaki Tsuchiya, "The Japanese Firm as a Capsule," *Japanese Economic Studies* (Fall 1984), pp. 8–41.

9. See Stanley Milgram, *Obedience to Authority* (New York, NY: Harper and Row, 1974).

10. Reinhold Niebuhr, *Moral Man and Immoral Society: A Study in Ethics and Politics* (New York, NY: C. Scribner's Sons, 1932), p. xi.

11. G. B. Richardson, "The Organization of Industry," *Economic Journal* (October 1972), p. 883.

18. Ethical Leadership and the Psychology of Decision Making

David M. Messick/Max H. Bazerman

Changes in today's business environment pose vexing ethical challenges to executives. We propose that unethical business decisions may stem not from the traditionally assumed trade-off between ethics and profits or from a callous disregard of other people's interests or welfare, but from psychological tendencies that foster poor decision making, both from an ethical and a rational perspective. Identifying and confronting these tendencies, we suggest, will increase both the ethicality and success of executive decision making.

Executives today work in a moral mine field. At any moment, a seemingly innocuous decision can explode and harm not only the decision maker but also everyone in the neighborhood. We cannot forecast the ethical landscape in coming years, nor do we think that it is our role to provide moral guidance to executives. Rather, we offer advice, based on contemporary research on the psychology of decision making, to help executives identify morally hazardous situations and improve the ethical quality of their decisions.

Psychologists have discovered systematic weaknesses in how people make decisions and process information; these new discoveries and theories are the foundation for this paper. These discoveries involve insights into errors that people make when they estimate risks and likelihoods, as well as biases in the way they seek information to improve their estimates. There are new theories about how easily our preferences can be influenced by the consequences we consider and the manner in which we consider them. Social psychologists have new information about how people divide the world into "us" and "them" that sheds new light on how

discrimination operates. Finally, there has been important new research into the dimensions along which people think that they are different from other people, which helps explain why people might engage in practices that they would condemn in others.[1]

We focus on three types of theories that executives use in making decisions—theories about the world, theories about other people, and theories about ourselves. Theories about the world refer to the beliefs we hold about how the world works, the nature of the causal network in which we live, and the ways in which our decisions influence the world. Important aspects of our theories about the world involve our beliefs about the probabilistic (or deterministic) texture of the world and our perceptions of causation.

Theories about other people are our organized beliefs about how "we" are different from "they." Interestingly, "they" may be competitors, employees, regulators, or foreigners, and whoever is "we" today may be "them" tomorrow. Our beliefs about others influence the ways in which we make judgments and decisions about other people, and these influences are often unconscious.

Finally, we all correctly believe that we are unique individuals. However, theories about ourselves lead us to unrealistic beliefs about ourselves that may cause us to underestimate our exposure to risk, take more than our fair share of the credit for success (or too little for failure), or be too confident that our theory of the world is the correct one. If most of the executives in an organization think that they are in the upper 10 percent of the talent distribution, there is the potential for pervasive disappointment.

Our discussion of these three theories focuses on the ways they are likely to be incorrect. Our message, however, is not that executives are poor decision makers. We focus on problem areas because they are the danger zones where errors may arise. They are the places where improvements may be achieved, areas in which executives would like to change their decision making if only they better understood their existing decision processes.

THEORIES ABOUT THE WORLD

Successful executives must have accurate knowledge of their world. If they lack this knowledge, they must know how to obtain it. One typical challenge is how to assess the risk of a proposed strategy or policy, which involves delineating the policy's consequences and assessing the likelihood of various possibilities. If an executive does a poor assessment of a policy's consequences, the policy may backfire and cause financial as well as moral embarrassment to the firm and the decision maker. There are three components to our theories of the world: the consideration of possible consequences, the judgment of risk, and the perception of causes.

The Cascade of Consequences

A principle in ecology that Hardin has called the First Law of Ecology is, simply stated, "You can never do just one thing."[2] Major decisions have a spectrum of consequences, not just one, and especially not just the intended consequence. Everyday experience as well as psychological research suggests that, in making complex choices, people often simplify the decision by ignoring possible outcomes or consequences that would otherwise complicate the choice. In other words, there is a tendency to reduce the set of possible consequences or outcomes to make the decision manageable. In extreme cases, all but one aspect of a decision will be suppressed, and the choice will be made solely on the basis of the one privileged feature. The folly of ignoring a decision's possible consequences should be obvious to experienced decision makers, but there are several less obvious ways in which decision errors can create moral hazards. The tendency to ignore the full set of consequences in decision making leads to the following five biases: ignoring low-probability events, limiting the search for stakeholders, ignoring the possibility that the public will "find out," discounting the future, and undervaluing collective outcomes.

Ignoring Low-Probability Events.
If a new product has the potential for great acceptance but a possible drawback, perhaps for only a few people, there is a tendency to underestimate the importance of the risk. In the case of DES (diethylstilbestrol), a synthetic estrogen prescribed for women with problem pregnancies, there was some early indication that the drug was associated with a higher than normal rate of problems not only in pregnant women but also in their daughters. The importance of this information was insufficiently appreciated. Worrisome risks may be ignored if they threaten to impede large gains.

Limiting the Search for Stakeholders.
DES's most disastrous effects did not befall the consumers of the drug, namely, the women who took it; the catastrophe struck their daughters. When there is a tendency to restrict the analysis of a policy's consequences to one or two groups of visible stakeholders, the decision may be blind-sided by unanticipated consequences to an altogether different group. A careful analysis of the interests of the stakeholders (those persons or groups whose welfare may be affected by the decision under consideration) is essential to reasonably anticipating potential problems. A basic tenet of moral theories is to treat people with respect, which can be done only if the interests of all concerned people are honestly considered. Assessing others' interests would have required research, for instance, on the long-term effects of DES.

Ignoring the Possibility That the Public Will "Find Out." The stakeholder who should always be considered is the

public in general. Executives should ask, "What would the reaction be if this decision and the reasons for it were made public?" If they fear this reaction, they should reconsider the decision. One reason for the test is to alert executives that if the decision is made, they will have to conceal it to avoid adverse public response. The need to hide the decision, and the risk that the decision and its concealment might be disclosed, become other consequences to face. The outrage provoked by the revelation that a crippling disease, asbestosis, was caused by asbestos exposure was partly due to the fact that Johns Manville had known about and hidden this relationship for years while employees and customers were continuously exposed to this hazard. A decision or policy that must be hidden from public view has the additional risk that the secret might be revealed. Damage to self-respect and institutional respect of those who must implement and maintain the concealment should also be considered a consequence.

Discounting the Future.
The consequences that we face tomorrow are more compelling than those we must address next week or next year. The consequences of decisions cascade not only over people and groups, but also over time. Figuring out how to address the entire temporal stream of outcomes is one of the most challenging tasks executives face. Policy A will earn more money this year than Policy B, but a year from now, if we get there, Policy B will probably leave us stronger than Policy A. Theories of the world that fail to cope with the temporal distribution of consequences will not only leave executives puzzled about why they are not doing better; they will also expose executives to accusations that they squandered the future to exploit the present. The tendency to discount the future partly explains the decaying urban infrastructure, the U.S. budget deficit, the collapse of fisheries, global warming, and environmental destruction. While there is much debate about the destructiveness of these issues, in each instance, the key decision makers have clearly underweighed the future in making the appropriate balanced decisions.

Undervaluing Collective Outcomes.
Accurate theories of the world must also be sensitive to the collective consequences of decisions. When E. F. Hutton's managers decided to earn money by kiting checks, not only did they put the reputation of their own firm in jeopardy, they also endangered the reputation of the entire securities industry. When a chemical firm decides to discharge waste into a public lake, it pollutes two collective resources, the lake and the reputation of the chemical industry in general. There is a tendency to treat these collective costs as externalities and to ignore them in decision making. To do so, however, is to ignore a broad class of stakeholders whose response could be, "If they voluntarily ignore the collective interests, then it is in the collective interest to regulate their activity."

Ethical decisions must be based on accurate theories about the world. That means, at a minimum, examining the full spectrum of a decision's consequences. Our perspective suggests that a set of biases reduces the effectiveness of the search for all possible consequences. It is interesting to evaluate the infamous Pinto decision from this consequential perspective. Ford executives knew that the car had a fire risk, but the cost they associated with it was small. Their deliberations gave no consideration to their customers' interests. They made no effort to ask car buyers if they were willing to pay an extra $10 to shield the gas tank. The Pinto decision proved a colossal embarrassment to Ford; when the documents were released, the effort to conceal the decision failed, and public opinion, fueled by Ralph Nader's book *Unsafe at Any Speed*, ran deeply and strongly against Ford.[3] The public felt that there was a collective interest in automobile safety and that Ford and, by association, the other auto manufacturers, were indifferent to that concern. From the public's perspective, it would be stupid to permit unethical firms to police themselves.

Judgment of Risk
Theories of the world will be inaccurate if they systematically fail to account for the full spec-

trum of consequences associated with decisions. And they will be inaccurate if they systematically err in assessing the probabilities associated with the consequences. Let's first consider these two scenarios:

- A tough-minded executive wants to know if the company's current promotion practices have caused any specific case of demonstrated discrimination against a minority employee. He explains that he is not interested in vague possibilities of discrimination but is concerned that the firm not do anything that "really" causes discrimination.
- Edmund Muskie, a candidate in the 1972 U.S. presidential election, borrowed the words of President Harry Truman when he stated that what this country needed was a "one-armed" economist. When asked why, he responded that he was tired of economists who said "on the one hand . . . but on the other hand. . . ."

Denying Uncertainty. These decision makers are grasping for certainty in an uncertain world. They want to know what *will* or *did* happen, not what *may* or *might have* happen(ed). They illustrate the general principle that people find it easier to act as if the world were certain and deterministic rather than uncertain and often unpredictable. The executive in the first scenario wants to know about "real" discrimination, not the possibility of discrimination. Muskie expressed frustration with incessantly hearing about "the other hand." What people want to hear is not what *might* happen, but what *will* happen. When executives act as if the world is more certain than it is, they expose themselves to poor outcomes, for both themselves and others. It is simply foolish to ignore risk on one's own behalf, but it is unethical to do so on behalf of others.

There are some good reasons why people underestimate the importance of chance. One is that they misperceive chance events. When the market goes up on five consecutive days, people find a reason or cause that makes the world seem deterministic (for example, a favorable

economic report was published). If the market goes up four days and then down on the fifth, people say a "correction" was due. Statistical market analyses suggest that changes in indices such as the Dow Jones index are basically random. Yet each morning, we are offered an "explanation" in the financial pages of why the market went up or down.

One implication of the belief in a deterministic world is the view that evidence should and can be perfect. The fact that there is a strong statistical relationship between smoking and bad health, for instance, is insufficient to convince tobacco company executives that cigarettes are harmful, because the standard of proof they want the evidence to meet is that of perfection. Any deviation from this standard is used strategically as evidence that smoking is not harmful.

We believe in a deterministic world in some cases because we exaggerate the extent to which we can control it. This illusion of control shows up in many contexts, but it seems maximal in complex situations that play out in the future. The tendency appears in experimental contexts in which people prefer to bet on the outcome of a flip of a coin that has not yet been tossed rather than on one that has already been thrown but whose outcome is unknown to the bettor.[4] The illusory sense that a bet may influence the outcome is more acute for future than for past events.

The illusion of control undoubtedly plays a large role in many business decisions. Janis has suggested that President Kennedy's disastrous decision to invade Cuba at the Bay of Pigs was flawed by, among other things, an erroneous belief that the invasion forces, with U.S. support, could control the battle's outcome.[5] Evidently, the Russian military offered similar assurances to support their attack on Grozny.

One common response to the assertion that executives underestimate the importance of random events is that they have learned through experience how to process information about uncertainty. However, experience may not be a good teacher. In situations in which our expectations or predictions were wrong, we often misremember what our expectations, in fact, were. We commonly tend to adjust our memories of what we thought would happen to what we later came to know did happen. This phenomenon, called the "hindsight bias," insulates us from our errors.[6]

We fail to appreciate the role of chance if we assume that every event that occurred was, in principle, predictable. The response "I should have known . . ." implies the belief that some future outcome was inherently knowable, a belief incompatible with the fact that essentially random events determine many outcomes. If every effort has been made to forecast the result of a future event, and the result is very different from predictions, it may be ill-advised to blame ourselves or our employees for the failure. This, of course, assumes that we made every effort to collect and appropriately process all the information relevant to the prediction.

Risk Trade-offs. Uncertainty and risk are facts of executive life. Many risky decisions concern ethical dilemmas involving jobs, safety, environmental risks, and organizational existence. How risky is it to build one more nuclear power plant? How risky is it to expose assembly-line employees to the chemicals for making animal flea collars? At some point, our decisions are reduced to basic questions like: What level of risk is acceptable? How much is safety worth?

One unhelpful answer to the second question is "any price." That answer implies that we should devote all our efforts to highway improvement, cures for cancer, reducing product risks, and so on, to the exclusion of productivity. Throughout our lives, dealing with risk requires trading off benefits and costs; however, this is not a process that people find easy. It is much simpler, but completely unrealistic, to say "any price." The illusion that a riskless world can be created is a myth that is consistent with a theory of the world that minimizes the role of chance.

If we deal irrationally or superficially with risk, costly inconsistencies can occur in the ways we make risk trade-offs. Experts point out

that U.S. laws are less tolerant of carcinogens in food than in drinking water or air. In the United Kingdom, 2,500 times more money per life saved is spent on safety measures in the pharmaceutical industry than in agriculture. Similarly, U.S. society spends about $140,000 in highway construction to save one life and $5 million to save a person from death due to radiation exposure.

A special premium seems to get attached to situations in which all risk can be eliminated. Consider the following two scenarios:

Scenario A. There is a 20 percent chance that the chemicals in your company's plant might be causing ten cancer-related illnesses per year. Your company must decide whether to purchase a multimillion-dollar filtration system that would reduce this probability to a 10 percent chance.

Scenario B. There is a 10 percent chance that the chemicals in your company's plant might be causing ten cancer-related illnesses per year. Your company must decide whether to purchase a multimillion-dollar filtration system that would entirely eliminate this risk.

Evidence suggests that executives would be more likely to purchase the filtration system in scenario B than in scenario A.[7] It appears to be more valuable to eliminate the entire risk than to make an equivalent reduction from one uncertain level to another. Rationally, all reductions in a risk of 10 percent should have the same value for the decision maker. The "preference for certainty" suggests that a firm might be willing to spend more money to achieve a smaller risk reduction if that smaller reduction totally eliminated the risk. Were this the case, not only would the firm's decision be wasteful, it would be unethical because it failed to accomplish the greatest good with the budget allocated for it.

Perceptions of risk are often faulty, frequently resulting in public and private decision makers' misdirected risk-reduction efforts. Is it not a breach of ethics if incoherent policies save fewer lives at greater costs than other possible policies? Failure to explicitly deal with risk trade-offs may have created precisely such a situation.

Risk Framing.
Whether a glass is half-full or half-empty is a matter of risk framing. When the glass is described as half-full, it appears more attractive than when described as half-empty. Similarly, a medical therapy seems more desirable when described in terms of its cure rate than its failure rate. This finding probably occurs because the cure rate induces people to think of the cure (a good thing), whereas an equivalent description in terms of failures induces people to think of failures (not a good thing).

A less obvious effect has been found with regard to the framing of risks. Consider this example:

- A large car manufacturer has recently been hit with a number of economic difficulties. It appears that it needs to close three plants and lay off 6,000 employees. The vice president of production, who has been exploring alternative ways to avoid the crisis, has developed two plans.

Plan A will save one of the three plants and 2,000 jobs.

Plan B has a one-third probability of saving all three plants and all 6,000 jobs, but has a two-thirds probability of saving no plants and no jobs.

Which plan would you select? There are a number of things to consider in evaluating these options. For example, how will each action affect the union? How will each plan influence the motivation and morale of the retained employees? What is the firm's obligation to its shareholders? While all these questions are important, another important factor influences how executives respond to them. Reconsider the problem, replacing the choices provided above with the following choices.

Plan C will result in the loss of two of the three plants and 4,000 jobs.

Plan D has a two-thirds probability of resulting in the loss of all three plants and all 6,000 jobs, but has a one-third probability of losing no plants and no jobs.

Now which plan would you select? Close examination of the two sets of alternative plans finds the two sets of options to be *objectively* the same. For example, saving one of three plants and 2,000 of 6,000 jobs (plan A) offers the same objective outcome as losing two of three plants and 4,000 of 6,000 jobs (plan C). Likewise, plans B and D are objectively identical. Informal empirical investigation, however, demonstrates that *most* individuals choose plan A in the first set (more than 80 percent) and plan D in the second set (more than 80 percent).[8] While the two sets of choices are objectively the same, changing the description of the outcomes from jobs and plants *saved* to jobs and plants *lost* is sufficient to shift the prototypic choice from risk-averse to risk-seeking behavior.

This shift is consistent with research showing that individuals treat risks concerning perceived gains (e.g., saving jobs and plants— plans A and B) differently from risks concerning perceived losses (e.g., losing jobs and plants— plans C and D). The way in which the problem is "framed" or presented can dramatically change how executives respond. If the problem is framed in terms of losing jobs and plants, executives tend to take the risk to avoid any loss. The negative value placed on the loss of three plants and 6,000 jobs is usually perceived as not being three times as bad as losing one plant and 2,000 jobs. In contrast, if the problem is framed in terms of saving jobs and plants (plans A and B), executives tend to avoid the risk and take the sure "gain." They typically view the gain placed on saving three plants and 6,000 jobs as not being three times as great as saving one plant and 2,000 jobs.

This typical pattern of responses is consistent with a general tendency to be risk averse with gains and risk seeking with losses.[9] This tendency has the potential for creating ethical havoc. When thinking about layoffs, for instance, most employees surely focus on their potential job loss. If executives adopt a risk-prone attitude in such situations—that is, if they are willing to risk all to attempt to avoid any losses—they may be seen as reckless and immoral by the very people whose jobs they are trying to preserve. If different stakeholders have different frames, the potential for moral disagreement is great.

Perception of Causes

The final aspect of executives' theories of the world, perhaps the most important, is the beliefs that executives and other people cherish about the causal texture of the world, about *why* things happen or don't happen. Everyone holds beliefs about business successes and failures. As we mentioned earlier, every morning we're given a reason for why the stock market rose, fell, or stayed the same, thus reinforcing the theory that the world is deterministic. Moreover, judging causal responsibility is often a precursor to judging moral accountability and to blaming or praising a person, organization, or policy for an outcome. However, even under the best of circumstances, causation is usually complex, and ambiguity about causation is often at the heart of disputes about responsibility, blame, and punishment.

Consider, for example, the *Herald of Free Enterprise*, a ferry that carried automobiles from the Belgian port of Zeebrugge to Dover, England. Several years ago, it sank in a placid sea a few minutes after leaving Zeebrugge; 180 persons drowned. An investigation determined that the boat sank because the bow doors, through which the cars enter, had been left open, allowing water to pour into the vessel. The assistant bosun, who was responsible for closing the bow doors, had, tragically, taken a nap.

There were no alarm lights to warn the captain that the doors were open. The captain had requested such lights, but the company had denied his request; it felt warning lights were unnecessary because the first mate monitored the closing. On this occasion, the first mate

failed to monitor the bow-door closing because he was needed elsewhere on board due to a chronic manpower shortage. Furthermore, the monitoring system was a "negative" check system, which means that signals were sent only if problems were detected. The lack of a signal was construed as an indication that all was well; the captain did not have to wait for a "positive" signal from the boat deck. Finally, there was the question of why water entered the ship since the bow doors are normally several meters above sea level. The answer was that the ship had taken on ballast to enable it to take cars onto the upper car deck. The captain had not pumped out the ballast before departing because he needed to make up twenty minutes to get back on schedule. Thus the ship left harbor at full throttle, creating a bow wave, with the ship's bow unusually low in the water.

What caused the *Herald of Free Enterprise* to capsize? Who is to blame? We have many candidates for blame: the assistant bosun, the first mate, the captain, the person who refused to provide warning lights, the person who instituted the negative check system, and the owners of the line for failing to provide adequate crew for the boat.

Focus on People. A central issue in this case is the tendency of most people to *blame a person*. This principle is at the heart of the slogan of the National Rifle Association, a U.S. lobbying organization for gun manufacturers and users: "Guns don't kill people, people do." "Human error" becomes the cause assigned to many accidents involving complex technologies (such as ferries). We tend to blame people because it is easy to imagine them having done something to "undo" or prevent the accident. If the assistant bosun had not fallen asleep, if the first mate had stayed on the car deck to supervise the bow door closing, if the captain had not left the harbor at full speed before pumping the ballast, and so on.

It is less easy to imagine changing the ship's equipment and procedures, and these appear less salient as a cause of the disaster. The absence of warning lights allowed the ship to depart with the bow doors open. The negative check system invited a nonmessage to be misconstrued as an "all clear" signal. The point is that human "errors" occur within systems that may vary widely in the degree to which they are "error proof." Our theories about the world usually involve people as the causal agents, rather than environments either that influence people for good or bad or that can compensate for human weaknesses such as drowsiness. From an engineering viewpoint, what is easier to change—warning lights or periodic drowsiness?

Different Events. Theories about causes often lead people to disagree, because, as McGill has pointed out, they are explaining different events.[10] When Sears introduced a commission-based sales system at its automotive repair shops, there was an increase in consumer complaints, usually accusing the shop of performing unnecessary, expensive work. Sears acknowledged that there had been some "isolated abuses" but denied that the problem was widespread. In subsequent public discussions, some of the controversy confused two phenomena. The first is why a particular employee would recommend and perform unnecessary work. The question, "Why did Jack do this?" may lead to determining how Jack is different from Bill and other employees who did not recommend unnecessary work. These causes answer the question, "Why did Jack do this, while others did not?" Are there changes in Jack's situation that can explain his misconduct? "Why did Jack do this now, when he did not do it earlier?" is another way to construe this question.

The second question is why Sears had more complaints in the new system. The fact that there was a change raises an important issue: different systems may produce different levels of unethical conduct. If we focus only on Jack, or if we never change the system, we fail to see that the system itself can be a cause of problems. In many cases, something like the method of compensation appears in the background. If an employee behaves dishonestly, we tend to contrast him or her with honest workers, rather than ask if there is something encouraging dishonesty. When we change situations, we can sometimes see that an organization's features can have a causal impact on human actions, analogous to what happens when a community is exposed to a carcinogenic agent. The overall cancer rate in the community will increase, but it may be difficult to ever determine whether any specific individual's cancer was caused by the toxin. There may be convincing proof that the agent is a cause of cancer in the community generally, but not of any particular cancer.

Sins of Omission. We have no problem judging that the assistant bosun bears some responsibility for the passenger deaths on the *Herald of Free Enterprise*, even though his contribution to the disaster was a failure to act. In many other situations, in which expectations and duties are not as well defined as they were with the *Herald*, a failure to take an action is used to shield persons from causal and, hence, moral responsibility. Is a public health official who decides not to authorize mandatory vaccinations responsible for the deaths of those who succumb to the disease?[11] Is the executive who fails to disclose his knowledge of a colleague's incompetence responsible for the harm that the colleague causes the firm? Many people would answer these questions in the negative, largely because they perceive that the immediate cause of the deaths or harm is the virus or incompetence. But since the actions of the public health official and the executive could have prevented the harm, their actions are *logically* in the same category as those of the assistant bosun. It is an old adage that evil prevails when good people fail to act, but we rarely hold the "good" people responsible for the evil.

THEORIES ABOUT OTHER PEOPLE

An executive's social world is changing at least as fast as his or her physical world. The internationalization of manufacturing and marketing exposes executives to very different cultures and people, and they need to be tolerant of different customs, practices, and styles. More women are entering the work force. In the United States, both the African American and Latino populations are growing faster than the Anglo population, a demographic fact reflected in labor markets. Also, the United States, like many other nations, prohibits employment discrimination on the basis of religion, race, gender, age, and other types of social or personal information. This combination of factors—the increasing social diversity of the business world and the inappropriateness of using such social information in making decisions—creates many ethical hazards that executives must avoid. Incorrect theories about social groups—about women, ethnic minorities, or other nationalities—increase executives' danger markedly. In this section, we discuss how executives, like other people, are likely to harbor erroneous theories about other groups.[12]

Ethnocentrism

The characteristics of our nation, group, or culture appear to us to be normal and ordinary, while others appear foreign, strange, and curious. Implicit in this perception is the assumption that what is normal is good and what is foreign, different, and unusual is less good. This perception that "our" way is normal and preferred and that other ways are somehow inferior has been called ethnocentrism. In the ethnocentric view, the world revolves around our group, and our values and beliefs become the standard against which to judge the rest of the world.

Everyone is ethnocentric to some degree. We probably cannot escape the sense that our native tongue is "natural" while other languages are artificial, that our food is normal while others are exotic, or that our religion is the true one while others are misguided. The fact that ethnocentrism is basic and automatic also makes it dangerous. We do not have to harbor hostile views of members of other groups in order to subtly discriminate. We must merely believe that our own group is superior, a belief that is often actively and officially encouraged by the groups in question and that most of us find all too easy to maintain.

The consequences of ethnocentrism are pervasive. We may describe the same actions of "us" and "them" in words that are descriptively equivalent but evaluatively biased. We are loyal, hard-working, and proud; they are clannish, driven, and arrogant. We are fun loving; they are childish.

Furthermore, "we" tend to be like each other and quite different from "them." "We" come in all shapes and sizes, while "they" tend to be all alike. We take pleasure in "our" successes and grieve over "our" failures, while we are relatively uncaring about "their" outcomes. We expect aid and support from others of "us" and are more willing to support "us" than "them." We may not wish "them" harm but would not go out of our way to help "them." What is curious about this phenomenon is that today "we" may be residents of Chicago and "they" may be rural residents of Illinois, and tomorrow "we" may be Americans and "they" may be Europeans, or "we" may be men and "they" may be women.

Ethnocentric thinking exaggerates the differences between "us" and "them" in ways that can expose leaders to the risk of making ethically unsound decisions. Intensely competitive situations, such as military contexts, illustrate this type of distortion. Military strategies have often made different assumptions about how "we" and "they" will react to intensive attack. They seem to believe that the enemy's spirit can be broken by a prolonged artillery or bombing attack and associated deprivations. Their belief does not seem to have been weakened by the evidence of Leningrad, London, Dresden, Vietnam, or, more recently, Sarajevo. In all these cases, civilian populations were subjected to intensive, prolonged attack, the main consequence of which seems to have been to strengthen the afflicted people's resolve to resist the aggressors. U.S. leaders did not share the Japanese belief that a swift and decisive victory over the U.S. Pacific fleet at Pearl Harbor would destroy the American will to wage a Pacific war. These instances reflect the belief that "they" will be more discouraged by extreme hardship than "we" would be. These incorrect theories about "them" turned out to be seriously wrong and immeasurably costly.

It is an error to think that the effects of ethnocentrism are always as momentous or conspicuous as in these examples. Consider the charge of pervasive racial discrimination in mortgage lending. There is evidence that a higher proportion of minority applicants than white applicants are rejected. This difference in rejection rates remains after accounting for the effects of differences in income, employment stability, credit history, and other indicators of creditworthiness. Yet mortgage bankers vigorously deny that they are harder on minority applicants than on white ones.

Much research indicates that the way ethnocentrism often works is not by denigrating "them" but by rendering special aid to "us." This has been called the "in-group favoritism" hypothesis.[13] In mortgage lending, this hypothesis suggests that the difference in approval rates for whites and minorities may not reflect the fact that qualified minority applicants are denied, but that unqualified white applicants are given loans. This difference has important implications for banks that want to understand and correct the disparity. Establishing a review procedure for rejected minority loans would not be an advisable policy if the in-group favoritism hypothesis is correct, because there may be few, if any, qualified minorities who are rejected. Looking only at rejected minority loans would uncover no evidence of racial discrimination. To find where the discriminatory action lies, the bank needs to examine the marginally unqualified applicants. The in-group favoritism hypothesis predicts that, of this group, more white than minority applicants will be approved.

Stereotypes

In addition to the "theory" that "our" group is better than others, we often have specific beliefs about particular groups, which constitute implicit theories about people in these groups. We have stereotypes about different nationalities, sexes, racial groups, and occupations. To the extent that we rely on stereotypes rather than information about individuals, we risk making unfair, incorrect, and possibly illegal judgments. The issue here is not the extent to which stereotypes are accurate; the issue is whether people will be judged and evaluated on the basis of their individual qualities or on the basis of their group membership. The fact that women are generally smaller and weaker than men is irrelevant to the question of whether a particular woman is strong enough to perform a physically demanding job.

Like ethnocentrism, stereotypes are dangerous because we are often unaware of their influence. We tend to think that our beliefs about groups are accurate, and we can often draw on experience to support these beliefs. Experience, however, can be a misleading guide. Think about the people whom you consider to be the most effective leaders in your company. What qualities do they have that make them effective? For a purely historical reason, there is a good chance that the people who come to mind as effective leaders are men. For that reason, many of the qualities you associate with effective leadership may be masculine. Consequently, you may find it difficult to imagine a woman who could be an effective leader.

It is instructive to review the origins of the common belief that business leaders are masculine. First, there is the fact that twenty to thirty years ago, almost all businesspeople were men. Thus *successful* businesspeople today—those who have been in business twenty or thirty years—are also men. If we form our impressions of what it takes to succeed by abstracting the qualities of the successful people we know, a perfectly reasonable process, our impressions will have a distinctly masculine aura. It is not that we have evidence that women do not succeed; rather, we have little evidence about women at all. If you are asked to imagine people in your company who are notorious failures, the people you conjure up would probably also be men. The stereotypical failure is probably also a man.

How can we guard against the dangers of ethnocentric and stereotypical theories? Starting with ethnocentrism, we should question arguments based on the belief that "they" are different from "us." The safest assumption to make, in the absence of contrary evidence, is that "they" are essentially the same as "us" and that if we want to know how "they" will react to a situation, a wise first step is to ask how "we" would react. Historically, far more harm has been incurred by believing that different groups are basically different than by assuming that all people are essentially the same.

Many decisions that executives make involve promotion, hiring, firing, or other types of personnel allocations. These decisions are stereotypical when they use considerations about the group rather than information about the person. "Women can't handle this kind of stress" is a stereotypical statement about women, not an assessment of a particular individual. Executives should be especially alert for inappropriate theories about others when the criteria for evaluation and the qualifications under discussion are vague. Ethnocentric or stereotypical theories are unlikely to have a large impact if rules state that the person with the best sales record will be promoted. The criteria and qualifications are clear and quantified. However, vague criteria such as sociability, leadership skill, or insight make evaluation susceptible to stereotyping.

One of the most effective strategies for combating ethnocentrism and stereotypes is to have explicit corporate policies that discourage them, such as adopting and publishing equal opportunity principles and constantly reminding employees that group-based judgments and comments are unacceptable. Executives must be the ethical leaders of their organizations.

THEORIES ABOUT OURSELVES

Low self-esteem is not generally associated with successful executives. Executives need confidence, intelligence, and moral strength to make difficult, possibly unpopular decisions. However, when these traits are not tempered with modesty, openness, and an accurate appraisal of talents, ethical problems can arise. In other words, if executives' theories about themselves are seriously flawed, they are courting disaster. Research has identified several ways in which peoples' theories of themselves tend to be flawed.[14] We discuss three: the illusion of superiority, self-serving fairness biases, and overconfidence.

Illusion of Superiority

People tend to view themselves positively. When this tendency becomes extreme, it can lead to illusions that, while gratifying, distort reality and bias decision making. Scholars have identified three such illusions: favorability, optimism, and control.[15]

Illusion of Favorability. This illusion is based on an unrealistically positive view of the self, in both absolute and relative terms. For instance, people highlight their positive characteristics and discount their negative. In relative terms, they believe that they are more honest, ethical, capable, intelligent, courteous, insightful, and fair than others. People give themselves more responsibility for their successes and take less responsibility for their failures than they extend to others. People edit and filter information about themselves to maintain a positive image, just as totalitarian governments control information about themselves.

Illusion of Optimism. This illusion suggests that people are unrealistically optimistic about their future relative to others. People overestimate the likelihood that they will experience "good" future events and underestimate the likelihood of "bad" future events. In particular, people believe that they are less susceptible than others to risks ranging from the possibility of divorce or alcoholism to injury in traffic accidents. To the extent that executives believe themselves relatively immune from such risks, they may be willing to expose themselves and their organizations to hazards.

Illusion of Control. The illusion of optimism is supported by the illusion of control that we referred to earlier. One reason we think we are relatively immune to common risks is that we exaggerate the extent to which we can control random events. Experiments have demonstrated the illusion of control with MBA students from some top U.S. business schools, so there is no reason to think that executives who have attended these schools will be immune to them.[16] (Indeed, the belief that one is exempt from these illusions, while others are not, is an excellent illustration of the illusion of optimism.)

These illusions may also characterize peoples' attitudes about the organizations to which they belong. The result is a kind of organizational ethnocentrism, as we discussed earlier. Managers may feel that their company's contributions to society are more important than those of other companies, even when a neutral observer sees comparability. Similarly, executives may feel that the damage their firms cause society is not as harmful as that created by other organizations. Such a pattern of beliefs can create a barrier to societal improvement when each organization underestimates the damages that it causes. Often, however, firms and their executives genuinely believe that they are being fair and just in their positions (and that others are biased, an illustration of the illusion of favorability).

Self-Serving Fairness Biases

Most executives want to act in a just manner and believe they are fair people. Since they are also interested in performance and success, they often face a conflict between fairness and the desired outcome. They may want a spacious office, a large share of a bonus pool, or the lion's share of the market. Furthermore, they may believe that achieving these outcomes is fair because they deserve them. Different parties, when judging a fair allocation among them, will often make different judgments about what is fair, and those judgments will usually serve the party's interest. These judgments often reflect disagreements about deservedness based on contributions to the collective effort. It is likely that if you asked each division in your organization to estimate the percentage of the company's worth that is created by the division, the sum of the estimates would greatly exceed 100 percent. (Research has been shown this to be true with married couples. The researchers who did the study reported that they had to ask the questions carefully because spouses would often be amazed, and then angry, about the estimates that their mates gave to questions like, "What percentage of the time do you clean up the kitchen?"[17])

One important reason for these self-serving views about fairness is that people are more aware of their contributions to collective activities than others are likely to be; they have more information about their own efforts than others have or than they have about others. Executives may recall disproportionately more instances of *their* division helping the corporation, of *their* corporation helping the community, and of *their* industry helping society.

Furthermore, executives, like other people, credit themselves for their efforts, whereas they are more likely to credit others only for their achievements. They also credit themselves for the temptations that they resisted but judge others strictly by their actions, not by their lack of action. An executive who is offered a substantial bonus to misrepresent the financial well-being of her firm may feel proud of her honesty when she declines, but others may either not know of the temptation or, if they do, believe that she merely followed the rules. While she may feel that the firm owes her gratitude, the firm may not share that feeling.

These fairness biases are particularly problematic during negotiations, when costly delays and impasses result. Egocentric interpretations of fairness hinder conflict resolution because each party believes that its own demands are fair and thus is unwilling to agree to what it perceives as inequitable settlements. It is not just a matter of different interests, it is a matter of what is fair and proper. The difference in perspectives can lead parties to question each others' ethics and morality. The temptation to view the other side as immoral when they fail to agree with us is especially pronounced in situations in which ethnocentric impulses may be aroused—for instance, international negotiations, labor management negotiations, or negotiations that involve issues of race or gender. For example, PriceWaterhouse, a major accounting firm, was surprised when it lost a sexual discrimination suit. The firm's view of its procedures' fairness was at odds with the plaintiff's and judge's views.

Overconfidence

Most people are erroneously confident in their knowledge. In situations in which people are asked factual questions and then asked to judge the probability that their answers are true, the probability judgments far exceed the actual accuracy measures of the proportion of correct answers.[18] For instance, when asked, "Which city is farther north, Rome or New York?," most respondents choose New York and indicate a probability of about 90 percent that it is true. In fact, it is not true; Rome is slightly north of New York. Research has indicated that when people (including executives) respond to a large group of two-option questions for which they claim to be 75 percent certain, their answers tend to be correct only 60 percent of the time.[19] For confidence judgments of 100 percent, it is not uncommon for subjects to be correct only 85 percent of the time. Other research found that subjects who assign odds of 1,000:1 to their answers are correct only 90 to 96 percent of the time.[20] Overconfidence has been identified among members of the armed forces, executives, business students, and C.I.A. agents.[21]

The danger of overconfidence is, of course, that policies based on erroneous information may fail and harm others as well as the executive who established the policy. Overconfidence, as part of our theories about ourselves, coupled with flawed theories about the world or about other people, poses serious threats to rational and ethical decision making.

To the degree to which people are overconfident in their (conservative) risk assessments—in their beliefs about the availability of scarce resources or the character of people unlike themselves—they will fail to seek additional information to update their knowledge. One cost of overconfidence is a reluctance to learn more about a situation or problem before acting.

Even if people acknowledge the need for additional information, research has shown that their process for gaining that information may be biased to confirm prior beliefs and hypotheses.[22] This tendency was initially demonstrated in a series of studies in which the subjects were given a three-number sequence, 2-4-6. Their task was to discover the numeric rule to which the three numbers conformed. To determine the rule, they were allowed to generate other sets of three numbers that the experimenter would classify as either conforming or not conforming to the rule. At any point, subjects could stop when they thought that they had discovered the rule.

The rule is "any three ascending numbers." Suppose you thought the rule was "the difference between the first two numbers equals the difference between the last two numbers" (a common expectation). Testing confirming sequences, like 1-2-3, 10-15-20, or 122-126-130, will provide positive feedback and increase confidence in the original, but incorrect, hypothesis. To discover how the true rule differs from this rule, you must try sequences that do not conform to the hypothesized rule. You need to ask questions that, if answered positively, would disconfirm your rule. This is a less comfortable mode of acquiring information, partly because it may appear that you are not confident in your belief.

Transpose this idea to an executive questioning an engineer about the safety of a tool grip. The executive wants to and does believe that the grip is safe. If the executive asks questions like, "This really is a safe grip, isn't it?" or "Does this grip meet all the standards that have been set for this type of tool?," he is doing two things that may distort the information that he will receive. First, he is displaying the confirmation bias by asking questions he expects to be answered "yes." Second, he is unconsciously exploiting social politeness, because people are more likely to agree than disagree. So by asking these types of questions, the executive is less likely to learn if the engineer has misgivings about any design features than if he asked questions such as, "What are the advantages and disadvantages of the grip?" or "What are the things we have most to worry about with this design?"

These processes suggest that executives may be favorably biased toward themselves and their firms. Will feedback help to eliminate or reduce these biases? We believe that feedback may provide only limited help because of the tendency to seek and notice confirming information, which forms an additional barrier to learning through experience.

When we consider the combined impact of the three processes described in this section—the illusion of superiority, self-centered perceptions of fairness, and overconfidence—we can see the peril associated with erroneous theories of the self. The major peril is that we will come to see ourselves as people for whom the normal rules, norms, and obligations do not apply. The danger is that an executive, especially a successful executive, will hold himself above conventional ethical principles and subject himself only to self-imposed rules that others might judge to be self-serving. He might justify telling a lie on the ground that it permits him to achieve important benefits for others (such as shareholders or employees) even though the shareholders or employees are being duped. He might feel that inflating an expense account or using company property for personal ends is not "really" wrong because of the value that he contributes to the company. Finally, he may undertake an immoral or illegal act, convinced that he will never be caught. The tendencies to feel superior, to generate self-serving, on-the-spot moral rules, and to be overconfident about beliefs create the potential for moral shallowness and callowness.

IMPROVING ETHICAL DECISION MAKING

Our position is that the causes of poor ethical decisions are often the same as the causes of poor decisions generally; decisions may be based on inaccurate theories about the world, about other people, or about ourselves. We suggest that ethical decision making may be improved in the same way that general decision making is improved. In this final section, we outline three broad criteria that executives can focus on: quality, breadth, and honesty.

Quality

Executives who make higher-quality decisions will tend to avoid ethical mistakes. Improving the quality of decision making means ensuring that all the consequences of actions are considered. It implies having accurate assessments of the risks associated with possible strategies and being attuned to the pitfalls of egocentric biases.

A general principle is that the types of flaws and biases we have discussed are likely to influence decision making more when decisions are intuitive, impulsive, or subjective rather than concrete, systematic, and objective. Stereotypes, for instance, have less influence on personnel decisions or performance appraisals if the evaluation criteria are quantitative rather than subjective and vague. Managers often resist this suggestion because they feel that using quantitative procedures makes their judgment "mechanical" or superfluous. The argument in favor of such procedures is that they reduce, or at least identify, opportunities for inappropriate information to influence decisions. Using a quantitative process allows a manager to identify precisely the source of such inappropriate information. Often, systematic procedures result in the same decision as more subjective ones, but the results are more acceptable because the process is viewed as objective, fair, and less subject to bias.

Whenever possible, executives should base decisions on data rather than hunches. In uncertain situations, the best guide comes from close attention to the real world (e.g., data), not from memory and intuition. People worry more about death by murder than death by automobile accident, even though the latter is, statistically, a much greater threat than the former. Reasoning by anecdote—for example, "My engineering chief says he is convinced the product is safe, regardless of what the test results say"—not only wastes resources expended to gather the data but also irresponsibly exposes others to avoidable risks. A corollary is that getting high-quality data is obligatory. In business, as in science, passing off poor, unreliable data as good is fraudulent and inexcusable.

Sometimes executives cannot escape making decisions and judgments on subjective, intuitive bases. But they can take steps to prevent some of the biases from distorting judgment. To combat overconfidence, for instance, it is effective to say to yourself, "Stop and think of the ways in which you could be wrong." Similarly, to avoid minimizing risk, you can ask, "What are the relevant things that I don't know?" Often, a devil's advocate, who is given the role of scrutinizing a decision for false assumptions and optimistic projections, can play this role. A major difference between President Kennedy's Bay of Pigs fiasco and his skillful handling of the Cuban missile crisis was his encouragement of dissenting opinions and inclusion of people whose political orientations disagreed with his own.[23]

One threat to rational and ethical decision making that we noted earlier stems from the untrustworthiness of human memory. The first step in managing this threat is to acknowledge it. The second is to compensate for it with improved, detailed record keeping. This recommendation corresponds to a tenet of the total quality management movement—record keeping and benchmarking are central to measuring objectively how well a process is performing. Quality management and ethical management are close companions; what promotes one generally promotes the other. Erroneous theories threaten both.

Breadth

By breadth, we mean assessment of the full range of consequences that policies may entail.

An ethical audit of a decision must take into account the outcomes for all stakeholders. The first task is to compile a list of the stakeholders. The second is to evaluate a decision's likely outcomes from the stakeholders' perspective.

One approach to identifying stakeholders is to make the decision process as open as possible and invite input from interested parties. However, different groups may have different access to public information, so this technique risks overlooking important constituencies. A potential solution is to include representatives of the important groups on the decision-making team. Broad consultation, which requires an active search to enlist all affected parties into the decision-making process, is important. Openness itself is often a signal to potential opponents that nothing is being hidden and there is nothing to fear. For example, a few years ago, two relatively similar construction projects in Arizona differed greatly in the care they took to involve the active environmental groups in their communities. The project that worked continually with citizens gained their trust and support for the project, while the one that ignored environmentalists faced expensive legal challenges in court.

Socially responsible executive decision making recognizes that a company is part of a broader community that has an interest in its actions. A full accounting for decisions must include a community-impact assessment. If there is community opposition to a policy, it is far better to address it early on rather than risk being ambushed by it later.

Finally, executives' decisions affect those not only in the present but also in the future. Executives' responsibility is to manage so that the world's social and physical environments are not spoiled for future generations. The continual squandering of nonrenewable resources or overuse of renewable ones gives privileges to the current generation at the expense of later ones. Likewise, postponing the payment for what we enjoy today saddles future generations with paying for current consumption. None of us would intentionally make our own children worse off than we are, and we would not want others to do so either.

Breadth is an important quality of ethical decision making because it is both ethically proper *and* strategically sound. It means doing the right thing and doing the smart thing. Intentional decisions to exclude stakeholders' interests or input may not only violate their rights, which is an ethical infraction, but also invite opposition, resentment, and hostility, which is stupid.

Honesty

In discussing breadth, we urged openness. But executives can rarely divulge all the information involved in a decision. Much information is proprietary, gives competitors an unfair advantage, and is legally confidential. A policy of openness does not require executives to tell all. It is perfectly ethical and appropriate to withhold some types of information. It is inappropriate to withhold information about a project or policy merely because an executive is ashamed to make it public. We propose that, if an executive feels so embarrassed about some aspect of a project that she wants to hide the information, she probably should not undertake the project. Conscience, in short, is a good litmus test for a decision's ethicality. If an idea cannot stand the light of day or the scrutiny of public opinion, then it is probably a bad idea. A variant of this "sunshine test" is to imagine how you would feel if you saw the idea or decision on the front page of the *New York Times*.

As we pointed out earlier, you cannot always trust your reaction to a hypothetical test. It's easy to say, "I wouldn't mind it if my family knew that I misstated the firm's income by $20 million," when this is, in fact, completely untrue. As one scholar points out, we ourselves are the easiest audience that we have to play to and the easiest to fool.[24] Consequently, we should imagine whether our audience would accept the idea or decision. In particular, we should ask whether the people with the most to lose would accept the reasons for our actions. If not, we are probably on moral thin ice.

One risk often overlooked when practicing deceit is the continual need to maintain deception. Not only are original facts hidden, but the fact of hiding must also be hidden. In the notorious Watergate scandal, President Nixon was forced from office not for what occurred in the Watergate complex, but for the efforts the White House made to hide the offense.

While it is important to be honest with others, it is just as important to be honest with yourself. Self-deception—being unaware of the processes that lead us to form our opinions and judgments—is unavoidable. We think we remember things accurately, but careful studies show that we do not. We think we know why we make judgments about other people, but research shows us other reasons.

If we can accept the fact that the human mind has an infinite, creative capacity to trick itself, we can guard against irrational, unethical decisions. To deny this reality is to practice self-deception. We can learn to suspect our naive judgments. We can learn to calibrate ourselves to judge risk. We can examine our motives in judging others; are we using hard, reliable information to evaluate subordinates, or are we using stereotypes?

The topic of executive ethics has been dominated by the assumption that executives are constantly faced with an explicit trade-off between ethics and profits. We argue, in contrast, that unethical behavior in organizations is more commonly affected by psychological tendencies that create undesirable behavior from both ethical and rational perspectives. Identifying and confronting these psychological tendencies will increase the success of executives and organizations.

REFERENCES

1. For the research on which we based this article, see: M. H. Bazerman, *Judgment in Managerial Decision Making* (New York: John Wiley, 1994); R. M. Dawes, *Rational Choice in an Uncertain World* (San Diego, California: Harcourt Brace Jovanovich, 1988); T. Gilovich, *How We Know What Isn't So* (New York: Free Press, 1991); and S. Plous, *The Psychology of Judgment and Decision Making* (New York: McGraw-Hill, 1993). A forthcoming book will explore these and other topics in greater detail. See: D. M. Messick and A. Tenbrunsel, *Behavioral Research and Business Ethics* (New York: Russell Sage Foundation, forthcoming).

2. G. Hardin, *Filters Against Folly* (New York: Penguin, 1985).

3. R. Nader, *Unsafe at Any Speed* (New York: Grossmans Publishers, 1965).

4. M. Rothbart and M. Snyder, "Confidence in the Prediction and Postdiction of an Uncertain Outcome," *Canadian Journal of Behavioral Science* 2 (1970): 38–43.

5. I. L. Janis, *Groupthink: Psychological Studies of Policy Decisions and Fiascoes* (Boston: Houghton Mifflin, 1982).

6. B. Fischhoff, "Hindsight: Thinking Backward," *Psychology Today* 8 (1975): 71–76.

7. D. Kahneman and A. Tversky, "Prospect Theory: An Analysis of Decision under Risk," *Econometrica* 47 (1979): 263–291.

8. Bazerman (1994); and Kahneman and Tversky (1979).

9. Kahneman and Tversky (1979).

10. A. L. McGill, "Context Effects in the Judgment of Causation," *Journal of Personality and Social Psychology* 57 (1989): 189–200.

11. I. Ritov and J. Baron, "Reluctance to Vaccinate: Omission Bias and Ambiguity," *Journal of Behavioral Decision Making* 3 (1990): 263–277.

12. For further details on many of these issues, interested readers may consult: S. Worcheland and W. G. Austin, *Psychology of Intergroup Relations* (Chicago: Nelson-Hill, 1986).

13. M. B. Brewer, "In-Group Bias in the Minimal Intergroup Situation: A Cognitive-Motivational Analysis," *Psychological Bulletin* 86 (1979): 307–324.

14. For example, see: S. E. Taylor, *Positive Illusions* (New York: Basic Books, 1989).

15. S. E. Taylor and J. D. Brown, "Illusion and Well-Being: A Social Psychological Perspective," *Psychological Bulletin* 103 (1988): 193–210.

16. R. M. Kramer, E. Newton, and P. L. Pommerenke, "Self-Enhancement Biases and Negotiator Judgment: Effects of Self-Esteem and Mood," *Organizational Behavior and Human Decision Processes* 56 (1993): 110–133.

17. M. Ross and F. Sicoly, "Egocentric Biases in Availability and Attribution," *Journal of Personality and Social Psychology* 37 (1979): 322–336.

18. S. Lichtenstein, B. Fischhoff, and L. D. Phillips, "Calibration of Probabilities," in D. Kahneman, P. Slovic, and A. Tversky, eds., *Judgement under Uncertainty: Heuristics and Biases* (Cambridge: Cambridge University Press, 1982), pp. 306–334.

19. B. Fischoff, P. Slovic, and S. Lichtenstein, "Knowing with Certainty: The Appropriateness of Extreme Confidence," *Journal of Experimental Psychology: Human Perception and Performance* 3 (1977): 552–564.

20. Ibid.

21. R. M. Cambridge and R. C. Shreckengost, "Are You Sure? The Subjective Probability Assessment Test" (Langley, Virginia: Office of Training, Central Intelligence Agency, unpublished manuscript, 1980).

22. P. C. Wason, "On the Failure to Eliminate Hypotheses in a Conceptual Task," *Quarterly Journal of Experimental Psychology* 12 (1960): 129–140.

23. Janis (1982).

24. S. Bok, *Lying: Moral Choice in Public and Private Life* (New York: Vintage Books, 1989).

Dimension III

Interacting with Others: Social and Group Processes

Part A

Foundations of Conformity, Obedience, and Persuasion

19. Opinions and Social Pressure

Solomon E. Asch

*T*hat social influences shape every person's practices, judgments and beliefs is a truism to which anyone will readily assent. A child masters his "native" dialect down to the finest nuances; a member of a tribe of cannibals accepts cannibalism as altogether fitting and proper. All the social sciences take their departure from the observation of the profound effects that groups exert on their members. For psychologists, group pressure upon the minds of individuals raises a host of questions they would like to investigate in detail.

How, and to what extent, do social forces constrain people's opinions and attitudes? This question is especially pertinent in our day. The same epoch that has witnessed the unprecedented technical extension of communication has also brought into existence the deliberate manipulation of opinion and the "engineering of consent." There are many good reasons why, as citizens and as scientists, we should be concerned with studying the ways in which human beings form their opinions and the role that social conditions play.

Studies of these questions began with the interest in hypnosis aroused by the French physician Jean Martin Charcot (a teacher of Sigmund Freud) toward the end of the nineteenth century. Charcot believed that only hysterical patients could be fully hypnotized, but this view was soon challenged by two other physicians, Hyppolyte Bernheim and A. A. Liébault, who demonstrated that they could put most people under the hypnotic spell. Bernheim proposed that hypnosis was but an extreme form of a normal psychological process which became known as "suggestibility." It was shown that monotonous reiteration of instructions could induce in normal persons in the waking state involuntary bodily changes such as swaying or rigidity of the arms, and sensations such as warmth and odor.

It was not long before social thinkers seized upon these discoveries as a basis for explaining numerous social phenomena, from the spread of opinion to the formation of crowds and the following of leaders. The sociologist Gabriel Tarde summed it all up in the aphorism: "Social man is a somnambulist."

When the new discipline of social psychology was born at the beginning of this century, its first experiments were essentially adaptations of the suggestion demonstration. The technique generally followed a simple plan. The subjects, usually college students, were asked to give their opinions or preferences concerning various matters; some time later they were again asked to state their choices, but now they were also informed of the opinions held by authorities or large groups of their peers on the same matters. (Often the alleged consensus was fictitious.) Most of these studies had substantially the same result: confronted with opinions contrary to their own, many subjects apparently shifted their judgments in the direction of the views of the majorities or the experts. The late psychologist Edward L. Thorndike reported that he had succeeded in modifying the esthetic preferences of adults by this procedure. Other psychologists reported that people's evaluations of the merit of a literary passage could be raised or lowered by ascribing the passage to different authors. Apparently the sheer weight of numbers or authority sufficed to change opinions, even when no arguments for the opinions themselves were provided.

Now the very ease of success in these experiments arouses suspicion. Did the subjects actually change their opinions, or were the experimental victories scored only on paper? On grounds of common sense, one must question whether opinions are generally as watery as these studies indicate. There is some reason to wonder whether it was not the investigators who, in their enthusiasm for a theory, were suggestible, and whether the ostensibly gullible subjects were not providing answers which they thought good subjects were expected to give.

The investigations were guided by certain underlying assumptions, which today are common currency and account for much that is thought and said about the operations of propaganda and public opinion. The assumptions are that people submit uncritically and painlessly to external manipulation by suggestion or prestige, and that any given idea or value can be "sold" or "unsold" without reference to its merits. We should be skeptical, however, of the supposition that the power of social pressure necessarily implies uncritical submission to it: independence and the capacity to rise above group passion are also open to human beings. Further, one may question on psychological grounds whether it is possible as a rule to change a person's judgment of a situation or an object without first changing his knowledge or assumptions about it.

In what follows I shall describe some experiments in an investigation of the effects of group pressure which was carried out recently with the help of a number of my associates. The tests not only demonstrate the operations of group pressure upon individuals but also illustrate a new kind of attack on the problem and some of the more subtle questions that it raises.

A group of seven to nine young men, all college students, are assembled in a classroom for a "psychological experiment" in visual judgment. The experimenter informs them that they will be comparing the lengths of lines. He shows two large white cards. On one is a single vertical black line—the standard whose length is to be matched. On the other card are three vertical lines of various lengths. The subjects are to choose the one that is of the same length as the line on the other card. One of the three actually is of the same length; the other two are substantially different, the difference ranging from three quarters of an inch to an inch and three quarters. (See Figure 19.1.)

The experiment opens uneventfully. The subjects announce their answers in the order in which they have been seated in the room, and on the first round every person chooses the

FIGURE 19.1
Subjects were shown two cards. One bore a standard line. The other bore three lines, one of which was the same length as the standard. The subjects were asked to choose this line.

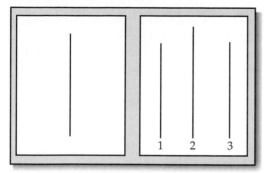

same matching line. Then a second set of cards is exposed; again the group is unanimous. The members appear ready to endure politely another boring experiment. On the third trial there is an unexpected disturbance. One person near the end of the group disagrees with all the others in his selection of the matching line. He looks surprised, indeed incredulous, about the disagreement. On the following trial he disagrees again, while the others remain unanimous in their choice. The dissenter becomes more and more worried and hesitant as the disagreement continues in succeeding trials; he may pause before announcing his answer and speak in a low voice, or he may smile in an embarrassed way.

What the dissenter does not know is that all the other members of the group were instructed by the experimenter beforehand to give incorrect answers in unanimity at certain points. The single individual who is not a party to this prearrangement is the focal subject of our experiment. He is placed in a position in which, while he is actually giving the correct answers, he finds himself unexpectedly in a minority of one, opposed by a unanimous and arbitrary majority with respect to a clear and simple fact. Upon him we have brought to bear two opposed forces: the evidence of his senses and the unanimous opinion of a group of his peers.

Also, he must declare his judgments in public, before a majority which has also stated its position publicly.

The instructed majority occasionally reports correctly in order to reduce the possibility that the naive subject will suspect collusion against him. (In only a few cases did the subject actually show suspicion; when this happened, the experiment was stopped and the results were not counted. There are 18 trials in each series, and on 12 of these the majority responds erroneously. How do people respond to group pressure in this situation? I shall report first the statistical results of a series in which a total of 123 subjects from three institutions of higher learning (not including my own, Swarthmore College) were placed in the minority situation described above. (See Figure 19.2.)

Two alternatives were open to the subject: he could act independently, repudiating the majority, or he could go along with the majority, repudiating the evidence of his senses. Of the 123 put to the test, a considerable percentage yielded

FIGURE 19.2
Error of 123 subjects, each of whom compared lines in the presence of six to eight opponents, is plotted in the gray curve. The accuracy of judgment not under pressure is indicated in black.

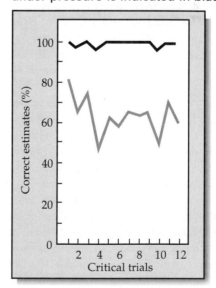

to the majority. Whereas in ordinary circumstances individuals matching the lines will make mistakes less than 1 percent of the time, under group pressure the minority subjects swung to acceptance of the misleading majority's wrong judgments in 36.8 percent of the selections.

Of course individuals differed in response. At one extreme, about one quarter of the subjects were completely independent and never agreed with the erroneous judgments of the majority. At the other extreme, some individuals went with the majority nearly all the time. The performances of individuals in this experiment tend to be highly consistent. Those who strike out on the path of independence do not, as a rule, succumb to the majority even over an extended series of trials, while those who choose the path of compliance are unable to free themselves as the ordeal is prolonged.

The reasons for the startling individual differences have not yet been investigated in detail. At this point we can only report some tentative generalizations from talks with the subjects, each of whom was interviewed at the end of the experiment. Among the independent individuals were many who held fast because of staunch confidence in their own judgment. The most significant fact about them was not absence of responsiveness to the majority but a capacity to recover from doubt and to reestablish their equilibrium. Others who acted independently came to believe that the majority was correct in its answers, but they continued their dissent on the simple ground that it was their obligation to call the play as they saw it.

Among the extremely yielding persons we found a group who quickly reached the conclusion: "I am wrong, they are right." Others yielded in order "not to spoil your results." Many of the individuals who went along suspected that the majority were "sheep" following the first responder, or that the majority were victims of an optical illusion; nevertheless, these suspicions failed to free them at the moment of decision. More disquieting were the reactions of subjects who construed their difference from the majority as a sign of some general deficiency in

themselves, which at all costs they must hide. On this basis they desperately tried to merge with the majority, not realizing the longer-range consequences to themselves. All the yielding subjects underestimated the frequency with which they conformed.

Which aspect of the influence of a majority is more important—the size of the majority or its unanimity? The experiment was modified to examine this question. In one series the size of the opposition was varied from one to fifteen persons. The results showed a clear trend. (See Figure 19.3.) When a subject was confronted with only a single individual who contradicted his answers, he was swayed little: he continued to answer independently and correctly in nearly all trials. When the opposition was increased to two, the pressure became substantial: minority subjects now accepted the wrong answer 13.6 percent

FIGURE 19.3
Size of majority that opposed them has an effect on the subjects. With a single opponent, the subject erred only 3.6 percent of the time; with two opponents he erred 13.6 percent; with three, 31.8 percent; with four, 35.1 percent; with six, 35.2 percent; with seven, 37.1 percent; with nine, 35.1 percent; with fifteen, 31.2 percent.

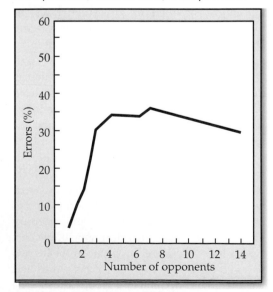

of the time. Under the pressure of a majority of three, the subjects' errors jumped to 31.8 percent. But further increases in the size of the majority apparently did not increase the weight of the pressure substantially. Clearly the size of the opposition is important only up to a point.

Disturbance of the majority's unanimity had a striking effect. In this experiment the subject was given the support of a truthful partner—either another individual who did not know of the prearranged agreement among the rest of the group, or a person who was instructed to give correct answers throughout.

The presence of a supporting partner depleted the majority of much of its power. Its pressure on the dissenting individual was reduced to one-fourth: that is, subjects answered incorrectly only one-fourth as often as under the pressure of a unanimous majority (Figure 19.4). The weakest persons did not yield as readily. Most interesting were the reactions to the partner. Generally the feeling toward him was one of warmth and closeness; he was

FIGURE 19.4

Two subjects supporting each other against a majority made fewer errors (gray curve) than one subject did against a majority (black curve).

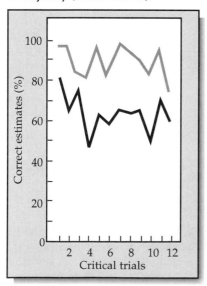

credited with inspiring confidence. However, the subjects repudiated the suggestion that the partner decided them to be independent.

Was the partner's effect a consequence of his dissent, or was it related to his accuracy? We now introduced into the experimental group a person who was instructed to dissent from the majority but also to disagree with the subject. In some experiments the majority was always to choose the worst of the comparison lines and the instructed dissenter to pick the line that was closer to the length of the standard one; in others the majority was consistently intermediate and the dissenter most in error. In this manner we were able to study the relative influence of "compromising" and "extremist" dissenters.

Again the results are clear. When a moderate dissenter is present, the effect of the majority on the subject decreases by approximately one-third, and extremes of yielding disappear. Moreover, most of the errors the subjects do make are moderate, rather than flagrant. In short, the dissenter largely controls the choice of errors. To this extent the subjects broke away from the majority even while bending to it.

On the other hand, when the dissenter always chose the line that was more flagrantly different from the standard, the results were of quite a different kind. The extremist dissenter produced a remarkable freeing of the subjects; their errors dropped to only 9 percent: Furthermore, all the errors were of the moderate variety. We were able to conclude that dissent *per se* increased independence and moderated the errors that occurred, and that the direction of dissent exerted consistent effects.

In all the foregoing experiments each subject was observed only in a single setting. We now turned to studying the effects upon a given individual of a change in the situation to which he was exposed. The first experiment examined the consequences of losing or gaining a partner. The instructed partner began by answering correctly on the first six trials. With his support the subject usually resisted pressure from the majority: eighteen of twenty-seven subjects were completely independent. But after six trials the partner joined the majority. As soon as he did so, there was an abrupt rise in the subjects' errors. Their submission to the majority was just about as frequent as when the minority subject was opposed by a unanimous majority throughout.

It was surprising to find that the experience of having had a partner and of having braved the majority opposition with him had failed to strengthen the individuals' independence. Questioning at the conclusion of the experiment suggested that we had overlooked an important circumstance; namely, the strong specific effect of "desertion" by the partner to the other side. We therefore changed the conditions so that the partner would simply leave the group at the proper point. (To allay suspicion it was announced in advance that he had an appointment with the dean.) In this form of the experiment, the partner's effect outlasted his presence. The errors increased after his departure, but less markedly than after a partner switched to the majority. (See Figure 19.5.)

In a variant of this procedure the trials began with the majority unanimously giving correct answers. Then they gradually broke away until on the sixth trial the naïve subject was alone and the group unanimously against him. As long as the subject had anyone on his side, he was almost invariably independent, but as soon as he found himself alone, the tendency to conform to the majority rose abruptly.

As might be expected, an individual's resistance to group pressure in these experiments depends to a considerable degree on how wrong the majority is. We varied the discrepancy between the standard line and the other lines systematically, with the hope of reaching a point where the error of the majority would be so glaring that every subject would repudiate it and choose independently. In this we regretfully did not succeed. Even when the difference between the lines was seven inches, there were still some who yielded to the error of the majority.

The study provides clear answers to a few relatively simple questions, and it raises many

FIGURE 19.5
Partner left subject after six trials in a single experiment. The gray curve shows the error of the subject when the partner "deserted" to the majority. The black curve shows error when the partner merely left the room.

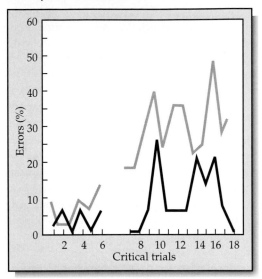

others that await investigation. We would like to know the degree of consistency of persons in situations which differ in content and structure. If consistency of independence or conformity in behavior is shown to be a fact, how is it functionally related to qualities of character and personality? In what ways is independence related to sociological or cultural conditions? Are leaders more independent than other people, or are they adept at following their followers? These and many other questions may perhaps be answerable by investigations of the type described here.

Life in society requires consensus as an indispensable condition. But consensus, to be productive, requires that each individual contribute independently out of his experience and insight. When consensus comes under the dominance of conformity, the social process is polluted and the individual at the same time surrenders the powers on which his functioning as a feeling and thinking being depends. That we have found the tendency to conformity in our society so strong that reasonably intelligent and well-meaning young people are willing to call white black is a matter of concern. It raises questions about our ways of education and about the values that guide our conduct.

Yet anyone inclined to draw too pessimistic conclusions from this report would do well to remind himself that the capacities for independence are not to be underestimated. He may also draw some consolation from a further observation: those who participated in this challenging experiment agreed nearly without exception that independence was preferable to conformity.

REFERENCES

Asch, S. E. Effects of group pressure upon the modification and distortion of judgments. *Groups, leadership, and men.* Harold Guetzdow (ed.). Carnegie Press, 1951.

Asch, S. E. *Social psychology.* Prentice Hall, Inc., 1952.

Miller, N. E., and Dollard, J. *Social learning and imitation.* Yale University Press, 1941.

20. Behavioral Study of Obedience

Stanley Milgram

Obedience is as basic an element in the structure of social life as one can point to. Some system of authority is a requirement of all communal living, and it is only the man dwelling in isolation who is not forced to respond, through defiance or submission, to the commands of others. Obedience, as a determinant of behavior, is of particular relevance to our time. It has been reliably established that from 1933–1945 millions of innocent persons were systematically slaughtered on command. Gas chambers were built, death camps were guarded, daily quotas of corpses were produced with the same efficiency as the manufacture of appliances. These inhumane policies may have originated in the mind of a single person, but they could only be carried out on a massive scale if a very large number of persons obeyed orders.

Obedience is the psychological mechanism that links individual action to political purpose. It is the dispositional cement that binds men to systems of authority. Facts of recent history and observation in daily life suggest that for many persons obedience may be a deeply ingrained behavior tendency, indeed, a prepotent impulse overriding training in ethics, sympathy, and moral conduct. C. P. Snow (1961) points to its importance when he writes:

> When you think of the long and gloomy history of man, you will find more hideous crimes have been committed in the name of rebellion. If you doubt that, read William Shirer's "Rise and Fall of the Third Reich." The German Officer Corps were brought up in the most rigorous code of obedience . . . in the name of obedience they were party to, and assisted in, the most wicked

> large scale actions in the history of the world [p. 24].

While the particular form of obedience dealt with in the present study has its antecedents in these episodes, it must not be thought all obedience entails acts of aggression against others. Obedience serves numerous productive functions. Indeed, the very life of society is predicated on its existence. Obedience may be ennobling and educative and refer to acts of charity and kindness, as well as to destruction.

GENERAL PROCEDURE

A procedure was devised which seems useful as a tool for studying obedience (Milgram, 1961). It consists of ordering a naive subject to administer electric shock to a victim. A simulated shock generator is used, with 30 clearly marked voltage levels that range from 15 to 450 volts. The instrument bears verbal designations that range from Slight Shock to Danger: Severe Shock. The responses of the victim, who is a trained confederate of the experimenter, are standardized. The orders to administer shocks are given to the naive subject in the context of a "learning experiment" ostensibly set up to study the effects of punishment on memory. As the experiment proceeds the naive subject is commanded to administer increasingly more intense shocks to the victim, even to the point of reaching the level marked Danger: Severe Shock. Internal resistances become stronger, and at a certain point the subject refuses to go on with the experiment. Behavior prior to the rupture is considered "obedience," in that the subject complies with the commands of the

Reprinted with permission from Alexandra Milgram.

This research was supported by a grant (NSF G-17916) from the National Science Foundation. Exploratory studies conducted in 1960 were supported by a grant from the Higgins Fund at Yale University. The research assistance of Alan E. Elms and Jon Wayland is gratefully acknowledged.

experimenter. The point of rupture is the act of disobedience. A quantitative value is assigned to the subject's performance based the maximum intensity shock he is willing to administer before he refuses to participate further. Thus for any particular subject and for any particular experimental condition the degree of obedience may be specified with a numerical value. The crux of the study is to systematically vary the factors believed to alter the degree of obedience to the experimental commands.

The technique allows important variables to be manipulated at several points in the experiment. One may vary aspects of the source of command, content and form of command, instrumentalities for its execution, target object, general social setting, etc. The problem, therefore, is not one of designing increasingly more numerous experimental conditions, but of selecting those that best illuminate the *process* of obedience from the sociopsychological standpoint.

RELATED STUDIES

The inquiry bears an important relation to philosophic analyses of obedience and authority (Arendt, 1958; Friedrich, 1958; Weber, 1947), an early experimental study of obedience by Frank (1944), studies in "authoritarianism" (Adorno, Frankel-Brunswik, Levinson, and Sanford, 1950; Rokeach, 1961), and a recent series of analytic and empirical studies in social power

(Cartwright, 1959). It owes much to the long concern with *suggestion* in social psychology, both in its normal forms (e.g., Binet, 1900) and in its clinical manifestations (Charcot, 1881). But it derives, in the first instance, from direct observation of a social fact; the individual who is commanded by a legitimate authority ordinarily obeys. Obedience comes easily and often. It is a ubiquitous and indispensable feature of social life.

METHOD

Subjects

The subjects were 40 males between the ages of 20 and 50, drawn from New Haven and the surrounding communities. Subjects were obtained by a newspaper advertisement and direct mail solicitation. Those who responded to the appeal believed they were to participate in a study of memory and learning at Yale University. A wide range of occupations is represented in the sample. Typical subjects were postal clerks, high school teachers, salesmen, engineers, and laborers. Subjects ranged in educational level from one who had not finished elementary school, to those who had doctorate and other professional degrees. They were paid $4.50 for their participation in the experiment. However, subjects were told that payment was simply for coming to the laboratory, and that the money was theirs no matter what happened after they arrived. Table 20.1

TABLE 20.1
Distribution of Age and Occupational Types in the Experiment

OCCUPATIONS	20–29 YEARS n	30–39 YEARS n	40–50 YEARS n	PERCENTAGE OF TOTAL (OCCUPATIONS)
Workers, skilled and unskilled	4	5	6	37.5
Sales, business, and white-collar	3	6	7	40.0
Professional	1	5	3	22.5
Percentage of total (age)	20	40	40	

shows the proportion of age and occupational types assigned to the experimental condition.

Personnel and Locale

The experiment was conducted on the grounds of Yale University in the elegant interaction laboratory. (This detail is relevant to the perceived legitimacy of the experiment. In further variations, the experiment was dissociated from the university, with consequences for performance.) The role of experimenter was played by a 31-year-old high school teacher of biology. His manner was impassive, and his appearance somewhat stern throughout the experiment. He was dressed in a gray technician's coat. The victim was played by a 47-year-old accountant, trained for the role; he was of Irish-American stock, whom most observers found mild-mannered and likable.

Procedure

One naive subject and one victim (an accomplice) performed in each experiment. A pretext had to be devised that would justify the administration of electric shock by the naive subject. This was effectively accomplished by the cover story. After a general introduction on the presumed relation between punishment and learning, subjects were told:

> But actually, we know very little *about the effect of punishment on learning, because almost no truly scientific studies have been made of it in human beings.*
>
> *For instance, we don't know how much punishment is best for learning—and we don't know how much difference it makes as to who is giving the punishment, whether an adult learns best from a younger or an older person than himself—or many things of that sort.*
>
> *So in this study we are bringing together a number of adults of different occupations and ages. And we're asking some of them to be teachers and some of them to be learners.*
>
> *We want to find out just what effect different people have on each other as teachers and learners, and also what effect punishment will have on learning in this situation.*

> *Therefore, I'm going to ask one of you to be the teacher here tonight and the other one to be the learner.*
>
> *Does either of you have a preference?*

Subjects then drew slips of paper from a hat to determine who would be the teacher and who would be the learner in the experiment. The drawing was rigged so that the naive subject was always the teacher and the accomplice always the learner. (Both slips contained the word "Teacher.") Immediately after the drawing the teacher and learner were taken to an adjacent room and the learner was strapped into an "electric chair" apparatus.

The experimenter explained that the straps were to prevent excessive movement while the learner was being shocked. The effect was to make it impossible for him to escape from the situation. An electrode was attached to the learner's wrist, and electrode paste was applied "to avoid blisters and burns." Subjects were told that the electrode was attached to the shock generator in the adjoining room.

In order to improve credibility the experimenter declared, in response to a question by the learner: "Although the shocks can be extremely painful, they cause no permanent tissue damage."

Learning Task. The lesson administered by the subject was a paired-associate learning task. The subject read a series of word pairs to the learner, and then read the first word of the pair along with four terms. The learner was to indicate which of the four terms had originally been paired with the first word. He communicated his answer by pressing one of four switches in front of him, which in turn lit up one of four numbered quadrants in an answer-box located atop the shock generator.

Shock Generator. The instrument panel consists of 30 lever switches set in a horizontal line. Each switch is clearly labeled with a voltage designation that ranges from 15 to 450 volts. There is a 15-volt increment from one switch to the next going from left to right. In addition, the following verbal designations are clearly indicated for groups of four switches going from left to right: Slight Shock, Moderate Shock, Strong Shock, Very Strong Shock, Intense Shock, Extreme Intensity Shock, Danger: Severe Shock. (Two switches after this last designation are simply marked XXX.)

Upon depressing a switch: a pilot light corresponding to each switch is illuminated in bright red; an electric buzzing is heard; an electric blue light, labeled "voltage energizer," flashes; the dial on the voltage meter swings to the right; various relay clicks are sounded.

The upper left-hand corner of the generator is labeled Shock Generator, Type ZLB, Dyson Instrument Company, Waltham, Mass. Output 15 Volts–450 Volts.

Details of the instrument were carefully handled to ensure an appearance of authenticity. The panel was engraved by precision industrial engravers, and all components were of high quality. No subject in the experiment suspected that the instrument was merely a simulated shock generator.[1]

Sample Shock.
Each naive subject is given a sample shock on the shock generator, prior to beginning his run as teacher. This shock is always 45 volts, and is applied by pressing the third switch of the generator. The shock is applied to the wrist of the naive subject, and has its source in a 45-volt battery wired into the generator. This further convinces the subject of the authenticity of the generator.

Shock Instructions.
The subject is told to administer a shock to the learner each time he gives a wrong response. Moreover—and this is the key command—the subject is instructed to "move one lever higher on the shock generator each time the learner flashes a wrong answer." He is also instructed to announce the voltage level before administering a shock. This serves to continually remind subjects of the increasing intensity of shocks administered to the learner.

Preliminary and Regular Run.
Pretests revealed that the procedure of reading words and administering shocks requires some practice before it can be handled smoothly. Therefore, immediately preceding the regular run, the teacher is given a preliminary series of 10 words to read to the learner. There are 3 neutral words in the practice series (i.e., words that the learner answers correctly), so that shocks are administered for 7 of the words, with the maximum shock at 105 volts (moderate shock). Almost all subjects master the procedure by the time the preliminary run is over.

Subjects are then presented with a second list, and are told that the procedure is the same as for the first list; the experimenter adds, however:

When you get to the bottom of the list, repeat it over again, and continue giving shocks, until the learner has learned all the pairs correctly.

The experimenter instructs the subject to

start from 15 volts and increase the shock level one step each time the learner gives a wrong answer.

Feedback from the Victim.
In all conditions the learner gives a predetermined set of responses to the word pair test, based on a schedule of approximately three wrong answers to one correct answer. In the present experimental condition no vocal response or other sign of protest is heard from the learner until Shock Level 300 is reached. When the 300-volt shock is administered, the learner pounds on the wall of the room in which he is bound to the electric chair. The pounding can be heard by the subject. From this point on, the learner's answers no longer appear on the four-way panel.

At this juncture, subjects ordinarily turn to the experimenter for guidance. The experimenter instructs the subject to treat the absence of a response as a wrong answer, and to shock the subject according to the usual schedule. He advises the subjects to allow 5–10 seconds before considering no response as a wrong answer, and to increase the shock level one step each time the learner fails to respond correctly. The learner's pounding is repeated after the 315-volt shock is administered; afterwards he is not heard from, nor do his answers reappear on the four-way signal box.

Experimenter Feedback.

At various points in the experiment the subject may turn to the experimenter for advice on whether he should continue to administer shocks. Or he may indicate that he does not wish to go on. It was important to standardize the experimenter's responses to these inquiries and reactions.

If the subject indicated his unwillingness to go on, the experimenter responded with a sequence of "prods," using as many as necessary to bring the subject into line.

> Prod 1: *Please continue.* or *Please go on.*
> Prod 2: *The experiment requires that you continue.*
> Prod 3: *It is absolutely essential that you continue.*
> Prod 4: *You have no other choice, you* must *go on.*

The prods were always made in sequence: Only if Prod 1 had been unsuccessful could Prod 2 be used. If the subject refused to obey the experimenter after Prod 4, the experiment was terminated. The experimenter's tone of voice was at all times firm, but not impolite. The sequence was begun anew on each occasion that the subject balked or showed reluctance to follow orders.

Special prods. If the subject asked if the learner was liable to suffer permanent physical injury, the experimenter said:

> *Although the shocks may be painful, there is no permanent tissue damage, so please go on. [Followed by Prods 2, 3, and 4 if necessary.]*

If the subject said that the learner did not want to go on, the experimenter replied:

> *Whether the learner likes it or not, you must go on until he has learned all the word pairs correctly. So please go on. [Followed by Prods 2, 3, and 4 if necessary.]*

Dependent Measures

The primary dependent measure for any subject is the maximum shock he administers before he refuses to go any further. In principle this may vary from 0 (for a subject who refuses to administer even the first shock) to 30 (for a subject who administers the highest shock on the generator). A subject who beaks off the experiment at any point prior to administering the thirtieth shock level is termed a *defiant* subject. One who complies with experimental commands fully, and proceeds to administer all shock levels commanded, is termed an *obedient* subject.

Further Records.

With few exceptions, experimental sessions were recorded on magnetic tape. Occasional photographs were taken through one-way mirrors. Notes were kept on any unusual behavior occurring during the course of the experiments. On occasion, additional observers were directed to write objective descriptions of the subjects' behavior. The latency and duration of shocks were measured by accurate timing devices.

Interview and Dehoax.

Following the experiment, subjects were interviewed; open-ended questions, projective measures, and attitude scales were employed. After the interview, procedures were undertaken to assure that the subject would leave the laboratory in a state of well-being. A friendly reconciliation was arranged between the subject and the victim, and an effort was made to reduce any tensions that arose as a result of the experiment.

RESULTS
Preliminary Notions

Before giving an account of the experimental results, it is instructive to consider how persons predict others will perform when commanded to administer powerful shocks to another person. Fourteen Yale seniors, all psychology majors, were provided with a detailed description of the experimental situation. They were asked to reflect carefully on it, and to predict the behavior of 100 hypothetical subjects. More specifically, they were instructed to plot the distribution of obedience of "100 Americans of diverse occupations, and ranging in age from 20 to 50 years," who were placed in the experimental situation.

There was considerable agreement among the respondents on the expected behavior of hypothetical subjects. All respondents predicted that only an insignificant minority would go through to the end of the shock series. (The estimates ranged from 0 to 3 percent; i.e., the most "pessimistic" member of the class predicted that of 100 persons, 3 would continue through to the most potent shock available on the shock generator—450 volts.) The class mean was 1.2 percent. The question was also posed informally to colleagues of the author, and the most general feeling was that few if any subjects would go beyond the designation Very Strong Shock.

Result of Experiment I

Subjects Accept Situation.
With few exceptions subjects were convinced of the reality of the experimental situation, that they were administering shocks to another person, and the most potent shocks were extremely painful. In the post-experimental interview subjects were asked: "How painful to the learner were the last few shocks that you administered to him?" Subjects were instructed to indicate their answers on a printed 14-point scale ranging from "Not at all painful" to "Extremely painful." The modal response was 14 (Extremely painful) with the mean at 13.42.

Signs of Extreme Tension.
Many subjects showed signs of nervousness in the experimental situation, and especially upon administering the more powerful shocks. In a large number of cases the degree of tension reached extremes that are rarely seen in sociopsychological laboratory studies. Subjects were observed to sweat, tremble, stutter, bite their lips, groan, and dig their fingernails into their flesh. These were characteristic rather than exceptional responses to the experiment.

One sign of tension was the regular occurrence of nervous laughing fits. Fourteen of the 40 subjects showed definite signs of nervous laughter and smiling. The laughter seemed entirely out of place, even bizarre. Full-blown, uncontrollable seizures were observed for 3 subjects. On one occasion we observed a seizure so violently convulsive that it was necessary to call a halt to the experiment. The subject, a 46-year-old encyclopedia salesman, was seriously embarrassed by his untoward and uncontrollable behavior. In the post-experimental interviews subjects took pains to point out that they were not sadistic types, and that the laughter did not mean they enjoyed shocking the victims.

Distribution of Scores.
It had been conjectured that persons would not, in general, agree to administer shocks beyond the level designated as Very Strong Shock. The distribution of maximum shocks for this experiment is shown in Table 20.2. The obtained distribution of scores deviates radically from the prediction.

Upon command of the experimenter, each of the 40 subjects went beyond the expected breakoff point. No subject stopped prior to administering Shock Level 20. (At this level—300 volts—the victim kicks on the wall and no longer provides answers to the teacher's multiple-choice questions.)

Of the 40 subjects, 5 refused to obey the experimental commands beyond the 300-volt level. Four more subjects administered one further shock, and then refused to go on. Two broke off at the 330-volt level, and 1 each at 345, 360, and 375 volts. Thus a total of 14 subjects defied the experimenter. It is instructive to reprint their remarks at the point of defiance, as transcribed from the tape recordings:

[0124] I think he's trying to communicate, he's knocking . . . Well it's not fair to shock the guy . . . these are terrific volts. I don't think this is very humane . . . Oh, I can't go on with this; no, this isn't right. It's a hell of an experiment. The guy is suffering in there. No, I don't want to go on. This is crazy. [Subject refused to administer more shocks.]

Table 20.2
Distribution of Breakoff Points

Verbal Designation and Voltage Indication	Number of Subjects for Whom This Was Maximum Shock
Slight Shock	
15	0
30	0
45	0
60	0
Moderate Shock	
75	0
90	0
105	0
120	0
Strong Shock	
135	0
150	0
165	0
180	0
Very Strong Shock	
195	0
210	0
225	0
240	0
Intense Shock	
255	0
270	0
285	0
300	5
Extreme Intensity Shock	
315	4
330	2
345	1
360	1
Danger: Severe Shock	
375	1
390	0
405	0
420	0
XXX	
435	0
450	26

[0123] He's banging in there. I'm gonna chicken out. I'd like to continue, but I can't do that to a man . . . I'm sorry I can't do that to a man. I'll hurt his heart. You take your check . . . No really, I couldn't do it.

These subjects were frequently in a highly agitated and even angered state. Sometimes, verbal protest was at a minimum, and the subject simply got up from his chair in front of the shock generator, and indicated that he wished to leave the laboratory.

Of the 40 subjects, 26 obeyed the orders of the experimenter to the end, proceeding to punish the victim until they reached the most potent shock available on the shock generator. At that point, the experimenter called a halt to the session. (The maximum shock is labeled 450 volts, and is two steps beyond the designation: Danger: Severe Shock.) Although obedient subjects continued to administer shocks, they often did so under extreme stress. Some expressed reluctance to administer shocks beyond the 300-volt level, and displayed fears similar to those who defied the experimenter; yet they obeyed.

After the maximum shocks had been delivered, and the experimenter called a halt to the proceedings, many obedient subjects heaved sighs of relief, mopped their brows, rubbed their fingers over their eyes, or nervously fumbled cigarettes. Some shook their heads, apparently in regret. Some subjects had remained calm throughout the experiment, and displayed only minimal signs of tension from beginning to end.

DISCUSSION

The experiment yielded two findings that were surprising. The first finding concerns the sheer strength of obedient tendencies manifested in this situation. Subjects have learned from childhood that it is a fundamental breach of moral conduct to hurt another person against his will. Yet, 26 subjects abandon this tenet in following the instructions of an authority who has no special powers to enforce his commands. To disobey would bring no material loss to the subject; no punishment would ensue. It is clear from the remarks and outward behavior of many participants that in punishing the victim they are often acting against their own values. Subjects often expressed deep disapproval of shocking a man in the face of his objections, and others denounced it as stupid and senseless. Yet the majority complied with the experimental commands. This outcome was surprising from two perspectives: first, from the standpoint of predictions made in the questionnaire described earlier. (Here, however, it is possible that the remoteness of the respondents from the actual situation, and the difficulty of conveying to them the concrete details of the experiment, could account for the serious underestimation of obedience.)

But the results were also unexpected to persons who observed the experiment in progress, through one-way mirrors. Observers often uttered expressions of disbelief upon seeing a subject administer more powerful shocks to the victim. These persons had a full acquaintance with the details of the situation, and yet systematically underestimated the amount of obedience that subjects would display.

The second unanticipated effect was the extraordinary tension generated by the procedures. One might suppose that a subject would simply break off or continue as his conscience dictated. Yet, this is very far from what happened. There were striking reactions of tension and emotional strain. One observer related:

I observed a mature and initially poised businessman enter the laboratory smiling and confident. Within 20 minutes he was reduced to a twitching, stuttering wreck, who was rapidly approaching a point of nervous collapse. He constantly pulled on his earlobe, and twisted his hands. At one point he pushed his fist into his forehead and muttered: "Oh God, let's stop it." And yet he continued to respond to every word of the experimenter, and obeyed to the end.

Any understanding of the phenomenon of obedience must rest on an analysis of the particular conditions in which it occurs. The following features of the experiment go some distance in explaining the high amount of obedience observed in the situation.

1. The experiment is sponsored by and takes place on the grounds of an institution of unimpeachable reputation, Yale University. It may be reasonably presumed that the personnel are competent and reputable. The importance of this background authority is now being studied by conducting a series of experiments outside of New Haven, and without any visible ties to the university.

2. The experiment is, on the face of it, designed to attain a worthy purpose—advancement of knowledge about learning and memory. Obedience occurs not as an end in itself, but as an instrumental element in a situation that the subject construes as significant, and meaningful. He may not be able to see its full significance, but he may properly assume that the experimenter does.

3. The subject perceives that the victim has voluntarily submitted to the authority system of the experimenter. He is not (at first) an unwilling captive impressed for involuntary service. He has taken the trouble to come to the laboratory presumably to aid the experimental research. That he later becomes an involuntary subject does not alter the fact that, initially, he consented to participate without qualification. Thus he has in some degree incurred an obligation toward the experimenter.

4. The subject, too, has entered the experiment voluntarily, and perceives himself under obligation to aid the experimenter. He has made a commitment, and to disrupt the experiment is a repudiation of this initial promise of aid.

5. Certain features of the procedure strengthen the subject's sense of obligation to the experimenter. For one, he has been paid for coming to the laboratory. In part this is canceled out by the experimenter's statement that:

Of course, as in all experiments, the money is yours simply for coming to the laboratory. From this point on, no matter what happens, the money is yours.[2]

6. From the subject's standpoint, the fact that he is the teacher and the other man the learner is purely a chance consequence (it is determined by drawing lots) and he, the subject, ran the same risk as the other man in being assigned the role of learner. Since the assignment of positions in the experiment was achieved by fair means, the learner is deprived of any basis of complaint on this count. (A similar situation obtains in Army units, in which—in the absence of volunteers—a particularly dangerous mission may be assigned by drawing lots, and the unlucky soldier is expected to bear his misfortune with sportsmanship.)

7. There is, at best, ambiguity with regard to the prerogatives of a psychologist and the corresponding rights of his subject. There is a vagueness of expectations concerning what a psychologist may require of his subject, and when he is overstepping acceptable limits. Moreover, the experiment occurs in a closed setting, and thus provides no opportunity for the subject to remove these ambiguities by discussion with others. There are few standards that seem directly applicable to the situation, which is a novel one for most subjects.

8. The subjects are assured that the shocks administered to the subject are "painful but not dangerous." Thus they assume that the discomfort caused the victim is momentary, while the scientific gains resulting from the experiment are enduring.

9. Through Shock Level 20 the victim continues to provide answers on the signal box. The subject may construe this as a sign that the victim is still willing to "play the game." It is only after Shock Level 20 that the victim repudiates the rules completely, refusing to answer further.

These features help to explain the high amount of obedience obtained in this experiment. Many of the arguments raised need not remain matters of speculation, but can be reduced to testable propositions to be confirmed or disproved by further experiments.[3]

The following features of the experiment concern the nature of the conflict which the subject faces.

10. The subject is placed in a position in which he must respond to the competing demands of two persons: the experimenter and the victim. The conflict must be resolved by meeting the demands of one or the other; satisfaction of the victim and the experimenter are mutually exclusive. Moreover, the resolution must take the form of a highly visible action, that of continuing to shock the victim or breaking off the experiment. Thus the subject is forced into a public conflict that does not permit any completely satisfactory solution.

11. While the demands of the experimenter carry the weight of scientific authority, the demands of the victim spring from his personal experience of pain and suffering. The two claims need not be regarded as equally pressing and legitimate. The experimenter seeks an abstract scientific datum; the victim cries out for relief from physical suffering caused by the subject's actions.

12. The experiment gives the subject little time for reflection. The conflict comes on rapidly. It is only minutes after the subject has been seated before the shock generator that the victim begins his protests. Moreover, the subject perceives that he has gone through but two-thirds of the shock levels at the time the subject's first protests are heard. Thus he understands that the conflict will have a persistent aspect to it, and may well become more intense as increasingly more powerful shocks are required. The rapidity with which the conflict descends on the subject, and his realization that it is predictably recurrent may well be sources of tension to him.

13. At a more general level, the conflict stems from the opposition of two deeply ingrained behavior dispositions: first, the disposition not to harm other people, and second, the tendency to obey those whom we perceive to be legitimate authorities.

REFERENCES

Adorno, T., Frenkel-Brunswik, Else, Levinson, D. J., and Sanford, R. N. *The authoritarian personality.* New York: Harper, 1950.

Arendt, H. What was authority? In C. J. Friedrich (ed.), *Authority.* Cambridge: Harvard Univer. Press, 1958, pp. 81–112.

Binet, A. *La suggestibilité.* Paris: Schleicher, 1900.

Buss, A. H. *The psychology of aggression.* New York: Wiley, 1961.

Cartwright, S. (ed.) *Studies in social power.* Ann Arbor: University of Michigan Institute for Social Research, 1959.

Charcot, J. M. *Oeuvres complètes.* Paris: Bureaux du Progrès Médical, 1881.

Frank, J. D. Experimental studies of personal pressure and resistance. *J. Gen. Psychol.,* 1944, *30,* 23–64.

Friedrich, C. J. (ed.) *Authority.* Cambridge: Harvard Univer. Press, 1958.

Milgram, S. Dynamics of obedience. Washington: National Science Foundation, 25 January 1961. (Mimeo)

Milgram, S. Some conditions of obedience and disobedience to authority. *Hum. Relat.,* 1965, *18,* 57–76.

Rokeach, M. Authority, authoritarianism, and conformity. In I. A. Berg and B. M. Bass (eds.), *Conformity and deviation.* New York: Harper, 1961, pp. 230–257.

Snow, C. P. Either-or. *Progressive,* 1961 (Feb.), 24.

Weber, M. *The theory of social and economic organization.* Oxford: Oxford Univer. Press, 1947.

1. A related technique, making use of a shock generator, was reported by Buss (1961) for the study of aggression in the laboratory. Despite the considerable similarity of technical detail in the experimental procedures, each investigator proceeded in ignorance of the other's work. Milgram provided plans and photographs of his shock generator, experimental procedure, and first results in a report to the National Science Foundation in January 1961. This report received only limited circulation. Buss reported his procedure six months later, but to a wider audience. Subsequently, technical information and reports were exchanged. The present article was first received in the editor's office on December 27, 1961; it was resubmitted with deletions on July 27, 1962.

2. Forty-three subjects, undergraduates at Yale University, were run in the experiment without payment. The results are very similar to those obtained with paid subjects.

3. A series of recently completed experiments employing the obedience paradigm is reported in Milgram (1965).

21. *Harnessing the Science of Persuasion*

Robert B. Cialdini

A lucky few have it; most of us do not. A handful of gifted "naturals" simply know how to capture an audience, sway the undecided, and convert the opposition. Watching these masters of persuasion work their magic is at once impressive and frustrating. What's impressive is not just the easy way they use charisma and eloquence to convince others to do as they ask. It's also how eager those others are to do what's requested of them, as if the persuasion itself were a favor they couldn't wait to repay.

The frustrating part of the experience is that these born persuaders are often unable to account for their remarkable skill or pass it on to others. Their way with people is an art, and artists as a rule are far better at doing than at explaining. Most of them can't offer much help to those of us who possess no more than the ordinary quotient of charisma and eloquence but who still have to wrestle with leadership's fundamental challenge: getting things done through others. That challenge is painfully familiar to corporate executives, who every day have to figure out how to motivate and direct a highly individualistic work force. Playing the "Because I'm the boss" card is out. Even if it weren't demeaning and demoralizing for all concerned, it would be out of place in a world where cross-functional teams, joint ventures, and intercompany partnerships have blurred the lines of authority. In such an environment, persuasion skills exert far greater influence over others' behavior than formal power structures do.

Which brings us back to where we started. Persuasion skills may be more necessary than ever, but how can executives acquire them if the most talented practitioners can't pass them along? By looking to science. For the past five decades, behavioral scientists have conducted experiments that shed considerable light on the way certain interactions lead people to concede, comply, or change. This research shows that persuasion works by appealing to a limited set of deeply rooted human drives and needs, and it does so in predictable ways. Persuasion, in other words, is governed by basic principles that can be taught, learned, and applied. By mastering these principles, executives can bring scientific rigor to the business of securing consensus, cutting deals, and winning concessions. In the pages that follow, I describe six fundamental principles of persuasion and suggest a few ways that executives can apply them in their own organizations.

THE PRINCIPLE OF PEOPLE LIKE THOSE WHO LIKE THEM
The Application: Uncover Real Similarities and Offer Genuine Praise

The retailing phenomenon known as the Tupperware party is a vivid illustration of this principle in action. The demonstration party for Tupperware products is hosted by an individual, almost always a woman, who invites to her home an array of friends, neighbors, and relatives. The guests' affection for their hostess predisposes them to buy from her, a dynamic that was confirmed by a 1990 study of purchase decisions made at demonstration parties. The researchers, Jonathan Frenzen and Harry Davis, writing in the *Journal of Consumer Research,* found that the guests' fondness for their hostess weighed twice as heavily in their purchase decisions as their regard for the products they bought. So when guests at a Tupperware party buy something, they aren't just buying to please themselves. They're buying to please their hostess as well.

What's true at Tupperware parties is true for business in general: If you want to influence people, win friends. How? Controlled research has identified several factors that reliably increase liking, but two stand out as especially compelling—similarity and praise. Similarity literally draws people together. In one experiment, reported in a 1968 article in the *Journal of Personality*, participants stood physically closer to one another after learning that they shared political beliefs and social values. And in a 1963 article in *American Behavioral Scientists*, researcher F. B. Evans used demographic data from insurance company records to demonstrate that prospects were more willing to purchase a policy from a salesperson who was akin to them in age, religion, politics, or even cigarette-smoking habits.

Managers can use similarities to create bonds with a recent hire, the head of another department, or even a new boss. Informal conversations during the workday create an ideal opportunity to discover at least one common area of enjoyment, be it a hobby, a college basketball team, or reruns of *Seinfeld.* The important thing is to establish the bond early because it creates a presumption of good-will and trustworthiness in every subsequent encounter. It's much easier to build support for a new project when the people you're trying to persuade are already inclined in your favor.

Praise, the other reliable generator of affection, both charms and disarms. Sometimes the praise doesn't even have to be merited. Researchers at the University of North Carolina writing in the *Journal of Experimental Social Psychology* found that men felt the greatest regard for an individual who flattered them unstintingly even if the comments were untrue. And in their book *Interpersonal Attraction* (Addison-Wesley, 1978), Ellen Berscheid and Elaine Hatfield Walster presented experimental data showing that positive remarks about another person's traits, attitude, or performance reliably generates liking in return, as well as

willing compliance with the wishes of the person offering the praise.

Along with cultivating a fruitful relationship, adroit managers can also use praise to repair one that's damaged or unproductive. Imagine you're the manager of a good-sized unit within your organization. Your work frequently brings you into contact with another manager—call him Dan—whom you have come to dislike. No matter how much you do for him, it's not enough. Worse, he never seems to believe that you're doing the best you can for him. Resenting his attitude and his obvious lack of trust in your abilities and in your good faith, you don't spend as much time with him as you know you should; in consequence, the performance of both his unit and yours is deteriorating.

The research on praise points toward a strategy for fixing the relationship. It may be hard to find, but there has to be something about Dan you can sincerely admire, whether it's his concern for the people in his department, his devotion to his family, or simply his work ethic. In your next encounter with him, make an appreciative comment about that trait. Make it clear that in this case at least, you value what he values. I predict that Dan will relax his relentless negativity and give you an opening to convince him of your competence and good intentions.

THE PRINCIPLE OF RECIPROCITY: PEOPLE REPAY IN KIND
The Application: Give What You Want to Receive

Praise is likely to have a warming and softening effect on Dan because, ornery as he is, he is still human and subject to the universal human tendency to treat people the way they treat him. If you have ever caught yourself smiling at a coworker just because he or she smiled first, you know how this principle works.

Charities rely on reciprocity to help them raise funds. For years, for instance, the Disabled American Veterans organization, using only a well-crafted fund-raising letter, garnered a very respectable 18% rate of response to its appeals.

But when the group started enclosing a small gift in the envelope, the response rate nearly doubled to 35%. The gift—personalized address labels—was extremely modest, but it wasn't what prospective donors received that made the difference. It was that they had gotten anything at all.

What works in that letter works at the office, too. It's more than an effusion of seasonal spirit, of course, that impels suppliers to shower gifts on purchasing departments at holiday time. In 1996, purchasing managers admitted to an interviewer from *Inc.* magazine that after having accepted a gift from a supplier, they were willing to purchase products and services they would have otherwise declined. Gifts also have a startling effect on retention. I have encouraged readers of my book to send me examples of the principles of influence at work in their own lives. One reader, an employee of the State of Oregon, sent a letter in which she offered these reasons for her commitment to her supervisor:

He gives me and my son gifts for Christmas and gives me presents on my birthday. There is no promotion for the type of job I have, and my only choice for one is to move to another department. But I find myself resisting trying to move. My boss is reaching retirement age, and I am thinking I will be able to move out after he retires. . . . [F]or now, I feel obligated to stay since he has been so nice to me.

Ultimately, though, gift giving is one of the cruder applications of the rule of reciprocity. In its more sophisticated uses, it confers a genuine first-mover advantage on any manager who is trying to foster positive attitudes and productive personal relationships in the office: Managers can elicit the desired behavior from coworkers and employees by displaying it first. Whether it's a sense of trust, a spirit of cooperation, or a pleasant demeanor, leaders should model the behavior they want to see from others.

The same holds true for managers faced with issues of information delivery and resource allocation. If you lend a member of your staff to a colleague who is shorthanded and staring at a fast-approaching deadline, you will significantly increase your chances of getting help when you need it. Your odds will improve even more if you say, when your colleague thanks you for the assistance, something like, "Sure, glad to help. I know how important it is for me to count on your help when I need it."

THE PRINCIPLE OF SOCIAL PROOF: PEOPLE FOLLOW THE LEAD OF SIMILAR OTHERS

The Application: Use Peer Power Whenever It's Available

Social creatures that they are, human beings rely heavily on the people around them for cues on how to think, feel, and act. We know this intuitively, but intuition has also been confirmed by experiments, such as the one first described in 1982 in the *Journal of Applied Psychology*. A group of researchers went door-to-door in Columbia, South Carolina, soliciting donations for a charity campaign and displaying a list of neighborhood residents who had already donated to the cause. The researchers found that the longer the donor list was, the more likely those solicited would be to donate as well.

To the people being solicited, the friends' and neighbors' names on the list were a form of social evidence about how they should respond. But the evidence would not have been nearly as compelling had the names been those of random strangers. In an experiment from the 1960s, first described in the *Journal of Personality and Social Psychology*, residents of New York City were asked to return a lost wallet to its owner. They were highly likely to attempt to return the wallet when they learned that another New Yorker had previously attempted to do so. But learning that someone from a foreign country had tried to return the wallet didn't sway their decision one way or the other.

The lesson for executives from these two experiments is that persuasion can be extremely effective when it comes from peers. The science supports what most sales professionals already know: Testimonials from satisfied customers work best when the satisfied customer and the prospective customer share similar circumstances. That lesson can help a manager faced with the task of selling a new corporate initiative. Imagine that you're trying to streamline your department's work processes. A group of veteran employees is resisting. Rather than try to convince the employees of the move's merits yourself, ask an old-timer who supports the initiative to speak up for it at a team meeting. The compatriot's testimony stands a much better chance of convincing the group than yet another speech from the boss. Stated simply, influence is often best exerted horizontally rather than vertically.

THE PRINCIPLE OF CONSISTENCY: PEOPLE ALIGN WITH THEIR CLEAR COMMITMENTS

The Application: Make Their Commitments Active, Public, and Voluntary

Liking is a powerful force, but the work of persuasion involves more than simply making people feel warmly toward you, your idea, or your product. People need not only to like you but to feel committed to what you want them to do. Good turns are one reliable way to make people feel obligated to you. Another is to win a public commitment from them.

My own research has demonstrated that most people, once they take a stand or go on record in favor of a position, prefer to stick to it. Other studies reinforce that finding and go on to show how even a small, seemingly trivial commitment can have a powerful effect on future actions. Israeli researchers writing in 1983 in the *Personality and Social Psychology Bulletin* recounted how they asked half the residents of a large apartment complex to sign a petition favoring the establishment of a recreation center for the handicapped. The cause was good and the request was small, so almost everyone who was asked agreed to sign. Two weeks later, on National Collection Day for the Handicapped,

all residents of the complex were approached at home and asked to give to the cause. A little more than half of those who were not asked to sign the petition made a contribution. But an astounding 92% of those who did sign donated money. The residents of the apartment complex felt obligated to live up to their commitments because those commitments were active, public, and voluntary. These three features are worth considering separately.

There's strong empirical evidence to show that a choice made actively—one that's spoken out loud or written down or otherwise made explicit—is considerably more likely to direct someone's future conduct than the same choice left unspoken. Writing in 1996 in the *Personality and Social Psychology Bulletin*, Delia Cioffi and Randy Garner described an experiment in which college students in one group were asked to fill out a printed form saying they wished to volunteer for an AIDS education project in the public schools. Students in another group volunteered for the same project by leaving blank a form stating that they didn't want to participate. A few days later, when the volunteers reported for duty, 74% of those who showed up were students from the group that signaled their commitment by filling out the form.

The implications are clear for a manager who wants to persuade a subordinate to follow some particular course of action: Get it in writing. Let's suppose you want your employee to submit reports in a more timely fashion. Once you believe you've won agreement, ask him to summarize the decision in a memo and send it to you. By doing so, you'll have greatly increased the odds that he'll fulfill the commitment because, as a rule, people live up to what they have written down.

Research into the social dimensions of commitment suggests that written statements become even more powerful when they're made public. In a classic experiment, described in 1955 in the *Journal of Abnormal and Social Psychology*, college students were asked to estimate the length of lines projected on a screen. Some students were asked to write down their choices on a piece of paper, sign it, and hand the paper to the experimenter. Others wrote their choices on an erasable slate, then erased the slate immediately. Still others were instructed to keep their decisions to themselves.

The experimenters then presented all three groups with evidence that their initial choices may have been wrong. Those who had merely kept their decisions in their heads were the most likely to reconsider their original estimates. More loyal to their first guesses were the students in the group that had written them down and immediately erased them. But by a wide margin, the ones most reluctant to shift from their original choices were those who had signed and handed them to the researcher.

This experiment highlights how much most people wish to appear consistent to others. Consider again the matter of the employee who has been submitting late reports. Recognizing the power of this desire, you should, once you've successfully convinced him of the need to be more timely, reinforce the commitment by making sure it gets a public airing. One way to do that would be to send the employee an e-mail that reads, "I think your plan is just what we need. I showed it to Diane in manufacturing and Phil in shipping, and they thought it was right on target, too." Whatever way such commitments are formalized, they should never be like the New Year's resolutions people privately make and then abandon with no one the wiser. They should be publicly made and visibly posted.

More than 300 years ago, Samuel Butler wrote a couplet that explains succinctly why commitments must be voluntary to be lasting and effective: "He that complies against his will/Is of his own opinion still." If an undertaking is forced, coerced, or imposed from the outside, it's not a commitment; it's an unwelcome burden. Think how you would react if your boss pressured you to donate to the campaign of a political candidate. Would that make you more apt to opt for that candidate in the privacy of a voting booth? Not likely. In fact, in their 1981 book *Psychological Reactance* (Academic Press), Sharon S. Brehm and Jack W. Brehm present data

that suggest you'd vote the opposite way just to express your resentment of the boss's coercion.

This kind of backlash can occur in the office, too. Let's return again to that tardy employee. If you want to produce an enduring change in his behavior, you should avoid using threats or pressure tactics to gain his compliance. He'd likely view any change in his behavior as the result of intimidation rather than a personal commitment to change. A better approach would be to identify something that the employee genuinely values in the workplace—high-quality workmanship, perhaps, or team spirit—and then describe how timely reports are consistent with those values. That gives the employee reasons for improvement that he can own. And because he owns them, they'll continue to guide his behavior even when you're not watching.

THE PRINCIPLE OF AUTHORITY: PEOPLE DEFER TO EXPERTS

The Application: Expose Your Expertise; Don't Assume It's Self-Evident

Two thousand years ago, the Roman poet Virgil offered this simple counsel to those seeking to choose correctly: "Believe an expert." That may or may not be good advice, but as a description of what people actually do, it can't be beaten. For instance, when the news media present an acknowledged expert's views on a topic, the effect on public opinion is dramatic. A single expert-opinion news story in the *New York Times* is associated with a 2% shift in public opinion nationwide, according to a 1993 study described in the *Public Opinion Quarterly*. And researchers writing in the *American Political Science Review* in 1987 found that when the expert's view was aired on national television, public opinion shifted as much as 4%. A cynic might argue that these findings only illustrate the docile submissiveness of the public. But a fairer explanation is that, amid the teeming complexity of contemporary life, a well-selected expert offers a valuable and efficient shortcut to good decisions. Indeed, some questions, be they legal, financial, medical, or technological, require so much specialized knowledge to answer, we have no choice but to rely on experts.

Since there's good reason to defer to experts, executives should take pains to ensure that they establish their own expertise before they attempt to exert influence. Surprisingly often, people mistakenly assume that others recognize and appreciate their experience. That's what happened at a hospital where some colleagues and I were consulting. The physical therapy staffers were frustrated because so many of their stroke patients abandoned their exercise routines as soon as they left the hospital. No matter how often the staff emphasized the importance of regular home exercise—it is, in fact, crucial to the process of regaining independent function—the message just didn't sink in.

Interviews with some of the patients helped us pinpoint the problem. They were familiar with the background and training of their physicians, but the patients knew little about the credentials of the physical therapists who were urging them to exercise. It was a simple matter to remedy that lack of information: We merely asked the therapy director to display all the awards, diplomas, and certifications of her staff on the walls of the therapy rooms. The result was startling: Exercise compliance jumped 34% and has never dropped since.

What we found immensely gratifying was not just how much we increased compliance, but how. We didn't fool or browbeat any of the patients. We *informed* them into compliance. Nothing had to be invented; no time or resources had to be spent in the process. The staff's expertise was real—all we had to do was make it more visible.

The task for managers who want to establish their claims to expertise is somewhat more difficult. They can't simply nail their diplomas to the wall and wait for everyone to notice. A little subtlety is called for. Outside the United States, it is customary for people to spend time interacting socially before getting down to business for the first time. Frequently they gather for dinner the

night before their meeting or negotiation. These get-togethers can make discussions easier and help blunt disagreements—remember the findings about liking and similarity—and they can also provide an opportunity to establish expertise. Perhaps it's a matter of telling an anecdote about successfully solving a problem similar to the one that's on the agenda at the next day's meeting. Or perhaps dinner is the time to describe years spent mastering a complex discipline—not in a boastful way but as part of the ordinary give-and-take of conversation.

Granted, there's not always time for lengthy introductory sessions. But even in the course of the preliminary conversation that precedes most meetings, there is almost always an opportunity to touch lightly on your relevant background and experience as a natural part of a sociable exchange. This initial disclosure of personal information gives you a chance to establish expertise early in the game, so that when the discussion turns to the business at hand, what you have to say will be accorded the respect it deserves.

THE PRINCIPLE OF SCARCITY: PEOPLE WANT MORE OF WHAT THEY CAN HAVE LESS OF

The Application: Highlight Unique Benefits and Exclusive Information

Study after study shows that items and opportunities are seen to be more valuable as they become less available. That's a tremendously useful piece of information for managers. They can harness the scarcity principle with the organizational equivalents of limited-time, limited-supply, and one-of-a-kind offers. Honestly informing a coworker of a closing window of opportunity—the chance to get the boss's ear before she leaves for an extended vacation, perhaps—can mobilize action dramatically.

Managers can learn from retailers how to frame their offers not in terms of what people stand to gain but in terms of what they stand to lose if they don't act on the information. The power of "loss language" was demonstrated in a 1988 study of California home owners written up in the *Journal of Applied Psychology*. Half were told that if they fully insulated their homes, they would save a certain amount of money each day. The other half were told that if they failed to insulate, they would lose that amount each day. Significantly more people insulated their homes when exposed to the loss language. The same phenomenon occurs in business. According to a 1994 study in the journal *Organizational Behavior and Human Decision Processes*, potential losses figure far more heavily in managers' decision making than potential gains.

In framing their offers, executives should also remember that exclusive information is more persuasive than widely available data. A doctoral student of mine, Amram Knishinsky, wrote his 1982 dissertation on the purchase decisions of wholesale beef buyers. He observed that they more than doubled their orders when they were told that, because of certain weather conditions overseas, there was likely to be a scarcity of foreign beef in the near future. But their orders increased 600% when they were informed that no one else had that information yet.

The persuasive power of exclusivity can be harnessed by any manager who comes into possession of information that's not broadly available and that supports an idea or initiative he or she would like the organization to adopt. The next time that kind of information crosses your desk, round up your organization's key players. The information itself may seem dull, but exclusivity will give it a special sheen. Push it across your desk and say, "I just got this report today. It won't be distributed until next week, but I want to give you an early look at what it shows." Then watch your listeners lean forward.

Allow me to stress here a point that should be obvious. No offer of exclusive information, no exhortation to act now or miss this opportunity forever should be made unless it is genuine. Deceiving colleagues into compliance is not only ethically objectionable, it's foolhardy. If the deception is detected—and it certainly

will be—it will snuff out any enthusiasm the offer originally kindled. It will also invite dishonesty toward the deceiver. Remember the rule of reciprocity.

PUTTING IT ALL TOGETHER

There's nothing abstruse or obscure about these six principles of persuasion. Indeed, they neatly codify our intuitive understanding of the ways people evaluate information and form decisions. As a result, the principles are easy for most people to grasp, even those with no formal education in psychology. But in the seminars and workshops I conduct, I have learned that two points bear repeated emphasis.

First, although the six principles and their applications can be discussed separately for the sake of clarity, they should be applied in combination to compound their impact. For instance, in discussing the importance of expertise, I suggested that managers use informal, social conversations to establish their credentials. But that conversation affords an opportunity to gain information as well as convey it. While you're showing your dinner companion that you have the skills and experience your business problem demands, you can also learn about your companion's background, likes, and dislikes— information that will help you locate genuine similarities and give sincere compliments. By letting your expertise surface and also establishing rapport, you double your persuasive power. And if you succeed in bringing your dinner partner on board, you may encourage other people to sign on as well, thanks to the persuasive power of social evidence.

The other point I wish to emphasize is that the rules of ethics apply to the science of social influence just as they do to any other technology. Not only is it ethically wrong to trick or trap others into assent, it's ill-advised in practical terms. Dishonest or high-pressure tactics work only in the short run, if at all. Their long-term effects are malignant, especially within an organization, which can't function properly without a bedrock level of trust and cooperation.

That point is made vividly in the following account, which a department head for a large textile manufacturer related at a training workshop I conducted. She described a vice president in her company who wrung public commitments from department heads in a highly manipulative manner. Instead of giving his subordinates time to talk or think through his proposals carefully, he would approach them individually at the busiest moment of their workday and describe the benefits of his plan in exhaustive, patience-straining detail. Then he would move in for the kill. "It's very important for me to see you as being on my team on this," he would say. "Can I count on your support?" Intimidated, frazzled, eager to chase the man from their offices so they could get back to work, the department heads would invariably go along with his request. But because the commitments never felt voluntary, the department heads never followed through, and as a result the vice president's initiatives all blew up or petered out.

This story had a deep impact on the other participants in the workshop. Some gulped in shock as they recognized their own manipulative behavior. But what stopped everyone cold was the expression on the department head's face as she recounted the damaging collapse of her superior's proposals. She was smiling.

Nothing I could say would more effectively make the point that the deceptive or coercive use of the principles of social influence is ethically wrong and pragmatically wrong-headed. Yet the same principles, if applied appropriately, can steer decisions correctly. Legitimate expertise, genuine obligations, authentic similarities, real social proof, exclusive news, and freely made commitments can produce choices that are likely to benefit both parties. And any approach that works to everyone's mutual benefit is good business, don't you think? Of course, I don't want to press you, into it, but, if you agree, I would love it if you could just jot me a memo to that effect.

Part B

Organizational Socialization and Commitment

22. Commitment and the Control of Organizational Behavior and Belief

Gerald R. Salancik

*M*ost articles on organizational commitment extol the virtues of commitment. In them, you will find that the committed employee is the happy employee, the success of the organization is a matter of its members sacrificing their time and effort, and commitment to the values of the organization gives meaning to a person's life. In them commitment enhances productivity, assures quality in the final product, and guarantees the flow of adaptive innovation. In them, you will find, in short, a lot of nonsense mixed with a lot of common sense. But from them your understanding of commitment may not be enhanced. . . .

The view of commitment we present in this paper is one which is grounded in behavior and the implications of behavior in one situation for behavior in another. The view derives primarily from the model of commitment developed by Kiesler (1971), with intellectual roots going back to Festinger (1957, 1964) and Lewin (1947). We borrow considerably from Keisler's work, and deviate in significant ways. As a working definition, "commitment is the binding of the individual to behavioral acts" (Kiesler & Sakumura, 1966). The important words are "binding" and "acts."

To act is to commit oneself. A person may talk about how important it is to keep the population growth rate down, but to be sterilized is to give eloquent, unshakeable force to the statement. An adulterer may proclaim unrelenting devotion to a lover, but to give up children, home, and joint bank accounts is to put meaning into the proclamation. Thus, at a minimum, a concept of commitment implies that behavior, or action, be a central focus.

DETERMINANTS OF COMMITMENT

While action is a necessary ingredient in commitment, all behaviors are not equally committing. There are degrees of commitment. A statement of a belief or attitude is a less committing action than the signing of a petition in favor of the belief, which in turn is less committing than actively advocating the belief to a hostile or skeptical audience.

The degree of commitment derives from the extent to which a person's behaviors are binding. Four characteristics of behavioral acts make them binding, and hence determine the extent of commitment: explicitness; revocability; volition; and publicity. The first is the *explicitness* or deniability of the act, and concerns the extent to which an action can be said to have taken place. Two contributors to explicitness are the observability of the act and the unequivocality of the act. Some acts are not observable and we may know them only by inference from assumed consequences. You leave a dollar bill on a checkout counter, turn away for a moment, then find it missing. The consequence is obvious, but do you know if the customer next to you took it or if it was carried away by a draft from the open door? Acts themselves can be equivocal, forgotten, or otherwise intractable. A person who says, "I sometimes think . . ." is behaving more equivocally than one who says, "I think. . . ."

A second characteristic of behavior affecting commitment is the *revocability* or reversibility of the action. Some actions are like trials. We try them out, see how they fit with us, and if they don't suit us we change our minds and do something else. Few actions are really irreversible. Even a vasectomy can be undone. Promises can be made and broken. Jobs can be quit. Marriages can be dissolved; engagements, broken. Contracts can be torn up. On the other hand, some actions are permanent and having occurred, they cannot be undone. They are

committing. Slapping someone in the face can be excused, forgiven, forgotten or reciprocated, but it cannot be taken back. Consumption of food or drink may be regretted but not reversed. Pulling the trigger of a loaded gun pointed at a friend commits all to its gross reality.

The explicitness and irrevocability of an act link action to an indelible reality. *Volition,* a third characteristic of committing behaviors, links action to the individual. This is one of the more difficult characteristics of human action to define precisely, and is frequently associated with such concepts as freedom and personal responsibility. What makes definition difficult is that all human action is both free and constrained, being done under one's own volition and in response to contingencies. Even the most seemingly free and personal action can be perceived as constrained. Artists and writers, such as Dostoevski and George Bernard Shaw, describe their acts of creation as the result of compulsions and external forces. And even the most seemingly constrained acts can be considered free. A person with a gun to his head ultimately is free to choose, whether to comply or accept the consequences of noncompliance. The perception of volition, moreover, can vary with the consequences that follow acts. A manager who takes a decision which turns out to be a disaster for his firm may make every effort to divest himself of responsibility. And one can observe in the annual reports of most corporations the following simple relationship. When sales increase from the previous year, the annual report points out how management's ingenious investments and development programs are paying off; when, the next year, sales decrease, an astounding downturn in the economy is lugubriously noted.

Despite difficulties in developing a precise concept of volition, volition wields powerful influences on the attitudes and behaviors of people, at least in Western culture. Some major characteristics found to relate to the degree of perceived volition of action are: (1) choice; (2) the presence of external demands for action;

(3) the presence of extrinsic bases for action; and (4) the presence of other contributors to action. Thus a person who works hard in order to make a lot of money is not perceived as having as much volition as a person who works hard for nothing. A person who works hard because his superior stands over him constantly is not perceived as having as much volition as one who does as much on his own. With regard to choice, a person who buys a Ford because that is the only car available for sale is not perceived as having as much volition as one who passes over a hundred other models to make the same purchase. . . .

A fourth characteristic of action affecting commitment is the *publicity* or publicness of the act. This characteristic links the action into a social context. While all action and behavior is by definition observable, publicity refers to the extent to which others know of the action and the kinds of persons who know of it. Some audiences are unimportant to us, as are their observations of our behavior. One of the simplest ways to commit yourself to a course of action is to go around telling all your friends that you are definitely going to do something. You will find yourself bound by your own statements. The same commitment will not develop from proclamations to strangers you meet on trains. The publicity of one's action places the action in a social context which is more or less binding and, as we shall describe, contributes to directing the effect of those behaviors on subsequent behaviors. . . .

COMMITMENT TO ORGANIZATIONS

A careless interpretation of the consistency assumption might lead one to infer that having chosen to join an organization or to do a job, individuals will be willing to stay with it and be quite satisfied. After all, one implication of taking a job is that the person likes it. Choice, however, is not enough. The choice itself must be committing. The person must be bound to this choice. . . .

Sacrifice and Initiation Rites

Some organizations prefer not to leave a member's commitment to the happenstance of his own decision process. Corporations frequently publicize the decisions of their new managers. The *Wall Street Journal* is crammed with advertisements by companies announcing that a particular individual has joined their firm, an act giving instant status to the manager's new role. Friends and past associates call in their congratulations and set into motion a climate of expectation that he is part of that firm. In recent years, insurance companies have been taking full spreads in such magazines as *Time* and *Newsweek* to publish the pictures of their sales personnel. Western Electric has done the same with television scans of their employees working on the job. For a few hundred dollars, an individual is identified with the organization. Next-door neighbors rush to ask, "Say, is this you?" One implication of the advertisement to both the employee and his friends is that the company really cares about its employees, and as a consequence it becomes more and more difficult to complain about it to friends. Harvard Business School uses a particularly effective method of maintaining long-term commitment from its graduates. Entering MBAs are immediately assigned to a group of classmates. This class does everything together from then on. They live in the same dormitories, hear the same lectures, and take the same exams. Virtually everything is scheduled for the class as a whole. Within each class, individuals are identified by namecards so that everyone knows the name of everyone else and is referred to by name in classroom discussions. Twenty years later, when the individuals have long departed the ivy-draped halls, the social network created there continues to operate. One of the things it is used for is to drum donations to the "B School," as it is fondly called.

In addition to advertising a person's commitment, some organizations take pains to make sure the individual is aware he has made a decision. Like the experiments with a well-constructed social psychological choice manipulation, the new employer commits the beginner: "Now, we want to be sure you're taking this job because you want to. We know you've given up a lot to come here and we're grateful. You left your home, your old friends. It must have been very difficult for you. And the salary we're offering, while more than you were making, is never enough to compensate for that."

The idea of giving up something to join the organization is one exploited in many ways. A common form is the initiation rites which still persist in college fraternities and sororities, fraternal clubs like the Masons or Elks, prisons, military organizations, revolutionary cadres, communal living experiments, police academies and religious organizations, orders and cults. An important part of the initiation process is the forcing of a sacrifice, in which members are asked to give up something as a price of membership (Karter, 1968). College fraternities require pledges to do hours of push-ups, to take verbal abuse, to have their privileges restricted, to accept subservient roles; in the end, those who endure love it. The effect is obvious. The individual in order to give meaning to his sacrifices is left to conclude they were made because of his devotion to the organization, a conclusion made more likely by his public pledge to enter the organization out of his own choosing. Other organizations have less colorful forms of sacrifice. Exclusive country clubs require their new members to make large initial donations in addition to yearly fees. The donations themselves provide for no services, and members pay for almost all services. But having given up an initial thousand, or a few thousand dollars, members feel a certain compulsion to spend $3.00 for a martini at the club's bar rather than half that at a public lounge.

Investments and Tenure

Many organizations do not exploit the idea of sacrifice as a price of membership. Instead they emphasize the instrumental or exchange bases for participation. Members are hired rather than invited into the organization. Commitment under such circumstances will obviously be more difficult.

Studies on commitment to organizations that emphasize the instrumental bases for membership—work organizations—have consistently found two factors as most reliably related to commitment. The two factors are position in the organization and tenure with the organization. Study after study on the issue comes down to: People with good jobs are willing to stay in them, and, the longer a person has been with an organization, the more he wants to stay. Unfortunately, most of the studies were done in such ways that it is difficult, and in many cases impossible, to interpret the meaning of the findings.

The relationship of tenure to organizational commitment is predictable from the model of commitment presented in this chapter and has been discussed in a related manner. Howard Becker (1960) suggested that individuals build up commitment over time through certain "sidebets" they make in the organization. One obvious form of accumulation investments in an organization is the build-up of pension benefits and credits over the course of a lifetime. Until recently, such employee benefits, often called the "golden padlock," were not transferable from one organization to another. If an individual terminated in one organization he lost some of his future wealth or security and had to begin accumulating it again in another organization. The costs of leaving the organization thus increase the longer one's involvement and one becomes more and more likely to continue where one is.

Regardless of financial investments, mobility also declines with tenure in an organization. As time goes by, one becomes less employable. And one's expertise becomes increasingly specific to one's current organization. Some organizations purposely manipulate the costs of leaving for some individuals. Universities will promote some of their assistant professors at rapid rates, making it more costly for other organizations to entice them away. Some business organizations will give young managers attractive positions unusual for their age, knowing it would be difficult for them to obtain equivalent offers elsewhere and also knowing it is cheaper to buy their commitment at an early age than it would be when they become industry hot-shots. . . .

WORK ENVIRONMENTS AND ORGANIZATIONAL COMMITMENT

Thus far we have discussed commitment to the organization as the result of the constraints on an individual's ability to leave the organization, and the extent to which the individual himself has made a definite and committing choice. In reading this over, one gets the feeling that commitment to an organization is an entrapment: an individual is either cut off from other alternatives because no one else wants him or because his own situation doesn't allow him to change it. Thus, individuals rarely make job changes involving moves when their children are entrenched in a school. In all, it is a rather negative view of commitment. You are committed because the facts of your life have bound you.

What about more positive features? Do people become committed to their jobs because they are attracted to them and find them enjoyable? The research on this issue is unimpressive. Much is based on termination interviews which find that workers who quit or say they quit because they didn't like the job or the pay. Having taken so decisive a step, it would be rather amusing to find them saying that they loved the job. Studies attempting to predict employee turnover or absenteeism from prior reports of job satisfaction have been notoriously unsuccessful from a practical point of view; that is, the studies report statistically reliable relationships of so low a magnitude that they predict little about behavior. Even superior measurement techniques do poorly (Newman, 1974).

The typical relationship found between job attitudes and turnover or absenteeism is clouded by other factors. We have already discussed that one of these factors is the tenure of the employee. Job satisfaction increases with age and tenure, as does commitment to the organization (see Grupp & Richards, 1975; Organ & Greene, 1974; Gow, Clark, & Dossett,

1974, for illustrative studies). Where investigators have bothered to make the necessary causal analyses, they have found that the change is a "real" one and not simply a function of changes in position, jobs, or salary (Stagner, 1975). As a person becomes more experienced in what he does he becomes more able to cope with the negative and positive features of his job. . . .

Commitment and Job Features

Despite the rather unpredictable relationship between job attitudes, absenteeism, turmoil, and turnover, the model of commitment presented here does suggest that certain features of a person's job situation will affect his commitment. In general, any characteristic of a person's job situation which reduces his felt responsibility will reduce his commitment. As for the relationship between commitment and satisfaction, our own view is that enjoyment is more likely to follow commitment than the reverse.

Many characteristics of job situations can affect a person's perception of responsibility. Some positions simply carry more responsibility, and persons in higher positions tend to be more committed. Similarly, some jobs offer more discretion and self-determination to their occupants, and it has been found that employees in autonomous positions generally have more favorable attitudes than those with little freedom to decide how to do their jobs (Hackman & Lawler, 1971; Hackman & Oldham, 1974).

In addition to the job and the freedom it permits, the manner by which the job is supervised or monitored can affect perceptions of responsibility. The supervisor who stands over a subordinate provides an excuse for the subordinate's behavior. When unpleasant aspects of the job become apparent, rather than coping with them, and finding some joy in the job, the subordinate can attribute his endurance to the supervisor's tenacious pressure. Lepper and Greene (1975) found that surveillance deteriorates interest in a task. Zanna (1970) found that when students are led to believe they worked very hard for a nasty supervisor, they enjoyed the task more than when they worked very hard for a nice supervisor. When they work for a nice person they attribute their effort to their liking for him, not the job. This would be an unrealistic attribution to a nasty boss, so they like the job more.

If a supervisor merely stands by without taking an active part in determining the subordinate's behavior, his presence may serve to reinforce the subordinate's felt responsibility. Maguire and Ouchi (1975) found that close output supervision improves employee satisfaction but that close behavioral supervision does not. Monitoring and providing an individual with feedback about his work performance can increase a person's felt responsibility. The person, knowing his outcomes and knowing his outcomes are known by others, may become more aware that the outcomes are his responsibility. Hackman and Oldham (1974) found workers' perception of responsibility was in part a function of feedback about their performance. While the precise effects of various supervisory conditions on commitment have not been well studied, we would expect that high output monitoring coupled with low behavioral control would lead to the greatest felt responsibility on the part of the worker. Whether or not these conditions will lead to greater satisfaction would depend on whether or not the worker can handle the task. Maguire and Ouchi (1975) found more satisfaction among monitored workers who could do their jobs without depending on others (i.e., low interdependence) than those who could not.

Commitment also derives from the relation of an employee's job to those of others in the organization. Some jobs are rather isolated and can be done independently of other jobs in the organization. It has been found that jobs which are not integrated with the work activities of others tend to be associated with less favorable attitudes (Sheperd, 1973). Gow, Clark, and Dossett (1974), for instance, find that telephone operators who quit tend to be those who are not integrated into the work group.

Work integration can affect commitment by the fact that integrated jobs are likely to be associated with salient demands from others in the organization. If a person has a job which affects the work of others in the organization, it is likely that those others will communicate their expectations for performance of that job. Such expectations can be committing in that the other people implicitly or explicitly hold the person accountable for what he does. Earlier we mentioned that when individuals did not know what was expected of them they tended to be less committed to the organization. One reason an individual will not know what is expected is because no one is telling him. In general, we would expect that anything which contributes to creating definite expectations for a person's behavior would enhance his felt responsibility, and hence commitment. Integration may be one such contributor.

Perhaps the most pervasive condition of a job which affects commitment is its instrumentality, the fact that work is a means to some other end. While all jobs in industrial and commercial organizations are done in exchange for salary, there are perhaps great variations in the extent to which the instrumental basis for the work is salient or not. In general, we would expect that when the instrumental basis for work is salient it will reduce a person's felt responsibility. The attribution, "I am doing this job only for the money," should inhibit commitment. A similar point was raised by Ingham (1970), who analyzed absenteeism and turnover in light engineering firms in Bradford, England. Observing that larger organizations had more absenteeism (but lower turnover), he argued that workers were attracted to large firms because of the higher pay offered, but that this instrumental orientation led to little personal involvement with the organization. . . .

There is far too little empirical work on the nature of commitment to jobs, and how features of the work situation lead to or detract from feelings of personal responsibility for work. Much more detailed accountings of the particulars of job situations need to be made.

REFERENCES

Becker, H. S. Notes on the concept of commitment. *American Journal of Sociology,* 1960, 66, 32–40.

Festinger, L. *A theory of cognitive dissonance.* Stanford, Calif.: Stanford University Press, 1957.

Festinger, L. *Conflict, decision, and dissonance.* Stanford, Calif.: Stanford University Press, 1964.

Gow, J. S., Clark, A. W., & Dossett, G. S. A path analysis of variables influencing labour turnover. *Human Relations,* 1974, 27, 703–19.

Hackman, J. R., & Lawler, E. E. Employee reactions to job characteristics. *Journal of Applied Psychology,* 1971, 55, 259–86.

Hackman, J. R., & Oldham, G. R. Motivation through the design of work: Test of a theory. Technical Report no. 6, Administrative Sciences, Yale University, 1974.

Ingham, G. K. *Size of industrial organizations and worker behavior.* Cambridge: Cambridge University Press, 1970.

Kanter, R. M. Commitment and social organizations. *American Sociological Review,* 1968.

Kiesler, C. A. *The psychology of commitment: Experiments linking behavior to belief.* New York: Academic Press, 1971.

Kiesler, C. A., & Sakumura, J. A test of a model for commitment. *Journal of Personality and Social Psychology,* 1966, 3, 349–53.

Lepper, M. R., Greene, D., & Nisbett, R. E. Undermining children's intrinsic interest with extrinsic rewards: A test of the "overjustification" hypothesis. *Journal of Personality and Social Psychology,* 1973, 28, 129–37.

Lewin, K. Group decision and social change. In T. M. Newcomb and E. L. Hartley (Eds.), *Readings in social psychology.* New York: Holt, Reinhart, & Winston, 1947, pp. 330–44.

Maguire, M. A., & Ouchi, W. Organizational control and work satisfaction. Research Paper no. 278, Graduate School of Business, Stanford University, 1975.

Newman, J. E. Predicting absenteeism and turnover: A field comparison of Fishbein's model and traditional job attitude measures. *Journal of Applied Psychology,* 1974, 59, 610–15.

Organ, D. W., & Greene, N. The perceived purposefulness of job behavior: Antecedents and consequences. *Academy of Management Journal,* 1974, 17, 69–78.

Stagner, R. Boredom on the assembly line: Age and personality variables. *Industrial Gerontology,* 1975, 21, 23–44.

Zanna, M. P. Attitude inference in a low choice setting. Ph.D. dissertation, Yale University, 1970.

23. *The Smile Factory: Work at Disneyland*

John Van Maanen

Part of Walt Disney Enterprises includes the theme park Disneyland. In its pioneering form in Anaheim, California, this amusement center has been a consistent money maker since the gates were first opened in 1955. Apart from its sociological charm, it has, of late, become something of an exemplar for culture vultures and has been held up for public acclaim in several best-selling publications as one of America's top companies, most notably by Peters and Waterman (1982). To outsiders, the cheerful demeanor of its employees, the seemingly inexhaustible repeat business it generates from its customers, the immaculate condition of park grounds, and, more generally, the intricate physical and social order of the business itself appear wondrous.

Disneyland as the self-proclaimed "Happiest Place on Earth" certainly occupies an enviable position in the amusement and entertainment worlds as well as the commercial world in general. Its product, it seems, is emotion— "laughter and well-being." Insiders are not bashful about promoting the product. Bill Ross, a Disneyland executive, summarizes the corporate position nicely by noting that "although we focus our attention on profit and loss, day-in and day-out we cannot lose sight of the fact that this is a feeling business and we make our profits from that."[1]

The "feeling business" does not operate, however, by management decree alone. Whatever services Disneyland executives believe they are providing to the 60 to 70 thousand visitors per day that flow through the park during its peak summer season, employees at the bottom of the organization are the ones who most provide them. The work-a-day practices that employees adopt to amplify or dampen customer spirits are therefore a core concern of this feeling business. The happiness trade is an interactional one. It rests partly on the symbolic resources put into place by history and park design but it also rests on an animated workforce that is more or less eager to greet the guests, pack the trams, push the buttons, deliver the food, dump the garbage, clean the streets, and, in general, marshal the will to meet and perhaps exceed customer expectations. False moves, rude words, careless disregard, detected insincerity, or a sleepy and bored presence can all undermine the enterprise and ruin a sale. The smile factory has its rules.

IT'S A SMALL WORLD

The writing that follows[2] represents Disneyland as a workplace. It is organized roughly as an old-fashioned realist ethnography that tells of a culture in native categories (Van Maanen, 1988). The culture of interest is the Disneyland culture but it is not necessarily the same one invented, authorized, codified, or otherwise approved by park management. Thus the culture I portray here is more of an occupational than a strictly organizational one (Van Maanen & Barley, 1985).

This rendition is of course abbreviated and selective. I focus primarily on such matters as the stock appearance (vanilla), status order

From: Peter J. Frost, Larry F. Moore, Meryl Reis Lois, Craig C. Lundberg, and Joanne Martin (Eds.). *Reframing Organizational Culture.* Newbury Park, CA: Sage Publications, pp. 58–76.

Author's Note: This paper has been cobbled together using three-penny nails of other writings. Parts come from a paper presented to the American Anthropological Association Annual Meetings in Washington, D.C., on November 16, 1989, called "Whistle While You Work." Other parts come from Van Maanen and Kunda (1989). In coming to this version, I've had a good deal of help from my friends Steve Barley, Nicole Biggart, Michael Owen Jones, Rosanna Hertz, Gideon Kunda, Joanne Martin, Maria Lydia Spinelli, Bob Sutton, and Bob Thomas.

(rigid), and social life (full), and swiftly learned codes of conduct (formal and informal) that are associated with Disneyland ride operators. These employees comprise the largest category of hourly workers on the payroll. During the summer months, they number close to four thousand and run the 60-odd rides and attractions in the park.

They are also a well-screened bunch. There is—among insiders and outsiders alike—a rather fixed view about the social attributes carried by the standard-make Disneyland ride operator. Single, white males and females in their early twenties, without facial blemish, of above average height and below average weight, with straight teeth, conservative grooming standards, and a chin-up, shoulder-back posture radiating the sort of good health suggestive of a recent history in sports are typical of these social identifiers. There are representative minorities on the payroll but because ethnic displays are sternly discouraged by management, minority employees are rather close copies of the standard model Disneylander, albeit in different colors.

This Disneyland look is often a source of some amusement to employees who delight in pointing out that even the patron saint, Walt himself, could not be hired today without shaving off his trademark pencil-thin mustache. But, to get a job in Disneyland and keep it means conforming to a rather exacting set of appearance rules. These rules are put forth in a handbook on the Disney image in which readers learn, for example, that facial hair or long hair is banned for men as are aviator glasses and earrings and that women must not tease their hair, wear fancy jewelry, or apply more than a modest dab of makeup. Both men and women are to look neat and prim, keep their uniforms fresh, polish their shoes, and maintain an upbeat countenance and light dignity to complement their appearance—no low spirits or cornball raffishness at Disneyland.

The legendary "people skills" of park employees, so often mentioned in Disneyland publicity and training materials, do not amount to very much according to ride operators. Most tasks require little interaction with customers and are physically designed to practically ensure that is the case. The contact that does occur typically is fleeting and swift, a matter usually of only a few seconds. In the rare event sustained interaction with customers might be required, employees are taught to deflect potential exchanges to area supervisors or security. A Training Manual offers the proper procedure: "On misunderstandings, guests should be told to call City Hall . . . In everything from damaged cameras to physical injuries, don't discuss anything with guests . . . there will always be one of us nearby." Employees learn quickly that security is hidden but everywhere. On Main Street, security cops are Keystone Kops; in Frontierland, they are Town Marshalls; on Tom Sawyer's Island, they are Cavalry Officers, and so on.

Occasionally, what employees call "line talk" or "crowd control" is required of them to explain delays, answer direct questions, or provide directions that go beyond the endless stream of recorded messages coming from virtually every nook and cranny of the park. Because such tasks are so simple, consisting of little more than keeping the crowd informed and moving, it is perhaps obvious why management considers the sharp appearance and wide smile of employees so vital to park operations. There is little more they could ask of ride operators whose main interactive tasks with visitors consist of being, in their own terms, "information booths," "line signs," "pretty props," "shepherds," and "talking statues."

A few employees do go out of their way to initiate contact with Disneyland customers but, as a rule, most do not and consider those who do to be a bit odd. In general, one need do little more than exercise common courtesy while looking reasonably alert and pleasant. Interactive skills that are advanced by the job have less to do with making customers feel warm and welcome than they do with keeping each other amused and happy. This is, of course, a more complex matter.

Employees bring to the job personal badges of status that are of more than passing interest to peers. In rough order, these include: good looks, college affiliation, career aspirations, past achievements, age (directly related to status up to about age 23 or 24 and inversely related thereafter), and assorted other idiosyncratic matters. Nested closely alongside these imported status badges are organizational ones that are also of concern and value to employees.

Where one works in the park carries much social weight. Postings are consequential because the ride and area a person is assigned provide rewards and benefits beyond those of wages. In-the-park stature for ride operators turns partly on whether or not unique skills are required. Disneyland neatly complements labor market theorizing on this dimension because employees with the most differentiated skills find themselves at the top of the internal status ladder, thus making their loyalties to the organization more predictable.

Ride operators, as a large but distinctly middle-class group of hourly employees on the floor of the organization, compete for status not only with each other but also with other employee groupings whose members are hired for the season from the same applicant pool. A loose approximation of the rank ordering among these groups can be constructed as follows:

1. The upper-class prestigious Disneyland Ambassadors and Tour Guides (bilingual young women in charge of ushering—some say rushing—little bands of tourists through the park);
2. Ride operators performing coveted "skilled work" such as live narrations or tricky transportation tasks like those who symbolically control customer access to the park and drive, the costly entry vehicles such as the antique trains, horse-drawn carriages, and Monorail);
3. All other ride operators;
4. The proletarian Sweepers (keepers of the concrete grounds);
5. The sub-prole or peasant status Food and Concession workers (whose park sobriquets reflect their lowly social worth—"pancake

ladies," "peanut pushers," "coke blokes," "suds divers," and the seemingly irreplaceable "soda jerks").

Pay differentials are slight among these employee groups. The collective status adheres, as it does internally for ride operators, to assignment or functional distinctions. As the rank order suggests, most employee status goes to those who work jobs that require higher degrees of special skill, relative freedom from constant and direct supervision, and provide the opportunity to organize and direct customer desires and behavior rather than to merely respond to them as spontaneously expressed.

The basis for sorting individuals into these various broad bands of job categories is often unknown to employees—a sort of deep, dark secret of the casting directors in personnel. When prospective employees are interviewed, they interview for "a job at Disneyland," not a specific one. Personnel decides what particular job they will eventually occupy. Personal contacts are considered by employees as crucial in this job-assignment process as they are in the hiring decision. Some employees, especially those who wind up in the lower ranking jobs, are quite disappointed with their assignments as is the case when, for example, a would-be Adventureland guide is posted to a New Orleans Square restaurant as a pot scrubber. Although many of the outside acquaintances of our pot scrubber may know only that he works at Disneyland, rest assured, insiders will know immediately where he works and judge him accordingly.

Uniforms are crucial in this regard for they provide instant communication about the social merits or demerits of the wearer within the little world of Disneyland workers. Uniforms also correspond to a wider status ranking that casts a significant shadow on employees of all types. Male ride operators on the Autopia wear, for example, untailored jumpsuits similar to pit mechanics and consequently generate about as much respect from peers as the grease-stained outfits worn by pump jockeys generate from real motorists in gas stations. The ill-fitting and homogeneous "whites" worn by Sweepers signify lowly institutional work tinged, perhaps, with a reminder of hospital orderlies rather than street cleanup crews. On the other hand, for males, the crisp, officer-like Monorail operator stands alongside the swashbuckling Pirate of the Caribbean, the casual cowpoke of Big Thunder Mountain, or the smartly vested Riverboat pilot as carriers of valued symbols in and outside the park. Employees lust for these higher status positions and the rights to small advantages such uniforms provide. A lively internal labor market exists wherein there is much scheming for the more prestigious assignments.

For women, a similar market exists although the perceived "sexiness" of uniforms, rather than social rank, seems to play a larger role. To wit, the rather heated antagonisms that developed years ago when the ride "It's a Small World" first opened and began outfitting the ride operators with what were felt to be the shortest skirts and most revealing blouses in the park. Tour Guides, who traditionally headed the fashion vanguard at Disneyland in their above-the-knee kilts, knee socks, tailored vests, black English hats, and smart riding crops were apparently appalled at being upstaged by their social inferiors and lobbied actively (and, judging by the results, successfully) to lower the skirts, raise the necklines, and generally remake their Small World rivals.

Important, also, to ride operators are the break schedules followed on the various rides. The more the better. Work teams develop inventive ways to increase the number of "time-outs" they take during the work day. Most rides are organized on a rotational basis (e.g., the operator moving from a break, to queue monitor, to turnstile overseer, to unit loader, to traffic controller, to driver, and, again, to a break). The number of break men or women on a rotation (or ride) varies by the number of employees on duty and by the number of units on line. Supervisors, foremen, and operators also vary as to what they regard as appropriate break standards (and, more importantly, as to the value of the many situational factors that can enter the calculation of break rituals—crowd size, condition of ride, accidents, breakdowns, heat, operator absences, special occasions, and so forth). Self-monitoring teams with sleepy supervisors and lax (or savvy) foremen can sometimes manage a shift comprised of 15 minutes on and 45 minutes off each hour. They are envied by others and rides that have such a potential are eyed hungrily by others who feel trapped by their more rigid (and observed) circumstances.

Movement across jobs is not encouraged by park management but some does occur (mostly within an area and job category). Employees claim that a sort of "once a sweeper, always a sweeper" rule obtains but all know of at least a few exceptions to prove the rule. The exceptions offer some (not much) hope for those working at the social margins of the park and perhaps keep them on the job longer than might otherwise be expected. Dishwashers can dream of becoming Pirates, and with persistence and a little help from their friends, such dreams just might come true next season (or the next).

These examples are precious, perhaps, but they are also important. There is an intricate pecking order among very similar categories of employees. Attributes of reward and status tend to cluster, and there is intense concern about the cluster to which one belongs (or would like to belong). To a degree, form follows function in Disneyland because the jobs requiring the most abilities and offering the most interest also offer the most status and social reward. Interaction patterns reflect and sustain this order. Few Ambassadors or Tour Guides, for instance, will stoop to speak at length with Sweepers who speak mostly among themselves or to Food workers. Ride operators, between the poles, line up in ways referred to above with only ride proximity (i.e., sharing a break area) representing a potentially significant intervening variable in the interaction calculation.

These patterns are of more than slight concern because Disneyland, especially in the summer, can be compared quite usefully to a college mixer where across-sex pairing is of great concern (Schwartz & Lever, 1976). More to the point, what Waller (1937) so accurately called the "rating and dating complex" is in full bloom among park employees. The various modern forms of mating games are valued pastimes among Disneyland employees and are often played with corporate status markers in mind. Thus, when Yvone, the reigning Alice in Wonderland, moved in one summer with Ted, a lowly Sweeper, heads were scratched in puzzlement even though most knew that Yvone was, in her other life, a local junior college student and Ted was in premed at USC. The more general point is that romance flourishes in the park and, at least, if folklore is our guide, marriages made in Disneyland are not uncommon.

Even when not devoted strictly to pairing-off objectives, employee pastimes usually involve other employees. Disneyland's softball and volleyball leagues, its official picnics, canoe races, employee nights at the park, beach parties, and so on provide a busy little social scene for those interested. Areas and rides, too, offer social excitement and bonuses such as when kegs of beer are rolled out at an off-site party after work crews break turnstile records ("We put 33,147 on the mountain today"). During the summer, some night crews routinely party in the early morning while day shift crews party at night. Sleep is not a commodity greatly valued by many employees caught up in a valued social whirl.

The so-called youth culture is indeed celebrated in and out of the park. Many employees, for example, live together in the large and cheap (by Los Angeles standards) apartment complexes that surround Disneyland. Employees sometimes refer to these sprawling, pastel, and slightly seedy structures as "the projects" or "worker housing." Yet, the spirited attractiveness of the collective, low-rent lifestyle for those living it is easily grasped by a few landlords in the area who flatly refuse to rent to Disneyland employees during the summer as a matter of principle and, maybe, sorry experience because these short-term rentals serve as amusement parks for off-duty Disneylanders who, as they say, "know how to party."

A fusion of work and play is notable, however, even when play seems to be the order of the occasion. Certainly no Disneyland get-together would be complete without ride operators launching into their special spiel practiced (or heard continuously on tape) at work:

Welcome aboard the African Queen, folks. My name is John and I'll be your guide and skipper for our trip down these rivers of adventure. As we pull away from the loading dock, turn around and take a last look at the people standing there, it may be the last time you ever see them . . . Please keep your hands inside the boat as we go past these hungry alligators, they're always looking for a handout . . . And now we return to civilization and the greatest danger of all, the California freeways.

The figurative parallel of this party is, of course, the atmosphere of a most collegial college. It has a literal parallel as well.

Paid employment at Disneyland begins with the much renowned University of Disneyland whose faculty runs a day-long orientation program (Traditions I) as part of a 40-hour apprenticeship program, most of which takes place on the rides. In the classroom, however, newly hired ride operators are given a very thorough introduction to matters of managerial concern and are tested on their absorption of famous Disneyland fact, lore, and procedure. Employee demeanor is governed, for example, by three rules:

First, we practice the friendly smile.
Second, we use only friendly and courteous phrases.
Third, we are not stuffy—the only Misters in Disneyland are Mr. Toad and Mr. Smee.

Employees learn too that the Disneyland culture is officially defined. The employee handbook put it in this format:

Dis-ney Cor-po-rate Cul-ture (diz´ne kor´pr'it kul´cher) n 1. Of or pertaining to the Disney organization, as a: the philosophy underlying all business decisions; b: the commitment of top leadership and management to that philosophy;

c: the actions taken by individual cast members that reinforce the image.

Language is also a central feature of university life and new employees are schooled in its proper use. Customers at Disneyland are, for instance, never referred to as such, they are "guests." There are no rides at Disneyland, only "attractions." Disneyland itself is a "Park," not an amusement center, and it is divided into "back-stage," "on-stage," and "staging" regions. Law enforcement personnel hired by the park are not policemen, but "security hosts." Employees do not wear uniforms but check out fresh "costumes" each working day from "wardrobe." And, of course, there are no accidents at Disneyland, only "incidents."

So successful is such training that Smith and Eisenberg (1987) report that not a single Disneyland employee uttered the taboo and dread words "uniform," "customer," or "amusement park" during the 35 half-hour interviews they conducted as part of a study on organizational communication. The *Los Angeles Times* (July 28, 1988) also gives evidence on this matter, quoting a tour guide's reaction to the employees' annual canoe races. "It's a good release," she says, "it helps you see the other cast members (park employees) go through the same thing you do." Whether or not employees keep to such disciplined talk with one another is, of course, a moot point because the corporate manual is concerned only with how employees talk to customers or outsiders.

The university curriculum also anticipates probable questions ride operators may someday face from customers and they are taught the approved public response. A sample:

Question (posed by trainer): What do you tell a guest who requests a rain check?

Answer (in three parts): We don't offer rain checks at Disneyland because (1) the main attractions are all indoors; (2) we would go broke if we offered passes; and (3) sunny days would be too crowded if we gave passes.

Shrewd trainees readily note that such an answer blissfully disregards the fact that waiting areas of Disneyland are mostly outdoors and that there are no subways in the park to carry guests from land to land. Nor do they miss the economic assumption concerning the apparent frequency of Southern California rains. They discuss such matters together, of course, but rarely raise them in the training classroom. In most respects, these are recruits who easily take the role of good student.

Classes are organized and designed by professional Disneyland trainers who also instruct a well-screened group of representative hourly employees straight from park operations on the approved newcomer training methods and materials. New-hires seldom see professional trainers in class but are brought on board by enthusiastic peers who concentrate on those aspects of park procedure thought highly general matters to be learned by all employees. Particular skill training (and "reality shock") is reserved for the second wave of socialization occurring on the rides themselves as operators are taught, for example, how and when to send a mock bobsled caroming down the track or, more delicately, the proper ways to stuff an obese adult customer into the midst of children riding the Monkey car on the Casey Jones Circus Train or, most problematically, what exactly to tell an irate customer standing in the rain who, in no uncertain terms, wants his or her money back and wants it back now.

During orientation, considerable concern is placed on particular values the Disney organization considers central to its operations. These values range from the "customer is king" verities to the more or less unique kind, of which "everyone is a child at heart when at Disneyland" is a decent example. This latter piety is one few employees fail to recognize as also attaching to everyone's mind as well after a few months of work experience. Elaborate checklists of appearance standards are learned and gone over in the classroom and great efforts are spent trying to bring employee emotional responses in line with such standards.

Employees are told repeatedly that if they are happy and cheerful at work, so, too, will the guests at play. Inspirational films, hearty pep talks, family imagery, and exemplars of corporate performance are all representative of the strong symbolic stuff of these training rites.

Another example, perhaps extreme, concerns the symbolic role of the canonized founder in the corporate mythology. When Walt Disney was alive, newcomers and veterans alike were told how much he enjoyed coming to the park and just how exacting he was about the conditions he observed. For employees, the cautionary whoop, "Walt's in the park," could often bring forth additional energy and care for one's part in the production. Upon his death, trainers at the University were said to be telling recruits to mind their manners because, "Walt's in the park all the time now."

Yet, like employees everywhere, there is a limit to which such overt company propaganda can be effective. Students and trainers both seem to agree on where the line is drawn for there is much satirical banter, mischievous winking, and playful exaggeration in the classroom. As young seasonal employees note, it is difficult to take seriously an organization that provides its retirees "Golden Ears" instead of gold watches after 20 or more years of service. All newcomers are aware that the label "Disneyland" has both an unserious and artificial connotation and that a full embrace of the Disneyland role would be as deviant as its full rejection. It does seem, however, because of the corporate imagery, the recruiting and selection devices, the goodwill trainees hold toward the organization at entry, the peer-based employment context, and the smooth fit with real student calendars, the job is considered by most ride operators to be a good one. The University of Disneyland, it appears, graduates students with a modest amount of pride and a considerable amount of fact and faith firmly ingrained as important things to know (if not always accept).

Matters become more interesting as new hires move into the various realms of Disneyland enterprise. There are real customers "out there" and employees soon learn that these good folks do not always measure up to the typically well mannered and grateful guest of the training classroom. Moreover, ride operators may find it difficult to utter the prescribed "Welcome Voyager" (or its equivalent) when it is to be given to the 20-thousandth human being passing through the Space Mountain turnstile on a crowded day in July. Other difficulties present themselves as well, but operators learn that there are others on-stage to assist or thwart them.

Employees learn quickly that supervisors and, to a lesser degree, foremen are not only on the premises to help them, but also to catch them when they slip over or brazenly violate set procedures or park policies. Because most rides are tightly designed to eliminate human judgment and minimize operational disasters, much of the supervisory monitoring is directed at activities ride operators consider trivial: taking too long a break; not wearing parts of one's official uniform such as a hat, standard-issue belt, or correct shoes; rushing the ride (although more frequent violations seem to be detected for the provision of longer-than-usual rides for lucky customers); fraternizing with guests beyond the call of duty; talking back to quarrelsome or sometimes merely querisome customers; and so forth. All are matters covered quite explicitly in the codebooks ride operators are to be familiar with, and violations of such codes are often subject to instant and harsh discipline. The firing of what to supervisors are "malcontents," "trouble-makers," "bumblers," "attitude problems," or simply "jerks" is a frequent occasion at Disneyland, and among part-timers, who are most subject to degradation and being fired, the threat is omnipresent. There are few workers who have not witnessed firsthand the rapid disappearance of a co-worker for offenses they would regard as "Mickey Mouse." Moreover, there are few employees who themselves have not violated a good number of operational and demeanor standards and anticipate, with just cause, the violation of more in the future.[3]

In part, because of the punitive and what are widely held to be capricious supervisory practices in the park, foremen and ride operators are usually drawn close and shield one another from suspicious area supervisors. Throughout the year, each land is assigned a number of area supervisors who, dressed alike in short-sleeved white shirts and ties with walkie-talkies hitched to their belts, wander about their territories on the lookout for deviations from park procedures (and other signs of disorder). Occasionally, higher level supervisors pose in "plainclothes" and ghost-ride the various attractions just to be sure everything is up to snuff. Some area supervisors are well-known among park employees for the variety of surreptitious techniques they employ when going about their monitoring duties. Blind observation posts are legendary, almost sacred, sites within the park ("This is where Old Man Weston hangs out. He can see Dumbo, Storybook, the Carousel, and the Tea Cups from here"). Supervisors in Tomorrowland are, for example, famous for their penchant of hiding in the bushes above the submarine caves, timing the arrivals and departures of the supposedly fully loaded boats making the 8½ minute cruise under the polar icecaps. That they might also catch a submarine captain furtively enjoying a cigarette (or worse) while inside the conning tower (his upper body out of view of the crowd on the vessel) might just make a supervisor's day—and unmake the employee's. In short, supervisors, if not foremen, are regarded by ride operators as sneaks and tricksters out to get them and representative of the dark side of park life. Their presence is, of course, an orchestrated one and does more than merely watch over the ride operators. It also draws operators together as cohesive little units who must look out for one another while they work (and shirk).

Supervisors are not the only villains who appear in the park. The treachery of co-workers, while rare, has its moments. Pointing out the code violations of colleagues to foremen and supervisors—usually in secret—provides one avenue of collegial duplicity. Finks, of all sorts, can be found among the peer ranks at Disneyland, and although their dirty deeds are uncommon, work teams on all rides go to some effort to determine just who they might be and, if possible, drive them from their midst. Although there is little overt hazing or playing of pranks on newcomers, they are nonetheless carefully scrutinized on matters of team (and ride) loyalty, and those who fail the test of "member in good standing" are subject to some very uncomfortable treatment. Innuendo and gossip are the primary tools in this regard, with ridicule and ostracism (the good old silent treatment) providing the backup. Since perhaps the greatest rewards working at Disneyland offered its ride operator personnel are those that come from belonging to a tight little network of like-minded and sociable peers where off-duty interaction is at least as vital and pleasurable as the on-duty sort, such mechanisms are quite effective. Here is where some of the most powerful and focused emotion work in the park is found, and those subject to negative sanction, rightly or wrongly, will grieve, but grieve alone.

Employees are also subject to what might be regarded as remote controls. These stem not from supervisors or peers but from thousands of paying guests who parade daily through the park. The public, for the most part, wants Disneyland employees to play only the roles for which they are hired and costumed. If, for instance, Judy of the Jets is feeling tired, grouchy, or bored, few customers want to know about it. Disneyland employees are expected to be sunny and helpful; and the job, with its limited opportunities for sustained interaction, is designed to support such a stance. Thus, if a ride operator's behavior drifts noticeably away from the norm, customers are sure to point it out—"Why aren't you smiling?" "What's wrong with you?" "Having a bad day?" "Did Goofy step on your foot?" Ride operators learn swiftly from the constant hints, glances, glares, and tactful (and tactless) cues sent by their audience what their role in the park is to be, and as long as they keep to it, there will be no objections from those passing by.

> I can remember being out on the river looking at the people on the Mark Twain looking down on the people in the Keel Boats who are looking up at them. I'd come by on my raft and they'd all turn and stare at me. If I gave them a little wave and a grin, they'd all wave back and smile; all ten thousand of them. I always wondered what would happen if I gave them the finger? (Ex-ride operator, 1988)

Ride operators also learn how different categories of customers respond to them and the parts they are playing on-stage. For example, infants and small children are generally timid, if not frightened, in their presence. School-age children are somewhat curious, aware that the operator is at work playing a role but sometimes in awe of the role itself. Nonetheless, these children can be quite critical of any flaw in the operator's performance. Teenagers, especially males in groups, present problems because they sometimes go to great lengths to embarrass, challenge, ridicule, or outwit an operator. Adults are generally appreciative and approving of an operator's conduct provided it meets their rather minimal standards, but they sometimes overreact to the part an operator is playing (positively) if accompanied by small children. A recent study of the Easter Bunny points out a similar sort of response on the part of adults to fantasy (Hickey, Thompson, & Foster, 1988). It is worth noting too that adults outnumber children in the park by a wide margin. One count reports an adult-to-children ratio of four-to-one (King, 1981).

The point here is that ride operators learn what the public (or, at least, their idealized version of the public) expects of their role and find it easier to conform to such expectations than not. Moreover, they discover that when they are bright and lively others respond to them in like ways. This Goffmanesque balancing of the emotional exchange is such that ride operators come to expect good treatment. They assume, with good cause, that most people will

react to their little waves and smiles with some affection and perhaps joy. When they do not, it can ruin a ride operator's day.

With this interaction formula in mind, it is perhaps less difficult to see why ride operators detest and scorn the ill-mannered or unruly guest. At times, these grumpy, careless, or otherwise unresponsive characters insult the very role the operators play and have come to appreciate—"You can't treat the Captain of the USS Nautilus like that!" Such out-of-line visitors offer breaks from routine, some amusement, consternation, or the occasional job challenge that occurs when remedies are deemed necessary to restore employee and role dignity.

By and large, however, the people-processing tasks of ride operators pass good naturedly and smoothly, with operators hardly noticing much more than the bodies passing in front of view (special bodies, however, merit special attention as when crew members on the subs gather to assist a young lady in a revealing outfit on board and then linger over the hatch to admire the view as she descends the steep steps to take her seat on the boat). Yet, sometimes, more than a body becomes visible, as happens when customers overstep their roles and challenge employee authority, insult an operator, or otherwise disrupt the routines of the job. In the process, guests become "dufusses," "ducks," and "assholes" (just three of many derisive terms used by ride operators to label those customers they believe to have gone beyond the pale). Normally, these characters are brought to the attention of park security officers, ride foremen, or area supervisors who, in turn, decide how they are to be disciplined (usually expulsion from the park).

Occasionally, however, the alleged slight is too personal or simply too extraordinary for a ride operator to let it pass unnoticed or merely inform others and allow them to decide what, if anything, is to be done. Restoration of one's respect is called for and routine practices have been developed for these circumstances. For example, common remedies include: the "seatbelt squeeze," a small token of appreciation given to a deviant customer consisting of the rapid cinching-up of a required seatbelt such that the passenger is doubled-over at the point of departure and left gasping for the duration of the trip; the "break-toss," an acrobatic gesture of the Autopia trade whereby operators jump on the outside of a norm violator's car, stealthily unhitching the safety belt, then slamming on the brakes, bringing the car to an almost instant stop while the driver flies on the hood of the car (or beyond); the "seatbelt slap," an equally distinguished (if primitive) gesture by which an offending customer receives a sharp, quick snap of a hard plastic belt across the face (or other parts of the body) when entering or exiting a seat-belted ride; the "break-up-the-party" gambit, a queuing device put to use in officious fashion whereby bothersome pairs are separated at the last minute into different units, thus forcing on them the pain of strange companions for the duration of a ride through the Haunted Mansion or a ramble on Mr. Toad's Wild Ride; the "hatch-cover ploy," a much beloved practice of Submarine pilots who, in collusion with mates on the loading dock, are able to drench offensive guests with water as their units pass under a waterfall; and, lastly, the rather ignoble variants of the "Sorry-I-didn't-see-your-hand" tactic, a savage move designed to crunch a particularly irksome customer's hand (foot, finger, arm, leg, etc.) by bringing a piece of Disneyland property to bear on the appendage, such as the door of a Thunder Mountain railroad car or the starboard side of a Jungle Cruise boat. This latter remedy is, most often, a "near miss" designed to startle the little criminals of Disneyland.

All of these unofficial procedures (and many more) are learned on the job. Although they are used sparingly, they are used. Occasions of use provide a continual stream of sweet revenge talk to enliven and enrich colleague conversation at break time or after work. Too much, of course, can be made of these subversive practices and the rhetoric that surrounds their use. Ride operators are quite aware that there are limits beyond which they dare not

pass. If they are caught, they know that restoration of corporate pride will be swift and clean.

In general, Disneyland employees are remarkable for their forbearance and polite good manners even under trying conditions. They are taught, and some come to believe, for a while at least, that they are really "on-stage" at work. And, as noted, surveillance by supervisory personnel certainly fades in light of the unceasing glances an employee receives from the paying guests who tromp daily through the park in the summer. Disneyland employees know well that they are part of the product being sold and learn to check their more discriminating manners in favor of the generalized countenance of a cheerful lad or lassie whose enthusiasm and dedication is obvious to all.

At times, the emotional resources of employees appear awesome. When the going gets tough and the park is jammed, the nerves of all employees are frayed and sorely tested by the crowd, din, sweltering sun, and eye-burning smog. Customers wait in what employees call "bullpens" (and park officials call "reception areas") for up to several hours for a $3\frac{1}{2}$ minute ride that operators are sometimes hell-bent on cutting to $2\frac{1}{2}$ minutes. Surely a monument to the human ability to suppress feelings has been created when both users and providers alike can maintain their composure and seeming regard for one another when in such a fix.

It is in this domain where corporate culture and the order it helps to sustain must be given its due. Perhaps the depth of a culture is visible only when its members are under the gun. The orderliness—a good part of the Disney formula for financial success—is an accomplishment based not only on physical design and elaborate procedures, but also on the low-level, part-time employees who, in the final analysis, must be willing, even eager, to keep the show afloat. The ease with which employees glide into their kindly and smiling roles is, in large measure, a feat of social engineering. Disneyland does not pay well; its supervision is arbitrary and skin-close; its working conditions are chaotic; its jobs require minimal amounts of intelligence or judgment; and asks a kind of sacrifice and loyalty of its employees that is almost fanatical. Yet, it attracts a particularly able workforce whose personal backgrounds suggest abilities far exceeding those required of a Disneyland traffic cop, people stuffer, queue or line manager, and button pusher. As I have suggested, not all of Disneyland is covered by the culture put forth by management. There are numerous pockets of resistance and various degrees of autonomy maintained by employees. Nonetheless, adherence and support for the organization are remarkable. And, like swallows returning to Capistrano, many part-timers look forward to their migration back to the park for several seasons.

THE DISNEY WAY

Four features alluded to in this unofficial guide to Disneyland seem to account for a good deal of the social order that obtains within the park. First, socialization, although costly, is of a most selective, collective, intensive, serial, sequential, and closed sort.[4] These tactics are notable for their penetration into the private spheres of individual thought and feeling (Van Maanen & Schein, 1979). Incoming identities are not so much dismantled as they are set aside as employees are schooled in the use of new identities of the situational sort. Many of these are symbolically powerful and, for some, laden with social approval. It is hardly surprising that some of the more problematic positions in terms of turnover during the summer occur in the food and concession domains where employees apparently find little to identify with on the job. Cowpokes on Big Thunder Mountain, Jet Pilots, Storybook Princesses, Tour Guides, Space Cadets, Jungle Boat Skippers, or Southern Belles of New Orleans Square have less difficulty on this score. Disneyland, by design, bestows identity through a process carefully set up to strip away the job relevance of other sources of identity and learned response and replace them with others of organizational relevance. It works.

Second, this is a work culture whose designers have left little room for individual experimentation. Supervisors, as apparent in their focused wandering and attentive looks, keep very close tabs on what is going on at any moment in all the lands. Every bush, rock, and tree in Disneyland is numbered and checked continually as to the part it is playing in the park. So too are employees. Discretion of a personal sort is quite limited while employees are "on-stage." Even "back-stage" and certain "off-stage" domains have their corporate monitors. Employees are indeed aware that their "off-stage" life beyond the picnics, parties, and softball games is subject to some scrutiny for police checks are made on potential and current employees. Nor do all employees discount the rumors that park officials make periodic inquiries on their own as to a person's habits concerning sex and drugs. Moreover, the sheer number of rules and regulations is striking, thus making the grounds for dismissal a matter of multiple choice for supervisors who discover a target for the use of such grounds. The feeling of being watched is, unsurprisingly, a rather prevalent complaint among Disneyland people and it is one that employees must live with if they are to remain at Disneyland.

Third, emotional management occurs in the park in a number of quite distinct ways. From the instructors at the university who beseech recruits to "wish every guest a pleasant good day," to the foremen who plead with their charges to, "say thank you when you herd them through the gate," to the impish customer who seductively licks her lips and asks, "what does Tom Sawyer want for Christmas?" appearance, demeanor, and etiquette have special meanings at Disneyland. Because these are prized personal attributes over which we normally feel in control, making them commodities can be unnerving. Much self-monitoring is involved, of course, but even here self-management has an organizational side. Consider ride operators who may complain of being "too tired to smile" but, at the same time, feel a little guilty for uttering such a confession. Ride operators who have worked an early morning shift on the Matterhorn (or other popular rides) tell of a queasy feeling they get when the park is opened for business and they suddenly feel the ground begin to shake under their feet and hear the low thunder of the hordes of customers coming at them, oblivious of civil restraint and the small children who might be among them. Consider, too, the discomforting pressures of being "on-stage" all day and the cumulative annoyance of having adults ask permission to leave a line to go to the bathroom, whether the water in the lagoon is real, where the well-marked entrances might be, where Walt Disney's cryogenic tomb is to be found,[5] or—the real clincher—whether or not one is "really real."

The mere fact that so much operator discourse concerns the handling of bothersome guests suggests that these little emotional disturbances have costs. There are, for instance, times in all employee careers when they put themselves on "automatic pilot," "go robot," "can't feel a thing," "lapse into a dream," "go into a trance," or otherwise "check out" while still on duty. Despite a crafty supervisor's (or curious visitor's) attempt to measure the glimmer in an employee's eye, this sort of willed emotional numbness is common to many of the "on-stage" Disneyland personnel. Much

of this numbness is, of course, beyond the knowledge of supervisors and guests because most employees have little trouble appearing as if they are present even when they are not. It is, in a sense, a passive form of resistance that suggests there still is a sacred preserve of individuality left among employees in the park.

Finally, taking these three points together, it seems that even when people are trained, paid, and told to be nice, it is hard for them to do so all of the time. But, when efforts to be nice have succeeded to the degree that is true of Disneyland, it appears as a rather towering (if not always admirable) achievement. It works at the collective level by virtue of elaborate direction. Employees—at all ranks—are stage-managed by higher ranking employees who, having come through themselves, hire, train, and closely supervise those who have replaced them below. Expression rules are laid out in corporate manuals. Employee time-outs intensify work experience. Social exchanges are forced into narrow bands of interacting groups. Training and retraining programs are continual. Hiding places are few. Although little sore spots and irritations remain for each individual, it is difficult to imagine work roles being more defined (and accepted) than those at Disneyland. Here, it seems, is a work culture worthy of the name.

NOTES

1. The quote is drawn from a transcript of a speech made to senior managers of Hurrah's Club by Bill Ross, Vice President for Human Relations at Disneyland, in January 1988. Elsewhere in this account I draw on other in-house publications to document my tale. Of use in this regard are: "Your Role in the Show" (1982), "Disneyland: The First Thirty Years" (1985), "The Disney Approach to Management" (1986), and Steven Birnbaum's semi-official travel guide to Disneyland (1988). The best tourist guide to the park I've read is Sehlinger's (1987) adamantly independent *The Unofficial Guide to Disneyland*.

2. This account is drawn primarily on my three-year work experience as a "permanent part-time" ride operator at Disneyland during the late 1960s. Sporadic contacts have been maintained with a few park employees and periodic visits, even with children in tow, have proved instructive. Also, lengthy, repeated beach interviews of a most informal sort have been conducted over the past few summers with ride operators (then) employed at the park. There is a good deal written about Disneyland, and I have drawn from these materials as indicated in the text. I must note finally that this is an unsponsored and unauthorized treatment of the Disneyland culture

and is at odds on several points with the views set forth by management.

3. The author serves as a case in point for I was fired from Disneyland for what I still consider a Mickey Mouse offense. The specific violation—one of many possible—involved hair growing over my ears, an offense I had been warned about more than once before the final cut was made. The form my dismissal took, however, deserves comment for it is easy to recall and followed a format familiar to an uncountable number of ex-Disneylanders. Dismissal began by being pulled off the ride after my work shift had begun by an area supervisor in full view of my cohorts. A forced march to the administration building followed where my employee card was turned over and a short statement read to me by a personnel officer as to the formal cause of termination. Security officers then walked me to the employee locker room where my work uniforms and equipment were collected and my personal belongings returned to me while an inspection of my locker was made. The next stop was the time shed where my employee's time card was removed from its slot, marked "terminated" across the top in red ink, and replaced in its customary position (presumably for Disneylanders to see when clocking on or off the job over the next few days). As now an ex-ride operator, I was escorted to the parking lot where two security officers scraped off the employee parking sticker attached to my car. All these little steps of status degradation in the Magic Kingdom were quite public and, as the reader might guess, the process still irks. This may provide the reader with an account for the tone of this narrative, although it shouldn't since I would also claim I was ready to quit anyway since I had been there far too long. At any rate, it may just be possible that I now derive as much a part of my identity from being fired from Disneyland as I gained from being employed there in the first place.

4. These tactics are covered in some depth in Van Maanen (1976, 1977) and Van Maanen and Schein (1979). When pulled together and used simultaneously, a people processing system of some force is created that tends to produce a good deal of conformity among recruits who, regardless of background, come to share very similar occupational identities, including just how they think and feel on the job. Such socialization practices are common whenever recruits are bunched together and processed as a batch and when role innovation is distinctly unwanted on the part of the agents of such socialization.

5. The unofficial answer to this little gem of a question is: "Under Sleeping Beauty's castle." Nobody knows for sure since the immediate circumstances surrounding Walt Disney's death are vague—even in the most careful accounts (Mosley, 1983; Schickel, 1985). Officially, his ashes are said to be peacefully at rest in Forest Lawn. But the deep freeze myth is too good to let go of because it so neatly complements all those fairy tales Disney expropriated and popularized when alive. What could be more appropriate than thinking of Walt on ice, waiting for technology's kiss to restore him to life in a hidden vault under his own castle in the Magic Kingdom?

Part C

Organizational Culture

24. Corporations, Culture, and Commitment: Motivation and Social Control in Organizations

Charles O'Reilly

*C*orporate culture is receiving much attention in the business press. A recent article in *Fortune* describes how the CEO at Black & Decker "transformed an entire corporate *culture,* replacing a complacent manufacturing mentality with an almost manic, market-driven way of doing things."[1] Similarly, the success of Food Lion (a $3 billion food-market chain that has grown at an annual rate of 37% over the past 20 years with annual returns on equity of 24%) is attributed to a culture which emphasizes "hard work, simplicity, and frugality."[2] Other well-known firms such as 3M, Johnson & Johnson, Apple, and Kimberly-Clark have been routinely praised for their innovative cultures.[3] Even the success of Japanese firms in the U.S. has been partly attributed to their ability to change the traditional culture developed under American managers. Peters and Waterman report how a U.S. television manufacturing plant, under Japanese management, reduced its defect rate from 140 to 6, its complaint rate from 70% to 7%, and the turnover rate among employees from 30% to 1%, all due to a changed management philosophy and culture.[4]

Even more dramatic is the turnaround at the New United Motors Manufacturing Incorporated (NUMMI) plant in Fremont, California. When General Motors closed this facility in 1982, it was one of the worst plants in the GM assembly division with an 18 percent daily absenteeism rate and a long history of conflict in its labor relations. The plant reopened as a joint venture between Toyota and GM in 1983. Over 85 percent of the original labor force was rehired, and workers are still represented by the UAW. Although the technology used is vintage 1970s and the plant is not as automated as many others within GM and Toyota, productivity is almost double what GM gets in other facilities. In 1987, it took an estimated 20.8 hours to produce a car at NUMMI versus 40.7 in other GM plants and 18.0 at Toyota. Quality of the NUMMI automobiles is the highest in the GM system, based on both internal audits and owner surveys, and absenteeism is at 2 percent compared to 8 percent at other GM facilities. What accounts for this remarkable success? According to one account, "At the system's core is a *culture* in which the assembly line workers maintain their machines, ensure the quality of their work, and improve the production process."[5]

But a culture is not always a positive force. It has also been implicated when firms run into difficulties. The CEO of financially troubled Computerland, William Tauscher, has attempted to restructure the firm, noting that "a low-cost culture is a must."[6] Henry Wendt, CEO of SmithKline Beecham, has attributed his firm's current difficulties to complacency. "We've been victims of our own success. . . . I want to create a new culture."[7] Corporate culture has also been implicated in problems faced by Sears, Caterpillar, Bank of America, Polaroid, General Motors, and others. Even difficulties in mergers and acquisitions are sometimes attributed to cultural conflicts which make integration of separate units difficult. Failure to merge two cultures can lead to debilitating conflict, a loss of talent, and an inability to reap the benefits of synergy.

But what is really meant when one refers to a firm's "culture"? Do all organizations have them? Are they always important? Even if we can identify cultures, do we know enough about how they work to manage them? Four major questions need to be answered:

- What is culture?
- From a manager's perspective, when is culture important?

- What is the process through which cultures are developed and maintained?
- How can cultures be managed?

WHAT IS CULTURE?

If culture is to be analyzed and managed, it is important that we be clear about what is meant by the term. Failure to clearly specify what "culture" is can result in confusion, misunderstanding, and conflict about its basic function and importance.

Culture as Control

Clearly, little would get done by or in organizations if some control systems were not in place to direct and coordinate activities. In fact, organizations are often seen to be efficient and effective solely because control systems operate.[8]

But what is a "control system"? A generic definition might be that a control system is "the knowledge that someone who knows and cares is paying close attention to what we do and can tell us when deviations are occurring?" Although broad, this definition encompasses traditional formal control systems ranging from planning and budgeting systems to performance appraisals. According to this definition, control systems work when those who are monitored are aware that someone who matters, such as a boss or staff department, is paying attention and is likely to care when things aren't going according to plan.

Several years ago a large toy manufacturer installed, at considerable expense, a management-by-objectives (MBO) performance appraisal system. After a year or so, top management became aware that the system was working well in one part of the organization but not another. They conducted an investigation and discovered the reason for the failure. In the part of the organization where MBO was working well, senior management was enthusiastic and committed. They saw real benefits and conveyed their belief up and down the chain of command. In the part of the organization where the system had failed, senior management saw

MBO as another bureaucratic exercise to be endured. Subordinate managers quickly learned to complete the paperwork but ignore the purpose. The lesson here was that a control system, no matter how carefully designed, works only when those being monitored believe that people who matter care about the results and are paying close attention. When Jan Carlzon became head of SAS Airline, he was concerned about the poor on-time record. To correct this, he personally requested a daily accounting of the on-time status of all flights. In the space of two years, SAS on-time record went from 83% to 97%.[9]

In designing formal control systems, we typically attempt to measure either outcomes or behaviors. For example, in hospitals it makes no sense to evaluate the nursing staff on whether patients get well. Instead, control systems rely on assessing behaviors. Are specified medical procedures followed? Are checks made at appropriate times? In other settings, behavior may not be observable. Whenever possible, we then attempt to measure outcomes. Salespeople, for instance, are usually measured on their productivity, since the nature of their job often precludes any effective monitoring of their behavior. In other situations, control systems can be designed that monitor both behaviors and outcomes. For example, for some retail sales jobs both behaviors (how the customer is addressed, how quickly the order is taken, whether the sales floor is kept stocked) and outcomes (sales volume) can be measured.

However, it is often the case that neither behavior nor outcomes can be adequately monitored.[10] These are the activities that are non-routine and unpredictable, situations that require initiative, flexibility, and innovation. These can be dealt with only by developing social control systems in which common agreements exist among people about what constitutes appropriate attitudes and behavior.

Culture may be thought of as a potential social control system. Unlike formal control systems that typically assess outcomes or behaviors only intermittently, social control

systems can be much more finely tuned. When we care about those with whom we work and have a common set of expectations, we are "under control" whenever we are in their presence. If we want to be accepted, we try to live up to their expectations. In this sense, social control systems can operate more extensively than most formal systems. Interestingly, our response to being monitored by formal and social control systems may also differ. With formal systems people often have a sense of external constraint which is binding and unsatisfying. With social controls, we often feel as though we have great autonomy, even though paradoxically we are conforming much more.

Thus, from a management perspective, culture in the form of shared expectations may be thought of as a social control system. Howard Schwartz and Stan Davis offer a practical definition of culture as "a pattern of beliefs and expectations shared by the organization's members. These beliefs and expectations produce norms that powerfully shape the behavior of individuals and groups."[11]

Culture as Normative Order

What Schwartz and Davis are referring to as culture are the central norms that may characterize an organization. Norms are expectations about what are appropriate or inappropriate attitudes and behaviors. They are socially created standards that help us interpret and evaluate events. Although their content may vary, they exist in all societies and, while often unnoticed, they are pervasive. For instance, in our society we have rather explicit norms about eye-contact. We may get uncomfortable when these are violated. Consider what happens when someone doesn't look at you while speaking or who continues to look without pause. In organizations we often find peripheral or unimportant norms around issues such as dress or forms of address. In the old railroads, for example, hats were a must for all managers, while everyone addressed each other with a formal "mister."

More important norms often exist around issues such as quality, performance, flexibility, or how to deal with conflict. In many organizations, it is impolite to disagree publicly with others. Instead, much behind-the-scenes interaction takes place to anticipate or resolve disputes. In other organizations, there may be norms that legitimate and encourage the public airing of disputes. Intel Corporation has an explicit policy of "constructive confrontation" that encourages employees to deal with disagreements in an immediate and direct manner.

In this view, the central values and styles that characterize a firm, perhaps not even written down, can form the basis for the development of norms that attach approval or disapproval to holding certain attitudes or beliefs and to acting in certain ways. For instance, the fundamental value of aggressiveness or competition may, if widely held and supported, be expressed as a norm that encourages organizational participants to stress winning competition. Pepsico encourages competition and punishes failure to compete.[12] Service is a pivotal norm at IBM; innovation is recognized as central at 3M. It is through norms—the expectations shared by group members and the approval or disapproval attached to these expectations—that culture is developed and maintained.

However, there is an important difference between the guiding beliefs or vision held by top management and the daily beliefs or norms held by those at lower levels in the unit or organization. The former reflect top managements' beliefs about how things ought to be. The latter define how things actually are. Simply because top management is in agreement about how they would like the organization to function is no guarantee that these beliefs will be held by others. One CEO spoke at some length about the glowing corporate philosophy that he believed in and felt characterized his firm's culture. After spending some time talking to mid-level managers in the organization, a very different picture emerged. A central norm shared by many of these managers was "Good people don't stay here." It is a common occurrence to find a noble sounding statement of corporate values framed on the wall and a very different and cynical interpretation of this creed held by people who have been around long enough to realize what is really important.

Moreover, norms can vary on two dimensions: the intensity or amount of approval/disapproval attached to an expectation; and the crystallization or degree of consensus or consistency with which a norm is shared. For instance, when analyzing an organization's culture it may be that for certain values there can be wide consensus but no intensity. Everyone understands what top management values, but there is no strong approval or disapproval attached to these beliefs or behaviors. Or, a given norm, such as innovation, can be positively valued in one group (e.g., marketing or R&D) and negatively valued in another (manufacturing or personnel). There is intensity but no crystallization.

It is only when there exist both intensity and consensus that strong cultures exist. This is why it is difficult to develop or change culture. Organizational members must come to know and share a common set of expectations. These must, in turn, be consistently valued and reinforced across divisions and management levels.[13] Only when this is done will there be both intensity and consensus. Similarly, a failure to share the central norms or to consistently reinforce them may lead to vacuous norms, conflicting interpretations, or to microcultures that exist only within subunits.

To have a strong culture, an organization does not have to have very many strongly held values. Only a few core values characterize strong culture firms such as Mars, Marriott, Hewlett-Packard, and Wal-Mart. What is critical is that these beliefs be widely shared and strongly held; that is, people throughout the organization must be willing to tell one another when a core belief is not being lived up to.

The Role of Culture in Promoting Innovation

How is it that firms such as Intel, Hewlett-Packard, Cray Research, 3M, and Johnson &

Johnson successfully develop both new products and new ways of doing things? How can culture help or hinder this process? The answer lies in those norms that, if they were widely shared and strongly held by members of the organization, would actively promote the generation of new ideas and would help in the implementation of new approaches.

What are these norms? This question was put to over 500 managers in firms as diverse as pharmaceuticals, consumer products, computers and semiconductors, and manufacturing.

Table 24.1 contains a list of the norms that were most frequently cited. Several things are notable about this list. First, regardless of the industry or technology, managers identified virtually the same sets of norms as important. While the progress of innovation varies widely across efforts to discover new drugs, improve oil exploration, build new electronic devices, or develop a new toilet bowl cleaner, the norms that facilitate these efforts are remarkably consistent. Second, these norms all function to facilitate the process of introducing new ways of

TABLE 24.1
Norms That Promote Innovation

A. Norms to Promote Creativity	B. Norms to Promote Implementation
1) Risk Taking	1) Common goals
• freedom to try things and fall	• sense of pride in the organization
• acceptance of mistakes	• teamwork
• allow discussion of "dumb" ideas	• willingness to share the credit
• no punishments for failure	• flexibility in jobs, budgets, functional areas
• challenge the status quo	• sense of ownership
• forget the past	• eliminate mixed messages
• willingness *not* to focus on the short term	• manage interdependencies
• expectation that innovation is part of your job	• shared visions and a common direction
• positive attitudes about change	• build consensus
• drive to improve	• mutual respect and trust
	• concern for the whole organization
2) Rewards for Change	2) Autonomy
• ideas are valued	• decision-making responsibility at lower levels
• respect for beginning ideas	• decentralized procedures
• build into the structure:	• freedom to act
• budgets • opportunities	• expectation of action
• resources • tools	• belief that *you* can have an impact
• time • promotions	• delegation
• top management attention and support	• quick, flexible decision making
• celebration of accomplishments	• minimize the bureaucracy
• suggestions are implemented	
• encouragement	
3) Openness	3) Belief in Action
• open communication and share information	• don't be obsessed with precision
• listen better	• emphasis on results
	• meet your commitments

continued

TABLE 24.1

Norms That Promote Innovation *(continued)*

• open access	• anxiety about timeliness
• bright people, strong egos	• value getting things done
• scanning, broad thinking	• hard work is expected and appreciated
• force exposure outside the company	• empower people
• move people around	• emphasis on quality
• encourage lateral thinking	• eagerness to get things done
• adopt the customer's perspective	• cut through the bureaucracy
• accept criticism	
• don't be too sensitive	
• continuous training	
• intellectual honesty	
• expect and accept conflict	
• willing to consult others	

doing things and to help people implement them. For example, when people share the expectation that it is not only permissible but also desirable to challenge the status quo, the likelihood of innovation is increased.

At Cray Research, a prime example of a firm whose success depends on its ability to innovate, creativity and diversity are seen as virtues. Similarly, at Intel Corporation, a company whose strategy has long been to be a first-mover and innovator, all employees are told to expect conflict and to deal with it directly. To resolve conflicts, employees are trained in a process called "constructive confrontation," which helps them deal with the conflict in productive rather than destructive ways. At Johnson & Johnson a similar belief is referred to as "creative conflict."

To appreciate how critical the norms shown in Table 24.1 can be to innovation, envision an organization that is characterized by norms the opposite of those listed. Imagine an organization where failure is punished severely, where no recognition or rewards are provided for those doing things differently, where the past is venerated and only ideas generated internally are considered worthwhile, where "dumb" ideas are ridiculed and people are never encouraged to take risks, and where there is no drive to change or improve things. In this environment, one would be amazed to see any change.

Contrast this with an organization such as 3M in which a basic financial goal is to have 25 percent of annual sales come from products developed over the last five years. Allen Jacobsen, 3M's CEO, says, "People ask me how do you get people to be innovative. It's simple. You give them responsibility for their own destinies and encourage them to take risks."[14] The secret to 3M's success isn't in Mr. Jacobsen's words but in the norms that form 3M's culture. These norms are widely shared and strongly held because management up and down the line provides the resources and encouragement to sustain them. It is the expectations held by people throughout the company, not just in R&D, that makes 3M and similar firms so innovative.

There is nothing magical or elusive about corporate culture. One has only to be clear about the specific attitudes and behaviors that are desired, and then to identify the norms or expectations that promote or impede them.

WHY CULTURE IS IMPORTANT

There are two reasons why a strong culture is valuable:

- the fit of culture and strategy, and
- the increased commitment by employees to the firm.

Both these factors provide a competitive edge, giving a strong culture firm an advantage over its competitors.[15]

Strategy and Corporate Culture

Every firm has, implicitly or explicitly, a competitive strategy which dictates how it attempts to position itself with respect to its competitors. Once established, a firm's strategy dictates a set of critical tasks or objectives that must be accomplished through a congruence among the elements of people, structure, and culture. For example, a decision to compete on innovation rather than price requires an appropriate formal structure and control system which then indicates the types of people required to accomplish the objectives and to fit the structure. The choice of a strategy also has significant implications for the informal organization or culture; that is, the norms of the organization must help execute the strategy.

An illustration of the importance of fit between strategy, people, structure, and culture can be seen in the history of the three major Silicon Valley firms that manufacture integrated circuits. Although operating in the same product market, Intel, National Semiconductor, and Advanced Micro Devices have each pursued a different strategy that is reflected in their people, structures, and cultures. National Semiconductor has chosen to compete largely as a low-cost manufacturer. To do this, it emphasizes strict cost control, a functional organizational structure, and a culture emphasizing numbers, a lack of frills, and a certain ruthlessness that has earned its people the sobriquet of "animals of the valley." Intel, however, has chosen to compete on product innovation. It has a looser formal organization with a culture valuing collegial interaction and the development of new technologies and products. Advanced Micro Devices has chosen a marketing strategy offering very high quality products, often as second source. Its strength has been in its marketing, and its culture reflects the value placed on selling, service, and quality.

For a strategy to be successfully implemented, it requires an appropriate culture. When firms change strategies, and often structures, they sometimes fail because the underlying shared values do not support the new approach. For example, a large, integrated electronics firm with a very strong culture based on technical excellence decided to enter the word processing market. Although they already made equipment that could easily be used as a basis for a word processor, the culture that made them successful in the design and manufacture of satellites and other sophisticated equipment ultimately sabotaged their efforts to design a word processor. The firm's engineers had a strong ethic of "getting it right" and would not release the machine. The window of opportunity for entry into the market passed, leaving the firm with a $40 million write-off of their investment. The point is both simple and important. As firms grow and strategies change, the culture or social control system also needs to be realigned to reflect the new direction.

Culture and Commitment

Culture is critical in developing and maintaining levels of intensity and dedication among employees that often characterizes successful firms. This strong attachment is particularly valuable when the employees have knowledge that is instrumental to the success of the organization or when very high levels of motivation are required. When IBM bought ROLM, the critical resource was not the existing product line but the design and engineering expertise of ROLM's staff. A failure to gain the commitment of employees during mergers and acquisitions can diminish or destroy the value of the venture. In contrast, a highly dedicated workforce represents a significant competitive advantage. Under turbulent or changing conditions, relying on employees who wait to be told exactly what to do can be a liability.

How, then, do strong culture organizations develop intensity and commitment? A 20-year veteran of IBM was quoted in a *Wall Street Journal* article as saying "I don't know what a cult is and what it is those bleary-eyed kids selling poppies really do, but I'm probably that deeply committed to the IBM company."[16] To understand this process, we need to consider what commitment is and how it is developed. By understanding the underlying psychology of commitment, we can then think about how to design systems to develop such an attachment among employees.

Organizational Commitment. What is meant by the term "organizational commitment"? It is typically conceived of as an individual's psychological bond to the organization, including a sense of job involvement, loyalty, and a belief in the values of the organization. There are three processes or stages of commitment: *compliance, identification,* and *internalization.*[17] In the first stage, *compliance,* a person accepts the influence of others mainly to obtain something from others, such as pay. The second stage is *identification,* in which the individual accepts influence in order to maintain a satisfying, self-defining relationship. People feel pride in belonging to the firm. The final stage of commitment is *internalization* in which the individual finds the values of the organization to be intrinsically rewarding and congruent with personal values.

Conceiving of commitment as developing in this manner allows us to understand how a variety of organizations—ranging from cults to strong culture corporations—generate commitment among their members. In fact, these organizations can be categorized based on the type of commitment displayed by their members. Cults and religious organizations, for example, typically have members who have internalized the values of the organization and who become "deployable agents," or individuals who can be relied upon to go forth and proselytize.[18] Japanese organizations, Theory Z, and strong culture firms are characterized by members who have a strong identification with the organization. These employees identify with the firm because it stands for something they value. In typical corporations, members comply with directions but may have little involvement with the firm beyond

self-interest; that is, there is no commitment with the firm beyond that of a fair exchange of effort for money and, perhaps, status.

HOW CULTURE IS DEVELOPED

How do people become committed to organization? Why, for example, would someone choose to join a cult? How do firms such as NUMMI get the incredible levels of productivity from their employees (as one team member said, "I like the new system so much it scares me. I'm scared because it took me 18 years to realize that I blew it at GM. Now we have a chance to do things a different way.")? The answer to this puzzle is simultaneously simple and nonobvious. As Jerry Salancik has noted, "commitment is too easy," yet it relies on an understanding of human motivation that is counter-intuitive.[19]

Constructing Social Realities

Most discussions of motivation assume a stable set of individual needs and values.[20] These are seen as shaping expectations, goals, and attitudes. In turn, these are presumed to guide behavior and people's responses to situations. In Maslow's theory, for instance, people are assumed to have a hierarchy of needs.[21] The managerial consequence of this view can be seen in our theories of job design in which jobs are supposed to be designed to take advantage of the desire of people to grow and self-actualize.[22] But are such theories correct? The empirical evidence is weak at best.[23] In spite of numerous efforts to demonstrate the effect of needs and personality, there is little support for the power of individual differences to predict behavior.

Consider the results of two experiments. In the first, Christian seminary students were approached and given one of two requests. Both asked them to extemporaneously address a visiting class in a discussion of the parable of the Good Samaritan. They were told to walk over to a classroom building to do this. In one condition they were informed that the class was already there and that they should hurry. In the other condition they were told that the class would arrive in several minutes. As they walked to the classroom, all subjects passed an old man (the "victim") dressed in shabby clothes and in obvious need of help. The experimenters were interested in what proportion of Christian seminarians thinking of the Good Samaritan would stop and help this person. Surprisingly, in the condition in which the subjects were told to hurry, only 30 percent paid any attention. Think about this. Seventy percent of a group of individuals with religious values who were training to be ministers failed to stop. Ninety-five percent of those who were not in a hurry stopped to help.

In another experiment, researchers observed when students using a campus restroom washed their hands. They discovered that when another person was visible in the restroom, 90 percent washed their hands. When no other person was visible, less than 20 percent did so.

What explains these and other findings? What often seems to account for behavior are the expectations of others. As individuals, we are very susceptible to the informational and normative influence of others. We pay attention to the actions of others and learn from them. "In actuality, virtually all learning phenomena resulting from direct experience occur on a vicarious basis by observing other people's behavior and its consequences for them." We watch others and form expectations about how and when we should act.[24]

Yet, we are not sensitive to how much of our world is really a social construction—one that rests on shared agreements. We often tend to underestimate the degree to which situations and the expectations of others can constrain and shape behavior. Strong situations—ones in which there are very clear incentives and expectations about what constitutes appropriate attitudes and behavior—can be very powerful. When we care what others think, the power of these norms or social expectations can be heightened.

Mechanisms for Developing Culture

How can cultures be developed and managed in organizations? All organizations—from cults to strong culture corporations—draw on the same underlying psychology and create

situations characterized by strong norms that focus people's attention, provide clear guidance about what is important, and provide for group reinforcement of appropriate attitudes and behavior. Four common mechanisms are used to accomplish this. What varies across these organizations is not what is done but only the degree to which these mechanisms are used.

Participation. The first mechanism that is critical in developing or changing a culture are systems that provide for participation. These systems encourage people to be involved and send signals to the individual that he or she is valued. These may range from formal efforts such as quality circles and advisory boards to less formal efforts such as suggestion systems and opportunities to meet with top managers and informal social gatherings. What is important about these processes is that people are encouraged to make incremental choices and develop a sense of responsibility for their actions. In some cases, such as work design, the specific choices made may be less important for future success than the fact that people had the chance to make them.

From a psychological perspective, choice is often associated with commitment. When we choose of our own volition to do something, we often feel responsible.[25] When the choice is volitional, explicit, public, and irrevocable, the commitment is even more binding. For instance, direct sales companies have learned that by getting the customer to fill out the order sheet, they can cut cancellations dramatically. A large number of psychological experiments have convincingly shown that participation can lead to both commitment and enjoyment, even when people are induced to engage in physically and emotionally stressful activities such as eating earthworms and becoming bone marrow donors.[26]

How do organizations use participation? Marc Galanter has documented how members of the Unification Church use processes of incremental commitment to recruit cult members.[27] Individuals are invited to dinner, convinced to spend the weekend for a seminar, and in some cases, induced to remain permanently with their new found "friends." Interestingly, there is no evidence that people who join cults under these circumstances are suffering from any psychopathology. Religious organizations often use elaborate systems of incremental choice and participation leading to greater and greater involvement. Japanese-managed automobile companies in the U.S. also have elaborate systems of selection and orientation that rely heavily on these approaches, as do American "strong culture" firms.

Management as Symbolic Action.

The second mechanism commonly seen in strong culture organizations is that of clear, visible actions on the part of management in support of the cultural values.[28] In organizations, participants typically want to know what is important. One way we gain this information is to carefully watch and listen to those above us. We look for consistent patterns. When top management not only says that something is important but also consistently behaves in ways that support the message, we begin to believe what is said. When the CEO of Xerox, David Kearns, began his quest for improved quality, there was some initial uncertainty about whether he meant it. Over time, as the message was repeated again and again, and as resources continued to be devoted to the quality effort, norms developed setting expectations about the role and importance of quality throughout the corporation.[29]

An important function of management is to provide interpretations of events for the organization's members. Without a shared meaning, confusion and conflict can result. Managers need to be sensitive to how their actions are viewed. Interpreting (or reinterpreting) history, telling stories, the use of vivid language, spending time, and being seen as visible in support of certain positions are all potential ways of shaping the organization's culture. This does not mean that managers need to be charismatic. However, managers need to engage in acts of "mundane symbolism." By this they can ensure

that important issues get suitable amounts of time, that questions are continually asked about important topics, and that the subject gets on the agenda and it is followed up.

The appropriate use of symbols and ceremonies is also important. When Jerry Sanders, CEO of Advanced Micro Devices, decided to shift the firm's strategy toward innovation, he not only made substantive changes in budget, positions, and organizational structure, he also used a symbol. As a part of the many talks he had with employees describing the need to change, Sanders would also describe how important it was to invest in areas that others could not easily duplicate—such as investing in proprietary products. He would describe how a poor farmer would always need a cash crop at the end of the year if he was to survive. But if he began to prosper, a smart farmer would begin to plant crops that others might not be able to afford—crops, for example, that took more than a year to come to fruition; crops like asparagus. The notion of asparagus became a visible and important symbol for change within AMD, even to the point where managers begin referring to revenues from new proprietary products as "being measured on asparagus."

Symbols are not a substitute for substance, and ceremonies cannot replace content. Rather, many of the substantive changes that occur in organizations, such as promotions or reorganizations, have multiple meanings and interpretations. Over time, people may lose a clear sense for what the superordinate goals are and why their jobs are important. In strong culture organizations, managers frequently and consistently send signals helping to renew these understandings. They do this by continually calling attention to what is important, in word and in action.

Information from Others.

While clear messages from management are an important determinant of a culture, so too are consistent messages from coworkers. If control comes from the knowledge that someone who matters is paying attention, then the degree to which we care about our coworkers also gives them a certain control over us. Years ago, several researchers conducted an experiment in which subjects were placed in a room to complete a questionnaire. While they were doing this, smoke began to flow from an air vent. While 75% of the subjects who were alone responded by notifying the experimenter of a possible fire, only 38% did so when in the company of two other subjects. When these other two were confederates of the experimenter and deliberately said nothing, only 10% of the subjects responded. One conclusion from this and other similar experiments is that we often take our cue from others when we are uncertain what to do.

In organizations, during periods of crisis or when people are new to the situation, they often look to others for explanations of what to do and how to interpret events. Strong cultures are typically characterized by consensus about three questions. In these settings there are often attempts made to insure a consistency of understanding and to minimize any us–them attitudes between parts of the organization. For instance, strong culture firms often pride themselves on the equality of treatment of all employees. At Mars, all employees punch a time clock and no one has a private secretary. At Gore-Tex, Wal-Mart, Disney, and others there are no employees or managers, only associates, team members, and hosts. At NUMMI, Honda, and Nissan there are no private dining rooms for managers and both managers and workers often wear uniforms. In the Rajneesh Commune, everyone wore clothes with the color magenta.

The goal here is to create a strong social construction of reality by minimizing contradictory interpretations. In cults, this is often done by isolating the members from the family and friends. Some religious organizations do this by encouraging extensive involvement in a variety of church activities and meetings. Japanese firms expect after work socializing. At NUMMI, for instance, each work team is given a semiannual budget to be spent only on team-sponsored activities where the entire team participates. In corporations, 60 hour work weeks can also isolate people from competing interpretations. Some electronics firms in Silicon Valley have provided employee T-shirts with slogans such as "Working 80 hours a week and loving it." With this commitment of time, workers may be as isolated as if they had joined a cult.

Comprehensive Reward Systems.

A final mechanism for promoting and shaping culture is the reward system, but not simply monetary rewards. Rather, these systems focus on rewards such as recognition and approval which can be given more frequently than money. These rewards also focus on the intrinsic aspects of the job and a sense of belonging to the organization. Recognition by your boss or coworkers for doing the right thing can be more potent in shaping behavior than an annual bonus. In the words of a popular management book, the trick is to catch someone doing something right and to reward it on the spot. While tokens such as scrolls or badges can be meaningless, under the right circumstances they can also be highly valued.

It is easy to desire one type of behavior while rewarding another. Often management professes a concern for quality while systematically rewarding only those who meet their goals, regardless of the quality. Innovation may be espoused but even the slightest failure is punished. At its simplest, people usually do what they are rewarded for and don't do what they're punished for. If this is true and to be taken seriously, then a simple analysis of what gets management's attention should give us a sense for what the culture supports. Who gets promoted? At 3M, one important aspect of success is to be associated with a new product introduction. If innovation is espoused, but doing things by-the-book is what is rewarded, it doesn't take a psychologist to figure out what the firm actually values. In fact, if there are inconsistencies between what top management says and what is actually rewarded, the likely outcome will be confusion and cynicism.

MANAGING CULTURE

Each of these can affect the development of a shared set of expectations. As shown in Figure 24.1, the process begins with words and actions on the part of the group's leaders. Even if no explicit statements are made, subordinates will attempt to infer a pattern. If management is credible and communicates consistently, members of the group may begin to develop consistent expectations about what is important. When this consensus is also rewarded, clear norms can then emerge.

Whether or not these norms constitute a desirable culture depends on the critical tasks to be accomplished and whether the formal control system provides sufficient leverage to attain these. If culture *is* important, four steps can help a manager understand how to manage it.

- Identify the strategic objectives of the unit. Once identified, specify the short-term objectives and critical actions that need to be accomplished if the strategic objectives are to be accomplished.
- Analyze the existing values and norms that characterize the organization. This can be done by focusing on what people in the unit feel is expected of them by their peers and bosses and what is actually rewarded. What does it take to get ahead? What stories are routinely told? Who are the people who exemplify the group? Look for norms that are widely shared and strongly felt.
- Once these are identified, look for norms that may hinder the accomplishment of critical tasks; norms that would help but are not currently present; and conflicts between what is needed and what is currently rewarded.
- Once these are identified, programs can be designed to begin to shape or develop the

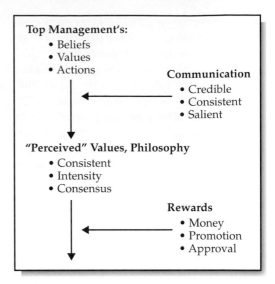

FIGURE 24.1
Employees' beliefs, attitudes, and behaviors expressed as norms

desired norms. These can draw upon the psychological mechanisms discussed previously.

The logic here is straightforward and links culture to those activities critical for the implementation of strategy and for generating widespread understanding and commitment among the organization's members. Obviously, these actions take time and management resources to accomplish. However, to ignore them is to ignore a social control system that may already be operating in the organization. The issue is whether this system is helping or hindering. Managers need to be sensitive to what the central organizational norms are and how they can affect them. To not be sensitive to these issues is to ignore the advice of a CEO who said, "We will either be a victim or a successful result of our culture."

REFERENCES

1. *Fortune,* January 2, 1989.
2. *Fortune,* August 15, 1988.
3. *Fortune,* June 6, 1988.
4. T. Peters and R. H. Waterman, *In Search of Excellence: Lessons From America's Best-Run*

Companies (New York, NY: Harper & Row, 1982), p. 32.
5. *Fortune,* January 30, 1989.
6. *BusinessWeek,* October 10, 1988.
7. *BusinessWeek,* October 10, 1988.

8. A. Wilkins and W. Ouchi, "Efficient Cultures: Exploring the Relationship Between Culture and Organizational Performance," *Administrative Science Quarterly,* 28 (1983): 468–481; O. Williamson, *Markets and Hierarchies* (New York, NY: Free Press, 1975).

9. J. Carlzon, *Moments of Truth* (Cambridge, MA: Ballinger, 1987).

10. S. Dornbusch and W. R. Scott, *Evaluation and the Exercise of Authority* (San Francisco, CA: Jossey-Bass, 1975).

11. H. Schwartz and S. Davis, "Matching Corporate Culture and Business Strategy," *Organizational Dynamics* (1981), pp. 30–48.

12. *Fortune,* April 10, 1989.

13. D. Feldman, "The Development and Enforcement of Group Norms," *Academy of Management Review,* 9 (1984): 47–53.

14. *Fortune,* June 6, 1988.

15. For example, see S. Davis, *Managing Corporate Culture* (Cambridge, MA: Ballinger, 1984); T. Deal and A. Kennedy, *Corporate Cultures* (Reading, MA: Addison-Wesley, 1982); Peters and Waterman, op. cit.

16. *Wall Street Journal,* April 7, 1986.

17. C. O'Reilly and J. Chatman, "Organizational Commitment and Psychological Attachment: The Effects of Compliance, Identification and Internalization on Prosocial Behavior," *Journal of Applied Psychology,* 71 (1986): 492–499.

18. W. Appel, *Cults in America* (New York, NY: Holt, Rinehart and Winston, 1983); D. Gerstel, *Paradise Incorporated: Synanon* (San Francisco, CA: Presidio Press, 1982).

19. G. Salancik, "Commitment Is Too Easy!" *Organizational Dynamics* (Summer 1977), pp. 62–80.

20. For example, see F. Herzberg, B. Mausner, and B. Snyderman, *The Motivation to Work* (New York, NY: John Wiley, 1959); A. Maslow, *Motivation and Personality* (New York, NY: Harper & Row, 1970).

21. Maslow, op. cit.

22. For example, see J. R. Hackman and G. Oldham, *Work Redesign* (Reading, MA: Addison-Wesley, 1980).

23. For example, see G. Salancik and J. Pfeffer, "A Social Information Processing Approach to Job Attitudes and Task Design," *Administrative Science Quarterly,* 23 (1978): 224–253.

24. For example, see S. Milgram, *Obedience to Authority* (New York, NY: Harper & Row, 1969); A. Bandura, *Social Learning Theory* (Englewood Cliffs, NJ: Prentice-Hall, 1977).

25. Salancik, op. cit.

26. For example, see I. Janis and L. Mann, *Decision Making: A Psychological Analysis of Conflict, Choice, and Commitment* (New York, NY: Free Press, 1977).

27. M. Galanter, "Psychological Induction into the Large Group: Findings from a Modern Religious Sect," *American Journal of Psychiatry,* 137 (1980): 1574–1579.

28. J. Pfeffer, "Management as Symbolic Action: The Creation and Maintenance of Organizational Paradigms," in L. Cummings and B. Staw, eds., *Research in Organizational Behavior,* Vol. 3 (Greenwich, CT: JAI Press, 1981).

29. G. Jacobsen and J. Hillkirk, *Xerox: American Samurai* (New York, NY: Collier Books, 1986).

25. The Role of the Founder in Creating Organizational Culture

Edgar H. Schein

How do the entrepreneur/founders of organizations create organizational cultures? And how can such cultures be analyzed? These questions are central to this article. First I will examine what organizational culture is, how the founder creates and embeds cultural elements, why it is likely that first-generation companies develop distinctive cultures, and what the implications are in making the transition from founders or owning families to "professional" managers.

The level of confusion over the term *organizational culture* requires some definitions of terms at the outset. An organizational culture depends for its existence on a definable organization, in the sense of a number of people interacting with each other for the purpose of accomplishing some goal in their defined environment. An organization's founder simultaneously creates such a group and, by force of his or her personality, begins to shape the group's culture. But that new group's culture does not develop until it has overcome various crises of growth and survival, and has worked out solutions for coping with its external problems of adaptation and its internal problems of creating a workable set of relationship rules.

Organizational culture, then, is the pattern of basic assumptions that a given group has invented, discovered, or developed in learning to cope with its problems of external adaptation and internal integration—a pattern of assumptions that has worked well enough to be considered valid and, therefore, to be taught to new members as the correct way to perceive, think, and feel in relation to those problems.

In terms of external survival problems, for example, I have heard these kinds of assumptions in first-generation companies:

The way to decide on what products we will build is to see whether we ourselves like the product; if we like it, our customers will like it.

The only way to build a successful business is to invest no more than 5 percent of your own money in it.

The customer is the key to our success, so we must be totally dedicated to total customer service.

In terms of problems of internal integration the following examples apply:

Ideas can come from anywhere in this organization, so we must maintain a climate of total openness.

The only way to manage a growing business is to supervise every detail on a daily basis.

The only way to manage a growing business is to hire good people, give them clear responsibility, tell them how they will be measured, and then leave them alone.

Several points should be noted about the definition and the examples. First, culture is not the overt behavior or visible artifacts one might observe on a visit to the company. It is not even the philosophy or value system that the founder may articulate or write down in various "charters." Rather, it is the assumptions that underlie the values and determine not only behavior patterns, but also such visible artifacts as architecture, office layout, dress codes, and so on. This distinction is important because founders bring many of these assumptions with them when the organization begins; their problem is how to articulate, teach, embed, and in other ways get their own assumptions across and working in the system.

Founders often start with a theory of how to succeed; they have a cultural paradigm in their heads, based on their experience in the culture in which they grew up. In the case of a founding *group*, the theory and paradigm arise from the way that group reaches consensus on their assumptions about how to view things. Here, the evolution of the culture is a multi-stage process reflecting the several stages of group formation. The ultimate organizational culture will always reflect the complex interaction between (1) the assumptions and theories that founders bring to the group initially and (2) what the group learns subsequently from its own experiences.

WHAT IS ORGANIZATIONAL CULTURE ABOUT?

Any new group has the problem of developing shared assumptions about the nature of the world in which it exists, how to survive in it, and how to manage and integrate internal relationships so that it can operate effectively and make life livable and comfortable for its members. These external and internal problems can be categorized as shown in Table 25.1.

TABLE 25.1
External and Internal Problems

Problems of External Adaptation and Survival

1. Developing consensus on the *primary task, core mission, or manifest and latent functions of the group*—for example, strategy.
2. Consensus on *goals*, such being the concrete reflection of the core mission.
3. Developing consensus on the *means to be used* in accomplishing the goals—for example, division of labor, organization structure, reward system, and so forth.
4. Developing consensus on the *criteria to be used in measuring how well the group is doing against its goals and targets*—for example, information and control systems.
5. Developing consensus on *remedial or repair strategies* as needed when the group is not accomplishing its goals.

Problems of Internal Integration

1. *Common language and conceptual categories*. If members cannot communicate with and understand each other, a group is impossible by definition.
2. Consensus on *group boundaries and criteria for inclusion and exclusion*. One of the most important areas of culture is the shared consensus on who is in, who is out, and by what criteria one determines membership.
3. Consensus on *criteria for the allocation of power and status*. Every organization must work out its pecking order and its rules for how one gets, maintains, and loses power. This area of consensus is crucial in helping members manage their own feelings of aggression.
4. Consensus on *criteria for intimacy, friendship, and love*. Every organization must work out its own rules of the game for peer relationships, for relationships between the sexes, and for the manner in which openness and intimacy are to be handled in the context of managing the organization's tasks.
5. Consensus on *criteria for allocation of rewards and punishments*. Every group must know what its heroic and sinful behaviors are: what gets rewarded with property, status, and power; and what gets punished through the withdrawal of rewards and, ultimately, excommunication.
6. Consensus on *ideology and "religion."* Every organization, like every society, faces unexplainable events that must be meaning so that members can respond to them and avoid the anxiety of dealing with the unexplainable and uncontrollable.

The external and internal problems are always intertwined and acting simultaneously. A group cannot solve its external survival problem without being integrated to some degree to permit concerted action, and it cannot integrate itself without some successful task accomplishment vis-à-vis its survival problem or primary task.

The model of organizational culture that then emerges is one of shared solutions to problems which work well enough to begin to be taken for granted—to the point where they drop out of awareness, become unconscious assumptions, and are taught to new members as a reality and as the correct way to view things. If one wants to identify the elements of a given culture, one can go down the list of issues and ask how the group views itself in relation to each of them: What does it see to be its core mission, its goals, the way to accomplish those goals, the measurement systems and procedures it uses, the way it remedies actions, its particular jargon and meaning system, the authority system, peer system, reward system, and ideology? One will find, when one does this, that there is in most cultures a deeper level of assumptions which

ties together the various solutions to the various problems, and this deeper level deals with more ultimate questions. The real cultural essence, then, is what members of the organization assume about the issues shown in Table 25.2.

In a fairly "mature" culture—that is, in a group that has a long and rich history—one will find that these assumptions are patterned and interrelated into a "cultural paradigm" that is the key to understanding how members of the group view the world. In an organization that is in the process of formation, the paradigm is more likely to be found only in the founder's head, but it is important to try to decipher it in order to understand the biases or directions in which the founder "pushes" or "pulls" the organization.

HOW DO ORGANIZATIONAL CULTURES BEGIN?
The Role of the Founder

Groups and organizations do not form accidentally or spontaneously. They are usually created because someone takes a leadership role in seeing how the concerted action of a number of

TABLE 25.2
Basic Underlying Assumptions Around Which Paradigms Form

1. *The organization's relationship to its environment.* Reflecting even more basic assumptions about the relationship of humanity to nature, one can assess whether the key members of the organization view the relationship as one of dominance, submission, harmonizing, finding an appropriate niche, and so on.

2. *The nature of reality and truth.* Here are the linguistic and behavioral rules that define what is real and what is not, what is a "fact," how truth is ultimately to be determined, and whether truth is "revealed" or "discovered"; basic concepts of time as linear or cyclical, monochronic or individual; and so forth.

3. *The nature of human nature.* What does it mean to be "human," and what attributes are considered intrinsic or ultimate? Is human nature good, evil, or neutral? Are human beings perfectible or not? Which is better, Theory X or Theory Y?

4. *The nature of human activity.* What is the "right" thing for human beings to do, on the basis of the above presumptions about reality, the environment, and human nature; to be active, passive, self-developmental, fatalistic, or what? What is work and what is play?

5. *The nature of human relationships.* What is considered to be the "right" way for people to relate to each other, to distribute power and love? Is life cooperative or competitive; individualistic, group collaborative, or communal; based on traditional lineal authority, law, or charisma, or what?

people could accomplish something that would be impossible through individual action alone. In the case of social movements or new religions, we have prophets, messiahs, and other kinds of charismatic leaders. Political groups or movements are started by leaders who sell new visions and new solutions. Firms are created by entrepreneurs who have a vision of how a concerted effort could create a new product or service in the marketplace. The process of culture formation in the organization begins with the founding of the group. How does this happen?

In any given firm the history will be somewhat different, but the essential steps are functionally equivalent:

1. A single person (founder) has an idea for a new enterprise.
2. A founding group is created on the basis of initial consensus that the idea is a good one: workable and worth running some risks for.
3. The founding group begins to act in concert to create the organization by raising funds, obtaining patents, incorporating, and so forth.
4. Others are brought into the group according to what the founder or founding group considers necessary, and the group begins to function, developing its own history.

In this process the founder will have a major impact on how the group solves its external survival and internal integration problem. Because the founder had the original idea, he or she will typically have biases on how to get the idea fulfilled—biases based on previous cultural experiences and personality traits. In my observation, entrepreneurs are very strong-minded about what to do and how to do it. Typically they already have strong assumptions about the nature of the world, the role their organization will play in that world, the nature of human nature, truth, relationships, time, and space.

Three Examples

Founder A, who built a large chain of supermarkets and department stores, was the dominant ideological force in the company until he died in his seventies. He assumed that his organization could be dominant in the market and that his primary mission was to supply his customers with a quality, reliable product. When A was operating only a corner store with his wife, he built customer relations through a credit policy that displayed trust in the customer, and he always took products back if the customer was not satisfied. Further, he assumed that stores had to be attractive and spotless, and that the only way to ensure this was by close personal supervision. He would frequently show up at all his stores to check into small details. Since he assumed that only close supervision would teach subordinates the right skills, he expected all his store managers to be very visible and very much on top of their jobs.

A's theory about how to grow and win against his competition was to be innovative, so he encouraged his managers to try new approaches, to bring in consulting help, to engage in extensive training, and to feel free to experiment with new technologies. His view of truth and reality was to find it wherever one could and, therefore, to be open to one's environment and never take it for granted that had all the answers. If new things worked, A encouraged their adoption.

Measuring results and fixing problems was, for A, an intensely personal matter. In addition to using traditional business measures, he went to the stores and, if he saw things not to his liking, immediately insisted that they be corrected. He trusted managers who operated on the basis of similar kinds of assumptions and clearly had favorites to whom he delegated more.

Authority in this organization remained very centralized; the ultimate source of power, the voting shares of stock, remained entirely in the family. A was interested in developing good managers throughout the organization, but he never assumed that sharing ownership through some kind of stock option plan would help in that process. In fact, he did not even share ownership with several key "lieutenants" who had been with the company through most of its life but were not in the family. They were well paid, but received no stock. As a result, peer relationships were officially defined as competitive. A liked managers to compete for slots and felt free to get rid of "losers."

A also introduced into the firm a number of family members who received favored treatment in the form of good developmental jobs that would test them for ultimate management potential. As the firm diversified, family members were made division heads even though they often had relatively little general management experience. Thus peer relationships were highly politicized. One had to know how to stay in favor, how to deal with family members, and how to maintain trust with nonfamily peers in the highly competitive environment.

A wanted open communication and high trust levels, but his own assumptions about the role of the family, the effect of ownership, and the correct way to manage were, to some degree, in conflict with each other, leading many of the members of the organization to deal with the conflicting signals by banding together to form a kind of counter-culture within the founding culture. They were more loyal to each other than to the company.

Without going into further detail. I want to note several points about the "formation" of this organization and its emerging culture. By definition, something can become part of the culture only if it works. A's theory and assumptions about how things "should be" worked, since his company grew and prospered. He personally received a great deal of reinforcement for his own assumptions, which undoubtedly gave him increased confidence that he had a correct view of the world. Throughout his lifetime he steadfastly adhered to the principles with which he started, and did everything in his power to get others to accept them as well. At the same time, however, A had to share concepts and assumptions with a great many other people. So as his company grew and learned from its own experience, A's assumptions gradually had to be modified, or A had to withdraw from certain areas of running the business. For

example, in their diversification efforts, the management bought several production units that would permit backward integration in a number of areas—but, because they recognized that they knew little about running factories, they brought in fairly strong, autonomous managers and left them alone.

A also had to learn that his assumption did not always lead to clear signals. He thought he was adequately rewarding his best young general managers, but could not see that for some of them the political climate, the absence of stock options, and the arbitrary rewarding of family members made their own career progress too uncertain. Consequently, some of his best people left the company—a phenomenon that left A perplexed but unwilling to change his own assumptions in this area. As the company matured, many of these conflicts remained and many sub-cultures formed around groups of younger managers who were functionally or geographically insulated from the founder.

Founder B built a chain of financial service organizations using sophisticated financial analysis techniques in an urban area where insurance companies, mutual funds, and banks were only beginning to use these techniques. He was the conceptualizer and the salesman in putting together the ideas for these new organizations, but he put only a small percentage of the money up himself, working from a theory that if he could not convince investors that there was a market, then the idea was not sound. His initial assumption was that he did not know enough about the market to gamble with his own money—an assumption based on experience, according to a story he told about the one enterprise in which he had failed miserably. With this enterprise, he had trusted his own judgment on what customers would want, only to be proven totally wrong the hard way.

B did not want to invest himself heavily in his organizations, either financially or personally. Once he had put together a package, he tried to find people whom he trusted to administer it. There were usually people who, like himself, were fairly open in their approach to business and not too hung up on previous assumptions about how things should be done. One can infer that B's assumptions about concrete goals, the means to be used to achieve them, measurement criteria, and repair strategies were pragmatic: Have a clear concept of the mission, test it by selling it to investors, bring in good people who understand what the mission is, and then leave them alone to implement and run the organization, using only ultimate financial performance as a criterion.

B's assumptions about how to integrate a group were, in a sense, irrelevant since he did not inject himself very much into any of his enterprises. To determine the cultures of those enterprises, one had to study the managers put into key positions by B—matters that varied dramatically from one enterprise to the next. This short example illustrates that there is nothing automatic about an entrepreneur's process of inserting personal vision or style into his or her organization. The process depends very much on whether and how much that person wants to impose himself or herself.

Founder C, like A, was a much more dominant personality with a clear idea of how things should be. He and four others founded a manufacturing concern several years ago, one based on the founder's product idea along with a strong intuition that the market was ready for such a product. In this case, the founding group got together because they shared a concept of the core mission, but they found after a few years that the different members held very different assumptions about how to build an organization. These differences were sufficient to split the group apart and leave C in control of the young, rapidly growing company.

C held strong assumptions about the nature of the world—how one discovers truth and solves problems—and they were reflected in his management style. He believed that good ideas could come from any source; in particular, he believed that he himself was not wise enough to know what was true and right, but that if he heard an intelligent group of people debate an idea and examine it from all sides, he could judge accurately whether it was sound or not. He also knew that he could solve problems best in a group where many ideas were batted around and where there was a high level of mutual confrontation around those ideas. Ideas came from individuals, but the testing of ideas had to be done in a group.

C also believed very strongly that even if he knew what the correct course of action was, unless the parties whose support was critical to implementation were completely sold on the idea, they would either misunderstand or unwittingly sabotage the idea. Therefore, on any important decision, C insisted on wide debate, many group meetings, and selling the idea down and laterally in the organization; only when it appeared that everyone understood and was committed would he agree to going ahead. C felt so strongly about this that he often held up important decisions even when he personally was already convinced of the course of action to take. He said that he did not want to be out there leading all by himself if he could not count on support from the troops; he cited past cases in which, thinking he had group support, he made a decision and, when it failed, found his key subordinates claiming that he had been alone in the decision. These experiences, he said, taught him to ensure commitment before going ahead on anything, even if doing so was time-consuming and frustrating.

While C's assumptions about how to make decisions led to a very group-oriented organization, his theory about how to manage led to a strong individuation process. C was convinced that the only way to manage was to give clear and simple individual responsibility and then to measure the person strictly on those responsibilities. Groups could help make decisions and obtain commitment, but they could not under any circumstance be responsible or accountable. So once a decision was made, it had to be carried out by individuals. If the decision was complex, involving a reorganization of functions, C always insisted that the new organization had to be clear and simple enough to permit the assignment of individual accountabilities.

C believed completely in a proactive model of man and in man's capacity to master nature; hence he expected of his subordinates that they would always be on top of their jobs. If a budget had been negotiated for a year, and if after three months the subordinate recognized that he would overrun the budget, C insisted that the subordinate make a clear decision either to find a way to stay within the budget or to renegotiate a larger budget. It was not acceptable to allow the overrun to occur without informing others and renegotiating, and it was not acceptable to be ignorant of the likelihood that there would be an overrun. The correct way to behave was always to know what was happening, always to be responsible for what was happening, and always to feel free to renegotiate previous agreements if they no longer made sense. C believed completely in open communications and the ability of people to reach reasonable decisions and compromises if they confronted their problems, figured out what they wanted to do, were willing to marshal arguments for their solution, and scrupulously honored any commitments they made.

On the interpersonal level, C assumed "constructive intent" on the part of all members of the organization, a kind of rational loyalty to organizational goals and to shared commitments. This did not prevent people from competitively trying to get ahead—but playing politics, hiding information, blaming others, or failing to cooperate on agreed-upon plans were defined as sins. However, C's assumptions about the nature of truth and the need for every individual to keep thinking out what he or she thought was the correct thing to do in any given situation led to frequent interpersonal tension. In other words, the rule of honoring commitments and following through on consensually reached decision was superseded by the rule of doing only what you believed sincerely to be the best thing to do in any given situation. Ideally, there would be time to challenge the original decision and renegotiate, but in practice time pressure was such that the subordinate, in doing what was believed to be best, often had to be insubordinate. Thus people in the organization frequently complained that decisions did not "stick," yet had to acknowledge that the reason they did not stick was that the assumption that one had to do the correct thing was even more important. Subordinates learned that insubordination was much less likely to be punished than doing something that the person knew to be wrong or stupid.

C clearly believed in the necessity of organization and hierarchy, but he did not trust the authority of position nearly so much as the authority of reason. Hence bosses were granted authority only to the extent that they could sell their decisions; as indicated above, insubordination was not only tolerated, but actively rewarded if it led to better outcomes. One could infer from watching this organization that it thrived on intelligent, assertive, individualistic people—and, indeed, the hiring policies reflected this bias.

So, over the years, the organization C headed had a tendency to hire and keep the people who fit into the kind of management system I am describing. And those people who fit the founder's assumptions found themselves feeling increasingly like family members in that strong bonds of mutual support grew up among them, with C functioning symbolically as a kind of benign but demanding father figure. These familial feelings were very important, though quite implicit, because they gave subordinates a feeling of security that was needed to challenge each other and C when a course of action did not make sense.

The architecture and office layout in C's company reflected his assumptions about problem solving and human relationships. He insisted on open office landscaping; minimum status differentiation in terms of office size, location, and furnishings (in fact, people were free to decorate their offices any way they liked); open cafeterias instead of executive dining rooms; informal dress codes; first-come, first-serve systems for getting parking spaces; many conference rooms with attached kitchens to facilitate meetings and to keep people interacting with each other instead of going off for meals; and so forth.

In summary, C represents a case of an entrepreneur with a clear set of assumptions about how things should be, both in terms of the formal business arrangements and in terms of internal relationships in the organization—and these assumptions still reflect themselves clearly in the organization some years later.

Let us turn next to the question of how a strong founder goes about embedding his assumptions in the organization.

HOW ARE CULTURAL ELEMENTS EMBEDDED?

The basic process of embedding a cultural element—a given belief or assumption—is a "teaching" process, but not necessarily an explicit one. The basic model of cultural formation, it will be remembered, is that someone must propose a solution to a problem the group faces. Only if the group shares the perception that the solution is working will that element be adopted, and only if it continues to work will it come to be taken for granted and taught to newcomers. It goes without saying, therefore, that only elements that solve group problems will survive, but the previous issue of "embedding" is how a founder or leader gets the group to do things in a certain way in the first place, so that the question of whether it will work can be settled. In other words, embedding a cultural element in this context means only that the founder/leader has ways of getting the group to try out certain responses. There is no guarantee that those responses will, in fact, succeed in solving the group's ultimate problem. How do founder/leaders do this? I will describe a number of mechanisms ranging from very explicit teaching to very implicit messages of which even the founder may be unaware. These mechanisms are shown in Table 25.3.

As the above case examples tried to show, the initial thrust of the messages sent is very much a function of the personality of the founder; some founders deliberately choose to build an organization that reflects their own personal biases while others create the basic organization but then turn it over to subordinates as soon as it has a life of its own. In both cases, the process of culture formation is complicated by the possibility that the founder is "conflicted," in the sense of having in his or her own personality several mutually contradictory assumptions.

The commonest case is probably that of the founder who states a philosophy of delegation but who retains tight control by feeling free to intervene, even in the smallest and most trivial decisions, as A did. Because the owner is granted the "right" to run his or her own company, subordinates will tolerate this kind of contradictory behavior and the organization's culture will develop complex assumptions about how one runs the organization "in spite of" or "around" the founder. If the founder's conflicts are severe to the point of interfering with the running of the organization, buffering layers of management may be built in or, in the extreme, the board of directors may have to find a way to move the founder out altogether.

The mechanisms listed in Table 25.3 are not equally potent in practice, but they can reinforce each other to make the total message more potent than individual components. In my observation the most important or potent messages are role modeling by leaders (item 3), what leaders pay attention to (item 6), and leader reactions to critical events (item 7). Only if we observe these leader actions can we begin to decipher how members of the organization "learned" the right and proper things to do, and what model of reality they were to adopt.

To give a few examples, A demonstrated his need to be involved in everything at a detailed level by frequent visits to stores and detailed inspections of what was going on in them. When he went on vacation, he called the office every single day at a set time and wanted to know in great detail what was going on. This behavior persisted into his period of semi-retirement,

TABLE 25.3
How Is Culture Embedded and Transmitted?

Each of the mechanisms listed below is used by founders and key leaders to embed a value or assumption they hold, though the message may be very implicit in the sense that the leader is not aware of sending it. Leaders also may be conflicted, which leads to conflicting messages. A given mechanism may convey the message very explicitly, ambiguously, or totally implicitly. The mechanisms are listed below from more or less explicit to more or less implicit ones.

1. *Formal statements of organizational philosophy, charters, creeds, materials used for recruitment and selection, and socialization.*

2. *Design of physical spaces, facades, buildings.*

3. *Deliberate role modeling, teaching, and coaching by leaders.*

4. *Explicit reward and status system, promotion criteria.*

5. *Stories, legends, myths, and parables about key people and events.*

6. *What leaders pay attention to, measure, and control.*

7. *Leader reactions to critical incidents and organizational crises* (times when organizational survival is threatened, norms are unclear or challenged, insubordination occurs, threatening or meaningless events occur, and so forth).

8. *How the organization is designed and structured.* (The design of work, who reports to whom, degree or decentralization, functional or other criteria for differentiation, and mechanisms used for integration carry implicit messages of what leaders assume and value.)

9. *Organizational systems and procedures.* (The types of information, control, and decision support systems in terms of categories of information, and when and how performance appraisal and other review processes are conducted carry implicit messages of what leaders assume and value.)

10. *Criteria used for recruitment, selection, promotion, leveling off, retirement, and "excommunication" of people.* (The implicit and possibly unconscious criteria that leaders use to determine who "fits" and who doesn't "fit" membership roles and key slots in the organization.)

when he would still call *daily* from his retirement home, where he spent three winter months.

A's loyalty to his family was quite evident: He ignored bad business results if a family member was responsible, yet punished a non-family member involved in such results. If the family member was seriously damaging the business, A put a competent manager in under him, but did not always give that manager credit for subsequent good results. If things continued to go badly, A would finally remove the family member, but always with elaborate rationalizations to protect the family image. If challenged on this kind of blind loyalty, A would assert that owners had certain rights that could not be challenged. Insubordination from a family member was tolerated and excused, but the same kind of

insubordination from a non-family member was severely punished.

In complete contrast, B tried to find competent general managers and turn a business over to them as quickly as he could. He involved himself only if he absolutely had to in order to save the business, and he pulled out of businesses as soon as they were stable and successful. B separated his family life completely from his business and had no assumptions about the rights of a family in a business. He wanted a good financial return so that he could make his family economically secure, but he seemed not to want his family involved in the businesses.

C, like B, was not interested in building the business on behalf of the family; his preoccupation with making sound decisions overrode all other concerns. Hence C set out to find the right kinds of managers and then "trained" them through the manner in which he reacted to situations. If managers displayed ignorance or lack of control of an area for which they were responsible, C would get publicly angry at them and accuse them of incompetence. If managers overran a budget or had too much inventory and did not inform C when this was first noticed, they would be publicly chided, whatever the reason was for the condition. If the manager tried to defend the situation by noting that it developed because of actions in another part of the same company, actions which C and others had agreed to, C would point out strongly that the manager should have brought that issue up much earlier and forced a rethinking or renegotiation right away. Thus C made it clear through his reactions that poor ultimate results could be excused, but not being on top of one's situation could never be excused.

C taught subordinates his theory about building commitment to a decision by systematically refusing to go along with something until he felt the commitment was there, and by punishing managers who acted impulsively or prematurely in areas where the support of others was critical. He thus set up a very complex situation for his subordinates by demanding on the one hand a strong individualistic orientation (embodied in official company creeds and public relations literature) and, on the other, strong rules of consensus and mutual commitment (embodied in organizational stories, the organization's design, and many of its systems and procedures).

The above examples highlighted the differences among the three founders to show the biases and unique features of the culture in their respective companies, but there were some common elements as well that need to be mentioned. All three founders assumed that the success of their business(es) hinged on meeting customer needs: their most severe outbursts at subordinates occurred when they learned that a customer had not been well treated. All of the official message highlighted customer concern, and the reward and control systems focused heavily on

such concerns. In the case of A, customer needs were even put ahead of the needs of the family; one way a family member could really get into trouble was to mess up a customer relationship.

All three founders, obsessed with product quality, had a hard time seeing how some of their own managerial demands could undermine quality by forcing compromises. This point is important because in all the official messages, commitment to customers and product quality were uniformly emphasized—making one assume that this value was a clear priority. It was only when one looked at the inner workings of A's and C's organizations that one could see that other assumptions which they held created internal conflicts that were difficult to overcome—conflicts that introduced new cultural themes into the organizations.

In C's organization, for example, there was simultaneously a concern for customers and an arrogance toward customers. Many of the engineers involved in the original product designs had been successful in estimating what customers would really want—a success leading to their assumption that they understood customers well enough to continue to make product designs without having to pay too much attention to what sales and marketing were trying to tell them. C officially supported marketing as a concept, but his underlying assumption was similar to that of his engineers, that he really understood what his customers wanted; this led to a systematic ignoring of some inputs from sales and marketing.

As the company's operating environment changed, old assumptions about the company's role in that environment were no longer working. But neither C nor many of his original group had a paradigm that was clearly workable in the new situation, so a period of painful conflict and new learning arose. More and more customers and marketing people began to complain, yet some parts of the organization literally could not hear or deal with these complaints because of their belief in the superiority of their products and their own previous assumptions that they knew what customers wanted.

In summary, the mechanisms shown in Table 25.3 represent *all* of the possible ways in which founder messages get communicated and embedded, but they vary in potency. Indeed, they may often be found to conflict with each other—either because the founder is internally conflicted or because the environment is forcing changes in the original paradigm that lead different parts of the organization to have different assumptions about how to view things. Such conflicts often result because new, strong managers who are not part of the founding group begin to impose their own assumptions and theories. Let us look next at how these people may differ and the implications of such differences.

FOUNDER/OWNERS VS. "PROFESSIONAL MANAGERS"

Distinctive characteristics or "biases" introduced by the founder's assumptions are found in first-generation firms that are still heavily influenced by founders and in companies that continue to be run by family members. As noted above, such biases give the first-generation firm its distinctive character, and such biases are usually highly valued by first-generation employees because they are associated with the success of the enterprise. As the organization grows, as family members or non-family managers begin to introduce new assumptions, as environmental changes force new responses from the organization, the original assumptions begin to be strained. Employees begin to express concern that some of their "key" values will be lost or that the characteristics that made the company an exciting place to work are gradually disappearing.

Clear distinctions begin to be drawn between the founding family and the "professional" managers who begin to be brought into key positions. Such "professional" managers are usually identified as non-family and as non-owners and, therefore, as less "invested" in the company. Often they have been specifically educated to be managers rather than experts in whatever is the company's particular product or market. They are perceived, by virtue of these facts, as being less loyal to the original values and assumptions that guided the company, and as being more concerned with short-run financial performance. They are typically welcomed for bringing in much needed organizational and functional skills, but they are often mistrusted because they are not loyal to the founding assumptions.

Though these perceptions have strong stereotypic components, it's possible to see that much of the stereotype is firmly based in reality if one examines a number of first-generation and family-owned companies. Founders and owners do have distinctive characteristics that derive partly from their personalities and partly from their structural position as owners. It is important to understand these characteristics if one is to explain how strongly held many of the values and assumptions of first-generation or family-owned companies are. Table 25.4 examines the "stereotype" by polarizing the founder/owner and "professional" manager along a number of motivational, analytical, interpersonal, and structural dimensions.

The main thrust of the differences noted is that the founder/owner is seen as being more self-oriented, more willing to take risks and pursue non-economic objectives and, by virtue of being the founder/owner, more *able* to take risks and to pursue such objectives. Founder/owners, are more often intuitive and holistic in their thinking, and they are able to take a long-range point of view because they are building their own identities through their enterprises. They are often more particularistic in their orientation, a characteristic that results in the building of more of a community in the early organizational stages. That is, the initial founding group and the first generation of employees will know each other well and will operate more on personal acquaintance and trust than on formal principles, job descriptions, and rules.

The environment will often be more political than bureaucratic, and founder-value biases will be staunchly defended because they will form the basis for the group's initial identity. New members who don't fit this set of assumptions

TABLE 25.4
How Do Founder/Owners Differ from Professional Managers?

MOTIVATION AND EMOTIONAL ORIENTATION	
ENTREPRENEURS/FOUNDERS/OWNERS ARE . . .	*PROFESSIONAL MANAGERS ARE . . .*
Oriented toward creating, building.	Oriented toward consolidating, surviving, growing.
Achievement-oriented.	Power- and influence-oriented.
Self-oriented, worried about own image; needs for "glory" high.	Organization-oriented, worried about company image.
Jealous of own perogatives, needs for autonomy high.	Interested in developing the organization and subordinates.
Loyal to own company, "local."	Loyal to profession of management, "cosmopolitan."
Willing and able to take moderate risks on own authority.	Able to take risks, but more cautious and in need of support.

Analytical Orientation

Primarily intuitive, trusting of own intuitions.	Primarily analytical, more cautious about intuitions.
Long-range time horizon.	Short-range time horizon.
Holistic; able to see total picture, patterns.	Specific; able to see details and their sequences.

Interpersonal Orientation

"Particularistic," in the sense of seeing individuals as individuals.	"Universalistic," in the sense of seeing individuals as members of categories like employees, customers, suppliers, and so on.
Personal, political, involved.	Impersonal, rational, uninvolved.
Centralist, autocratic.	Participative, delegation-oriented.
Family ties count.	Family ties are irrelevant.
Emotional, impatient, easily bored.	Unemotional, patient, persistent.

Structural/Positional Differences

Have the privileges and risks of owership.	Have minimal ownership; hence fewer privileges and risks.
Have secure position by virtue of ownership.	Have less secure position, must constantly prove themselves.
Are generally highly visible and get close attention.	Are often invisible and do not get much attention.
Have the support of family members in the business.	Function alone or with the support of non-family members.
Have the obligation of dealing with family members and deciding on the priorities family issues should have relative to company issues.	Do not have to worry about family issues at all, which are by definition irrelevant.
Have weak bosses, Boards that are under their own control.	Have strong bosses, Boards that are not under their own control.

and values are likely to leave because they will be uncomfortable, or they will be ejected because their failure to confirm accepted patterns is seen as disruptive.

Founder/owners, by virtue of their position and personality, also tend to fulfill some *unique functions* in the early history of their organizations:

1. *Containing and absorbing anxiety and risk.* Because they are positionally more secure and personally more confident, owners more than managers absorb and contain the anxieties and risks that are inherent in creating, developing, and enlarging an organization. Thus in time of stress, owners play a special role in reassuring the organization that it will survive. They are the stakeholders; hence they do have the ultimate risk.

2. *Embedding non-economic assumptions and values.* Because of their willingness to absorb risk and their position as primary stakeholders, founder/owners are in a position to insist on doing things which may not be optimally efficient from a short-run point of view, but which reflect their own values and biases on how to build an effective organization and/or how to maximize the benefits to themselves and their families. Thus founder/owners often start with humanistic and social concerns that become reflected in organizational structure and process. Even when "participation," or "no layoffs," or other personnel practices such as putting marginally competent family members into key slots are "inefficient," owners can insist that this is the only way to run the business and make that decision stick in ways that professional managers cannot.

3. *Stimulating innovation.* Because of their personal orientation and their secure position, owners are uniquely willing and able to try new innovations that are risky, often with no more than an intuition that things will improve. Because managers must document, justify, and plan much more carefully, they have less freedom to innovate.

As the organization ages and the founder becomes less of a personal force, there is a trend away from this community feeling toward more of a rational, bureaucratic type of organization dominated by general managers who may care less about the original assumptions and values, and who are not in a position to fulfill the unique functions mentioned above. This trend is often feared and lamented by first- and second-generation employees. If the founder introduces his or her own family into the organization, and if the family assumptions and values perpetuate those of the founder, the original community feeling may be successfully perpetuated. The original culture may then survive. But at some point there will be a complete transition to general management, and at that point it is not clear whether the founding assumptions survive, are metamorphosed into a new hybrid, or are displaced entirely by other assumptions more congruent with what general managers as an occupational group bring with them.

4. *Originating evolution through hybridization.* The founder is able to impose his or her assumptions on the first-generation employees, but these employees will, as they move up in the organization and become experienced managers, develop a range of new assumptions based on their own experience. These new assumptions will be congruent with some of the core assumptions of the original cultural paradigm, but will add new elements learned from experience. Some of these new elements or new assumptions will solve problems better than the original ones because external and internal problems will have changed as the organization matured and grew. The founder often recognizes that these new assumptions are better solutions, and will delegate increasing amounts of authority to those managers who are the best "hybrids": those who maintain key old assumptions yet add relevant new ones.

The best example of such hybrid evolution comes from a company that was founded by a very freewheeling, intuitive, pragmatic entrepreneur: "D" who, like C in the example above, believed strongly in individual creativity, a high degree of decentralization, high autonomy for each organizational unit, high internal competition for resources, and self-control mechanisms rather than tight, centralized organizational controls. As this company grew and prospered, coordinating so many autonomous units became increasingly difficult, and the frustration that resulted from internal competition made it increasingly expensive to maintain this form of organization.

Some managers in this company, notably those coming out of manufacturing, had always operated in a more disciplined, centralized manner—without, however, disagreeing with core assumptions about the need to maximize individual autonomy. But they had learned that in order to do certain kinds of manufacturing tasks, one had to impose some discipline and tight controls. As the price of autonomy and decentralization increased, D began to look increasingly to these manufacturing managers as potential occupants of key general management positions. Whether he was conscious of it or not, what he needed was senior general managers who still believed in the old system but who had, in addition, a new set of assumptions about how to run things that were more in line with what the organization now needed. Some of the first-generation managers were quite nervous at seeing what they considered to be their "hardnosed" colleagues groomed as heirs apparent. Yet they were relieved that these potential successors were part of the original group rather than complete outsiders.

From a theoretical standpoint, evolution through hybrids is probably the only model of culture change that can work, because the original culture is based so heavily on community assumptions and values. Outsiders coming into such a community with new assumptions are likely to find the culture too strong to budge, so they either give up in frustration or find themselves ejected by the organization as being too foreign in orientation. What makes this scenario especially likely is the fact that the *distinctive* parts of the founding culture are often based on biases that are not economically justifiable in the short run.

As noted earlier, founders are especially likely to introduce humanistic, social service, and other non-economic assumptions into their paradigm of how an organization should look, and the general manager who is introduced from the outside often finds these assumptions to be the very thing that he or she wants to change in the attempt to "rationalize" the organization and make it more efficient. Indeed, that is often the reason the outsider is brought in. But if the current owners do not recognize the positive functions their culture plays, they run the risk of throwing out the baby with the bath water or, if the culture is strong, wasting their time because the outsider will not be able to change things anyway.

The ultimate dilemma for the first-generation organization with a strong founder-generated culture is how to make the transition to subsequent generations in such a manner that the organization remains adaptive to its changing external environment without destroying cultural elements that have given it its uniqueness, and that have made life fulfilling in the internal environment. Such a transition cannot be made effectively if the succession problem is seen only in power or political terms. The thrust of this analysis is that the *culture* must be analyzed and understood, and that the founder/owners must have sufficient insight into their own culture to make an intelligent transition process possible.

ACKNOWLEDGMENTS
AND SELECTED BIBLIOGRAPHY

The research on which this paper is based was partly sponsored by the Project on the Family Firm, Sloan School of Management, M.I.T., and by the Office of Naval Research, Organizational Effectiveness Research Programs, under Contract No. N00014-80-C-0905, NR 170-911.

The ideas explored here have been especially influenced by my colleague Richard Beckhard and by the various entrepreneurs with whom I have worked for many years in a consulting relationship. Their observations of themselves and their colleagues have proved to be an invaluable source of ideas and insights.

Earlier work along these lines has been incorporated into my book *Career Dynamics* (Addison-Wesley, 1978). Further explication of the ideas of an organizational culture can be found in Andrew M. Pettigrew's article "On Studying Organizational Cultures" (*Administrative Science Quarterly*, December 1979), Meryl Louis's article "A Cultural Perspective on Organizations" (*Human Systems Management*, 1981, 2, 246–258), and in H. Schwartz and S. M. Davis's "Matching Corporate Culture and Business Strategy" (*Organizational Dynamics*, Summer 1981).

The specific model of culture that I use was first published in my article "Does Japanese Management Style Have a Message for American Managers?" (*Sloan Management Review*, Fall 1981) and is currently being elaborated into a book on organizational culture.

Managing Person–Organization Conflicts

26. Unexpected Connections: Considering Employees' Personal Lives Can Revitalize Your Business

Lotte Bailyn/Joyce K. Fletcher/Deborah Kolb

*A*t a corporate retreat on organizational learning, the vice president of finance for a major manufacturer leads a discussion to raise the "real" issues that inhibit learning and growth. He promises to listen and asks his people to talk honestly, to "tell it like it is" instead of telling management what it wants to hear. To his surprise, nearly all the issues raised in each group—regardless of level or function—relate to work and family.

The director of a strategic business unit at a large high-tech company says, "After my heart attack at age thirty-seven, my doctor told me, 'Get a new job or you won't make forty.' I knew the important things in my life were health and family, but I loved my work and I couldn't face the prospect of giving it up. Isn't there any way to have a life and still do what I love to do?"

The president of a financial services company muses that past routes to success seem to be dead-ends. He notes, "We've been tremendously successful, largely because of the hard work, energy, and commitment of our people. But I have the sense that we have pushed about as far as we can. The creative ideas and the energy to work on them seem to be coming from the top, and I know we can't sustain growth this way. We need to re-energize people and get those creative juices flowing from the bottom up if we are going to get to the next level of growth. And I am just not sure how to do that."

What can we make of this? It seems as if corporate America is caught in a dilemma. On the one hand, employees' personal lives are clearly an important issue. Integrating work and personal life is not just something that affects a small group of lower and mid-level workers for a short time but is an issue that affects many people—even at the highest levels in the organization—for a major portion of their lives. On the other hand, future growth depends on "getting more" from these same people. It is no wonder that leaders are bewildered and seem to say one thing and do another. As recent articles and commentaries in the popular press suggest, organizations like to *say* they are "family friendly," but, in fact, their internal workings indicate they don't "care" about family. Is it fair to say companies don't care? Or is it that organizations' current definition of the problem offers few alternatives?

Indeed, traditional thinking tends to pit employee goals and business goals against each other. Obvious responses to either goal seem to make the other worse: If you try to help families by putting in some benefits and special programs, there is a fear that too many people will use the benefits, costs will increase, and productivity will suffer. If you try to help the business by increasing demands for employee commitment and involvement, there is a fear that people will tune out and do only what is asked rather than bring new energy to their work. They might even leave and take needed skills and expertise with them.

The plethora of articles do little more than describe the situation and call for "fundamental change." Employee advocates long for socially responsible organizations; management longs for committed employees who have the passion and energy to stimulate new growth. Is it a trade-off? Must we choose between the goals of the business and people's needs? We argue that the answer is a resounding *no*. Our research shows that the solution to this dilemma lies in *connecting* the two issues—people's personal lives and strategic business issues—rather than treating them as a trade-off. It may seem strange and counterintuitive. But we have found that there is an untapped source of strategic innovation and growth that comes from making an explicit connection between personal needs and business goals. The payoff, it turns out, comes from refusing an either/or choice and instead connecting the two issues at the concrete level of local, everyday work practices at all organizational levels.

ONE COMPANY'S EXPERIENCES

A multiyear action research project, supported by the Ford Foundation, enabled us to work with a company known for its leading-edge employee benefits. Although the company had a full array of policies and procedures for flexible work arrangements, employees were barely using the policies and benefits for two reasons: first, employees assumed that family benefits applied only to a few people for part of their work lives (primarily women with young children), and, second, there were career repercussions for those employees who did take advantage of them. The result was that the benefits were underutilized, particularly by men, single workers, and career-oriented mothers.

We negotiated with the company to try a different approach that was not based on benefits and policies. We wanted to connect work to personal life (broadly defined to include both family and community) and to use this connection as a catalyst for changing work practices. We worked jointly with a corporate team to define:

- A current state—The culture unnecessarily creates conflict between work and personal life, which has negative consequences for the business and for the equitable treatment of employees.
- A desired state—The culture capitalizes on work–personal life issues as an opportunity to create innovative, productive work practices.

Using an action research method, we worked at a number of sites in the company that represented the major parts of the business. At each site, we collaborated with different groups to see if together we could change aspects of work to meet a double goal: enable employees to better integrate their work with their personal lives *and* help the site meet its business goals. And in each case, we were able to make this productive connection.

Less Stressful On-Time Product Launch

The first group we worked with was a product development team that had a tough task: produce a new product, using new technology, in a much shorter time than they'd ever done, but with no additional resources.[1] The group consisted of engineers, both men and women, single and married, with and without children. The engineers wanted very much to meet the ambitious schedule. They knew that this product was important for the company and that their careers were tied to its success. So they were working hard. In this group, working hard meant working long hours and coming in evenings and weekends. There seemed to be an unquestioned belief that, given the situation they were in and the importance of the product, they had no choice but to work additional hours.

People told us that they needed to put in long hours because they couldn't get their individual work done during the normal workday. Meetings, other engineers' requests for help, schedule checks, and management reviews—all deprived them of continuous, concentrated time needed to produce the systems that the product required. The result was that they were working in a continual crisis mode. Although people were aware that there were problems with this way of working, their attempts to address the issue through detailed process redesign usually made the situation worse.

Looking at the work patterns from the viewpoint of the engineers' personal lives

uncovered different aspects of the problem. Many "interruptions" turned out to be unnecessary or unproductive. We also began to understand why the unit continued to work this way, even though almost everyone saw that it was less than efficient. For example, people noted that the norm was to reward individual heroics: someone would get kudos for solving a visible problem even if that person had caused it in the first place! So there was no incentive in the system to prevent problems or to evaluate what were true emergencies and what could wait. Having a crisis to respond to actually helped a person be seen as a team player; it was an opportunity to demonstrate that he or she cared about the work.

We worked with the team in designing an experiment to change some of the work practices. With the double goal of changing work norms so the team members could get their individual work done during the day and reduce the tendency to proliferate emergencies, they came up with a plan to restructure their daily activities into "quiet times" and "interactive times." The results of the experiment were remarkable. The team achieved an on-time launch of the new product *and* received several excellence awards for quality. On the personal side, team members and their supervisor reported feeling more in control of their own time, less stressed, and less likely to take work and worries home with them at night. They also found themselves thinking twice before interrupting someone, even when it wasn't quiet time, and found that the interactions they did have were more productive and focused. Managers, trying to respect quiet time, reduced the number of status reports they requested and found that this made the engineers more, not less, productive.

What we learned at this site is that looking at work through the lens of employees' personal lives raised aspects of work that not only were creating individual stress but were also interfering with the attempt to shorten the time to market. Once everyone understood this connection, it was possible to introduce changes

TABLE 26.1
Product Development Team

Type of work	Software engineering
Employees	Professional; the majority are men.
Business issue	Shorten time to market.
Personal issues	Long hours
	Stress
Diagnosis	Team operates in continual crisis situation.
	Rewarding of individual heroics undermines teamwork.
Experimental intervention	Analyze how time is used.
	Create quiet times and interaction times.
Business results	Launch product on time, despite contrary expectations.
	Mitigate oversupervision by managers. Help engineers use time more effectively by distinguishing between interruptions and critical interactions.
Personal results	Less stress and pressure
	Less work during nonwork hours for some engineers
	More control over work and personal life

that helped both personal and business goals (see Table 26.1).

Reduced Absenteeism and Improved Customer Service

The second site, a customer administration center, dealt with customers on billing, scheduling, and so on, via computer.[2] To increase customer satisfaction, the site was trying to become an organization of multi-skilled, self-managed work groups. The employees had had cross-functional training and had been reorganized into multi-functional groups, but management didn't know where to go next and was waiting for corporate empowerment training to make the change.

The workers were nonexempt, and their hours were not long, but rigid. The result was a lot of absenteeism and lateness, which, according to managers, reduced their ability to serve customers. So managers tightly monitored the way people worked, resulting in a highly controlled environment.

When we asked people what made the work difficult to integrate with their personal lives, they mentioned the rigidity. For example, despite the expressed need of many employees and an array of flexible policies on the books, very few of them were actually used. Most requests for flexibility were restricted to changing the beginning and end of the workday by a half hour or so. Since managers felt they always had to oversee their employees, they were understandably reluctant to give more leeway. Moreover, employees who wanted to take advantage of the benefits had to submit a plan to management indicating their need and documenting how they would meet business goals. Reluctant to relinquish control, management typically sat on these plans or returned them, requesting more detailed documentation. Few requests were granted, and fewer and fewer requests were made, in a self-reinforcing cycle that systematically disempowered employees.

When we reported our findings to the senior team, it became clear that we had raised aspects of the work culture that not only made the working conditions difficult for the employees, but also undermined the managers' efforts to improve the unit's effectiveness. Their highly controlled, individualistic way of managing partly explained why they were having difficulty moving toward empowerment and self-managed teams.

In response, senior management proposed a three-month experiment: each employee could establish any schedule that he or she wanted, as long as the work got done. After some confusion about what this meant, some dramatic changes occurred. First, almost everyone asked for different hours, men and women, single and married, managers and front-line workers. Given the various schedules proposed, managers realized they could no longer deal with the requests on an individual basis and had to bring the groups together to decide how to get the work done. Obviously, the groups had to compromise, which gave them their first experience in self-management.

A 30 percent reduction in absenteeism made managers see the value in relinquishing some of the control they had felt was necessary. Customer service improved as service hours were extended due to more liberal employee schedules. The organization was on its way toward the transformation it had sought but had not been able to achieve. And employees now had the flexibility to manage pressing issues in their lives.

What we learned from this example is that using a personal lens to understand working conditions helps to identify ways in which old cultural assumptions undermine new initiatives. In this situation, we found that letting work groups manage their own schedules helped them to develop as self-managed teams and serve their customers better (see Table 26.2).

Cross-Functional Synergies and Predictable Schedules

Our work at the third site also produced benefits to both the employees and business goals, but in a different way. In a sales and service district set up to sell and service all the company's products, one product group in particular was consistently below target.[3]

The group was organized as a partnership, but the functions were quite independent. Salespeople, both men and women who were paid on commission, had very difficult selling targets and thus worked long hours. Service people, primarily blue-collar men, had to respond to service calls at all hours and were beset by uncertainty about their schedules. Neither group had much respect for the other and had had little experience working together.

Our analysis indicated that there were unrealized synergies between the two groups. Not only could they help each other be more productive, but they could support each other in ways that would ease the stresses in their lives.

TABLE 26.2
Customer Administration Center

Type of work	Routine, clerical
Employees	White-collar: the majority are women
Business issues	Improve customer service
	Move to self-managed, empowered teams
Personal issue	Rigid schedules
Diagnosis	Culture of control leads to zero-sum view of flexibility and productivity.
	Culture of conservatism interferes with the risk-taking required to move to self-managed teams
Experimental intervention	All employees have flexible work arrangements
	Teams learn about self-management by taking control of flexible arrangements
Business results	Absenteeism reduced by 30 percent
	Improved customer service from more coverage.
	Teams learn to work in empowered ways.
Personal results	Less stress and pressure
	Time to attend to family and community issues
	More control over work and personal life

In collaboration with the district leadership, we decided to experiment with a cross-functional team. The team met for nine months and made a dramatic turnaround.

At first, all the old antagonisms surfaced, and the members did not understand how they could help each other. But when one service manager reported that three of his people were planning to retire, the salespeople realized that this would adversely affect their own ability to plan installations. Thus began a slow realization that working together could improve their performance. They discovered further synergies when the service people did the groundwork so the salespeople could close a big sale.

As a result, the group, which had not been able to meet its sales targets for some time, was among the highest revenue-producing units in the district. Further, the members found ways to support each other that led to more control and predictability in their lives.

What we learned from this site was that creativity and commitment are best mobilized in response to people's personal needs. This became clear when we discovered that management had once before tried to form a cross-functional team around this same product group, without positive results. What, the managers wondered, was different about what we had done? The significant difference was that we *began* by looking at the stresses in people's *personal* lives. We brought the members together to consider how they could ease their work situation to make their lives more livable, which motivated them to engage the issues more creatively (see Table 26.3).

Since this initial project, we have worked with many other work teams, at many different levels, and in many different organizations. The results are similar. Whether the situation involves scientists, purchasing agents, loan processors, line workers, or researchers, connecting the two seemingly incompatible aims of better integrating personal lives and more effectively meeting business goals leads to a win all around. When we reexamine work practices and organizational cultures through the lens of employees' personal lives, not only do formerly invisible inefficiencies and dysfunctional work practices surface, but creative, unforeseen solutions emerge. Making this unexpected connection is a powerful way to engage employee involvement and creativity. By adding personal payoff to organizational changes, employees are energized and motivated to undertake them. The bottom line is that implementing these innovations not only helps employees integrate work and personal life, but also leads to increases in productivity and effectiveness.

TABLE 26.3
Sales and Service District

Type of work	Sales—individual, based on commission
	Service—individual, driven by calls
Employees	Sales—equal number of men and women
	Service—the majority are men.
Business issue	Increase revenues for poorly performing product group.
Personal issues	Sales—long hours driven by ever-increasing stretch goals in bad economic climate.
	Service—unpredictability of hours driven by promised fast response time.
Diagnosis	Sales and service work at cross-purposes.
	Failure to realize synergies in working with the same customers.
Experimental intervention	Cross-functional product team
Business results	Highest revenues in district
	Synergies recognized (service can help sell and sales can help on routine service).
Personal results	More control over hours
	More mutual support

HOW TO CAPTURE THE BENEFITS OF CONNECTION: A DUAL AGENDA

To capture the benefits of connection, managers need to develop a dual agenda: identify and change work practices that have unintended negative consequences both for employees' personal lives *and* for the business. The approach has three major phases: viewing work through the lens of personal life, identifying leverage points for change, and designing and implementing work-practice interventions that meet the dual agenda of productivity benefits to the business and personal benefits to employees.

Viewing Work Through the Lens of Personal Life

People tend to see their work and personal lives as separate spheres. While they recognize the conflicts between these spheres, they usually see them as their private responsibility to manage and contain. The purpose of the first phase is to challenge this tendency by making an explicit connection between work and personal life. We accomplish this by asking people to consider the impact of their work and how it is performed on their personal lives. One useful question is "What is it about how work is done in your area that makes it difficult for you to integrate your work and personal life?" The question applies to individuals and to work groups from the lowest to highest levels of the organization.

Starting from the perspective of personal life generates a different kind of response from asking the same question with only a work redesign perspective. Typically, people focus on work practices they personally find unnecessary or inefficient—constant interruptions, rigid and inflexible rules, competitive approaches that lead to duplicated efforts, emergency meetings called late in the day, and so on. In probing deeper, people begin to discuss why they think the work continues to get done this way, despite the inefficiencies. At this point, some of the cultural assumptions that drive the work begin to surface, and people start to talk about how emergencies are glorified and the people who respond to them are seen as heroes, how staying late is a way to show you care about the work, how solving crises is rewarded while preventing them is not, or how a willingness to sacrifice personal time signals commitment.

As people explore how work interferes with personal life, the strategic benefits of changing these practices become obvious. As the group probes for underlying causes, it

becomes apparent that the very same assumptions and work practices that make integrating work and personal life difficult are also a problem in meeting business goals.

People begin to see these issues as systemic. They realize that what they are experiencing— stress, overcommitment, family conflict—is not an individual problem that they can solve by themselves. Instead, they begin to appreciate how the structure of work contributes to those dilemmas. The frustrations they feel at being unable to deal with their own problems now are seen in a different context. People also realize that their issues are not unique; others in the work group or management team experience similar problems. Recognizing that identifiable features of the work contribute to these personal concerns increases the team's commitment to move to the next step and consider the leverage points for change.

Identifying Leverage Points

In the second phase, the group considers ways of changing work practices to meet the dual agenda of improving effectiveness and enhancing the integration of work and personal life. The kinds of connections that a group makes depends on many factors—the type of work the team does; the team's size, composition, and level; and the specific pressures, opportunities, and resource constraints that the team is experiencing. Whatever leverage points the team considers, it is important that the members evaluate them in terms of the dual agenda. If a certain change is made, how will it improve the group's ability to meet a key strategic challenge? How will it enhance the group's ability to integrate work and personal lives?

Identifying leverage points for change is not easy. It requires looking at unexamined practices and assumptions about how work is done, where it is done, when it is done, and who does it. The first step is to think expansively about how changing particular work practices would help the business and help employees. The purpose at this stage is to brainstorm and, for the moment, not let questions about feasibility overwhelm the discussion. Thinking out of the box on work issues is difficult because we tend to accept that there is no other way to do things. It is important to let ideas flow.

For example, in a purchasing organization, when the members looked at their work through the lens of personal life, they realized that they were operating in a continual state of crisis, leading to extremely long hours and unpredictability. With the business goal to cut costs, delays in getting supplies to the line organization were a big problem. Crises exacerbated the problem. Probing deeper, they began to understand the underlying causes of the crises. They saw that how they worked with suppliers contributed to the very crises that created business and personal life problems. Some of the negative practices included giving bonuses to managers who solved crises and ignoring suppliers who warned about problems because the group feared the suppliers would routinely ask for extensions. New understanding allowed the group to design a process to distinguish among suppliers, detect and respond to early warning signals, and map out a reward system based on the absence of crises.

Considering the possibility that there are other ways of working leads naturally to thinking about experiments. We found some critical factors to think about when designing experiments that will achieve the benefits we've described:

1. The experiments must focus on organizational, not individual, issues. It is not enough to hold the work as a constant and find a way to give certain individuals more time or flexibility to meet current demands. The work itself—and the organizational assumptions driving the way the work gets done—must be the focus.
2. The experiments must meet the dual agenda of business and personal life. It is not enough to find obvious solutions that favor one over the other. An on-site day care facility might help some people meet work demands. A reduction in head count might

meet a cost-cutting goal. But an experiment that meets the dual agenda must move to nonobvious solutions that affect both personal and business goals.
3. The experiments must be connected to the deeper issues they are addressing. It is not enough to say, "Let's reduce the number of meetings," without understanding how norms governing meetings are connected to broader issues such as reward systems, idealized behavior, promotion policies, or other organizational norms.
4. The group needs to define evaluation criteria for both parts of the agenda. If the change is implemented, what business measures should be affected? What personal life issues?

Implementing Work-Practice Interventions

In the third phase, the group tries to implement different ways of working. Invariably, some kinks need to be ironed out as the intervention runs into obstacles. While many interventions can seem simple and straightforward, in fact, they are by definition violating some basic assumptions and taken-for-granted norms. Had they been truly simple, they probably would have been implemented already! While this approach unleashes energy, creativity, and innovation, it can seem risky to those involved. It is important to deal with these risks to protect the intervention and enhance its chances for success.

Some team members may fear they will seem less committed or dependable if they suggest a change that would make it easier to integrate their work and personal life. They may have been unable to discuss problems in this area, so sharing them is difficult. At the same time, managers may fear that any suggested change is likely to incur productivity losses. Therefore, senior management must indicate that it is willing to suspend, if only temporarily, some of the operating procedures that were identified as barriers to the dual agenda.

For example, at one manufacturing site, a work group identified an inflexible operations review procedure as one factor that made it difficult for them to meet business and personal goals. The vice president's willingness to suspend some of the procedure's requirements for the duration of the experiment was important for many reasons. Not only did it help people see that management was serious about giving them authority to control significant conditions that affected their productivity, but it also helped them realize that change was possible and worth the effort. In addition, it protected the work group manager from bearing all the risks of innovation. In another organization, senior managers, who had previously insisted on unreachable stretch goals to motivate researchers, allowed them to establish and work toward "realistic" targets. At still another site, management agreed to modify some aspects of a short-term productivity measure. Senior management's willingness to create the conditions for success is important to this approach. Without support, even the best ideas that come from the dual agenda are unlikely to succeed.

As the group implements work-practice improvements and the benefits to the business become evident, a company may be tempted to keep the benefits for itself by increasing workloads or reducing head count. For example, one unit proposed realigning work responsibilities between on-site and remote personnel to reduce excessive travel demands on scientists. However, as the proposal moved forward, the company was tempted to increase the number of projects assigned to each scientist, thereby replicating both the business problem (missed opportunities from lack of time for reflection and analysis) and the personal issue (no time for nonwork activities). Only by evaluating the proposed change against the dual criteria did the company reexamine the indiscriminate increase in workload and preserve the dual goals. All experiments are fragile; without tangible benefits to employees and the visible support of key decision makers, they are likely to be only transitory.

CONCLUSION

The dual agenda makes it possible to increase productivity and effectiveness in the business, while enabling employees to better integrate their work and personal lives. But it is not easy to achieve. Connecting these issues is not the typical response. Faced with the business issues in our examples, most managers would try to reengineer work processes, throw more time at the problem, or reduce the workforce to cut costs. Faced with the personal life issues, most human resource personnel would ask for additional benefits—like bringing in evening meals or giving extra vouchers for child care—to help people cope. But these accommodations might leave both the workplace and families and communities worse off. When firms develop family-friendly policies and benefits that leave existing work practices and cultural assumptions about work and good workers intact, the conflict between the demands of the new workplace and the needs of families and communities is exacerbated. Only by connecting work and personal lives through a dual agenda can companies reframe the conflict into an opportunity for innovation and change.

How can an organization determine if it would benefit from a dual agenda approach? First and most obvious is to find out whether people are having difficulty juggling their work and personal lives. Signs of stress and fatigue, complaints about work demands and time, and dissatisfaction with work and family policies may emerge in satisfaction surveys, exit interviews, and off-line retreats. More critical may be the loss of valued employees or the sudden change in the performance of people who seemed to have great potential.

Such indicators may suggest that a company is ready for the dual agenda approach. They may explain why creative ideas are coming only from the top of the organization, or why repeated new initiatives show great promise but then disappoint. If companies undertake new initiatives to increase productivity, revenues, and general performance without looking at them through the lens of personal life, the very goals of the initiatives may be undermined.

Some typical work practices and assumptions are dysfunctional for both business and personal goals: more time necessarily leads to greater productivity; time is an unlimited resource; the most committed workers are those who work the longest hours; individual competition and heroics are the best way to get the most out of people. When work is performed in an atmosphere of continual crisis or when the response to problems is to do the same thing, only harder, there are clear opportunities for innovation and change that can meet the criteria of the dual agenda.

Linking personal lives with strategic issues is an unexpected connection. But if we continue to deal with each area separately, in the long run, both individuals and organizations—if not society—will suffer. What we have outlined, however, is not a one-time fix. Rather, it describes a process of continually looking at the intersection of work and personal lives and using the connection as a lever to challenge work practices on an ongoing basis. The solution to one set of issues raises other issues that a company can subject to the same analysis and experimentation. Such an ongoing process results in changed mind-sets and, ultimately, in the culture change that most companies seek but find so difficult to achieve.

This unexpected connection can revitalize your business.

REFERENCES

This paper is based on a research project supported by the Ford Foundation. For a full report, see: R. Rapoport, L. Bailyn, D. Kolb, J. K. Fletcher, et al., Relinking Life and Work: Toward a Better Future *(New York: The Ford Foundation, 1996). Others involved in the research project were Susan Eaton, Maureen Harvey, Robin Johnson, and Leslie Perlow. Rhona Rapoport was the consultant to the project. The Ford Foundation, in conjunction with the Xerox Corporation and* Working Mother *magazine, is hosting a CEO Summit in New York on 15 September 1997 to discuss this report.*

Our names are listed in alphabetical order. This article was a fully collaborative effort, as was, with other team members, the project itself.

1. For a full description of the work at this site, see: L. Perlow, "The Time Famine: An Un- intended Consequence of the Way Time Is Used at Work" (Cambridge, Massachusetts: MIT Sloan School of Management, Ph.D. dissertation, 1995).

2. For a full description of this site, see: R. Johnson, "Where's the Power in Em- powerment? Definition, Difference, and Dilemmas of Empowerment in the Context of Work-Family Management" (Boston, Massachusetts: Harvard Business School, Ph.D. dissertation, 1994).

3. For a full description of this case, see: the appendix by S. Eaton and M. Harvey, in "Re-linking Work and Family: A Catalyst for Organizational Change" (Cambridge, Massachusetts: MIT Sloan School of Man- agement, working paper #3892-96, 1996).

27. Managing Attraction and Intimacy at Work

Marcy Crary

In recent years the number of women in management and professional positions has increased, so men and women are working together more frequently than ever before. As a result, we now have a relatively new and unstudied phenomenon in organizations: attraction and intimacy at work.

A large part of the writing to date on this topic has dealt with the "office romance," the ways in which managers can deal with these romances, and the problems these relationships create for others in the organization. However, little attention has been devoted to the two people actually involved in a relationship (whether sexual, nonsexual, or assumed by others to be sexual) and to understanding what it is like to be attracted to a co-worker of the opposite sex. There has been little discussion of the ways in which people deal with these feelings and the intense emotional responses that frequently can accompany them.

The label of "office romance" often trivializes the range and complexity of the issues faced by people in a close relationship at work. Outsiders' views of the attraction between two people typically oversimplify the experiences those individuals may be struggling with. These views may also be distorted by the viewer's projection of his or her own concerns into the situation.

Whether one is the person who feels attracted, the one who is the object of attraction, or the manager who is faced with the situation, all three individuals can profit from a better understanding of attractions and close relationships between men and women in organizations. Furthermore, this understanding should

emerge from the perspective of the individual involved.

The observations in this article are drawn from the author's research on individuals' experiences of attraction and closeness in the workplace. This work has involved conversations with professional men and women whose workplaces include financial services companies, consulting groups, mental health clinics, state agencies, hospitals, and universities. These people have primarily been individuals in their thirties or forties, married or single, in either the early or the middle stages of their careers. The issues covered include (1) what "intimacy" at work means to different people, (2) what it is like to feel attracted to someone at work, (3) the choice between closeness and distance in female–male work relationships, and (4) the tensions and dilemmas of being in an "intimate" relationship at work (see Table 27.1). The final section of this article discusses the broader implications of these data for people and their organizations.

DIFFERENT MEANINGS OF ATTRACTION AND INTIMACY AT WORK

Part of the complexity of male–female relationships in the workplace is that individuals may experience the phenomena of attraction and intimacy in very different ways. (The discussions in this article can apply to same-gender work relationships in which there is a conscious component of sexuality present. There are obviously further complexities in people's experiences with homosexual relationships, given the organizational and cultural taboos against

Marcy Crary, "Managing Attraction and Intimacy at Work" from *Organizational Dynamics*, Spring 1987.

TABLE 27.1
Questionnaire on Attraction and Intimacy at Work

Think of a time when you felt attracted to someone of the opposite sex at work . . .

What did you do with these feelings?
a. I ignored them, hoping they would go away.
b. I talked about them with someone else.
c. I talked about them with the person to whom I was attracted.

How did you behave with the person?
a. I avoided him/her.
b. I continued to work with him/her, but I stayed distant emotionally.
c. I tried to get to know him/her better personally.
d. I sought out more opportunities to work with him/her.

Think of a close relationship you have with a colleague of the opposite sex . . .

How would you define/describe the closeness of the relationship?
a. Purely professional.
b. Emotional.
c. Spiritual.
d. Sexual.
e. None of the above.
f. Some of the above.
g. All of the above.
h. Other.

What tensions or dilemmas have you had about this relationship at work?
a. I felt vulnerable around him/her.
b. I worried about what other people would be thinking.
c. I worried about what would happen if something/someone came between us.
d. It was hard to balance work and personal time.
e. All of the above.
f. Some of the above.

What effect did the relationship have upon your work?
a. I felt more productive.
b. It interfered with my work.
c. It had no impact on my work.

The questions reflect a sampling of the issues encountered by people who are attracted to or have close relationships with work colleagues of the opposite sex. Deciding how to manage one's own feelings and behavior in these situations is not often easy, and the norms of most workplaces do not make it any easier.

homosexuality.) Being "attracted" to or feeling "intimate" with a member of the opposite sex at work can have a variety of meanings. Attraction is not always based on physical attractiveness; it can be based upon any number of factors, including one's attraction to the other's competence, power, values and beliefs, and so forth.

Similarly, "intimacy" at work can refer to relationships that are close but not necessarily sexual. If people's experiences are to be guides in our thinking about male–female relationships at work, intimacy and sexuality need to be treated as separate dimensions of such relationships.

What then do people mean by "intimacy" at work? The individuals who were interviewed gave a wide range of comments:

> It's being able to exchange honest, straightforward, constructive feedback on our work.
>
> We have very creative, free exchanges of ideas about the things we are working on.
>
> I can share any or all of the "backstage" thoughts and feelings that come up for me in this place or in my life outside work.
>
> I have the feeling that she is always looking out for me, always ready to help me out or make suggestions.

Some people describe intimate work relationships that are or have been sexual, but the experience of intimacy at work is not as automatically associated with sexuality as one might think.

In brief, the experience of "intimacy" at work varies from person to person, and ranges in the depth of self shared, the degree to which it involves the task at hand, and the extent to which a sexual relationship is involved. These variations undoubtedly reflect the differences in the needs and interests that people bring to cross-gender relationships at work, the nature of their work and the degree of interaction it requires, their position in the organization, and the organization's norms about closeness at work.

DEALING WITH ATTRACTIONS AT WORK

Individuals have different ways of managing their feelings of attraction and closeness to the opposite sex; the interview data bear this out. Some of the aspects involved are the degree of awareness of the attraction, feelings about attraction, and problems with expressing attraction.

The Degree of Awareness of One's Attractions

There are significant differences in people's ability to observe and talk about their experiences of attraction (often the first stage in the development of a close relationship). Some people seem very aware of their feelings when they are drawn to another person. For example, one woman who was interviewed about her experiences of attraction was able to describe 11 different steps in her typical attraction experience (see Table 27.2). Her response shows a strong familiarity with the experience of attraction to others in her work setting, as well as an unusual ability to describe her own experience in the process. Most people find it difficult to step back and make such observations about their own experiences. The people who have a greater awareness of these feelings are probably also more skilled in discussing and managing their feelings of attraction.

Feelings About Attraction: Positive or Negative?

Feeling attracted to a member of the opposite sex at work can be very stimulating and productive for some people. However, attraction is also associated with a range of negative feelings. A number of people talked about feeling intensely distracted by their feelings of attraction, to the point where they were unable to attend to their work. In some cases such a feeling leads to uncertainty, confusion, and frustrations. For example, one woman said, "For me, attraction equals tension. I don't know what he is thinking or feeling—it makes me feel *really* insecure. I hope I look okay, I can't be casual with him or around him. I'm on eggshells!"

One male professor described the difficulties he experienced when he felt attracted to one of his students:

> I had a young woman in two of my classes this semester who was strikingly beautiful and, I thought, quite sexy. I found I noticed her more than others in the classroom. As a result, I also felt more uptight when I was around her. In some way I felt disempowered by her, or maybe it was that I was empowering her. It felt like our relationship was cluttered by my sexual fantasies. Some of my uptightness was in response to my assumption that I was not equally attractive to her. Plus, I assumed she

TABLE 27.2

One Woman's Description of the Process of "Getting Attracted" to Someone in the Workplace

1. I'm first attracted to the person-as-a-person—noticing his intelligence, the way he talks, etc. I'll find myself noticing something about his physical appearance (clothes, jewelry, hair) in the midst of a conversation.

2. Apart from his physical self, I may find myself remembering or ruminating over some personal data about him. I find myself thinking about something that is interesting about him, something that has piqued my curiosity.

3. The person may appear in my dreams. (This is an indication to me that I'm using him psychically, as a symbol of something in myself; he is becoming a source of my own growth.)

4. At this point I start really to pay attention to him. I'm interested in him on a psychic level, interested in him as a person; I want to relate to him apart from the work context. I've moved into a more active process at this point.

5. I begin to ask him questions about himself, watching how he is with other people, perhaps getting into conversations with friends at work about who's cute or not and thinking of him. This kind of talk with others helps to crystallize my feelings, making me aware of my own internal "ranking" of this person. The opinion of others also affects my interest in the other, perhaps magnifying my attraction.

6. I am consciously paying attention to his clothing, watching how he moves, perhaps giggling at his jokes more. I noticed what I like about his personality and his abilities.

7. I'll initiate more conversations with him. At meetings that he attends, I find myself stretching the "inclusion stage," the initial warm-up time in the meeting, by asking questions about his weekend, seeking more personal data.

8. At this point, if I'm really interested in him, I may covertly pass on information about my availability by not mentioning that I was with another person when I went to the movie over the weekend. I notice whom he mentions and whom he doesn't mention in his discussions of his weekend.

9. I move into a more personal state. I seek contact with him outside the workplace, or we might celebrate a work event by going somewhere outside the workplace.

10. Another signal of the intensifying of the relationship is his frequent appearance in my dreams. I may also be physically turned on by something he tells me about himself.

11. At this point, I'm usually clear that I want to develop a friendship with this person. I may or may not seek a sexual relationship with him. I can nurse such attractions and not act on them, but just enjoy them as they unfold.

could see my interest in her given how strongly I felt attracted to her. My vulnerability in this situation is that if she knows I'm attracted to her, she can somehow use that against me.

Attraction can also be associated with fear, or even with resentment or anger. Obvious difficulties can arise when a person feels attraction but also resents these very feelings (and the person who evokes them) because of the internal tensions they generate. One organizational con-sultant who was interviewed said, "If you show me some avoidance or punitive behavior between a man and a woman in a workplace that needs to be addressed or resolved—and that is not tied to some specific incident—my bet is that they have some attraction to each other that they can't deal with." His observation was confirmed by other comments by a number of the people interviewed. Feelings of attraction can, ironically, be a reason for distancing oneself from a colleague at work.

Problems with Expressing One's Attraction

Many people struggle with the question of whether to discuss an attraction with the other person. The difficulty with *not* discussing the attraction is that one can end up with pent-up energy, which can in turn lead to a preoccupation with the attraction and sometimes even to counterproductive behavior. (Some people seek the aid of a close but neutral party to help them sort out their feelings and gain some perspective on their attraction—particularly when the costs of directly expressing that attraction to the person seem too high.)

Often, people are afraid that discussing the attraction will propel them into acting on it, thus causing them to lose control of the situation. They worry that revealing their feelings will galvanize the relationship with the other person, making the situation even more difficult to manage because they then have the other person's feelings to deal with as well as their own.

There are also fears that their intentions will be misunderstood by the other individual. One woman consultant said:

> I chose to tell him that I was attracted to him but that for a number of reasons I was not going to act on it. This was in response to his telling me that he found me very attractive. Well, it turned out that in telling him I was attracted to him I had made the situation much worse. He continued to pursue the issue, so much so that it almost felt like sexual harassment. I then chose to back off from working with him because he was making it so difficult.

This woman went on to talk about how painful she found the issue of managing attraction. All of her experiences to date had been very difficult, and none of them had had happy endings. She now feels scared when she feels attracted to a man at work.

The decision of whether to express one's attraction to the other person can have ramifications far beyond the literal act of self-expression.

There are often other "publics" to keep in mind. The complexity of this decision making can be seen in one man's description of the process he goes through before deciding whether to be open about his feelings.

> I may have the feeling of "Wow, that person excites me." Depending on the environment, I am cautious about acting on the excitement. . . . If there is enough energy so that the attraction is not just fleeting, and I think about it beyond our last face-to-face contact . . . I start wondering if I should make the statement publicly or privately to her. The more I feel at risk, the more likely I am to make the statement publicly. It gives it less power, diffuses it.
>
> The risk here is that if I make the statement to a woman who is part of a minority in the organization, she may feel undermined. If you make a public statement that demonstrates affection or intimacy, it can be undermining because it may be seen as turfstaking, a signal of ownership, thus decreasing her power and influence among men in the room. My own risk is that if we don't have enough of a relationship to support my statement, she may misconstrue it and use it against me. By making the statement publicly, I make sure that there are other versions of it available.

For this man, managing the internal tension is closely linked to his concerns about the interpersonal, group, and organizational "fallout" concerning the expression of his attraction. He was particularly aware of the political implications of his behavior and had many different ways of managing his feelings in relation to others' needs and behaviors. For others, less skilled in managing their own attractions, however, the question of how, when, where, and if to express their attraction becomes an emotional maze. The effective resolution of the "attraction question" between two people can make a noticeable contribution to the development of a more productive work relationship. However, the way to achieve this resolution is not always readily apparent to those involved.

THE CHOICE OF "GETTING CLOSER" VS. "KEEPING ONE'S DISTANCE"

Whether there is initial attraction or not, and whether this attraction is sexual or not, people differ in terms of the amount of distance they consider appropriate in their relationships with the opposite sex at work. Degrees of closeness versus distance in work relationships can generally be seen in (1) the amount and quality of self-disclosure shared with the other person, (2) the kinds of shared activities and interactions on and off the job, and (3) the extent to which these interactions are solely work-role related. But how and why individuals choose to shape the distance between themselves and their colleagues of the opposite sex varies a great deal from person to person.

Crane, one of the bank managers interviewed, was a strong believer in the "keep your distance" orientation. He described his own attitudes and behaviors toward women in his work setting as follows:

> I can see nothing more damaging than getting involved with someone at work. I don't do it, ever. It can demoralize staff and add complications to your personal life.
>
> I have no attractions. I keep myself as tightly controlled as I possibly can. My eyes don't rove.
>
> It's a litigious society. Others' perceptions rule. I'd rather err on the side of being fearful of others' perceptions than be overly supportive to my women subordinates.

To Crane, keeping distance between himself and other employees at work meant, among other things, never discussing his personal life with anyone. He took pride in the fact that his boss did not know where he lived. For a number of different reasons, Crane also felt it particularly appropriate to keep women apart from his personal self at work. While he might have lunch or play squash with a male colleague, he would avoid such situations with women colleagues. He characterized women in their twenties and thirties as "seething with emotion"—emotions that in turn might affect him. He expressed a preference for working with older women whose emotions had "cooled off with age" and were therefore more stable to work with. By choosing to keep a distance between himself and his female colleagues, he hoped to preclude the dangers of attractions at work.

Ben provides a sharp contrast to Crane's orientation toward women at work. Ben, a psychologist, described his relationships with women with whom he has worked in this way:

> In every job I've had, I have always been attracted to one woman in a "monogamous," sexually tinged, intense, emotionally seductive relationship. We usually show a lot of physical attention and give a lot of emotional support to each other.

The intimacy Ben developed in a number of his cross-gender work relationships was very functional to the work he did. These pairings provided an important emotional and political base of operations within the highly charged situations in which he worked. Ben indicated that none of these relationships were physically sexual ones; the "monogamy" he refers to evolved from his tendency to pair with one woman in the organization with whom he could share emotional, professional, and organizational secrets. (Their pairing was often thought to be sexual by others, given the frequency with which they met and the intensity of their emotional connectedness.)

These two cases provide very different examples of how people resolve the dilemma of whether to be close to fellow workers or to keep them at a distance. Most people's work relationships with the opposite sex are variations on the patterns found in the experiences of these two men.

People seem to have different reasons for seeking closeness or keeping distance in these relationships. These differences may partly stem from different levels of the need for intimacy. In his book *Power, Intimacy and the Life Story* (Dorsey Press, 1985), D. P. McAdams found that "individuals high on intimacy motivation have been shown to spend more time thinking about relationships with others, to engage in more conversations with others, and to experience more positive effects when interacting with others than individuals scoring low on intimacy motivation."

Issues of power and/or sexuality are also likely to influence peoples' orientations toward closeness or distance at work. For some, having power may enable them to create close relationships and not have to worry about the ramifications; for others, having power may lead them to avoid closeness with work colleagues. On the other hand, people may seek distance to avoid dealing with issues of sexuality. As one woman put it,

I find it difficult to deal with intimacy and professionalism together because I link intimacy and sexuality. I can't separate the two. I am more likely to choose distance in most situations because of this.

For whatever reasons, each of us makes choices about this fundamental question—to be close or to be distant—whether we are conscious of it or not.

BEING IN AN INTIMATE RELATIONSHIP AT WORK

Many of the close relationships described by the individuals interviewed were obviously of enormous importance to them—whether it be to their personal, social, professional, or physical well-being. Descriptions of the positive side of these relationships include the following:

I delight in our ability to think together; we have "sophisticated" communication between us. We shoot metalevel analyses of what is going on in the work situation back and forth at each other in meetings. We're both good at systems thinking.

When I'm with him I feel centered, fully alive, more resourceful. I feel more generous to the world. I am the "better half" of myself.

When we work together I feel effective, centered—almost like I'm "tripping out" on myself and on him.

At the same time many of the professionals interviewed were explicit about the personal difficulties they experience when they are in an "intimate" relationship (whether sexual or nonsexual) with another person at work. Four different categories of problems can be isolated in these people's experiences: (1) the tension of balancing intimacy with work, (2) the feeling of increased vulnerability both inside and outside the relationship, (3) dealing with outsiders' views and feelings about the relationship, and (4) dealing with ongoing changes in the definition of the relationship.

Balancing Intimacy and Work with the Same Person

Most of us have been socialized into thinking of intimacy and work as two separate compartments in our lives; intimacy takes place at home and work takes place at our place of employment. But for many people the realities of day-to-day experiences at work belie these rational arrangements of our worlds. Working closely together can create a sense of intimacy between people, or the creation of intimate relationships may be essential to performing the task itself. One woman's success as a consultant depended on establishing good relationships with the line managers she worked with; she saw these close connections as essential to the quality of their mutual effort, stating that "our intimacy makes for a better business relationship."

But the combination of intimacy and work is not an easy blend for many people; it presents significant emotional challenges. Romantic relationships at work require balancing the roles of boyfriend/girlfriend with one's organizational responsibilities. For some, the conflicting demands are too much, while for others the challenge is stimulating.

Allen, who worked in a financial services firm, talked about a romantic relationship he developed with one of his female co-workers. Having his girlfriend in his work group became problematic over time:

She walks into my office unannounced, and I don't have the time to be with her. When I'm in the office I'm always very short with people— and I was with her on a number of occasions as

well. I also felt that I couldn't comfortably talk about what we were going to do that night. This was interfering with my performance at work. I felt I should spend time with her and I couldn't; she didn't like that.

For Allen, the experience of having a girlfriend in his workplace felt too complicated and jeopardized the quality of his work. He expressed a strong preference, after having had this experience, for keeping his personal and professional lives separate. Putting them together created too many emotional and psychological stresses for him. According to his theory, keeping them separate would allow him to express his "work self" at work and his intimate self at home. These two selves seemed incompatible in a single setting.

A contrasting example came from David, who stated that he had little difficulty in having a romantic relationship in his company. He talked about his decision to start up a sexual relationship with a younger woman in his own company. Both of them kept this secret. His initial attraction to the woman had in fact distracted him from work, but once he developed an intimate, sexual relationship with her, he reported little difficulty in keeping his attention on his work. (However, he did not rule out possible difficulties in the future if others found out about the relationship.)

Part of the relative ease he experienced, in contrast to Allen, may have come from his position as president of the company and his years of experience on the job. His external power and established expertise may have minimized the internal anxieties that are usually associated with such a relationship at work.

The tensions of people caught in the dilemmas of balancing an intimate relationship with a working relationship may stem partly from their difficulties in sorting out their own needs as they relate to the other person. The difficulties seemed particularly great when people's work attitudes and behaviors were significantly different from the kinds of attitudes and behaviors they exhibited when they were with that other person. In effect, the work self collided

with the intimate self. Putting their two different "selves" together in the same physical space was dysfunctional for them, for the relationship, and in some cases for the organization. There are other people, however, for whom the intimate and work selves are in less intense conflict; for these individuals, managing intimacy at work may be less difficult.

Increased Vulnerability Within and Outside of the Relationship

Maintaining a close relationship at work makes some people feel more vulnerable both to the other person involved and to others in the work environment. Things shared within the relationship can be misused by that other person. This kind of vulnerability may be illustrated by an incident involving one man's interaction with a female employee to whom he had felt quite close. They shared a common outlook on many different issues, worked very well together, and shared a lot of personal feelings. One day he walked past her as she was talking with some of his other employees. As he passed by, she remarked, "You look like a sad little boy." Although he kept walking and did not respond, a number of strong feelings welled up in him. He said, "She was exactly right. She cut me to the quick with her remark. I was surprised; I didn't know I was so accessible to others. I felt really exposed." He felt she had misused knowledge she had gained through their friendship to embarrass him in front of his other employees. She had made a public observation about what he felt was a private part of himself. This was double vulnerability, both inside and outside of the relationship.

Dealing with Outsiders' Views of the Relationship

An increased vulnerability to outsiders' attitudes often accompanies an intimate relationship at work. Everyone is aware of the taboo against sexual intimacy at work; indeed, many people have their own rules about not having a sexual relationship with colleagues or clients. But an obvious closeness to a colleague of the opposite sex invites outsiders to make their own interpretations about the nature of the relationship. They will usually suspect that the relationship is sexual, whether or not this is actually true.

Some of the women interviewed talked about their fears of being disempowered by outsiders' perceptions (or misperceptions) of their closeness to a male colleague or client. They feared the classic accusation that associates a woman's rise in an organization with her sexual activity rather than with her competence. As a result these women have learned to be very discreet in managing their close relationships, whether these relationships are sexual or not. They also feel that they must always be aware of how others perceive their relationships. One single female consultant stated that she wished she were married, if only to be rid of other people's constant assumptions that her relationships with male clients were sexual. (Interestingly enough, very few of the people interviewed mentioned concerns about their being unfair or unobjective as a result of their close relationships. Ironically, these are the concerns expressed most often by outsiders.)

Dealing with Changes in the Relationship

The development and maintenance of any close relationship involves various changes in the relationship over time. The degrees of involvement in, commitment to, and dependence on the relationship are significant dimensions that are subject to change. Many of the difficulties reported by people in close relationships at work involve coping with the ongoing issues raised by such changes. Because these relationships develop in a work setting, the changes in them are apt to have organizational as well as personal implications.

In ongoing intimate relationships, many women and men struggle with the issue of sexual involvement. When there is a lack of reciprocal interest in exploring such involvement, it can be very difficult for one of the pair to respond to this issue and not hurt the other's feelings, the quality of the relationship, or the quality of their work together.

One woman commented, "If you pay attention to men at certain levels emotionally and develop a close relationship, they often sexualize it. I have to be careful about this." Her statement was based on the experience she had had with a male manager in her organization who was her boss's peer. They had built a relationship based on their conversations about company management styles and a variety of outside interests that they shared. She had sometimes gone to his office to chat with him. Finally one day he told her that if they wanted to have a personal relationship they should have it outside work, or people might talk. She knew that this statement was also an invitation. She was surprised by his comment because she had never wanted to develop a personal relationship with him outside the company. She cut down on the amount of contact they had in order to keep their relationship on a more professional basis. As a result of this experience, she became more careful of her interactions with men in the work environment.

A male manager reported a similar experience in which his female boss thought he wanted to begin a more personal and potentially sexual relationship. He did not share her needs and interests, and he had to communicate this to her very delicately in order to maintain both their professional relationship and his career.

Another difficulty with work relationships is the question of how deeply the intimacy should be carried into the individuals' projects. One woman reported an incident in which she worked closely with a man she was employing as a consultant on her art project. They had been working intensely together for a number of months and had achieved a special intimacy from their similar spiritual and aesthetic orientations. They were agonizing over a particularly difficult decision when the man drew back and said, "Well, it's your project, you decide." At that moment, the woman felt confronted with the deep division between their respective personal investments in the project. The limits to their intimacy were exposed to her in a very abrupt, raw fashion.

Subtle shifts in interest and investment in a relationship may seem relatively unimportant to outsiders. For the people in the relationship, however, these changes can have a substantial impact.

CONCLUSION

The data presented in this paper have implications not only for individual employees, but for the organizations in which they work as well.

Issues for Employees

Figure 27.1 lists some common questions a person may have as he or she deals with the issues of attraction and intimacy at work. How one deals with these questions will have an obvious

FIGURE 27.1
Attraction and Intimacy Questions for the Employee

impact on the kinds of experiences a person will encounter. Negative and positive responses lead one in different directions.

For example, people who always respond negatively to the question will probably not experience the problems that arise from attempting to get closer to another person. Being unaware of one's feelings, having negative reactions to one's feeling of attraction, and avoiding the person to whom one is attracted can distance one from the emotional complexity of managing closeness in a work relationship. To these people, such distance from one's feelings and from colleagues of the opposite sex seems safer. In remaining distant, one avoids potential misunderstandings that may lead to charges of sexual harassment or other volatile outcomes. But there are potential costs to the choice of distance from one's feelings and one's colleagues. These costs are highlighted in a 1981 *Wall Street Journal* article that quoted a female manager for AT&T who was 29 years old and single:

> I build an iron fence around myself for twelve hours a day. That isn't really me, but I feel it's a responsibility I have to take as a woman, to make clear I'm not available. I'm sociable; lunch or a drink after work is fine because it's work related. But if I find myself attracted to a colleague, I just don't allow it to go anywhere, and I don't let myself get into a situation with that person in which it might be hard to control my feelings.

Though no more detail is given about this woman and her life apart from her career, one must wonder about the potential costs of her choice of behavior: (1) Might she be keeping herself from forming interpersonal friendships that could contribute to her own personal development? (2) Might she be keeping herself from opportunities to form close relationships with male colleagues, connections that might help to advance her career? (3) Might she be keeping herself from experiencing and expressing her own emotional needs? Several women interviewed mentioned their experience of feeling neutered in their workplace. This may work insofar as suppressing one's sexuality is one way of resolving the problem of attractions at work—but again, at what cost?

Choosing closeness in a cross-gender work relationship, however, leads a person into a challenging set of personal and interpersonal issues. One must manage a more complex set of needs and concerns in relation to both one's self and the other person. One risks feelings of increased vulnerability; one must manage outsiders' interpretations of the relationship; one has to meet the changing needs and concerns of both people involved. But if the result of one's efforts is a good working relationship with a colleague of the opposite sex, one has a precious commodity.

Issues for Organizations

What is the significance of employee attraction and intimacy for organizations and their managers? Experiences in these areas involve strong feelings; for better or for worse, these feelings affect people's behavior and performance on the job. Because there is such variation in the way people deal with these issues, managers need a better understanding of how people experience these situations and how their behavior is affected by them. Managers also need to become more aware of their own attitudes on these issues.

Managers themselves face a number of risks in assuming that all people's experiences are similar, or in not understanding how those involved in the situation actually feel. If they don't understand differences between people, or if they have a simplistic or negative view of intimacy at work, they will often react negatively to such intimate relationships, including some in which intimacy could be very productive both for the involved individuals and the organization.

These negative reactions can also make managers avoid relationships in which they themselves anticipate "intimacy problems." In this case, these people may miss out on the potential growth that develops out of working through complex issues with close colleagues. Moreover, the organization risks losing the potential synergy and creativity that these relationships may bring to the work environment.

Organizations as a whole need to develop constructive standards about close male–female relationships. As Edgar H. Schein has pointed out in his article "Coming to a New Awareness of Organizational Culture" (*Sloan Management Review*, Winter 1984), one of the major issues of internal integration within an organization's culture is the problem of intimacy, friendship, and love. Organizations need to develop a consensus regarding closeness among their members. But if the consensus-building process (and the rules that result from it) is to be effective as a cultural "solution" for the organization, it must include the perceptions, thoughts, and feelings of that organization's members. Managers cannot merely legislate "solutions" to attraction and intimacy by making rules that prohibit romantic involvements. Such formal rules and sanctions only drive emotions underground, thus preventing people from dealing more constructively with the issues involved.

A consensus-building process requires open conversation and active participation. Companies can make it easier for people to learn about and manage issues of attraction and intimacy at work by making conversations about these issues easier. Internal training programs can make employees more sensitive to differences in people's experiences in these areas, as well as to the tensions and dilemmas associated with close male–female relationships at work. Skill-building sessions can help people assess the costs and benefits of their own ways of managing these issues (both for themselves and for others in the organization), and they can teach people alternative strategies. Role models of close, effective male–female relationships in management can have an obvious impact on people's hopes and fears concerning attraction and intimacy at work. With a more open climate in which to approach these issues, men and women should be freer to create high-quality working relationships that contribute to both their personal and professional development. Organizations will be rewarded in turn with the energy and creativity these relationships may contribute to the resolution of organizational problems.

ACKNOWLEDGMENT

I would like to thank Fernando Bartolomé, Tim Hall, Meryl Louis, Carolyn Lukensmeyer, Asya Pazy, Duncan Spelman, and Peter Vaill for their feedback on earlier versions of this paper. I am especially indebted to the people who were willing to talk with me about their own experiences with attraction and intimacy at work.

SELECTED BIBLIOGRAPHY

Issues of attraction and intimacy at work must be understood in terms of the development of working relationships. For an excellent overview of the literature on this subject, see John J. Gabarro's chapter on "The Development of Working Relationships" in *The Handbook of Organizational Behavior*, edited by Jay W. Lorsch (Prentice Hall, 1986). Kathy E. Kram's *Mentoring at Work* (Scott Foresman, 1985) provides a very thorough discussion of the complexities of close working relationships.

A knowledge of the role of intimacy in adult development contributes a very different perspective to the issues of intimacy at work. Capacities for understanding and managing intimacy can be linked to stages of adult development. Robert Kegan describes different stages in the evolution of one's understanding of the self and one's relations to others in *The Evolving Self* (Harvard University Press, 1982). *Communication, Intimacy, and Close Relationships* (Academic Press, 1984), edited by Valerian J. Derlega, presents a rich compilation of theories and research on intimate relationships. The chapter by Dan McAdams, "Human Motives and Personal Relationships," explores the roles of power and intimacy in close relationships.

For a discussion of intimacy and its relation to organizational culture, see Edgar H. Schein's article, "Coming to a New Awareness of Organizational Culture" (*Sloan Management Review*, Winter 1984).

An excellent general reference for issues relating to sexuality in the workplace is *Sexuality in Organizations*, edited by Dale A. Neugarten and Jay M. Shafritz (Moore, 1980). This book addresses the overall complexity of managing attraction in hierarchical structures. Of particular interest are the articles "The Executive Man and Woman: The Issue of Sexuality" by David L. Bradford, Alice G. Sargent, and Melinda Sprague, and "Coping with Cupid: The Formation, Impact and Management of Romantic Relationships in Organizations" by Robert E. Quinn. Bradford et al. examine how the issues of sexuality *per se* influence male–female working relationships. Quinn's article presents his research on the effects of office affairs on superiors', co-workers', and other employees' attitudes and behaviors. A more recent treatment of sexual politics at work is Robert E. Quinn and Patricia L. Lees' article "Attraction and Harassment: Dynamics of Sexual Politics in the Workplace" (*Organizational Dynamics*, Autumn 1984).

A number of interesting articles have been written on managing attraction in the workplace. An article by Lynn R. Cohen, "Minimizing Communication Breakdowns Between Male and Female Managers" (*Personnel Administrator*, 1982) offers an explanation of nonverbal cues that create sexual tension in the office. James G. Clawson and Kathy E. Kram examine the dilemmas of intimacy versus distance in male–female developmental work relationships in their article "Managing Cross-Gender Mentoring" (*Business Horizons*, May/June 1984). In the *Harvard Business Review* (September/October 1983), Eliza G. C. Collins examines the impact of love relationships between top executives in a company and explores the options of dealing with them in ways to maintain organizational stability. In the article "Sexual Relationships at Work: Attraction, Transference, Coercion or Strategy" (*Personnel Administrator*, March 1982), Natasha Josefowitz describes the stages of attraction and the different reasons why people have sexual relationships at work. In the article "Managing Sexual Attraction in the Workplace" (*Personnel Administrator*, August 1983), Kaleel Jamison makes suggestions about what the manager can do to deal with incidents of sexual attraction in his or her company. Duncan Spelman, Marcy Crary, Kathy Kram, and James Clawson discuss the range of forces within the individual, work group, and organization that influence the development and management of attractions at work in their chapter "Sexual Attractions at Work: Managing the Heart" in *Not As Far as You Think* (Lexington Books, 1986), edited by Lynda L. Moore.

For a fascinating discussion of managing emotional expression on the job and its effects on the individual, see Arlene R. Hochschild's *The Managed Heart* (University of California Press, 1983).

28. Executive Women and the Myth of Having It All

Sylvia Ann Hewlett

There is a secret out there—a painful, well-kept secret: At midlife, between a third and a half of all successful career women in the United States do not have children. In fact, 33% of such women (business executives, doctors, lawyers, academics, and the like) in the 41-to-55 age bracket are childless—and that figure rises to 42% in corporate America. These women have not chosen to remain childless. The vast majority, in fact, yearn for children. Indeed, some have gone to extraordinary lengths to bring a baby into their lives. They subject themselves to complex medical procedures, shell out tens of thousands of dollars, and derail their careers—mostly to no avail, because these efforts come too late. In the words of one senior manager, the typical high-achieving woman childless at midlife has not made a choice but a "creeping nonchoice."

Why has the age-old business of having babies become so difficult for today's high-achieving women? In January 2001, in partnership with the market research company Harris Interactive and the National Parenting Association, I conducted a nationwide survey designed to explore the professional and private lives of highly educated, high-earning women. The survey results are featured in my new book, *Creating a Life: Professional Women and the Quest for Children*.

In this survey, I target the top 10% of women—measured in terms of earning power—and focus on two age groups: an older generation, ages 41 to 55, and their younger peers, ages 28 to 40, as defined for survey purposes. I distinguish between high achievers (those who are earning more than $55,000 in the younger group,

$65,000 in the older one) and ultra-achievers (those who are earning more than $100,000). I include a sample of high-potential women—highly qualified women who have left their careers, mainly for family reasons. In addition, I include a small sample of men.

The findings are startling—and troubling. They make it clear that, for many women, the brutal demands of ambitious careers, the asymmetries of male–female relationships, and the difficulties of bearing children late in life conspire to crowd out the possibility of having children. In this article, I lay out the issues underlying this state of affairs, identify the heavy costs involved, and suggest some remedies, however preliminary and modest. The facts and figures I relate are bleak. But I think that they can also be liberating, if they spur action. My hope is that this information will generate workplace policies that recognize the huge costs to businesses of losing highly educated women when they start their families. I also hope that it will galvanize young women to make newly urgent demands of their partners, employers, and policy makers and thus create more generous life choices for themselves.

THE CONTINUING INEQUITY

When it comes to career and fatherhood, high-achieving men don't have to deal with difficult trade-offs: 79% of the men I surveyed report wanting children—and 75% have them. The research shows that, generally speaking, the more successful the man, the more likely he will find a spouse and become a father. The opposite holds true for women, and the disparity is

---

Sylvia Ann Hewlett, "Executive Women and the Myth of Having It All" from *Harvard Business Review*, July 2002, pp. 66–73.

particularly striking among corporate ultra-achievers. In fact, 49% of these women are childless. But a mere 19% of their male colleagues are. (See Figure 28.1.) These figures underscore the depth and scope of the persisting, painful inequities between the sexes. Women face all the challenges that men do in working long hours and withstanding the up-or-out pressure of high-altitude careers. But they also face challenges all their own.

Slim Pickings in Partners

Let's start with the fact that professional women find it challenging even to *be* married—for most, a necessary precondition for childbearing. Only 60% of high-achieving women in the older age group are married, and this figure falls to 57% in corporate America. By contrast, 76% of older men are married, and this figure rises to 83% among ultra-achievers.

Consider Tamara Adler, 43, a former managing director of Deutsche Bank in London. She gave her take on these disturbing realities when I interviewed her for the study. Adler was the bank's most senior woman, and her highly successful career had left no room for family. She mentioned the obvious reasons—long hours and travel—but she also spoke eloquently about how ambitious careers discriminate against women: "In the rarified upper reaches of high-altitude careers where the air is thin . . . men have a much easier time finding oxygen. They find oxygen in the form of younger, less driven women who will coddle their egos." She went on to conclude, "The hard fact is that most successful men are not interested in acquiring an ambitious peer as a partner."

It's a conclusion backed up by my data: Only 39% of high-achieving men are married to women who are employed full time, and 40% of these spouses earn less than $35,000 a year. Meanwhile, nine out of ten married women in the high-achieving category have husbands who are employed full time or self-employed, and a quarter are married to men who earn more than $100,000 a year. Clearly, successful women professionals have slim pickings in the marriage department—particularly as they age. Professional men seeking to marry typically reach into a large pool of younger women, while professional women are limited to a shrinking pool of eligible peers. According to U.S. Census Bureau data, at age 28 there are four college-educated, single men for every three college-educated, single women. A decade later, the situation is radically changed. At age 38, there is one man for every three women.

The Time Crunch

Now add to that scarcity of marriage candidates a scarcity of time to spend nurturing those relationships. My survey results show that women are dealing with long and lengthening workweeks. Twenty-nine percent of high achievers and 34% of ultra-achievers work more than 50 hours a week, and a significant proportion of these women are on the job ten to 20 more hours a week than they were five years ago. Among ultra-achievers, a quarter are away on business at least five nights every three months. According to research by sociologists Jerry Jacobs and Kathleen Gerson, the percentage of women working at least 50 hours a week is now higher in the United States than in any other country.

Think of what a 55-hour week means in terms of work–life balance. If you assume an hour lunch and a 45-minute round-trip commute (the national average), the workday stretches to almost 13 hours. Even without "extras" (out-of-town trips, client dinners, work functions), this kind of schedule makes it extremely difficult for any professional to maintain a relationship. Take Sue Palmer, 49, managing director of Grant Thornton, the London-based global accounting firm, and the only woman on its management committee. "Ten years ago," she said, "an assistant of mine told me at the end of a particularly grueling 70-hour week, 'You know, Sue, you couldn't have a torrid love affair if you wanted to.' And I shot back, 'I couldn't have a *tepid* love affair if I wanted to.' "

FIGURE 28.1
The Sobering Facts

In January 2001, in partnership with Harris Interactive and the National Parenting Association, I conducted a nationwide survey targeting the top 10% of women—measured in terms of earning power—and a small sample of men for comparative purposes. Responding were 1,168 high-achieving career women ages 28 to 55; 479 high-achieving, noncareer women ages 28 to 55; and 472 high-achieving men ages 28 to 55. (The group of ultra-achieving men was not large enough to disaggregate.) The sample was drawn from the Harris Poll on-line database of cooperative respondents. Data were weighted for key demographic variables to reflect each sample's national population. My analysis delineated an older generation, 41 to 55, and that group's younger peers, 28 to 40. I also distinguished between high achievers (those earning more than $65,000 or $55,000, depending on age), ultra-achievers (those earning more than $100,000), and high-potential women—highly qualified women who have left their careers, mainly for family reasons. Corporate women were defined as working in companies with more than 5,000 employees. The two charts below contain some of the startling—and sobering—findings.

Percentage of professionals childless at ages 41 to 55

Percentage of married professionals at ages 41 to 55

The survey was carried out by Harris Interactive under the auspices of the National Parenting Association, a nonprofit research organization. Funding for the survey and the associated research was provided by Ernst & Young, Merck, the Annie E. Casey Foundation, and the David and Lucile Packard Foundation. For more about the methodology and findings, go to www.parentsunite.org.

Of course, long hours aren't unique to women. They're a fact of life in corporate America, where management is under intense pressure to use its professional workforce for as many hours a week as possible. The reasons for this go back to 1938 when Congress passed the Fair Labor Standards Act, which institutionalized the 40-hour workweek and required employers to pay overtime for additional hours worked. One provision, however, exempted managers and professionals and still does. For those workers, extra hours carry no marginal costs to employers. The temptation for companies to take advantage of that provision might not have been so problematic back in 1938 when only 15% of employees were exempt, and most of them were men with stay-at-home spouses. But it produces significant overload today when close to 30% of employees are in the exempt category, many of them women who rarely have the luxury of a spouse at home tending to domestic responsibilities.

An Unforgiving Decade

Women pay an even greater price for those long hours because the early years of career building overlap—almost perfectly—the prime years of childbearing. It's very hard to throttle back during that stage of a career and expect to catch up later. As policy analyst Nancy Rankin points out, the career highway has all kinds of off-ramps but few on-ramps.

In fact, the persistent wage gap between men and women is due mainly to the penalties women incur when they interrupt their careers to have children. In a recent study, economists Susan Harkness and Jane Waldfogel compared that wage gap across seven industrialized countries and found it was particularly wide in the United States. For example, in France, women earn 81% of the male wage, in Sweden 84%, and in Australia 88%, while in the United States, women continue to earn a mere 78% of the male wage. These days, only a small portion of this wage gap can be attributed to discrimination (getting paid less for doing the same job or being denied access to jobs, education, or

capital based on sex). According to recent studies, an increasingly large part of the wage gap can now be explained by childbearing and child rearing, which interrupt women's—but not men's—careers, permanently depressing their earning power. If the gap between what men and women earn in this country is wider than elsewhere, it isn't because this country has done an inferior job combating discrimination. It is because it has failed to develop policies—in the workplace and in society as a whole—that support working mothers.

Ironically, this policy failure is to some extent the fault of the women's movement in the United States. Going back to the mid-nineteenth century, feminists in this country have channeled much of their energy into the struggle to win formal equality with men. More recently, the National Organization for Women has spent 35 years fighting for a wide array of equal rights, ranging from educational and job opportunities to equal pay and access to credit. The idea is that once all the legislation that discriminates against women is dismantled, the playing field becomes level and women can assume a free and equal place in society by simply cloning the male competitive model.

In Europe, various groups of social feminists have viewed the problem for women quite differently. For them, it is not a woman's lack of legal rights that constitutes her main handicap, or even her lack of reproductive freedom. Rather, it is her dual burden—taking care of a home and family as well as holding down a job—that leads to her second-class status.

The Second Shift

The problem with the notion that American women should be able to successfully clone the male competitive model is that husbands have not picked up a significant share of women's traditional responsibilities on the home front. Even high-achieving women who are married continue to carry the lion's share of domestic responsibilities. (See Figure 28.2.) Only 9% of their husbands assume primary responsibility for meal preparation, 10% for the laundry, and

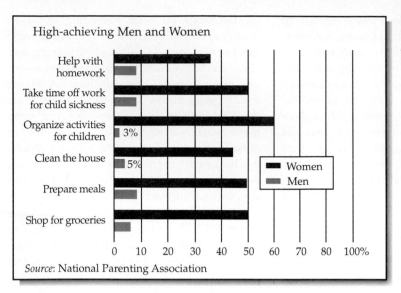

FIGURE 28.2
Primary Child Care and Household Responsibilities

High-achieving Men and Women

- Help with homework
- Take time off work for child sickness
- Organize activities for children — 3%
- Clean the house — 5%
- Prepare meals
- Shop for groceries

■ Women
■ Men

0 10 20 30 40 50 60 70 80 100%

Source: National Parenting Association

5% for cleaning the house. When it comes to children, husbands don't do much better. Only 9% of them take time off from work when a child is sick, 9% take the lead in helping children with homework, and 3% organize activities such as play dates and summer camp.

Yes, these percentages have grown over the years—but not much. At the end of the day, the division of labor at home boils down to one startling fact: 43% of the older, high-achieving women and 37% of the younger, high-achieving women feel that their husbands actually create more household work for them than they contribute. (Thirty-nine percent of ultra-achieving women also feel this way, despite the fact that half of them are married to men who earn less than they do.)

Stubborn Biology

So this is the difficult position in which women find themselves. According to Lisa Benenson, former editor of *Working Woman* and *Working Mother* magazines, "The signals are very clear. Young women are told that a serious person needs to commit to her career in her 20s and devote all her energies to her job for at least ten years if she is to be successful." But the fact is, if you take this advice you might well be on the wrong side of 35 before you have time to draw

breath and contemplate having a child—exactly the point in life when infertility can—and overwhelmingly does—become an issue.

Media hype about advances in reproductive science only exacerbates the problem, giving women the illusion that they can delay childbearing until their careers are well established. My survey tells us that 89% of young, high-achieving women believe that they will be able to get pregnant deep into their 40s. But sadly, new reproductive technologies have not solved fertility problems for older women. The research shows that only 3% to 5% of women who attempt in vitro fertilization in their 40s actually succeed in bearing a child. This kind of information is hard to come by because the infertility industry in this country likes to tout the good news—with dire consequences. Too many career women put their private lives on the back burner, assuming that children will eventually happen for them courtesy of high-tech reproduction—only to discover disappointment and failure.

A COSTLY IMBALANCE

I can't tell you how many times over the course of this research the women I interviewed apologized for "wanting it all." But it wasn't as though these women were looking for special treatment. They were quite prepared to shoulder more than their fair share of the work involved in having both career and family. So why on earth shouldn't they feel entitled to rich, multidimensional lives? At the end of the day, women simply want the choices in love and work that men take for granted.

Instead, they operate in a society where motherhood carries enormous economic penalties. Two recent studies lay out these penalties in very specific terms. In her study, economist Waldfogel finds that mothers earn less than other women do even when you control for marital status, experience, and education. In fact, according to her research, one child produces a "penalty" of 6% of earnings, while two children produce a wage penalty of 13%. In a more recent study, economists Michelle Budig and Paula England find that motherhood results in a penalty of 7% per child.

Given such a huge disincentive, why do women persist in trying to "have it all"? Because, as a large body of research demonstrates, women are happier when they have both career and family. In a series of books and articles that span more than a decade, University of Michigan sociologist Lois Hoffmann has examined the value of children to parents and finds that, across cultures, parents see children as enormously important in providing love and companionship and in warding off loneliness. Children also help parents deal with the questions of human existence: How do I find purpose beyond the self? How do I cope with morality?

Thus, the fact that so many professional women are forced to sacrifice motherhood is patently unfair, and it also has immense implications for American business, since it causes women intent on motherhood to cut short their careers. This is, of course, the flip side of the same coin. For if a large proportion

Creeping Nonchoice Reality and Regret

The findings presented in this article are compelling in the way that brutal statistics can be. But for me, the most powerful evidence of a problem came from the personal stories I heard while conducting the research. Going into the interviews, I had assumed that if accomplished women were childless, surely they had chosen to be. I was prepared to believe that the exhilaration and challenge of a megawatt career made it easy to opt out of motherhood.

Nothing could be further from the truth. When I surveyed these women about children, their sense of loss was palpable. Consider Lisa Polsky, who joined Morgan Stanley in 1995 as a managing director after successful stints at Citibank and Bankers Trust; she managed to make it on Wall Street, the ultimate bastion of male market power. But when we met in 1999, our conversation focused on what she had missed. Polsky was 44 then, and her childbearing days were over. She said, "What gnaws at me is that I always assumed I would have children. Somehow I imagined that having a child was something I would get to in a year or so, after the next promotion, when I was more established."

Kate, 52, a member of the medical faculty at the University of Washington, felt the same way. "Looking back, I can't think why I allowed my career to obliterate my 30s," she told me. "I just didn't pay attention. I'm only just absorbing the consequences."

And there is Stella Parsons, 45, who had just been offered a chairmanship at Ohio State University the day I interviewed her. But she waved my congratulations away. "I wish some of this career success had spilled over to my private life. I just didn't get it together in time." Then she whispered, "I'm almost ashamed to admit it, but I still ache for a child."

of women who stay on track in their careers are forced to give up family, an equally large proportion who opt for family are forced to give up their careers. According to my survey, 66% of high-potential women would like to return to full-time jobs.

The cost to corporations and to our economy becomes monumental in the aggregate. Our nation needs professional women to stay in the labor force; we can ill afford to have a quarter of the female talent pool forced out of their jobs when they have children. But in 2000 at the height of the labor crunch, Census Bureau data showed that fully 22% of all women with professional degrees (MBAs, MDs, PhDs, and so on) were not in the labor market at all. What an extraordinary waste of expensively educated talent!

At the same time, we need adults at all income levels to become committed, effective parents. When a parent devotes time, attention, and financial resources to help a child become a well-adjusted person—one who succeeds in school and graduates from college—not only do parents feel deeply fulfilled, but society, of course, is graced with productive workers who boost the GDP, obey the law, and pay their taxes. Thus, we are all stakeholders in parents' ability to come through for their children.

And when women come to understand the value of parenthood to the wider community, they can quit apologizing for wanting both a career and a family. A woman can hold her head high when she goes into her boss and asks for a schedule that fits her needs.

THE CHALLENGE TO BUSINESS

The statistics I've laid out here would be bearable if they were purely historical—the painful but isolated experience of a pioneering generation—but they are not. My survey shows that younger women are facing even more difficult trade-offs. (The sidebar "The Delusions of a Younger Generation" suggests that younger women may be more dangerously complacent than their elders.) Can we reverse these pernicious trends and finally create the possibility of true work–life balance? I believe we can.

The first challenge is to employers, to craft more meaningful work–life policies. Professional women who want both family and career know that conventional benefit packages are insufficient. These women need reduced-hour jobs and careers that can be interrupted, neither of which is readily available yet. And more than anything, they need to be able to partake of such benefits without suffering long-term damage to their careers.

High-achieving women make it abundantly clear that what they want most are work–life policies that confer on them what one woman calls "the gift of time." Take Joanna, for example. At 39, Joanna had worked for five years as an account executive for a Chicago head-hunter. She believed her company had great work–life policies—until she adopted a child. "My main problem," Joanna said, "is the number of hours I am expected to put in. I work 60 hours a week 50 weeks of the year, which leaves precious little time for anything else." Joanna asked for a reduced schedule, but it was a "no go. The firm didn't want to establish a precedent," she said. Joanna began looking for another job.

According to my survey, some employers take family needs into account: 12% offer paid parenting leave and 31% job sharing. Many more, however, provide only time flexibility: 69% allow staggered hours, and 48% have work-at-home options. These less ambitious policies seem to be of limited use to time-pressed, high-achieving women.

So, what do professionals want? The high-achieving career women who participated in my survey were asked to consider a list of policy options that would help them achieve balance in their lives over the long haul. They endorsed the following cluster of work–life policies that would make it much easier to get off conventional career ladders and eventually get back on:

A Time Bank of Paid Parenting Leave. This would allow for three months of paid leave, which could be taken as needed, until the child turned 18.

Restructured Retirement Plans. In particular, survey respondents want to see the elimination of penalties for career interruptions.

Career Breaks. Such a leave of absence might span three years—unpaid, of course, but with the assurance of a job when the time came to return to work.

Reduced-Hour Careers. High-level jobs should be created that permit reduced hours and workloads on an ongoing basis but still offer the possibility of promotion.

Alumni Status for Former Employees. Analogous to active retirement, alumni standing would help women who have left or are not active in their careers stay in the loop. They might be tapped for advice and guidance, and the company would continue to pay their dues and certification fees so they could maintain professional standing.

Policies like these are vital—though in themselves not enough to solve the problem. In particular, companies must guard against the perception that by taking advantage of such policies, a woman will tarnish her professional image. Outside the fiction of human resource policies, a widespread belief in business is that a woman who allows herself to be accommodated on the family front is no longer choosing to be a serious contender. Top management must work to banish this belief from the corporate culture.

The good news is that, where top management supports them, work–life policies like the

The Delusions of a Younger Generation

One professional woman, a 29-year-old lawyer, told me: "The pioneer women of the 1970s and 1980s paid some kind of special price for their careers. For us, things are different. We plan on having it all."

But is such easy confidence warranted? I think not. In fact, women in their 20s and 30s are dealing with the same cruel trade-offs. If anything, the choices younger women must make are more difficult than ever. Let's start with the fact that they are marrying even later. My data show that the high-achieving women of the older generation tended to marry young: 75% of them were married by 25, but only 54% of the younger generation are married by that age.

Young women are delaying childbirth even longer, too. If you compare women in the two age groups by calculating what proportion had a child by 35, younger women seem to be in worse shape. Only 45% of the younger women have had a child by 35, while 62% of the older women had a child by that age. (Indeed, among ultra-achievers, no one in the older group had her first child after 36.)

It's easy to speculate that these women are delaying childbirth because they don't feel a sense of biological urgency. The hype around the miracle babies of high-tech reproduction is falling on eager ears. Amy, 29, is just embarking on her career. Her story is probably typical. "I figure I've got 14, 15 years before I need worry about making babies," she e-mailed me. "In my mid-30s, I'll go back to school, earn an MBA, and get myself a serious career. At 40, I'll be ready for marriage and family. I can't tell you how glad I am that this new reproductive technology virtually guarantees that you can have a baby until 45. Or maybe it's even later. Go doctors!"

Modern medicine notwithstanding, the chances of Amy's getting pregnant in her 40s are tiny—in the range of 3% to 5%. The luxury of time she feels is, unfortunately, an illusion.

ones I've listed do pay off. My survey data show that companies offering a rich array of work–life policies are much more likely to hang on to their professional women than companies that don't. High-achieving mothers who have been able to stay in their careers tend to work for companies that allow them access to generous benefits: flextime, telecommuting, paid parenting leave, and compressed workweeks. In contrast, high-achieving mothers who have been forced out of their careers tended to work for companies with inadequate work–life benefits.

I heard a wonderful example of the loyalty these kinds of policies engender when I spoke with Amy, 41, a marketing executive for IBM. Her son had just turned three, and Amy was newly back at work. "People don't believe me when I tell them that my company offers a three-year personal leave of absence," she said. As she described the policy, it applies not only to mothers; others have used it to care for elderly parents or to return to school. The leave is unpaid but provides continuation of benefits and a job-back guarantee. "IBM gave me this gift," she said, "and I will always be grateful." Clearly, in the aggregate, business leaders hold the power to make important and constructive change.

Because companies can't be expected to craft all the policies that will make a difference in women's lives, government should also take action. I have urged policy makers at the national level, for example, to extend the Family and Medical Leave Act to workers in small companies and turn it into paid leave. State and federal governments could also accomplish much by providing tax incentives to companies that offer employees flextime and various reduced-hour options. And we should promote legislation that eliminates perverse incentives for companies to subject their employees to long-hour weeks.

THE CHALLENGE TO WOMEN

My book focuses on what women themselves can do to expand their life choices. In a nutshell, if you're a young woman who wants both career and family, you should consider doing the following:

Figure out what you want your life to look like at 45. If you want children (and between 86% and 89% of high-achieving women do), you need to become highly intentional—and take action now.

Give urgent priority to finding a partner. My survey data suggest that high-achieving women have an easier time finding partners in their 20s and early 30s.

Have your first child before 35. The occasional miracle notwithstanding, late-in-life childbearing is fraught with risk and failure. Even if you manage to get one child "under the wire," you may fail to have a second. This, too, can trigger enormous regret.

Choose a career that will give you the gift of time. Certain careers provide more flexibility and are more forgiving of interruptions. Female entrepreneurs, for example, do better than female lawyers in combining career and family—and both do better than corporate women. The key is to avoid professions with rigid career trajectories.

Choose a company that will help you achieve work–life balance. Look for such policies as reduced-hour schedules and job-protected leave.

That's an easy list to compile, but I have no illusions that it will change the world, because identifying what each woman can do is only half the battle. The other half is convincing women that they are entitled to both a career and children. Somehow the perception persists that a woman isn't a woman unless her life is riddled with sacrifice.

AN END TO SELF-SACRIFICE

In February 2001, I conducted an informal focus group with young professionals at three consulting firms in Cambridge, Massachusetts. During that session, a young woman named

Natalie commented, "This is the third consulting firm I've worked for, and I've yet to see an older, more senior woman whose life I would actually want."

Natalie's colleague Rachel was shocked and asked her to explain. She responded, "I know a few hard-driving women who are climbing the ladder at consulting firms, but they are single or divorced and seem pretty isolated. And I know a handful of working mothers who are trying to do the half-time thing or the two-thirds–time thing. They work reduced hours so they can see their kids, but they don't get the good projects, they don't get the bonuses, and they also get whispered about behind their backs. You know, comments like, 'If she's not prepared to work the client's hours, she has no business being in the profession.'"

This is the harsh reality behind the myth of having it all. Even in organizations whose policies support women, prevailing attitudes and unrelenting job pressures undermine them. Women's lives have expanded. But the grudging attitudes of most corporate cultures weigh down and constrain what individual women feel is possible.

Power, Influence, and Interpersonal Attraction

29. Who Gets Power—And How They Hold On to It: A Strategic-Contingency Model of Power

Gerald R. Salancik/Jeffrey Pfeffer

*P*ower is held by many people to be a dirty word or, as Warren Bennis has said, "It is the organization's last dirty secret."

This article will argue that traditional "political" power, far from being a dirty business, is, in its most naked form, one of the few mechanisms available for aligning an organization with its own reality. However, institutionalized forms of power—what we prefer to call the cleaner forms of power: authority, legitimization, centralized control, regulations, and the more modern "management information systems"—tend to buffer the organization from reality and obscure the demands of its environment. Most great states and institutions declined, not because they played politics, but because they failed to accommodate to the political realities they faced. Political processes, rather than being mechanisms for unfair and unjust allocations and appointments, tend toward the realistic resolution of conflicts among interests. And power, while it eludes definition, is easy enough to recognize by its consequences—the ability of those who possess power to bring about the outcomes they desire.

The model of power we advance is an elaboration of what has been called strategic-contingency theory, a view that sees power as something that accrues to organizational subunits (individuals, departments) that cope with critical organizational problems. Power is used by subunits, indeed, used by all who have it, to enhance their own survival through control of scarce critical resources, through the placement of allies in key positions, and through the definition of organizational problems and policies. Because of the processes by which power develops and is used, organizations become both more aligned and more misaligned with their environments. This contradiction is the most interesting aspect of organizational power and one that makes administration one of the most precarious of occupations.

WHAT IS ORGANIZATIONAL POWER?

You can walk into most organizations and ask without fear of being misunderstood, "Which are the powerful groups of people in this organization?" Although many organizational informants may be *unwilling* to tell you, it is unlikely they will be *unable* to tell you. Most people do not require explicit definitions to know what power is.

Power is simply the ability to get things done the way one wants them to be done. For a manager who wants an increased budget to launch a project that he thinks is important, his power is measured by his ability to get that budget. For an executive vice president who wants to be chairman, his power is evidenced by his advancement toward his goal.

People in organizations not only know what you are talking about when you ask who is influential but they are likely to agree with one another to an amazing extent. Recently, we had a chance to observe this in a regional office of an insurance company. The office had 21 department managers; we asked 10 of these managers to rank all 21 according to the influence each one had in the organization. Despite the fact that ranking 21 things is a difficult task, the managers sat down and began arranging the names of their colleagues and themselves in a column. Only one person

bothered to ask, "What do you mean by influence?" When told "power," he responded, "Oh," and went on. We compared the rankings of all ten managers and found virtually no disagreement among them in the managers ranked among the top five or the bottom five. Differences in the rankings came from department heads claiming more influence for themselves than their colleagues attributed to them.

Such agreement on those who have influence, and those who do not, was not unique to this insurance company. So far we have studied over 20 very different organizations—universities, research firms, factories, banks, retailers, to name a few. In each one we found individuals able to rate themselves and their peers on a scale of influence or power. We have done this both for specific decisions and for general impact on organizational policies. Their agreement was unusually high, which suggests that distributions of influence exist well enough in everyone's mind to be referred to with ease—and we assume with accuracy.

WHERE DOES ORGANIZATIONAL POWER COME FROM?

Earlier we stated that power helps organizations become aligned with their realities. This hopeful prospect follows from what we have dubbed the strategic-contingencies theory of organizational power. Briefly, those subunits most able to cope with the organization's critical problems and uncertainties acquire power. In its simplest form, the strategic-contingencies theory implies that when an organization faces a number of lawsuits that threaten its existence the legal department will gain power and influence over organizational decisions. Somehow other organizational interest groups will recognize its critical importance and confer upon it a status and power never before enjoyed. This influence may extend beyond handling legal matters and into decisions about product design, advertising production, and so on. Such extensions undoubtedly would be accompanied by appropriate, or acceptable, verbal justifications. In time, the head of the legal department may become the head of the corporation, just as in times past the vice president for marketing had become the president when market shares were a worrisome problem and, before him, the chief engineer, who had made the production line run as smooth as silk.

Stated in this way, the strategic-contingencies theory of power paints an appealing picture of power. To the extent that power is determined by the critical uncertainties and problems facing the organization and, in turn, influences decisions in the organization, the organization is aligned with the realities it faces. In short, power facilitates the organization's adaptation to its environment—or its problems.

We can cite many illustrations of how influence derives from a subunit's ability to deal with critical contingencies. Michael Crozier described a French cigarette factory in which the maintenance engineers had a considerable say in the plant-wide operation. After some probing he discovered that the group possessed the solution to one of the major problems faced by the company, that of trouble-shooting the elaborate, expensive, and irascible automated machines that kept breaking down and dumbfounding everyone else. It was the one problem that the plant manager could in no way control.

The production workers, while troublesome from time to time, created no insurmountable problems; the manager could reasonably predict their absenteeism or replace them when necessary. Production scheduling was something he could deal with since, by watching inventories and sales, the demand for cigarettes was known long in advance. Changes in demand could be accommodated by slowing down or speeding up the line. Supplies of tobacco and paper were also easily dealt with through stockpiles and advance orders.

The one thing that management could neither control nor accommodate to, however, was the seemingly happenstance breakdowns. And the foremen couldn't instruct the workers what to do when emergencies developed since the maintenance department kept its records or problems and solutions locked up in a cabinet or in its members' heads. The breakdowns were, in truth, a critical source of uncertainty for the organization, and the maintenance engineers were the only ones who could cope with the problem.

The engineers' strategic role in coping with breakdowns afforded them a considerable say on plant decisions. Schedules and production quotas were set in consultation with them. And the plant manager, while formally their boss, accepted their decisions about personnel in their operation. His submission was to his credit, for without their co-operation he would have had an even more difficult time in running the plant.

Ignoring Critical Consequences

In this cigarette factory, sharing influence with the maintenance workers reflected the plant manager's awareness of the critical contingencies. However, when organizational members are not aware of the critical contingencies they face and do not share influence accordingly, the failure to do so can create havoc. In one case, an insurance company's regional office was having problems with the performance of one of its departments, the coding department. From the outside, the department looked like a disaster area. The clerks who worked in it were somewhat dissatisfied; their supervisor paid little attention to them, and they resented the hard work. Several other departments were critical of this manager, claiming that she was inconsistent in meeting deadlines. The person most critical was the claims manager. He resented having to wait for work that was handled by her department, claiming that it held up his claims adjusters. Having heard the rumors about dissatisfaction among her subordinates, he attributed the situation to poor supervision. He was second in command in the office and therefore took up the issue with her immediate boss, the head of administrative services. They consulted with the personnel manager, and the three of them concluded that the manager needed leadership training to improve her relations with her subordinates. The coding manager objected, saying it was a waste of time, but agreed to go along with the training and also agreed to give more priority to the claims department's work. Within a week after the training, the results showed that her workers were happier but that the performance of her department had decreased, save for the people serving the claims department.

About this time, we began, quite independently, a study of influence in this organization. We asked the administrative services director to draw up flow charts of how the work of one department moved onto the next department. In the course of the interview, we noticed that the coding department began or interceded in the work flow of most of the other departments and casually mentioned to him, "The coding manager must be very influential." He said, "No, not really. Why would you think so?" Before we could reply, he recounted the story of her leadership training and the fact that things were worse. We then told him that it seemed obvious that the coding department would be influential from the fact that all the other departments depended on it. It was also clear why productivity had fallen. The coding manager took the training seriously and began spending more time raising her workers' spirits than she did worrying about the problems of all the departments that depended on her. Giving priority to the claims area only exaggerated the problem, for their work was getting done at the expense of the work of the other departments. Eventually the company hired a few more clerks to relieve the pressure in the coding department and performance returned to a more satisfactory level.

Originally we got involved with this insurance company to examine how the influence of each manager evolved from his or her department's handling of critical organizational contingencies. We reasoned that one of the most important contingencies faced by all profit-making organizations was that of generating income. Thus we expected managers would be influential to the extent to which they contributed to this function. Such was the case. The underwriting managers, who wrote the policies that committed the premiums, were the most influential; the claims managers, who kept a lid on the funds flowing out, were a close second. Least influential were the managers of functions unrelated to revenue, such as mailroom and payroll managers. And contrary to what the administrative services manager believed, the third most powerful department head (out of 21) was the woman in charge of the coding function, which consisted of rating, recording, and keeping track of the codes of all policy applications and contracts. Her peers attributed more influence to her than could have been inferred from her place on the organization chart. And it was not surprising, since they all depended on her department. The coding department's records, their accuracy, and the speed with which they could be retrieved, affected virtually every other operating department in the insurance office. The underwriters depended on them in getting the contracts straight; the typing department depended on them in preparing the formal contract document; the claims department depended on them in adjusting claims; and accounting depended on them for billing. Unfortunately, the "bosses" were not aware of these dependences, for unlike the cigarette factory, there were no massive breakdowns that made them obvious, while the coding manager, who was a hardworking but quiet person, did little to announce her importance.

The cases of this plant and office illustrate nicely a basic point about the source of power in organizations. The basis for power in an organization derives from the ability of a person or subunit to take or not take actions that are desired by others. The coding manager was seen as influential by those who depended on her department, but not by the people at the top. The engineers were influential because of their role in keeping the plant operating. The two cases differ in these respects: The coding supervisor's source of power was not as widely recognized as that of the maintenance engineers, and she did not use her source of power to influence decisions; the maintenance engineers did. Whether power is used to influence anything is a separate issue. We should not confuse this issue with the fact that power derives from a social situation in which one person has a capacity to do something and another person does not but wants it done.

POWER SHARING IN ORGANIZATIONS

Power is shared in organizations; and it is shared out of necessity more than out of concern for principles of organizational development or participatory democracy. Power is shared because no one person controls all the desired activities in the organization. While the factory owner may hire people to operate his noisy machines, once hired they have some control over the use of the machinery. And thus they have power over him in the same way he has power over them. Who has more power over whom is a mooter point than that of recognizing the inherent nature of organizing as a sharing of power.

Let's expand on the concept that power derives from the activities desired in an organization. A major way of managing influence in organizations is through the designation of activities. In a bank we studied, we saw this principle in action. This bank was planning to install a computer system for routine credit evaluation. The bank, rather progressive-minded, was concerned that the change would have adverse effects on employees and therefore surveyed their attitudes.

The principal opposition to the new system came, interestingly, not from the employees who performed the routine credit checks, some of whom would be relocated because of the change, but from the manager of the credit department. His reason was quite simple. The manager's primary function was to give official approval to the applications, catch any employee mistakes before giving approval, and arbitrate any difficulties the clerks had in

deciding what to do. As a consequence of his role, others in the organization, including his superiors, subordinates, and colleagues, attributed considerable importance to him. He, in turn, for example, could point to the low proportion of credit approvals, compared with other financial institutions, that resulted in bad debts. Now, to his mind, a wretched machine threatened to transfer his role to a computer programmer, a man who knew nothing of finance and who, in addition, had ten years less seniority. The credit manager eventually quit for a position at a smaller firm with lower pay, but one in which he would have more influence than his redefined job would have left him with.

Because power derives from activities rather than individuals, an individual's or subgroup's power is never absolute and derives ultimately from the context of the situation. The amount of power an individual has at any one time depends, not only on the activities he or she controls, but also on the existence of other persons or means by which the activities can be achieved and on those who determine what ends are desired and, hence, on what activities are desired and critical for the organization. One's own power always depends on other people for these two reasons. Other people, or groups or organizations, can determine the definition of what is a critical contingency for the organization and can also undercut the uniqueness of the individual's personal contribution to the critical contingencies of the organization.

Perhaps one can best appreciate how situationally dependent power is by examining how it is distributed. In most societies, power organizes around scarce and critical resources. In the United States, a person doesn't become powerful because he or she can drive a car. There are simply too many others who can drive with equal facility. In certain villages in Mexico, on the other hand, a person with a car is accredited with enormous social status and plays a key role in the community. In addition to scarcity, power is also limited by the need for one's capacities in a social system. While a racer's ability to drive a car around a 90° turn at 80 mph may be sparsely distributed in a society, it is not likely to lend the driver much power in the society. The ability simply does not play a central role in the activities of the society.

The fact that power revolves around scarce and critical activities, of course, makes the control and organization of those activities a major battleground in struggles for power. Even relatively abundant or trivial resources can become the bases for power if one can organize and control their allocation and the definition of what is critical. Many occupational and professional groups attempt to do just this in modern economies. Lawyers organize themselves into associations, regulate the entrance requirements for novitiates, and then get laws passed specifying situations that require the services of an attorney. Workers had little power in the conduct of industrial affairs until they organized themselves into closed and controlled systems. In recent years, women and blacks have tried to define themselves as important and critical to the social system, using law to reify their status.

In organizations there are obviously opportunities for defining certain activities as more critical than others. Indeed, the growth of managerial thinking to include defining organizational objectives and goals has done much to foster these opportunities. One sure way to liquidate the power of groups in the organization is to define the need for their services out of existence. David Halberstam presents a description of how just such a thing happened to the group of correspondents that evolved around Edward R. Murrow, the brilliant journalist, interviewer, and war correspondent of CBS News. A close friend of CBS chairman and controlling stockholder William S. Paley, Murrow, and the news department he directed, were endowed with freedom to do what they felt was right. He used it to create some of the best documentaries and commentaries ever seen on television. Unfortunately, television became too large, too powerful, and too suspect

in the eyes of the federal government that licensed it. It thus became, or at least the top executives believed it had become, too dangerous to have in-depth, probing commentary on the news. Crisp, dry, uneditorializing headliners were considered safer. Murrow was out and Walter Cronkite was in.

The power to define what is critical in an organization is no small power. Moreover, it is the key to understanding why organizations are either aligned with their environments or misaligned. If an organization defines certain activities as critical when in fact they are not critical, given the flow of resources coming into the organization, it is not likely to survive, at least in its present form.·

Most organizations manage to evolve a distribution of power and influence that is aligned with the critical realities they face in the environment. The environment, in turn, includes both the internal environment, the shifting situational contexts in which particular decisions are made, and the external environment that it can hope to influence but is unlikely to control.

THE CRITICAL CONTINGENCIES

The critical contingencies facing most organizations derive from the environmental context within which they operate. This determines the available needed resources and thus determines the problems to be dealt with. That power organizes around handling these problems suggests an important mechanism by which organizations keep in turn with their external environments. The strategic-contingencies model implies that subunits that contribute to the critical resources of the organization will gain influence in the organization. Their influence presumably is then used to bend the organization's activities to the contingencies that determine its resources. This idea may strike one as obvious. But its obviousness in no way diminishes its importance. Indeed, despite its obviousness, it escapes the notice of many organizational analysts and managers, who all too frequently think of the organization in terms of a descending pyramid, in which all the departments in one tier hold equal power and status. This presumption denies the reality that departments differ in the contributions they are believed to make to the overall organization's resources, as well as to the fact that some are more equal than others.

Because of the importance of this idea to organizational effectiveness, we decided to examine it carefully in a large midwestern university. A university offers an excellent site for studying power. It is composed of departments with nominally equal power and is administered by a central executive structure much like other bureaucracies. However, at the same time it is a situation in which the departments have clearly defined identities and face diverse external environments. Each department has its own bodies of knowledge, its own institutions, its own sources of prestige and resources. Because the departments operate in different external environments, they are likely to contribute differentially to the resources of the overall organization. Thus a physics department with close ties to NASA may contribute substantially to the funds of the university; and a history department with a renowned historian in residence may contribute to the intellectual credibility or prestige of the whole university. Such variations permit one to examine how these various contributions lead to obtaining power within the university.

We analyzed the influence of 29 university departments throughout an 18-month period in their history. Our chief interest was to determine whether departments that brought more critical resources to the university would be more powerful than departments that contributed fewer or less critical resources.

To identify the critical resources each department contributed, the heads of all departments were interviewed about the importance of seven different resources to the university's success. The seven included undergraduate students (the factor determining size of the state allocations by the university), national prestige, administrative expertise, and so on. The most critical resource was found to be contract and grant monies received by a department's faculty for research or consulting services. At this university, contract and grants contributed somewhat less than 50 percent of the overall budget, with the remainder primarily coming from state appropriations. The importance attributed to contract and grant monies, and the rather minor importance of undergraduate students, was not surprising for this particular university. The university was a major center for graduate education; many of its departments ranked in the top ten of their respective fields. Grant and contract monies were the primary source of discretionary funding available for maintaining these programs of graduate education, and hence for maintaining the university's prestige. The prestige of the university itself was critical both in recruiting able students and attracting top-notch faculty.

From university records it was determined what relative contributions each of the 29 departments made to the various needs of the university (national prestige, outside grants, teaching). Thus, for instance, one department may have contributed to the university by teaching 7 percent of the instructional units, bringing in 2 percent of the outside contracts and grants, and having a national ranking of 20. Another department, on the other hand, may have taught one percent of the instructional units, contributed 12 percent to the grants, and be ranked the third best department in its field within the country.

The question was: Do these different contributions determine the relative power of the departments within the university? Power was measured in several ways; but regardless of how measured, the answer was "Yes." Those three resources together accounted for about 70 percent of the variance in subunit power in the university.

But the most important predictor of departmental power was the department's contribution to the contracts and grants of the university. Sixty percent of the variance in power was due to this one factor, suggesting that the power of departments derived primarily from the dollars they provided for graduate education, the activity believed to be the most important for the organization.

THE IMPACT OF ORGANIZATIONAL POWER ON DECISION MAKING

The measure of power we used in studying this university was an analysis of the responses of the department heads we interviewed. While such perceptions of power might be of interest in their own right, they contribute little to our understanding of how the distribution of power might serve to align an organization with its critical realities. For this we must look to how power actually influences the decisions and policies of organizations.

While it is perhaps not absolutely valid, we can generally gauge the relative importance of a department of an organization by the size of the budget allocated to it relative to other departments. Clearly it is of importance to the administrators of those departments whether they are squeezed in a budget crunch or are given more funds to strike out after new opportunities. And it should also be clear that when those decisions are made and one department can go ahead and try new approaches while another must cut back on the old, then the deployment of the resources of the organization in meeting its problems is most directly affected.

Thus our study of the university led us to ask the following question: Does power lead to influence in the organization? To answer this question, we found it useful first to ask another one, namely: Why should department heads try to influence organization decisions to favor their own departments to the exclusion of other departments? While this second question may seem a bit naive to anyone who has witnessed the political realities of organizations, we posed it in a context of research on organizations that sees power as an illegitimate threat to the neater rational authority of modern bureaucracies. In this context, decisions are not believed to be made because of the dirty business of politics but because of the overall goals and purposes of the organization. In a university, one reasonable basis for decision making is the teaching workload of departments and the demands that follow from that workload. We would expect, therefore, that departments with heavy student demands for courses would be able to obtain funds for teaching. Another reasonable basis for decision making is quality. We would expect, for that reason, that departments with esteemed reputations would be able to obtain funds both because their quality suggests they might use such funds effectively and because such funds would allow them to maintain their quality. A rational model of bureaucracy intimates, then, that the organizational decisions taken would favor those who perform the stated purposes of the organization—teaching undergraduates and training professional and scientific talent—well.

The problem with rational models of decision making, however, is that what is rational to one person may strike another as irrational. For most departments, resources are a question of survival. While teaching undergraduates may seem to be a major goal for some members of the university, developing knowledge may seem so to others; and to still others, advising governments and other institutions about policies may seem to be the crucial business. Everyone has his own idea of the proper priorities in a just world. Thus goals rather than being clearly defined and universally agreed upon are blurred and contested throughout the organization. If such is the case, then the decisions taken on behalf of the organization as a whole are likely to reflect the goals of those who prevail in political contests, namely, those with power in the organization.

Will organizational decisions always reflect the distribution of power in the organization? Probably not. Using power for influence requires a certain expenditure of effort, time, and resources. Prudent and judicious persons are not likely to use their power needlessly or wastefully. And it is likely that power will be used to influence organizational decisions primarily under circumstances that both require and favor its use. We have examined three conditions that are likely to affect the use of power in organizations: scarcity, criticality, and uncertainty. The first suggests that subunits will try to exert influence when the resources of the organization are scarce. If there is an abundance of resources, then a particular department or a particular individual has little need to attempt influence. With little effort, he can get all he wants anyway.

The second condition, criticality, suggests that a subunit will attempt to influence decisions to obtain resources that are critical to its own survival and activities. Criticality implies that one would not waste effort, or risk being labeled obstinate, by fighting over trivial decisions affecting one's operations.

An office manager would probably balk less about a threatened cutback in copying machine usage than about a reduction in typing staff. An advertising department head would probably worry less about losing his lettering artist than his illustrator. Criticality is difficult to define because what is critical depends on people's beliefs about what is critical. Such beliefs may or may not be based on experience and knowledge and may or may not be agreed upon by all. Scarcity, for instance, may itself affect conceptions of criticality. When slack resources drop off, cutbacks have to be made— those "hard decisions," as congressmen and resplendent administrators like to call them. Managers then find themselves scrapping projects they once held dear.

The third condition that we believe affects the use of power is uncertainty: When individuals do not agree about what the organization should do or how to do it, power and other social processes will affect decisions. The reason for this is simply that, if there are no clear-cut criteria available for resolving conflict of interest, then the only means for resolution is some form of social process, including power, status, social ties, or some arbitrary process like flipping a coin or drawing straws. Under conditions of uncertainty, the powerful manager can argue his case on any grounds and usually win it. Since there is no real consensus, other contestants are not likely to develop counterarguments or amass sufficient opposition. Moreover, because of his power and their need for access to the resources he controls, they are more likely to defer to his arguments.

Although the evidence is slight, we have found that power will influence the allocations of scarce and critical resources. In the analysis of power in the university, for instance, one of the most critical resources needed by departments is the general budget. First granted by the state legislature, the general budget is later allocated to individual departments by the university administration in response to requests from the department heads. Our analysis of the factors that contribute to a department getting more or less of this budget indicated that subunit power was the major predictor, overriding such factors as student demand for courses, national reputations of departments, or even the size of a department's faculty. Moreover, other research has shown that when the general budget has been cut back or held below previous uninflated levels, leading to monies becoming more scarce, budget allocations mirror departmental powers even more closely.

Student enrollment and faculty size, of course, do themselves relate to budget allocations, as we would expect since they determine a department's need for resources, or at least offer visible testimony of needs. But departments are not always able to get what they need by the mere fact of needing them. In one analysis it was found that high-power departments were able to obtain budget without regard to their teaching loads and, in some cases, actually in inverse relation to their teaching loads. In contrast, low-power departments could get increases in budget only when they could justify the increases by a recent growth in teaching load, and then only when it was far in excess of norms for other departments.

General budget is only one form of resource that is allocated to departments. There are others such as special grants for student fellowships or faculty research. These are critical to departments because they affect the ability to attract other resources, such as outstanding faculty or students. We examined how power influenced the allocations of four resources department heads had described as critical and scarce.

When the four resources were arrayed from the most to the least critical and scarce, we found that departmental power best predicated the allocations of the most critical and scarce resources. In other words, the analysis of how power influences organizational allocations leads to this conclusion: Those subunits most likely to survive in times of strife are those that are most critical to the organization. Their importance to the organization gives them power to influence resource allocations that enhance their own survival.

HOW EXTERNAL ENVIRONMENT IMPACTS EXECUTIVE SELECTION

Power not only influences the survival of key groups in an organization, it also influences the selection of individuals to key leadership positions, and by such a process further aligns the organization with its environmental context.

We can illustrate this with a recent study of the selection and tenure of chief administrators in 57 hospitals in Illinois. We assumed that since the critical problems facing the organization would enhance the power of certain groups at the expense of others, then the leaders to emerge should be those most relevant to the context of the hospitals. To assess this we asked each chief administrator about his professional background and how long he had been in office. The replies were then related to the hospitals' funding, ownership, and competitive conditions for patients and staff.

One aspect of a hospital's context is the source of its budget. Some hospitals, for instance, are run much like other businesses. They sell bed space, patient care, and treatment services. They charge fees sufficient both to cover their costs and to provide capital for expansion. The main source of both their operating and capital funds is patient billings. Increasingly, patient billings are paid for, not by patients, but by private insurance companies. Insurers like Blue Cross dominate and represent a potent interest group outside a hospital's control but critical to its income. The insurance companies, in order to limit their own costs, attempt to hold down the fees allowable to hospitals, which they do effectively from their positions on state rate boards. The squeeze on hospitals that results from fees increasing slowly while costs climb rapidly more and more demands the talents of cost accountants or people trained in the technical expertise of hospital administration.

By contrast, other hospitals operate more like social service institutions, either as government healthcare units (Bellevue Hospital in New York City and Cook County Hospital in Chicago, for example) or as charitable institutions. These hospitals obtain a large proportion of their operating and capital funds, not from privately insured patients, but from government subsidies or private donations. Such institutions rather than requiring the talents of a technically efficient administrator are likely to require the savvy of someone who is well integrated into the social and political power structure of the community.

Not surprisingly, the characteristics of administrators predictably reflect the funding context of the hospitals with which they are associated. Those hospitals with larger proportions of their budget obtained from private insurance companies were most likely to have administrators with backgrounds in accounting and least likely to have administrators whose professions were business or medicine. In contrast, those hospitals with larger proportions of their budget derived from private donations and local governments were most likely to have administrators with business or professional backgrounds and least likely to have accountants. The same held for formal training in hospital management. Professional hospital administrators could easily be found in hospitals drawing their incomes from private insurance and rarely in hospitals dependent on donations or legislative appropriations.

As with the selection of administrators, the context of organizations has also been found to affect the removal of executives. The environment, as a source of organizational problems, can make it more or less difficult for executives to demonstrate their value to the organization. In the hospitals we studied, long-term administrators came from hospitals with few problems. They enjoyed amicable and stable relations with their local business and social communities and suffered little competition for funding and staff. The small city hospital director who attended civic and Elks meetings while running the only hospital within a 100-mile radius, for example, had little difficulty holding on to his job. Turnover was highest in hospitals with the most problems, a phenomenon similar to that observed in a study of industrial organizations in which turnover was highest among executives in industries with competitive environments and unstable market conditions. The interesting thing is that instability characterized the industries rather than the individual firms in them. The troublesome conditions in the individual firms were attributed, or rather misattributed, to the executives themselves.

It takes more than problems, however, to terminate a manager's leadership. The problems themselves must be relevant and critical. This is clear from the way in which an administrator's tenure is affected by the status of the hospital's operating budget. Naively we might assume that all administrators would need to show a surplus. Not necessarily so. Again, we must distinguish between those hospitals that depend on private donations for funds and those that do not. Whether an endowed budget shows a surplus or deficit is less important than the hospital's relations with benefactors. On the other hand, with a budget dependent on patient billing, a surplus is almost essential; monies for new equipment or expansion must be drawn from it, and without them

quality care becomes more difficult and patients scarcer. An administrator's tenure reflected just these considerations. For those hospitals dependent upon private donations, the length of an administrator's term depended not at all on the status of the operating budget but was fairly predictable from the hospital's relations with the business community. On the other hand, in hospitals dependent on the operating budget for capital financing, the greater the deficit the shorter was the tenure of the hospital's principal administrators.

CHANGING CONTINGENCIES AND ERODING POWER BASES

The critical contingencies facing the organization may change. When they do, it is reasonable to expect that the power of individuals and subgroups will change in turn. At times the shift can be swift and shattering, as it was recently for powerholders in New York City. A few years ago it was believed that David Rockefeller was one of the ten most powerful people in the city, as tallied by *New York* magazine, which annually sniffs out power for the delectation of its readers. But that was before it was revealed that the city was in financial trouble, before Rockefeller's Chase Manhattan Bank lost some of its own financial luster, and before brother Nelson lost some of his political influence in Washington. Obviously David Rockefeller was no longer as well positioned to help bail the city out. Another loser was an attorney with considerable personal connections to the political and religious leaders of the city. His talents were no longer in much demand. The persons with more influence were the bankers and union pension fund executors who fed money to the city; community leaders who represent blacks and Spanish-Americans, in contrast, witnessed the erosion of their power bases.

One implication of the idea that power shifts with changes in organizational environments is that the dominant coalition will tend to be that group that is most appropriate for the organization's environment, as also will the leaders of an organization. One can observe this historically in the top executives of industrial firms in the United States. Up until the early 1950s, many top corporations were headed by former production line managers or engineers who gained prominence because of their abilities to cope with the problems of production. Their success, however, only spelled their demise. As production became routinized and mechanized, the problem of most firms became one of selling all those goods they so efficiently produced. Marketing executives were more frequently found in corporate boardrooms. Success outdid itself again, for keeping markets and production steady and stable requires the kind of control that can only come from acquiring competitors and suppliers or the invention of more and more appealing products—ventures that typically require enormous amounts of capital. During the 1960s, financial executives assumed the seats of power. And they, too, will give way to others. Edging over the horizon are legal experts, as regulation and antitrust suits are becoming more and more frequent in the 1970s, suits that had their beginnings in the success of the expansion generated by prior executives. The more distant future, which is likely to be dominated by multinational corporations, may see former secretaries of state and their minions increasingly serving as corporate figureheads.

THE NONADAPTIVE CONSEQUENCES OF ADAPTATION

From what we have said thus far about power aligning the organization with its own realities, an intelligent person might react with a resounding ho-hum, for it all seems to obvious: Those with the ability to get the job done are given the job to do.

However, there are two aspects of power that make it more useful for understanding organization and their effectiveness. First, the "job" to be done has a way of expanding itself until it becomes less and less clear what the job is. Napoleon began by doing a job for France in the war with Austria and ended up Emperor,

convincing many that only he could keep the peace. Hitler began by promising an end to Germany's troubling postwar depression and ended up convincing more people than is comfortable to remember that he was destined to be the savior of the world. In short, power is a capacity for influence that extends far beyond the original bases that created it. Second, power tends to take on institutionalized forms that enable it to endure well beyond its usefulness to an organization.

There is an important contradiction in what we have observed about organizational power. On the one hand we have said that power derives from the contingencies facing an organization and that when those contingencies change so do the bases for power. On the other hand we have asserted that subunits will tend to use their power to influence organizational decisions in their own favor, particularly when their own survival is threatened by the scarcity of critical resources. The first statement implies that an organization will tend to be aligned with its environment since power will tend to bring to key positions those with capabilities relevant to the context. The second implies that those in power will not give up their positions so easily; they will pursue policies that guarantee their continued domination. In short, change and stability operate through the same mechanism, and as a result, the organization will never be completely in phase with its environment or its needs.

The study of hospital administrators illustrates how leadership can be out of phase with reality. We argued that privately funded hospitals needed trained technical administrators more so than did hospitals funded by donations. The need as we perceived it was matched in most hospitals, but by no means in all. Some organizations did not conform with our predictions. These deviations imply that some administrators were able to maintain their positions independent of their suitability for those positions. By dividing administrators into those with long and short terms of office, one finds that the characteristics of longer-termed administrators were virtually unrelated to the hospital's content. The shorter-termed chiefs on the other hand had characteristics more appropriate for the hospital's problems. For a hospital to have a recently appointed head implies that the previous administrator had been unable to endure by institutionalizing himself.

One obvious feature of hospitals that allowed some administrators to enjoy a long tenure was a hospital's ownership. Administrators were less entrenched when their hospitals were affiliated with and depended upon larger organizations, such as governments or churches. Private hospitals offered more secure positions for administrators. Like private corporations, they tend to have more diffused ownership, leaving the administrator unopposed as he institutionalizes his reign. Thus he endures, sometimes at the expense of the performance of the organization. Other research has demonstrated that corporations with diffuse ownership have poorer earnings than those in which the control of the manager is checked by a dominant shareholder. Firms that overload their boardrooms with more insiders than are appropriate for their context have also been found to be less profitable.

A word of caution is required about our judgment of "appropriateness." When we argue some capabilities are more appropriate for one context than another, we do so from the perspective of an outsider and on the basis of reasonable assumptions as to the problems the organization will face and the capabilities they will need. The fact that we have been able to predict the distribution of influence and the characteristics of leaders suggests that our reasoning is not incorrect. However, we do not think that all organizations follow the same pattern. The fact that we have not been able to predict outcomes with 100 percent accuracy indicates they do not.

MISTAKING CRITICAL CONTINGENCIES

One thing that allows subunits to retain their power is their ability to name their functions as critical to the organization when they may not

be. Consider again our discussion of power in the university. One might wonder why the most critical tasks were defined as graduate education and scholarly research, the effect of which was to lend power to those who brought in grants and contracts. Why not something else? The reason is that the more powerful departments argued for those criteria and won their case, partly because they were more powerful.

In another analysis of this university, we found that all departments advocate self-serving criteria for budget allocation. Thus a department with large undergraduate enrollments argued that enrollments should determine budget allocations, a department with a strong national reputation saw prestige as the most reasonable basis for distributing funds, and so on. We further found that advocating such self-serving criteria actually benefited a department's budget allotments but, also, it paid off more for departments that were already powerful.

Organizational needs are consistent with a current distribution of power also because of a human tendency to categorize problems in familiar ways. An accountant sees problems with organizational performances as cost accountancy problems or inventory flow problems. A sales manager sees them as problems with markets, promotional strategies, or just unaggressive salespeople. But what is the truth? Since it does not automatically announce itself, it is likely that those with prior credibility, or those with power, will be favored as the enlightened. This bias, while not intentionally self-serving, further concentrates power among those who already possess it, independent of changes in the organization's content.

INSTITUTIONALIZING POWER

A third reason for expecting organizational contingencies to be defined in familiar ways is that the current holders of power can structure the organization in ways that institutionalize themselves. By institutionalization we mean the establishment of relatively permanent structures and policies that favor the influence of a particular subunit. While in power, dominant coalition has the ability to institute constitutions, rules, procedures, and information systems that limit the potential power of others while continuing their own.

The key to institutionalizing power always is to create a device that legitimates one's own authority and diminishes the legitimacy of others. When the "Divine Right of Kings" was envisioned centuries ago it was to provide an unquestionable foundation for the supremacy of royal authority. There is generally a need to root the exercise of authority in some higher power. Modern leaders are no less affected by this need. Richard Nixon, with the aid of John Dean, reified the concept of executive privilege, which meant in effect that what the President wished not to be discussed need not be discussed.

In its simpler form, institutionalization is achieved by designating positions or roles for organizational activities. The creation of a new post legitimizes a function and forces organization members to orient to it. By designating how this new post relates to older, more established posts, moreover, one can structure an organization to enhance the importance of the function in the organization. Equally, one can diminish the importance of traditional functions. This is what happened in the end with the insurance company we mentioned that was having trouble with its coding department. As the situation unfolded, the claims director continued to feel dissatisfied about the dependency of his functions on the coding manager. Thus he instituted a reorganization that resulted in two coding departments. In so doing, of course, he placed activities that affected his department under his direct control, presumably to make the operation more effective. Similarly, consumer-product firms enhance the power of marketing by setting up a coordinating role to interface production and marketing functions and then appoint a marketing manager to fill the role.

The structures created by dominant powers sooner or later become fixed and unquestioned features of the organization. Eventually, this can

be devastating: It is said that the battle of Jena in 1806 was lost by Frederick the Great, who died in 1786. Though the great Prussian leader had no direct hand in the disaster, his imprint on the army was so thorough, so embedded in its skeletal underpinnings, that the organization was inappropriate for others to lead in different times.

Another important source of institutionalized power lies in the ability to structure information systems. Setting up committees to investigate particular organizational issues and having them report only to particular individuals or groups facilitates their awareness of problems by members of those groups while limiting the awareness of problems by the members of other groups. Obviously, those who have information are in a better position to interpret the problems of an organization, regardless of how realistically they may, in fact, do so.

Still another way to institutionalize power is to distribute rewards and resources. The dominant group may quiet competing interest groups with small favors and rewards. The credit for this artful form of co-optation belongs to Louis XIV. To avoid usurpation of his power by the nobles of France and the Fronde that had so troubled his father's reign, he built the palace at Versailles to occupy them with hunting and gossip. Awed, the courtiers basked in the reflected glories of the "Sun King" and the overwhelming setting he had created for his court.

At this point, we have not systematically studied the institutionalization of power. But we suspect it is an important condition that mediates between the environment of the organization and the capabilities of the organization for dealing with that environment. The more institutionalized power is within an organization, the more likely an organization will be out of phase with the realities it faces. President Richard Nixon's structuring of his White House is one of the better documented illustrations. If we go back to newspaper and magazine descriptions of how he organized his office from the beginning in 1968, most of what occurred subsequently follows almost as an afterthought. Decisions flowed through virtually only the small White House staff; rewards, small presidential favors of recognition, and perquisites were distributed by this staff to the loyal; and information from the outside world—the press, Congress, the people on the streets—was filtered by the staff and passed along only if initiated "bh." Thus it was not surprising that when Nixon met war protestors in the early dawn, the only thing he could think to talk about was the latest football game, so insulated had he become from their grief and anger.

One of the more interesting implications of institutionalized power is that executive turnover among the executives who have structured the organization is likely to be a rare event that occurs only under the most pressing crisis. If a dominant coalition is able to structure the organization and interpret the meaning of ambiguous events like declining sales and profits or lawsuits, then the "real" problems to emerge will easily be incorporated into traditional molds of thinking and acting. If opposition is designed out of the organization, the interpretations will go unquestioned. Conditions will remain stable until a crisis develops, so overwhelming and visible that even the most adroit rhetorician would be silenced.

IMPLICATIONS FOR THE MANAGEMENT OF POWER IN ORGANIZATIONS

While we could derive numerous implications from this discussion of power, our selection would have to depend largely on whether one wanted to increase one's power, decrease the power of others, or merely maintain one's position. More important, the real implications depend on the particulars of an organizational situation. To understand power in an organization one must begin by looking outside it—into the environment—for those groups that mediate the organization's outcomes but are not themselves within its control.

Instead of ending with homilies, we will end with a reversal of where we began. Power, rather than being the dirty business it is often made out to be, is probably one of the few mechanisms for reality testing in organizations. And the cleaner forms of power, the institutional forms, rather than having the virtues they are often credited with, can lead the organization to become out of touch. The real trick to managing power in organizations is to ensure somehow that leaders cannot be unaware of the realities of their environments and cannot avoid changing to deal with those realities. That, however, would be like designing the "self-liquidating organization," an unlikely event since anyone capable of designing such an instrument would be obviously in control of the liquidations.

Management would do well to devote more attention to determining the critical contingencies of their environments. For if you conclude, as we do, that the environment sets most of the structure influencing organizational outcomes and problems, and that power derives from the organization's activities that deal with those contingencies, then it is the environment that needs managing, not power. The first step is to construct an accurate model of the environment, a process that is quite difficult for most organizations. We have recently started a project to aid administrators in systematically understanding their environments. From this, experience, we have learned that the most critical blockage to perceiving an organization's reality accurately is a failure to incorporate those with the relevant expertise into the process. Most organizations have the requisite experts on hand but they are positioned so that they can be comfortably ignored.

One conclusion you can, and probably should, derive from our discussion is that power—because of the way it develops and the way it is used—will always result in the organization suboptimizing its performance. However, to this grim absolute, we add a comforting caveat: If any criteria other than power were the basis for determining an organization's decisions, the results would be even worse.

SELECTED BIBLIOGRAPHY

The literature on power is at once both voluminous and frequently empty of content. Some is philosophical musing about the concept of power, while other writing contains popularized palliatives for acquiring and exercising influence. Machiavelli's *The Prince*, if read carefully, remains the single best perspective treatment of power and its use. Most social scientists have approached power descriptively, attempting to understand how it is acquired, how it is used, and what its effects are. Mayer Zald's edited collection *Power in Organizations* (Vanderbilt University Press, 1970) is one of the more useful sets of thoughts about power from a sociological perspective, while James Tedeschi's edited book, *The Social Influence Processes* (Aldine-Atherton, 1972) represents the social psychological approach to understanding power and influence. The strategic contingencies's approach, with its emphasis on the importance of uncertainty for understanding power in organizations, is described by David Hickson and his colleagues in "A Strategic Contingencies Theory of Intraorganizational Power" (*Administrative Science Quarterly*, December 1971, pp. 216–29).

Unfortunately, while many have written about power theoretically, there have been few empirical examinations of power and its use. Most of the work has taken the form of case studies. Michel Crozier's *The Bureaucratic Phenomenon* (University of Chicago Press, 1964) is important because it describes a group's source of power as control over critical activities and illustrates how power is not strictly derived from hierarchical position. J. Victor Baldridge's *Power and Conflict in the University* (John Wiley & Sons, 1971) and Andrew Pettigrew's study of computer purchase decisions in one English firm (*Politics of Organizational Decision Making*, Tavistock, 1973) both present insights into the acquisition and use of power in specific instances. Our work has been more empirical and comparative, testing more explicitly the ideas presented in this article. The study of university decision making is reported in articles in the June 1974, pp. 135–51, and December 1974, pp. 453–73, issues of the *Administrative Science Quarterly*, the insurance firm study in J. G. Hunt and L. L. Larson's collection, *Leadership Frontiers* (Kent State University Press, 1975), and the study of hospital administrator succession appeared in 1977 in the *Academy of Management Journal*.

30. Influence Without Authority: The Use of Alliances, Reciprocity, and Exchange to Accomplish Work

Allan R. Cohen/David L. Bradford

Bill Heatton is the director of research at a $250 million division of a large West Coast company. The division manufactures exotic telecommunications components and has many technical advancements to its credit. During the past several years, however, the division's performance has been spotty at best; multimillion dollar losses have been experienced in some years despite many efforts to make the division more profitable. Several large contracts have resulted in major financial losses, and in each instance the various parts of the division blamed the others for the problems. Listen to Bill's frustration as he talks about his efforts to influence Ted, a colleague who is marketing director, and Roland, the program manager who reports to Ted.

> Another program is about to come through. Roland is a nice guy, but he knows nothing and never will. He was responsible for our last big loss, and now he's in charge of this one. I've tried to convince Ted, his boss, to get Roland off the program, but I get nowhere. Although Ted doesn't argue that Roland is capable, he doesn't act to find someone else. Instead, he comes to me with worries about my area.
>
> I decided to respond by changing my staffing plan, assigning to Roland's program the people they wanted. I had to override my staff's best judgment about who should be assigned. Yet I'm not getting needed progress reports from Roland, and he's never available for planning. I get little argument from him, but there's no action to correct the problem. That's bad because I'm responding but not getting any response.

> There's no way to resolve this. If they disagree, that's it. I could go to a tit-for-tat strategy, saying that if they don't do what I want, we'll get even with them next time. But I don't know how to do that without hurting the organization, which would feel worse than getting even!
>
> Ted, Roland's boss, is so much better than his predecessor that I hate to ask that he be removed. We could go together to our boss, the general manager, but I'm very reluctant to do that. You've failed in a matrix organization if you have to go to your boss. I have to try hard because I'd look bad if I had to throw it in his lap.
>
> Meanwhile, I'm being forceful, but I'm afraid it's in a destructive way. I don't want to wait until the program has failed to be told it was all my fault.

Bill is clearly angry and frustrated, leading him to behave in ways that he does not feel good about. Like other managers who very much want to influence an uncooperative co-worker whom they cannot control, Bill has begun to think of the intransigent employee as the enemy. Bill's anger is narrowing his sense of what is possible; he fantasizes revenge but is too dedicated to the organization to actually harm it. He is genuinely stuck.

Organizational members who want to make things happen often find themselves in this position. Irrespective of whether they are staff or line employees, professionals or managers, they find it increasingly necessary to influence colleagues and superiors. These critical others control needed resources, possess required information,

---

Allan R. Cohen and David L. Bradford, "Influence Without Authority: The Use of Alliances, Reciprocity, and Exchange to Accomplish Work," *Organizational Dynamics*, Winter 1989.

set priorities on important activities, and have to agree and cooperate if plans are to be implemented. They cannot be ordered around because they are under another area's control and can legitimately say no because they have many other valid priorities. They respond only when they choose to. Despite the clear need and appropriateness of what is being asked for (certainly as seen by the person who is making the request), compliance may not be forthcoming.

All of this places a large burden on organizational members, who are expected not only to take initiatives but also to respond intelligently to requests made of them by others. Judgment is needed to sort out the value of the many requests made of anyone who has valuable resources to contribute. As Robert Kaplan argued in his article "Trade Routes: The Manager's Network of Relationships" (*Organizational Dynamics*, Spring 1984), managers must now develop the organizational equivalent of "trade routes" to get things done. Informal networks of mutual influence are needed. In her book *The Change Masters* (Simon & Schuster, 1983) Rosabeth Moss Kanter showed that developing and implementing all kinds of innovations requires coalitions to be built to shape and support new ways of doing business.

A key current problem, then, is finding ways to develop mutual influence without the formal authority to command. A peer cannot "order" a colleague to change priorities, modify an approach, or implement a grand new idea. A staff member cannot "command" his or her supervisor to back a proposal, fight top management for greater resources, or allow more autonomy. Even Bill Heatton, in dealing with Roland (who was a level below him in the hierarchy but in another department), could not dictate that Roland provide the progress reports that Bill so desperately wanted.

EXCHANGE AND THE LAW OF RECIPROCITY

The way influence is acquired without formal authority is through the "law of reciprocity"—the almost universal belief that people should be paid back for what they do, that one good (or bad) deed deserves another. This belief is held by people in primitive and not-so-primitive societies all around the world, and it serves as the grease that allows the organizational wheels to turn smoothly. Because people expect that their actions will be paid back in one form or another, influence is possible.

In the case of Bill Heatton, his inability to get what he wanted from Roland and Ted stemmed from his failure to understand fully how reciprocity works in organizations. He therefore was unable to set up mutually beneficial exchanges. Bill believed that he had gone out of his way to help the marketing department by changing his staffing patterns, and he expected Roland to reciprocate by providing regular progress reports. When Roland failed to provide the reports, Bill believed that Ted was obligated to remove Roland from the project. When Ted did not respond, Bill became angry and wanted to retaliate. Thus Bill recognized the appropriateness of exchange in making organizations work. However, he did not understand how exchange operates.

Before exploring in detail how exchange can work in dealing with colleagues and superiors, it is important to recognize that reciprocity is the basic principle behind all organizational transactions. For example, the basic employment contract is an exchange ("an honest day's work for an honest day's pay"). Even work that is above and beyond what is formally required involves exchange. The person who helps out may not necessarily get (or expect) immediate payment for the extra effort requested, but some eventual compensation is expected.

Think of the likely irritation an employee would feel if his or her boss asked him or her to work through several weekends, never so much as said thanks, and then claimed credit for the extra work. The employee might not say anything the first time this happened, expecting or hoping that the boss would make it up somehow. However, if the effort were never acknowledged in any way, the employee, like most people, would feel that something important had been violated.

The expectation of reciprocal exchanges occurs between an employee and his or her supervisor, among peers, with higher-level managers in other parts of the organization, or all of the above. The exchange can be of tangible goods, such as a budget increase, new equipment, or more personnel; of tangible services, such as a faster response time, more information, or public support; or of sentiments, such as gratitude, admiration, or praise. Whatever form exchanges take, unless they are roughly equivalent over time, hard feelings will result.

Exchanges enable people to handle the give-and-take of working together without strong feelings of injustice arising. They are especially important during periods of rapid change because the number of requests that go far beyond the routine tends to escalate. In those situations, exchanges become less predictable, more free-floating and spontaneous. Nevertheless, people still expect that somehow or other, sooner or later, they will be (roughly) equally compensated for the acts they do above and beyond those that are covered by the formal exchange agreements in their job. Consequently, some kind of "currency" equivalent needs to be worked out, implicitly if not explicitly, to keep the parties in the exchange feeling fairly treated.

CURRENCIES: THE SOURCE OF INFLUENCE

If the basis of organizational influence depends on mutually satisfactory exchanges, then people are influential only insofar as they can offer something that others need. Thus power comes from the ability to meet others' needs.

A useful way to think of how the process of exchange actually works in organizations is to use the metaphor of "currencies." This metaphor provides a powerful way to conceptualize what is important to the influencer and the person to be influenced. Just as many types of currencies are traded in the world financial market, many types are "traded" in organizational life. Too often people think only of money

or promotion and status. Those "currencies," however, usually are available only to a manager in dealing with his or her employees. Peers who want to influence colleagues or employees who want to influence their supervisors often feel helpless. They need to recognize that many types of payments exist, broadening the range of what can be exchanged.

Some major currencies that are commonly valued and traded in organizations are listed in Table 30.1. Although not exhaustive, the list makes evident that a person does not have to be at the top of an organization or have hands on the formal levers of power to command multiple resources that other may value.

Part of the usefulness of currencies comes from their flexibility. For example, there are many ways to express gratitude and to give assistance. A manager who most values the currency of appreciation could be paid through verbal thanks, praise, a public statement at a meeting, informal comments to his peers, and/or a note to her boss. However, the same note of thanks seen by one person as a sign of appreciation may be seen by another person as an attempt to brownnose or by a third person as a cheap way to try to repay extensive favors and service. Thus currencies have value not in some abstract sense but as defined by the receiver.

Although we have stressed the interactive nature of exchange, "payments" do not always have to be made by the other person. They can be self-generated to fit beliefs about being virtuous, benevolent, or committed to the organization's welfare. Someone may respond to another person's request because it reinforces cherished values, a sense of identity, or feelings of self-worth. The exchange is interpersonally stimulated because the one who wants influence has set up conditions that allow this kind of self-payment to occur by asking for cooperation to accomplish organizational goals. However, the person who responds because "it is the right thing to do" and who feels good about being the "kind of person who does not act out of narrow self-interest" is printing currency (virtue) that is self-satisfying.

TABLE 30.1
Commonly Traded Organizational Currencies

Inspiration-Related Currencies	
Vision	Being involved in a task that has larger significance for the unit, organization, customers, or society.
Excellence	Having a chance to do important things really well.
Moral/Ethical Correctness	Doing what is "right" by a higher standard than efficiency.
Task-Related Currencies	
Resources	Lending or giving money, budget increases, personnel, space, and so forth.
Assistance	Helping with existing projects or undertaking unwanted tasks.
Cooperation	Giving task support, providing quicker response time, approving a project, or aiding implementation.
Information	Providing organizational as well as technical knowledge.
Position-Related Currencies	
Advancement	Giving a task or assignment that can aid in promotion.
Recognition	Acknowledging effort, accomplishment, or abilities.
Visibility	Providing chance to be known by higher-ups or significant others in the organization.
Reputation	Enhancing the way a person is seen.
Importance/Insiderness	Offering a sense of importance, of "belonging."
Network/Contacts	Providing opportunities for linking with others.
Relationship-Related Currencies	
Acceptance/Inclusion	Providing closeness and friendship.
Personal Support	Giving personal and emotional backing.
Understanding	Listening to others' concerns and issues.
Personal-Related Currencies	
Self-Concept	Affirming one's values, self-esteem, and identity.
Challenge/Learning	Sharing tasks that increase skills and abilities.
Ownership/Involvement	Letting others have ownership and influence.
Gratitude	Expressing appreciation or indebtedness.

Of course, the five categories of currencies listed in Table 30.1 are not mutually exclusive. When the demand from the other person is high, people are likely to pay in several currencies across several categories. They may, for example stress the organizational value of their request, promise to return the favor at a later time, imply that it will increase the other's prestige in the organization, and express their appreciation.

ESTABLISHING EXCHANGE RATES

What does it take to pay back in a currency that the other party in an exchange will perceive as equivalent? In impersonal markets, because everything is translated into a common monetary currency, it generally is easy to say what a fair payment is. Does a ton of steel equal a case of golf clubs? By translating both into dollar equivalents, a satisfactory deal can be worked out.

In interpersonal exchanges, however, the process becomes a bit more complicated. Just how does someone repay another person's willingness to help finish a report? Is a simple thank-you enough? Does it also require the recipient to say something nice about the helper to his or her boss? Whose standard of fairness should be used? What if one person's idea of fair repayment is very different from the other's?

Because of the natural differences in the way two parties can interpret the same activity, establishing exchanges that both parties will perceive as equitable can be problematic. Thus it is critical to understand what is important to the person to be influenced. Without a clear understanding of what that person experiences and values, it will be extremely difficult for anyone to thread a path through the minefield of creating mutually satisfactory exchanges.

Fortunately, the calibration of equivalent exchanges in the interpersonal and organizational worlds is facilitated by the fact that approximations will do in most cases. Occasionally, organizational members know exactly what they want in return for favors or help, but more often they will settle for very rough equivalents (providing that there is reasonable goodwill).

THE PROCESS OF EXCHANGE

To make the exchange process effective, the influencer needs to (1) think about the person to be influenced as a potential ally, not an adversary; (2) know the world of the potential ally, including the pressures as well as the person's needs and goals; (3) be aware of key goals and available resources that may be valued by the potential ally; and (4) understand the exchange transaction itself so that win-win outcomes are achieved. Each of these factors is discussed below.

Potential Ally, Not Adversary

A key to influence is thinking of the other person as a potential ally. Just as many contemporary organizations have discovered the importance of creating strategic alliances with suppliers and customers, employees who want influence within the organization need to create internal allies. Even though each party in an alliance continues to have freedom to pursue its own interests, the goal is to find areas of mutual benefit and develop trusting, sustainable relationships. Similarly, each person whose cooperation is needed inside the organization is a potential ally. Each still has self-interests to pursue, but those self-interests do not preclude searching for and building areas of mutual benefit.

Seeing other organizational members as potential allies decreases the chance that adversarial relationships will develop—an all-too-frequent result (as in the case of Bill Heatton) when the eager influencer does not quickly get the assistance or cooperation needed. Assuming that even a difficult person is a potential ally makes it easier to understand that person's world and thereby discover what that person values and needs.

The Potential Ally's World

We have stressed the importance of knowing the world of the potential ally. Without awareness of what the ally needs (what currencies are valued), attempts to influence that person can only be haphazard. Although this conclusion may seem self-evident, it is remarkable how often people attempt to influence without adequate information about what is important to the potential ally. Instead, they are driven by their own definition of "what should be" and "what is right" when they should be seeing the world from the other person's perspective.

For example, Bill Heatton never thought about the costs to Ted of removing Roland from the project. Did Ted believe he could coach Roland to perform better on this project? Did Ted even agree that Roland had done a poor job on the previous project, or did Ted think Roland had been hampered by other departments' shortcomings? Bill just did not know.

Several factors can keep the influencer from seeing the potential ally clearly. As with Bill Heatton, the frustration of meeting resistance from a potential ally can get in the way of really understanding the other person's world. The desire to influence is so strong that only the need for cooperation is visible to the influencer. As a result of not being understood, the potential ally digs in, making the influencer repeat an inappropriate strategy or back off in frustration.

When a potential ally's behavior is not understandable ("Why won't Roland send the needed progress report?"), the influencer tends to stereotype that person. If early attempts to influence do not work, the influencer is tempted to write the person off as negative, stubborn, selfish, or "just another bean counter/whiz kid/sales-type" or whatever pejorative label is used in that organizational culture to dismiss those organizational members who are different.

Although some stereotypes may have a grain of truth, they generally conceal more than they reveal. The actuary who understands that judgment, not just numbers, is needed to make decisions disappears as an individual when the stereotype of "impersonal, detached number machine" is the filter through which he or she is seen. Once the stereotype is applied, the frustrated influencer is no longer likely to see what currencies that particular potential ally actually values.

Sometimes, the lack of clear understanding about a potential ally stems from the influencer's failure to appreciate the organizational forces acting on the potential ally. To a great extent, a person's behavior is a result of the situation in which that person works (and not just his or her personality). Potential allies are embedded in an organizational culture that shapes their interests and responses. For example, one of the key determinants of anyone's behavior is likely to be the way the person's performance is measured and rewarded. In many instances, what is mistaken for personal orneriness is merely the result of the person's doing something that will be seen as good performance in his or her function.

The salesperson who is furious because the plant manager resists changing priorities for a rush order may not realize that part of the plant manager's bonus depends on holding unit costs down—a task made easier with long production runs. The plant manager's resistance does not necessarily reflect his or her inability to be flexible or lack of concern about pleasing customers or about the company's overall success.

Other organizational forces that can affect the potential ally's behavior include the daily time demands on that person's position; the amount of contact the person has with customers, suppliers, and other outsiders, the organization's information flow (or lack of it); the style of the potential ally's boss; the belief and assumptions held by that person's co-workers; and so forth. Although some of these factors cannot be changed by the influencer, understanding them can be useful in figuring out how to frame and time requests. It also helps the influencer resist the temptation to stereotype the noncooperator.

Self-Awareness of the Influencer

Unfortunately, people desiring influence are not always aware of precisely what they want. Often their requests contain a cluster of needs (a certain product, arranged in a certain way, delivered at a specified time). They fail to think through which aspects are more important and which can be jettisoned if necessary. Did Bill Heatton want Roland removed, or did he want the project effectively managed? Did he want overt concessions from Ted, or did he want better progress reports?

Further, there is a tendency to confuse and intermingle the desired end goal with the means of accomplishing it, leading to too many battles over the wrong things. In *The Change Masters*, Kanter reported that successful influencers in organizations were those who never lost sight of the ultimate objective but were willing to be flexible about means.

Sometimes influencers underestimate the range of currencies available for use. They may assume, for example, that just because they are low in the organization they have nothing that others want. Employees who want to influence their boss are especially likely not to realize all of the supervisor's needs that they can fulfill. They become so caught up with their feelings of powerlessness that they fail to see the many ways they can generate valuable currencies.

In other instances, influencers fail to be aware of their preferred style of interaction and its fit with the potential ally's preferred style. Everyone has a way of relating to others to get work done. However, like the fish who is unaware of the water, many people are oblivious of their own style of interaction or see it as the only way to be. Yet interaction style can cause problems with potential allies who are different.

For example, does the influencer tend to socialize first and work later? If so, that style of interaction will distress a potential ally who likes to dig right in to solve the problem at hand and only afterward chat about sports, family, or office politics. Does the potential ally want to be approached with answers, not problems? If so, a tendency to start influence attempts with open-ended, exploratory problem solving can lead to rejection despite good intentions.

Nature of the Exchange Transaction

Many of the problems that occur in the actual exchange negotiation have their roots in the failure to deal adequately with the first three factors outlined above. Failure to treat other people as potential allies, to understand a potential ally's world, and to be self-aware are all factors that interfere with successful exchange. In addition, some special problems commonly arise when both parties are in the process of working out a mutually satisfactory exchange agreement.

Not Knowing How to Use Reciprocity.
Using reciprocity requires stating needs clearly without "crying wolf," being aware of the needs of an ally without being manipulative, and seeking mutual gain rather than playing "winner takes all." One trap that Bill Heatton fell into was not being able to

"close on the exchange." That is, he assumed that if he acted in good faith and did his part, others would automatically reciprocate. Part of his failure was not understanding the other party's world; another part was not being able to negotiate clearly with Ted about what each of them wanted. It is not even clear that Ted realized Bill was altering his organization as per Ted's requests, that Ted got what he wanted, or that Ted knew Bill intended an exchange of responses.

Preferring to Be Right Rather than Effective.
This problem is especially endemic to professionals of all kinds. Because of their dedication to the "truth" (as their profession defines it), they stubbornly stick to their one right way when trying to line up potential allies instead of thinking about what will work given the audience and conditions. Organizational members with strong technical backgrounds often chorus the equivalent of "I'll be damned if I'm going to sell out and become a phony salesman, trying to get by on a shoeshine and smile." The failure to accommodate to the potential ally's needs and desires often kills otherwise sound ideas.

Overusing What Has Been Successful.
When people find that a certain approach is effective in many situations, they often begin to use it in places where it does not fit. By overusing the approach, they block more appropriate methods. Just as a weight lifter becomes muscle-bound from overdeveloping particular muscles at the expense of others, people who have been reasonably successful at influencing other people can diminish that ability by overusing the same technique.

For example, John Brucker, the human resources director at a medium-size company, often cultivated support for new programs by taking people out to fancy restaurants for an evening of fine food and wine. He genuinely derived pleasure from entertaining, but at the same time he created subtle obligations. One time, a new program he wanted to introduce required the agreement of William Adams, head of engineering. Adams, an old-timer, perceived Brucker's proposal as an unnecessary frill, mainly because he did not perceive the real benefits to the overall organization. Brucker responded to Adams's negative comments as he always did in such cases—by becoming more friendly and insisting that they get together for dinner soon. After several of these invitations, Adams became furious. Insulted by what he considered to be Brucker's attempts to buy him off, he fought even harder to kill the proposal. Not only did the program die, but Brucker lost all possibility of influencing Adams in the future. Adams saw Brucker's attempts at socializing as a sleazy and crude way of trying to soften him up. For his part, Brucker was totally puzzled by Adams's frostiness and assumed that he was against all progress. He never realized that Adams had a deep sense of integrity and a real commitment to the good of the organization. Thus Brucker lost his opportunity to sell a program that, ironically, Adams would have found valuable had it been implemented.

As the case above illustrates, a broad repertoire of influence approaches is needed in modern organizations. Johnny-one-notes soon fall flat.

THE ROLE OF RELATIONSHIPS

All of the preceding discussion needs to be conditioned by one important variable: the nature of the relationship between both parties. The greater the extent to which the influencer has worked with the potential ally and created trust, the easier the exchange process will be. Each party will know the other's desired currencies and situational pressures, and each will have developed a mutually productive interaction style. With trust, less energy will be spent on figuring out the intentions of the ally, and there will be less suspicion about when and how the payback will occur.

A poor relationship (based on previous interactions, on the reputation each party has in the organization, and/or on stereotypes and animosities between the functions or departments that each party represents) will impede an otherwise easy exchange. Distrust of the goodwill, veracity, or reliability of the influencer can lead to the demand for "no credit; cash up front," which constrains the flexibility of both parties.

The nature of the interaction during the influencer process also affects the nature of the relationship between the influencer and the other party. The way that John Brucker attempted to relate to William Adams not only did not work but also irreparably damaged any future exchanges between them.

Few transactions within organizations are one-time deals. (Who knows when the other person may be needed again or even who may be working for him or her in the future?) Thus in most exchange situations two outcomes matter: success in achieving task goals and success in improving the relationship so that the next interaction will be even more productive. Too often, people who want to be influential focus only on the task and act as if there is no tomorrow. Although both task accomplishment and an improved relationship cannot always be realized at the same time, on some occasions the latter can be more important than the former. Winning the battle but losing the war is an expensive outcome.

INCONVERTIBLE CURRENCIES

We have spelled out ways organizational members operate to gain influence for achieving organizational goals. By effectively using exchange, organizational members can achieve their goals and at the same time help others achieve theirs. Exchange permits organizational members to be assertive without being antagonistic by keeping mutual benefit a central outcome.

In many cases, organizational members fail to acquire desired influence because they do not use all of their potential power. However, they sometimes fail because not all situations are amenable to even the best efforts at influencing. Not everything can be translated into compatible currencies. If there are fundamental differences in what is valued by two parties, it may not be possible to find common ground, as illustrated in the example below.

The founder and chairman of a high-technology company and the president he had hired five years previously were constantly displeased with one another. The president was committed to creating maximum shareholder value, the currency he valued most as a result of his M.B.A. training, his position, and his temperament. Accordingly, he had concluded that the company was in a perfect position to cash in by squeezing expenses to maximize profits and going public. He could see that the company's product line of exotic components was within a few years of saturating its market and would require massive, risky investment to move to sophisticated end-user products.

The president could not influence the chairman to adopt this direction, however, because the chairman valued a totally different currency, the fun of technological challenge. An independently wealthy man, the chairman had no interest in realizing the $10 million or so he would get if the company maximized profits by cutting research and selling out. He wanted a place to test his intuitive, creative research hunches, not a source of income.

Thus the president's and chairman's currencies were not convertible into one another at an acceptable exchange rate. After they explored various possibilities but failed to find common ground, they mutually agreed that the president should leave—on good terms and only after a more compatible replacement could be found. Although this example acknowledges that influence through alliance, currency conversion, and exchange is not always possible, it is hard to be certain that any situation is hopeless until the person desiring influence has fully applied all of the diagnostic and interpersonal skills we have described.

Influence is enhanced by using the model of strategic alliances to engage in mutually beneficial exchanges with potential allies. Even though it is not always possible to be successful, the chances of achieving success can be greatly increased. In a period of rapid competitive, technological, regulative, and consumer change, individuals and their organizations need all the help they can get.

SELECTED BIBLIOGRAPHY

Some of the classic work on exchange as a process of influence was done by Peter Blau. His book *The Dynamics of Bureaucracy* (University of Chicago Press, 1963) was a landmark study of how tax assessors traded gratitude for expert assistance. When exchange is added to notions about the universality of reciprocity, as outlined by Alvin Gouldner in his pioneering article "The Norm of Reciprocity: A Preliminary Statement" (*American Sociological Review*, 25, 1960), a powerful way of thinking about influence is created.

David Berlew picked up on these ideas and wrote an interesting piece addressed to people who want more influence: "What You Can Do When Persuasion Doesn't Work" (*NTL Connection*, 1986). He discussed three types of exchange that can be used by those attempting to get things done.

The case for managers needing to build alliances in order to accomplish work was made by Robert Kaplan in his article "Trade Routes: The Manager's Network of Relationships" (*Organization Dynamics*, 1984). John Kotter found in his study of successful general managers (*The General Managers*, Free Press, 1982) that they had wide networks of contacts in their organizations, which helped them find the right person(s) when trying to make things happen. Rosabeth Moss Kanter's *The Change Masters* (Simon & Schuster, 1983) is the best examination of the ways organization members go about achieving major innovations through alliances. It shows the steps that innovative members go through, including the many ways they use influence to build coalitions and overcome resistance. We have built on her work by looking with a microscope at the mechanisms behind the processes she describes.

Other researchers have explored influence processes from many angles. David Kipnis and his collaborators found that they can categorize influence styles along seven dimensions. In "Patterns of Managerial Influence: Shotgun Managers, Tacticians, and Bystanders" (*Organizational Dynamics*, 1984), they identify the problem of managers who lack organizational power (and by implication what to do about it) and therefore give up attempting to influence. John Kotter addressed ways of increasing influence in *Power in Management: How to Understand, Acquire and Use It* (AMACOM, 1979). He shows the advantages and disadvantages of different methods.

Our own book *Managing for Excellence: The Guide to High Performance in Contemporary Organizations* (John Wiley & Sons, 1984) addresses influence downward by arguing that shared responsibility is needed with subordinates in order to get the best from them and that treating them as full partners in the unit's management is necessary even though formal authority rests with the manager. We also show that mutual influence is needed to allow both parties to use their full strength. These ideas translate directly into lessons for influence when formal authority is lacking.

Finally, the literature of negotiations has many applications for using exchange for influence. Although there are popular books on negotiating that overlook important issues of trust when relationships are ongoing within the same organization, there is much to be learned from applying negotiating insights. Roger Fisher's and William Ury's book *Getting to Yes* (Houghton Mifflin, 1981) is helpful on ways to approach someone to look for common interests despite having differing specific objectives. An excellent overview of the issues involved in any kind of negotiation can be found in Roy Lewicki and Joseph Litterer's test *Negotiation* (R. D. Irwin, 1985). Their discussion of exchange and equity is particularly relevant to influence as we have described it. In addition, Roy Lewicki's comments on an earlier draft of this article were particularly helpful, and we are grateful for his wisdom and generosity.

31. Who Tempered Radicals Are and What They Do

Debra Meyerson

tempered\\'tem-perd\\adj 1 a: having the elements mixed in satisfying proportions: TEMPER-
ATE b: qualified, lessened, or diluted by the mix-
ture or influence of an additional ingredient:
MODERATED

radical\\ra-di-kel\\adj 1: of, relating to, or proceeding from a root . . . 2: of or relating to the
origin: FUNDAMENTAL 3 a: marked by a considerable departure from the usual or traditional:
EXTREME 4 b: tending or disposed to make
extreme changes in existing views, habits, conditions, or institutions[1]

Martha Wiley sits in her tenth-floor office in a
prestigious high-rise building in downtown
Seattle. Decorated with earth-tone sofa and
chair, overgrown ivies, and floor-to-ceiling ficus
tree, her office looks as if she has inhabited it for
years. Traditional management books line her
bookshelves, interrupted only by a few recog-
nizable volumes on women and management, a
stone abstract carving of a woman and child,
and a half-dozen silver-framed pictures of her
two children and husband. Neatly stacked piles
of paper cover her desk, suggesting that an
orderly and busy executive sits behind it.
Only running shoes and sweats in the corner
disrupt the traditional mood of this office.

At 44, Martha has spent the past ten years
working her way up to her current position as
senior vice president and highest-ranking
woman in the real estate division of Western
Financial. She shows no sign of slowing down.
From the time Martha walked into her office at
7:00 A.M. until this last meeting of the day at
5:30 P.M., she has sprinted from one meeting to
the next, stopping only for a one-hour midday
workout. This last meeting, before she rushes

home to relieve her nanny, was requested by
one of her most valued employees to talk about
"the future." Her employee nervously explains
that since returning from maternity leave with
her second child, she has found it increasingly
difficult to be in the office five long days each
week. She needs to find an alternative way to
continue performing her job.

After thirty minutes, the two women agree
to a plan: The employee will work two days from
home and three days in the office, and every
other week she will take one day off. Martha's
only request is that the employee remain flexible
and be willing to come into the office when it is
absolutely necessary for her work.

Martha is pleased that she can meet this
employee's needs. In fact, she has actively
looked for opportunities to initiate changes that
accommodate working parents and that make
her department more hospitable to women and
people of color. A full 30 percent of her staff now
have some sort of flexible work arrangement,
despite a lack of formal policy to guide these
initiatives. Martha has little doubt that her
experiments in work arrangements, even
though she has kept them quiet, have been
slowly paving the way for broader changes at
Western. She had heard that word of her
successes was spreading, and that it was only a
matter of time before the institution caught up to
her lead. (Eventually, the organization did
initiate some policies that have given employees
more flexibility in arranging their work
schedules.)

This example is typical of Martha's
approach to change at Western. Though her
agenda for change is bold—she wants nothing

less than to make the workplace more just and humane—her method of change is modest and incremental. Martha constantly negotiates the path between her desire to succeed within the system and her commitment to challenge and change it; she navigates the tension between her desire to fit in and her commitment to act on personal values that often set her apart. As a result, she continues to find ways to rock the boat, but not so hard that she falls out of it.

All types of organizations—from global corporations to small neighborhood schools—have Marthas. They occupy all sorts of jobs and stand up for a variety of ideals. They engage in small local battles rather than wage dramatic wars, at times operating so quietly that they may not surface on the cultural radar as rebels or change agents. But these men and women of all colors and creeds are slowly and steadily pushing back on conventions, creating opportunities for learning, and inspiring change within their organizations.

Sometimes these individuals pave alternative roads just by quietly speaking up for their personal truths or by refusing to silence aspects of themselves that make them different from the majority. Other times they act more deliberately to change the way the organization does things. They are not heroic leaders of revolutionary change; rather, they are cautious and committed catalysts who keep going and who slowly make a difference. They are "tempered radicals."[2]

COMPETING PULLS

Tempered radicals are people who operate on a fault line. They are organizational insiders who contribute and succeed in their jobs. At the same time, they are treated as outsiders because they represent ideals or agendas that are somehow at odds with the dominant culture.[3]

People operate as tempered radicals for all sorts of reasons. To varying extents, they feel misaligned with the dominant culture because their social identities—race, gender, sexual orientation, age, for example—or their values and beliefs mark them as different from the organizational majority. A tempered radical may, for example, be an African American woman trying to make her company more hospitable to others like herself. Or he may be a white man who holds beliefs about the importance of humane and family-friendly working conditions—or someone concerned for social justice, human creativity, environmental sustainability, or fair global trade practices that differ from the dominant culture's values and interests.

In all cases they struggle between their desire to act on their "different" selves and the need to fit into the dominant culture. Tempered radicals at once uphold their aspiration to be accepted insiders and their commitment to change the very system that often casts them as outsiders. As Sharon Sutton, an African American architect, has explained, "We use our right hand to pry open the box so that more of us can get into it while using our left hand to be rid of the very box we are trying to get into."[4]

Tempered radicals are therefore constantly pulled in opposing directions: toward conformity and toward rebellion. And this tension almost always makes them feel ambivalent toward their organizations.* This ambivalence is not uncommon. Psychologists have found that people regularly feel ambivalent about their social relations, particularly toward institutions and people who constrain their freedom. Children, for example, regularly hold strong opposing feelings, such as love and hate, towards their parents.[5] Sociologists have observed a comparable response in employees toward their organizations. They frequently counter organizational attempts to induce conformity and define their identities with efforts to express their individuality.[6] People

---

* Though this is a pervasive state, it is nonetheless a simplification that people are pulled only in two directions. The nature of the "self" is complex and people are pulled in multiple directions. Here, I emphasize this general stance that results from two types of pulls that are at odds with each other. Later, we discuss the specific content of the pulls toward difference and ways people respond to them.

who differ from the majority are the most likely targets of organizational pressures toward conformity, and at the same time they have the greatest reason to resist them.

A RANGE OF RESPONSES

If ambivalence is the psychological reaction to being pulled in opposing directions, how does it lead people to behave? Some people make a clear choice, relieving their ambivalence by moving clearly in one direction or the other.[7] Others become paralyzed and ultimately so frustrated that escaping the situation is their only relief. Some people flame out in anger. They grow to feel unjustly marginalized and focus on how to avenge perceived wrongs. They feel victimized by their situation and ultimately come to be at the mercy of their own rage. While the pain and anger are often justified, they can become debilitating.

Tempered radicals set themselves apart by successfully navigating a middle ground. They recognize modest and doable choices in between, such as choosing their battles, creating pockets of learning, and making way for small wins.

Tempered radicals also become angry, but they mitigate their anger and use it to fuel their actions. In the world of physics, when something is "tempered" it is toughened by alternately heating and cooling. Tempered steel, for example, becomes stronger and more useful through such a process. In a similar way, successfully navigating the seemingly incongruous extremes of challenging and upholding the status quo can help build the strength and organizational significance of tempered radicals.[8]

Note, though, that *tempered* radicals are not radicals. The distinction is important. The word *radical* has several meanings: "of, relating to, or proceeding from a root," or fundamental, as well as "marked by a considerable departure from the usual or traditional," or extreme.[9] Tempered radicals may believe in questioning fundamental principles (e.g., how to allocate resources) or root assumptions, but they do not advocate extreme measures. They work *within* systems, not against them.

Martha, for example, could stridently protest her firm's employment policies or could take a job within an activist organization and advocate for legalistic remedies to the inequities she perceives. But she has chosen the tempered path, in part because she believes that she can personally make more of a difference by working within the system. Her success has created a platform from which to make changes—often seemingly small and almost invisible—which over time have the potential to affect many people.

Martha also has chosen her course because she likes it. She is quick to admit that she loves her job, takes pride and pleasure in moving up the corporate ladder, and enjoys the status and spoils of her success. She likes living in a comfortable home and taking summer vacations in Europe. While Martha clearly enjoys the privileges that come with success, she believes that the criteria by which the system distributes these privileges need to be changed. Does this belief make her a hypocrite? Or does it simply speak to a duality she and other tempered radicals constantly straddle?

A SPECTRUM OF STRATEGIES

Martha makes choices every day, some conscious, some not, in order to strike a balance. She is committed to chipping away at her "radical" agenda, but not so boldly as to threaten her own legitimacy and organizational success. What is the right balance to strike? More generally, how do tempered radicals navigate the often murky organizational waters to pursue their ideals while fitting in enough to succeed? How do they successfully rock the organizational boat without falling out?

These questions drove my research and form the heart of this book. Not surprisingly, there is no single formula for finding a successful course. Rather, tempered radicals draw on a wide variety of strategies to put their ideals into practice, some more forceful and open, others subtler and less threatening. By choosing among these strategies, each tempered radical creates the balance that is appropriate for him or her in a given situation.

Figure 31.1 presents a spectrum of strategies. It is anchored on the left side by a collection of strategies I have labeled "resisting quietly and staying true to one's 'self,'" which includes acts that quietly express people's "different" selves and acts that are so subtle that they are often not visible to those they would threaten. The other end of the spectrum, "organizing collective action," reflects actions people take to get others involved in deliberate efforts to advance change. Martha's initiatives around flexible work arrangements and similar strategies fall in the category of "leveraging small wins," between the two endpoints.[10]

The spectrum varies along two primary dimensions. First, it speaks to the immediate scope of impact of a tempered radical's actions. At the far left, only the individual actor and a few people in his or her immediate presence are likely to be directly affected by the action. At the opposite end of the spectrum, tempered radicals' actions are meant to provoke broader learning and change. At the far left, the action is invisible or nearly so and therefore provokes little opposition; at the far right, the action is very public and is more likely to encounter resistance.

The second overlapping dimension is the intent underlying a person's actions. At the left, people primarily strive to preserve their "different" selves. Many of these people who operate quietly are not trying to drive broad-based change; they simply want to be themselves and

act on their values within an environment where that may feel difficult. Others who resist quietly do intend to provoke some change, but they do it from so far behind the scenes that the actions are not visible. At the right end of the spectrum, people are motivated by their desire to advance broader organizational learning and change. In reality, of course, no one person sits on a specific point on the spectrum, and the strategies themselves blur and overlap. I've distinguished them for the purpose of contrast, rather than to suggest that they reflect distinct responses. A few examples may help bring this spectrum to life.

Sheila Johnson is a black woman from a working-class family. She has worked her way up to senior vice president in the private equity division at Western Financial. Even though she is one of only a handful of black women in Western's professional ranks, she thought that she would have a reasonable chance of succeeding here because of Western's stated commitment to "diversity." Sheila has tried over the years to keep a low profile, but when she has a chance to help other minorities, or when she feels she must speak up, she usually does so.

Sheila recalls a period when her division's human resource manager complained about the inability to find and hire "qualified minorities" at every level. She knew that standard recruiting procedures at elite college and graduate schools did not constitute the kind of pipeline that would bring in enough diverse candidates to change the face of Western. So she took it upon herself to post descriptions of entry-level

FIGURE 31.1
How Tempered Radicals Make a Difference

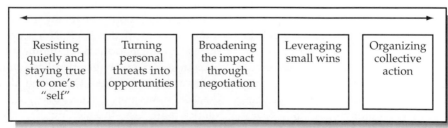

| Resisting quietly and staying true to one's "self" | Turning personal threats into opportunities | Broadening the impact through negotiation | Leveraging small wins | Organizing collective action |

jobs throughout minority communities. She did not call attention to her intervention—she didn't ask for permission or insist that the practice become recruiting policy. But through her quiet efforts, she helped create a more diverse pool of candidates, many of whom were hired into entry-level jobs.

Sheila could have broadened the impact of her actions by talking openly about them to enable others to recognize why their standard recruiting practices had failed to fill the bill. Had she made this link clear, she would have pushed others to learn from her actions, which might have led to additional adaptations. Although taking these additional steps could have broadened the impact of her actions, Sheila probably would have had to overcome opposition and assume a potentially greater risk. Because she undertook her actions so quietly, and outside the scope of the organization, I see her behind-the-scenes efforts as an example of "quiet resistance."

John Ziwak is a tempered radical of a different sort. On the surface, he seems to have little in common with Sheila. John has enjoyed all the privileges of growing up in a white middle-class family. He attended an elite university, went to business school at a branch of the University of California, and landed a plum job at a local high-technology company. Six years later, now married with two children, John accepted his current post as manager of business development at Atlas Tech. Although he wants to continue to rise within Atlas, he has no intention of shirking his duties as parent and partner. He can't. His wife also works in a demanding career, and they have always shared responsibilities—and plan to continue.

But it isn't that easy. John, like his wife, faces ongoing pressure from his organization to choose between his commitment to his work and his commitment to his family. John doesn't think that this choice is reasonable; he doesn't believe that he should have to give up his duties at home to prove his commitment and to succeed at Atlas. So in both big and small ways he resists pressure to make such choices and, when appropriate, he challenges prevailing expectations.

One morning John's boss told him that he needed to get on that night's red-eye flight to New York to meet with an important candidate for acquisition. His wife was already out of town and he did not want to ask the babysitter to stay overnight, so he told his boss that he couldn't go: "I told him that I was sorry I would miss this meeting because I would have brought a lot to the discussion." At the same time, John made sure to point out that he usually can travel, but that he needs some advance notice owing to his wife's travel schedule. John hoped that his boss would understand the broader implications of his resistance—that only a subset of employees can be available on such short notice and that the boss's expectations penalize those who can't pick up and go at the last minute. Whether the boss understood the bigger issue or not, he did begin to give John advance notice about travel whenever possible.

John's act was not dramatic or proactive. A normal reaction in a normal encounter between himself and his boss, it illustrates the strategy I have called "turning threats into opportunities." In this instance, John turned an immediate threat to his personal values and priorities—a request to meet organizational expectations that clash with personal values—into an opportunity for learning. Though John cannot tell how much his boss actually learned, he thinks he made at least a start.

The actions taken by John, Sheila, and Martha fall at different points on the spectrum shown in Figure 31.1. On another day, any one of them might take another action that might fall elsewhere on the spectrum, depending on the opportunity, the situation, the importance of the issue to them, and—as Sheila admitted— "how much sleep [I] had on a given day." Though the actions of some tempered radicals tend toward one end of the spectrum versus the other, most take different actions at different times. It is important to understand that *the spectrum represents different strategies for acting, not different types of people.*

The spectrum does not imply that the quiet responses on the left are in any way less important than those on the right. As we will see, a lifetime of quiet resistance can require enormous patience, conviction, and fortitude. And sometimes persistent behind-the-scenes actions cumulate over time for lasting change or set the context for more public and revolutionary acts.

GUIDING MODELS

Tempered radicals face two primary sets of challenges: those related to the preservation of their "selves" and those that involve advancing an agenda for change from within. Given the centrality of these themes, I want to make explicit my assumptions about how organizations change, the nature of the "self," and how the two are connected through action. These ideas are supported by my own research and guided by the research of others.

How Organizations Change

My "theory" of change begins with the notion that organizations are always changing, continually adapting in response to an ongoing flow of inputs and activities.[11] Since most changes are small, incremental adaptations scattered throughout organizations, it may be difficult to recognize this movement as *change*, except retrospectively when small effects have had time to accumulate. In addition, because this process is diffuse, specific *causes* of change are often difficult to pinpoint. Indeed, the change process looks more like random events and chaos than it does rational cause–effect sequences.

Here's an example of the difficulty of pointing to the source of change: Four years after my first interview at Western, a senior human resources officer explained that during the previous five years, the culture had shifted dramatically to be more hospitable to working parents. Whereas once a 5:30 P.M. staff meeting would have been the norm, now it would be seen as completely inappropriate to schedule meetings that late. She was at a loss to point to

the specific cause of this shift. The change evolved, she concluded, because many employees, over a period of years, pushed back on the old expectations and set examples for new ones.

This image of change as a continuous and fragmented process bears little resemblance to portraits of episodic and revolutionary change processes you read in many best-selling management texts. These more dramatic pictures of transformation see organizational change occurring not continuously, but periodically as a result of specific trigger events, such as crises, technological innovations, top-down strategic mandates, or bottom-up revolutions. These moments of large-scale transformation are the "figure" against the "ground" of periods of stability.[12] While I do not deny the significance of the occasional crisis, technological innovation, or dramatic intervention, there is significant evidence that such events do not drive much of the adaptation that occurs in organizations.[13]

Many mundane processes that play a part in incremental adaptation disappear as organizational noise if we think of organizational change strictly as episodic and revolutionary. If, however, we look at change as emergent and ongoing, little prods like Sheila's recruiting efforts, which redirect organizational momentum slightly, suddenly appear as significant catalysts of adaptation. So too are small, local accommodations that accumulate into something bigger, such as Martha's flexible work initiative. Interpretation and learning are also pivotal components of this adaptive change process. As people understand things differently, they act differently, and different actions inspire more change.

This view of organizational and social change makes room for lots of normal people to effect change in the course of their everyday actions and interactions. It is an inclusive model that sees people on the margin as well as the center making a difference in a wide variety of ways. Change agents are not just those characterized by bold visions and strategic savvy, but also those characterized by patience, persistence, and resourcefulness. In this model, change agents are sensitive improvisers who are able to recognize and act on opportunities as they arise.

This view of change and change agents is less dramatic, less inspiring, and less breathless than portraits of grand transformation and revolutionary leaders. It is also more inclusive, more realistic, and more hopeful for most people who care to make a difference in their worlds. I believe it is also more reflective of how most real and lasting change occurs.

The "Self"

My assumptions about the "self" also follow from theories that emphasize fluidity. I begin with the notion that who we are—our "selves"—is at the same time stable and mutable.[14] Some aspects of our core identities remain relatively stable, and other, more mercurial aspects are highly sensitive to social cues.[15] For example, some people may want to downplay a part of their identities, but if colleagues see and reinforce those aspects of their identities, they will be compelled to acknowledge these aspects of themselves more explicitly.[16] High-level women who want to ignore their gender identity, for example, are often forced by others who interact with them *as women* to acknowledge and address this aspect of themselves. The reverse is also true. Say an individual defines his religion as a core part of his identity. If, however, others challenge or criticize him when he acts on his faith by, say, reading the Bible in public or praying in a group setting or even talking about being a regular churchgoer, he may be less inclined to express that part of his "self" explicitly in the future. In this context, he may completely suppress it.

Thus the "self" is not immune to external cues; it is built and sustained in relationships with others. Accordingly, both sides of a tempered radical's competing "selves" develop in interactions with others. Since work life tends to be full of relationships that enforce the part of the "self" that identifies with the majority culture, the social cues that lure the "self"

toward conformity are strong. It is crucial, then, for people to interact with people inside and outside their organizations who affirm the nonconforming parts of their "selves." These relationships help keep their threatened identities alive.

Action, the "Self," and Change

So what is the connection between people's "selves" and the outcomes of organizational learning and change? One piece, as I mentioned earlier, is that asserting the nonconforming aspects of oneself can pave the way for learning and change by questioning current practice and expectations and providing an alternative.

This dynamic can also be self-reinforcing. When people act in ways that outwardly express a valued part of their selves, they make that part of their selves "real." The act of putting this part of themselves out in the world for affirmation and challenge often reminds them, and others, that they will not silence these valued parts of their selves and that they will not allow the dominant culture to define who they are. Not only is action driven by people's valued selves, but it helps construct and fortify those selves.

Actions produce other consequences as well. When people act on their different selves, they make it possible for others who share their social identities and values to find each other. When environmentalists do something *as environmentalists*, for instance, they become visible to other environmentalists. Gay people report that once they come out of the closet, they suddenly discover dozens of other coworkers who are gay. In this way, people's actions have the unintended effect of creating relationships with similar others, thus making the context more friendly.

Actions can also bolster people's sense of efficacy, proving to themselves and to others that they can make a difference, even if the direct consequences of their actions are small.[17] When people believe they can make a difference, they are more likely to search for opportunities to act, which makes it more likely that they will locate opportunities. When people recognize opportunities for action, their environment will seem less threatening and more amenable to action.[18]

This self-fulfilling cycle suggests the crucial importance of *action* as a starting point and trigger for a wide range of outcomes. Actions help develop sustaining relationships with similar others, affirm threatened "selves," generate organizational learning and change, fuel a sense of efficacy, and heighten attention to opportunities. The first and last of these create a context more amenable to action.[19] (See Figure 31.2.) While most people talk about action being driven by people who see themselves as change agents, I've observed how the reverse is true—and very powerful; actions transform people from the stance of passive bystander or victim to that of constructive agent.

WHY PEOPLE ACT AS TEMPERED RADICALS

Why do people bother to navigate such a difficult maze of conformity and rebellion? Why might you want to do so? Given the multitude of organizational processes that steer people toward conformity, wouldn't it be easier to go along, at least until you have "enough" power to make "real" change without jeopardizing your job? Challenging the status quo can be very risky, which puts an extra burden on tempered radicals to perform well in their jobs. Wouldn't it be simpler to find an organization

where all parts of your core "self" are valued, where you don't face extra pressures? It certainly is not easy to act in ways that keep these competing selves alive, nor is it comfortable psychologically to remain in an ongoing state of ambivalence. So why do people take this path?

The most straightforward answer is that they don't like the alternatives. While the lures toward conformity can be overwhelming in some contexts, for some people this route is unacceptably demoralizing and draining. If they conform completely, they essentially silence a core part of their selves. Some people feel that they are "selling out" on their values and turning their backs on their communities. This route can also enervate people, as they come to see themselves as victims of their situations. For many of the tempered radicals I interviewed, complete conformity was not an option.

A person could also stay consistently true to his or her self, and simply start fresh when the friction gets too great to bear or when he or she is forced from the organization. But most people have neither the desire nor the luxury to risk the alienation (and displacement) that would likely result. Those who end in this direction don't survive in conventional organizations; they are often the ones better suited to the role of pure radical, advocating from outside the organization, from a position closer to their ideals.

With these alternatives, we might ask the opposite question: Why aren't more people

FIGURE 31.2
The Action Cycle: How Action Transforms Self and Others

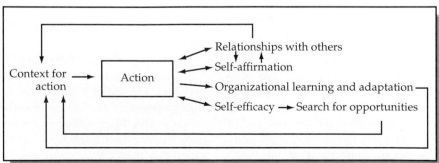

tempered radicals? The obvious answer, as I mentioned earlier, is that it creates a difficult ambivalence to tolerate and manage. And for many, the rewards of conformity—combined with the risk of exclusion—are too great to pass up. While this simple answer is undoubtedly true, I suggest that in fact *many people are tempered radicals and just don't realize it*. They struggle silently with their ambivalence, reluctant to acknowledge it and uncertain how they might make it work better for themselves and constructively for their organizations.

Fortunately, when people do act on their convictions, they set in motion a powerful cycle (see Figure 31.2) and make a start at managing the ambiguity of their situations. Even small acts can have far-reaching effects, affirming an actor's sense of self, fueling their sense of efficacy, and making a difference for others.

TEMPERED RADICALS AS EVERYDAY LEADERS

Few of the tempered radicals mentioned in these pages see themselves as heroes or champions of organizational revolutions. They often are not the CEOs, presidents, or senior professionals in their organizations, and yet they sometimes play a role in organizational adaptation as crucial as that of their colleagues with more authority. They have become the "everyday leaders" in their organizations, often unrecognized but nevertheless essential agents of organizational learning and change.

When these individuals push back on conventional expectations, challenge assumptions about what is "normal," and revise work practices to meet unaddressed needs, they push others to learn and force systems to adapt to impending challenges. Martha's initiatives, for example, have responded to the needs of certain employees who cannot continue to work effectively in traditional, full-time work arrangements. As word of her successes has spread, the organization has been challenged to confront this issue in a more systemic way. John's push back on his boss' expectations about travel brought into focus entrenched practices and

assumptions that inadvertently penalized certain groups of employees and made them less effective at work. Sheila's efforts to hire from the community addressed an immediate recruiting challenge her group was facing. Had she intervened more visibly, she could have pointed to the limitations of the organizationally endorsed approach to recruiting. To different extents, each of these relatively small actions took steps toward surfacing and addressing an important adaptive challenge facing the system.[20]

Tempered radicals also provoke learning and adaptation through the perspective they bring as people who are not fully assimilated into the system. Tempered radicals are more likely to think "out of the box" because they are not fully in the box. As "outsiders within," they have both a critical and a creative edge.[21] They speak new "truths."

For example, someone concerned about environmental sustainability probably has a different view of time than others, seeing the long-term effects of current actions. That person thus brings an entirely new set of perspectives, asks different questions, and might pose different solutions to problems such as urban growth and development. In the film industry, we have the example of Robert Redford, who is both an insider and yet a self-appointed outsider, an atypical member of the film community. His innovations in independent filmmaking, born as an alternative to Hollywood, have been an influential force for creativity *inside* Hollywood. His stance as an "outsider within" gives him a critical edge that both questions "normal" ways of doing things in his profession and offers new possibilities. Redford is, in many ways, a quintessential tempered radical and, whether he intends to be or not, a leader within his industry.

CONCLUSION

Tempered-radical-as-leader is a more inclusive, realistic, and inspiring way to think about leadership—and life—than are images of leadership found in fairy tales and the popular business press. To gauge the efficacy of one's efforts against portraits of leaders as lone crusaders at the helm of dramatic transformation is to resign oneself to falling short, to feeling that one's efforts have not made a *real* difference. The depiction of tempered-radical-as-leader provides more compelling metrics and ideals. It allows that through a wide range of ways people make a difference for others, create new truths, and live lives of integrity, meaning, and purpose.

Tempered radicals exist at all levels in all kinds of organizations. Not only do they exist, but they persist and, to varying extents, succeed. Even if they don't feel "radical" or have an explicit agenda for change, countless people act as tempered radicals, at least over some portions of their careers and under certain circumstances. They know that the challenges they pose may bring some risk to their careers, yet many feel that going along in silence can bring even greater costs to their souls.

While John Ziwak, Martha Wiley, and Sheila Johnson face similar challenges, their experiences as tempered radicals, particularly their experiences of being "different," are not the same at all. Most of this book focuses on common tensions and action strategies for people who differ from the norm in any multitude of ways. But before we move on to that focus, we'll explore how different kinds of tempered radicals experience their differences.

REFERENCES

1. *Merriam-Webster's Collegiate Dictionary*, 10th ed. (Springfield, MA: Merriam-Webster, 1998).
2. Debra Meyerson and Maureen Scully, "Tempered Radicalism and the Politics of Ambivalence and Change," *Organizational Science* 6, no. 5 (1995): 585–601.
3. In her autobiographical account, *Trespassing: My Sojourn in the Halls of Privilege* (New York: Houghton Mifflin, 1997), Gwendolyn Parker describes the feeling of being an outsider even as she climbed up the ladder of success at American Express Company.
4. Sharon Sutton, *Finding Our Voice in a Dominant Key* (unpublished manuscript, University of Michigan, 1991).
5. See Sigmund Freud, *Civilization and Its Discontents* (New York: Norton, 1961).
6. On ambivalence see Gideon Kunda's *Engineering Culture* (Philadelphia: Temple University Press, 1991). Kunda describes the way people construct their selves in relation to a culture that attempts to be all-consuming. See also Ken Smith and David Berg, *Paradoxes of Group Life* (San Francisco: Jossey-Bass, 1987) and Blake Ashforth and Fred Mael, "The Power of Resistance: Sustaining Valued Identities," in *Power and Influence in Organizations*, ed. Roderick Kramer and Margaret Neale (Thousand Oaks, CA: Sage, 1998), 89–102.

Both these works speak to the opposing inclinations of self in relation to conformity-inducing social institutions. See also Neil Smelsner's 1998 Presidential Address to the American Sociological Association: Neil J. Smelsner, "The Rational and the Ambivalent in the Social Sciences," *American Sociological Review* 63 (1998): 1–15 for a discussion of the ubiquity of ambivalence in social life and the conditions that foster it.
7. These two strategies are comparable to the strategies of "exit" and "loyalty" described by Albert Hirschman, *Exit, Voice and Loyalty* (Cambridge, MA: Harvard University Press, 1970), in this classic treatment of people's ambivalence toward the state and constraining social institutions.
8. Meyerson and Scully, "Tempered Radicalism."
9. *Merriam-Webster's New Collegiate Dictionary*, 10th ed. (Springfield, MA: Merriam-Webster, 1998).
10. Karl E. Weick, "Small Wins," *American Psychologist* 39, no. 1 (1984): 40–49.
11. Karl E. Weick and Robert E. Quinn, "Organizational Change and Development," *Annual Review of Psychology* 50 (1999): 361–386 and Karl E. Weick, "Emergent Change as a Universal in

Organizations," in *Breaking the Code of Change*, eds. Michael Beer and Nitin Noria (Boston: Harvard Business School Press, 2000), 223–241.

12. Michael Tushman and Elaine Romanelli, "Organizational Determinants of Technological Change: Toward a Sociology of Technological Evolution," in *Research in Organizational Behavior* 14, eds. Barry Staw and Larry Cummings (Greenwich, CT: JAI, 1992), 311–347.

13. Weick and Quinn, "Organizational Change and Development."

14. One's identity—and therefore one's deviance based on identity—is defined in part by one's cultural and historical situation. What being an Indian woman means is different in the United States than it is in India. After an Indian woman spends time in the United States, it means something different to be a woman when she returns to her home country. The point is, it is hard to answer the question "who am I?" in a vacuum. People's identities change over time and place, and they change as their place in a web of relations changes. This notion is relatively alien to Western notions of the "self" as autonomous and stable, but it is familiar within Eastern conceptions of self as defined relationally. See Dorinne Kondo, *Crafting Selves: Power, Gender, and Discourses of Identity in a Japanese Workplace* (Chicago: University of Chicago Press, 1990) and Hazel Marcus and Shinobu Kitayama, "Culture and the Self: Implications for Cognition, Emotion, and Motivation," *Psychological Review* 98, no. 2 (1991): 224–253. What this means for tempered radicals is that the tensions they experience and their feelings of deviance are specific to time and context. And, although I view ambivalence as a starting point, how people experience ambivalence, the extent to which their selves are at odds, and what they do with these felt tensions can vary enormously over time and situation.

15. It has also been found that people's conception of the "self" is culturally specific, e.g., Marcus and Kitayama, "Culture and the Self."

16. William B. Swann, Jr., "Identity Negotiation: Where Two Roads Meet," *Journal of Personality and Social Psychology* 53, no. 6 (1987): 1038–1051; Viktor Gecas, "The Self-concept," *Annual Review of Sociology* 8 (1982): 1–33. See also Erving Goffman, *The Presentation of Self in Everyday Life* (New York: Doubleday, 1959).

17. Karl E. Weick, "Small Wins."

18. Jane E. Dutton, "The Making of Organizational Opportunities: An Interpretive Pathway to Organizational Change," in *Research in Organizational Behavior* 15, eds. Barry Staw and Larry Cummings (Greenwich, CT: JAI, 1992), 195–226. Dutton describes the psychological mechanisms by which "opportunity framing" motivates action. The first of these is the suppression of perceived threat, which lowers anxiety and allows for greater search for response options. The second is a "positive gloss" effect, which heightens one's sense of mastery and efficacy, which in turn provides motivation for action.

19. Ibid.

20. Ronald Heifetz, *Leadership Without Easy Answers* (Cambridge, MA: Harvard University Press, 1994). Heifetz, who teaches a popular leadership course at Harvard's Kennedy School of Government, argues that enabling a system to meet its adaptive challenges is the most crucial component of leadership.

21. Patricia Hill Collins, "Learning from the Outsider Within," *Journal of Social Problems* 33, no. 6 (1986): 53. Sociologists have made similar observations about the creativity and insight black women bring to the field of sociology as a result in part of their "outsider within" status in the field. Outsiders within occupy a special place—they become different people, and their difference sensitizes them to patterns that may be more difficult for established sociological insiders to see.

Part

F

Group Processes

32. Suppose We Took Groups Seriously . . .

Harold J. Leavitt

INTRODUCTION

This chapter is mostly a fantasy, but not a utopian fantasy. As the title suggests, it tries to spin out some of the things that might happen if we really took small groups seriously; if, that is, we really used groups, rather than individuals, as the basic building blocks for an organization.

This seems an appropriate forum for such a fantasy. It was fifty years ago, at Hawthorne, that the informal face-to-face work group was discovered. Since then groups have been studied inside and out; they have been experimented with, observed, built, and taken apart. Small groups have become the major tool of the applied behavioral scientist. Organizational development methods are group methods. Almost all of what is called participative management is essentially based on group techniques.

So the idea of using groups as organizational mechanisms is by no means new or fantastic. The fantasy comes in proposing to start with groups, not add them in; to design organizations from scratch around small groups, rather than around individuals.

But right from the start, talk like that appears to violate a deep and important value, individualism. But, this fantasy will not really turn out to be anti-individualistic in the end.

The rest of this chapter will briefly address the following questions: (1) Is it fair to say that groups have not been taken very seriously in organizational design? (2) Why are groups even worth thinking about as organizational building materials? What are the characteristics of

Reprinted by permission of AT&T Corp.

groups that might make them interesting enough to be worth serious attention? (3) What would it mean "to take groups seriously?" Just what kinds of things would have to be done differently? (4) What compensatory changes would probably be needed in other aspects of the organization, to have groups as the basic unit? And finally, (5) is the idea of designing the organization around small face-to-face groups a very radical idea, or is it just an extension of a direction in which we are already going?

HAVEN'T GROUPS BEEN TAKEN SERIOUSLY ENOUGH ALREADY?

The argument that groups have not been taken "seriously" doesn't seem a hard one to make. The contemporary ideas about groups didn't really come along until the 30s and 40s. By that time a logical, rationalistic tradition for the construction of organizations already existed. That tradition was very heavily based on the notion that the individual was the construction unit. The logic moved from the projected task backward. Determine the task, the goal, then find an appropriate structure and technology, and last of all fit individual human beings into predefined man-sized pieces of the action. That was, for instance, what industrial psychology was all about during its development between the two world wars. It was concerned almost entirely with individual differences and worked in the service of structuralists, fitting square human pegs to predesigned square holes. The role of the psychologist was thus ancillary to the role of the designers of the whole organization. It was a backup, supportive role that followed more than it led design.

It was not just the logic of classical organizational theory that concentrated on the individual. The whole entrepreneurial tradition of American society supported it. Individuals, at least male individuals, were taught achievement motivation. They were taught to seek individual evaluation, to compete, to see the world, organizational or otherwise, as a place in which to strive for individual accomplishment and satisfaction.

In those respects the classical design of organizations was consonant with the then existent cultural landscape. Individualized organizational structures blended with the environment of individualism. All the accessories fell into place: individual incentive schemes for hourly workers, individual merit rating and assessment schemes, tests for selection of individuals.

The unique characteristic of the organization was that it was not simply a racetrack within which individuals could compete, but a system in which somehow the competitive behavior of individuals could be coordinated, harnessed and controlled in the interest of the common tasks. Of course one residual of all that was a continuing tension between individual and organization, with the organization seeking to control and coordinate the individual's activities at the same time that it tried to motivate him, while the competitive individual insisted on reaching well beyond the constraints imposed upon him by the organization. One product of this tension became the informal organization discovered here at Western; typically an informal coalition designed to fight the system.

Then it was discovered that groups could be exploited for what management saw as positive purposes, *toward* productivity instead of away from it. There followed the era of experimentation with small face-to-face groups. We learned to patch them on to existing organizations as bandaids to relieve tensions between individual and organization. We promoted coordination through group methods. We leaned that groups were useful to discipline and control recalcitrant individuals.

Groups were fitted onto organizations. The group skills of individual members improved so that they could coordinate their efforts more effectively, control deviants more effectively and gain more commitment from subordinate individuals. But groups were seen primarily as tools to be tacked on and utilized in the preexisting individualized organizational system. With a few notable exceptions, like Renis Likert

(1961), most did not design organizations around groups. On the contrary, as some of the ideas about small groups began to be tacked onto existing organizational models, they generated new tensions and conflicts of their own. Managers complained not only that groups were slow, but that they diffused responsibility, vitiated the power of the hierarchy because they were too "democratic and created small in-groups empires which were very hard for others to penetrate." There was the period, for example, of the great gap between T-group training (which had to be conducted on "cultural islands") and the organization back home. The T-groups therefore talked a lot about the "reentry problem," which meant in part the problem of movement from a new culture (the T-group culture) designed around groups back into the organizational culture designed around individuals.

But of course groups didn't die despite their difficulties. How could they die? They had always been there, though not always in the service of the organization. They turned out to be useful, indeed necessary, though often unrecognized tools. For organizations were growing, and professionalizing, and the need for better coordination grew even as the humanistic expectations of individuals also grew. So "acknowledged" groups (as distinct from "natural," informal groups) became fairly firmly attached even to conservative organizations, but largely as compensating addenda very often reluctantly backed into by organizational managers.

Groups have never been given a chance. It is as though someone had insisted that automobiles be designed to fit the existing terrain rather than build roads to adapt to automobiles.

ARE GROUPS WORTH CONSIDERING AS FUNDAMENTAL BUILDING BLOCKS?

Why would groups be more interesting than individuals as basic design units around which to build organizations? What are the prominent characteristics of small groups? Why are they interesting? Here are several answers:

First, small groups seem to be good for people. They can satisfy important membership needs. They can provide a moderately wide range of activities for individual members. They can provide support in times of stress and crisis. They are settings in which people can learn not only cognitively but empirically to be reasonably trusting and helpful to one another. Second, groups seem to be good problem finding tools. They seem to be useful in promoting innovation and creativity. Third, in a wide variety of decision situations, they make better decisions than individuals do. Fourth, they are great tools for implementation. They gain commitment from their members so that group decisions are likely to be willingly carried out. Fifth, they can control and discipline individual members in ways that are often extremely difficult through more impersonal quasi-legal disciplinary systems. Sixth, as organizations grow large, small groups appear to be useful mechanisms for fending off many of the negative effects of large size. They help to prevent communication lines from growing too long, the hierarchy from growing too steep, and the individual from getting lost in the crowd.

There is a seventh, but altogether different kind of argument for taking groups seriously. Thus far the designer of organizations seemed to have a choice. He could build an individualized *or* a groupy organization. A groupy organization will, de facto, have to deal with individuals; but what was learned here so long ago is that individual organizations, must, de facto, deal with groups. Groups are natural phenomena, and facts of organizational life. They can be created but their spontaneous development cannot be prevented. The problem is not shall groups exist or not, but shall groups be planned or not? If not, the individualized organizational garden will sprout groupy weeds all over the place. By defining them as weeds instead of flowers, they shall continue, as in earlier days, to be treated as pests, forever fouling up the beauty of rationally designed individualized organizations, forever forming informally (and irrationally) to harass and outgame the planners.

It is likely that the reverse could also be true, that if groups are defined as the flowers and individuals as the weeds, new problems will crop up. Surely they will, but that discussion can be delayed for at least a little while.

WHO USES GROUPS BEST?

So groups look like interesting organizational building blocks. But before going on to consider the implications of designing organizations around groups, one useful heuristic might be to look around the existing world at those places in which groups seem to have been treated somewhat more seriously.

One place groups have become big is in Japanese organizations (Johnson & Ouchi, 1974). The Japanese seem to be very groupy, and much less concerned than Americans about issues like individual accountability. Japanese organizations, of course, are thus consonant with Japanese culture, where notions of individual aggressiveness and competitiveness are deemphasized in favor of self-effacement and group loyalty. But Japanese organizations seem to get a lot done, despite the relative suppression of the individual in favor of the group. It also appears that the advantages of the groupy Japanese style have really come to the fore in large technologically complex organizations.

Another place to look is at American conglomerates. They go to the opposite extreme, dealing with very large units. They buy large organizational units and sell units. They evaluate units. In effect they promote units by offering them extra resources as rewards for good performance. In that sense conglomerates, one might argue, are designed around groups, but the groups in question are often themselves large organizational chunks.

GROUPS IN AN INDIVIDUALISTIC CULTURE

An architect can design a beautiful building which either blends smoothly with its environment or contrasts starkly with it. But organization designers may not have the same choice. If we design an organization which is structurally dissonant with its environment, it is conceivable that the environment will change to adjust to the organization. It seems much more likely, however, that the environment will reject the organization. If designing organizations around groups represents a sharp counterpoint to environmental trends, maybe we should abort the idea.

Our environment, one can argue, is certainly highly individualized. But one can also make a less solid argument in the other direction; an argument that American society is going groupy rather than individual this year. Or at least that it is going groupy as well as individual. The evidence is sloppy at best. One can reinterpret the student revolution and the growth of anti-establishment feelings at least in part as a reaction to the decline of those institutions that most satisfied social membership needs. One can argue that the decline of the Church, of the village and of the extended family is leaving behind a vacuum of unsatisfied membership and belongingness motives. Certainly popular critics of American society have laid a great deal of emphasis on the loneliness and anomie that seem to have resulted not only from materialism but from the emphasis on individualism. It seems possible to argue that, insofar as there has been any significant change in the work ethic in America, the change has been toward a desire for work which is socially as well as egoistically fulfilling, and which satisfies human needs for belongingness and affiliation as well as needs for achievement.

In effect, the usual interpretation of Abraham Maslow's need hierarchy may be wrong. Usually the esteem and self-actualization levels of motivation are emphasized. Perhaps the level that is becoming operant most rapidly is neither of those, but the social–love–membership level.

The rising role of women in American society also has implications for the groupiness of organizations. There is a moderate amount of evidence that American women have been socialized more strongly into affiliative and relational sorts of attitudes than men. They probably can, in general, more comfortably work in direct achievement roles in group settings, where there are strong relational bonds among members, than in competitive, individualistic settings. Moreover it is reasonable to assume that as women take a more important place in American society, some of their values and attitudes will spill over to the male side.

Although the notion of designing organizations around groups in America in 1974 may be a little premature, it is consonant with cultural trends that may make the idea much more appropriate ten years from now.

But groups are becoming more relevant for organizational as well as cultural reasons. Groups seem to be particularly useful as coordinating and integrating mechanisms for dealing with complex tasks that require the inputs of many kinds of specialized knowledge. In fact the development of matrix-type organizations is high technology industry is perhaps one effort to modify individually designed organizations toward a more groupy direction; not for humanistic reasons but as a consequence of tremendous increase in the informational complexity of the jobs that need to be done.

WHAT MIGHT A SERIOUSLY GROUPY ORGANIZATION LOOK LIKE?

Just what does it mean to design organizations around groups? Operationally how is that different from designing organizations around individuals? One approach to an answer is simply to take the things organizations do with individuals and try them out with groups. The idea is to raise the level from the atom to the molecule, and *select* groups rather than individuals; *train* groups rather than individuals, *pay* groups rather than individuals, *promote* groups rather than individuals, *design jobs* for groups rather than for individuals, *fire* groups rather than individuals, and so on down the list of activities which organizations have traditionally

carried on in order to use human beings in their organizations.

Some of the items on that list seem easy to handle at the group level. For example, it doesn't seem terribly hard to design jobs for groups. In effect that is what top management already does for itself to a great extent. It gives specific jobs to committees, and often runs itself as a group. The problem seems to be a manageable one: designing job sets which are both big enough to require a small number of persons and also small enough to require only a small number of persons. Big enough in this context means not only jobs that would occupy the hands of group members but that would provide opportunities for learning and expansion.

Ideas like evaluating, promoting, and paying groups raise many more difficult but interesting problems. Maybe the best that can be said for such ideas is that they provide opportunities for thinking creatively about pay and evaluation. Suppose, for example, that as a reward for good work the group gets a larger salary budget than it got last year. Suppose the allocation for increases within the group is left to the group members. Certainly one can think up all sorts of difficulties that might arise. But are the potential problems necessarily any more difficult than those now generated by individual merit raises? Is there any company in America that is satisfied with its existing individual performance appraisal and salary allocation schemes? At least the issues of distributive justice within small groups would presumably be open to internal discussion and debate. One might even permit the group to allocate payments to individuals differentially at different times, in accordance with some criteria of current contribution that they might establish.

As far as performance evaluation is concerned, it is probably easier for people up the hierarchy to assess the performance of total groups than it is to assess the performance of individual members well down the hierarchy. Top managers of decentralized organizations do it all the time, except that they usually reward the formal leader of the decentralized unit rather than the whole unit.

The notion of promoting groups raises another variety of difficulties. One thinks of physically transferring a whole group, for example, and of the costs associated with training a whole group to do a new job, especially if there are no bridging individuals. But there may be large advantages too. If a group moves, its members already know how to work with one another. Families may be less disrupted by movement if several move at the same time.

There is the problem of selection. Does it make sense to select groups? Initially, why not? Can't means be found for selecting not only for appropriate knowledge and skill but also for potential ability to work together? There is plenty of groundwork in the literature already.

After the initial phase, there will of course be problems of adding or subtracting individuals from existing groups. We already know a good deal about how to help new members get integrated into old groups. Incidentally, I was told recently by a plant manager in the midwest about an oddity he had encountered: the phenomenon of groups applying for work. Groups of three or four people have been coming to his plant seeking employment together. They wanted to work together and stay together.

COSTS AND DANGER POINTS

To play this game of designing organizations around groups, what might be some important danger points? In general, a group-type organization is somewhat more like a free market than present organizations. More decisions would have to be worked out ad hoc, in a continually changing way. So one would need to schedule more negotiation time both within and between groups.

One would encounter more issues of justice, for the individual vis-à-vis the group and for groups vis-à-vis one another. More and better arbitration mechanisms would probably be needed along with highly flexible and rapidly adaptive record keeping. But modern record-keeping technology is, potentially, both highly flexible and rapidly adaptive.

Another specific issue is the provision of escape hatches for individuals. Groups have been know to be cruel and unjust to their deviant members. One existing escape route for the individual would of course continue to exist: departure from the organization. Another might be easy means of transfer to another group.

Another related danger of a strong group emphasis might be a tendency to drive away highly individualistic, nongroup people. But the tight organizational constraints now imposed do the same thing. Indeed might not groups protect their individualists better than the impersonal rules of present-day large organizations?

Another obvious problem: If groups are emphasized by rewarding them, paying them, promoting them, and so on, groups may begin to perceive themselves as power centers, in competitive conflict with other groups. Intergroup hostilities are likely to be exacerbated unless we can design some new coping mechanisms into the organization. Likert's proposal for solving that sort of problem (and others) is the linking pin concept. The notion is that individuals serve as members of more than one group, both up and down the hierarchy and horizontally. But Likert's scheme seems to me to assume fundamentally individualized organizations in the sense that it is still individuals who get paid, promoted and so on. In a more groupy organization, the linking pin concept has to be modified so that an individual might be a part-time member of more than one group, but still a real member. That is, for example, a portion of an individual's pay might come from each group in accordance with that group's perception of his contribution.

Certainly much more talk, both within and between groups, would be a necessary accompaniment of group emphasis; though we might argue about whether more talk should be classified as a cost or a benefit. In any case careful design of escape hatches for individuals and connections among groups would be as important in this kind of organization as would stairways between floors in the design of a private home.

There is also a danger of overdesigning groups. All groups in the organization need not look alike. Quite to the contrary. Task and technology should have significant effects on the shapes and sizes of different subgroups within the large organization. Just as individuals end up adjusting the edges of their jobs to themselves and themselves to their jobs, we should expect flexibility within groups, allowing them to adapt and modify themselves to whatever the task and technology demand.

Another initially scary problem associated with groups is the potential loss of clear formal individual leadership. Without formal leaders how will we motivate people? Without leaders how will we control and discipline people? Without leaders how will we pinpoint responsibility? Even as I write those questions I cannot help but feel that they are archaic. They are questions which are themselves a product of the basic individual building block design of old organizations. The problem is not leaders so much as the performance of leadership functions. Surely groups will find leaders, but they will emerge from the bottom up. Given a fairly clear job description, some groups, in some settings, will set up more or less permanent leadership roles. Others may let leadership vary as the situation demands, or as a function of the power that individuals within any group may possess relative to the group's needs at that time. A reasonable amount of process time can be built in to enable groups to work on the leadership problem, but the problem will have to be resolved within each group. On the advantage side of the ledger, this may even get rid of a few hierarchical levels. There should be far less need for individuals who are chiefly supervisors of other individuals' work. Groups can serve as hierarchical leaders of other groups.

Two other potential costs: With an organization of groups, there may be a great deal of infighting, and power and conflict issues will come even more to the fore than they do now. Organizations of groups may become highly political, with coalitions lining up against one another on various issues. If so, the rest of the organizational system will have to take those political problems into account, both by setting up sensible systems of intercommunications among groups, and by allocating larger amounts of time and expertise to problems of conflict resolution.

But this is not a new problem unique to groupy organizations. Conflict among groups is prevalent in large organizations which are political systems now. But because these issues have not often been foreseen and planned for, the mechanisms for dealing with them are largely ad hoc. As a result, conflict is often dealt with in extremely irrational ways.

But there is another kind of intergroup power problem that may become extremely important and difficult in groupy organizations. There is a real danger that relatively autonomous and cohesive groups may be closed, not only to other groups but more importantly to staff advice or to new technological inputs.

These problems exist at present, of course, but they may be exacerbated by group structure. I cannot see any perfect way to handle those problems. One possibility may be to make individual members of staff groups part-time members of line groups. Another is to work harder to educate line groups to potential staff contributions. Of course the reward system, the old market system, will probably be the strongest force for keeping groups from staying old-fashioned in a world of new technologies and ideas.

But the nature and degree of many of the second order spinoff effects are not fully knowable at the design stage. We need to build more complete working models and pilot plants. In any case it does not seem obvious that slowdowns, either at the work place or in decision-making processes, would necessarily accompany group based organizational designs.

SOME POSSIBLE ADVANTAGES TO THE ORGANIZATION

Finally, from an organizational perspective, what are the potential advantages to be gained from a group-based organization? The first might be a sharp reduction in the number of units that need to be controlled. Control would not have to be carried all the way down to the individual level. If the average group size is five, the number of blocks that management has to worry about is cut to 20 percent of what it was. Such a design would also probably cut the number of operational levels in the organization. In effect, levels which are now primarily supervisory would be incorporated into the groups that they supervise.

By this means many of the advantages of the small individualized organization could be brought back. These advantages would occur within groups simply because there would be a small number of blocks, albeit larger blocks, with which to build and rebuild the organization.

But most of all, and this is still uncertain, despite the extent to which we behavioral scientists have been enamoured of groups, there would be increased human advantages of cohesiveness, motivation, and commitment, and via that route, both increased productivity, stronger social glue within the organization, and a wider interaction between organization and environment.

SUMMARY

Far and away the most powerful and beloved tool of applied behavioral scientists is the small face-to-face group. Since the Western Electric researches, behavioral scientists have been learning to understand, exploit and love groups. Groups attracted interest initially as devices for improving the implementation of decisions and to increase human commitment and motivation. They are not loved because they are also creative and innovative, they often make better quality decisions than individuals, and because they make organizational life more livable for people. One can't hire an applied behavioral scientist into an organization who within ten minutes will not want to call a group meeting and talk things over. The group meeting is his primary technology, his primary tool.

But groups in organizations are not an invention of behavioral types. They are a natural phenomenon of organizations. Organizations develop informal groups, like it or not. It is both possible and sensible to describe most large organizations as collections of groups in interaction with one another; bargaining with one another, forming coalitions with one another, cooperating and competing with one another. It is possible and sensible, too, to treat the decisions that emerge from large organizations as a resultant of the interplay of forces among groups within the organization, and not just the resultant of rational analysis.

On the down side, small face-to-face groups are great tools for disciplining and controlling their members. Contemporary China, for example, has just a fraction of the number of lawyers in the United States. Partially this is a result of the lesser complexity of Chinese society and lower levels of education. But a large part of it, surprisingly enough, seems to derive from the fact that modern China is designed around small groups. Since small groups take responsibility for the discipline and control of their members, many deviant acts which would be considered illegal in the United States never enter the formal legal system in China. The law controls individual deviation less, the group controls it more (Li, 1971).

Control of individual behavior is also a major problem of large complex western organizations. This problem has driven many organizations into elaborate bureaucratic quasi-legal sets of rules, ranging from job evaluation schemes to performance evaluations to incentive systems; all individually based, all terribly complex, all creating problems of distributive justice. Any organizational design that might eliminate much of the legalistic superstructure therefore begins to look highly desirable.

Management should consider building organizations using a material now understood very well and with properties that look very promising, the small group. Until recently, at least, the human group has primarily been used for patching and mending organizations that were originally built of other materials.

The major unanswered questions in my mind are not in the understanding of groups, not in the potential utility of the group as a building block. The more difficult answered question is whether or not the approaching era is one in which Americans would willingly work in such apparently contra-individualistic units. I think we are.

REFERENCES

Johnson, Richard T., and Ouchi, William G. "Made in America (under Japanese Management)." *Harvard Business Review*, September–October 1974.

Li, Victor. "The Development of the Chinese Legal System." *China: The Management of a Revolutionary Society*, edited by John Lindbeck. Seattle: University of Washington Press, 1971.

Likert, Rensis. *New Patterns of Management*, New York: McGraw-Hill, 1961.

33. Groupthink

Irving L. Janis

The U.S. road to disaster—in Vietnam, the Bay of Pigs, Korea, and Pearl Harbor—is paved with the desperate drive for consensus at any cost that suppresses dissent among the mighty in the corridors of power.

"How could we have been so stupid?" President John F. Kennedy asked after he and a close group of advisers had blundered into the Bay of Pigs invasion. For the last two years I have been studying that question, as it applies not only to the Bay of Pigs decision makers but also to those who led the United States into such other major fiascos as the failure to be prepared for the attack on Pearl Harbor, the Korean War stalemate, and the escalation of The Vietnam War.

Stupidity certainly is not the explanation. The men who participated in making the Bay of Pigs decision, for instance, comprised one of the greatest arrays of intellectual talent in the history of American Government—Dean Rusk, Robert McNamara, Douglas Dillon, Robert Kennedy, McGeorge Bundy, Arthur Schlesinger, Jr., Allen Dulles, and others.

It also seemed to me that explanations were incomplete if they concentrated only on disturbances in the behavior of each individual within a decision-making body: temporary emotional states of elation, fear, or anger that reduce a man's mental efficiency, for example, or chronic blind spots arising from a man's social prejudices or idiosyncratic biases.

I preferred to broaden the picture by looking at the fiascos from the standpoint of group dynamics as it has been explored over the past three decades, first by the great social psychologist Kurt Lewin and later in many experimental situations by myself and other behavioral scientists. My conclusion after poring over hundreds of relevant documents—historical reports about formal group meetings and informal conversations among the members—is that the groups that committed the fiascos were victims of what I call "groupthink."

"GROUPY"

In each case study, I was surprised to discover the extent to which each group displayed the typical phenomena of social conformity that are regularly encountered in studies of group dynamics among ordinary citizens. For example, some of the phenomena appear to be completely in line with findings from social–psychological experiments showing that powerful social pressures are brought to bear by the members of a cohesive group whenever a dissident begins to voice his objections to a group consensus. Other phenomena are reminiscent of the shared illusions observed in encounter groups and friendship cliques when the members simultaneously reach a peak of "groupy" feelings.

Above all, there are numerous indications pointing to the development of group norms that bolster morale at the expense of critical thinking. One of the most common norms appears to be that of remaining loyal to the group by sticking with the policies to which the group has already committed itself, even when those policies are obviously working out badly and have unintended consequences that disturb the conscience of each member. This is one of the key characteristics of groupthink.

1984

I use the term *groupthink* as a quick and easy way to refer to the mode of thinking that persons engage in when *concurrence seeking* becomes so dominant in a cohesive ingroup that it tends to override realistic appraisal of alternative course of action. Groupthink is a term of the same order as the words in the newspeak vocabulary George Orwell used in his dismaying world of *1984*. In that context, groupthink takes on an invidious connotation. Exactly such a connotation is intended, since the term refers to a deterioration in mental efficiency, reality testing, and moral judgments as a result of group pressures.

The symptoms of groupthink arise when the members of decision-making groups become motivated to avoid being too harsh in their judgments of their leaders' or their colleagues' ideas. They adopt a soft line of criticism, even in their own thinking. At their meetings, all the members are amiable and seek complete concurrence on every important issue, with no bickering or conflict to spoil the cozy, "we-feeling" atmosphere.

KILL

Paradoxically, soft-headed groups are often hard-hearted when it comes to dealing with outgroups or enemies. They find it relatively easy to resort to dehumanizing solutions—they will readily authorize bombing attacks that kill large numbers of civilians in the name of the noble cause of persuading an unfriendly government to negotiate at the peace table. They are unlikely to pursue the more difficult and controversial issues that arise when alternatives to a harsh military solution come up for discussion. Nor are they inclined to raise ethical issues that carry the implication that *this fine group of ours, with its humanitarianism and its high-minded principles, might be capable of adopting a course of action that is inhumane and immoral.*

NORMS

There is evidence from a number of social–psychological studies that as the members of a group feel more accepted by the others, which is a central feature of increased group cohesiveness, they display less overt conformity to group norms. Thus we would expect that the more cohesive a group becomes, the less the members will feel constrained to censor what they say out of fear of being socially punished for antagonizing the leader or any of their fellow members.

In contrast, the groupthink type of conformity tends to increase as group cohesiveness increases. Groupthink involves nondeliberate suppression of critical thoughts as a result of internalization of the group's norms, which is quite different from deliberate suppression on the basis of external threats of social punishment. The more cohesive the group, the greater the inner compulsion on the part of each member to avoid creating disunity, which inclines him to believe in the soundness of whatever proposals are promoted by the leader or by a majority of the group's members.

In a cohesive group, the danger is not so much that each individual will fail to reveal his objections to what the others propose but that he will think the proposal is a good one, without attempting to carry out a careful, critical scrutiny of the pros and cons of the alternatives. When groupthink becomes dominant, there also is considerable suppression of deviant thoughts, but it takes the form of each person's deciding that his misgivings are not relevant and should be set aside, that the benefit of the doubt regarding any lingering uncertainties should be given to the group consensus.

STRESS

I do not mean to imply that all cohesive groups necessarily suffer from groupthink. All ingroups may have a mild tendency toward groupthink, displaying one or another of the symptoms from time to time, but it need not be so dominant as to influence the quality of the group's final decision. Neither do I mean to imply that there is anything necessarily inefficient or harmful about group decisions in general. On the contrary, a group whose members have properly defined roles, with traditions concerning the procedures to follow in pursuing a critical inquiry, probably is capable of making better decisions than any individual group member working alone.

The problem is that the advantages of having decisions made by groups are often lost because of powerful psychological pressures that arise when the members work closely together, share the same set of values, and, above all, face a crisis situation that puts everyone under intense stress.

The main principle of groupthink, which I offer in the spirit of Parkinson's Law, is this: *The more amiability and esprit de corps there is among the members of a policy-making ingroup, the greater the danger that independent critical thinking well be replaced by groupthink, which is likely to result in irrational and dehumanizing actions directed against outgroups.*

SYMPTOMS

In my studies of high-level governmental decision makers, both civilian and military, I have found eight main symptoms of groupthink.

1. Invulnerabilty

Most or all of the members of the ingroup share an *illusion* of invulnerability that provides for them some degree of reassurance about obvious dangers and leads them to become overoptimistic and willing to take extraordinary risks. It also causes them to fail to respond to clear warnings of danger.

The Kennedy ingroup, which uncritically accepted the Central Intelligence Agency's disastrous Bay of Pigs plan, operated on the false assumption at they could keep secret the fact that the United States was responsible for the invasion of Cuba. Even after news of the plan began to leak out, their belief remained unshaken. They failed even to consider the danger that awaited them: a worldwide revulsion against the U.S.

A similar attitude appeared among the members of President Lyndon B. Johnson's ingroup, the "Tuesday Cabinet," which kept escalating the Vietnam War despite repeated setbacks and failures. "There was a belief," Bill Moyers commented after he resigned, "that if we indicated a willingness to use our power, they [the North Vietnamese] would get the

message and back away from an all-out confrontation. . . . There was a confidence—it was never bragged about, it was just there—that when the chips were really down, the other people would fold."

A most poignant example of an illusion of invulnerability involves the ingroup around Admiral H. E. Kimmel, which failed to prepare for the possibility of a Japanese attack on Pearl Harbor despite repeated warnings. Informed by his intelligence chief that radio contact with Japanese aircraft carriers had been lost, Kimmel joked about it: "What, you don't know where the carriers are? Do you mean to say that they could be rounding Diamond Head (at Honolulu) and you wouldn't know it?" The carriers were in fact moving full-steam toward Kimmel's command post at the time. Laughing together about a danger signal, which labels it as a purely laughing matter, is a characteristic manifestation of groupthink.

2. Rationale

As we see, victims of groupthink ignore warnings; they also collectively construct rationalizations in order to discount warnings and other forms of negative feedback that, taken seriously, might lead the group members to reconsider their assumptions each time they recommit themselves to past decisions. Why did the Johnson ingroup avoid reconsidering its escalation policy when time and again the expectations on which they based their decisions turned out to be wrong? James C. Thompson, Jr., a Harvard historian who spent five years as an observing participant in both the State Department and the White House, tells us that the policymakers avoided critical discussion of their prior decisions and continually invented new rationalizations so that they could sincerely recommit themselves to defeating the North Vietnamese.

In the fall of 1964, before the bombing of North Vietnam began, some of the policymakers predicted that six weeks of air strikes would induce the North Vietnamese to seek peace talks. When someone asked, "What if they don't?" the answer was that another four weeks certainly would do the trick.

Later, after each setback, the ingroup agreed that by investing just a bit more effort (by stepping up the bomb tonnage a bit, for instance), their course of action would prove to be right. *The Pentagon Papers* bear out these observations.

In *The Limits of Intervention*, Townsend Hoopes, who was acting Secretary of the Air Force under Johnson, says that Walt W. Rostow in particular showed a remarkable capacity for what has been called "instant rationalization." According to Hoopes, Rostow buttressed the group's optimism about being on the road to victory by culling selected scraps of evidence from news reports or, if necessary, by inventing "plausible" forecasts that had no basis in evidence at all.

Admiral Kimmel's group rationalized away their warnings, too. Right up to December 7, 1941, they convinced themselves that the Japanese would never dare attempt a full-scale surprise assault against Hawaii because Japan's leaders would realize that it would precipitate an all-out war which the United States would surely win. They made no attempt to look at the situation through the eyes of the Japanese leaders—another manifestation of groupthink.

3. Morality

Victims of groupthink believe unquestioningly in the inherent morality of their ingroup; this belief inclines the members to ignore the ethical or moral consequences of their decisions.

Evidence that this symptom is at work usually is of a negative kind—the things that are left unsaid in group meetings. At least two influential persons had doubts about the morality of the Bay of Pigs adventure. One of them, Arthur Schlesinger, Jr., presented his strong objections in a memorandum to President Kennedy and Secretary of State Rusk but suppressed them when he attended meetings of the Kennedy team. The other, Senator J. William Fulbright, was not a member of the group, but the President invited him to express his misgivings in a speech to the policymakers. However, when Fulbright finished speaking the President moved on to other agenda items without asking for reactions of the group.

David Kraslow and Stuart H. Loory, in the *The Secret Search for Peace in Vietnam*, report that during 1966 President Johnson's ingroup was concerned primarily with selecting bomb targets in North Vietnam. They based their selections on four factors—the military advantage, the risk to American aircraft and pilots, the danger of forcing other countries into the fighting, and the danger of heavy civilian casualties. At their regular Tuesday luncheons, they weighed these factors the way school teachers grade examination papers, averaging them out. Though evidence on this point is scant, I suspect that the group's ritualistic adherence to a standardized procedure induced the members to feel morally justified in their destructive way of dealing with the Vietnamese people—after all, the danger of heavy civilian casualties from U.S. air strikes was taken into account on their checklists.

4. Stereotypes

Victims of groupthink hold stereotyped views of the leaders of enemy groups; they are so evil that genuine attempts at negotiating differences with them are unwarranted, or they are too weak or too stupid to deal effectively with whatever attempts the ingroup makes to defeat their purposes, no matter how risky the attempts are.

Kennedy's groupthinkers believed that Premier Fidel Castro's air force was so ineffectual that obsolete B-26s could knock it out completely in a surprise attack before the invasion began. They also believed that Castro's army was so weak that a small Cuban-exile brigade could establish a well-protected beachhead at the Bay of Pigs. In addition, they believed that Castro was not smart enough to put down any possible internal uprisings in support of the exiles. They were wrong on all three assumptions. Though much of the blame was attributable to faulty intelligence, the point is that none of Kennedy's advisers even questioned the CIA planners about these assumptions.

The Johnson advisers' sloganistic thinking about "the Communist apparatus" that was "working all around the world" (as Dean Rusk put it) led them to overlook the powerful nationalistic strivings of the North Vietnamese government and its efforts to ward off Chinese domination. The crudest of all stereotypes used by Johnson's inner circle to justify their policies was the domino theory ("If we don't stop the Reds in South Vietnam, tomorrow they will be in Hawaii and next week they will be in San Francisco," Johnson once said). The group so firmly accepted this stereotype that it became almost impossible for any adviser to introduce a more sophisticated viewpoint.

In the documents on Pearl Harbor, it is clear to see that the Navy commanders stationed in Hawaii had a naive image of Japan as a midget that would not dare to strike a blow against a powerful giant.

5. Pressure

Victims of groupthink apply direct pressure to any individual who momentarily expresses doubts about any of the group's shared illusions or who questions the validity of the arguments supporting a policy alternative favored by the majority. This gambit reinforces the concurrence-seeking norm that loyal members are expected to maintain.

President Kennedy probably was more active than anyone else in raising skeptical questions during the Bay of Pigs meetings, and yet he seems to have encouraged the group's docile, uncritical acceptance of defective arguments in favor of the CIA's plan. At every meeting, he allowed the CIA representatives to dominate the discussion. He permitted them to give their immediate refutations in response to each tentative doubt that one of the others expressed, instead of asking whether anyone shared the doubt or wanted to pursue the implications of the new worrisome issue that had just been raised. And at the most crucial meeting, when he was calling on each member to give his vote

for or against the plan, he did not call on Arthur Schlesinger, the one man there who was known by the President to have serious misgivings.

Historian Thompson informs us that whenever a member of Johnson's ingroup began to express doubts, the group used subtle social pressures to "domesticate" him. To start with, the dissenter was made to feel at home, provided that he lived up to two restrictions: (1) that he did not voice his doubts to outsiders, which would play into the hands of the opposition; and (2) that he kept his criticisms within the bounds of acceptable deviation, which meant not challenging any of the fundamental assumptions that went into the group's prior commitments. One such "domesticated dissenter" was Bill Moyers. When Moyers arrived at a meeting, Thompson tells us, the President greeted him with, "Well, here comes Mr. Stop-the-Bombing."

6. Self-Censorship

Victims of groupthink avoid deviating from what appears to be group consensus; they keep silent about their misgivings and even minimize to themselves the importance of their doubts.

As we have seen, Schlesinger was not at all hesitant about presenting his strong objections to the Bay of Pigs plan in a memorandum to the President and the Secretary of State. But he became keenly aware of his tendency to suppress objections at the White House meetings. "In the months after the Bay of Pigs I bitterly reproached myself for having kept so silent during those crucial discussions in the cabinet room," Schlesinger writes in *A Thousand Days*. "I can only explain my failure to do more than raise a few timid questions by reporting that one's impulse to blow the whistle on this nonsense was simply undone by the circumstances of the discussion."

7. Unanimity

Victims of groupthink share an *illusion* of unanimity within the group concerning almost all judgments expressed by members who speak in favor of the majority view. This symptom results partly from the preceding one, whose effects are augmented by the false assumption that any individual who remains silent during any part of the discussion is in full accord with what the others are saying.

When a group of persons who respect each other's opinions arrives at a unanimous view, each member is likely to feel that the belief must be true. This reliance on consensual validation within the group tends to replace individual critical thinking and reality testing, unless there are clear-cut disagreements among the members. In contemplating a course of action such as the invasion of Cuba, it is painful for the members to confront disagreements within their group, particularly it it becomes apparent that there are widely divergent views about whether the preferred course of action is too risky to undertake at all. Such disagreements are likely to arouse anxieties about making a serious error. Once the sense of unanimity is shattered, the members no longer can feel complacently confident about the decision they are inclined to make. Each man must then face the annoying realization that there are troublesome uncertainties and he must diligently seek out the best information he can get in order to decide for himself exactly how serious the risks might be. This is one of the unpleasant consequences of being in a group of hardheaded, critical thinkers.

To avoid such an unpleasant state, the members often become inclined, without quite realizing it, to prevent latent disagreements from surfacing when they are about to initiate a risky course of action. The group leader and the members support each other in playing up the areas of convergence in their thinking, at the expense of fully exploring divergencies that might reveal unsettled issues.

"Our meetings took place in a curious atmosphere of assumed consensus," Schlesinger writes. His additional comments clearly show that, curiously, the consensus was an illusion— an illusion that could be maintained only because the major participants did not reveal their own reasoning or discuss their idiosyncratic assumptions and vague reservations.

Evidence from several sources makes it clear that even the three principals—President Kennedy, Rusk, and McNamara—had widely differing assumptions about the invasion plan.

8. Mindguards

Victims of groupthink sometimes appoint themselves as mindguards to protect the leader and fellow members from adverse information that might break the complacency they shared about the effectiveness and morality of past decisions. At a large birthday party for his wife, Attorney General Robert F. Kennedy, who had been constantly informed about the Cuban invasion plan, took Schlesinger aside and asked him why he was opposed. Kennedy listened coldly and said, "You may be right or you may be wrong, but the President has made his mind up. Don't push it any further. Now is the time for everyone to help him all they can."

Rusk also functioned as a highly effective mindguard by failing to transmit to the group the strong objections of three "outsiders" who had learned of the invasion plan—Undersecretary of State Chester Bowles, USIA Director Edward R. Murrow, and Rusk's intelligence chief, Roger Hilsman. Had Rusk done so, their warnings might have reinforced Schlesinger's memorandum and jolted some of Kennedy's ingroup, if not the President himself, into reconsidering the decision.

PRODUCTS

When a group of executives frequently displays most or all of these interrelated symptoms, a detailed study of their deliberations is likely to reveal a number of immediate consequences. These consequences are, in effect, products of poor decision-making practices because they lead to inadequate solutions to the problems under discussion.

First, the group limits its discussions to a few alternative courses of action (often only two) without an initial survey of all the alternative that might be worthy of consideration.

Second, the group fails to reexamine the course of action initially preferred by the majority after they learn of risks and drawbacks they had not considered originally.

Third, the members spend little or no time discussing whether there are nonobvious gains they may have overlooked or ways of reducing the seemingly prohibitive costs that made rejected alternatives appear undesirable to them.

Fourth, members make little or no attempt to obtain information from experts within their own organizations who might be able to supply more precise estimates of potential losses and gains.

Fifth, members show positive interest in facts and opinions that support their preferred policy; they tend to ignore facts and opinions that do not.

Sixth, members spend little time deliberating about how the chosen policy might be hindered by bureaucratic inertia, sabotaged by political opponents, or temporarily derailed by common accidents. Consequently, they fail to work out contingency plans to cope with foreseeable setbacks that could endanger the overall success of their chosen course.

SUPPORT

The search for an explanation of why groupthink occurs had led me through a quagmire of complicated theoretical issues in the murky area of human motivation. My belief, based on recent social psychological research, is that we can best understand the various symptoms of groupthink as a mutual effort among the group members to maintain self-esteem and emotional equanimity by providing social support to each other, especially at times when they share responsibility for making vital decisions.

Even when no important decision is pending, the typical administrator will begin to doubt the wisdom and morality of his past decisions each time he receives information about setbacks, particularly if the information is accompanied by negative feedback from prominent men who originally had been his supporters. It should not be surprising, therefore, to find that individual members strive to develop unanimity and esprit de corps that will help bolster each other's morale, to create an optimistic outlook about the success of pending decisions, and to reaffirm the positive value of past policies to which all of them are committed.

PRIDE

Shared illusions of invulnerability, for example, can reduce anxiety about taking risks. Rationalizations help members believe that the risks are really not so bad after all. The assumption of inherent morality helps the members to avoid feelings of shame or guilt. Negative stereotypes function as stress-reducing devices to enhance a sense of moral righteousness as well as pride in a lofty mission.

The mutual enhancement of self-esteem and morale may have functional value in enabling the members to maintain their capacity to take action, but it has maladaptive consequences insofar as concurrence-seeking tendencies interfere with critical, rational capacities and lead to serious errors of judgment.

While I have limited my study to decision-making bodies in government, groupthink symptoms appear in business, industry and any other field where small, cohesive groups make the decisions. It is vital, then, for all sorts of people—and especially group leaders—to know what steps they can take to prevent groupthink.

REMEDIES

To counterpoint my case studies of the major fiascos, I have also investigated two highly successful group enterprises, the formulation of the Marshall Plan in the Truman Administration and the handling of the Cuban missile crisis by President Kennedy and his advisers. I have found it instructive to examine the steps Kennedy took to change his group's decision-making processes. These changes ensured that the mistakes made by his Bay of Pigs ingroup were not repeated by the missile-crisis ingroup, even though the membership of both groups was essentially the same.

The following recommendations for preventing groupthink incorporate many of the good practices I discovered to be characteristic of the Marshall Plan and missile-crisis groups:

1. The leader of a policy-forming group should assign the role of critical evaluation to each member, encouraging the group to give high priority to open airing of objections and doubts. This practice needs to be reinformed by the leader's acceptance of criticism of his own judgments in order to discourage members from soft-pedaling their disagreements and from allowing their striving for concurrence to inhibit critical thinking.
2. When the key members of a hierarchy assign a policy-planning mission to any group within their organization, they should adopt an impartial stance instead of stating preferences and expectations at the beginning. This will encourage open inquiry and impartial probing of a wide range of policy alternatives.
3. The organization routinely should set up several outside policy-planning and evaluation groups to work on the same policy question, each deliberating under a different leader. This can prevent the insulation of an ingroup.
4. At intervals before the group reaches a final consensus, the leader should require each member to discuss the group's deliberations with associates in his own unit of the organization—assuming that those associates can be trusted to adhere to the same security regulations that govern the policymakers—and then to report back their reactions to the group.
5. The group should invite one or more outside experts to each meeting on a staggered basis and encourage the experts to challenge the views of the core members.
6. At every general meeting of the group, whenever the agenda calls for an evaluation of policy alternatives, at least one member should play devil's advocate, functioning as a good lawyer in challenging the testimony of those who advocate the majority position.
7. Whenever the policy issue involves relations with a rival nation or organization, the group should devote a sizable block of time, perhaps an entire session, to a survey of all warning signals from the rivals and should write alternative scenarios on the rivals' intentions.
8. When the group is surveying policy alternatives for feasibility and effectiveness, it should from time to time divide into two or more subgroups to meet separately, under different chairmen, and then come back together to hammer out differences.
9. After reaching a preliminary consensus about what seems to be the best policy, the group should hold a "second-chance" meeting at which every member expresses as vividly as he can all his residual doubts, and rethinks the entire issue before making a definitive choice.

HOW

These recommendations have their disadvantages. To encourage the open airing of objections, for instance, might lead to prolonged and costly debates when a rapidly growing crisis requires immediate solution. It also could cause rejection, depression and anger. A leader's failure to set a norm might create cleavage between leader and members that could develop into a disruptive power struggle if the leader looks on the emerging consensus as anathema. Setting up outside evaluation groups might increase the risk of security leakage. Still, inventive executives who know their way around the organizational maze probably can figure out how to apply one or another of the prescriptions successfully, without harmful side effects.

They also could benefit from the advice of outside experts in the administrative and behavioral sciences. Though these experts have much to offer, they have had few chances to work on policy-making machinery within large organizations. As matters now stand, executives innovate only when they need new procedures to avoid repeating serious errors that have deflated their self-images.

In this era of atomic warheads, urban disorganization and ecocatastrophes, it seems to me that policymakers should collaborate with behavioral scientists and give top priority to preventing groupthink and its attendant fiascos.

34. The Design of Work Teams

J. Richard Hackman

In an essay written to commemorate the fiftieth anniversary of the well-known Hawthorne studies at Western Electric Corporation, Harold Leavitt (1975, 76) observed:

Far and away the most powerful and beloved tool of applied behavioral scientists is the small face-to-face group. Since the Western Electric research, behavioral scientists have been learning to understand, exploit and love groups. Groups attracted interest initially as devices for improving the implementation of decisions and to increase human commitment and motivation. They are now loved because they are also creative and innovative, they often make better quality decisions than individuals, and because they make organizational life more livable for people. One can't hire an applied behavioral scientist into an organization who within ten minutes will not want to call a group meeting and talk things over.

Leavitt's paper, entitled "Suppose We Took Groups Seriously . . . ," raises the possibility that both people and organizations would be better off if groups, rather than individuals, were the basic building blocks in the design and management of organizations. Recent trends in organizational practice—such as the increasing use of quality circles, autonomous work groups, project teams, and management task forces—suggest that groups are indeed becoming a popular way to get things done in organizations.

While groups can yield the kinds of benefits Leavitt discusses, they also have a shady side, at least as they typically are designed and managed in contemporary organizations. They can, for example, waste the time and energy of members, rather than use them well. They can enforce norms of low rather than high productivity (Whyte 1955). They sometimes make notoriously bad decisions (Janis 1982). Patterns of destructive conflict can arise, both within and between groups (Alderfer 1977). And groups can exploit, stress, and frustrate their members—sometimes all at the same time (Hackman 1976).

Clearly, if Leavitt's vision is to be realized, we must expand what we know about how to design, manage, and consult to work groups in organizations. There is currently no well-tested and accepted body of research and theory to guide practitioners in using groups to do work, nor do we have a documented record of success in using behavioral-science techniques to help groups become more effective.

This chapter . . . provides a conceptual model for integrating and extending that knowledge, and offers some action guidelines for structuring, supporting, and managing groups in contemporary organizations.

A NORMATIVE MODEL OF GROUP EFFECTIVENESS

The model of work-group effectiveness described in this section is an attempt to bridge between *understanding group behavior* and *doing something to improve it* (the topic of the final section of this chapter).[1] The intent of the normative model is to identify the factors that most powerfully enhance or depress the task effectiveness of a group and to do so in a way that increases the possibility that change can occur. This requires that the variables used in

"The Design of Work Teams" in *Handbook of Organizational Behavior*, J. W. Lorsch, ed. (1987) © 1987, pp. 315, 322, 323–331, 332, 338, 339. Reprinted by permission of Prentice Hall Inc., Englewood Cliffs, New Jersey.

the model be powerful (i.e., they make nontrivial differences in how a group performs), potentially manipulable (i.e., it is feasible to change them in an organization), and accessible (i.e., people can understand them and use them). Moreover, they must be arranged sensibly: the model is not a naturalistic chronological description of what leads to what as a group goes about its work; yet if it is to be useful, it must be plausible.

That is a reasonably tall order, and if we are to have a chance of filling it, we must be very clear about both the kinds of groups to which the model applies and what we mean by "group effectiveness."

SCOPE OF THE MODEL
Domain

The normative model focuses exclusively on *work groups in organizations*. This means that the model applies only to (1) real groups (that is, intact social systems complete with boundaries and differentiated roles among members); (2) groups that have one or more *tasks* to perform, resulting in discernible and potentially measurable group products; and (3) groups that operate within an *organizational context*.

This turns out to be a fairly inclusive statement. The model would apply, for example, to a group of executives charged with deciding where to locate a new plant, a team of rank-and-file workers assembling a product, a group of students writing a case assigned by their instructor, a health-care team tending to the needs of a group of patients, and a group of economists analyzing the budgetary implications of a proposed new public policy.

Nonetheless, many sets of people commonly referred to as "groups" are excluded. Social groups are out (no task), as are reference groups (not an intact social system), coacting groups (i.e., people who may report to the same manager but who have their own, individual tasks to perform—no *group* task), and freestanding groups (no organizational context).

This statement of domain may seem relatively straightforward, but it often is difficult to determine what is a "real" group, a "group task," and an "organizational context." For a detailed and more formal discussion of these issues, see Hackman (1983).

GROUP EFFECTIVENESS DEFINED

In conducting experiments on group performance, researchers try to select tasks for which it is relatively easy to tell how well a group has performed: one can count the number of right answers, or measure how long it takes the group to finish, or see if the group solved the problem correctly. For teams in organizations, effectiveness criteria are more complex. Most organizational tasks do not have clear right-or-wrong answers, for example, nor do they lend themselves to quantitative measures that validly indicate how well a group has done its work. Moreover, one needs to be concerned about more than raw productivity or decision quality when assessing groups in organizations. Unlike participants in laboratory experiments (who come in, do the task, and go home), members of work groups and committees usually continue to relate to one another long after the group task is completed; what happens in the work group can substantially affect their willingness (and their ability) to do so.

For these reasons, we use three criteria to assess team effectiveness. The first deals with the actual output of the group, the second with the state of the group as a performing unit, and the third with the impact of the group experience on individual members.

1. *The productive output of the work group should meet or exceed the performance standards of the people who receive and/or review the output*. If a group's output is not acceptable to its "clients" and/or to managers charged with evaluating its performance, then it cannot be considered effective. An effectiveness criterion that relies explicitly on assessments made by organization members or clients (rather than on "objective" indexes of performance) was chosen for two reasons. First,

reliable and valid objective criteria are available for only a small proportion of work teams in organizations; to deal only with those teams would restrict radically the domain of the model. In addition, what *happens* to a group and its members usually depends far more on others' assessments of the group's output than on any objective performance index (even though such assessments may be based, in part, on whatever objective measures happen to be available).[2]

2. *The social processes used in carrying out the work should maintain or enhance the capability of members to work together on subsequent team tasks.* Some groups operate in such a way that the integrity of the group as a performing unit is destroyed; the group "burns itself up" in the process of performing the task. Even if the product of such a group is acceptable, it would be difficult to argue that the group has been a fully effective performing unit.

3. *The group experience should, on balance, satisfy rather than frustrate the personal needs of group members.* If the primary effect of group membership is to keep individuals from doing what they want and need to do, or if members' predominant reactions to the group experience are disgust and disillusionment, then the costs of generating the group product, at least those borne by individual members, are probably too high.

The inclusion of social and personal criteria in a definition of effectiveness is a departure from tradition—as is the use of system-defined (rather than researcher-defined) assessments of a group's output. Yet the criteria themselves require neither extraordinary accomplishment nor exemplary social processes. All that is necessary is output judged acceptable by those who receive it, a team that winds up its work at least as healthy as when it started, and members who are at least as satisfied as they are frustrated by what has transpired. The challenge for researchers and practitioners is to develop ways of understanding, designing, and managing groups that help them meet or exceed these modest standards of team effectiveness.

The Basic Proposition

The normative model presented in the pages that follow rests on the validity of one key proposition. If this proposition is valid (and if its implications are appropriately developed), it should be possible to explain why some groups perform better than others, to assess the strengths and weaknesses of specific groups in organizations, and to determine what needs to be done to help a group become more effective.

Specifically, it is proposed that the overall effectiveness of work groups in organizations is a joint function of

- The level of *effort* group members collectively expend carrying out task work,
- The amount of *knowledge and skill* members bring to bear on the group task, and
- The appropriateness to the task of the *performance* strategies used by the group in its work.[3]

We will refer to effort, knowledge and skill, and performance strategies as *process criteria of effectiveness*. They are the hurdles a group must surmount to be effective. To assess the adequacy of a group's task processes, then, we might ask: Is the group working hard enough to get the task done well and on time? Do members have the expertise required to accomplish the task, and are they using their knowledge and skill efficiently? Has the group developed an approach to the work that is fully appropriate for the task being performed, and are they implementing that strategy well?

Answers to these questions provide diagnostic data about a group's strengths and weaknesses as a performing unit, and they should enable us to predict with some confidence a group's eventual performance effectiveness. But, as strongly implied by research on interventions that focus exclusively on improving group processes, direct attempts to *manipulate* a group's standing on the process criteria (e.g., by exhortation or instruction) are likely to fail.

A more promising approach is to design and manage a group so that task-effective group processes emerge naturally. Several features of the group and its context can potentially lead to improvements in a group's level of effort, its application of member knowledge and skill, and the appropriateness of its task performance strategies. In particular, we will examine the impact of the following three classes of variables on each of the process criteria:[4]

- The *design of the group* as a performing unit: the structure of the group task, the composition of the group, and group norms that regulate member behavior
- The *organizational context* of the group: the reward, education, and information systems that influence the group, and the material resources that are put at the group's disposal.
- *Group synergy* resulting from members' interactions as they carry out the task.[5]

Throughout, we will emphasize aspects of group design, context, and synergy that foster both high-quality task behavior and eventual team effectiveness. After completing this analysis, we will explore ways of assessing the standing of a group on the variables in the normative model, and speculate about the implications of the model for the creation and management of work teams in organizations.[6]

CONDITIONS THAT SUPPORT EFFORT

Group members are most likely to work hard on their task if (1) the task itself is motivationally engaging, (2) the organizational reward system provides challenging performance objectives and reinforces their achievement, and (3) interaction among members minimizes "social loafing" and instead promotes a shared commitment among members to the team and its work. These factors are illustrated in Figure 34.1 and discussed below.

FIGURE 34.1
Conditions That Foster Hard Work on a Group Task

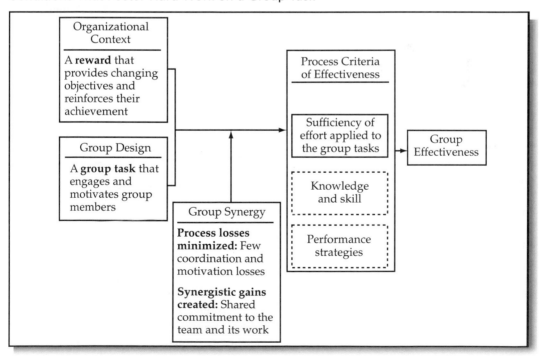

Design of the Group

We would expect a group to work especially hard on its tasks when the following conditions are met:

- The group task requires members to use a variety of relatively high-level skills.
- The group task is a whole and meaningful piece of work, with a visible outcome.
- The outcomes of the group's work on the task have significant consequences for other people (e.g., other organization members or external clients).
- The task provides group members with substantial autonomy for deciding about how they do the work—in effect, the group "owns" the task and is responsible for the work outcomes.
- Work on the task generates regular, trustworthy feedback about how well the group is performing.

If a group task meets these criteria, it is likely that members will experience their work as meaningful, they will feel collectively responsible for the products they create, and they will know, on a more or less continuous basis, how they are doing. And, extrapolating from Hackman and Oldham's (1980, chap. 4) model of individual task motivation, a group task with these properties should result in high built-in motivation for a group to try hard to do well (see, for example, Wall and Clegg 1981).

This emphasis on the group task runs counter to traditional wisdom about motivated work behavior. One often hears managers report that some group is "filled with lazy [or hard-working] people," or that group members "have a norm of not working very hard [or of always giving their best]." It is true that people have different chronic energy levels, but there is not much one can do about that. And while norms do emerge in groups that encourage especially high or low effort, such norms usually develop as a reaction to how things are set up, as a means of coping with the group task and work situation.

Thus, if a group's work is routine and unchallenging, of dubious importance, and wholly preprogrammed with no opportunity for feedback, members are likely to develop antiproductivity norms. But if a group task is challenging, important to the organization or its clients, "owned" by the group, and consequential for group members, then a norm encouraging high effort on the task is likely to emerge. Improving the design of a group's work is usually a better way to foster high collective effort than directly addressing group norms about productivity.

Organizational Context

A supportive organizational reward system can reinforce the motivational benefits of a well-designed team task, and a poorly structured reward system can undermine and erode those benefits. Reward systems that support high effort by work teams tend to have the following three features:

Challenging, Specific Performance Objectives.

There is a great deal of research evidence that goal-directed effort is greater when a group accepts moderately difficult performance objectives and receives feedback about its progress in attaining those objectives (Zander 1971, 1980). When the organization specifies a challenging performance target (e.g., a date by which the work must be done, the number of items to be produced, a quality level to be achieved), members often mobilize their efforts to achieve that target. Objectives, however, should supplement rather than replace task-based motivation. A group is unlikely to persist in working toward challenging objectives if its task is inherently frustrating and alienating.

Positive Consequences for Excellent Performance.

A reward system that recognizes and reinforces excellent group performance can complement and amplify the motivational incentives of a well-designed group task. People tend to engage in behaviors that are rewarded, and people in groups are no exception (Glaser and Klaus 1966). Which specific kinds of rewards will work best, of course, depends on what group members value. Sometimes simple recognition of excellence will suffice; in other cases, more tangible rewards will be required. But whatever the content of the consequences, their impact on team effort will be greater if members understand that they are contingent on performance—that is, that the group will receive them only if it earns them by performing well.

Rewards and Objectives that Focus on Group, Not Individual, Behavior.
When rewards are given to individuals on the basis of managers' judgments about who has contributed most to a group product, dissension and conflict often develop within the group. This is the dilemma of the athletic coach, who must try to motivate the team as a whole while simultaneously cultivating and reinforcing individual performance. And it is a problem routinely faced by managers of work teams in organizations where the reward system has traditionally focused on the identification and recognition of excellent *individual* performers.

The destructive effects of rewarding individual contributions rather than team performance can be considerable. Therefore, if it is not feasible to provide performance-contingent rewards to the group as a unit, it may be better to base rewards on the performance of even larger groups (such as a department or division) or not to use contingent rewards at all than to invite the divisiveness that can develop when members of a team are put into competition with one another for scarce and valued rewards (Lawler 1981).

Group Synergy
Group synergy can contribute to effective task behavior in two ways. First, group members can find innovative ways to avoid "process losses," and thereby minimize waste and misuse of members' time, energy, and talent. Second, members can interact synergistically to create *new* internal resources that can be used in their work—capabilities that did not exist before the group created them. Process losses and synergistic gains that affect how much effort a group applies to its task are discussed below.

Minimizing Coordination and Motivation Losses.
There are always some "overhead costs" to be paid when groups perform tasks. The need to coordinate member activities, for example, takes time and energy away from productive work, resulting in a level of actual productivity that is less than what theoretically would be possible with optimum use of member resources (Steiner 1972). In addition, group productivity often is compromised by what Steiner terms "motivation decrements" and what Latané (e.g., Latané, Williams, and Harkins 1979) has called "social loafing." As groups get larger, the amount of effort *each member* contributes to the group task decreases— perhaps because each individual feels less responsible for the outcome than would be the case in a smaller group or if one person were doing the task alone.

Some groups suffer much greater coordination and motivation losses than others. And group members can cultivate process skills that help them behave in ways that minimize such losses. But if the group is large or if the task is ill defined or alienating, it may be impossible for the group to avoid serious coordination and motivation losses.

Creating Shared Commitment to the Team and Its Work.
Some groups show great "spirit": everyone is committed to the team, proud of it, and willing to work hard to make it one of the best. When individuals value their membership in the group and find it rewarding to work collaboratively with their teammates, they may work considerably harder than they would otherwise. Managers often engage in group-building activities (such as encouraging members of an ongoing team to give the group a name, to decorate their work area, or to participate in an athletic league as a team) in the hope of increasing members' commitment to the group and their willingness to work especially hard on the group task.[7]

Commitment to a team sometimes can result in high effort on the group task even when objective performance conditions are highly unfavorable (e.g., a team that develops a "can do" attitude and comes to view each new adversity as yet another challenge to be met). It is questionable, however, whether such commitment is sustainable if performance conditions remain poor (e.g., a frustrating or alienating group task, or a reward system that does not recognize excellence).

CONDITIONS THAT SUPPORT KNOWLEDGE AND SKILL

A group is most likely to bring sufficient talent and expertise to bear on its task when (1) the group has an appropriate number of members with a good mix of skills, (2) the education system of the organization offers training or consultation as needed to supplement members' existing knowledge, and (3) group interaction avoids inappropriate "weighting" of members' contributions and instead fosters sharing of expertise and collective learning. These factors are illustrated in Figure 34.2 and discussed below.

Design of the Group

A group's composition is the most important condition affecting the amount of knowledge and skill members apply to their tasks. Well-composed groups have the following four characteristics:

Individual Members Have High Task-Relevant Expertise. The most efficient way to make sure a group has the expertise it needs for its work is simply to assign talented individuals to it. This seemingly

FIGURE 34.2
Conditions That Foster Effective Use of Talent and Expertise in Task Work

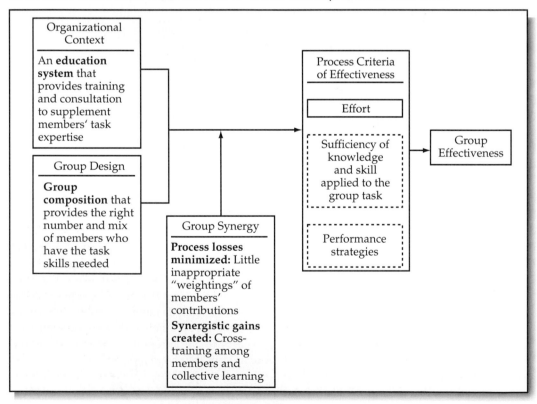

obvious principle, however, is not always straightforward in practice. Even when people with ample task-relevant knowledge and skill are available, they may be overlooked—for example, when groups are composed with only political considerations in mind. This can result in a team whose members cover all the right bases, but one that is not capable of carrying out well the work it was created to do.

The Group Is Just Large Enough to Do the Work.

If a task required four sets of hands, then there should be four people in the group—but no more than that. The research literature offers abundant evidence documenting the dysfunctions that occur in large groups (see Steiner 1972, chap. 4 for a review) and establishing the advantages of groups that are slightly *smaller* than the task technically requires (Wicker et al. 1976). Yet large work groups (especially decision-making committees) are widely used in organizations. Often the decision to put additional people in a group allows managers to avoid difficult personnel choices or sensitive political issues (e.g., how to involve a department in the work of a task force on which it has no representatives), but the cost may be losses in the quality of the group product and the efficiency with which it is produced.

Members Have Interpersonal as Well as Task Skills.

If a group task is well designed (i.e., it provides the group considerable autonomy in managing a challenging piece of work), then at least moderate interpersonal skills are required to bring the *task* skills of members to bear on the group's work—especially if members are diverse (i.e., they come from different demographic groups, represent different organizational units, or have divergent personal views on the matter at hand). Some individuals have little competence in working collaboratively with other people, especially if those people differ from themselves in important ways. Even one or two such individuals can significantly impede the ability of a group to bring members' expertise effectively to bear on the group task.

Membership Is Moderately Diverse.

Members of an excessively homogeneous group may get along well together but lack the resources needed to perform the task because the members essentially replicate one another. An excessively heterogeneous group, on the other hand, may have a rich complement of talent within the group but be unable to use that talent well because members are so diverse in values or perspective that they cannot work together effectively. The aspiration in composing a group is to strike just the right balance between homogeneity and heterogeneity: members should have a variety of talents and perspective, yet be similar enough that they can understand and coordinate with one another.[8]

Organizational Context

Sometimes a group has within its bounds all the knowledge and skill needed for optimum task performance. More commonly there are aspects of the work for which additional talent or expertise would be helpful. The educational system of the organization can play a useful role in helping the group obtain the outside expertise it needs for its work.

For this potential to be realized, two conditions must be met. First, relevant educational resources (which can include technical consultation as well as training) must exist somewhere in the organization. Second, some sort of "delivery system" must be in place to make those resources accessible to the group. This may not be a simple matter for rank-and-file teams in organizations where employees have never had the right to call on staff resources.

The particular kind of assistance required will, of course, depend on both the task requirements and the specific needs of the group. And the appropriate form of assistance will vary as well. Sometimes a one-shot technical consultation will suffice; sometimes a continuing consulting relationship will be needed; and sometimes a training program for group members will be more appropriate, to build the relevant expertise into the group itself. Whatever the content of the assistance and the vehicle used to provide it, the role of the educational system is the same: to help groups obtain the full complement of knowledge and skill required for excellent task performance.

Group Synergy

Minimizing Inappropriate Weighting of Member Contributions. The knowledge and skill of group members can be wasted if the group solicits and weights contributions in a way that is incongruent with members' expertise—as when the credence given a member's idea depends on such task-irrelevant considerations as his or her demographic attributes (e.g., gender, ethnicity, or age) or behavioral style (e.g., talkativeness or verbal dominance). This process loss has been well documented in the research literature (e.g., Johnson and Torcivia 1967; Thomas and Fink 1961; Torrance 1954). Groups often have trouble assessing which members have the special expertise needed for the task, and they appear to have even more difficulty explicitly acknowledging these differences and weighting members' contributions in accord with them. To the extent a group is able to minimize this problem, it will take better advantage of the expertise that was put in the group when it was composed.

Fostering Collective Learning. When members of a group interact in ways that help them learn from one another, they can increase the total pool of talent available for task work—a synergistic gain from group interaction. The practice of "cross-training," often encouraged in autonomous work groups in industry, is an example of such behavior, as are more informal activities that involve the sharing of knowledge, expertise, and experience among members. A group that orients itself to collective learning and whose members share what is learned with each other should be far better able to exploit the educational resources of an organization than a group that takes a laissez-faire stance toward the development of its internal talent.

CONDITIONS THAT SUPPORT APPROPRIATE PERFORMANCE STRATEGIES

The likelihood that the group will employ a task-appropriate performance strategy increases when (1) group norms support explicit assessment of the performance situation and active consideration of alternative ways of proceeding with the work; (2) the information system of the organization provides members with the data they need to assess the situation and evaluate alternative strategies; and (3) group interaction results in little "slippage" when performance plans are executed and instead prompts creative new ideas about ways to proceed with the work. These factors are illustrated in Figure 34.3 and discussed below.

Design of Group

Group members typically reach agreement on how they will go about performing their task relatively early in their time together. Indeed, for familiar tasks, members may not talk about their strategy at all, because it is obvious to everyone how the task should be done. Once a strategy is agreed to, whether implicitly or explicitly, members tend to behave in accord with it and enforce adherence to it (March and Simon 1958, chap. 6). Performance strategies thus become part of the fabric of the group, a "given" that is no more open to question than the task of the group or who is in the group.

The specific strategies that will be most appropriate for a given group depend both on the task to be done and on the imperatives and resources in the performance situation. No "one best strategy" can be specified in advance for most task-performing groups in organizations. It is possible, however, to build group norms that increase the likelihood that members will develop task-appropriate performance strategies and execute them well. Such norms have two properties, the first being a prerequisite for the second.[9]

Group Norms Support Self-Regulation. Behavior in some groups is so chaotic and subject to individual whim as to approach

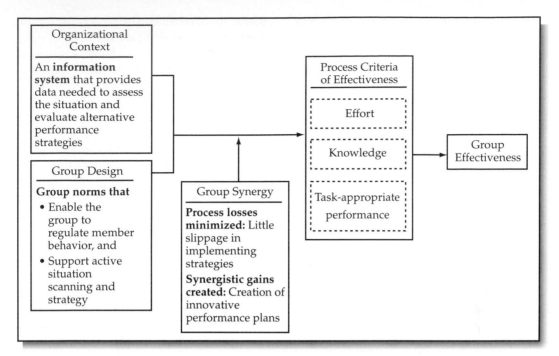

FIGURE 34.3
Conditions That Encourage the Use of Task-Appropriate Performance Strategies

anarchy. Such groups are unlikely to be able to execute any performance strategy in an orderly fashion, even one that has been specified in detail by management. Thus, a normative structure that enables a group to regulate member behavior is essential to the efficient execution of performance strategies. This requires that behavioral norms be sufficiently crystallized (i.e., members have consensus about them) and intense (i.e., compliance results in substantial approval or avoidance of substantial disapproval by other members) that individuals will wish to behave in accord with them (Jackson 1965).

Group Norms Support Situation Scanning and Strategy Planning.

Groups that actively assess the demands and opportunities in the performance situation and that consider several alternative ways of proceeding with the work tend to develop more appropriate performance strategies than groups

that do not (Hackman, Brousseau, and Weiss 1976; Maier 1963). Yet such activities tend not to take place spontaneously. Instead, it appears that the general disinclination of group members to "talk about process" extends even to discussions about how the work of the group will be carried out.[10]

For this reason, it is necessary somehow to prompt or encourage group members to engage in situation scanning and strategy planning activities. Group norms provide an efficient and powerful way to accomplish this. Such norms focus attention on opportunities and constraints that might otherwise be overlooked and make it difficult for members to fall into familiar or habitual patterns of behavior that may be inappropriate for the particular task at hand.[11]

Group norms governing performance processes can be established when a group is first formed or can be introduced during a hiatus in the work, when members are ready to reconsider how they operate as a team. Regardless of how and when they are developed, the norms that guide a group's performance processes are an important structural feature of the group—an aspect of group design that often has been overlooked by both scholars and managers interested in work-team effectiveness.

Organizational Context

The information system of an organization is critical to a group's ability to plan and execute a task-appropriate performance strategy. If a group cannot obtain clear information about its performance situation, or if it does not have access to data about the likely outcomes of alternative approaches to the task, it may develop a way of proceeding that seems reasonable to group members but that turns out, when executed, to be grossly inappropriate.

Clarity About the Parameters of the Performance Situation.

To develop a task-appropriate performance strategy, a group needs a relatively clear map of the performance situation. Of special importance is information about (1) task requirements and constraints that may limit strategic options, (2) the material resources available for use, and (3) the people who will receive, review, and/or use the group product, and the standards they are likely to employ in assessing its adequacy.

Access to Data About Likely Consequences of Alternative Strategies.

The information system also should make available to a group the data and analytic tools members need to compare and evaluate the probable consequences of alternative performance strategies. Consider, for example, a manufacturing team that is attempting to decide how to approach a complex assembly task. One possibility might be a cyclic strategy, in which all members build components for a period of time, then assemble final products (producing a relative flood of output), followed by another component-building period, and so on. How would this strategy compare to one in which some members build components continuously while others are dedicated to final assembly? To

choose between these strategies, the group needs information about the timing of demand for their product, the availability of space for storing components and completed products, and the cost of obtaining and holding parts for use in batch-component production. It would be quite risky for a group to choose a strategy without data about such matters.

How much information a group needs depends in part on how much latitude it has to manage its own affairs. Groups that have the authority to invent their own strategies and manage their own performance processes will need relatively complete data on both the parameters of the performance situation and the likely consequences of alternative ways of proceeding. Groups with less authority for setting their own directions will have less need for such data.

Managers who control access to performance-relevant information must make sure that data needed by a team are realistically available to it. This is not always easy: the relevant data may not exist, they may be costly to obtain, or the manager may be unable to convince his or her colleagues that it is appropriate to share with the group politically or competitively sensitive information. In such circumstances, the group needs to know *that*—that it will have to make do with imperfect or incomplete data.[12] Care also must be taken not to flood the group with excess or irrelevant information, data that members must process but for which they have no present use. Some organizations minimize this risk by initially providing teams only with basic data about the parameters of the performance situation and a guide to other information available. The group has the responsibility for deciding what additional data it requires and for determining when and how to obtain it.

Group Synergy

Minimizing Slippage in Strategy Implementation.

Plans are never perfectly implemented—there is always a slip or two, something that wastes or misdirects the time and energy of group members, compromising even well-conceived plans. To the extent a group minimizes this process loss, the opportunities provided by norms that foster strategy planning and by a supportive information system can be well used. But if slippage is high, the group may fail to exploit even a highly favorable performance situation.[13]

Creating Innovative Strategic Plans.

On the positive side, groups can develop ways of interacting that occasionally result in truly original or insightful ways of proceeding with the work. For example, a group might find a way to exploit some resources that everyone else has overlooked; it might invent a way to get around a seemingly insurmountable performance obstacle; or it might come up with a novel way to generate ideas for solving a difficult problem. When group members get in the habit of thinking creatively about how they will do their work, interesting and useful ideas can emerge—ideas that did not exist before the group invented them.

OVERVIEW AND SUMMARY

An overview of the normative model is presented in Figure 34.4. It shows three major points of leverage for fostering group effectiveness: (1) the design of the group as a performing unit, (2) the supports provided by the organizational context in which the group operates, and (3) the synergistic outcomes of the interaction among group members. The contributions of each of these classes of variables are summarized next in brief.

Design

The design of a group—task structure, group composition, and group norms—should

FIGURE 34.4
An Overview of the Normative Model of Group Effectiveness

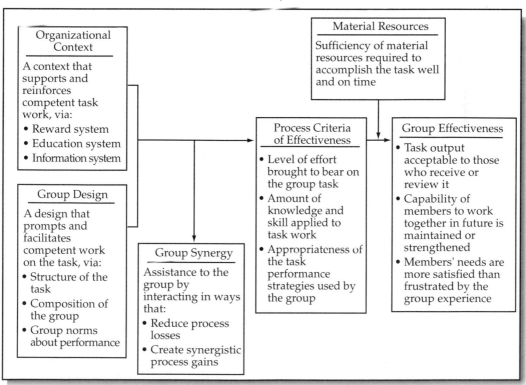

promote effective task behavior and lessen the chances that members will encounter built-in obstacles to good performance. While a good group design cannot guarantee competent group behavior, it does create conditions that make it easier and more natural for task-effective behaviors to emerge and persist.

Context

The organizational context of a group—the reward, education, and information systems of the organization—should support and reinforce the design features. A supportive organizational context gives a group what it needs to exploit the potential of a good basic design (although it probably cannot compensate for a fundamentally flawed design). An unsupportive organizational context can easily undermine the positive features of even a well-designed team. Excellent group performance requires *both* a good design for the team and a supportive organizational context.

Figure 34.4 shows one important contextual feature not previously discussed—the *material resources* required to do the work. If a group lacks the tools, equipment, space, raw materials, money, or human resources it needs, its performance surely will suffer—even if it stands high on the process criteria of effectiveness. A talented, well-motivated production team, for example, will not perform well if the raw materials it needs to make its products are not available, or if production tools are unsatisfactory. Similarly, a committee formed to select a new agency manager cannot be successful if there are no qualified candidates available. And a group that provides human services to clients may have performance problems if members' work stations are so spread about that they cannot coordinate their activities, or if money is so scarce that needed support staff cannot be obtained.[14]

Synergy

Group synergy "tunes" the impact of design and contextual factors. Positive synergy—that is, when the synergistic gains from group interaction exceed group process losses—can help a group overcome the limitations of a poor performance situation (e.g., a badly designed group task or an unsupportive reward system). And if performance conditions are favorable, positive synergy can help a group exploit the opportunities those conditions provide. Negative synergy, when process losses exceed synergistic gains, has opposite effects. It can amplify the negative impact of a poor performance situation, and it can prevent a group from taking advantage of favorable circumstances. The relationship between performance conditions (i.e., the group design and the organizational context) and group synergy is illustrated in Figure 34.5.[15]

IMPLICATIONS FOR THE MANAGEMENT OF TEAMS

Because this chapter represents a departure from traditional thinking about group performance, it may be appropriate to conclude by briefly highlighting some of the broader management implications of what has been proposed.

On Leadership

The research literature is rich with studies of leadership in groups (for reviews, see Hare 1976, chap. 13, and Stogdill 1974). Most of this research assesses what leaders do *within* groups or tests propositions about what leader traits and styles are most effective under what circumstances. Such questions are derivative in the approach taken here, because leaders are viewed as exercising influence primarily through the decisions they make about how to frame the group task, how to structure the group and its context, and how to help the group get started up well and headed in an appropriate direction.

Indeed, we have not even discussed whether an internal group leader should be named—let alone how he or she should behave. It often does make sense to have such a role, especially when substantial coordination among members is required, when there is lots of information to be processed (Maier 1967), or when it is advisable to have one person be the liaison with other groups or with higher management.

		Unfavorable	Favorable
Group Synergy	Predominantly Negative	Amplification of the impact of performance-depressing conditions	Failure by the group to exploit opportunities in the performance situation
	Predominantly Positive	Damping of the negative impact of performance conditions; perhaps transcending their effects for a limited period of time	Full exploitation of favorable performance conditions

FIGURE 34.5
Consequences for Task Behavior of the Interaction Between Performance Conditions and Group Synergy

Yet it is rarely a good idea to decide in advance about the leadership structure of a work group. If a group has been designed well and helped to begin exploring the group norms and member roles it wishes to have, questions of internal leadership should appear naturally. And while there invariably will be a good deal of stress and strain in the group as leadership issues are dealt with, when a resolution comes it will have the considerable advantage of being the group's own.

The manager's role, then, is to make sure a group confronts the leadership issue directly (even if members would prefer to deal with it implicitly or avoid it entirely), not to resolve it for the group. To do the latter is to short-circuit an important developmental task in the life of a team and to rob the group of a significant opportunity to organize and develop its own internal resources.

On Creating Redundant Conditions

There are many ways for a group to be effective in performing a task, and even more ways for it to be ineffective. Moreover, different task and organizational circumstances involve vastly different demands and opportunities. Thus it is impossible to specify in detail what specific behaviors managers should adopt to help groups perform effectively. There are simply too many ways a group can operate and still wind up with the same outcome.[16] Attempts to specify contingencies for managerial behavior do not help much, in that they usually result in prescriptions too complex for anyone to follow (Hackman 1984).

Thus, while many models of leadership call for the active manipulation of "causes" that are assumed to be tightly linked to "effects," our view of group behavior suggests that the key to effective group management may be to create redundant conditions that support good performance, leaving groups ample room to develop and enact their own ways of operating within those conditions.

A manager interested in encouraging a group to work hard, for example, would try to make the group task more motivationally engaging. *And* he or she would try to provide more (or more potent) positive consequences contingent on hard, effective work. *And* he or she would work with the group members to improve the efficiency of their internal processes and to build a positive team spirit. And if there were other steps that could be taken to create conditions supportive of high effort, these would be attempted as well.

Group performance does not have clean, unitary causes. To help a group improve its effectiveness involves doing whatever is possible to create multiple, redundant conditions that together may nudge the group toward more competent task behavior and, eventually, better performance.[17]

On Managerial Authority

The approach taken in this chapter clearly favors the creation of conditions that empower groups, that increase their authority to manage their own work. While this does not imply a diminution of managerial authority, it does suggest that it be redirected.

One critical use of authority, already discussed at some length, is in creating organizational conditions that foster and support effective group behavior. Managers must not view design and contextual features as "givens" over which they have little control. Instead, influence must be wielded upward and outward in the organization to make organizational structures and systems as supportive of team effectiveness as possible. If a manager does not have the authority to initiate discussions about making such changes, he or she should consider trying to get it, because it will be hard to be a good team manager without it.

Managerial authority also should be used to establish and enforce standards of group behavior and acceptable performance. When a manager defines a piece of work to be done, sets performance standards, and is clear about the bounds of acceptable group behavior, he or she is exercising managerial authority—and concurrently empowering the group that will do the work. To be vague about what is required and expected can be just as debilitating to a group as traditional, hands-on supervision. To enable groups to use their authority well, managers must not be afraid to exercise their own.

On Knowing Some Things

The management behaviors implied by the model of team effectiveness explored in this chapter will seem unfamiliar and awkward to some managers, and may be hard for them to perform well. But any new endeavor can be difficult. Trying to make sense of a balance sheet, for example, or figuring out a good design for a production process can feel just as awkward and be just as hard for an unpracticed manager to do well. Yet for some reason we are far more willing to acknowledge the need for training and experience in these areas than we are in aspects of managerial work related to the effective use of human resources.

Managing work groups is every bit as tough as figuring out what to do about the numbers on a balance sheet. To manage teams well, one needs to know some things, have some skills, and have opportunities to practice. The sooner those requirements are acknowledged, the sooner we will be able to develop a cadre of managers who are expert in creating work teams, developing them, and harvesting the considerable contributions they have to make to organizational effectiveness.

REFERENCES

1. The work of Cummings (e.g., 1978, 1981) on the design and management of work groups from a sociotechnical-systems perspective has much in common with what is presented here, although it comes from a rather different intellectual tradition. For an overview of that tradition, see Trist (1981).
2. There are, however, occasions when it may not be sensible to rely on client assessments of a group's output. Consider, for example, a situation in which the legitimate clients of the group are seriously disturbed, ethnocentric, or competitive with the group. The very meaning of "good performance" under these circumstances is problematic.
3. For example, a group might decide to divide itself into two sub-groups, each of which would do part of the overall task, with the

final product to be assembled later. Or it might choose to free associate about task solutions in the first meeting, reflect for a week about the ideas that came up, and then meet to draft the product. Or it might decide to spend considerable time checking and rechecking for errors after learning that its client cares a great deal about product quality. All of these are choices about task performance strategy.

4. For simplicity, feedback loops among classes of variables in the framework (e.g., how the organizational context may change in response to a team's level of effectiveness) are not shown or discussed here.

5. As applied to group behavior in this chapter, "synergy" refers to group-level phenomena that (1) emerge from the interaction among members, and (2) affect how well a group is able to deal with the demands and opportunities in its performance situation.

6. Some of the material that follows is adapted from Hackman and Oldham (1980), chaps. 7–8.

7. Such activities are not risk free. "Team spirit" can evolve into group ethnocentrism and can prompt dysfunctional competition and conflict between groups.

8. A number of scholars have examined the impact of member compatibility on task behavior and performance. See, for example, Belbin (1981); Hewett, O'Brien, and Hornik (1974); and Schutz (1958, 1961).

9. Following Jackson (1965), norms are conceptualized as structural features of a group that summarize members' shared approval (or disapproval) of various behaviors. Norms simplify group influence processes because they make it possible for members to count on certain things being done and other things not being done. For more detailed discussion of how norms structure and channel behavior in a group, see Hackman (1976).

10. Spontaneous strategy planning does, of course, occur if a task is so novel that members are at a loss about how to proceed with it, and is generally more likely when the task is unfamiliar.

11. This analysis presumes that a team has at least some latitude for planning its own strategy. Usually this is the case. In some groups, however, behavior is so completely preprogrammed or closely supervised that members have essentially no strategy choices to make. For such groups, there is little need for a norm supporting scanning and planning, because those activities are someone else's responsibility. All that is needed is the orderly execution of the strategy that has been supplied. The implications of giving a team the authority to devise its own strategies (rather than reserving that authority for management) are explored later in this chapter.

12. Particularly unfortunate are occasions when a manager deliberately withholds performance-relevant information from a group, to make sure the group remains dependent on him or her. While this may preserve a manager's feelings of personal power, it can result in inappropriate performance strategies and needlessly poor team performance.

13. One particularly virulent form of this process loss bears special mention. Members of some groups collude with each other in a way that makes it impossible ever to implement performance plans. Such a group may have ample information about the performance situation and may develop a fully task-appropriate performance strategy. But once the plans are complete they are ignored. When members reconvene, they develop new plans and a new resolve, and the cycle repeats itself. The group acts as if a good strategy is all that is needed for team effectiveness, and its inevitable failures are always well-wrapped in new and better plans for the future. This kind of synergy often is driven by unconscious forces, it is not uncommon in groups that have high-pressure work environments, and it can be lethal to team effectiveness.

14. The importance of mundane aspects of the performance situation such as these are increasingly being recognized as critical to effective work performance (see, for example, Peters and O'Connor 1980, and Peters,

O'Connor, and Rudolf 1980). To overlook them is to jeopardize the effort expended to design a team well and provide it with appropriate contextual supports.

15. Although performance conditions and group synergy are placed on separate axes in the figure, they are not independent: positive synergy is more likely under favorable conditions, and negative synergy is more likely under unfavorable conditions. Thus performance spirals can develop. For example, good group performance can lead to management decisions that improve the group's performance situation, which promotes positive synergy, which results in even better performance, and so on. Equally plausible is a negative spiral, in which poor performance begets organizational "tightening up," resulting in negative synergy, and so on.

16. Systems theorists call this aspect of organized endeavor "equifinality" (Katz and Kahn 1978, 30). According to this principle, a social system can reach the same outcome from a variety of initial conditions and by a variety of methods.

17. We see here a key difference between descriptive and action models of behavior in organization. A descriptive model parcels up the world for conceptual clarity: in contrast, a good action model parcels up the world to increase the chances that something can be created or changed. Rather than seek to isolate unitary causes, an action model attempts to identify clusters of covarying factors that can serve as useful levers for change. For related views, see Hackman (1984), Mohr (1982), and Weick (1977).

ADDITIONAL READINGS

C. P. Alderfer (1977) "Group and Intergroup Relations" in J. R. Hackman and J. L. Suttle, eds., *Improving Life at Work*. Santa Monica, Calif.: Goodyear.

C. Argyris (1969) "The Incompleteness of Social Psychological Theory: Examples from Small Group, Cognitive Consistency, and Attribution Research." *American Psychologist*, 24, pp. 893–908.

———. (1980) *The Inner Contradictions of Rigorous Research*. New York: Academic Press.

———. (1983) "Action Science and Intervention." *Journal of Applied Behavioral Science*, 19, pp. 115–35.

R. F. Bales (1950) *Interaction Process Analysis: A Method for the Study of Small Groups*. Cambridge, Mass.: Addison-Wesley.

———. (1970) *Personality and Interpersonal Behavior*. New York: Holt, Rinehart and Winston.

R. F. Bales and S. P. Cohen (1979) *SYMLOG: A System for the Multiple Level Observation of Groups*. New York: Free Press.

M. Beer (1976) "The Technology of Organization Development" in M. D. Dunnette, ed., *Handbook of Industrial and Organizational Psychology*. Chicago: Rand McNally.

R. M. Belbin (1981) *Management Teams: Why They Succeed or Fail*. London: Heinemann.

H. J. Bertcher and F. F. Maple (1977) *Creating Groups*. Beverly Hills, Calif.: Sage.

R. R. Blake and J. S. Mouton (1969) *Building a Dynamic Corporation Through Grid Organization Development*. Reading, Mass.: Addison-Wesley.

A. D. Colman and W. H. Bexton (1975) *Group Relations Reader*. Sausalito, Calif.: GREX.

C. L. Cooper (1975), ed., *Theories of Group Processes*. London: Wiley.

T. G. Cummings (July 1978) "Self-Regulating Work Groups: A Socio-Technical Synthesis." *Academy of Management Review*, 2, no. 3, pp. 625–34.

———. (1981) "Designing Effective Work Groups" in P. C. Nystrom and W. H. Starbuck, eds., *Handbook of Organizational Design*, vol. 2. London: Oxford University Press.

N. C. Dalkey (1967) *Delphi*. Santa Monica, Calif.: Rand.

J. H. Davis (1973) "Group Decision and Social Interaction: A Theory of Social Decision Schemes." *Psychological Review*, 80, pp. 97–125.

J. H. Davis and V. B. Hinsz (1982) "Current Research Problems in Group Performance and Group Dynamics" in H. Brandstätter, J. H. Davis, and G. Stocker-Kreichgauer, eds., *Group Decision Making*. London: Academic Press.

A. L. Delbecq, A. H. Van de Ven, and D. H. Gustafson (1975) *Group Techniques for Program Planning*. Glenview, Ill.: Scott, Foresman.

M. D. Dunnette, J. Campbell, and K. Jaastad (1963) "The Effect of Group Participation on Brainstorming Effectiveness for Two Industrial Samples." *Journal of Applied Psychology*, 47, pp. 30–37.

W. G. Dyer (1977) *Team Building: Issues and Alternatives*. Reading, Mass.: Addison-Wesley.

F. Friedlander and L. D. Brown (1974) "Organization Development" in M. R. Rosenzweig and L. W. Porter, eds., *Annual Review of Psychology*, vol. 25. Palo Alto, Calif.: Annual Reviews.

C. J. G. Gersick (1983) "Life Cycles of *Ad Hoc* Groups." Technical report no. 3, Group Effectiveness Research Project, School of Organization and Management, Yale University.

R. Glaser and D. J. Klaus (1966) "A Reinforcement Analysis of Group Performance." *Psychological Monographs*, 80, whole no. 621, pp. 1–23.

P. Goodman, R. Atkin, and E. Ravlin (1982) "Some Observations on Specifying Models of Group Performance." Paper delivered at a symposium on Productive Work Teams and Groups, American Psychological Association Convention, Washington, D.C.

T. B. Green (1975) "An Empirical Analysis of Nominal and Interacting Groups." *Academy of Management Journal*, 18, pp. 63–73.

J. R. Hackman (1969) "Toward Understanding the Role of Tasks in Behavioral Research." *Acta Psychologica,* 31, pp. 97–128.

———. (1976) "Group Influences on Individuals" in M. D. Dunnette, ed., *Handbook of Industrial and Organizational Psychology*. Chicago: Rand McNally.

———. (1982) "A Set of Methods for Research on Work Teams." Technical report no. 1, Group Effectiveness Research Project, School of Organization and Management, Yale University.

———. (1983) "A Normative Model of Work Team Effectiveness." Technical report no. 2, Group Effectiveness Research Project, School of Organization and Management, Yale University.

———. (1984) "Psychological Contributions to Organizational Productivity: A Commentary" in A. P. Brief, ed., *Productivity Research in the Behavioral and Social Sciences*. New York: Praeger.

J. R. Hackman, K. R. Brousseau, and J. A. Weiss (1976) "The Interaction of Task Design and Group Performance Strategies in Determining Group Effectiveness." *Organizational Behavior and Human Performance*, 16, pp. 350–65.

J. R. Hackman and C. G. Morris (1975) "Group Tasks, Group Interaction Process, and Group Performance Effectiveness: A Review and Proposed Integration" in L. Berkowitz, ed., *Advances in Experimental Social Psychology*. New York: Academic Press.

J. R. Hackman and G. R. Oldham (1980) *Work Redesign*. Reading, Mass.: Addison-Wesley.

A. P. Hare (1976) *Handbook of Small Group Research*. 2d ed. New York: Free Press.

———. (1982) *Creativity in Small Groups*. Beverly Hills, Calif.: Sage.

J. S. Heinen and E. Jacobson (1976) "A Model of Task Group Development in Complex Organizations and a Strategy of Implementation." *Academy of Management Review*, 1, pp. 98–111.

D. M. Herold (1978) "Improving the Performance Effectiveness of Groups Through a Task-Contingent Selection of Intervention Strategies." *Academy of Management Review*, 3, pp. 315–25.

T. T. Hewett, G. E. O'Brien, and J. Hornik (1974) "The Effects of Work Organization, Leadership Style, and Member Compatibility

Upon the Productivity of Small Groups Working on a Manipulative Task." *Organizational Behavior and Human Performance*, 11, pp. 283–301.

L. R. Hoffman (1979a) "Applying Experimental Research on Group Problem Solving to Organizations." *Journal of Applied Behavioral Science*, 15, pp. 375–91.

————. (1979b), ed., *The Group Problem Solving Process: Studies of a Valence Model*. New York: Praeger.

J. Jackson (1965) "Structural Characteristics of Norms" in I. D. Steiner and M. Fishbein, eds., *Current Studies in Social Psychology*. New York: Holt, Rinehart and Winston.

I. L. Janis (1982) *Groupthink*. 2d ed. Boston: Houghton Mifflin.

H. H. Johnson and J. M. Torcivia (1967) "Group and Individual Performance on a Single-Stage Task as a Function of Distribution of Individual Performance." *Journal of Personality and Social Psychology*, 3, pp. 266–73.

R. E. Kaplan (1979) "The Conspicuous Absence of Evidence that Process Consultation Enhances Task Performance." *Journal of Applied Behavioral Science*, 15, pp. 346–60.

D. Katz and R. L. Kahn (1978) *The Social Psychology of Organizations*. 2d ed. New York: Wiley.

R. Katz (1982) "The Effects of Group Longevity on Project Communication and Performance." *Administrative Science Quarterly*, 27, pp. 81–104.

B. Latané, K. Williams, and S. Harkins (1979) "Many Hands Make Light the Work: The Causes and Consequences of Social Loafing." *Journal of Personality and Social Psychology*, 37, pp. 822–32.

E. E. Lawler (1981) *Pay and Organization Development*. Reading, Mass.: Addison-Wesley.

H. J. Leavitt (1975) "Suppose We Took Groups Seriously . . ." in E. L. Cass and F. G. Zimmer, eds., *Man and Work in Society*. New York: Van Nostrand Reinhold.

N. R. F. Maier (1963) *Problem Solving Discussions and Conferences: Leadership Methods and Skills*. New York: McGraw-Hill.

————. (1967) "Assets and Liabilities in Group Problem Solving: The Need for an Integrative Function." *Psychological Review*, 74, pp. 239–49.

J. G. March and H. A. Simon (1958) *Organizations*. New York: Wiley.

J. E. McGrath (1964) *Social Psychology: A Brief Introduction*. New York: Holt, Rinehart and Winston.

————. (1984) *Groups: Interaction and Performance*. Englewood Cliffs, N.J.: Prentice Hall.

J. E. McGrath and I. Altman (1966) *Small Group Research: A Synthesis and Critique of the Field*. New York: Holt, Rinehart and Winston.

J. E. McGrath and D. A. Kravitz (1982) "Group Research." *Annual Review of Psychology*, 33, pp. 195–230.

U. Merry and M. E. Allerhand (1977) *Developing Teams and Organizations*. Reading, Mass.: Addison-Wesley.

L. B. Mohr (1982) *Explaining Organizational Behavior*. San Francisco: Jossey-Bass.

D. C. Myers and H. Lamm (1976) "The Group Polarization Phenomenon." *Psychological Bulletin*, 83, pp. 602–27.

D. H. Nagao, D. A. Vollrath, and J. H. Davis (1978) "Group Decision Making: Origins and Current Status" in H. Brandstätter, J. H. Davis, and H. C. Schuler, eds., *Dynamics of Group Decisions*. Beverly Hills, Calif.: Sage.

A. F. Osborn (1957) *Applied Imagination*. Rev. ed. New York: Scribner's.

R. Payne and C. L. Cooper (1981) eds., *Groups at Work*. Chichester, England: Wiley.

L. H. Peters and E. J. O'Connor (1980) "Situational Constraints and Work Outcomes: The Influences of a Frequently Overlooked Construct." *Academy of Management Review*, 5, pp. 391–97.

L. H. Peters, E. J. O'Connor, and C. J. Rudolf (1980) "The Behavioral and Affective Consequences of Performance-Relevant Situational Variables." *Organizational Behavior and Human Performance*, 25, pp. 79–96.

E. J. Poza and M. L. Marcus (1980) "Success Story: The Team Approach to Work Restructuring." *Organizational Dynamics*, Winter, pp. 3–25.

T. B. Roby and J. T. Lanzetta (1958) "Considerations in the Analysis of Group Tasks." *Psychological Bulletin*, 55, pp. 88–101.

I. M. Rubin, M. S. Plovnick, and R. E. Fry (1977) *Task-Oriented Team Development*. New York: McGraw-Hill.

P. J. Runkel and J. E. McGrath (1972) *Research on Human Behavior*. New York: Holt, Rinehart and Winston.

E. H. Schein (1969) *Process Consultation*. Reading, Mass.: Addison-Wesley.

W. C. Schutz (1958) *FIRO: A Three-Dimensional Theory of Interpersonal Behavior*. New York: Holt, Rinehart and Winston.

———. (1961) "On Group Composition." *Journal of Abnormal and Social Psychology*, 62, pp. 275–81.

G. Stasser and J. H. Davis (1981) "Group Decision Making and Social Influence: A Social Interaction Sequence Model." *Psychological Review*, 88, pp. 523–51.

M. I. Stein (1975) *Stimulating Creativity*, Vol. 2. New York: Academic Press.

I. D. Steiner (1972) *Group Process and Productivity*. New York: Academic Press.

R. M. Stogdill (1974) *Handbook of Leadership*. New York: Free Press.

S. A. Stumpf, D. E. Zand, and R. D. Freedman (1979) "Designing Groups for Judgmental Decisions." *Academy of Management Review*, 4, pp. 589–600.

E. J. Thomas and C. F. Fink (1961) "Models of Group Problem Solving." *Journal of Abnormal and Social Psychology*, 63, pp. 53–63.

———. (1963) "Effects of Group Size." *Psychological Bulletin*, 60, pp. 371–84.

E. P. Torrance (1954) "Some Consequences of Power Differences on Decision Making in Permanent and Temporary Three-Man Groups." *Research Studies, State College of Washington*, 22, pp. 130–40.

E. L. Trist (1981) "The Evolution of Sociotechnical Systems as a Conceptual Framework and as an Action Research Program" in A. H. Van de Ven and W. F. Joyce, eds., *Perspectives on Organization Design and Behavior*. New York: Wiley.

B. W. Tuckman (1965) "Developmental Sequence in Small Groups." *Psychological Bulletin*, 63, pp. 384–99.

N. Vidmar and J. R. Hackman (1971) "Interlaboratory Generalizability of Small Group Research: An Experimental Study." *Journal of Social Psychology*, 83, pp. 129–39.

T. D. Wall and C. W. Clegg (1981) "A Longitudinal Field Study of Group Work Design." *Journal of Occupational Behavior*, 2, pp. 31–49.

R. E. Walton and L. S. Schlesinger (1979) "Do Supervisors Thrive in Participative Work Systems?" *Organizational Dynamics*, Winter, pp. 24–38.

K. E. Weick (1965) "Laboratory Experimentation with Organizations" in J. G. March, ed., *Handbook of Organizations*. Chicago: Rand McNally.

———. (1977) "Organization Design: Organizations as Self-Designing Systems." *Organizational Dynamics*, Autumn, pp. 31–46.

W. F. Whyte (1955) *Money and Motivation: An Analysis of Incentives in Industry*. New York: Harper.

A. Wicker, S. L. Kirmeyer, L. Hanson, and D. Alexander (1976) "Effects of Manning Levels on Subjective Experiences, Performance, and Verbal Interaction in Groups." *Organizational Behavior and Human Performance*, 17, pp. 251–74.

R. W. Woodman and J. J. Sherwood (1980) "The Role of Team Development in Organizational Effectiveness: A Critical Review." *Psychological Bulletin*, 88, pp. 166–86.

A. Zander (1971) *Motives and Goals in Groups*. New York: Academic Press.

———. (1980) "The Origins and Consequences of Group Goals" in L. Festinger, ed., *Retrospections on Social Psychology*. New York: Oxford University Press.

Dimension IV

Facing the Future: Creativity, Innovation, and Organizational Leadership

Part A

Foundations of Creativity

35. Within You, Without You: The Social Psychology of Creativity, and Beyond

Teresa M. Amabile

I study creativity because I'm still trying to figure out something that happened in kindergarten. That's when I first heard the word *creativity*. My teacher had come to our home for the end-of-the-year conference with my mother. While eavesdropping, I heard Mrs. Bollier say, "I think Teresa shows a lot of potential for artistic creativity, and I hope that's something she really develops over the years." I remember feeling thrilled but, sadly, my pride was premature. I haven't done anything even vaguely artistic in the years since; I still draw the way I did in kindergarten. I'd really like to know why.

There are at least two obvious explanations. Mrs. Bollier might have been wrong; maybe I had no particular talent for artwork. I, however, prefer the alternative explanation: I *did* have the beginnings of artistic talent, but my later experiences with art squelched its development. In kindergarten, we had plenty of free access to art materials—easels, paper, lots of paint, clay, and crayons—and plenty of encouragement to experiment with them. The following year, I entered a strict, traditional parochial school where experience with art was limited to an hour every Friday afternoon when, I think, the nuns were too tired to do anything else with us.

Week after week, we were given the same task. Each child would receive a small index-card-sized copy of one of the great masterworks in painting. In second grade, one week, we had Da Vinci's *Adoration of the Magi*. From third grade I remember Chagall's *I and the Village*. Rather than discussing these paintings and artists with us, our teachers instead told us to *copy* them. Given our limited skill development, and our limited materials (loose-leaf paper

Teresa M. Amabile, *Theories of Creativity*, Mark A. Runco, Robert S. Albert, (editors), pp. 61–91, copyright © 1990 by Sage Publications, Inc. Reprinted by permission of Sage Publications, Inc.

and a few broken crayons), "art" became an experience in frustration. I couldn't even get all those horses and angels to fit on the page! But, worse than that, we were strictly graded on our monstrosities. I felt my interest in artwork waning, and I no longer pestered my mother to let me draw and color when I was at home.

Only once in those school years did I hear the word *creative*. Inexplicably one day, our teacher told us to take out our art materials and do whatever we wanted. Eager as a prisoner set free, I began drawing a brightly colored abstract mosaic. Sister Carmelita, pacing the aisles, stopped by my desk, lowered her head, and said, "I think maybe we're being a little *too* creative!"

I wondered often what happened to my promised artistic creativity, but my interest in the problem stayed underground for many years. Meanwhile, I was experiencing frustration of a different sort. I had been interested in science throughout high school, but had no idea *which* science to major in once I entered college. I chose chemistry because it looked the hardest. Although I did well, earning A's in my chemistry, physics, and calculus courses, it all left me cold. I worked as a research assistant during the summers, which gave me ample opportunity to observe what I lacked. Each day, our small band of professors and research assistants would troop off to lunch in the cafeteria and seat ourselves around a large table. Each day, the professors could talk of little else but their work—what was going nicely, what had taken a bad turn, what new ideas they had. They spoke with passion and excitement, and by the time we left the table each day, it was strewn with napkins showing hastily sketched equations and models. That passion was what I lacked, and I knew I'd never have it for chemistry; I never found myself wanting to think about my research outside of the laboratory.

I did discover that passion when I took my first psychology course as an elective in college. *Here* was a science I could care about—an exciting science of people, not a boring science of molecules. I had found my true interest, and everything else began to fall into place.

One important piece fell into place when I started the graduate program in psychology at Stanford and learned about Mark Lepper's work on intrinsic motivation. Lepper defined *intrinsic motivation* as the motivation to do an activity for its own sake, because it was intrinsically interesting, enjoyable or satisfying. In contrast, extrinsic motivation was defined as the motivation to do an activity primarily in order to achieve some extrinsic goal, such as a reward. Lepper and his colleagues had investigated the phenomenon they called the "overjustification effect": If an individual who is initially intrinsically interested in an activity engages in that activity in order to meet some extrinsic goal, that individual's intrinsic motivation to engage in that activity in the future will be undermined (e.g., Deci, 1971; Lepper, Greene, & Nisbett, 1973). That certainly sounded like what had happened to me and my artistic potential. Could it be that intrinsic motivation is necessary for creativity?

The overjustification research, however, had not examined creativity or other aspects of performance. It had focused on subsequent interest to engage in an activity. To clarify my hypotheses about the impact of intrinsic/extrinsic motivation on creativity, and to renew my old curiosity about creativity, I began to read the creativity literature—both psychological theory and research, and the self-report writings of individuals recognized for their creativity.

In the psychological literature, I found that little attention had been paid to motivation. Instead, research (most of it done after 1950) had focused on personality characteristics of outstanding creative individuals (e.g., Baron, 1955; Helson, 1965; MacKinnon, 1962), cognitive abilities involved in creative achievement (e.g., Guilford, 1956), the development of creativity tests (e.g., Torrance, 1966), or methods for training creativity skills (e.g., Gordon, 1961; Parnes, 1967; Stein, 1974).

However, there was some psychological literature outside of the "creativity camp" that provided strong suggestive evidence of a link between intrinsic motivation and creativity.

Crutchfield's (1955, 1959, 1962) work on conformity found that individuals who had been identified as highly creative were much less likely to conform in the Asch situation than were those identified as less creative. According to Crutchfield, conformity pressures can lead to extrinsic, "ego-involved" motivation, in which finding a solution is simply a means to an ulterior end. This contrasts sharply with intrinsic, "task-involved" motivation, in which the creative act is an end in itself.

McGraw (1978) reviewed a vast literature on problem solving and concluded that reward (an extrinsic motivator) has very different effects on performance, depending on the type of task. *Algorithmic* tasks are those having a clear, straightforward path to solution. *Heuristic* tasks are those with no such clear, straightforward path; some exploration is required. McGraw concluded that performance on algorithmic tasks should be enhanced by increases in extrinsic motivation, but performance on heuristic tasks should be adversely affected. McGraw's descriptions of heuristic tasks clearly included tasks that require creativity.

In his pioneering work on enjoyment, Csikszentmihályi (1975) studied people who were deeply intrinsically involved in activities ranging from chess to musical composition to rock climbing to dancing to surgery. He described the *flow experience* in such individuals, the experience of being totally involved in the activity, where one action flows smoothly into the next and extrinsic concerns disappear.

Csikszentmihályi's description of the flow experience, along with McGraw's assertions about the effect of extrinsic motivation on heuristic tasks, and Crutchfield's discussion of ego-involved and task-involved motivation all fit remarkably well with first-person descriptions of the creative process by widely recognized creative individuals. In reading the autobiographies, letters, and journals of people such as Albert Einstein and Sylvia Plath, I discovered a recurring theme: They felt most inhibited in their creative work when focusing on extrinsic concerns such as expected evalua-tion, surveillance, or promised reward. They did their most creative work when they experienced the "flow" of deep intrinsic motivation. Using this support from the psychological literature, the phenomenological literature, and my own (limited) experience, I formulated what I then called the intrinsic motivation hypothesis of creativity: intrinsic motivation is conducive to creativity, and extrinsic motivation is detrimental. I planned to test this hypothesis by having subjects do creativity tasks in the presence or absence of extrinsic constraints—clearly, a social–psychological paradigm.

When I told my graduate advisers that I wanted to do research in the social psychology of creativity, they informed me that there was no such thing. But, just weeks after that conversation, I opened the new *Journal of Personality and Social Psychology* to find an article by Dean Simonton (1975) with the phrase "social psychology of creativity" splashed boldly about. That was all the encouragement I needed.

ASSUMPTIONS, DEFINITIONS, AND ASSESSMENTS

Before beginning any creativity experiments, of course, I had to figure out what I was studying and how I was going to measure it. I venture to say that this is the single most difficult problem shared by all creativity researchers. A perusal of previous research revealed that the majority of creativity studies relied on some sort of standardized tests, such as the Torrance Tests of Creative Thinking. Apart from reservations I had about calling performance on these tests "creativity," I was concerned that these tests had all been formulated to pinpoint individual differences in creative ability. To the extent that they were indeed sensitive to such individual differences, these tests were quite appropriate for personality studies of creativity, but quite inappropriate for social–psychological studies of creativity. In my planned studies, I intended to identify social factors that could undermine *any* person's creativity, no matter what that person's baseline level of skill in creative activity. In such studies, individual differences would be error variance, and measures sensitive to such differences would contribute to error.

I decided, instead of using creativity tests for my studies, to simply have subjects make products in response to clearly defined tasks; the tasks would be designed so as not to depend heavily on special skills in drawing, verbal fluency, mathematical ability, or the like. Some such tasks that my students and I have used include making paper collages and writing haiku poems. Once these products have been made in the context of our studies, we have them rated on creativity and other dimensions by experts—people who are familiar with the domain; for example, we ask studio artists to rate the paper collages. This approach to creativity assessment was used by a few previous researchers (e.g., Getzels & Csikszentmihályi, 1976; Kruglanski, Friedman, & Zeevi, 1971), with apparent success. We call it the consensual assessment technique.

The consensual assessment technique for creativity is based on this operational definition: *A product or response is creative to the extent that appropriate observers independently agree it is creative. Appropriate observers are those familiar with the domain in which the product was created or the response articulated* (Amabile, 1982b). Interjudge agreement, clearly, is the most important requirement of this technique. But mere statistical agreement would be suspect without certain precautions: We do not train the judges in any way; we ask them to use their own subjective definitions of creativity; and we ensure that they work independently. Repeatedly, in dozens of studies with small groups of judges, we have found interjudge reliabilities ranging above .70, and often above .80. Moreover, we have found that creativity ratings are statistically separable from other rated product dimensions, such as technical quality or aesthetic appeal.

Although it may be necessary to specify an operational definition of creativity that relies solely on subjective criteria, such a definition is not, by itself, sufficient for a comprehensive theory of creativity—or even for a social psychology of creativity. Any theoretical formulation must make guesses about what judges are responding to when they rate products as more or less creative. For this reason, we have been guided by a conceptual definition of creativity that is closely aligned with many previous definitions (e.g., Barron, 1955; MacKinnon, 1975; Stein, 1974): A product or response will be judged as creative to the extent that (a) it is both a novel and appropriate, useful, correct, or valuable response to the task at hand, and (b) the task is heuristic rather than algorithmic (Amabile, 1983b).

Our approach to creativity definition and measurement rests on several assumptions about key creativity issues. Indeed, either implicitly or explicitly, all creativity researchers must make assumptions about these issues. I defend mine only by saying that I have not seen persuasive evidence to the contrary. These are the issues: Can creativity be recognized as a quality of products? I believe that the assessment of creativity is much like the judgment of attitude statements on degrees of favorability (Thurstone & Chave, 1929) or the identification of individuals as physically attractive (Walster, Aronson, Abrahams, & Rottman, 1966). Although creativity may be very difficult for judges to define (I have asked them!), it is something they can recognize when they see it. Moreover, experts can agree on the extent to which a given product is creative. And not only can judges recognize creativity in products; I believe they can also recognize it in persons and processes. However, a focus on the *product* seems to me the most straightforward and scientifically conservative; products are the most easily observed discrete units and probably the least subject to disagreement.

Certainly, this approach cannot be used for assessing creativity in products that may be at the frontiers of a domain, where there is bound to be great disagreement as to whether a new idea is highly creative or simply bizarre. But then, *no* approach to creativity assessment will work at those levels. Only the passage of time, and an eventual social consensus, can yield a proper assessment.

Is creativity a continuous or discontinuous quality? I believe that the highest levels of creativity that we see in the world—the greatest scientific advances, the most startling artistic achievements—lie on the high end of the same continuum on which we see everyday "garden variety" creativity—ideas and responses that are more modestly novel and less earth-shattering. I do not believe that there is a discontinuous break in the abilities or thought processes behind differing levels of creativity. The difference seems to lie instead in vastly differing abilities, cognitive styles, motivational levels, and circumstances. The difference in *kind*. Thus I believe it is appropriate to ask expert judges to rate degrees of creativity in products. And I also believe it is justifiable to say that experiments using "ordinary" subjects doing relatively low-level tasks are informative even about Einstein's creativity.

Is the creative process different in different domains? I believe that it is basically the same—that a scientist attempting to develop a new process in her laboratory is going through essentially the same process as an artist in his studio or a poet at her desk. Certainly, different cognitive processes will be differentially important in the various domains. However, in general, the creative process will depend on the same components and be affected by the same social factors. Thus it is appropriate to use tasks from a variety of domains in establishing a social psychology of creativity, or any psychology of creativity.

EVIDENCE ON THE INTRINSIC MOTIVATION PRINCIPLE OF CREATIVITY

Using the consensual technique for creativity assessment, my students and I have conducted dozens of studies over the past 12 years to test the intrinsic motivation hypothesis of creativity. We find our results sufficiently compelling that we now refer to the intrinsic motivation *principle* of creativity: Intrinsic motivation is conducive to creativity, but extrinsic motivation is detrimental. In other words, people will be most creative when they feel motivated primarily by the inter-

est, enjoyment, satisfaction, and challenge of the work itself—and not by external pressures.

The Phenomenology of Creativity

The first source of evidence on the intrinsic motivation principle is rather a source of hypotheses about specific social factors that may lead to decrements in intrinsic motivation and creativity: the first-person account. We have studied a great many autobiographies, personal journals, letters, biographies, and interviews of widely recognized creative individuals in a variety of fields. These include writers T. S. Eliot, Anne Sexton, Sylvia Plath, Thomas Wolfe, Fyodor Dostoyevski, D. H. Lawrence, Joyce Carol Oates, Charles Dickens, Gertrude Stein, George Eliot, Isaac Asimov, and John Irving; scientists Albert Einstein, Marie Curie, and James Watson; musician/composers W. A. Mozart and Pablo Casals; artists Pablo Picasso and Ansel Adams; social scientist Margaret Mead; and filmmaker Woody Allen.

Richly complex as they are, these sources strongly suggest the validity of the intrinsic motivation principle in two ways. First, repeatedly, these individuals express high levels of intrinsic motivation for doing their work. The novelist John Irving (*The World According to Garp*) is just one of many examples:

> *The unspoken factor here is love. The reason I can work so hard at my writing is that it's not work to me. Or, as I said before, my work is pleasure to me. (Amabile, in press)*

In addition, these creative individuals report numerous incidents in which their intrinsic motivation and creativity were undermined by salient extrinsic constraints. The constraints cited include expected evaluation, strictly regimented educational methods, surveillance, competition, reward, restricted choice, and deadlines. The poet Sylvia Plath provides perhaps the clearest lay-person's statement of the intrinsic motivation principle of creativity in action:

> *Editors and publishers and critics and the world . . . I want acceptance there, to feel my work good and well-taken. Which ironically freezes me at*

my work, corrupts my nunnish labor of work-for-itself-as-its-own-reward. (Hughes & McCullough, 1982, p. 305)

Experimental Evidence

The second and most important source of evidence on the intrinsic motivation principle is the laboratory experiment. My students and I have used the basic overjustification paradigm in our research: subjects work on an interesting creativity task either in the presence or in the absence of a specific extrinsic constraint. Subsequently, their products are rated on creativity by several independent experts. We have carried out such experiments with a wide range of independent variables (extrinsic constraints), subject groups ranging in age from preschool children to working adults, and a variety of artistic, verbal and problem-solving creativity tasks. Though they are not without their complexities, our results reveal consistent patterns in strong support of the intrinsic motivation hypothesis:

Evaluation. Expected evaluation has a detrimental effect on creativity (Amabile, 1979; Amabile, Goldfarb, & Brackfield, in press; Hennessey, 1989). Actual prior positive evaluation has a detrimental effect on subsequent creativity (Berglas, Amabile, & Handel, 1979).

Surveillance. Being watched while working has a detrimental effect on creativity (Amabile, Goldfarb, & Brackfield, in press).

Reward. Contracted-for reward has a detrimental effect on creativity (Amabile, Hennessey, & Grossman, 1986; Hennessey, 1989). "Bonus" reward (not contracted for) has a positive effect on creativity (Amabile, Hennessey, & Grossman, 1986).

Competition. Competing for prizes has a detrimental effect on creativity (Amabile, 1982a, 1987).

Restricted choice. Restricted choice in how to do an activity has a detrimental

effect on creativity (Amabile & Gitomer, 1984; Hennessey, 1989).

Each of the social–environmental factors shown in our research to negatively affect creativity has also been shown, in overjustification research, to negatively affect intrinsic motivation. In an effort to provide a more direct link between intrinsic motivation and creativity within the same study, we attempted a motivational induction with creative writers. I will describe the study in some detail as a way of illustrating our basic paradigm.

This study (Amabile, 1985) was designed to directly create an extrinsic motivational state in some subjects without going through the intermediate step of first imposing an extrinsic constraint. And the same method was used to directly create an intrinsically motivated state in other subjects. For this purpose, we borrowed a technique from Salancik (1975). We asked subjects to complete a questionnaire about their attitudes toward the target creativity task (writing). Some were given an intrinsic questionnaire, on which all of the items dealt with the intrinsically interesting aspects of the activity. Other subjects completed an extrinsic questionnaire, which dealt with only extrinsic reasons for doing the activity. The purpose of the questionnaire was simply to lead subjects to think about the activity in intrinsic terms or in extrinsic terms. Then, immediate effects of this intrinsic or extrinsic orientation could be directly observed.

It was important in this study to find subjects who were already involved in this type of creative activity on a regular basis so that we might temporarily influence their orientation toward that activity. To this end, we recruited creative writers, using advertisements such as this: "Writers: If you are involved in writing, especially poetry, fiction, or drama, you can make three dollars for about an hour of your time. We are studying people's reasons for writing."

Most of those who responded to the advertisements were undergraduates or graduate students in English or creative writing at

Brandeis University or Boston University, although a few were not affiliated with any university. The most important characteristic of these participants, for our purposes, is that they identified themselves as *writers*—they came to us with a high level of involvement in writing. On a prescreening questionnaire, we discovered that they spent an average of 6.3 hours of their own time per week writing poetry, fiction, or drama; the range was 3 to 18 hours.

Upon arrival at our laboratory, each writer completed a questionnaire on "reasons for writing"—reasons for being involved in writing. (Some subjects, in a control condition, did not complete any questionnaire.) On the intrinsic questionnaire, subjects were asked to rank-order (in terms of importance to them personally) seven reasons for writing; all of these reasons had been consistently rated as intrinsic on a pretest. Two of the intrinsic items were these: "You get a lot of pleasure out of reading something good that you have written"; and "You like to play with words." By contrast, the extrinsic questionnaire asked subjects to rank-order seven reasons that had pretested as strongly extrinsic, such as "You have heard of cases where one bestselling novel or collection of poems has made the author financially secure"; and "You enjoy public recognition of your work." After completing the questionnaire, the writers were asked to write a short haikustyle poem. (Those in the control group were simply asked to write the poem.)

After the study was completed, we asked several poets to judge the poems, using the consensual assessment technique. The results were quite dramatic. As might be expected, the writers in the control group wrote poems that were judged fairly high on creativity; these were, after all, creative writers. The writers in the intrinsic group wrote poems that were judged as somewhat higher in creativity than those in the control group, but the difference was not large. The most important result comes from the extrinsic group. Those writers produced poems that were judged as significantly lower in creativity than the poems produced by either of the other groups.

Consider the implications of this study for "real-world" work environments. These writers entered our laboratory with an intrinsic motivational orientation toward writing. Apparently, we were not able to increase that intrinsic orientation much; the creativity of the intrinsic group isn't notably higher than the creativity of the control group. On the other hand, with a terribly brief and simple manipulation, we significantly reduced the creativity of writers in the extrinsic group. People who had been writing creatively for years, who had long-standing interests in creative writing, suddenly found their creativity blocked after spending barely five minutes thinking about the extrinsic reasons for doing what they do. (A note about the ethics of this experiment: We fully debriefed all of our participants before they left the lab, and we had all of the extrinsic subjects fill out the intrinsic questionnaire at the end of their experimental sessions.)

In this study, a brief and subtle written manipulation had a significant impact on the creativity of highly motivated individuals. Consider, then, the potential effects of extrinsic constraints in everyday work environments on the creativity of people who work in those environments every day.

Observational Data

It is one thing to assume that the social–environmental factors we manipulate in the laboratory play an important role in real-world creativity. It is another thing to actually find out. In an attempt to do so, I worked with colleagues at the Center for Creative Leadership to interview a large number of research and development scientists about creative and noncreative events in their work experience (Amabile & Gryskiewicz, 1988). We asked the participants, who were 120 R&D scientists from over 20 corporations, to tell us about an example of high creativity and an example of low creativity from their work experience (defining *creativity* as they saw fit). We told them that we were particularly interested in anything about the events that stood out in their minds—anything about the person or persons involved and anything about the work environment. We felt that, by using this critical incident technique, we would be more likely to avoid the interjection of personal beliefs about creativity than if we simply asked interviewees what they thought was important for supporting or undermining creativity in organizations.

In our search for information about the major influences on creativity and innovation, we did a detailed content analysis of verbatim transcripts of these tape-recorded interviews. The types of things our interviewees talked about fell into four major categories. Rank-ordered by frequency, they are as follows: (a) qualities of environments that promote creativity, (b) qualities of environments that inhibit creativity, (c) qualities of problem-solvers that promote creativity, and (d) qualities of problem-solvers that inhibit creativity. In our system, "qualities of environments" are any factors outside of the problem-solvers themselves (including other people) that appeared to consistently influence creativity positively, as in the high-creativity stories, or negatively, as in the low-creativity stories. "Qualities of problem-solvers" are any factors of ability, personality, or mood within the problem-solvers themselves that seemed to consistently influence creativity either positively or negatively. We found that environmental factors were mentioned much more frequently than personal qualities. Because this finding appeared in both the high- and low-creativity stories, and because a large percentage of the stories did not involve the interviewee as a central character (problem-solver), we feel that this preponderance of environmental factors cannot be dismissed as a simple attributional bias.

The prominence of the environment in these interviews is an important finding for the social psychology of creativity. It suggests that our laboratory research on the effects of social constraints has produced not only statistically significant findings but ecologically significant ones as well. The *environment* was a much more salient factor than the *individual* for these R&D scientists

in their experience of specific creative and uncreative events. Does this mean that, in an absolute sense, environmental factors account for more of the variance in creative output than individual difference factors? Does this mean that the forces *within you* are less significant than the forces *without you* in determining the creativity of your behavior? Not necessarily, and not even probably. Certainly, at a macroscopic level, personal factors such as general intelligence, experience in the field, and ability to think creatively are the major influences on output of creative ideas by R&D scientists. But, assuming that hiring practices at major corporations select individuals who exhibit relatively high levels of these personal qualities, the variance above this baseline may well be accounted for primarily by factors in the work environment.

Social factors may be responsible for only a small part of the total variance in creative behavior, but they may account for the lion's share of the variance that anyone can do anything about! It is almost always easier to change the social environment (or one's perception of it) than to change traits and abilities.

Our detailed content analysis of the interviews, done by independent coders, revealed several environmental factors that inhibit creativity. Among these are many that we had already studied in experimental paradigms: constrained choice, an overemphasis on tangible reward, evaluation expectation, and competition. There were other inhibiting factors, however, that remain for future experimental investigation: perceived apathy toward the target project, unclear goals, distraction, insufficient resources, overemphasis on the status quo, and time pressure.

BEYOND THE INTRINSIC MOTIVATION PRINCIPLE

Clearly, there's much more to the social psychology of creativity than just the intrinsic motivation principle. While I have worked within mainstream social–psychological paradigms to study the effects of specific social constraints on the immediate creative performance of ordinary individuals, Dean Simonton has used pioneering historiometric techniques to study the effects of complex social phenomena (such as cultural diversity, warfare, and zeitgeist) on historically recognized creative achievements (see Simonton, 1984, in press). A comprehensive social psychology of creativity must include this work, as well as the work of others who have studied social influences at the macroscopic level (e.g., Albert, 1980; Andrews, 1975).

The data from the R&D interview study suggest a number of environmental variables that may *enhance* creativity. In our previous devotion to the overjustification paradigm and the intrinsic motivation hypothesis, we *de facto* eliminated an investigation of such variables. It may, in fact, be true that undermining creativity is much easier than stimulating it. But that's no reason not to try.

Recently, our own experimental research has begun moving beyond the simplicity of the intrinsic motivation principle. Nearly all of our previous experiments assumed *a hydraulic* relationship between intrinsic and extrinsic motivation: As extrinsic motivation increases, intrinsic motivation (and creativity) must decrease. However, it seems clear from anecdotal evidence that extrinsic motivators such as reward and competition need not undermine creativity. In fact, for some people, there seems to be an *additive* relationship: not only does their intrinsic motivation remain high, but their creativity may actually be enhanced in the face of extrinsic motivators.

For example, the filmmaker Woody Allen seems to have managed to maintain both a high level of intrinsic motivation and a high level of creativity in an extremely extrinsically oriented profession. He more or less ignores both the awards and the critics, continuing to innovate with new styles and themes. As another example, the scientists Watson and Crick clearly felt strong competitive pressure in their race to discover the structure of DNA (Watson, 1968). Yet, at the moments that they made their greatest breakthroughs, they were so single-mindedly

focused on the puzzle before them that they temporarily forgot not only about their competitors and the prizes awaiting the victors but also about the time of day and their own need for food. In another feat of cognitive distancing, the poet Anne Sexton told her agent that, although she would love to make a great deal of money from her books, she knew that she had to forget all about that while actually writing her poems.

Two of our recent studies provide some exciting evidence suggestive of an additive effect of intrinsic and extrinsic motivators. In one study (Hennessey, Amabile, & Martinage, in press), we set out to determine if it would be possible to immunize people against the negative effects of constraint on intrinsic motivation and creativity by training them to think of intrinsic and extrinsic motivation in the way that Allen, Watson, Crick, and Sexton seemed to: I am well aware of my strong intrinsic interest in my work, and that can't be easily shaken; I certainly enjoy the benefits of wealth, fame, and critical acclaim, but I place all that secondary to my own passion for what I do.

Planning to do this training study with children, we made a set of videotapes in which two attractive children answered an adult's questions about their work. The script was written so as to portray these children as models of intrinsic motivation. They spoke excitedly about different aspects of their schoolwork that interested them, and, while acknowledging the importance of good grades and praise from parents, they firmly stated that "those are not what's really important." After the children watched these videotapes, the experimenter led the children to discuss what had been said, and to describe their own intrinsic interests or ways of dealing with constraint. In later testing sessions with a different experimenter, we found that children who had watched the intrinsic motivation training tapes scored higher on a measure of intrinsic motivation (Harter, 1981) than children who had watched tapes on other topics. In addition, although the control-group children exhibited lower creativity when offered a reward, the trained children showed no such decrement. This was what we had predicted. But we got more than we'd bargained for. The trained children produced *higher* levels of creativity under contracted-for reward—a clearly additive effect.

Another, earlier study of ours may provide a clue about the mechanism at work in this surprising additive effect (surprising, at least, to those of us who expected only hydraulic effects). With both adults and children, we found (as expected) that contracted-for reward leads to lower levels of creativity (Amabile, Hennessey, & Grossman, 1986). The design was a basic 2×2 factorial, where reward was crossed with choice. Thus, subjects in the choice-reward condition had previously chosen to do the activity in order to obtain a reward. Subjects in the no-choice/reward condition, however, were simply given the reward as something that went along with the activity. They were given no choice in the matter; they made no contract with the experimenter. We expected that subjects in this condition would show no decrement in creativity, because they should not have had the self-perception of working on the activity in order to gain the reward (extrinsic motivation). Not only did we find no decrement, we found an *increment*: Subjects in this "bonus" reward condition showed higher levels of creativity than in any of the other three conditions.

We speculate that perhaps the bonus reward enhances *positive affect*, which may simply add on to the conductive effect of intrinsic motivation on creativity. Not only did subjects in this condition *not* have their intrinsic motivation undermined, they were led to feel even better about what they were doing because of the unexpected bonus. Indeed, a postexperimental questionnaire assessing affect lends some support to this speculation.

So it may be that the children in the training study's intrinsic motivation condition learned to interpret extrinsic constraints such as reward in a way that did not detract from intrinsic motivation but instead added to positive affect about task engagement. This possibility seems likely when we consider the kind of statements that appeared in the intrinsic motivation training videotape:

Adult: *It sounds like both of you do the work in school because you like it, but what about getting good grades from your teacher or presents from your parents for doing well? Do you think about those things?*

Tommy: *Well, I like to get good grades, and when I bring home a good report card, my parents always give me money. But that's not what's really important. I like to learn a lot. There are a lot of things that interest me, and I want to learn about them, so I work hard because I enjoy it.*

It appears, then, that the intrinsic motivation principle of creativity, in its simple form, is incomplete. It implies that extrinsic constraints will always undermine creativity. But both observational evidence and experimental evidence suggest that this isn't so. Individual differences in people's *interpretation* of the constraints can significantly affect the outcomes on creativity, whether those individual differences arise through explicit training (as in our study) or occur naturally as personality characteristics.

BEYOND THE SOCIAL PSYCHOLOGY OF CREATIVITY: WITHIN YOU AND WITHOUT YOU

The intense study of social–environmental influences on creativity, which has flourished over the past dozen years, was a necessary correction to the almost exclusive focus on creative *persons* in preceding decades. Clearly, however, in any comprehensive psychology of creativity, both person influences and environment influences must appear prominently. Even in our own research on the social psychology of creativity, we have repeatedly been led to consider the influence of personality, ability, and experience. The R&D scientists we interviewed (Amabile & Gryskiewicz, 1988) may have mentioned work environment factors more frequently than person factors in their stories of high and low creativity, but person factors certainly did appear prominently. Positive personal factors mentioned frequently in the high-creativity stories included personality traits such as persistence, curiosity, energy, and intellectual honesty; self-motivation, the intrinsic motivation of being excited by the work itself; special cognitive abilities; risk orientation; expertise in the area; diverse experience; social skill; and brilliance. Negative personal factors mentioned frequently in the low-creativity stories included being unmotivated, unskilled, inflexible, externally motivated, or socially unskilled.

Earlier, I argued: "Social factors may be responsible for only a small part of the total variance in creative behavior, but they may account for the lion's share of the variance that anyone can do anything about!" I believe this is true and vitally important for anyone wishing to enhance creativity in practice. However, for purposes of theory building, we must pay heed to all factors contributing significantly to the *total variance* in creative behavior.

The componential model of creativity, which we have been using as a theoretical guide in our research, attempts to include all such factors. The model is described in more detail

elsewhere (Amabile, 1983a, 1983b, 1988a, 1988b). Figure 35.1 outlines the three major components of creativity included in the model. It is not surprising that intrinsic task motivation is featured as one prominent component, but the factors of talent, personality, and cognitive style that have been so extensively investigated by other researchers are also included. As a way of illustrating the components and their role in the creative process, let me describe the hypothetical (and highly simplified) case of an artist creating a sculpture.

Domain-Relevant Skills

Domain-relevant skills are the basis from which any performance must proceed. They include memory for factual knowledge, technical proficiency, and special talents in the domain in question. A sculptor's domain-relevant skills include her innate talent for visual imagery and realistic rendering of that imagery, her factual knowledge of art history and the properties of the clay she has chosen, her familiarity with the subject she wishes to depict, and the technical skill she has acquired in her craft.

This component can be viewed as the set of cognitive pathways that may be followed to solve

FIGURE 35.1
Components of Creative Performance

1 Domain-relevant Skills	2 Creativity-relevant Skills	3 Task Motivation
Includes: –Knowledge about the domain –Technical skills required –Special domain-relevant "talent" Depends on: –Innate cognitive abilities –Innate perceptual and motor skills –Formal and informal education	Includes: –Appropriate cognitive style –Implicit or explicit knowledge of heuristics for generating novel ideas –Conducive work style Depends on: –Training –Experience in idea generation –Personality characteristics	Includes: –Attitudes toward the task –Perceptions of own motivation for undertaking the task Depends on: –Initial level of intrinsic motivation toward the task –Presence or absence of salient extrinsic constraints in the social environment –Individual ability to cognitively minimize extrinsic constraints

Source: From Amabile, T. M. Social psychology of creativity: A componential conceptualization. *Journal of Personality and Social Psychology* 45 (1983): 357–77.

a given problem or do a given task. As Newell and Simon (1972, p. 82) poetically describe it, this component can be considered the problem-solver's "network of possible wanderings."

Creativity-Relevant Skills

Herein lies the "something extra" of creative performance. Assuming that an individual has some incentive to perform an activity, performance will be "technically good" or "adequate" or "acceptable" if the requisite domain-relevant skills are there. However, even with these skills at an extraordinarily high level, an individual will not produce creative work if creativity-relevant skills are lacking. Creativity-relevant skills include a cognitive style favorable to taking new perspectives on problems, an application of heuristics for the exploration of new cognitive pathways, and a working style conducive to persistent, energetic pursuit of one's work.

Creativity-relevant skills, depend to some extent on personality characteristics related to independence, self-discipline, orientation toward risk taking, tolerance for ambiguity, perseverance in the face of frustration, and a relative unconcern for social approval (Barron, 1955; Feldman, 1980; Golann, 1963; Hogarth, 1980; MacKinnon, 1962; Stein, 1974).

Our sculptor's arsenal of creativity skills might include her ability to break perceptual set when observing physical objects, her tolerance for ambiguity in the process of deciding on a theme and how to render it, her ability to suspend judgment as she plays around with different approaches, and her ability to break out of strict algorithms for sculpting. She might also have learned to employ some of the creativity heuristics described by theorists: "When all else fails, try something counterintuitive" (Newell, Shaw, & Simon, 1962); or "Make the familiar strange" (Gordon, 1961). Finally, if she is productively creative, her work style is probably marked by an ability to concentrate effort for long periods of time (Campbell, 1960; Hogarth, 1980) and an ability to abandon unproductive strategies, temporarily putting aside stubborn problems (Simon, 1966).

Intrinsic Task Motivation

A person can have no motivation for doing a task, a primarily intrinsic motivation, or a primarily extrinsic motivation; obviously, intrinsic and extrinsic motivation for the same task may coexist. However, one is likely to be primary. As I have argued on the basis of our empirical results, a primarily intrinsic motivation will be more conducive to creativity than a primarily extrinsic motivation. For practical purposes, there are two ways in which motivation can be considered the most important of the three creativity components. First, as I've noted, it may be the easiest to affect in a straightforward way because intrinsic/extrinsic motivation is strongly subject to even subtle social influences. Second, no amount of skill in the domain or in methods of creative thinking can compensate for a lack of intrinsic motivation to perform an activity. Without intrinsic motivation, an individual either will not perform the activity at all or will do it in a way that simply satisfies the extrinsic goals. But, to some extent, a high degree of intrinsic motivation *can* make up for a deficiency of domain-relevant skills or creativity-relevant skills. A highly intrinsically motivated individual is likely to draw skills from other domains or apply great effort to acquire necessary skills in the target domain.

Task motivation makes the difference between what our sculptor *can* do and what she *will* do. The former depends on her levels of domain-relevant skills and creativity-relevant skills. But it is her task motivation that determines the extent to which she will fully engage her domain-relevant skills and creativity-relevant skills in the service of creative performance.

Within the componential model, task motivation includes two elements: the individual's baseline attitude toward the task and the individual's perceptions of his or her reasons for undertaking the task in a given instance. For example, the sculptor approaches each task with a baseline level of interest—probably quite high for most sculpture tasks but perhaps quite low for print-making. For any given sculpture task, however, her interest will vary from the baseline as a function of any extrinsic constraints imposed on her (such as competition) *and* her own strategies for dealing with those constraints.

Stages of the Creative Process

The three components of domain-relevant skills, creativity-relevant skills, and task motivation are the building blocks for the componential model of creativity. The model is, conceptually, a multiplicative one: Each of the components is necessary for some level of creativity to be produced; the higher the level of each of the three components, the higher the overall level of creativity should be.

The three components appear to operate at different levels of specificity. Creativity-relevant skills operate at the most general level; they may influence responses in any content domain. Thus, if the sculptor has a rich store of creativity-relevant skills, she may indeed appear to be a cre-ative "type," in the sense that she produces unusual responses in many domains of behavior. Domain-relevant skills operate at an intermediate level of specificity. This component includes all skills relevant to a general domain, such as sculpture, rather than skills relevant to only a specific task within a domain, such as sculpting a clay bust of Beethoven. Obviously, within a particular domain, skills relevant to any given specific task will overlap with skills relevant to any other task. Finally, task motivation operates at the most specific level. In terms of impact on creativity, motivation may be very specific to particular tasks within domains, and may even vary over time for a particular task. Our artist may be highly intrinsically motivated to sculpt a friend's head, but she may be singularly uninterested in a commissioned job to sculpt the head of the city's mayor.

How do these building blocks figure into the overall process of individual creativity? Figure 35.2 presents a schematic representation

FIGURE 35.2
Componential Model of Individual Creativity

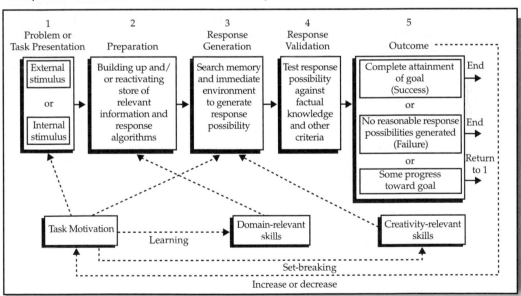

Source: From Amabile, T. M. Social psychology of creativity: A componential conceptualization. *Journal of Personality and Social Psychology* 45 (1983): 357–77.

Note: Broken lines indicate the typical sequence of steps in the process. Only direct and primary influences are depicted here.

of the componential model of the creative process (Amabile, 1983a, 1983b). This model describes the way in which an individual (such as the sculptor) might assemble and use information in attempting to arrive at a solution, response, or product. In information-processing terms, task motivation is responsible for initiating and sustaining the process; it determines whether the artist even undertakes the task, and it also determines some aspects of her response generation. Domain-relevant skills are the raw materials that feed the process. They determine what approaches the sculptor will take initially and what criteria she will use to assess the response possibilities that are generated. Creativity-relevant skills act as an executive controller; they can influence the way in which the artist searches for possibilities.

The process outlined in Figure 35.2 applies to both high and low levels of creativity; the level of creativity of a product or response varies as a function of the levels of each of the three components. This model resembles previous theories of creativity in the specification of the stages of problem presentation, preparation, response generation, and response validation (e.g., Hogarth, 1980; Nystrom, 1979; Wallas, 1926)—although there are a number of variations in the exact number and naming of stages in the sequence. This model is more detailed than previous ones, however, in its inclusion of the impact of each of the three components of creativity at each stage in the process. (Note that only direct and primary influences are depicted in the figure.)

The initial step in this sequence is the presentation of the task or the problem. Task motivation has an important influence at this stage. If the sculptor has a high level of intrinsic interest in the task, this interest will often be sufficient to begin the creative process. Under these circumstances, in essence, she poses the problem to herself. For example, she may decide that she wishes to sculpt the head of a friend. In other situations, however, the problem is presented by someone else. The problem might, of course, be intrinsically interesting under

these circumstances as well. If that friend came up with the idea and asked the artist to sculpt his head, she might still be intrinsically interested in the task. However, in general, an externally posed problem is less likely to be intrinsically interesting than an internally generated one.

The second stage is preparatory to the actual generation of responses or solutions. At this point, the sculptor builds up or reactivates her store of information about the task, including her knowledge of response algorithms for doing tasks like this. If her domain-relevant skills are rather impoverished at the outset, this stage may be quite a long one during which a great deal of learning takes place. On the other hand, if her domain-relevant skills are already sufficiently rich to afford an ample set of possibilities to explore, the reactivation of this already stored set of information and algorithms may be almost instantaneous.

Note one important implication of this model: Contrary to popular belief, it is not possible to have *too much* knowledge about a task domain. According to this belief, people who have the smallest knowledge base in a domain are able to produce the most creative ideas. Certainly, people who are new to a field often do exhibit a higher level of creativity than those who have a longer work history. But it is clear from empirical research (e.g., Findlay & Lumsden, 1988) that the important distinction is not the *amount* of knowledge but the way in which that knowledge is stored and the ease with which it can be accessed. If the artist stores her information and techniques according to rigid algorithms (which may be more likely for an old-timer than a new arrival), creativity is less probable. But if she stores information in wide categories with easy access of association, increased information should only lead to increased creativity. It is not possible to have too much knowledge; it *is* possible to have algorithms that are applied too inflexibly.

The novelty of the product or response is determined in the third stage. Here, the individual generates response possibilities by searching through the available pathways and exploring features of the environment that are relevant to the task at hand. Both creativity-relevant skills and task motivation play an important role at this stage. The sculptor's existing repertoire of creativity-relevant skills determines her flexibility in exploring cognitive pathways, the attention she gives to particular aspects of the task, and the extent to which she follows a particular pathway in pursuit of a product. In addition, creativity-relevant skills can influence the sub-goals of the response-generation stage by determining whether she will generate a large number of response possibilities through a temporary suspension of judgment. Finally, and most important, if the artist's task motivation is intrinsic rather than extrinsic, it can add to her existing repertoire of creativity-relevant skills a willingness to take risks with this particular task and to notice aspects of the task that might not be obviously relevant to creating the final product.

Domain-relevant skills again figure prominently in the fourth stage—the validation of the response possibility that has been chosen on a particular trial. Using her knowledge of the domain, the artist tests the response possibility for correctness or appropriateness, given her particular set of goals. Thus it is this stage that determines whether the product or response will be appropriate, useful, correct, or valuable—the second response characteristic that, together with novelty, is essential for the product to be considered creative according to the conceptual definition of creativity.

The fifth stage represents the decision making that must be carried out on the basis of the test performed in stage four. If the artist feels that this test has been passed—if she believes she has attained her goal—the process terminates. If she sees complete failure—if no reasonable response possibility has been generated—the process will also terminate. If she senses some progress toward the goal—if at least a reasonable response possibility has been generated (or if, in Simon's 1978, terms, there is some evidence of "getting warmer")—the process returns to the first stage, where the problem is

once again posed. In any case, information gained from the trial is added to the artist's existing repertoire of domain-relevant skills. If her intrinsic task motivation remains sufficiently high, she will try again, perhaps with information gained from the previous trial being used to pose the problem in a somewhat different form. If, however, her task motivation drops below some critical minimum, she will give up.

For complex tasks, the application of this model to the production of creative responses also becomes complex. Work on any given task or problem may involve a long series of loops through the process until success in a final product is achieved. Indeed, work on what seems to be one task may actually involve a series of rather different subtasks, each with its own separate solution. And, of course, the sequence represented in Figure 35.2 is an idealized one. In actuality, for example, the sculptor may attempt to generate ideas on how to render her subject, have difficulty, go immediately back to the preparation stage to gather more information or learn new techniques, and then continue on with idea generation.

The Feedback Cycle
The outcome of one cycle of the creative process can directly influence task motivation, thereby setting up a feedback cycle through which future engagement in the same or similar tasks can be affected. If the sculptor has been completely successful, in her view, she will have no motivation to undertake exactly the same task again, because that task has truly been completed. However, with success, her intrinsic motivation for similar sculpting tasks should increase. If complete failure has occurred—if no reasonable response were generated—her intrinsic motivation for the task should decrease. If partial success has been met, intrinsic motivation will increase if she has the sense of getting warmer in approaching her goal. However, it will decrease when she finds herself essentially no closer to the goal than at the outset.

Harter's theory of "effectance motivation" (1978) suggests this influence of process outcome on task motivation. Harter built on White's (1959) definition of the "urge toward competence," a definition proposing a motivational construct that "impels the organism toward competence and is satisfied by a feeling of efficacy" (Harter, 1978, p. 34). According to Harter's theory, failure at mastery attempts eventually leads to decreases in intrinsic motivation striving for competence. However, success (which will be more probable the higher the level of skills) leads to intrinsic gratification, feelings of efficacy, and increases in intrinsic motivation, which, in turn, lead to more mastery attempts. In essential agreement with Harter, a number of social–psychological theorists (e.g., Deci & Ryan, 1985) have proposed that success (confirmation of competence) leads to increased intrinsic motivation.

Through its influence on task motivation, outcome assessment can also indirectly affect domain-relevant and creativity-relevant skills. If the sculptor ends up with a higher level of intrinsic task motivation, set-breaking and cognitive risk taking may become more habitual with her, thereby increasing her permanent repertoire of creativity skills. Also, a higher level of motivation may motivate learning about the task and related subjects, thereby increasing her domain-relevant skills.

A MAP FOR THE FUTURE

In nearly all of my previous research, I have focused on establishing one link in the model depicted in Figure 35.2: the influence of intrinsic/extrinsic task motivation on response generation. Now, with a bit more information and a great deal less hubris, my students, colleagues, and I are moving beyond the simple establishment of the intrinsic motivation principle of creativity to a broader examination of the social psychology of creativity. At the same time, we are moving beyond the social psychology of creativity toward a more integrated social–personality–cognitive psychology of creativity.

A More Inclusive Social Psychology of Creativity

Within the social psychology of creativity, we are attempting a more macroscopic look at social influences—both negative *and* positive. For example, we are beginning to think of ways in which intrinsic motivation training may be incorporated into school curricula (Hennessey & Amabile, 1987).

In addition, building on the results of the R&D interview study, we have developed an instrument called the Work Environment Inventory (WEI). Designed to assess the presence of factors in the work environment that inhibit or stimulate individual creativity, the WEI is being tested with data collected in dozens of different organizations. As a guide in this work, I have articulated a preliminary model of organizational innovation that incorporates and builds on the componential model of individual creativity depicted in Figure 35.2 (Amabile, 1988a, 1988b). The ultimate goal is to develop and test a comprehensive model of organizational innovation that meets four criteria. First, the entire process of individual creativity must be considered as a crucial element in the process of organizational innovation. Second, the model must attempt to incorporate all aspects of organizations that influence innovation, with innovation being defined as *the successful implementation of creative ideas within an organization*. Third, the model must show the major stages of the organizational innovation process. Fourth, it must describe the influence of organizational factors on individual creativity.

While we are expanding our social–psychological perspective at macroscopic levels above the intrinsic motivation phenomenon, we are also beginning to take a more microscopic look within that phenomenon to discover mechanisms by which it occurs. Specifically, we are addressing three questions: How does motivational state (intrinsic versus extrinsic) influence creative thinking? What is the role of affect? What is the role of individual differences?

How Motivation Influences Creative Thinking

In his classic paper on creative thinking, Campbell (1960) describes the process as involving a consideration of widely varying, blindly generated ideas, followed by a selective retention of those ideas that best fit some criteria. Simonton (1988) suggests much the same process in his "chance-configuration" theory of creativity. And, in his analysis of motivation and cognition, Simon (1967) asserts that the most important function of motivation is the control of attention.

We have used these theories to suggest a model of the way in which motivational orientation might influence creativity. The metaphor for this model is a maze with several exits; performing a task is represented as attempting to find a way out of the maze. The task can be done by rote, using familiar algorithms, and resulting in an uncreative solution; in the maze metaphor, the individual can take the straight, well-worn, familiar pathway out of the maze. This is the route most likely to be taken by extrinsically motivated individuals (those motivated primarily by factors outside of the task itself, outside of the maze). Because they view the task as merely a means to an end, their attention has been narrowed to doing the minimum necessary to meet the extrinsic constraint (see Kruglanski, Stein, & Riter, 1977). However, finding a creative solution requires exploration through the maze, a more heuristic approach to the task. Individuals will only be likely to take this more creative approach if they are initially intrinsically interested in the activity itself *and* if their social environment does not demand a narrowing of behavior into the familiar algorithm.

This model leads to several specific predictions about differences in the ways intrinsically and extrinsically motivated individuals will process tasks, leading ultimately to the more creative outcomes under intrinsic motivation. (Notice, however, that the model would predict no decrements in the more algorithmic *technical quality* of work under extrinsic motivation.) Compared with extrinsically motivated individuals, intrinsically motivated persons should generate and examine a larger number of ideas and possibilities while engaged in the task; make associations and juxtapositions that are more unusual; spend a longer period of time on the activity; become more deeply involved cognitively in the activity, as evidenced by several attention measures; experience more positive affect when *anticipating* working on the task, as well as when actually working on it; depart more frequently from familiar algorithms for task engagement; spend more time thinking about the task after they have finished it; and produce more creative end products. Some previous studies with various cognitive tasks offer suggestive evidence (e.g., Kruglanski, Stein & Riter, 1977; McGraw & Fiala, 1982; Pittman, Emery, & Boggiano, 1982). We have planned a series of studies to examine these predictions directly.

The Role of Affect

We will also be investigating the role of affect in the motivation–creativity link. Several theorists (e.g., Csikszentmihályi, 1975; Deci & Ryan, 1985; Izard, 1977) have suggested that intrinsic motivation involves positive affective experience, and extrinsic motivation involves negative affect. There is considerable empirical support for this suggestion (e.g., Pretty & Seligman, 1983; Reeve, Cole, & Olsen, 1986; Ryan, 1982). As I described earlier, we have suggested affect as a possible explanation for the unexpectedly high creativity of subjects in the "bonus" reward condition of our choice-reward study (Amabile, Hennessey, & Grossman, 1986).

Isen and her colleagues have demonstrated that induced positive affect increases the probability of unusual associations, set-breaking responses, heuristic problem-solving strategies, and inclusive categorization of stimuli (e.g., Isen, Daubman, & Nowicki, 1987; Isen, Johnson, Mertz, & Robinson, 1985; Isen, Means, Patrick, & Nowicki, 1982). We have planned a series of studies to examine affect as a possible mediator of the effects of motivational orientation on creativity. Do differences in motivational orientation correspond to differences in affect? Are motivational orientation differences causally prior to affective differences? Are the effective differences necessary to produce differences in creativity? Is there a difference between trait (chronic) and state (temporary) motivation, and between chronic and situation-specific affective states in these effects?

We predict a link between intrinsic motivation, positive affect, and high creativity, but we will attempt to determine the causal direction of this link and whether this link might be found only for state intrinsic motivation. It may be that the more enduring trait intrinsic motivation of individuals actively committed to a creative pursuit in their daily lives is not marked by the kind of positive affect studied by Isen but by a more "sober" positive affect—a sense of intimate involvement with and dedication to the work.

Toward a Comprehensive Psychology of Creativity

In beginning to examine specific mechanisms and subtle interactions within the intrinsic motivation phenomenon, we have, of necessity, moved beyond the social psychology of creativity toward a broader view of the creative process. We will be looking at reaction times, attentional measures, memory tests, and the use of algorithms, all taken from cognitive psychology. We are beginning to inform our work with concepts from personality psychology as well. We recognize the significant roles of both situation-induced *and* chronic affective states. We realize that intrinsic/extrinsic motivational orientation is not only a state that can be influenced by the presence or absence of extrinsic social constraints. It is also a *trait*, an enduring attitude that an individual has toward tasks within a domain. We have even developed a questionnaire (the Work Preference Inventory, or WPI) designed to assess individual differences in adults' motivational orientation. Our preliminary results are most encouraging.

This, I believe, is what all of us creativity researchers must do in mapping our future courses. In delving more deeply into the details of the phenomena that interest us, we must constantly attempt to integrate our own perspectives with those offered by others. A comprehensive psychology of creativity *is* within our grasp.

In moving toward that comprehensive understanding, I would still like, somehow, someday, to study the impact of telling subjects that they are "maybe being a little too creative." Then I would like to track down Sister Carmelita and thank her for getting me involved in all of this.

REFERENCES

Albert, R. S. (1980). Family positions and the attainment of eminence: A study of special family experiences. *Gifted Child Quarterly, 24*, 87–95.

Amabile, T. M. (1979). Effects of external evaluation on artistic creativity. *Journal of Personality and Social Psychology, 37*, 221–223.

Amabile, T. M. (1982a). Children's artistic creativity: Detrimental effects of competition in a field setting. *Personality and Social Psychology Bulletin, 8*, 573–578.

Amabile, T. M. (1982b). Social psychology of creativity: A consensual assessment technique. *Journal of Personality and Social Psychology, 43*, 997–1013.

Amabile, T. M. (1983a). *The social psychology of creativity*. New York: Springer-Verlag.

Amabile, T. M. (1983b). Social psychology of creativity: A componential conceptualization. *Journal of Personality and Social Psychology, 45*, 357–377.

Amabile, T. M. (1985). Motivation and creativity: Effects of motivational orientation on creative writers. *Journal of Personality and Social Psychology, 48*, 393–399.

Amabile, T. M. (1987). The motivation to be creative. In S. Isaksen (Ed.), *Frontiers in creativity: Beyond the basics*. Buffalo, NY: Bearly Limited.

Amabile, T. M. (1988a). From individual creativity to organizational innovation. In

K. Gronhaug & G. Kaufman (Eds.), *Achievement and motivation: A social-developmental perspective*. New York: Cambridge University Press.

Amabile, T. M. (1988b). A model of organizational innovation. In B. M. Staw & L. L. Cummings (Eds.), *Research in organizational behavior* (Vol. 10). Greenwich, CT: JAI.

Amabile, T. M. (in press). *Growing up creative*. New York: Crown.

Amabile, T. M., & Gitomer, J. (1984). Children's artistic creativity: Effects of choice in task materials. *Personality and Social Psychology Bulletin, 10,* 209–215.

Amabile, T. M., Goldfarb, P., & Brackfield, S. (in press). Social influences on creativity: Evaluation, coaction, and surveillance. *Creativity Research Journal.*

Amabile, T. M., & Gryskiewicz, S. S. (1988). Creative human resources in the R&D laboratory: How environment and personality impact innovation. In R. L. Kuhn (Ed.), *Handbook for creative and innovative managers.* New York: McGraw-Hill.

Amabile, T. M., Hennessey, B. A., & Grossman, B. S. (1986). Social influences on creativity: The effects of contracted-for reward. *Journal of Personality and Social Psychology, 50,* 14–23.

Andrews, F. M. (1975). Social and psychological factors which influence the creative process. In I. A. Taylor & J. W. Getzels (Eds.), *Perspectives in creativity.* Chicago: Aldine.

Barron, F. (1955). The disposition toward originality. *Journal of Abnormal and Social Psychology, 51,* 478–485.

Berglas, S., Amabile, T. M., & Handel, M. (1979). *An examination of the effects of verbal reinforcement on creativity.* Paper presented at the meeting of the American Psychological Association, New York.

Campbell, D. (1960). Blind variation and selective retention in creative thought as in other knowledge processes. *Psychological Review, 67,* 380–400.

Crutchfield, R. S. (1955). Conformity and character. *American Psychologist, 10,* 191–198.

Crutchfield, R. S. (1959). Personal and situational factors in conformity to group pressure. *Acta Psychologica, 15,* 386–388.

Crutchfield, R. S. (1962). Conformity and creative thinking. In H. Gruber, G. Terrell, & M. Wertheimer (Eds.), *Contemporary approaches to creative thinking.* New York: Atherton.

Csikszentmihályi, M. (1975). *Beyond boredom and anxiety.* San Francisco: Jossey-Bass.

Deci, E. L. (1971). Effects of externally mediated rewards on intrinsic motivation. *Journal of Personality and Social Psychology, 18,* 105–115.

Deci, E. L., & Ryan, R. M. (1985). *Intrinsic motivation and self-determination in human behavior.* New York: Plenum.

Feldman, D. (1980). *Beyond universals in cognitive development.* Norwood, NJ: Ablex.

Findlay, C. S., & Lumsden, C. J. (1988). The creative mind: Toward an evolutionary theory of discovery and innovation. *Journal of Social and Biological Structures.*

Getzels, J., & Csikszentmihályi, M. (1976). *The creative vision: A longitudinal study of problem-finding in art.* New York: Wiley Interscience.

Golann, S. E. (1963). Psychological study of creativity. *Psychological Bulletin, 60,* 548–565.

Gordon, W. W. (1961). *Synectics: The development of creative capacity.* New York: Harper & Row.

Guilford, J. P. (1956). The structure of intellect. *Psychological Bulletin, 53,* 267–293.

Harter, S. (1978). Effectance motivation reconsidered: Toward a developmental model. *Human Development, 21,* 34–64.

Harter, S. (1981). A new self-report scale of intrinsic versus extrinsic orientation in the classroom. *Developmental Psychology, 17,* 300–312.

Helson, R. (1965). Childhood interest clusters related to creativity in women. *Journal of Consulting Psychology, 29,* 352–361.

Hennessey, B. A. (1989). The effect of extrinsic constraints on children's creativity while using a computer. *Creativity Research Journal, 2,* 151–168.

Hennessey, B. A., & Amabile, T. M. (1987). *Creativity and learning.* Washington, DC: National Education Association.

Hennessey, B. A., Amabile, T. M., & Martinage, M. (in press). Immunizing children against the negative effects of reward. *Contemporary Educational Psychology*.

Hogarth, R. (1980). *Judgement and choice.* Chichester: John Wiley.

Hughes, T., & McCullough, F. (Eds.). (1982). *The journals of Sylvia Plath.* New York: Dial.

Isen, A. M., Daubman, K. A., & Nowicki, G. P. (1987). Positive affect facilitates creative problem solving. *Journal of Personality and Social Psychology, 52,* 1122–1131.

Isen, A. M., Johnson, M. M. S., Mertz, E., & Robinson, G. F. (1985). The influence of positive affect on the unusualness of word associations. *Journal of Personality and Social Psychology, 48,* 1–14.

Isen, A. M., Means, B., Patrick, R., & Nowicki, G. P. (1982). Some factors influencing decision-making strategy and risk-taking. In M. S. Clark & S. T. Fiske (Eds.), *Affect and cognition: The 17th Annual Carnegie Symposium on Cognition.* Hillsdale, NJ: Lawrence Erlbaum.

Izard, C. (1977). *Human emotions.* New York: Plenum.

Kruglanski, A. W., Friedman, I., & Zeevi, G. (1971). The effects of extrinsic incentive on some qualitative aspects of task performance. *Journal of Personality, 39,* 606–617.

Kruglanski, A. W., Stein, C., & Riter, A. (1977). Contingencies of exogenous reward and task performance: On the "minimax" principle in instrumental behavior. *Journal of Applied Social Psychology, 7,* 141–148.

Lepper, M. R., & Greene, D. (1978). *The hidden costs of reward.* Hillsdale, NJ: Lawrence Erlbaum.

Lepper, M. R., Greene, D., & Nisbett, R. (1973). Undermining children's intrinsic interest with extrinsic rewards: A test of the "overjustification" hypothesis. *Journal of Personality and Social Psychology, 28,* 129–137.

MacKinnon, D. W. (1962). The nature and nurture of creative talent. *American Psychologist, 17,* 484–495.

McKinnon, D. W. (1975). IPAR's contribution to the conceptualization and study of creativity. In I. Taylor & J. Getzels (Eds.), *Perspectives in creativity.* Chicago: Aldine.

McGraw, K. O. (1978). The detrimental effects of reward on performance: A literature review and a prediction model. In M. R. Lepper & D. Greene (Eds.), *The hidden costs of reward.* Hillsdale, NJ: Lawrence Erlbaum.

McGraw, K. O., & Fiala, J. (1982). Undermining the Zeigamik effect: Another hidden cost of reward. *Journal of Personality, 50,* 58–66.

McGuire, W. (1973). The yin and yang of progress in social psychology. *Journal of Personality and Social Psychology, 26,* 446–456.

Newell, A., Shaw, J., & Simon, H. (1962). The processes of creative thinking. In H. Gruber, G. Terrell, & M. Wertheimer (Eds.), *Contemporary approaches to creative thinking.* New York: Atherton.

Newell, A., & Simon, H. (1972). *Human problem solving.* Englewood Cliffs, NJ: Prentice Hall.

Nystrom, H. (1979). *Creativity and innovation.* London: John Wiley.

Osborn, A. (1963). *Applied imagination: Principles and procedures of creative thinking.* New York: Scribner.

Pames, S. (1967). *Creative behavior guidebook.* New York: Scribner.

Pittman, T. S., Emery, J., & Boggiano, A. K. (1982). Intrinsic and extrinsic motivational orientations: Reward-induced changes in preference for complexity. *Journal of Personality and Social Psychology, 42,* 789–797.

Pretty, G. H., & Seligman, C. (1983). Affect and the overjustification effect. *Journal of Personality and Social Psychology, 46,* 1241–1253.

Reeve, J., Cole, S. G., & Olsen, B. C. (1986). Adding excitement to intrinsic motivation research. *Journal of Social Behavior and Personality, 1,* 349–363.

Ryan, R. M. (1982). Control and information in the intrapersonal sphere: An extension of cognitive evaluation theory. *Journal of Personality and Social Psychology, 43,* 450–461.

Salancik, G. (1975). *Retrospective attribution of past behavior and commitment to future behavior.* Unpublished manuscript, University of Illinois.

Simon, H. (1966). Scientific discovery and the psychology of problem solving. In *Mind and cosmos: Essays in contemporary science and phi-*

losophy. Pittsburgh: University of Pittsburgh Press.

Simon, H. (1967). Understanding creativity. In C. Gowan, G. D. Demos, & E. P. Torrance (Eds.), *Creativity: Its educational implications*. New York: John Wiley.

Simon, H. (1978). Information-processing theory of human problem-solving. In W. K. Estes (Ed.), *Handbook of learning and cognitive processes: Vol. 5. Human information processing*. Hillsdale, NJ: Lawrence Erlbaum.

Simonton, D. K. (1975). Sociocultural context of individual creativity: A transhistorical time-series analysis. *Journal of Personality and Social Psychology, 32,* 1119–1133.

Simonton, D. K. (1984). *Genius, creativity, and leadership: Historiometric inquiries*. Cambridge, MA: Harvard University Press.

Simonton, D. K. (1988). Creativity, leadership, and chance. In R. J. Sternberg (Ed.), *The nature of creativity*. New York: Cambridge University Press.

Simonton, D. K. (in press). *Scientific genius: A psychology of science*. Cambridge: Cambridge University Press.

Stein, M. I. (1974). *Stimulating creativity* (Vol. 1). New York: Academic Press.

Thurstone, L., & Chave, E. (1929). *The measurement of attitude*. Chicago: University of Illinois Press.

Torrance, E. P. (1966). *Torrance Tests of Creative Thinking: Norms-technical manual*. Princeton, NJ: Personnel.

Wallas, G. (1926). *The art of thought*. New York: Harcourt, Brace.

Walster, E., Aronson, V., Abrahams, D., & Rottman, L. (1966). Importance of physical attractiveness in dating behavior. *Journal of Personality and Social Psychology, 4,* 508–516.

Watson, J. D. (1968). *The double helix*. New York: Atheneum.

White, R. (1959). Motivation reconsidered: The concept of competence. *Psychological Review, 66,* 297–323.

36. Weirder Than Fiction: The Reality and Myths of Creativity

Joseph V. Anderson

WHEN OPPORTUNITY KNOCKS

A. C. Markkula had a nice life. As marketing manager for Intel Corporation, a major semi-conductor manufacturer, he had an interesting job, a cushy salary, and the recognition of his peers at conferences and conventions. Then one day in 1977 he opened his door and there stood Steve, a scruffy looking flake, who'd dropped out of college, flirted with fruitarianism and Hare Krishna, and spent a year in India contemplating his navel and the ultimate verities. Now Steve was storming back into reality with the claim that he'd discovered a bonafide wizard, plus a secret of the universe. He'd sold his VW bus for $1,300 and set up a venture to spread a special form of information across the globe and now, Steve said, he'd chosen Markkula to be his special agent. All Markkula had to do was quit his job, hand over a quarter of a million dollars, and get to work. And though Markkula wouldn't get paid, he'd have the right to be an equal partner in the venture.[1]

Creativity knocks on the door of our psyche every day. But it does so in the strangest forms: as flakes with messages from God, as weird ideas that wake us from slumber, and as strange visions that vaguely materialize when we're wide awake and otherwise quite sane. Sometimes, it even rises from a sea of numbers that stare back at us from a screen or printed page.

But more often than not, we send it away. We slam the door, go back to sleep, or rub our eyes incredulously, then return to what we were doing. That's a sane, and safe, response. But in doing so we rob ourselves of a part of ourselves—the part that's able to leap tall buildings at a single bound. Why do we do that?

We turn our back on creativity because, well frankly, because it's weird. It beckons us to the precipice of illogical danger, like turning over your life savings to a fruitarian on a quest. But ask yourself this—what makes such ventures weird? For the most part, we do. It's weird because no one else is doing it. Or because there's no guarantee it'll work. Or, most often, it's weird because "I can't do that, because . . .".

More often than not, the "because" we generate is a bunch of poppycock that we've been sucked into believing, such as, "I'm not creative enough to pull that off, no matter how good it sounds." Well if old A. C. Markkula had succumbed to that self-imposed obstacle, I'd still be writing my articles in longhand. Instead, he walked out the door with that odd-ball and took that grand leap of faith that carried him beyond the boundaries of vocation, family, and logic. That's how he hooked up with Steven Jobs and met the world's bonafide wizard, Stephen Wozniak. Markkula had just joined Apple computer company, which still operated out of Wozniak's garage. And Markkula made Steve's dream come to life. He chased that weird apparition because he believed he had it within himself to muster the creativity required. And he saw his own objections and timidity for what they were—poppycock. So he grabbed the poppy by its privates and gave it a heave. And the rest, as they say, is history. We can do the same.

All we need to do is separate reality from the myths that plague us. The biggest myth that constrains us is that creativity is too big for us to handle. The next biggest myth is that we only get creative by bearing down on a problem, through stringent systems, organizational re-design and personal struggle. As it turns out, these two grand myths are mostly hot air, and it is time to deflate them. We need to cut creativity down to size. And we need to substitute the commandment to be creative with the permission to do so.

First, a Look at Reality

Creativity is nothing more than going beyond the current boundaries, whether those are boundaries of technology, knowledge, social norms, or beliefs. So *Star Trek* (boldly going where no man has gone before) certainly qualifies. And so does Beethoven's 5th symphony. But we lose sight of the fact that a host of mundane acts are equally as creative. Lengthening a hem beyond what the pattern calls for is no less creative than Beethoven's transition to a new kind of music. Both started from an existing framework. And both take the existing practice a step farther than the norm. Think about that for a while.

Creativity is nothing more than seeing and acting on new relationships, thereby bringing them to life. Like combining man's two chief needs, sustenance and safety, into a single fruit that guards the house, is incredibly loyal and plops itself into your cereal bowl. Al Capp invented that prototype long ago in his comic strip "Li'l Abner." It was called a Schmoo. Odd? Yes. Unreasonable? Nope. Just new and shocking, because it violated the laws of nature.

That little poo-poo of Mother Nature is a central point. The laws of nature are merely boundaries. And they've been violated before. Like the law that one body can not occupy two places at the same time. In essence, that law was violated thousands of years ago, with the first letter. One's thoughts could be in Athens, and in Corinth, at the same time. And if we take Descartes at his word, "I think, therefore, I am" the person simultaneously existed in both places since their thoughts did. The telephone and live TV are simply better violations of the same law, because the thoughts are truly simultaneous whereas the letter writer had probably forgotten the thought by the time it got to Corinth. For letters, phones, telegraphs, and TV's to be invented someone had to believe that even the laws of nature could, in effect, be broken.

Yes, But Can I Do It? Now that we've established the concept of creativity, do you recognize it? Probably so. Have you experienced it? Most of us say "no" because we've never done anything big with it. We've never written a symphony, much less a hit song. We've never painted the Cystine [sic] Chapel, much less our own house. We never really invented anything. So we're likely to sit back and content ourselves with identifying creativity rather than practicing it. That makes us as useless as a drama critique . . . all talk and no action. The fact of the matter is we've all been creative. We just never labeled it as such, because we didn't understand the various types of creativity. We can rectify that problem pretty quickly.

The Types of Creativity. In essence, there are only three broad types of creativity. You can make things, you can combine things, or you can change things.

> **Creation** is the activity we usually think of when someone says creativity. It is the act of making something out of nothing. With fervid apologies to physicists and their theory of atomic displacement, it *is* possible to make something out of nothing. Beethoven faced a blank page and made the immortal 5th symphony spring to life. Shakespeare did the same with *Othello* and a host of other masterpieces. The Wright brothers filled an empty sky with planes. And on and on it goes. Creation is, without question, creativity. But it is not the whole,

nor is it even the most important type. There are others of equal importance.

Synthesis is the act of relating two or more previously unrelated phenomena. Take a cake. Take a shovel. Put them side by side and stare at them. Boom! The cake server is born. It's a miniature shovel. That's synthesis. The first wheel was the product of creation. So was the first axle and the first box. But until someone came along and synthesized them into the cart, mankind didn't get much good out of the three components. Synthesis is the core of society's advancement. Creation is nice, but synthesis is the real engine of survival and prosperity. Have you ever performed synthesis? Did you ever fill a pie tin with mud instead of batter? Ever fill a balloon with water instead of air. Did you ever put Tuesday together with going to the beach rather than going to work? Congratulations. You synthesized. And that puts you in the same league as Thomas Edison. He never created anything in his whole life. All he did was suck the brains of others and synthesized like crazy. So whadayathink? You creative?

Modification is the act of altering something that already exists so that it can: (a) perform its function better, (b) perform a new function, (c) perform in a different setting, or (d) be used by someone new. Putting pontoons on an airplane doesn't change the function of the plane (take off, fly, land), but it certainly broadens the settings in which it can perform its function. Moving a hose to the back end of a vacuum cleaner changes the whole function of the machine, from sucking to blowing. And something as simple as lowering a water fountain, or adding a foot stool opens its use to a whole new group, unattended children.

The remaining point to be made here is that creation, synthesis, and modification overlap so much that it is difficult to separate them in reality. The folks at Etonic aggressively stumbled on creativity by deciding to play barefoot in the park at midnight. There in the blackness of night their senses took over and rediscovered the incredible lightness of being naked of foot, and the ability to pivot equally well on toe or heel. And that unlocked their "Catalyst" shoe, the revolutionary light shoe with a two-piece sole. The Catalyst had never existed before. So in that respect it represented creation. But in essence it was just a modification, one that came via synthesis, putting tennis with bare feet, rather than with shoes.

The reality, therefore, is this. Each of us has the gift of creativity, in one form or another. So don't fret if a symphony isn't within you. You have one of the other gifts. And the only thing it takes to release them is for you to remove the self-imposed obstacles . . . the myths that confound us. And that just happens to be our next topic.

The Myths That Confound Us

The Missing Organ. Many people seem to think that creativity is like a mystic organ, say an extra pancreas or enlarged hypothalamus gland, that only a few people possess. In all honesty, they may be correct when it comes to true creation. However, that is a minuscule part of functional creativity, easily swamped by the contribution of synthesis and modification. And the latter two are not dependent on mysticism, revelation, or even an extra organ. All they require is open eyes and the willingness to act on what you see. If you ever hid food under your pillow you've got what it takes for those. You went beyond the boundary of Mom's social order, and you synthesized like crazy—associating food with a bed instead of with a table.

The Need for Genius. Many people also believe that creativity is the result of the *amount* of intelligence that one possesses. Clinical and field studies, however, fail to support this hypothesis. Verifiable geniuses (as measured by IQ tests and similar instruments) tend to do very well for themselves vocationally, but they usually do so as corporate vice presidents shuffling paper. They haven't made much of a dent in terms of making creative contributions to the world.[2] A solid "C" student with curiosity and determination usually makes a bigger impact on the world. Edison, Einstein, and even Theodore Geisel (otherwise known as "Dr. Seuss") were all lackluster students.

> *The key is not how much intelligence you have, but the type of intelligence, and your willingness to use it. Steven Jobs was a back alley hustler with street smarts, not an intellectual. His "genius" was the ability to dream dreams, then connive and cajole others into cooperation.*

Wozniak was his first victim, and once he was under wing Jobs convinced lawyers and ad agencies to work for nothing more than the promise of future payments, and Markkula to risk everything he had. Jobs rightfully earned the title as the father of Apple, despite the fact that he was neither a technical nor marketing wizard. He was just a jack-of-all-trades in both, with a whole lot of chutzpa.

The Need for Chutzpa.

The Need for Chutzpa. Does it follow then that chutzpa is a requirement for creativity? No. Walter Mitty, you may recall, was an outward milquetoast at the same time that his imagination was running rampant across the globe. Creativity can easily bloom without the social courage and hustle we call chutzpa. But there is a big difference between dreaming an idea and using it. And at that point chutzpa comes screaming back on stage. Without the outward hustle and courage it brings, ideas stay on the drawing board or get lost in the dark recesses of the mind. Consequently, we'd have to acknowledge that while creativity can bloom for anyone, it only bears fruit for the chutzpatic

gardener. So reality provides a simple truth. The meek creative simply needs to form a partnership with an adrenal hustler. "Steve Wozniak, meet Steve Jobs. Now go make millions."

The Solitary Magician. Another myth is that the creative person exists in a vacuum, locked in his garage with God as the only source of inspiration. It makes a great movie script, but usually misses the mark in terms of reality.

Take a look at electricity. Frenchmen came up with the first spark maker and discovered alternating current. Germans invented the Leyden jar and the vacuum pump. Italians came up with the wet-cell and storage batteries. A Dane was the intellectual source of much of electric theory. Then Ben Franklin, perhaps the world's most under-rated creator, was the world's foremost authority on electric theory for a considerable time. An Austrian invented the first electric-powered machine. And an academic just down the road from Edison at Rensselaer Institute of Technology was blissfully inventing capacitors, alternators, generators, and filters for his own entertainment.[3]

So when Thomas Edison sat alone in his workshop and "invented" the light bulb, he was hardly alone. Every one of those other folks was crammed into the shadows. They represented the ninety-nine percent perspiration Edison advocated—knowing the trail of research. In fact, Edison had been a regular visitor in Professor Henry Rowland's office, the American academic blissfully puttering away in his lab.

Creativity and Nobility. Since we tend to envision the creative person locked in his garage with God, we tend to see creativity as the progeny of sacred union. Sometimes it may be exactly that, but usually not. In fact, there are numerous indications that creativity is the product of someone you'd like to throw in jail.

In 1860 a group of investors paid young Johnnie to make a field investigation of the commercial viability of petroleum. He thought it was a sure fire winner. So he lied through his teeth. He told the investors it was a loser, put every penny of his own funds into petroleum, and aced them out of the market. Then he went on to invent most of the competitive practices that are now illegal. Before he was a philanthropist, John D. Rockefeller was a crook. But he was also marvelously creative, and the industry still bears his mark in terms of production, distillation, and distribution.

And if you want larceny with a grin, look at Samuel Slater. In 1790 he stole the trade secrets of mass production in England and sold himself to the highest bidder in America, boldly violating every aspect of British patent and copyright law, thereby putting America on the map as an industrial nation. But Sam redeemed himself. He and his wife were the originators of Sunday School in America. And ironically, at the same time he was violating the British, he was the leading advocate of the legislation that established America's own patent and copyright laws.[4] You have to sit back and admire that type of gall.

The list goes on and on, but the point is that creativity isn't very pristine. In fact, it sometimes emanates from the dark side of our personality. That's unsettling if you see business as a quaint tea party. It's intuitively obvious if you recognize it as trench warfare.

So with a nod to Freud, the first place you may want to check for ideas is your id. The second place you'll want to check is the id of thy neighbor. At its worst, creativity involves outright theft on a grand scale. At its best, it is a form of unconscious plagiarism. If God accompanies us to the garage, he usually sits there and tells us what our neighbors are doing. So don't be timid about where you look or what you use. Any idea is fair game as a starting point. Even if it's protected, it can inspire a useful offshoot. Apple hasn't really "created" anything. But it's been brilliant at synthesis and modification.

Purity of Heart Is to Will One Thing.

That's a quote from Kierkegaard, a prominent and very dead theologian. They might be wise words to a religious aesthetic but they are the kiss of death to someone trying to be creative. No matter how creative you might be, you need to pull your head out of the sand and see what else is going on.

Surprisingly enough, though, many firms don't use the ideas and technologies that are readily available. It has been suggested that this is due to an "NIH syndrome" (not invented here), which seems to be equal parts pompous disdain, proprietary fastidiousness, and uncertainty about how to exploit new knowledge.

Bell & Howell was once a major name in every upscale home. Its eight-millimeter movie cameras were the bane and blessing of every family gathering and the chronicler of American family history. By 1972 more than one million cameras were being sold each year, but by 1981, sales had plummeted by almost ninety percent and Bell & Howell became a name used only in nostalgia and *Trivial Pursuit*. The simplicity of video swept the marketplace and Bell & Howell ignored the new idea. Now the marketplace ignores Bell & Howell.[5]

Revelation and Creativity.

Michelangelo professed that he never created a sculpture. He simply stared at the block of marble until God showed him the statue that was trapped within. Then all Mike did was get the gravel out of the way. Wouldn't it be nice to have just such a direct line to the almighty? The fact of the matter is that Michelangelo's profession was probably on a par with Oral Roberts's recent proclamation that God said his supporters better cough up $8,000,000 or their favorite healer was kaput.

In reality, if a line exists at all, it's so indirect and convoluted that one is reminded of Mark Twain's words, "Lord, if you forgive the little jokes I play on you, I'll forgive the great big ones you play on me." The bulk of creativity comes to the surface by accident, or initially misdirected.

Alexander Graham Bell didn't get a direct commission from on high to create an instrument for carrying conversations between New York and Paris. He was dinking around trying to invent a hearing aid for his deaf fiancée. In 1795 Nicholas Joseph Cugnot dabbled with an abject failure, a steam-driven cannon carriage for the French army. Men comfortably walk at three to four miles per hour. The gun carriage zipped along at two miles per hour and had to stop every 300 yards to rebuild a head of steam. But it was the first automobile, in disguise. In 1842, Dr. John Gorrie became mentally ill and died, because the medical industry refused to embrace his cure for malaria, which happened to be the first air-conditioner. So keep your eyes open and realize that the best application of your idea might be worlds away from your current focus.

External Validity and Creativity.

The previous stories shoot a hole in a major myth that hamstrings us—if Mom doesn't tack it on the refrigerator, it doesn't count as art. More often than not we let others decree whether we are creative or not. And when that happens, we're in trouble. Either we stop trying, or we join John Gorrie in a padded cell.

> The fact of the matter is that most creative acts are initially rejected, ignored or belittled. Bell was laughed off the stage at his first demonstration of the phone. Van Gogh never sold a painting—the ones that now go for eight million dollars. It was just about a century before Cugnot's car resurfaced in Henry Ford's factory, and it took just as long for Gorrie's machine to become the air conditioner.

Simply put, the rest of the world doesn't immediately embrace creativity. So if you rely on their judgment you'll never get out of the starting blocks. Remember, creativity exists if:

a. a new thing comes into being (creation);
b. two previously unrelated things are joined (synthesis);
c. or, if a thing is improved or gains a new application (modification).

That's it. The total list of requirements. Notice that the list does not say "Creativity exists only if someone else says 'My how creative'." Once you realize that, you become your own arbiter of creativity. Blanch DuBois may have been "dependent on the kindness of strangers" in *A Streetcar Named Desire*, but you don't have to be.

In other words, stop chasing after the "moms" of the world looking for approval, and spend your time actually being creative. You'll stay sane, and the world will benefit from your work.

If It Ain't Big, It Ain't Creativity.

And now we get to the crux of the matter. We surgically gut our latent creativity by setting incredibly high benchmarks, such as "it's only creative if it changes the world." So if we've never written a symphony, or invented a product, or designed a marketing plan that captured seventy-seven percent of the yuppie market, we look despairingly in the mirror at the slack-jawed drone that gazes back, and condemn ourselves to a life of drab obedience to those who have.

In the process we forget that moving a desk so that work flows smoother is also creativity. It's modification. And creativity also blooms when we redesign a job description so that related tasks are given to the same person. That's synthesis. It's even creativity when we cut our losses on a worthless industrial adhesive by slapping it on the back of our secretary's note pad so she can stick our messages where we'll see them. We call that bit of creation the 3M "Post-It" notes.

And when you get right down to it, our notion of bigness and importance is usually the opposite of reality. The much ballyhooed creation of the Saturn car company by GM is small potatoes, infinitely unimportant. The car still has four wheels, still uses an internal combustion engine, people still ride inside it, and so on. It's big in terms of dollars, but frankly, it doesn't change the world a bit. What does? The lowly tin can. Now that's something to praise. It revolutionized the world. It changed food production and storage, made armies and individuals more mobile, and virtually eliminated botulism. The flush toilet is another one. Urban mortality rates plummeted as a result.

As it turns out, creativity usually resides in the seemingly small potatoes of corporate and individual life. Or should we say peanuts? George Washington Carver was probably the most prolific creator in America's history, making Edison look like a tortoise in terms of the number of products created. And Carver did it all by looking at one little insignificant thing—the peanut.

So start seeing creativity in your own peanuts: the reporting procedure that could be improved, the sales territory that can be redesigned, the new vendor or purchasing procedure, or the tasks that can be re-designed.

And Now for a Parting Shot

But what if you're trying to get creativity out of other people, and not just trying to be creative yourself? You start by confronting the reality and myths we've just covered. Then you add two more things.

First—realize that no structure, process, incentive system, or management reorganization is going to make your firm creative, unless you first help the individuals within those structures and systems unlock their willingness to try. And that isn't done at arm's length. You've got to crawl into the trenches and be a cheerleader and seducer. Hold up a mirror for your people and help them see their own creative potential by identifying it for them.

The best creativity motivator I ever met was an old curmudgeon that ran one of the production shops at a naval shipyard. When someone finished a job ahead of schedule (with no defects) he jumped on a workbench with airhorn and megaphone in hand and treated the entire shop to an absolutely obscene drinking song in celebration. The sight of the grumpy old S.O.B. making a fool of himself was so ridiculous, and the instigator received so many kudos and free drinks, that everyone busted a hump to be the next cause of hilarity. Creativity ravished the shop floor, and no problem was insurmountable. They had less down time, less turnover, and higher productivity than any other unit.

Sometimes, our desire for professionalism is so strong that we make the affirmation process needlessly convoluted and diluted. When a kid takes their artwork to Mom, they want a hug and a kiss—an emotional reaction. Given the current climate, a hug and kiss at work will land you in jail, or on the Supreme Court—but some other kind of emotional reaction is certainly called for. So loosen up. Managers prosper from borrowing some inspirational tactics from the art of leadership. And that, in itself, is the creative act of synthesis.

Second—while you're holding that mirror, keep a careful eye on the images they see, because they'll initially need some help separating the reality from the poppycock.

- Remind them that creativity exists in the small and mundane things of life, as well as in the big things.
- Remind them that creativity is more than creation. Celebrate synthesis and modification as well.
- Encourage them to look around—to transfer ideas from other areas, and to look for seemingly absurd applications of what they've already got.
- In short, help them see that they have the seed of creativity in themselves already.

And while you're at it, do the same for yourself.

NOTES

1. This, and subsequent information on Markkula and Apple, comes from Robert F. Hartley, *Marketing Successes* (New York: John Wiley & Sons Inc., 1985), 200–213.
2. Lewis Terman, father of the American IQ test, discovered this rather enlightening factoid in a 60-year study of 1,528 measurable geniuses. Cited by Leslie Dorman in "Original Spin," *Psychology Today*, August 1989, 47–52.
3. The historical information on electricity and other forms of technology comes from *The People's Chronology*, James Trager, ed. (New York: Holt, Rinehart and Winston, 1979). In addition to being an entertaining ammuni-

tion dump for *Trivial Pursuit*, it is a fascinating guide to the progression of knowledge. You'd be well served to buy a recent edition.

4. *The People's Chronology*, James Trager, ed. (New York: Holt, Rinehart and Winston, 1979), again.

5. Ann Hughey, "Sales of Home Movie Equipment Falling as Firms Abandon Market, Video Grows," *Wall Street Journal*, March 17, 1982, 25.

37. Why No One Really Wants Creativity

Barry M. Staw

For years I have been among the advocates of creativity—the usual set of academics who decry the status quo, argue the merits of being different, and push for organizational innovation. Well, I've had enough. The term *creativity* has a nice ring to it and nearly everyone thinks it is a good thing; but few people or organizations really want creativity. When they think it through, when the processes involved and their attendant costs are made clear, people and firms tend to back away from creativity, perhaps with just cause. Let me elaborate.

CELEBRATING THE VICTOR

It is very common in both the creativity literature and the organizational world to trot out the successful entrepreneur, inventor, or business venture to show off the benefits of creativity. We celebrate the victor—the person or organization that has pulled off the major coup or taken the market by storm. Interviews are given, biographies are written, and success stories printed. Copying the victor is also common practice. Self-help books proliferate on how to make us more creative, often modeled on characteristics of people known to be creative. Consultants abound, selling programs designed to renew, reorient, revitalize, or reinvent organizations, usually modeled on the practices of firms that have recently experienced success with a major new product or service. There are, of course, serious questions about whether the correlates of creativity actually cause creativity and, for sure, much of the research on creative people and innovative firms has lacked adequate controls or methodological rigor. But even if

we take these correlates at face value, assuming they are the real factors driving creativity, this still does not mean that people really want or need creativity. Would people, given the chance, make the choices and enact the behaviors necessary to become creative? I doubt it.

WHY INDIVIDUALS REJECT CREATIVITY

Although there are a multitude of creativity theories, most researchers in this area do agree on a short list of characteristics shared by many of those who are creative. Creatives are risk takers. They are willing to take their chances on an unproven solution rather than go with the tried and true. Creatives are nonconformists. They are willing to defy convention and even authority to explore new ideas and to get to the truth. Creatives are persistent. They don't give up when they get frustrated or rebuffed by a problem, they keep at it. Creatives are flexible. They are able to reformulate a problem when facing failure rather than just give up or continue down the same path. Finally, creatives put in long, hard hours. They become totally absorbed in their work, often to the exclusion of their family or personal life.

The picture of the creative individual does not mesh well with the proclivities of the average person. For example, research on decision making has repeatedly found that people are risk averse, at least when it comes to possible gains. That is, when given a choice between a large but uncertain reward (e.g., 10% chance to win $10,000) and a smaller and certain payoff (e.g., 100% chance to win $1,000), people will generally choose the sure thing. Only when they are in losing situations have people reliably been shown to choose the riskier alternative. Likewise, when given a chance to follow the majority or minority point of view, most people opt for the prevailing view. This is, of course, an adaptive strategy in most situations. Yet, evidence shows that people often choose to follow others even when that means abandoning the truth, and this is especially the case when the conformist strategy is backed by an authority or someone who seems to be in charge.

In terms of decision style, most people also fall short of the creative ideal. They are satisficers rather than searchers for the optimal or most desirable solution. They follow a number of energy-saving heuristics that generally lead to a set of systematic biases or inaccuracies in processing information. And, unless they are held accountable for their decision-making strategies, they tend to find the easy way out—either by not engaging in very careful thinking or by modeling their choices on the preferences of those who will be evaluating them.

The overall picture does not favor creativity. Most people do not follow a life pattern similar to that of the creative, nor would they want to. The average person may become intrigued when the glories of successful creativity are hailed by the media. But when confronted with the bald truth that most scientists never come up with any earthshaking findings, most new businesses end in failure, and most whistle-blowers get demoted or fired, it is not surprising that people generally opt for a safer, more normal life than that followed by the creative.

In defending creativity one can, of course, argue that creative acts are not really rational decisions in terms of a full calculus of costs, benefits, and the probabilities of various outcomes. Perhaps creatives are altruists, people who accept personal risks and costs that will only benefit the larger collective, such as an organization or society. Perhaps creatives are slightly tilted individuals who don't really mind the endless nights nursing a laboratory experiment or the social isolation that comes with taking the minority viewpoint. For a few, taking the creative route is something they must do, something that makes inherent sense. For some, the creative act is a bit like falling in love. Creative people can become so smitten with a project or venture that the simple calculation of costs and benefits seems downright inappropriate. My own father is a little like this. He frequently asks others what they think about his latest business deal. But when others look at the numbers and ask how he will turn a profit, he simply crosses out the offending figures, replacing them with more "realistic" estimates that are 20% higher.

So my point is this. Most people admire creative individuals, at least in retrospect. They admire the successful entrepreneur, scientist, writer, or musician. But this does not mean that the typical person would make the same choices in life, given the odds of failure, nor would that person really want to follow a pattern of social behavior and decision making that mimics those who are known to be creative. We should therefore consider ourselves lucky that there are a few people out there willing to take the creative route. We need them.

WHY ORGANIZATIONS REJECT INNOVATION

Much of the same logic pertains to organizational innovation. Although there is practically a cottage industry devoted to celebrating successful innovations and touting their characteristics as the "new solution," few managers really want to pay the price for innovation. To most managers, being innovative means that they have to do everything wrong.

First, instead of the normal recruitment process in which people are brought in who have the skills needed by the firm and the values it admires, innovative companies must let down their barriers. They must accommodate those whose skills are more peripheral and whose goals are suspect.

Second, instead of socializing new members of the organization to absorb the values and culture of the firm, the innovative corporation must encourage people not to listen, at least not too hard. There is nothing that kills innovation like everyone speaking in the same voice, even if it is a well-trained voice.

Third, instead of issuing directives and policy statements and hoping that they will be obeyed, innovative firms must encourage disobedience. In fact, those in power should go so far as to encourage active opposition. Innovative organizations are those that harbor multiple perspectives and objectives, not simply a variety of views about how a particular product should be designed and produced.

Fourth, instead of striving for lower costs and efficiency, innovative companies must opt for adaptiveness. They need to have excess capacity and personnel devoted to seemingly meaningless ventures. Because innovation requires investing in losers as well as winners, adaptive firms must be prepared to follow several competing designs simultaneously, and move through a sequence of product alternatives before settling on a single course of action.

Finally, to be truly innovative, firms must be industry leaders rather than followers. They must stick their necks out on untried products and technologies, not knowing if they will be successes or failures. They can't wait for other firms to launch the first products, only to come in late, making some adjustments to reap the profits. They must pursue projects that often appear to be more folly than wisdom.

Naturally, most organizations and their managers would hesitate in adopting these suggestions. They might consider a few items on the list interesting or worth long-term consideration, but that is a far cry from taking concrete action to accomplish them.

From what we know about organizations, they work very hard to recruit and select employees who look and act like those already in the firm. For those who might have slipped into the organization without the proper skills and values, socialization is usually the answer.

Creating clones of existing personnel is generally what management wants and gets. Those who deviate from the prevailing culture become dissatisfied and tend to leave the organization, leaving room for those who have been "properly socialized."

Research also shows that organizational power structures are difficult to change. Those in power set the agenda, they reward those who fall in line politically, who are willing to support the existing order. Power also begets power. Those who have power get the resources to maintain their positions, while others must struggle to survive. There are few known cases of those in power willingly giving up their influence or sharing it with the opposition.

Finally, almost by definition, the organizational world is populated by followers rather than leaders. Even the Japanese corporations currently touted as the world's most successful enterprises are not generally considered industry leaders. Though Japanese management is praised for its quality control techniques and novel inventory systems, little is made of the basic conservatism of Japanese industry. These companies generally let other firms do the innovating. Once a product has been developed and the market possibilities made clear, they enter the fray as efficient and effective producers.

In summary, organizations find it hard to see the logic of innovation. Being a creative organization may sound good, but when the details are described more fully, it is just not the path most corporations or their management want to take.

ASSESSING THE DAMAGE

Does the fact that few individuals or organizations really want creativity doom us to mediocrity, to a path without progress and hope? Certainly not. My point in writing this essay is simply to deflate the notion of creativity, to let the air out of some of the rhetoric usually seen in creativity manuals and texts. Creativity is not something we all strive to achieve, nor something we can all improve upon given proper effort and guidance. In my view, creativity suffers from a large case of false advertising. The popular press, along with the collusion of many consultants and academics, has sold us the notion that we can reap the rewards of a Galileo, Edison, or Picasso without paying the full price. Likewise, managers are told that they can convert their own organization into a slick Silicon Valley firm without losing something in the bargain. The reality is that only a few individuals and organizations really want to be creative, when all the details are known. We should appreciate the few takers of this questionable deal rather than scold the majority for its caution and common sense.

Managing Creativity and Innovation in Organizations

38. The Weird Rules of Creativity

Robert I. Sutton

*F*or the past decade at least, the holy grail for companies has been innovation. Managers have gone after it with all the zeal their training has instilled in them. They've focused on identifying the optimal incentives and inputs to the creative process, on bringing customers' and other important perspectives to bear, on investing in ideas according to their odds of success, and on slashing the percentage of losers. There's only one problem: None of that works very well.

What does foster creativity doesn't look at all like rational management to most experienced executives. The practices go beyond counterintuitive; they seem downright weird. For example, you might reasonably expect that creativity would flourish in a fun, low-stress workplace, where conflict is held in check and managers keep a close watch on how money is spent and people use their time. You'd be wrong. After studying creative companies and teams for more than a decade, I've found them to be remarkably inefficient and often terribly annoying places to work, where "managing by getting out of the way" is often the best approach of all.

Managing for creativity, I've discovered, means taking most of what we know about management and standing it on its head. It means placing bets on ideas without much heed to their projected ROI. It means ignoring what has worked before. It means taking perfectly happy people and goading them into fights among themselves. Good creativity management means hiring the candidate you have a gut feeling against. And as for those people who stick their fingers in their ears and chant, "I'm not listening, I'm not listening," when customers are making suggestions? It means praising and promoting them.

In this article, I advocate several ideas about managing creativity that are clearly odd but just as clearly effective. One set of ideas relates to hiring, another to management, and a third to risk and randomness. All of them have solid grounding in academic research. And here's what's really weird. I've actually found numerous companies and teams that use these ideas with great results.

WHY THESE WEIRD IDEAS WORK

The practices in this article succeed by increasing the range of a company's knowledge, by causing people to see old problems in new ways, and by helping companies break from the past. Decades of research show that these three conditions produce the richest soil for creative work. So why do ideas for promoting them seem so strange to managers?

It's because as important as innovation is to most companies, it isn't—and never will be—their primary activity. Quite the contrary, companies are overwhelmingly focused—and correctly so—on the more routine work of making money *right now* from tried-and-true products, services, and business models. The practices that are well suited for cashing in on old, proven ways are drastically different from those needed for innovation. Consider the contrast between how Disney organizes the work of cast members at its theme parks and that of "imagineers" at its research and development facility in Burbank, California. The job titles are revealing metaphors for the two kinds of work. Cast members in theme parks follow well-defined scripts; whether they are playing the role of Cinderella or Goofy, acting as guides on the Jungle Cruise, or sweeping the streets, precise guidelines are enforced to ensure that they stay in character. This is Disney's routine work. In contrast, Disney Imagineering is a place where people are expected to keep trying different things. Imagineers come to work each day to dream up wild ideas about new things a guest might experience. The best practices for imagineers can't be choreographed in the same

detail as those of cast members. After all, the management problem is to expand the possibilities of what an imagineer might do, not to constrain them.

The right balance of what organizational theorist James March has termed exploitation of proven knowledge versus exploration of new possibilities varies across industries. But even in companies that are much ballyhooed for innovation, only a small percentage of effort is usually devoted to generating and testing new products and services. This comparative rarity helps explain why practices that support innovation may seem odd and provoke discomfort and why managers hesitate to use them even when they should. Study after study shows that, independent of other factors, the more often people are exposed to something, the more positive they feel about it; rare and unfamiliar things provoke negative evaluations. This "mere exposure effect" has been found, as Stanford psychologist Robert Zajonc writes, for "geometric figures, random polygons, Chinese and Japanese ideographs, photographs of faces, numbers, letters of the alphabet, letters of one's own name, random sequences of tone, food, odors, flavors, colors, actual persons, stimuli that were initially liked and initially disliked stimuli." People are unaware of the effect and routinely deny it is happening, but still it persists.

Little wonder, then, that the best ideas for promoting and sustaining creativity seem strange, even wrong, to most managers. As we'll see, managing for innovation often means shifting your traditional, rational approaches to hiring, management, and risk 180 degrees.

IT STARTS WITH HIRING

The difference begins with hiring. What rational manager would intentionally hire someone who would be slow to learn the company culture or who would make coworkers feel uncomfortable? Who would waste a hire on a candidate whose skills the company doesn't even need? Or bring in a person without previous experience in solving the type of problem at hand? Yet these are all sound approaches for building companies that embrace innovation as a way of life.

Let's begin with those "slow learners." Most companies, of course, screen job candidates to pick out the fast learners—those gregarious people with social graces who can figure out quickly how to do things "the right way." But companies and teams that do innovative work need at least some members who are slow to learn how things are "supposed to be done." Otherwise, each newcomer will soon become a perfect imitation of everyone else in the company, and there won't be any new ideas around to develop and test.

Research in personality psychology suggests that people with certain traits are best able to avoid, ignore, or reject "the heat of the herd," as futurist George Gilder puts it. These include people who have high self-esteem and those who psychologist Mark Snyder calls "low self-monitors"—people who are especially insensitive to subtle, and even not so subtle, hints from others about how to act. For better or worse, low self-monitors are relatively unfettered by social norms. These mavericks and misfits can drive bosses and coworkers crazy, but they increase the range of what is thought, noticed, said, and done in a company. High self-monitors are likely to be yes-men and -women; they can't stop themselves from telling others what they think they want to hear. Low self-monitors can't stop themselves from saying and doing what they think is right because they don't notice—or don't care about—pressures to follow the herd. People with high self-esteem think and act independently as well; confident people continue to believe in their ideas despite rejection and criticism.

The Xerox researcher who invented the laser printer, Gary Starkweather, is a great example of someone who succeeded because he felt compelled to do what he felt was right and had enough self-confidence to reject the organizational code. As Michael Hiltzik recounts in his book *Dealers of Lightning*, Starkweather was hired in 1968 as an optics researcher by Xerox's main technical laboratory in Webster, New York. He kept insisting that the then new "technology of lasers could be used to 'paint' an image onto a xerographic drum with greater speed and precision than ordinary white light." The traditional "white light" researchers at the Webster lab repeatedly dismissed lasers as impractical and too expensive. Starkweather responded by doing one experiment after another that answered nearly every objection raised by his superiors and peers. When Starkweather's manager still tried to stop his research, he was confident enough to complain to a senior manager at Xerox about how "laboratory dogma" was ruining both a good idea and his career. He was then transferred to the new Xerox PARC research facility in Palo Alto, California; by 1974, he had developed his ideas into a commercially feasible product. When it was finally launched in 1977, the 9700 printer became one of Xerox's best-selling products.

Hiring people who make you uncomfortable, even those you don't like, is another way to find a few useful misfits who will ignore and reject the organizational code, increasing the variety in what people think, say, and do. A senior executive in a toy company once told me that her managers kept hiring people who pretended to "think like us" during job interviews but showed their true colors after being hired by pointing out how bad the company's products were. The behavior, in her words, "makes us hate them"—but, she admitted, some of those complainers were crucial to her company's success because they kept coming up with great ideas for new toys ("probably just to spite us"). Of course, the next step, which I recommended to her, is to intentionally hire people that she and others in the company dislike.

Another way to spark creativity is to hire people with skills you don't think you need. If this sounds ridiculous, consider that the practice is not uncommon among product design companies, which live or die on innovation. This attitude led IDEO to hire Craig Syverson because he seemed to have a lot of "cool" skills in areas like computers and the arts. When IDEO's managers offered him a position, they weren't quite sure what the job would entail or if they needed his skills at all. Syverson experimented with several jobs, but soon focused on video production work even though, at first, there was no demand for custom videos from IDEO clients. As IDEO's focus expanded, however, from designing products to designing user and customer experiences, Syverson's ability to capture how people use different products became a crucial—and profitable—service to clients.

Design Continuum is another product design company that brings in new ideas by hiring people with varied, even offbeat, backgrounds. It has hired engineers who moonlight or have worked as sculptors, carpenters, and rock musicians. The company likes to hire people such as Roy Thompson, who started out writing graffiti on the streets and subways of Brooklyn, and David Cohen, who worked as an aircraft mechanic. These diverse experiences give the company a broad palette of ideas to try in new ways and places.

If I were running a company that depended on innovation, I would go even further to import fresh knowledge: I would hire some people who had never tried to solve problems like the ones I was addressing. In the creative process, ignorance is bliss, especially in the early stages. People who don't know how things are "supposed to be" aren't blinded by preconceptions.

The easiest way to guarantee such naïveté is to hire novices, as Jane Goodall's groundbreaking research on chimpanzees shows. When anthropologist Louis Leakey offered Goodall the opportunity to do two years of intensive observations of these apes in Africa, Goodall hesitated to take the job because she had no scientific training. Leakey insisted that not only was university training unnecessary, it had serious drawbacks. Goodall explains in her book *In the Shadow of Man*, "He wanted someone with a mind uncluttered and unbiased by theory who would make the study for no other reason than a real desire for knowledge." Ultimately, Goodall and Leakey both believed that if she had not been ignorant of existing theories, she never would have been able to observe and explain so many new chimp behaviors.

Dyson Appliances, maker of the hottest-selling vacuum cleaner in the United Kingdom, takes much the same approach to hiring. Dyson's Dual Cyclone has a powerful and groundbreaking vacuum technology and requires no bag. The machine has a striking colorful design and see-through chamber that lets you view the cyclone inside as it spins at nearly 1,000 miles per hour. Founder and CEO James Dyson believes that one reason his company invents successful products is that it employs graduates straight from universities. He writes, "They are unsullied. They have not been strapped into a suit and taught to think by a company with nothing on its mind but short-term profit and early retirement."

Naïveté can also come in the form of people who are experts in some other area, which allows them to see—and perhaps solve—problems from a new perspective. This approach was used during the early days of Ballard Power Systems, whose innovative fuel cell technology might just replace the internal combustion engine. As Tom Koppell describes in his book *Powering the Future*, founder and then CEO Geoffrey Ballard hired a young chemistry professor named Keith Prater in 1974 to work on batteries the company was developing. Prater warned Ballard that he had no experience in batteries. "That's fine," said Ballard, "I don't want someone who knows batteries. They know what won't work. I want someone who is bright and creative and willing to try things that others might not try." And indeed, Prater played a key role in developing innovative batteries during the company's early days, and later, in making breakthroughs in fuel cells for powering buses and cars.

MANAGING FOR CREATIVE SPARKS

Once you've got your talent in the door, the next order of business is to do something with it. Again, my ideas will seem strange to people who believe that the best ways for managing routine tasks are equally well suited to innovative work, but they are supported by theory and practice. If it's creativity you want, you should encourage people to ignore and defy superiors and peers—and while you're at it, get them to fight among themselves. You should reassign people who have settled into productive grooves in their jobs. And you should start rewarding failure, not just success; reserve punishment only for inaction.

People who do what they think is right—rather than what they are told or what they anticipate their superiors want—can drive their bosses crazy and get their companies in deep trouble. But they also force companies to try ideas that some boss or powerful group may have rejected as a waste of time or money. 3M's former CEO William McKnight, for example, once ordered a young employee named Richard Drew to abandon a project he was working on, insisting it would never work. Drew disregarded the order and went on to invent masking tape, one of 3M's breakthrough products. Drew's perseverance also laid the foundation for 3M's defining product, Scotch tape.

Similarly, in *The HP Way*, David Packard brags about an employee who defied a direct order from him. "Some years ago," he writes, "at an HP laboratory in Colorado Springs devoted to oscilloscope technology, one of our bright, energetic engineers, Chuck House, was advised to abandon a display monitor he was developing. Instead he embarked on a vacation to California—stopping along the way to show potential customers a prototype." House was convinced he was on to something, so he persisted with the project, even persuading his R&D manager to rush the monitor into production. The resulting $35 million in revenue proved he was right. Packard continues: "Some years later, at a gathering of HP engineers, I presented Chuck with a medal for 'extraordinary contempt and defiance beyond the normal call of engineering duty.' "

I've never seen an organization with guidelines such as, "Ignore your boss if you think he or she is wrong." If you work in a place that actually enforces a rule like this, please contact me immediately. I have, however, found companies where managers provide vague encouragement for employees to work on what they want and don't demand to know the details. This "don't ask, don't tell" policy is made explicit at 3M, where technical people are expected to allocate up to 15% of their time to projects of their own choosing. The same attitude and similar practices are seen at Corning's Sullivan Park R&D lab, which churns out hundreds of kinds of experimental glass each year. Scientists there are required to spend 10% of their time on "Friday afternoon experiments" to develop "slightly crazy ideas." This policy not only allows scientists to work on pet projects that bosses don't know about but also frees them to work on pet projects that superiors have discontinued. For instance, an entire genomics-technology business is being built on an idea that was officially killed by the head of research but was pursued in Friday afternoon experiments.

In fact, creative work must be sheltered from the cold light of day, especially when ideas are incomplete and untested. William Coyne, former vice president of R&D at 3M, remarked in a speech at Motorola University, "After you plant a seed in the ground, you don't dig it up every week to see how it is doing." In an age of customer centricity, this may border on the heretical. But if you want to develop new products and services, I urge you to keep your creative people away from your biggest customers—and for that matter from critics and anyone whose primary concern is money.

Doing so helps creativity blossom. Psychological research shows that people are especially hesitant to try new things in front of "evaluative others" like critics and bosses. The virtues of doing innovative work in isolation are well documented. Tracy Kidder's Pulitzer Prize–winning book, *The Soul of a New Machine*, describes an engineering team that was sequestered in the basement offices of Data General. Kidder shows how the resulting lack of attention helped the "MicroKids" on this "Eagle Team" do a better and faster job of designing a minicomputer. Kiyoshi Kawashima, former president of Honda, used a similar approach in 1978. He was concerned that Honda was losing its vitality because senior managers couldn't understand what kinds of cars young people wanted. Kawashima assembled the youngest members of his staff (average age 27) to design a car that would appeal to younger customers and promised that senior managers would not interfere with the team's operation. The result was the hot-selling Honda City Car. Few companies, it seems, are able to innovate without shielding teams from the mainstream.

At the same time, a company shouldn't let a team get too cozy. One of my most well-supported ideas for managing creativity is that you should find some happy people and then get them to fight. Mind you, I'm not talking about provoking personality conflicts or relationship issues; battles between people who despise one another squelch innovation. The fights you need to cause are all about ideas. Bob Taylor, a psychologist turned research adminis-

Growing Up Is Hard To Do

The relative age of a company is no guide to its creativity level; start-ups are as vulnerable as established companies. Consider what happened at Lotus Development in the mid-1980s. Lotus, now part of IBM, was founded in 1982 by Mitchell Kapor and Jonathan Sachs to bring to market their "killer app," Lotus 1-2-3. In just two years, sales grew from $53 million to $156 million, which led to an urgent need for experienced professional managers. McKinsey consultant James Manzi was brought in as president in 1984 and became CEO in 1985. Manzi built enormously profitable marketing and sales operations, modeling them after those of *Fortune* 500 companies.

But Lotus started having trouble developing successful new products. Part of the problem was that management techniques suitable only for managing routine work were being used throughout the company. By 1985 or so, around the time the company had grown to more than 1,000 employees, many original members felt that they no longer fit in. Most of the new hires were MBAs cut from the "big-company cloth," many having worked for such organizations as Coca-Cola and Procter & Gamble.

In 1985, Kapor (then chairman of the board) and Freada Klein (then head of organizational development and training) tried an experiment. With Kapor's approval, Klein pulled together the résumés of the first 40 people to join the company. She disguised the names and put them into the applicant pool. Some of these people had the right technical and managerial skills for the jobs they applied for, but they also had done a lot of "wacko and risky things." They had been community organizers, clinical psychologists, and transcendental meditation teachers (Kapor included); several had lived at an ashram.

Not one of the applicants was called for an interview. Kapor and Klein viewed this as a sign that Lotus was unwittingly screening out innovative people. They seem to have been correct. Lotus Notes, the only hit product invented by the company after Lotus 1-2-3, was developed 20 miles from headquarters, so as Klein puts it, "the team could work unfettered by the narrow Lotus culture." Lotus did need a great marketing and sales organization to cash in on its innovative ideas. The narrowness that came along with these changes, however, was a double-edged sword.

trator, first encouraged this kind of conflict among the computer scientists from various universities he funded while at the U.S. Department of Defense's Advanced Research Projects Agency (ARPA) in the 1960s and later at Xerox PARC in the 1970s. These scientists and engineers, perhaps more than any others, are responsible for the technologies that made the computer revolution possible, including the personal computer, the Internet, and the laser printer. The computer scientists Taylor funded through ARPA met at an annual series of research conferences, as retold by Michael Hiltzik:

> The daily discussions unfolded in a pattern that remained peculiar to Taylor's management style throughout his career. Each participant got an hour or so to describe his work. Then he would be thrown to the mercy of the assembled court like a flank steak to a pack of ravenous wolves. "I got them to argue with each other," Taylor recalled with unashamed glee. . . . "These were people who cared about their work. . . . If there were technical weak spots, they would almost always surface under these conditions. It was very, very healthy."
>
> Enhancing innovation also has to do with how performance is rewarded. This, too, entails a dramatic departure from the management practices ingrained in most companies. Rather than rewarding success and punishing failure, companies should reward both.
>
> Again, I must distinguish between what is right for routine work and what is right for creative work. When known procedures are used by well-trained people, failure does signal improper training, weak motivation, or poor leadership. But applying this standard to innovative work stifles intelligent risks. Every bit of solid theory and evidence demonstrates that it is impossible to generate a few good ideas without also generating a lot of bad ideas. Former Time Warner chairman Steve Ross had a philosophy that people who didn't make enough mistakes should be fired. That's an anomaly, though. Few companies tolerate failure, let alone reward it.

If you want a creative organization, inaction is the worst kind of failure—and the only kind that deserves to be punished. Researcher Dean Keith Simonton provides strong evidence from multiple studies that creativity results from action. Renowned geniuses like Picasso, da Vinci, and physicist Richard Feynman didn't succeed at a higher rate than their peers. They simply produced more, which meant that they had far more successes *and failures* than their unheralded colleagues. In every occupation Simonton studied, from composers, artists, and poets to inventors and scientists, the story is the same: Creativity is a function of the quantity of work produced. These findings mean that measuring whether people are doing something—or nothing—is one of the ways to assess the performance of people who do creative work. Companies should demote, transfer, and even fire those who spend day after day talking about and planning what they are going to do but never do anything.

SOME IDEAS ABOUT RISK AND RANDOMNESS

One of the main reasons for rewarding both success and failure is that most managers, analysts, and other so-called experts (like everyone else) do a poor job of judging new ideas and predicting which ones will succeed. Organizations use all sorts of methods, such as "gates" in the product development process, to try to improve their odds of success. But there is little evidence that such practices actually reduce the proportion of flops. As James March writes, "Unfortunately, the difference between visionary genius and delusional madness is much clearer in history books than in experience."

Yet there is one simple, proven, and powerful thing you can do to increase the likelihood that a risky project will succeed: Commit to it wholeheartedly. Forget the slim odds; simply convince yourself and everyone else that, with determination and persistence, the project is destined to be a triumph.

More than 500 academic studies confirm the power of positive thinking. As the famous sociologist Robert Merton explained it:

> The self-fulfilling prophecy is, in the beginning, a false definition of the situation evoking a new

behavior which makes the originally false conception come true. The specious validity of the self-fulfilling prophecy perpetuates a reign of error. For the prophet will cite the actual course of events as proof that he was right from the very beginning. Such are the perversities of social logic.

Henry Ford put it more succinctly: "If you think you can, or if you think you can't, you are right."

Successful heretics tend to be confident and persistent. They believe deeply in what they are doing and are skilled at convincing everyone around them that they are right. Apple cofounder (and, once again, CEO) Steve Jobs does this with his widely touted "reality distortion field." Insiders recount how he casts a spell on those around him, convincing them that the success of an idea, project, or person is virtually certain. Aircraft designer and former test pilot Burt Rutan managed to do this with the team developing the Voyager, which became the first airplane to fly nonstop around the world without refueling. Numerous "experts" predicted that the Voyager was doomed to fail, just as they predicted that other experimental aircraft designed by Rutan wouldn't work. Rutan told his engineers, "Confidence in nonsense is required." This suggests that, if you can't decide which new projects or ideas to bet on based on their objective merits, pick those that will be developed by the most committed and persuasive heretics.

If predictions about which new ideas will succeed are so hard to make, and commitment to an idea, any idea, is one of the only surefire ways to increase the odds of success, does this mean that companies might as well use a random process to generate possibilities to explore? Actually, yes. Random selection is one of the best ways to ensure that new ideas will not be biased by knowledge of past successes. I got this idea from Karl Weick of the University of Michigan, who has described the ritual used by Naskapi Indians to determine where to hunt game. They placed the shoulder bone of a caribou over a fire

until it cracked—then read the cracks as a map. Weick asserts that the ritual was effective because plans for future hunts were not shaped by the results of past hunts. It kept the Naskapis from mindlessly returning to—and depleting—territory they had covered before.

The same logic is used by some companies to generate ideas about different paths they might take. Reactivity, a software company I advise, holds regular brainstorming sessions where employees talk about ideas for new technologies, products, and companies. After holding a few of these sessions, software designers Jeremy Henrickson, Graham Miller, and Bill Walker were becoming concerned that the ideas discussed were getting too narrow. So they invented a random selection process: Attendees at the sessions were given index cards and told to jot down on each a technology (one stack of cards) or an industry (a second stack). The stacks were then used to create random pairings of technologies to industries, and the group brainstormed for five minutes on the possibilities of each pair. Some seemed hopeless—how much could XML programming, for instance, reshape the funeral industry? But others—an idea about dynamic risk management in the shipping industry, for instance—seemed well worth researching in more detail. Most important, Miller reports, it "helped get us out of the rut we were in."

Companies that want to avoid getting stuck in a rut should be especially wary of opinions from customers who use their current products or services, and from the marketing and sales people who represent their views. Michael Eisner, CEO of Disney, put it this way in an interview in the January–February 2000 issue of *Harvard Business Review*: "Most audience—or customer—research is useless." Just because everyone loved *Titanic*, he argued, doesn't mean they want another movie "about a love affair and a sinking ship." Most of the mainframe computer users that IBM surveyed in the 1970s couldn't imagine why they would ever want a small computer on their desks. And Bob Metcalfe, the founder of 3Com, wrote in

MIT's *Technology Review* that the financial success of 3Com's Etherlink, a high-speed way to connect computers, happened because he ignored reports from salespeople that customers were clamoring for a slight improvement in a popular product.

A CONSTANT, CONSTRUCTIVE CONTEST

My aim here is not to convince your company to discard every routine it uses and devote all efforts to inventing new ways of thinking and acting. On the contrary, doing routine work with proven methods is the right thing to do most of the time. It is wise to manage most organizations as if the future will be a perfect imitation of the past: Hospitals want surgical residents to perform operations exactly as their experienced mentors do. Airlines want new pilots to fly 747s just like the experienced pilots who came before them did. McDonald's wants each new trainee to make Big Macs just the way they have always been made. Tried and true wins out over new and improved most of the time.

But if part of your mission is to explore new possibilities, then your goal must be to build a culture that supports constant mindfulness and experimentation. It isn't sufficient to generate new ideas now and then. Your company—or more likely a part of it—needs to be a place that generates and tests many disparate ideas. It should be an arena, a constant and constructive contest, where the best ideas win.

Will these ideas for innovation ever look anything but weird to the majority of managers? Probably not, because most companies will always devote more time, people, and money to exploiting old ideas than to exploring new ones. Exposure effects being what they are, managing for creativity will always require a conscious effort. However, if you read "Dilbert" or have friends in the arts, you know that exposure effects cut both ways. To people who spend their days doing creative work, the way that most companies are managed seems just as weird.

39. Managing Innovation: When Less Is More

Charlan Jeanne Nemeth

While a "good company" requires unsurpassed management, product quality, and financial soundness, the "most admired" companies are presumed to also have "a spark that ignites the work force and allows the enterprise to respond readily to change. That ingredient is innovation and all the top companies embrace it passionately."[1]

Is this really true? Do our most admired companies emphasize innovation as much as execution? I think not. Most companies, even those considered "visionary," emphasize mechanisms of social control rather than innovation. They recognize the power of clear goals, worker participation, consistent feedback, a cohesive work force, and a reward system that underscores desired behaviors and values. In fact, the "spark" that many companies are likely to ignite is not innovation or risk taking, but rather loyalty and commitment to the company. They attempt to create a cult-like culture involving passion and excitement. Through this path, they may achieve productivity and high morale, but at the same time can thwart creativity, innovation, and an ability "to respond readily to change."

Creativity and innovation may require a "culture" that is very different and, in a sense, diametrically opposed to that which encourages cohesion, loyalty, and clear norms of appropriate attitudes and behavior. It is wrong to assume that the mechanisms of social control that heighten adherence to company rules and expectations can also be easily used to enhance innovation. Desiring and expecting creativity—and even rewarding it—do not necessarily increase its appearance. Motivation and increased effort may permit new variations on a theme, but they are unlikely to stimulate major changes in perspective or reformulation. Quite the contrary. In fact, there is evidence that one must be removed from this social control. One must feel free to "deviate" from expectations, to question shared ways of viewing things, in order to evidence creativity. To use a metaphor from an actual creativity task, one must be able to look "outside the box" to find new insights, e.g., to see a new use for an old product or to recognize a new market.

Minority viewpoints have importance and power, not just for the value of the ideas themselves, but for their ability to stimulate creative thought. Thus, one must learn not only to respect and tolerate dissent, but to "welcome" it. The "trick" is to balance coordinated group activity with an openness to differing views—to create unity in the organization without uniformity.

THE "GOOD" AND THE "VISIONARY"

In a recent book, Collins and Porras attempted to analyze "visionary" companies, those so nominated by CEOs as not only "good" or successful, but enduring.[2] The criterion "endurance" was defined as a company that was founded prior to 1950 and that had multiple product or service life cycles. Examples of those nominated included Hewlett-Packard, IBM, Procter and Gamble, Wal-Mart, GE, Boeing, 3M, Nordstrom, Merck, and Walt Disney.

In their analysis, Collins and Porras tried to discern what distinguished "visionary companies" from their less successful counterparts. One particular characteristic stands out. Collins and Porras argue that the visionary companies are marked by a cult-like atmosphere which includes a fervently held ideology, indoctrination, a high degree of "fit" or uniformity, and elitism. Such comparisons between strong "corporate cultures" and "cults" have been noted by other authors as well.[3]

A fervently held ideology is assumed to be important because it provides the core values, the glue that will bind the organization. Table 39.1 illustrates the core values of the "visionary" companies and includes examples, e.g., Nordstrom's credo of "service to the customer above all else." Some companies have explicit rules as well as a general statement. Thomas Watson, Sr., founder of IBM, for example, not only had core values of "respect for the individual" and "listen to the customer," but he had rules. There was a dress code which included dark suits. Marriage was encouraged; smoking was discouraged and alcohol was forbidden. At Disneyland, there is a strict grooming code, one which does not permit facial hair or dangling jewelry.[4]

Newcomers to the organization are indoctrinated into this prevailing ideology by various socialization techniques. The ideology may be succinct. For example, Nordstrom's employee "handbook" consists of a single $5'' \times 8''$ card with the rule: "Use your good judgment in all situations. There will be no additional rules." While there may not be additional rules, there is considerable "on the job" socialization, including guidance in the form of approval and disapproval by peers and continual ranking and feedback as to performance. There are also intensive orientations, universities, and training centers.

Another common technique includes a mythology of "heroic deeds," which is essentially an oral history of people who have exemplified the ideology of the company—for example, extraordinary service to a customer. And, finally, there is the usage of unique language, mottoes, and corporate songs, all of which foster cohesion and a sense of group belonging.

WHY IT WORKS: MAJORITY POWER

That such a cult-like climate would enhance morale, loyalty, and adherence to normative prescriptions is not particularly surprising. These companies have used well-established principles of social control and, in so doing, recognize the importance of normative prescriptions, of the power of the judgments and of approval of peers. This power of peers is one of the most established findings in social psychology. When people are faced with a majority of others who agree on a particular attitude or judgment, they are very likely to adopt the majority judgment. Literally hundreds of studies have documented this finding.[5] Even when using objective issues (such as judging the length of lines) people will abdicate the information from their own senses and adopt an erroneous majority view. The question is: Why?

The available evidence suggests that there are two primary reasons for adopting normative or majority views, even when incorrect. One is that people assume that truth lies in numbers and are quick to infer that they themselves are incorrect when faced with a unanimous major-

TABLE 39.1
"Core Values" (as defined by Collins and Porras)

"Respect and concern for individual employees"	Hewlett-Packard
"Exceed customer expectations"	Wal-Mart
"Being on the leading edge of aviation; being pioneers"	Boeing
"Respect for individual initiative"	3M
"Service to the customer above all else"	Nordstrom
"We are in the business of preserving and improving human life"	Merck

ity. The other reason is that they fear disapproval and rejection for being different.[6]

It is difficult to overestimate the power of these majority views. In the early studies with unambiguous and easy judgments of line length, fully 35% of the judgments were against the individual's own senses and in conformity with the erroneous majority judgment.[7] In later studies using color judgments, conformity was as high as 70%.[8] Given that participants in these studies were relative strangers, one can only imagine the magnitude of this pressure when the majority members are valued co-workers, colleagues, and bosses.

People worry about being different, about not being accepted—and worse, about being ridiculed or rejected. The evidence suggest that this is not a baseless fear. It is a highly predictable reaction. When a person "differs," especially when the group is cohesive and is of importance to the members, that "deviate" can be certain of receiving the most communication, usually aimed at changing his or her opinion. If such persuasion is unsuccessful, the person is often disliked, made to feel unwelcome, and may ultimately be rejected.[9] Such reactions can be found in even temporary groups with little at stake in the issue. It is exacerbated when the group is important and the issue is relevant to the group itself.

Recent work shows that majorities not only shape judgments and behavior, but they also shape the ways in which individuals think. We now have numerous studies showing that, when faced with a majority view that differs from their own, people tend to view the issue from the majority perspective.[10] In an attempt to find the majority to be correct, they not only adopt the majority position, but they convince themselves of the truth of that position by how they think about the issue. They consider the issue only from the majority perspective, trying to understand why the majority takes the position it does.

Faced with a majority, people search for information in a biased manner. They consider primarily information that corroborates the majority position. They also tend to adopt the majority strategy for solving problems to the exclusion of other strategies. They are also relatively unable to detect original solutions to problems.[11] In some sense, they "brainwash" themselves by finding and focusing on information consistent with the majority view.

An important limitation to the power of the majority appears to lie in the issue of unanimity. Numerous studies have documented that a single dissenter can break the power of the majority. Further, the dissenter need not agree with anyone else. It is not a question of providing support for a given viewpoint; it is a question of the majority being fragmented and divided.[12] This element is one reason why dissent can have value.

ENHANCING THE POWER OF THE MAJORITY

Many "visionary" companies seek to enhance the power of the majority so as to increase adoption of company principles. They not only have clear values, goals, and indoctrination techniques, but they tend to promote interaction with like-minded individuals (i.e., within the company) and reinforce it with an intolerance for dissent. Much like cults, many of these companies tend to isolate the individual from the "outside world." They promote socializing *within* the organization and try to inhibit the maintenance of relationships outside the corporate family. These are powerful mechanisms for promoting cohesion and consolidating opinion.

One of the best documented findings in social psychology is that discussion among like-minded individuals increases both the extremeness of the views and the confidence in them. After discussion, groups of "risky" people become more risky; groups of "cautious" people become more cautious. Groups of people who favor segregation become more extreme and sure of their position. So do groups of people who favor integration.[13] They don't just become more "like" each other; they all become more extreme as well as more alike.

Furthermore, people are more likely to *act* on their beliefs after discussion with like-minded individuals. Thus, promoting interaction within the company and shielding people from dissenting views is likely to make the individuals adhere to the company ideology more strongly and to act in accordance with it.

The sense of identification with the organization is further enhanced by the usage of mottoes, slogans, and company songs such as those sung at IBM and Wal-Mart.[14] Some even invoke a special language. For example, Nordstrom employees are "Nordies." Disneyland employees use theatrical language, e.g., a job is a "part," being on duty is "onstage." Such promotions of the "ingroup"—especially when they are coupled with a definition of another corporate entity as an "outgroup"—further augment a sense of pride and even superiority relative to the other group. Many successful companies purposely imbue their employees with the belief that they are the "best." Procter and Gamble, IBM, and Nordstrom epitomize the type of company where such elitism reigns. With this sense of confidence and belonging can come a fervent adherence to company ideology and to the preservation and even enhancement of the basic company philosophy. Thus, many have argued that such cult-like atmospheres are highly productive and filled with enthusiasm.

A corresponding element of this "ingroup" promotion is a tendency to monitor and punish deviance. The "visionary" companies are particularly intolerant of dissent. They "eject like a virus" those who do not fit with the corporate culture. If you don't want to be "Procterized," you don't belong at P&G; if you are not dedicated to the clean living and service atmosphere at Marriott, then stay away. Diversity is tolerated—even welcomed—as long as it is accompanied by a belief in the company ideology.[15]

THE OTHER SIDE: CREATIVITY

One might ask how can you argue with a corporate culture, cult-like or not, that results in high morale, enthusiasm, a clear vision, a sense of belonging, and a dedication that translates into profits? How can you question the value of coordinated group activity which may account for the success of large-scale projects (e.g., Boeing's launch of the 747 or Disney's entry into Epcot Center and Disneyland)? But does this type of corporate culture also promote creativity? Or an ability to respond readily to change?

There are authors and executives who suggest that the same techniques of clear goals, indoctrination, cohesion, consistent feedback, and reward systems can be used to foster innovation—even a "cult-like culture of change." The premise is that one can have the camaraderie, a sense of "can do," and a dedicated commitment to the company's ideology while, at the same time, having flexibility, innovation, and an ability to adjust to changing circumstances.

Many companies recognize the need to "reinvent themselves,"[16] whether they call it "self renewal" (Motorola), "individual initiative" (Phillip Morris), or being a "pioneer" (Sony). However, can one create a culture that promotes creativity, openness to new ideas, and innovation while at the same time having people indoctrinated in a similar ideology? Can the ideology itself be innovation? With feedback and appropriate rewards, does it work? The available research on creativity suggests it may not be that easy. Good intentions and great effort do not necessarily result in creativity. One can work very hard while engaging in convergent (single perspective) thinking that is unlikely to produce anything original. In fact, there is evidence that the atmosphere most likely to induce creativity is one diametrically opposed to the "cult like" corporate culture.

The Nature of Creativity

Much of creativity starts with the proper posing of a question. And it seems aided by an ability to break premises, by being able to look "outside the box." Using that metaphor, the task of joining all the dots in Figure A in 4 straight lines without lifting pen from paper (and without retracing any lines) is made solvable by adding two hypothetical dots (•) outside the box

(Figure B). Who said that you can't connect more dots than required?

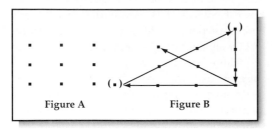

Figure A   Figure B

Though this task serves as a metaphor, there is ample evidence that the unreflective adoption of premises and old patterns of solving problems is detrimental to creativity. If individuals are given a series of problems for which a given solution "works," they will tend to use that solution even when it is no longer the best one. An obvious better solution will not be detected.[17]

In light of this, a firm might want to recruit relatively unconventional people and be careful about the extent to which it tames that unconventionality. Thomas Watson of IBM recognized this in his continual reference to "wild ducks." Borrowing from Kierkegaard, Watson was fond of telling the story of a man on the coast of Zealand who liked to watch the ducks fly south each fall. Well intentioned, he began to feed the ducks in a nearby pond only to find that, with time, they stopped flying south. They wintered in Denmark, feeding on what he provided. After several years, they grew so fat and lazy that they hardly flew at all. The message: You can make wild ducks tame, but you can never make tame ducks wild again.[18]

Many companies have recognized how easy it is to thwart creativity. As expressed by Enron's President Richard Kinder, a good idea is fragile "like a lighted match, easily blown out by the cold winds of rigid management."[19] In a good deal of literature, however, it isn't rigid management that thwarts creativity. It is much more basic and much more insidious. People in general are loathe to suggest an original idea for

fear of the ridicule and rejection. In fact, most attempts to raise the level of creativity explicitly understand that one must try to do two things: ensure that the individual's creativity is not stifled by conformity pressures or fears of social embarrassment; and take advantage of creativity enhancing forces (e.g., reinforcement for contributing or cross-stimulation).

Brainstorming, for example, explicitly asks people to generate as many ideas as possible, to refrain from evaluating or criticizing their own or others views, and to build on ideas that are proposed (piggybacking).[20] While there appears to be modest success with such a technique, the fear of disapproval and the reluctance to voice ideas remains. Even with these admonitions, groups are still less creative than individuals alone.[21] When people are in group interaction, it is not easy to lessen the concerns about embarrassment and ridicule. Status tends to make it worse. People are particularly unlikely to challenge persons of higher status. Prof. Bennis of the University of Southern California estimates that at least 7 out of 10 in American business hush up when their opinions are at odds with their superiors. Even when they know better, they allow their bosses to make mistakes.[22]

Such problems are apparent in many different kinds of decision-making groups. In studies of Cabinet level "fiascoes," such as the Bay of Pigs, Janis found that groups marked by cohesiveness and a strong directive leader are especially likely to seek "uniformity."[23] As a result, they suffer under the illusion that there is unanimity when, in fact, there is not. Silence is often assumed to indicate assent. Then, out of a fear of ridicule and a sense of futility, each individual is reluctant to voice a differing view. Dean Rusk, for example, had strong doubts about the Bay of Pigs invasion but did not express them at the Cabinet level meetings. Arthur Schlesinger later rebuked himself, writing: "In the months after the Bay of Pigs I bitterly reproached myself for having kept so silent during those crucial discussions though my feelings of guilt were tempered by the knowledge that a course of objection would have accomplished little save to gain me a name as a nuisance."[24]

Thus, managers need to be aware of the fact that most of us are quite fragile when it comes to expressing "differing" views. People usually test the waters to see what is acceptable and, in the process, may unwittingly censor their own thoughts as well as their verbal expressions. Contrary to what strong leaders with strong cultures may think, the directiveness and strength of the leader can actually thwart creative thought and the expression of divergent views. It is even more likely when the group is highly cohesive. These are precisely the elements that are believed to cause "groupthink," the strain to uniformity that overrides a realistic appraisal of alternatives."[25]

CREATIVITY AT THE TOP: IMPLEMENTATION VS. INNOVATION

Some of the admired companies—those reputed to have not only good management and financial success, but innovation—appear to be those whose *leader* had the creative idea. Under these conditions, a strong corporate culture emphasizing uniformity, loyalty, and adherence to company expectations would be advantageous. It is advantageous precisely because it can operate in a relatively monolithic way—full of energy, morale, and a tendency not to consider alternatives or problems. This is not the same as promoting creativity from within the organization. Cohesion, convergent thought, and loyalty help to *implement* an idea but tend not to enhance the *production* of a creative idea. Rather, flexibility, openness, and the welcoming of dissent are especially useful for stimulating creative thought.

Several companies showing creativity made the "most admired" list and illustrate creativity by top executives. One such example is Enron, whose CEO, Kenneth Lay, found himself with a large national network of gas lines. Trained as an economist, he favored free markets and disliked federal regulation. Yet, in viewing his national map differently than others, he saw it as a network to buy gas where it was cheap and sell it where it was needed. Thus, he found himself promoting deregulation. He created spot markets and, in the process, changed the industry. It paid off. Enron was named one of the "most admired" companies by *Fortune* magazine and ranked No. 1 in innovation.

Another example is Mirage Resorts, ranked No. 2 in innovation. CEO Steve Wynn had the idea: giving customers of the gambling industry outstanding service, food, and entertainment. His Treasure Island resort was the first designed to generate more income from non-gambling than gambling sources. And he found a way to make his employees enthusiastic about service. He spent as much on the employees' cafeteria and corridors as on those used by "guests." He essentially created a culture of cohesion and high morale, all adhering to his core ideology of service. Again, the idea appears to be an insight of an individual—and, importantly, of the CEO himself. In that context, the cohesive culture that he created is an advantage, primarily in terms of implementation.

Honda is still another example of creativity at the top. Two owners, Honda and Fujisawa, the former the motorcycle enthusiast, the latter the businessman, merged their talents and developed the Honda 50cc Supercub in 1958. It was a marketing success, strongly appealing to small commercial enterprises in Japan. It was lightweight, affordable, and yet had strong horsepower.

When they tried to enter the U.S. market, however, there were several problems. Motorcycle enthusiasts in the U.S. were a special breed and the emphasis was on size and power. Thus, Honda feared introducing their small bikes for fear of hurting their image in the macho U.S. market and, instead, introduced their larger motorcycles, the 250cc and 305cc bikes. However, it was the failure of these bikes that inadvertently led to the success of the smaller 50cc Supercub. Not content with using an intermediary, the Honda executives themselves drove the smaller 50cc bikes around Los

Angeles on errands and, in the process, attracted attention and enquiries, including one from Sears. It was the failure of their larger bikes that led to the willingness to permit distribution of the Supercub. And the rest is history.

Honda is said to have "redefined" the U.S. motorcycle industry. After their "You meet the nicest people on a Honda" campaign, nearly one of out every two motorcycles sold was a Honda.[26] The history of this invention is not dissimilar from most creative efforts. It is a combination of talent and drive, but also a series of miscalculations, serendipity, and learning. Again, however, it was the leadership that manifested the creativity.

The problem with creative ideas generated by the CEO and implemented by a cohesive, strong culture that promotes uniformity is that the beneficial outcomes are dependent on the CEO. He had better have the best ideas because his ideas are likely to be implemented—right or wrong—in such a culture. This is part of the reason why some worry a bit about Microsoft. While tied for third place in *Financial Executive*'s survey for "best boss,"[27] Bill Gates is seen as the quintessential "modern-day robber baron" who can create a monopoly without it appearing to be one, and who can make a product like Windows as addictive as the products of RJ Reynolds. Yet, Cusumano and Selby point out that Microsoft's weakness is precisely its dependence on Bill Gates.[28] He is the undisputed leader of Microsoft, but he is also one human being. With increasingly complex scenarios and potentials, Gates, brilliant though he may be, has limitations—be it time, attention span, motivation, or wisdom.

CREATIVITY WITHIN THE ORGANIZATION

For companies that attempt to foster innovation from within the ranks, a number recognize the importance of dissent or of being a "maverick." They often try to limit the fear of failure and promote risk taking. Anecdotal evidence abounds, such as when Robert Johnson (Johnson and Johnson) is reputed to have congratulated a manager who lost money on a failed new product by saying. "If you are making mistakes, that means you are making decisions and taking risks." Coca-Cola actually celebrates the failure of its sweet "New Coke," the venture in 1985 that proved to be ill-advised—except for the fact that Coca-Cola learned something important: Coke's strength was its image, not necessarily its flavor.[29]

Some companies even tout an ideology that permits employees to buck top management. Marriott says that "if managers can't explain why they're asking employees to do something, they don't have to do it."[30] DuPont grants employees money to pursue projects turned down by management. Hewlett-Packard instituted a "medal of defiance," presumably based on an employee (Chuck House) who defied David Packard in continuing to work on a computer graphics project, one that eventually turned out to be a big money maker.[31]

Even with such statements and medals, it is unlikely to reduce employees' concerns about defying management. While most of us would like to believe that we are tolerant of dissenting views, the initial inclination of anyone—whether they are management or workers—is to underestimate and resist viewpoints that differ from their own. The tendency is to consider them false, unworthy of reflection, and often indicative of poor intelligence or an undeveloped moral character.[32] With such a reaction from management, no matter how subtle, most would not "defy." One has only to wonder whether Chuck House would have been given a medal had his project turned out to be a failure.

Perhaps more effective are concrete mechanisms instituted by some companies that actually limit the control of upper management or that actively remove some of the inhibitions to creativity. For example, GE has work-out groups where employees voice their gripes—though it appears that the number who actually do so are in a minority. Pfizer under Edward Steer sent its R&D center overseas. Presumably this frees the researchers since they are removed from authorities in

New York; it also permits entry into overseas markets more readily. Other companies actively recruit heterogeneity in teams, hoping for diversity of viewpoints. Chrysler was one of the first to put together heterogeneous teams (manufacturing, marketing, and engineering) to work on the same automobile design.[33] Motorola and 3M regularly use "venture" teams of people from various disciplines,[34] a practice that research suggests will enhance the quality of decisions.[35]

Other companies have attempted to institute classic brainstorming techniques, the elements of which include refraining from criticism of an idea and attempting to build on the ideas of others. Raychem, for example, promotes the stealing of ideas, all for a good cause. Recognizing the employees often suffer from a "not invented here" syndrome—that is, if we didn't invent it, it's not very valuable—they give an award for adopting others' ideas from within the organization. The trophy and certificate say, "I stole somebody else's idea and I'm using it." And the originator of the idea? He or she gets a certificate saying, "I had a great idea and 'so and so' is using it."[36] This is a clever concrete mechanism for inducing the basic brainstorming tenet of building on others' ideas.

CREATIVITY WITHIN: THE CORPORATE CULTURE

Motorola is described as having an especially contentious corporate culture. Gary Tooker, CEO and Vice Chairman, is seen as "a master of the company's usually contentious, sometimes profane discussions that pit manager against manager and business unit against business unit, often in pursuit of conflicting technologies."[37] An example is the development by the Land Mobile sector of a combination cellular phone/pager/two way radio (MIRS), which utilizes specialized mobile radio frequencies (SMR). This competes directly with the alternative cellular duopolies and could undermine its other sector, General Systems. Do they worry about internal conflict? Motorola mainly believes in the free market and as Chris Galvin, President and COO explains, a "willingness to obsolete ourselves."[38]

3M is almost everyone's choice for a prototype of innovation. Well known is their "15 percent rule" where employees devote up to 15% of their time pursuing ideas of interest to them that may have potential value for the company. And equally known are their demands for performance—25% of sales coming from products introduced in the last 5 years plus 10% growth in sales and earnings, 20% return on equity, and 27% return on capital employed. With these demands, however, are support systems ranging from seed money, mechanisms for linking employees (e.g., through e-mail) and, apparently, a deeply held conviction by management that one needs to respect ideas coming from below and that people may need to fail in order to learn.[39]

One of 3M's classic stories is the development of Post-it notes—which, in fact, was aided by a failure. The glue eventually used for Post-it notes was a failed attempt by Spencer Silver to develop a super strong glue. Art Fry, singing in his church choir had trouble marking his hymnal with pieces of paper; they would slip out. Then came the idea: "What I need is a bookmark with Spence's adhesive along the edge."[40] And thus Post-it notes were conceived. It should also be mentioned that marketing was initially skeptical, but the case was made when they found that the notes were already being used extensively among 3M's internal staff.

DuPont actually tries to teach creativity skills. Using their own in-house training center, there is a recognition that creative ideas need to be implemented. Thus, a senior manager or department controls the funds and resources that will permit the translation of the idea into concrete action. Workshops not only include managers and employees who are knowledgeable about the technology under discussion, but they make sure that there are also individuals who, while competent, are not particularly knowledgeable about the issue. They are the hoped-for "wild cards" who will bring fresh perspectives. Finally, the individuals are taught to avoid the "inhibitors" of creativity. They are vigilant about indications of convergent thought; for example, they are "on guard" about

tendencies to make an idea fit with a precon-
ceived notion. Further, people are encouraged
to suspend their own knowledge, experience,
and expertise and to play with each idea.[41]

THE FIT WITH "CREATIVITY" RESEARCH

Many of the devices utilized by Motorola, 3M,
and DuPont are consistent with available
knowledge about good problem solving and
creativity. There are attempts to make groups
heterogeneous in the hopes of gaining diverse
views. There are cautions about convergent
thought, about premature criticism of an idea.
People are given time and resources to "play"
with ideas and yet are encouraged by clear goals.
Yet it is the recognition of a "contentious atmosphere," the "bickering, tension, and dissent"
described at Motorola that may provide better
insight into creativity than most executives and
researchers realize.[42]

   While the literature on creativity is somewhat mixed, the profile used to describe the
"highly creative" individual includes personality traits such as confidence and independence,
a preference for complexity over simplicity, for
some disorder rather than for everything neat
and tidy, a tendency for being "childlike though
not childish," and some indications of noncon-
formity and even rebellion in childhood.
Creative people are characterized as high on
personal dominance and forcefulness of opinion and, in addition, they tend to have a
distant or detached attitude in interpersonal
relations, though they are not without sensitiv-
ity or insight.[43] Play appears important, even
random variations of thought.[44] Such profiles
have also appeared in my own recent series of
interviews with Nobel laureates. Most were
aware of being "different" even as children.
Most had to buck conventional wisdom and
collegial skepticism in their continued
pursuits. And they were childlike, even at the
age of 70+, playing with metaphors from
completely different disciplines.[45]

   Such a portrait of the "highly creative"
would suggest that they would not be drawn to

nor nurtured by a highly cohesive corporate
culture, one that demanded strict adherence to
company norms, attitudes, and values or one
that demanded "belonging" and a high degree
of in-house socializing. Creative people and the
creative process need independence—at least
independence in thought. They need to be able
to break premises, to pose questions differently.
The need to be an "outsider," a person who can
effectively interact with others but who remains
a marginalized from the group. The research
often notes such outsider status on the part of
the highly creative and it is a persistent theme
among the Nobel laureates that I interviewed.

CREATIVITY IN GROUPS: THE ROLE OF DISSENT

While we often tend to think of creativity as an
individual phenomenon, it is important to recognize the importance of groups. First of all,
most discussion and decision making occurs in
groups and, thus, the influence processes and
interactions that occur become important in
their own right. Secondly, and more importantly, groups can strongly hinder *or* promote
individual creativity and the quality of individual judgments and solutions to problems.

   As noted, most of the research literature
emphasizes the negative aspects of groups—the
fact that groups can hinder creativity. In groups,
individuals have an overriding fear of social
embarrassment and ridicule and they are reluctant to voice differing views. Thus, most
attempts to raise the quality of group decision
making and creativity have concentrated on how
one might diminish these fears and thus give
"voice" to differing viewpoints. Encouraging
risk, asking people to refrain from criticism, and
promoting the idea that people should build on
the ideas of others are all attempts at "freeing"
the individual from the fears that silence him.

   Recent research, however, shows that
groups are not just inhibitors of good decision
making and creativity. Rather, groups can actually stimulate creativity and better problem
solving on the part of each of the individuals.
The key is the presence of dissent, of exposure

to minority viewpoints that are assumed to be incorrect, that are likely to be ridiculed, and that are likely to invoke rejection. Such minority views stimulate more complex thinking, better problem solving, and more creativity.[46]

One aspect of good problem solving is a willingness to search the available information and, importantly, to search it in a relatively unbiased way. When we are faced with a majority dissent, we tend to look for information that corroborates the majority view. However, when the dissent comes from the minority, it stimulates us to reassess the entire issue and, in the process, search for information on all sides of the issue.[47]

In addition to information search, minority views have also been found to stimulate what we call "divergent thought," where people are more likely to consider the issue from various perspectives. For example, when faced with a minority view, people utilize all strategies in the service of problem solving. They come at the problem from all possible directions and, in the process, find more solutions. In fact, stimulated by minority views, they perform much better than they would alone.[48]

Still other studies demonstrate that minority viewpoints stimulate original thought. Thoughts are more "unique"—that is, less conventional. People exposed to minority views are also more likely to come up with original solutions or judgments.[49]

What is important about these findings is that the benefits of minority viewpoints do *not* depend on the "truth" of the minority position. The findings mentioned above hold whether or not the minority is correct. It is not because the minority holds a correct position that decision making and problem solving are enhanced. It is because dissenting views by a minority of individuals—right or wrong—*stimulates* the kinds of thought processes that, on balance, lead to better decisions, better problem solving, and more originality.

CONCLUDING THOUGHTS

Many people are wary of dissent because it poses conflict and can strain the cohesion and camaraderie of a well-functioning group. Further, it can impede organizational goals by questioning the established routes to success. This concern is given further credence by the examples of companies who have thrived on strong corporate cultures that emphasized uniformity, loyalty, and cohesion as efficient mechanisms for achieving its goals. The problem with such efficiency is that it results in a lack of reflection. If the path to success changes, there is no provision for flexibility, adaptation to new circumstances, or innovation.

It is tempting to conclude that innovation can be achieved simply by using these same cultural norms—uniformity, loyalty, and cohesion—along with a system of rewards or encouragement from the top. Yet, creativity in individuals and innovation at the organizational level are not so easily produced. Rather, the ability to think "outside the box," to find truly original solutions to old problems, requires the freedom to break the rules and to consider different options without fear of reprisals or rejection. As the research findings show, dissent actually stimulates originality and better decision-making procedures. When challenged by minority views, people reappraise the situation. Without such stimulation, people tend to be complacent, relying on the agreement of their group. With exposure to minority views, people come to recognize that their own views may be incorrect, or at least partially incorrect. As a result, they search anew, they think anew, and, in the process, they consider new options and achieve greater clarity.

There needs to be a "welcoming" and not just a tolerating of dissent. Dissent is a very economical mechanism for producing innovation. By harnessing the power of conflict, one can limit complacency and even substitute robust thought. Complacency is the real danger. Even with the best of intentions, people are loathe to consider alternatives when convinced of the truth of their own position. They tend to search for confirming information, augment their own views, and punish dissenters. Dissent breaks up that complacency and sets in motion thought processes that ultimately result in better and more original solutions. If an existing idea is correct, it is likely to remain with even greater clarity as a result of the challenge of dissent; if it is flawed, most likely it will be replaced by a better one. Either way, the group and the organization will profit.

NOTES

1. B. O'Reilly, "The Secrets of America's Most Admired Corporations: New Ideas, New Products," *Fortune*, 135/4 (March 1997): 60–64.

2. J. C. Collins and J. L. Porras, *Built to Last: Successful Habits of Visionary Companies* (New York, NY: HarperCollins, 1994).

3. C. A. O'Reilly and J. A. Chatman, "Culture as Social Control: Corporations, Cults and Commitment," *Research in Organizational Behavior*, 18 (1996): 157–200.

4. T. Ehrenfeld, "Out of the Blue," *Inc.*, 117 (1995): 68–72.

5. V. L. Allen, "Situational Factors in Conformity," in L. Berkowitz, ed., *Advances in Experimental Social Psychology*, Vol. 2 (New York, NY: Academic Press, 1965), pp. 133–175; J. M. Levine, "Reaction to Opinion Deviance in Small Groups," in P. Paulus, ed., *Psychology of Group Influence: New Perspectives*, 2nd edition (Hillsdale, NJ: Erlbaum, 1989).

6. M. Deutsch and H. B. Gerard, "A Study of Normative and Informational Social Influence upon Individual Judgment," *Journal of Abnormal and Social Psychology*, 195/51 (1955): 629–636.

7. S. E. Asch, "Effects of Group Pressure upon the Modification and Distortion of Judgment," in H. Guetzkow, ed., *Groups, Leadership and Men* (Pittsburgh, PA: Carnegie Press, 1951).

8. C. Nemeth and C. Chiles, "Modeling Courage: The Role of Dissent in Fostering Independence," *European Journal of Social Psychology*, 18 (1988): 275–280.

9. S. Schachter, "Deviation, Rejection and Communication," *Journal of Abnormal and Social Psychology*, 46 (1951): 190–207.

10. C. J. Nemeth, "Dissent as Driving Cognition, Attitudes and Judgments," *Social Cognition* (1995), pp. 273–291; C. Nemeth and P. Owens, "Making Work Groups More Effective: The Value of Minority Dissent," in M. A. West, ed., *Handbook of Work Group Psychology* (London: John Wiley & Sons, 1996), pp. 125–141.

11. C. Nemeth and J. Wachtler, "Creative Problem Solving as a Result of Majority vs. Minority Influence," *European Journal of Social Psychology*, 13 (1983): 45–55.

12. Levine, op. cit.

13. D. G. Myers and H. Lamm, "The Group Polarization Phenomenon," *Psychological Bulletin*, 83 (1976): 602–627.

14. J. Pfeffer, "Management as Symbolic Action: The Creation and Maintenance of Organizational Paradigms," in L. L. Cummings and B. M. Staw, eds., *Research in Organizational Behavior*, Vol. 3 (Greenwich CT: JAI Press, 1981), pp. 1–52.

15. Collins and Porras, op. cit.

16. T. Peters, "Crazy Times Call for Crazy Organizations," *Working Woman*, 19 (1994): 1–8.

17. (Luchins, 1946) A. S. Luchins, "Classroom Experiments on Mental Set," *American Journal of Psychology*, 59 (1946): 295–298.

18. T. J. Watson, *A Business and Its Beliefs: The Ideas that Helped Build IBM* (New York, NY: McGraw-Hill, 1963).

19. B. O'Reilly, op. cit.

20. A. F. Osborne, *Applied Imagination* (New York, NY: Scribner, 1957).

21. J. E. McGrath, *Groups: Interaction and Performance* (Englewood Cliffs, NJ: Prentice Hall, 1984), p. 131.

22. F. Summerfield, "Paying the Troops to Buck the System," *Business Month* (May 1990), pp. 77–79.

23. I. L. Janis, *Groupthink: Psychological Studies of Policy Decisions and Fiascoes* (Boston, MA: Houghton Mifflin, 1972).

24. Ibid., p. 39.

25. Ibid.

26. See, generally, R. T. Pascale, "The Honda Effect," *California Management Review*, 38/4 (Summer 1996): 80–91.

27. "Who's the Best Boss?" *Financial Executive,* 12 (1996): 22–24.

28. M. A. Cusumano and R. W. Selby, "What? Microsoft Weak?" *Computerworld,* 29/40 (October 1995): 105–106.

29. G. Dutton, "Enhancing Creativity," *Management Review,* 85 (1996): 44–46.

30. Collins and Porras, op. cit.

31. Summerfield, op. cit.

32. Asch, op. cit., Nemeth and Wachtler, op. cit.

33. B. O'Reilly, op. cit.

34. A. K. Gupta and A. Singhal, "Managing Human Resources for Innovation and Creativity," *Research-Technology Management,* 36 (1993): 41–48.

35. S. E. Jackson, K. E. May, and K. Whitney. "Dynamics of Diversity in Decision Making Teams," in R. A. Guzzo and E. Salas, eds., *Team Decision Making Effectiveness in Organizations* (San Francisco, CA: Jossey-Bass, 1995).

36. Gupta and Senghal, op. cit.

37. R. Henkoff, "Keeping Motorola on a Roll," *Fortune,* 12 (1994): 67–78.

38. S. Cabana and J. Fiero, "Motorola, Strategic Planning and the Search Conference," *Journal for Quality and Participation,* 18 (1995): 22–31.

39. "Deeply Embedded Management Values at 3M," *Sloan Management Review,* 37 (1995): 20.

40. "Post-it: How a Maverick Got His Way," *Marketing,* October 28, 1993, p. 31.

41. L. K. Gundry, C. W. Prather, and J. R. Kickul, "Building the Creative Organization," *Organizational Dynamics,* 22 (1994): 22–37.

42. G. N. Smith, "Dissent in to the Future," *Financial World,* 162 (1993): 8.

43. F. Barron, *Creative Person and Creative Process* (New York, NY: Holt, Rinehart and Winston, 1969).

44. D. T. Campbell, "Variation and Selective Retention in Sociocultural," *General Systems: Yearboook of the Society for General Systems Research,* 16 (1969): 69–85.

45. C. J. Nemeth, *Those Noble Laureates* (1997, in progress).

46. C. J. Nemeth, "Differential Contributions of Majority and Minority Influence," *Psychological Review,* 93 (1986): 23–32; C. J. Nemeth, "Dissent as Driving Cognition, Attitudes and Judgment," *Journal of Social Cognition,* 13 (1995): 273–291.

47. C. J. Nemeth and J. Rogers, "Dissent and the Search for Information," *British Journal of Social Psychology,* 35 (1996): 67–76.

48. C. Nemeth and J. Kwan, "Originality of Word Associations as a Function of Majority vs. Minority Influence Processes," *Social Psychology Quarterly,* 48 (1985): 277–282.

49. Ibid.; C. K. W. DeDreu and N. K. DeVries, "Differential Processing and Attitude Change Following Majority and Minority Arguments," *British Journal of Social Psychology,* 35 (1996): 77–90; R. Martin, "Minority Influence and Argument Generation," *British Journal of Social Psychology,* 35 (1996): 91–113.

40. *The Political Nature of Innovation*

Peter J. Frost/Carolyn P. Egri

> *The innovator makes enemies of all those who prospered under the old order, and only lukewarm support is forthcoming from those who would prosper under the new . . . because men are generally incredulous, never really trusting new things unless they have tested them by experience.*
>
> —NICCOLO MACHIAVELLI
> *The Prince*

As observed long ago by Machiavelli, the introduction of an innovation or change continues to induce and become the focus of political activity in modern society and its organizations. It is in these disputes over the ambiguous means and ends of an envisioned change that the process of innovation becomes political. How then, does an innovation emerge and survive whatever conflict it engenders? Under what conditions and when does organizational politics flourish in the innovation process? Research evidence indicates that political gamesmanship is most likely to be positively linked with the degree of originality, with the degree of perceived risk, and with the complexity of the situation. Perhaps the most vulnerable time of the innovation process is during the implementation stage when the dysfunctional nature of organizational politics is most often highlighted. It is responsible for, among other things, unnecessary delays, excessive conflict, compromised outcomes, and sometimes, ultimate failure.

The main theme throughout studies in which these results are observed is on the "problem" of the social and political dynamics engendered by innovation. Consistent with the general pro-innovation bias found in society,

these resistances to innovation are generally regarded by managers as threats rather than opportunities. For those managers who are more entrenched in an organization (either by virtue of age, seniority or through the benefits accorded them by the status quo) the messiness, disorder and "muddling through" required of the innovation process can be particularly distasteful, thereby resulting in avoidance or resistance.

To illustrate the tangle and complexity of the innovation process and its political nature, we present several case studies which describe the process in some detail. There do not appear to be as many studies of innovation which deal with the politics of innovation. Most common treatments of innovation either do not address process or gloss over or truncate its detail in the interest of limited space or because the authors are addressing other questions.

THE TRIALS OF PRODUCT CHAMPIONS AND SPONSORS—NASA MOONLANDER MONITOR

The case of the development of the NASA Moonlander Monitor is one which illustrates

From P. Frost, V. Mitchell, & W. Nord (Eds.), *Organizational Reality: Reports from the Firing Line*, HarperCollins, 1992, pp. 449–460.

the integral role an innovation champion and his/her managerial sponsors can play in the development of a new product. It is also an example of how innovators can successfully be mavericks within an organizational culture which, while posing at the surface level a number of obstacles to such initiatives, is supportive of innovation and change in its deep structure.

As a young engineer at Hewlett-Packard, Chuck House proved to be instrumental in the development and application of oscilloscope technology for new venues (Pinchot, 1985). Initial impetus for the project was provided by the Federal Aviation Administration, which identified the need for an improved airport control tower monitor. Although the Hewlett-Packard monitor did not meet the FAA's specification for a high resolution picture and subsequently lost out to competitors, there were features of their prototype which struck House as worthy of further investigation. House believed that the size (smaller and lighter than other models), speed (20 times as fast), energy efficiency and brighter (but fuzzier) picture of his group's monitor was a significant technological breakthrough— although one which had yet to find its niche in the marketplace.

In the course of his efforts to demonstrate the merits of his team's model, House proved to be a political gamesman who operated as a maverick by violating a number of organizational rules and boundaries. His first foray into the political arena involved conducting his own market research on potential applications. To gather such information, House personally showed the monitor prototype to 40 computer manufacturers and potential customers in an organizationally unsanctioned trip from Colorado to California. In doing so, not only was he violating functional organizational boundaries by circumventing the marketing department but he was also violating a cardinal Hewlett-Packard security rule which forbade the showing of prototypes to customers. However, based on the marketing infor-

mation collected during his trip, House was able to gain a temporary reprieve from senior management for his project. During the next 18 months, the project team continued development work in the lab and on-site with customers.

The next obstacle to the continuation of the project came during the annual division review by senior management. This review was influenced to a large degree by a marketing department telephone survey which projected that there was only a total demand for 32 monitors. The resistance and lack of creative initiative of the marketing group (perhaps motivated by House's previous incursion into their territory) was evident in the manner in which the survey was conducted. As Pinchot (1985: 26–27) reports: "Chuck argued that marketing had failed to understand his strategy for marketing the product. They had called only upon oscilloscope customers, the only customers they knew. New applications required new customers, Chuck explained. Besides, the device was difficult to describe: Because it was new, only demonstrations could uncover its saleability." Marketing's forecast of demand for the monitor prevailed over House's group's projections which were based on direct operating feedback from customers (and were, to some extent, obtained through organizationally illegitimate means). Not only was House's project threatened by the lack of administrative innovation by the marketing group, his project did not have the support of the chief corporate engineer who favored an alternate technology.

The conclusion of the divisional review was that, in light of the apparent lack of market demand and technological support from others in the organization, the only rational action was to abort the project. In corporate founder David Packard's words: "When I come back next year I don't want to see that project in the lab!" (Pinchot, 1985: 27).

It is at this point that House's political gamesmanship was put to the test. Unwilling to accept this decision, House "chose" to reinterpret Packard's pronouncement to mean that the project would be out of the lab in one year's time but in production, not on the scrapheap. With the covert support of his boss Dar Howard, the tactic of covering up development costs of the project from budget restrictions started in earnest as House's team raced to complete the project in one year when the normal length of time would be two. In the face of continuing opposition from the marketing department, House gained additional support by convincing interested potential customers to personally call on his superiors and argue for the project.

Fortunately for House and his team, they made their deadline and when Packard returned one year later, the monitor was indeed in the marketplace. Packard was reported to be both amused and impatient with this obvious re-interpretation of his order but perhaps indicative of his own maverick origins, he now supported the obviously successful project. Rather than being punished for their insubordination, House and his team were now given permission to continue to develop additional applications, among them the eventual use of the oscilloscope monitor for the NASA Moon Mission, the medical monitor used in the first artificial heart transplant, and a large-screen oscilloscope which was used as part of an Emmy-award-winning special effects system. Without the committed championship of House and the sponsorship of his immediate superiors, these landmark innovations could have easily been the victims of opposing political forces.

DESIGNING POLITICAL BATTLES TO BUILD A NEW COMPUTER

In his Pulitzer-prize-winning book, *The Soul of a New Machine*, Tracy Kidder (1981) treats us to a detailed account of the trials of the design engineer in the highly competitive computer industry. He also gives us an inside look at how competitive political contests can be surreptitiously orchestrated by senior managers to promote innovation.

Data General prided itself on its maverick culture—a culture which could be directly traced back to its founding members, three young computer engineers who left DEC in 1968 to set up shop in a former beauty parlour. Within ten years, Data General was on the *Fortune* 500 list and had carved out its niche in the minicomputer market. However, by 1976, Data General was also sorely in need of a new product, namely, a 32-bit minicomputer which was comparable to, but better than, those recently introduced by their competitors.

The political stage was set by senior executives headed by CEO Ed de Castro when they announced that Data General would build a new research and development facility in North Carolina. It was here, they publicly announced, that major research would be conducted to develop the needed 32-bit minicomputer. The important Fountainhead Project (FHP) was transferred to the new location along with 50 of the most talented DG engineers and technicians. Meanwhile, among those who remained behind in Westborough, Massachusetts, were Tom West and his small Eclipse group. Their previous project had been cancelled in favor of the FHP—Data General could not afford to fund two major competing projects. Instead, West was assigned to revamp the lower priority 16-bit Eclipse. Although de Castro never put it in writing, West received tentative approval to transform the Eclipse into a 32-bit minicomputer as the rechristened Eagle project. Technically, the Eclipse group was not to do any groundbreaking developments—that was the territory of North Carolina's FHP. How West and his managers were able to do just that in record time is a testament to skillful team building and political acumen.

The first priority was to keep a low profile so as not to appear to be in competition with FHP. This political strategy was justified by West as follows:

You gotta distinguish between the internal promotion to the actual workers and the promoting we did externally to other parts of the company. Outside the group I tried to low-key the thing. I tried to dull the impression that this was a competing product with North Carolina. I tried to sell it externally as not much of a threat . . . It was just gonna be a fast, Eclipse-like machine. This was the only way it was gonna live. We had to get the resources quietly, without creating a big brouhaha, and it's difficult to get a lot of external cooperation under those circumstances." (Kidder, 1981: 47)

Part of this low profile strategy was physical. The Eclipse group was located in the cramped basement quarters of Westborough headquarters where even the air conditioning didn't work properly. This resulted in both physical and social isolation from the rest of the company, all the better to facilitate covering up their real agenda for the Eagle project. The Eclipse group's low profile was also facilitated by the type of engineers recruited for the project. West and his lieutenant Carl Alsing hired recent engineering graduates not only for their excellent academic credentials but also for their willingness to work long hours and their unbridled enthusiasm for computer design work. By doing so, the group was ensured a low profile in that there were few who would see them as competition for the higher priced and proven talent in North Carolina.

One example of the lengths to which Eclipse group members went to avoid appearing to be in competition with FHP or encroaching on their territory is how computer architect Steve Wallach got his job done. If there was a computer instruction which deviated from the approved parameters of the Eagle project and might be construed as infringing on the FHP project, Wallach would work with his friends in System Software on the item. When finished, he would then ask his friends to write a memo requesting inclusion of the controversial instruction into the Eagle—thus avoiding any charges that the Eclipse group was going outside of approved project parameters.

Throughout the project, team members were constantly negotiating with support groups for their assistance. The competition for resources was difficult for the Eclipse group as Kidder (1981: 112) relates: "The game was fixed for North Carolina and all the support groups

knew it." Through personal contacts and persuasive skills they were able to gain the needed resources.

What is particularly interesting in this case is that many of the engineers on the Eclipse team were unaware of the full extent of West's role in ensuring survival of the project. It was all part of his managerial style which was to stay separate from the team and to run interference with other corporate bodies in order that his engineering team could be creatively free. West also benefitted from having a management sponsor in Vice-President of Engineering Carl Carman who authorized the project and the money to recruit staff. Fortuitously, the FHP reported to a different Vice-President so there was no internal organizational conflict for Carman.

Finally, in a classic David vs. Goliath scenario, the small Eclipse group overcame all organizational and technical obstacles to deliver the 32-bit minicomputer ahead of North Carolina. This was a tale of a maverick group operating effectively within a maverick culture. For de Castro, it was a relatively low cost exercise in creative insurance so that Data General would have the desired product.

AN OUTSIDER DOING BATTLE WITH THE DEEP STRUCTURE: THE DVORAK SIMPLIFIED KEYBOARD

The case of the Dvorak Simplified Keyboard (DSK) is one which clearly demonstrates how self-interested political actors can effectively forestall a demonstrably beneficial technological change. When invented in 1873, the current universal "QWERTY" typewriter keyboard was designed to prevent typists from striking two adjoining keys in quick succession. Otherwise, the keys would "jam" together in the basket of a machine which relied on the forces of gravity to pull the keys back to their original positions. Technological improvements to the typewriter (the introduction of spring-loaded keys at the turn of the century and later, the invention of electric typewriters) overcame the jamming problem but the original keyboard remained. Enter Dr. August Dvorak, education professor, who through scientific time and motion studies developed a new keyboard configuration which would enable typists to work faster, more accurately (50% fewer mistakes) and with less physical strain to gain productivity improvements ranging from 35% to 100% (Dvorak, Merrick, Dealey, & Ford, 1936). Additionally, Dvorak proved that typists could learn their skill in one-third of the time it took to learn on the QWERTY keyboard. Why then, aren't we all (present authors included) typing on this technologically superior invention?

Perhaps the chief culprits in resisting this technological innovation were the typewriter manufacturers who had considerable financial interests in retaining the traditional keyboard. During the 1930s when Dvorak introduced his invention, there was little incentive for typewriter manufacturers to convert over to a keyboard which would increase typist productivity thereby conceivably resulting in fewer sales. Furthermore, they would be required to pay royalties on Dvorak's patented invention.

Rejected by the manufacturers, Dvorak then reasoned that publicity at the World Typewriting Championships would help generate public demand for his invention. From 1934 to 1941, DSK-trained typists did indeed win the top typing awards at these competitions. However, the championships were sponsored by the manufacturers who, faced with these embarrassing outcomes, worked to deny Dvorak the publicity he sought. When publishing contest results, they only listed the names of the winning typists, not the machines they used in competition. An attempt by contest officials to ban DSK typists from competition was aborted when Dvorak threatened to advise the newspapers. Dvorak was even forced to hire security guards to protect his machines during the contests when it was discovered that they had been sabotaged.

The manufacturers were also skillful in networking with the American National Standards Institute. As members of the ANSI Keyboard Committee, they were able to prevent inclusion of the DSK into the national standards manual. Dvorak's attempts to gain a government contract for his typewriters were also unsuccessful. Despite the demonstrated superiority of the DSK in experimental tests conducted in the U.S. Navy and the General Services Administration, both rejected the possibility of a conversion. The rationale was that the measurable costs of replacing obsolete equipment and retraining typists outweighed the intangible future benefits of productivity improvements. This was a surprising conclusion since the trial results showed an average productivity increase of 74% with retraining costs being amortized over 10 days. Then in the ultimate covering up political tactic, the U.S. Navy assigned the DSK test results a security classification.

It is no wonder that, after 30 years of political battles to fulfil his dream, a frustrated Dr. Dvorak told Parkinson: "I'm tired of trying to do something worthwhile for the human race. They simply don't want to change!" (Parkinson, 1972: 18)

But as this account of innovation politics suggests, it is not all humans who resist change but rather those interest groups who stand to lose their financial stake if the innovation is implemented.

THE POWER OF VESTED INTERESTS TO FRUSTRATE NEW IDEAS: HELPING AUTISTIC CHILDREN

As related by Graziano (1969) in his account of a mental health innovation, the realm of interorganizational innovation is often the scene for political action at the deep structural level. Set in the 1960s, this account shows how the entrenched interests of a medical establishment (expert in the psychoanalytic treatment of such patients) actively resisted acknowledging or experimenting with a new technique (behavioral modification) to treat autistic children. The power of the professional elite is demonstrated by their ability to effectively maintain the status quo of local mental health services while circumventing efforts of an opposing group to gain local funding for an alternative treatment.

At a fundamental level, the two opposing interest groups were aligned into one which was supported by the medical profession versus one which was community-based. On the side of the entrenched power elite in the mental health community were the private-practice psychiatrists who operated the local clinics and dominated the local Mental Health Association. How they were able to parlay their position to influence other institutional actors (the local university and the "United Agency" fund-raising organization) is particularly interesting in this drama of innovation. In opposition to this coalition for the status quo was the Association for Mentally Ill Children (ASMIC), which was a lay group comprised of the parents of those autistic children who had not been helped by the psychoanalytic methodology (either because they had not responded to this course of treatment or had parents who could not afford the expensive private clinics). The ASMIC had employed a psychologist skilled in this new approach (remember that the time was the early 1960s when behavior modification was still a relatively radical new theory) to assist them in their attempt to change the system. However the integral role which organizational politics plays in the course of innovation is highlighted by Graziano's (1969: 10) comment that: "The *conception* of innovative ideas in mental health depends upon creative humanitarian and scientific forces, while their *implementation* depends, not on science or humanitarianism, but on a broad spectrum of professional or social politics."

Although both groups initially worked together for four years in a local clinic offering both methodologies, the subsequent struggles over the resources to be allocated to each program and evaluation of the therapeutic effectiveness of each led to their separation.

Operating independently, the ASMIC tried repeatedly to gain financial support for their alternative approach. Once outside the mainstream of the medical establishment though, they encountered political resistance orchestrated by the local private clinics at both the surface and deep structure levels. An ASMIC proposal to the local university to try an experimental pilot project testing the merits of the behavioral modification methodology was rejected on two counts—it was too radical and it was not supported by the local mental health community.

Attempts to gain independent funding for their project from the local community funding agency ("United Agency") were first delayed and finally rejected after three years of efforts by the ASMIC to comply with the agency's demands. The influence of the established clinics (which were also funded by the United Agency) could be surmised to have played a role in the construction of these obstacles to implementation. Even though the ASMIC had garnered enough funds (from the parents of the autistic children and laterally from the State Department of Mental Health) to operate at a minimal level of service, the United Agency's rationale for withholding funds proved to be innovative in their own right. First there was the criticism that the program was first only a "paper proposal"; then after six months of operation, the United Agency contended that the program had been in operation "too brief a time on which to base a decision." After another year, the funding application was rejected because it had not been "professionally evaluated"; with a positive State Department of Mental Health evaluation in hand, the ASMIC program was then deemed to be a "duplication of services"; with state endorsement that it was a nonduplicated service, the United Agency declared that state financial support was required; and finally, with a state grant in hand, the United Agency rejected the application outright because the ASMIC had been "uncooperative" by not providing confidential information on clients' names, addresses, and fathers' places of employment.

AUTOMATICALLY CONTROLLED MACHINE TOOLS—AN OBJECT OF DEEP STRUCTURE POLITICS

That class conflict and the ideology of progress inform the institutions, ideas, and social groups which determine the design and use of a particular technology is the basic thesis of Noble's (1984) analysis of machine tool automation in manufacturing production. This case illustrates how deep structure politics were used to preserve and extend the control and power of the sectional interests of the owner/managerial, scientific technical and military communities at the expense of those of workers. The capacity of a societal ideology to influence not only the choice of a technology but also to frame (in a pre-emptive manner) that decision in terms of the criteria and assumptions which are used demonstrates the covert and subtle nature of deep structure power games.

Following WW II, there were two viable avenues by which machine tool automation could proceed. The first was Record Playback (R/P) which built on the skills and knowledge of machinist craftsmen thereby enhancing their traditional power base in the production process. In R/P, automatic control of a machine tool was achieved via a taped program which recorded the movements of the machine operator. It required a skilled machinist to make the initial program and any subsequent changes and adjustments to it. The second option was Numerical Control (N/C) technology in which the tape was programmed not by repeating a machinist's movements but by using scientific engineering methods. This in turn resulted in the assignment of machine programming responsibilities to staff engineers and technicians.

At a fundamental level, what did each technological approach represent? By removing the critical programming function from the shopfloor, N/C extended managerial control over production startup, pace, and maintenance. In contrast, the R/P approach would be a continuation of the current sharing of production control with the skilled workers on the shopfloor. The overwhelming choice of industrial management was to pursue the N/C technological approach. The primary motive for this managerial decision was that it enabled management to regain control over production.

This impetus for the assertion of managerial control was only reinforced by the growing unionization of the American blue-collar workforce during the 1950s which (when coupled with the union movement's ideological alliance with Communist ideals) served to elevate managerial perceptions of threat. Support for this observation can be found in the fate of R/P systems which were developed in a number of large firms such as General Electric and the Ford Motor Company. Despite positive preliminary test results (based on production efficiency and cost criteria) corporate management consistently cancelled these experiments in favor of more complex engineer controlled N/C systems. Significantly, the decision at GE was made during a period of labor union unrest.

Managerial interests were also influenced and supported by the actions of other societal interest groups which preferred the N/C technology. The power of the scientific and military communities in channeling the course of machine tool automation should not be underestimated. The military underwrote much of the research and development costs of N/C projects in the university labs. MIT, at the forefront of computer microelectronic research, was an early advocate of N/C technology. Not only did N/C research provide MIT with a promising venue for applications of their new-found computer technology, but it also was consistent with an ideological bias for the superiority of formal educational expertise (needed to program N/C tapes) over layman experience (the basis of R/P technology).

SOME LESSONS FROM THE TRENCHES

Very briefly, we can draw some inferences from the experiences of innovators in these organizations. These propositions need to be tested in other settings and under conditions in which their effects can be carefully identified and analyzed. For the time being, we think it is useful for managers and others to consider the following lessons.

> *Lesson 1:* Product innovation success within organizational settings requires a combination of both product *and* administrative innovation.

A good idea or product is simply not enough to guarantee successful implementation and diffusion within and outside an organization. For example, Hewlett-Packard's NASA Moon-lander Monitor was a technological innovation which was almost terminated by a lack of administrative innovation. The information House gained from hands-on development with customers enabled him to modify the monitor to meet their needs while generating demand for the end-product. In this case and others, reliance on standard operating procedures is often insufficient to meet the unique requirements of new products or ideas.

> *Lesson 2(a):* When a proposed innovation is congruent with the organizational and societal deep structure, political activity remains primarily on the surface, is benign or at a low level. Consequently, the probability of the acceptance and diffusion of such an innovation is enhanced with the support of the deep structure.
>
> *Lesson 2(b):* A proposed innovation which threatens power relationships at the deep structure level evokes the full breadth and depth of opposing political forces, strategies and tactics. Consequently, the probability of acceptance and diffusion of such an innovation is significantly reduced.

These propositions focus on the type and range of political tactics which emerge or are elicited when a proposed innovation either confirms or threatens existing power relationships. As evidenced in the cases of the Dvorak Simplified Keyboard, the mental health innovation and

those areas of ICI which resisted OD initiatives, when those interests which benefit from maintaining the status quo perceive an innovation to be a threat, the politics of change are both numerous and powerful. What results is a mismatched contest where the deep structure frames the rules of the game and to a large extent preordains the outcome. The metaphor of a "corporate immune system" is a useful one in understanding the dynamics of this response. As Pinchot (1985, p. 189) relates:

> *When you start something new, the system naturally resists it. It is almost as if the corporation had an immune system which detects anything that is not part of the status quo and surrounds it. If you are to survive, you will have to lull this immune system into ignoring you. You will have to appear to be part of the corporate self, rather than identified as a foreign body.*

Although Pinchot focuses on the intraorganizational arena, we believe that the same "immune system" can be activated in the interorganizational and societal realms. As outsiders or newcomers to the arenas in which they were trying to introduce their changes, Dvorak and the ASMIC were easily allocated the role of unwanted invaders by a system which perceived few, if any, benefits to influential system members through effecting a change to the status quo.

At ICI, the OD change agents were also perceived to be outsiders to the production process. However the success of Ripley and Bridge's program in the Agricultural Division could be traced to their strategy of first developing a strong, coherent program for change independent of the corporate system before attempting to enter it and then, to work within the system in a non-threatening manner. They started low in the organizational structure and built support in an incremental way. In contrast, the OD programs in the other areas were more visible and did not have the strength of unity in either philosophy or personnel to withstand the opposition.

When the proposed innovation or change is consistent and/or supports existing power relationships, the politics remain at the more manageable surface level. The contests at Hewlett-Packard and at Data General were against a backdrop of a unity of interests between innovators and the corporate ethic. These innovators were secure in the knowledge that the organizational mission was to be at the forefront of their technology—a deep structure which desired technological change for competitive purposes. They also benefitted from cultures with a deep structure mythology of hero-founders who were mavericks in their own right. By acting as mavericks themselves, they were only continuing the organizational tradition and could count on a degree of understanding of their actions at the highest corporate levels. Opposition to these product innovations were of a more traditional and restricted nature in terms of internal power plays, managing line vs. staff territories and gaining the necessary resources for development. As corporate insiders, these innovators could draw on their past experience and that of others in the organization to gauge how best to proceed—which political tactics had succeeded in the past, which had failed, the relative risks involved, who were the power players and who were not.

For administrative innovations, political gamesmanship played a major role in the eventual success or failure of the proposed change. Success often hinged on the innovator's ability to marshall a wide range of supportive political tactics at both the surface and deep structure levels. Ripley and Bridge at ICI's Agricultural Division proved to be politically adept at numerous influence tactics. Review of these successful administrative innovations reveals that there was a minimal number of opposing political games, either at the surface or deep structure levels.

Administrative failures at ICI present a contrasting picture. The tactics of appealing to higher authority and appealing to reason proved to be ineffective against the deep structure games of a resistant organization. These OD change agents were effectively pre-empted by divisional managements which denied that any change to the status quo was needed and

rejected the claim that these staff persons had a right to be involved in any change process.

Lesson 3: Within organizations, the political strategy of "asking for forgiveness" is limited to only the initial phases of the conception and development of a product innovation. For the adoption and diffusion of a new product, the innovator must "seek and secure permission" of the organization.

We note in these case studies of innovation there are two distinct types of political strategies—that of "asking for forgiveness" and that of "seeking and securing permission." "Asking for forgiveness" occurs when an innovator proceeds to the point of adoption without official organizational knowledge and/or sanction. It is an independent course of action often marked by secrecy and the furtive seconding or transfer of corporate resources. Alternatively, the strategy of "seeking and securing permission" usually encompasses the political strategies of developing champions and sponsors and of building networks and coalitions. Neglecting to do so may threaten the long term viability of an innovation.

In our view, asking for forgiveness is a viable strategy when pursuing product innovation. Seeking and securing permission is a more viable strategy when pursuing administrative innovations. It is possible to hide a product innovation from potential naysayers in the important fragile early phases of that innovation. Social and administrative innovations, on the other hand, depend more immediately on corporate interdependencies for their successful implementation. Thus it becomes important for the innovator to both seek *and* secure permission from organizational actors in a variety of positions and levels to ensure success. In the long run, product innovations move from the laboratory to implementation and thus to integration with other organizational routines and procedures. This entails a shift to a greater emphasis on the permission rather than the forgiveness strategy.

These accounts of innovation demonstrate the integral role political strategy plays in both promoting and suppressing innovation. If the proposed change threatens the self-interests of a powerful dominant coalition (as in the mental health innovation, the Dvorak keyboard, and machine tool automation), we find that the emergence of a technological innovation is a tenuous one. In these cases, the full breadth of deep structure and surface politics is elicited to preserve prevailing power relationships. Apparently, rationality is subsumed in these high stakes interorganizational and societal level battles for survival of the fittest. On the other hand, if there is no perceived fundamental threat, the political activity remains on the surface and can be more readily managed by prospective innovators.

REFERENCES

Dvorak, A.; Merrick, N. L.; Dealey, W. L.; and Ford, G. C. (1936). *Typewriting Behavior: Psychology Applied to Teaching and Learning Typewriting*. New York: American Book Company.

Graziano, A. M. (1969). "Clinical Innovation and the Mental Health Power Structure: A Social Case History," *American Psychologist* 24(1), 10–18.

Kidder, T. (1981). *The Soul of a New Machine*. New York: Avon Books.

Noble, D. F. (1984). *Forces of Production*. New York: Knopf.

Parkinson, R. (1972). "The Dvorak Simplified Keyboard: Forty Years of Frustration," *Computers and Automation* 21(11), 18–25.

Pinchot, J. III (1985). *Intrapreneuring*. New York: Harper and Row.

Part C

Leadership and Change

41. Pathfinding, Problem Solving, and Implementing: The Management Mix

Harold J. Leavitt

*E*very couple of decades managers and academics scratch their heads and once again ponder some tough old questions like these: What is managing *really* all about? What are managers doing right? What are they doing wrong? What should they *really* be trying to do?

Even though such questions will never be finally answered, they are healthy, indicative of a recurrent readiness to change and to experiment. This time around, they seem especially important, driven partly by anxiety and uncertainty about what it will take to cope with the volatile, complex, and fast-changing world that lies ahead.

This small book tries to focus more clearly on questions of this kind, and to suggest partial and temporary answers to some of them. It begins with a simple three-part description of what the managing process looks like in the late 1980s. Those three parts then serve as handles for examining where American management has gone right and gone wrong in recent years, and what kinds of corrections and changes seem to be in order.

The book's general argument is that we have unintentionally neglected the visionary, pathfinding part of the managing process over the last 20 years. We have, at our peril, put most of our energies into two other areas—into planful, analytic, systematic methods of problem solving and into the action and people-oriented implementing parts of managing. Only since the early 1980s have the bills from that neglect of pathfinding become obvious. We are right now in a healthy but hectic period of repayment, regrouping, and renewal.

This first chapter outlines the three-part model of the managing process and briefly describes each of the three parts. The main purpose of the chapter is to lay the groundwork for understanding why the neglect of pathfinding by managers and educators alike has come close to costing us our managerial shirts.

Reprinted from Harold Leavitt, *Corporate Pathfinders* (Homewood, Ill.: Dow Jones-Irwin, 1986), pp. 1–24.

The three parts into which this model divides managing are these: #1 pathfinding, #2 problem solving, and #3 implementing.

Consider them in reverse order, starting with #3 *implementing*, because that one is such a pervasive element of our image of the modern manager. For here lies the macho mover-and-shaker part of the managing process, as well as the office politics and manipulative parts, and even the participative, human relations parts. It is this implementing side of managing that shows up most often in soap opera managers and in movie versions of the manager. Implementing is about *action*, about getting things done through people, making things happen. Implementing is getting the bricks laid, the services rendered, and the product delivered. Implementing is *doing* things *through others*. Managers are people who get things done. They persuade, cajole, influence, command.

But managing is not just about implementing. It is also about *problem solving*. Managers have to organize, plan, and make decisions. Good managing takes some IQ points as well as some capacity to get things done. Managing means taking hold of complex, messy, ill-defined problems and converting them into organized, systematized forms. Managers have to make rational decisions about products, people, and markets; they have to allocate scarce resources sensibly. Managers must be thinkers as well as doers. They have to make order out of chaos.

Behind both the problem solving and implementing parts of managing, there lurks still another part of the process, the much fuzzier, less observable #1 part, here called *pathfinding*. Pathfinding is the major focus of this book, and while ephemeral and hard to measure, it is an incontrovertibly real and critical part of the managing process.

#1 Pathfinding is about getting the right questions rather than the right answers. It is about making problems rather than solving them. It is *not* about figuring out the best way to get there from here, nor even about making sure that we get there. It is rather about pointing to where we ought to try to go.

#1 Pathfinding, that is, is about mission, purpose, and vision; #2 problem solving is about analysis, planning, and reasoning; and #3 implementing is about doing, changing, and influencing. Our model of managing is about those three critical sets of activities and about the back-and-forth interactions among the three.

The model is pictured in Figure 41.1.

The wavy vertical lines are there to show that the boundaries between the pieces are often foggy, and to suggest that movement from any one to any other can be both difficult and critical. It is not enough, that is, for the manager to be competent in one of these three, or even in all three at once. The manager had also better be skillful at moving across the harsh terrain that often separates them.

That three-part view of managing can (and will) be applied at several levels. For the individual manager, the three parts can be treated as three styles of managing. Some managers, that is, use predominantly pathfinding styles; others are problem solvers; still others are implementers. Most of us mix the three styles, presumably to fit appropriate situations. But are we really that flexible? Can we learn

FIGURE 41.1
A Model of the Managing Process

A Model of the Managing Process		
#1	#2	#3
Pathfinding	Problem Solving	Implementing

new styles late in life? How? Aren't the three parts of managing mutually contradictory?

At that same individual level, educational questions arise. In the education of managers, should we try to teach a blend of all three and shoot for "balanced excellence"? Have business schools taught any pathfinding at all? Could they? Or should they try? Later chapters examine such questions from an individual perspective.

The three parts—pathfinding, problem solving, and implementing—can also be looked at from an organizational perspective. Do organizations need pathfinding individuals? In what proportions? At the top? Throughout the organization? Should the three parts of the process be specialized, with each the responsibility of a particular group or level? Should we let R&D, for example, do the pathfinding, while engineering does the problem solving and sales does the implementing? Or should the CEO be the pathfinder, with the staff people the problem solvers and all the rest the implementers?

Do large ongoing organizations need more pathfinding types? Won't that erode discipline and lead to anarchy? How can the individualistic, high-risk pathfinding style be integrated into the participative kind of implementation that has grown so prevalent in recent years?

This three-part model can be considered at a societal level as well. To what extent is pathfinding part of the heritage of most Western nations? Has some of that heritage been lost? Have recent educational policies and practices encouraged or suppressed pathfinding tendencies? Has the growth of very large organizations discouraged individualistic pathfinding? Do the cultures of most organizations, especially large and old ones, need a good shot of pathfinding style—a mood of urgency, a push toward innovation, a salient sense of mission?

IMPLEMENTING

Let's add a little meat to these bones by looking at each part of that three-part model in more depth. Again we start at the #3 end.

Implementing is not done by managers alone. Each of us implements all the time, whether or not we wear managerial hats. We mow the lawn, drive the car, fix the lamp, cook the dinner. But when implementing is part of the managing process, it has a couple of attributes that distinguish it from implementing in nonmanagerial settings.

First, managerial implementing is always done through other people. That's of course not at all a new idea. My old mentor Douglas McGregor used to define all of managing that way: "Managing is getting things done through people." While in other parts of life we can often implement our own decisions, managing human organizations invariably requires convincing other people to mow our lawns and cook our dinners. Implementing in organizations almost always requires the manager to persuade or command or manipulate or force other people to change their present behavior, to do what the manager wants done instead of what those people are now doing. *Managerial implementing is therefore a highly social activity.*

Second, managerial implementing involves changing other people's behavior, and therefore *it is a highly emotional activity.* Everything the social sciences know about changing behavior says that people change for emotional reasons far more than for rational reasons. It's love, hate, greed, loyalty, jealousy, and passion, much more than cool, pure reason, that drive us to change our ways. So the implementing part of managing has more to do with people's hearts than with their brains. It is not through logic and rationality that we persuade our employees to improve quality or increase productivity. It is through pride or ambition or loyalty. Getting people to do what you want them to do is much more a gutsy than an intellectual process.

But what's new? Hasn't that always been the case? Yes, but in our new world of knowledge and information, the role of emotionality has, paradoxically, gotten bigger, not smaller. In the old world of mostly physical arm-and-leg work, and in the social environment of those days, implementing was mostly focused on the fear-provoking emotionality of command and control or on the emotionality of paternalistic protectionism. In today's more professional, more educated, and more egalitarian organizational world, implementing becomes an issue of persuasion, negotiation, and inspiration rather than of command or protection.

Skill in working with human emotionality is not only rare in managers; it is often seen as "unmanagerial." Recent generations of young managers have, in general, been taught to use their heads much more than their hearts. They are supposed to learn to be rational, objective, hardheaded, professional. But when managers try to influence emotional human beings with exclusively rational tools, trouble starts.

Where and how, then, does one learn implementing skills? Imagine a teenager asking you something like that. "I really like that implementing stuff. I'd love to learn how to win friends and influence people. But how do I learn to become a great implementer? What should I study? What occupation should I try?"

It is not very difficult to identify some occupations in which implementing skills are critical to effective performance. How about direct selling? Or line supervision in a manufacturing plant? Surely platoon leaders in the Marine Corps had also better learn to be pretty good at implementing. They are helped along, of course, by rank, military structure, and all the rest, but in the last analysis it's the platoon leader who has to get those 50 marines to take that hill.

Litigating lawyers had better understand emotional implementing too. They have to persuade judges and jurors, to cajole and browbeat and sweet-talk witnesses. The litigators I have encountered in American law firms are killers, competitors. They are often singled out by other lawyers as a special subgenus of the legal species. Litigators worry about whether to select younger women for this jury or whether they would be better off with older men. They focus on the idiosyncrasies and characteristics of the opposing lawyers and on those of the judge. They work on people's prejudices and impulses, just as a very good salesperson does.

The band of occupations that can offer a young person practice in implementing is very broad indeed. It includes not only second lieutenants, lobbyists, and salespeople but also psychiatrists, counselors, organizational development people, and others in the "helping professions." Whether they acknowledge it or not, the members of these professions too try to change people's behavior by largely emotional means.

So what may seem like a collection of very strange bedfellows fits into this implementing part of the world of managing. Two bonds tie them all together. First, in all the varied kinds of managerial implementing, *human emotionality is the essence* from which change is made.

Second, most members of these implementing occupations think *small*. They think about people singly or in small numbers. For most skilled managerial implementers, human beings are *real*. They have names, faces, personalities, individual idiosyncrasies. They are not masses or statistics or hired hands, as they often are for extreme #2 problem solvers. So it should come as no surprise that when #3 implementers try to design large organizations, they usually want to use small groups as their building blocks, piling up pyramids composed of many small human units.

PROBLEM SOLVING

Let's turn now for a closer look at the #2 problem solving piece of the managing process. If the key word for #3 implementing is *action*, then the key word for #2 problem solving is *analysis*. Problem solving (at least as we in the Western world see it) is about reason and logic. It is about orderly, systematic approaches to problems. It is about planning and coordinating.

We know a good deal about how to teach problem solving skills, much more than we know about how to teach implementing skills. Indeed, that's what most education is all about. Reading, writing, and arithmetic are all analytic problem solving skills. A caricature of the complete #2 problem solver does not look at all like the fast-moving, fast-talking caricature of the implementer. The problem solver casts an intellectually reserved shadow. The image is of the steel-trap mind poring over the printout by lamp-light, figuring out the right answer, the logical solution, the defensible decision, the optimal strategy.

If that inquiring teenager likes the #2 problem solving image and asks you where a young person ought to go for training to become a great problem solver, the answer should be quite easy. One good place to go is the Modern American Business School. Something like 80 percent of the contemporary MBA curriculum has been focused on the #2 analytic problem solving part of managing. That's the place to learn about linear programming, systems analysis, operations research, and econometric methods, about how to build marketing models and how to do financial analyses. Look at the catalog of any MBA school. The course titles use the word *analysis* again and again: Financial Analysis, Market Analysis, Decision Analysis, Economic Analysis. Go to business school to learn to program what has previously been unprogrammable.

But business school is only one of the places where the young person can learn how to do analytic problem solving. He or she might also try engineering or accounting or management consulting or tax law. All of those professions require high levels of analytic skills. They require logic, consistency, and orderliness. While it's likely that members of those professions are sometimes talented in other ways too, analytic skill remains a sine qua non for competence in all of them.

Given all of that emphasis on analysis and logic, it is no surprise that all-out #2 types take a dim view of emotionality. While for #3 implementers emotionality is the raw material of change, for orthodox #2s that same emotionality is likely to be seen as noise in the system, as a sign of human imperfection. In a few million years the full rationality that God so clearly intended will evolve. Real men aren't emotional. So one of the trouble spots in the managing process is located at the junction of #2 and #3, where rational problem solvers meet emotional implementers.

Notice too that analytic occupations carry very high status in Western society, in contrast to the somewhat lower status usually ascribed to many of the implementing occupations, such as selling or manufacturing management. It's OK for your son or daughter to enter any one of them. And they pay well too. Among MBA students, for example, it has been the jobs in consulting and financial analysis that have been viewed as the most desirable ones, at least until recently. Selling has been viewed as low class, and manufacturing as too dirty.

A caveat: While much of the problem solving part of managing can be learned through quantitative, analytic training, not *all* of it can be picked up that easily. There is, as every manager knows, more to real-world problem solving than can be found in the problem sets at the end of the chapters in the accounting text. There is more uncertainty in the real world, more unforeseeable variability. So such words as *judgment, experience, wisdom*, and *good sense* have stayed on our recruiting checklists, even as #2-type academics seek ways of making them unnecessary.

PATHFINDING

If implementing includes large emotional components and if problem solving includes large rational and analytic components, how can one characterize the #1 pathfinding part of the managing process? The central issue of pathfinding is not influence or persuasion, nor is it reasoning or systematic analysis. The key word here is *mission*. The pathfinding part of managing is the homeland of the visionary, the dreamer, the innovator, the creator, the entrepreneur, and the charismatic leader. The central questions are very difficult and often unaddressed: How do I decide what I want to be when I grow up? What should this organization try to become if it could become anything imaginable? What do we really want to do with this company?

The #1 pathfinding world is highly personal and subjective, with answers, where there are any, emerging more from within the self than from a diagnosis of what's out there. Pathfinding is the ephemeral part of managing that deals with values, aesthetics, and beliefs. Putting faith before evidence, pathfinders often violate #2 problem solving precepts. But they also build new worlds.

Do we even need such soft, subjective stuff to manage the modern organization? The answer is unequivocally yes, whether we derive it from social or political or organizational observation. The pathfinding role has always been a critical driving force in the rise of human institutions. From the founding of the United States to the development of IBM to the birth pangs of that new little start-up company, the beliefs and visions of a few stubborn souls have always driven innovation and development.

By far the best illustration of a pathfinding statement that I can offer is familiar to all Americans. It is the second sentence of the American Declaration of Independence: "We hold these truths to be self-evident, that all men are created equal, that they are endowed by their Creator with certain unalienable Rights, that among these are Life, Liberty and the pursuit of Happiness."

What an assertive, pathfinding declaration that is! It must have driven the #2 problem solvers of the day absolutely wild. All men are created equal? How do you know? What's the genetic evidence? "Rights" like "Liberty" or "the pursuit of Happiness"? How do you measure such stuff? "Self-evident" truths? No evidence required? No data to support them? And could anyone, even armed with the most clear and potent evidence, have changed those Founding Fathers' minds? They weren't to be distracted by mere facts!

The pathfinders whom most of us would cite as memorable are also necessarily skillful as implementers. We only remember them if other people have joined up with their visions. Visionaries who do *not* influence others to follow them are simply forgotten. Or if they are remembered at all, they are remembered as impractical dreamers, not as men and women of vision. Indeed, that almost defines a *charismatic leader*. A charismatic leader is a #1 pathfinder who is also successful at #3 implementing— someone with a sense of mission who can also get others to join in.

Pathfinders need not be heroes. They are not always lovable or even smart. People with unusual ideas, strong commitments, and deep beliefs may also be intransigent, single-minded, unforgiving, or simply stupid. It's not just the good guys, the Jesus Christs and Martin Luther Kings, who qualify as pathfinders. Some great pathfinders were more than a bit unpleasant; some were very bad fellows. Adolf Hitler belongs in that set, as does Jim Jones of Jonestown in Guyana, and probably so too do many of the robber barons of European and American industrial history.

In business, the pathfinders are easiest to spot among entrepreneurs and founders of companies. Watson of IBM, Hewlett and Packard, Land of Polaroid, and Freddie Laker were all people dedicated to building their dreams into realities. Such pathfinders are not always pleasant or friendly, and they may not be successful in the long run, but they are all stubborn, committed believers with strong, clear notions of good and bad.

Pathfinders also turn up in old established companies, but less frequently. When they do, they inject new mission and purpose into old organizations. In the early 1980s Lee Iacocca, for example, may have done just that at Chrysler, and Carlson at SAS. In both cases they have turned around their companies' spirits as well as their P&Ls.

To what education and which professions, then, should we direct young people who decide that pathfinding is what excites them?

It's much harder to answer that question for #1 pathfinding than it was for #2 problem solving or #3 implementing. Pathfinders seem far easier to identify than to develop. Perhaps we should point young people in directions quite unrelated to the contemporary management scene. We could suggest that they seek their fortunes among artists and architects, or among philosophers and religionists, or among theoretical physicists; or perhaps we should recommend a broad liberal education, if such a thing still exists.

Indeed, one can argue that management education as we now practice it would do very little to enhance pathfinding abilities. Our methods of educating and developing new managers have not only neglected pathfinding; they have often downright clobbered it. While problem solvers and implementers, whether in companies or in universities, fight like the devil with one another, they also share a common interest (sometimes unconscious) in keeping the pathfinders out.

For obvious reasons, #2 problem solvers don't want stubborn, intractable, impractical visionaries around. Pathfinders can seldom offer (and seldom care to offer) hard evidence for their choices; and hard evidence is the essence of modern problem solving. Pathfinders often ignore the rules, or act impulsively, or wave off what they see as trivial details.

Here in northern California's Silicon Valley one version of the clash between #1 and #2 styles has occurred several times in recent years. It happens as small companies succeed and grow larger. At some point, the venture capitalists or other investors convince the #1-type founders that their now chaotic organization needs discipline and control. So a #2-type COO is brought aboard. Occasionally the marriage works, but frequently the freewheeling #1 style of the founder is just too disruptive for the control-oriented #2 manager (or vice versa), so sparks fly, heads roll, and energy is diverted from the main target just when it is needed most.

#3 Implementers are also likely to feel cool toward those unmalleable, individualistic pathfinders. Contemporary #3 types are particularly oriented toward teamwork, consensus, and cooperation among an organization's members. No matter how positively we may value such styles, they do not fit neatly with the stubborn, determined individualism of pathfinders. #1 Pathfinders often become team leaders, but they are seldom good team players.

OUTSTANDING PATHFINDERS, PROBLEM SOLVERS, AND IMPLEMENTERS: SOME EXAMPLES

Occasionally rare and unique personalities turn up who leave their mark in history almost entirely as implementers, or problem solvers, or pathfinders. They are so good at that one part of managing that it completely overshadows the other two. It's worth identifying a few such extraordinary people, people known to almost all of us, to help draw a clearer picture of the differences among the three parts.

Who, for example, among great public figures familiar to all of us, is the implementer par excellence? Who is preeminent among the problem solvers? Who are the outstanding pathfinders?

Certainly one ideal nominee for an Oscar among implementers would be Lyndon Baines Johnson, at least that part of him that keeps coming through in his biographies. Implementing can be done in many ways, and Johnson's was only one way. He was so good at it, however, and it was so central to his managing style that he serves as an excellent example.

As president, Johnson was certainly not considered by most observers to have been a particularly great #2 intellect, nor a great planner or organizer. Neither was he regarded as a great #1 visionary pathfinder. He did, the reader will remember, try to establish a mission for America, his Great Society, but that notion somehow never took hold, perhaps because many Americans weren't sure he really believed in it himself.

But Johnson will always be remembered as a top-notch implementer. His skill at twisting the arms and stroking the egos of congressmen was legendary. He could shuffle greed, love, fear, and sentimentality to get what he wanted. He could make compromises, negotiate workable solutions. He could get it done. In one sense, he was a very good planner too. He did his homework before taking on the people he wanted to influence. He learned all about their children and their lovers and their hobbies and their hangups. And he used whatever tactics were needed to do the job. He got things implemented through people.

The stories left behind from the Johnson presidency reflect those characteristics. Johnson's memorable quotations were invariably pragmatic and earthy. One of his favorites: "Don't spit in the soup; we all have to eat."

On one occasion, the story goes, an aide came to him to ask, "Mr. President, why are you climbing into bed with Joe Smith, who has always been your enemy? For years that guy has been trying to destroy you, and now you seem to be forming an alliance with him." Johnson is said to have replied, "I'd rather have him inside the tent pissing out than outside pissing in."

No statesmanlike rhetoric here. Those Johnsonisms are not likely to make *The World's Great Quotations*, but they catch Johnson's pragmatic emphasis on doing what one has to do to get the damn job done. And they surely also illustrate his awareness of the relevance of human emotionality in the implementing process. Typical of the approach of excellent implementers, these quotations illustrate two key characteristics of #3 skill—attention to emotionality and attention to the individual.

After some hesitation, I have decided to include one more remark that has been ascribed, truly or falsely, to President Johnson. The remark is worth reporting, not because it is off-color, but because it so clearly demonstrates Johnson's faith that implementing is what *really* counts. "When you grab 'em by the balls," the remark goes, "their hearts and minds will soon follow." Translated, that would read, "If you catch people where their #3 emotions are, then the #2 rationality and their #1 values will adapt themselves to fit." In this rather cynical ideology, emotionality dominates both logic and morality. While Johnson's application of that ideology looks especially manipulative, the ideology itself underlies the practice of many other types of implementers.

It's not too difficult to find other examples of excellent implementers. During World War II General George Patton was a flamboyant example, out there at the head of his troops, his twin pearl-handled revolvers at his side. And Ronald Reagan has shown extraordinary skill at social influence, both through his mastery of the media and in face-to-face dealings with congressmen. Remember, for example, how, early in his first term, he got those AWAC planes for the Saudis? While commentators were insisting that he couldn't possibly push the deal through, he did. And the newspapers talked about how his personal charm had swung the votes his way. Incidentally, was any #1 mission involved in that deal? Or was any of the deal part of a grand #2 plan? Most observers seemed to feel that in that case #3 was all there was.

Doesn't Lee Iacocca belong on any list of great recent managerial implementers? He may be good at #1 and #2 as well, but his affable personal implementing style and his effective exploitation of the emotional aspects of managing have been extraordinary.

Each of us could probably make a private list of "implementers I have known"—from a particular teacher who counseled and guided us, to the company tactician who always seemed to know just when to push hard and when to back off, to that extraordinary sales rep who somehow made those impossible sales, to the negotiator who always seemed to get a better deal than anyone else.

If Johnson serves as a caricature of the extreme and skillful implementer, who can similarly exemplify the far-out problem solver? The epitome of rational, analytic intelligence? The person who could decompose very complex problems and then reassemble them into a clear controllable form? Does your vice president for finance fit the mold? Or your chief industrial engineer? How about David Stockman, recently the director of the U.S. Budget Bureau?

One public figure of a couple of decades ago who fit that image perfectly, at least by media stereotype, was Robert McNamara during his tenure as U.S. secretary of defense. The later McNamara of the World Bank appears much more mellow than did the earlier Department of Defense version. McNamara in those early years was much admired by many of his contemporaries chiefly because of his brilliantly orderly, systematic, and rational mind. In contrast to the stories about LBJ (under whom McNamara served), the stories about McNamara reflect just those #2 qualities. Here's one:

McNamara is attending a presentation at which the presenter shows slide after slide full of graphs and charts and numbers. At the 105th slide, McNamara says, "Stop! Slide number 105 contradicts slide number 6." And sure enough, he is right! Everyone in attendance is awed by his capacity to order and process such massive quantities of information. Some Washington veterans still count McNamara as the greatest civil servant of his time. They usually cite his incisive, analytic, logical qualities as the main reason.

However, at least as the stories go, the McNamara of those DOD days was not nearly as effective in implementing his decisions as he was in making them, and history books are not likely to picture him as a great visionary (though that is probably quite unjust). There are Washington old-timers who still turn beet red with anger at the mention of his name. When they calm down enough to say why, it is almost always to complain that he tried to "take over," to reduce other people's autonomy. Some generals in Vietnam and some legislators in Washington, themselves pretty good #3 implementers, viewed him as an intruder into their autonomous territories and resisted those carefully worked-out controls imposed from the Pentagon.

While it is difficult to identify senior managers who manifest extreme #2 posture in these late 1980s, such managers were less rare in the 60s and 70s. In those years, executives like Roy Ash at Litton Industries and Harold Geneen at ITT were seen as the very model of modern managers—brilliant, tough, systematic, coldly rational.

Analytic think tanks like the Rand Corporation flourished in those decades too. And small analytic-planning groups played a powerful role in France. The stereotype of the cool analytic MBA also came into its own in that period too, and it became so popular with managers that the number of such MBAs multiplied, as did the number of business schools that produced them. The 1960s and 70s were the decades when corporate staffs grew fat and great conglomerates roamed the earth.

Examples of #1 pathfinders, however, seem to turn up throughout human history. They include great religious figures like Jesus and Mohammed; leaders of nations like Mahatma Gandhi, Vladimir Ilyich Lenin, Charles de Gaulle, Lee Kuan Yew, and Golda Meir; and pioneers in the professions like Florence Nightingale and Sigmund Freud.

Other less attractive personages also belong on the pathfinder list: Adolf Hitler, Muammar al-Qaddafi, Napoleon Bonaparte, and Attila the Hun. My favorite candidate for recent top-of-the-line pathfinder is Dr. Martin Luther King, Jr. His most remembered phrase is "I have a dream." That's as pathfinding a phrase as one can imagine. Of course, Dr. King must be counted as a great implementer as well. Followers flocked to act upon his dream. He too changed behavior by emotional means, though he used a style quite different from President Johnson's.

Just for practice, imagine how differently either Robert McNamara or Lyndon Johnson, given the same intent as King's, might have approached the same problem of changing race relations in America.

McNamara would have worked out a grand strategy, wouldn't he? He would have been sure that all of the staff work had been done, the information gathered and analyzed, the contingencies planned for. He would have done an admirably professional job.

President Johnson's approach? Perhaps he would have identified the key players, figured out which people really had the power. Then perhaps he would have worked on those people, one at a time, using every weapon that he could muster to line them up—from the prestige of his office, to promises of support for their pet projects, to personal persuasion.

Would either of them have shown the passionate, resolute, self-sacrificing style used by Dr. King? I think not.

In the corporate world, pathfinders are, thank heaven, not yet an entirely endangered species. They can most often (but not always) be found among founders of companies, in part because successful founders are apt to get more public attention than second- or third-generation managers.

Some recent examples: Messrs. Hewlett and Packard seem to have truly committed themselves to a clear set of organizational values. They have captured and transmitted much of their intent with the phrase "the H-P way." That phrase really means something to H-P people everywhere. It describes a style of openness, honesty, and mutual support and respect reminiscent of the best of small-town America. At Apple Computer, in contrast, Steve Jobs and Company tried to pursue a very different vision—a brash, innovative, almost arrogant organizational culture. Some observers saw that pursuit as a somewhat flaky new children's crusade; for others, it was a youthful cultural revolution, ideally appropriate to its time, its place, and its product.

But in older companies too, pathfinders arise. Pehr Gyllenhammer at Volvo has pushed long, hard, and effectively for a more humane and productive alternative to the old assembly line. He has argued saliently for keeping most of Volvo's operations in its native Sweden despite high labor costs, because he believes in fighting the productivity battle in more positive ways than by escaping to cheap labor overseas.

So Volvo has tried to stay competitive (and so far it has worked) by innovating in both the technology and the sociology of production—building quality cars and trucks with small teams, using appropriate tools, and even modifying the design of its products to fit coherently into the total system. So far, it's doing pretty well.

Ren McPherson, at Dana Corporation, has also successfully pushed his vision of people-based productivity into an otherwise unglamorous old auto parts company. He too did it by using personal passion and determination, injecting pride and enthusiasm into the organization.

In all of these cases the pathfinding leaders have backed up their own pathfinding leadership with effective #3 participative-type implementation, providing us with living examples of successful marriages between #1 and #3. In later chapters that #1–#3 relationship gets a closer look, and so do some of the obstacles that frequently beset such marriages.

Surely the reader can (and should) add to this list from personal experience. Pathfinders—dedicated, purposive people—are not to be found only among the famous and infamous, or only at the tops of large organizations. Small entrepreneurial companies are very often led by people with such dedication to particular visions and values, and deep within large organizations, often in the face of enormous bureaucratic roadblocks, the dedicated champions of new ideas and important causes still make their voices heard.

DOES THE MANAGERIAL WORLD NEED MORE PATHFINDING?

There are some persuasive arguments on both sides of the question of the importance of pathfinding, especially in large organizations. On the pro side:

- Innovations are almost always the products of pathfinding individuals and small groups, almost never the products of large, highly structured bureaucracies.
- Breakthroughs in any field typically emerge from a combination of thorough understanding of the existing rules *and* a risk-taking readiness to break out of them, to march to different drummers.
- One can also cite the usual broader arguments: the knowledge explosion, ever faster technological change, a crowded and small organizational world. For those reasons and more, organizations need both innovation and direction. They need a constant flow of innovations in products and services because competitors will kill them if they stand still. Intercontinental airplanes knock off passenger liners. Slide rules give way to calculators. Transistors not only destroy vacuum-tube makers but also displace old ways of building watches, radios, and computers. Organizations need direction and purpose lest they be lost in the buffeting storms of competition, regulation, and social change. And individuals need purpose lest *they* be lost in meaningless ennui. The pathfinding part of managing is about both innovation and purpose.

- But let's not try to justify #1 by using only #2-type arguments. There are powerful #1-type reasons for building more pathfinding into Western management. Pathfinding is our heritage, in the United States and almost all other Western countries. Our traditions and our self-esteem commit us to changing the world, to developing the new and the better. Independence, achievement, and daring are integral to our value systems. Pathfinding is what we claim to believe in. We should build it into ourselves and our organizations just because it is our heritage, and just because we believe it is good.
- Just in case the hardheaded reader wants a more practical reason to supplement all of that sentimental junk, here's one: Our traditions of individualism, of independent effort, of starting new fires may just constitute one of our few comparative advantages over the Japanese, with their traditions of conformity, obedience, and self-subordination.

Perhaps it's appropriate here to cite just a few arguments against pushing the pathfinding idea too far:

- How can you run a company full of independent, rule-breaking, intractable pathfinders? That's an invitation to anarchy.
- It's always (well, almost always) been the well-organized, disciplined army that wins the war. Precision and planfulness, not vision and stubbornness, make the difference between success and failure.
- Those imaginative dreamers are a dime a dozen. They're almost always unrealistic and impractical. They bite off more than they can chew, and they won't spit it out no matter how obvious it is that they're wrong. They can kill a company by stubbornly refusing to abandon their dogmatic beliefs.
- The job of managers is to understand the world as it exists and to deal with it, not to take on the impossible job of making it over.

42. *Managing with Power*

Jeffrey Pfeffer

It is one thing to understand power—how to diagnose it, what are its sources, what are the strategies and tactics for its use, how it is lost. It is quite another thing to use that knowledge in the world at large. And putting the knowledge of power and influence into action—managing with power—is essential for those who seek to get things accomplished:

> *"There's a thing you learn at Data General, if you work here for any period of time," said West's lieutenant of hardware, Ed Rasala, "that nothing happens unless you push it."*[1]

Computers don't get built, cities don't get rebuilt, and diseases don't get fought unless advocates for change learn how to develop and use power effectively. We saw that in the early 1980s the blood banks resisted testing for transfusion-transmitted AIDS, and even denied that a contaminated blood supply was a serious health risk. The 1980s saw an increase in the political skill of the AIDS lobby, and its tactics are now being borrowed by others:

> *Women with breast cancer are taking a lesson from AIDS advocacy groups and using political action to urge the Federal and state governments to pay more attention to their disease. "They showed us how to get through to the government. . . . They took on an archaic system and turned it around while we have been quietly dying."* [2]

Women's health issues are sorely underfunded compared to the proportion of women in the population, a situation that is likely to change if, and only if, power and influence are brought to bear on and, more importantly, *in* those organizations that fund medical research and regulate the pharmaceutical and medical industries.

In corporations, public agencies, universities, and government, the problem is how to get things done, how to move forward, how to solve the many problems facing organizations of all sizes and types. Developing and exercising power require having both will and skill. It is the will that often seems to be missing. Power and influence have a negative connotation. We hound politicians from office, and try to bring down those institutions or individuals that seek to do things differently or better. I wonder how many of us would have had the nerve or the courage to do what the young Henry Ford II did when the company that bears his name was in trouble in the 1940s?

Ford Motor Company was founded by Henry Ford II's grandfather. Although the elder Ford had tremendous engineering genius, and the Model T truly transformed the country, in his later years he was rigid, inflexible, autocratic, and virtually destroyed the company by failing to incorporate new technology and styling. Ford saw a criticism of the Model T as a criticism of him personally, so the competitive threat of Chevrolet was met with price cutting—eight times from 1920 to 1924, twice more in 1926.[3] Even after the Model A was introduced in 1927, the company continued to decline. Henry Ford, originally surrounded by bright engineers and innovative managers, soon surrounded himself with bodyguards and strongmen, including the notorious Harry Bennett, who carried a gun and who would, on occasion, take target practice while talking with visitors.

> *Even the brief triumph of the Model A did not halt the downward spiral of the company. Henry Ford remained locked in the past. He grew more erratic and finally senile. At the end of his life he*

believed that World War II did not exist, that it was simply a ploy made up by the newspapers to help the munitions industry. . . . It was a spectacular self-destruction, one that would never again be matched in a giant American corporation.[4]

By the time of World War II, the federal government actually considered taking over the company, because it was in such desperate managerial and financial condition that it could fail at any time, and the government badly needed its wartime production capabilities. In 1943, Secretary of the Navy Frank Knox discharged a 26-year-old Henry Ford II from the Navy. He had a bigger, more important job to do—to take over and then save the Ford Motor Company. Henry's father, Edsel Ford, had died of stomach cancer that same year at the age of 49. Although described as both gentle and brilliant, he had been totally dominated by the elder Ford, and had never played a major role in the company. The company had destroyed the second generation of Fords, and there were people who would have been quite happy to do the same thing with the third generation.

As Ford had grown older and more senile, effective control of the company had passed to the hands of Harry Bennett, head of the dreaded Ford Service Department, which was effectively a secret police force of hoodlums, gangsters, and ex-policemen, who exercised control through physical force. One story had it that when an employee violated the company's policy against smoking, Bennett personally shot the cigar from the man's mouth. With Edsel gone, and Henry Ford increasingly infirm, the only thing keeping Bennett from control of Ford was Henry Ford II.

Although Ford was in the company, with the title of vice president, Bennett constantly belittled him (as he had his father, Edsel). Moreover, the elder Ford had drawn up a codicil to his will, which stipulated that at his death, control of the company would pass to a 10-person board of directors, not including Henry Ford II, for 10 years. Henry was incensed, and threatened to resign unless the will was

changed. He also warned that he would inform the company's dealers about the firm's sorry condition. Henry's mother (Edsel's widow), Eleanor Clay Ford (related to the Hudson department store family), insisted that Henry II be given control of the company or she would sell her stock. Henry's grandmother (and the elder Ford's wife), Clara Bryant Ford, backed Eleanor. On September 20, 1945, Henry Ford II became president of Ford Motor Company. The next day this decision was ratified by the board of directors.

Henry Ford immediately fired Bennett—after 29 years in the company, much of it as its effective boss, he was out. Inheriting a company with no financial controls and in managerial disarray, losing $10 million a month, Ford hired financial experts, including Arjay Miller, to straighten out the company's books and records, and Ernie Breech, from Bendix, to help with the management. In the first several months in control, Ford fired more than 1,000 executives, including many of Bennett's cronies. By 1949, Ford had instituted a pension plan with the United Auto Workers Union, the first in the industry, and brought out an all-new automobile. In 1950, the company earned a profit of $265 million. Ford and his recent hires had turned the company around, but it had taken courage and a willingness to take on some pretty tough people inside the organization to do it. Henry Ford II had managed with power.

What does it mean, to manage with power?

First, it means recognizing that in almost every organization, there are varying interests. This suggests that one of the first things we need to do is to diagnose the political landscape and figure out what the relevant interests are, and what important political subdivisions characterize the organization. It is essential that we do not assume that everyone necessarily is going to be our friend, or agree with us, or even that preferences are uniformly distributed. There are clusters of interests within organizations, and we need to understand where these are and to whom they belong.

Next, it means figuring out what point of view these various individuals and subunits have on issues of concern to us. It also means understanding why they have the perspective that they do. It is all too easy to assume that those with a different perspective are somehow not as smart as we are, not as informed, not as perceptive. If that is our belief, we are likely to do several things, each of which is disastrous. First, we may act contemptuously toward those who disagree with us—after all, if they aren't as competent or as insightful as we are, why should we take them seriously? It is rarely difficult to get along with those who resemble us in character and opinions. The real secret of success in organizations is the ability to get those who differ from us, and whom we don't necessarily like, to do what needs to be done. Second, if we think people are misinformed, we are likely to try to "inform" them, or to try to convince them with facts and analysis. Sometimes this will work, but often it will not, for their disagreement may not be based on a lack of information; it may, instead, arise from a different perspective on what our information means. Diagnosing the point of view of interest groups as well as the basis for their positions will assist us in negotiating with them and in predicting their response to various initiatives.

Third, managing with power means understanding that to get things done, you need power—more power than those whose opposition you must overcome—and thus it is imperative to understand where power comes from and how these sources of power can be developed. We are sometimes reluctant to think very purposefully or strategically about acquiring and using power. We are prone to believe that if we do our best, work hard, be nice, and so forth, things will work out for the best. I don't mean to imply that one should not, in general, work hard, try to make good decisions, and be nice, but that these and similar platitudes are often not very useful in helping us get things accomplished in our organizations. We need to understand power and try to get it. We must be willing to do things to build our sources of power, or else we will be less effective than we might wish to be.

Fourth, managing with power means understanding the strategies and tactics through which power is developed and used in organizations, including the importance of timing, the use of structure, the social psychology of commitment and other forms of interpersonal influence. If nothing else, such an understanding will help us become astute observers of the behavior of others. The more we understand power and its manifestations, the better will be our clinical skills. More fundamentally, we need to understand strategies and tactics of using power so that we can consider the range of approaches available to us, and use what is likely to be effective. Again, as in the case of building sources of power, we often try not to think about these things, and we avoid being strategic or purposeful about employing our power. This is a mistake. Although we may have various qualms, there will be others who do not. Knowledge without power is of remarkably little use. And power without the skill to employ it effectively is likely to be wasted.

Managing with power means more than knowing the ideas discussed in this book. It means being, like Henry Ford, willing to do something with that knowledge. It requires political savvy to get things done, and the willingness to force the issue.

For years in the United States, there had been demonstrations and protests, court decisions and legislative proposals attempting to end the widespread discrimination against minority Americans in employment, housing, and public accommodations. The passage of civil rights legislation was a top priority for President Kennedy, but although he had charisma, he lacked the knowledge of political tactics, and possibly the will to use some of the more forceful ones, to get his legislation passed. In the hands of someone who knew power and influence inside out, in spite of the opposition of southern congressmen and senators, the legislation would be passed quickly.

In March 1965, the United States was wracked by violent reactions to civil rights marches in the South. People were killed and injured as segregationists attacked demonstrators, with little or no intervention by the local law enforcement agencies. There were demonstrators across from the White House holding a vigil as Lyndon Johnson left to address a joint session of Congress. This was the same Lyndon Johnson who, in 1948, had opposed federal anti-lynching legislation, arguing that it was a matter properly left to the states. This was the same Lyndon Johnson who, as a young congressional secretary and then congressman, had talked conservative to conservatives, liberal to liberals, and was said by many to have stood for nothing. This was the same Lyndon Johnson who in eight years in the House of Representatives had introduced not one piece of significant legislation and had done almost nothing to speak out on issues of national importance. This was the same Lyndon Johnson who, while in the House, had tried instead to enrich himself by influencing colleagues at the Federal Communications Commission to help him both obtain a radio station in Austin, Texas, and change the operating license to make the station immensely profitable and valuable. This was the same Lyndon Johnson who, in 1968, having misled the American people, would decide not to run for reelection because of both his association with the Vietnam War and a fundamental distrust of the presidency felt by many Americans. On that night Johnson was to make vigorous use of his power and his political skill to help the civil rights movement.

With almost the first words of his speech, the audience . . . knew that Lyndon Johnson intended to take the cause of civil rights further than it had ever gone before. . . . He would submit a new civil rights bill . . . and it would be far stronger than the bills of the past. . . . "their cause must be our cause, too," Lyndon Johnson said. "Because it is not just Negroes, but really it is all of us, who must overcome the crippling legacy of bigotry and injustice. . . . And we shall overcome."[5]

As he left the chamber after making his speech, Johnson sought out the 76-year-old chairman of the House Judiciary Committee, Emmanuel Celler:

"Manny," he said, "I want you to start hearings tonight."

"Mr. President," Celler protested, "I can't push that committee or it might get out of hand. I am scheduling hearings for next week."

. . . Johnson's eyes narrowed, and his face turned harder. His right hand was still shaking Celler's, but the left hand was up, and a finger was out, pointing, jabbing.

"Start them this week, Manny," he said. "And hold night sessions, too."[6]

Getting things done requires power. The problem is that we would prefer to see the world as a kind of grand morality play, with the good guys and the bad ones easily identified. Obtaining power is not always an attractive process, nor is its use. And it somehow disturbs our sense of symmetry that a man who was as sleazy, to use a term of my students, as Lyndon Johnson was in some respects, was also the individual who almost single-handedly passed more civil rights legislation in less time with greater effect than anyone else in U.S. history. We are troubled by the issue of means and ends. We are perplexed by the fact that "bad" people sometimes do great and wonderful things, and that "good" people sometimes do "bad" things, or often, nothing at all. Every day, managers in public and private organizations acquire and use power to get things done. Some of these things may be, in retrospect, mistakes, although often that depends heavily on your point of view. Any reader who always does the correct thing that pleases everyone should immediately contact me—we will get very wealthy together. Mistakes and opposition are inevitable. What is not inevitable is passivity, not trying, not seeking to accomplish things.

In many domains of activity we have become so obsessed with not upsetting anybody, and with not making mistakes, that we settle for doing nothing. Rather than rebuild San Francisco's highways, possibly in the wrong place, maybe even in the wrong way, we do nothing, and the city erodes economically without adequate transportation. Rather than possibly being wrong about a new product, such as the personal computer, we study it and analyze it, and lose market opportunities. Analysis and forethought are, obviously, fine. What is not so fine is paralysis or inaction, which arise because we have little skill in overcoming the opposition that inevitably accompanies change, and little interest in doing so.

Theodore Roosevelt, making a speech at the Sorbonne in 1910, perhaps said it best:

It is not the critic who counts; not the man who points out how the strong man stumbles, or where the doer of deeds could have done them better. The credit belongs to the man who is actually in the arena, whose face is marred by dust and sweat and blood; who strives valiantly; who errs, and comes short again and again; because there is not effort without error and shortcoming; but who does actually strive to do the deeds; who knows the great enthusiasms, the great devotions; who spends himself in a worthy cause, who at the best knows in the end the triumphs of high achievement and who at the worst, if he fails, at least fails while daring greatly, so that his place shall never be with

those cold and timid souls who know neither victory nor defeat.[7]

It is easy and often comfortable to feel powerless—to say, "I don't know what to do, I don't have the power to get it done, and besides, I can't really stomach the struggle that may be involved." It is easy, and now quite common, to say, when confronted with some mistake in your organization, "It's not really my responsibility, I can't do anything about it anyway, and if the company wants to do that, well, that's why the senior executives get the big money—it's their responsibility." Such a response excuses us from trying to do things; in not trying to overcome opposition, we will make fewer enemies and are less likely to embarrass ourselves. It is, however, a prescription for both organizational and personal failure. This is why power and influence are not the organization's last dirty secret, but the secret of success for both individuals and their organizations. Innovation and change in almost any arena require the skill to develop power, and the willingness to employ it to get things accomplished. Or, in the words of a local radio newscaster, "If you don't like the news, go out and make some of your own."

NOTES

1. Tracy Kidder, *Soul of a New Machine* (Boston: Atlantic-Little, Brown, 1981), 111.
2. Jane Gross, "Turning Disease Into a Cause: Breast Cancer Follows AIDS," *New York Times* (January 7, 1991): A1.
3. David Halberstam, *The Reckoning* (New York: William Morrow, 1986), 90.
4. Ibid., 91.
5. Robert A. Caro, *Means of Ascent: The Years of Lyndon Johnson* (New York: Alfred A. Knopf, 1990), xix–xx.
6. Ibid., xxi.
7. Richard M. Nixon, *Leaders* (New York: Warner Books, 1982), 345.

43. *Ambidextrous Organizations: Managing Evolutionary and Revolutionary Change*

Michael L. Tushman/Charles A. O'Reilly III

All managers face problems in overcoming inertia and implementing innovation and change. But why is this problem such an enduring one? Organizations are filled with sensible people and usually led by smart managers. Why is anything but incremental change often so difficult for the most successful organizations? And why are the patterns of success and failure so prevalent across industries and over time? To remain successful over long periods, managers and organizations must be ambidextrous—able to implement both incremental and revolutionary change.

PATTERNS IN ORGANIZATION EVOLUTION

Across industries there is a pattern in which success often precedes failure. But industry-level studies aren't very helpful for illustrating what actually went wrong. Why are managers sometimes ineffective in making the transition from strength to strength? To understand this we need to look inside firms and understand the forces impinging on management as they wrestle with managing innovation and change. To do this, let's examine the history of two firms, RCA semiconductors and Seiko watches, as they dealt with the syndrome of success followed by failure.

The stark reality of the challenge of discontinuous change can be seen in Table 43.1. This is a listing of the leading semiconductor firms over a forty-year period. In the mid-1950s, vacuum tubes represented roughly a $700 million market. At this time, the leading firms in the then state-of-the-art technology of vacuum tubes included great technology companies such as RCA, Sylvania, Raytheon, and Westinghouse. Yet between 1955 and 1995, there was almost a complete turnover in industry leadership. With the advent of the transistor, a major technological discontinuity, we see the beginnings of a remarkable shakeout. By 1965, new firms such as Motorola and Texas Instruments had become important players while Sylvania and RCA had begun to fade. Over the next 20 years still other upstart companies like Intel, Toshiba, and Hitachi became the new leaders while Sylvania and RCA exited the product class.

Why should this pattern emerge? Is it that managers and technologists in 1955 in firms like Westinghouse, RCA, and Sylvania didn't understand the technology? This seems implausible. In fact, many vacuum tube producers did enter the transistor market, suggesting that they not only understood the technology, but saw it as important. RCA was initially successful at making the transition. While from the outside it appeared that they had committed themselves to transistors, the inside picture was very different.

Within RCA, there were bitter disputes about whether the company should enter the transistor business and cannibalize their profitable tube business. On one side, there were reasonable arguments that the transistor business was new and the profits uncertain. Others, without knowing whether transistors would be successful, felt that it was too risky not to pursue the new technology. But even if RCA were to enter the solid-state business, there were thorny issues about how to organize it within the company. How could they manage both

TABLE 43.1
Semiconductor Industry, 1955–1995

1955 (Vacuum Tubes)	1955 (Transistors)	1965 (Semiconductors)	1975 (Integrated Circuits)	1982 (VLSI)	1995 (Submicron)
1. RCA	Hughes	TI	TI	Motorola	Intel
2. Sylvania	Transitron	Fairchild	Fairchild	TI	NEC
3. General Electric	Philco	Motorola	National	NEC	Toshiba
4. Raytheon	Sylvania	GI	Intel	Hitachi	Hitachi
5. Westinghouse	TI	GE	Motorola	National	Motorola
6. Amperex	GE	RCA	Rockwell	Toshiba	Samsung
7. National Video	RCA	Sprague	GI	Intel	TI
8. Rawland	Westinghouse	Philco	RCA	Philips	Fujitsu
9. Eimac	Motorola	Transitron	Philips	Fujitsu	Mitsubishi
10. Lansdale	Clevite	Raytheon	AMD	Fairchild	Philips

Source: Adapted from R. Foster, *Innovation: The Attacker's Advantage* (New York, NY: Summit Books, 1986).

technologies? Should the solid-state division report to the head of the electronics group, a person steeped in vacuum tube expertise?

With its great wealth of marketing, financial, and technological resources, RCA decided to enter the business. Historically, it is common for successful firms to experiment with new technologies.[1] Xerox, for example, developed user-interface and software technologies, yet left it to Apple and Microsoft to implement them. Western Union developed the technology for telephony and allowed American Bell (AT&T) to capture the benefits. Almost all relatively wealthy firms can afford to explore new technologies. Like many firms before them, RCA management recognized the problems of trying to play two different technological games but were ultimately unable to resolve them. In the absence of a clear strategy and the cultural differences required to compete in both markets, RCA failed.

In his study of this industry, Richard Foster (then a Director at McKinsey & Company) notes, "Of the 10 leaders in vacuum tubes in 1955 only two were left in 1975. There were three variants of error in these case histories. First is the decision not to invest in the new technology. The second is to invest but picking the wrong technology. The third variant is cultural. Companies failed because of their inability to play two games at once: To be both effective defenders of what quickly became old technologies and effective attackers with new technologies."[2] Senior managers in these firms fell victim to their previous success and their inability to play two games simultaneously. New firms, like Intel and Motorola, were not saddled with this internal conflict and inertia. As they grew, they were able to re-create themselves, while other firms remained trapped.

In contrast to RCA, consider Hattori-Seiko's watch business. While Seiko was the dominant Japanese watch producer in the 1960s, they were a small player in global markets (see Table 43.2). Bolstered by an aspiration to be a global leader in the watch business, and informed by internal experimentation between alternative oscillation technologies (quartz, mechanical, and tuning fork), Seiko's senior management team made a bold bet. In the mid-1960s, Seiko transformed itself from being merely a mechanical watch firm into being both a quartz and mechanical watch company. This move into low-cost, high-quality watches triggered wholesale change within Seiko and, in turn, within the world-wide watch

TABLE 43.2
Employment in the Swiss Watch Industry, 1955–1985

Year	No. of Firms	No. of Employees
1955	2300	70,000
1965	1900	84,000
1970	1600	89,000
1975	1200	63,000
1980	900	47,000
1985	600	32,000

industry. As transistors replaced vacuum tubes (to RCA's chagrin), quartz movement watches replaced mechanical watches. Even though the Swiss had invented both the quartz and tuning fork movements, at this juncture in history they moved to reinvest in mechanical movements. As Seiko and other Japanese firms prospered, the Swiss watch industry drastically suffered. By 1980, SSIH, the largest Swiss watch firm, was less than half the size of Seiko. Eventually, SSIH and Asuag, the two largest Swiss firms, went bankrupt. It would not be until after these firms were taken over by the Swiss banks and transformed by Nicholas Hayek that the Swiss would move to recapture the watch market.

The real test of leadership, then, is to be able to compete successfully by both increasing the alignment or fit among strategy, structure, culture, and processes, while simultaneously preparing for the inevitable revolutions required by discontinuous environmental change. This requires organizational and management skills to compete in a mature market (where cost, efficiency, and incremental innovation are key) *and* to develop new products and services (where radical innovation, speed, and flexibility are critical). A focus on either one of these skill sets is conceptually easy. Unfortunately, focusing on only one guarantees short-term success but long-term failure. Managers need to be able to do both at the same time, that is, they need to be ambidex-

trous. Juggling provides a metaphor. A juggler who is very good at manipulating a single ball is not interesting. It is only when the juggler can handle multiple balls at one time that his or her skill is respected.

These short examples are only two illustrations of the pattern by which organizations evolve: periods of incremental change punctuated by discontinuous or revolutionary change. Long-term success is marked by increasing alignment among strategy, structure, people, and culture through incremental or evolutionary change punctuated by discontinuous or revolutionary change that requires the simultaneous shift in strategy, structure, people, and culture. These discontinuous changes are almost always driven either by organizational performance problems or by major shifts in the organization's environment, such as technological or competitive shifts. Where those less successful firms (e.g., SSIH, RCA) react to environmental jolts, those more successful firms proactively initiate innovations that reshape their market (e.g., Seiko).[3]

WHAT'S HAPPENING? UNDERSTANDING PATTERNS OF ORGANIZATIONAL EVOLUTION

These patterns in organization evolution are not unique. Almost all successful organizations evolve through relatively long periods of incremental change punctuated by environmental shifts and revolutionary change. These discontinuities may be driven by technology, competitors, regulatory events, or significant changes in economic and political conditions. For example, deregulation in the financial services and airline industries led to waves of mergers and failures as firms scrambled to reorient themselves to the new competitive environment. Major political changes in Eastern Europe and South Africa have had a similar impact. The combination of the European Union and the emergence of global competition in the automobile and electronics industries has shifted the basis of competition in these markets. Technological change in microprocessors has altered the face of the computer industry.

The sobering fact is that the cliché about the increasing pace of change seems to be true. Sooner or later, discontinuities upset the congruence that has been a part of the organization's success. Unless their competitive environment remains stable—an increasingly unlikely condition in today's world—firms must confront revolutionary change. The underlying cause of this pattern can be found in an unlikely place: evolutionary biology.

Innovation Patterns Over Time

For many years, biological evolutionary theory proposed that the process of adaptation occurred gradually over long time periods. The process was assumed to be one of variation, selection, and retention. Variations occurred naturally within species across generations. Those variations that were most adapted to the environment would, over time, enable a species to survive and reproduce. This form would be selected in that it endured while less adaptable forms reproduced less productively and would diminish over time. For instance, if the world became colder and snowier, animals who were whiter and had heavier coats would be advantaged and more likely to survive. As climatic changes affected vegetation, those species with longer necks or stronger beaks might do better. In this way, variation led to adaptation and fitness, which was subsequently retained across generations. In this early view, the environment changed gradually and species adapted slowly to these changes. There is ample evidence that this view has validity.

But this perspective missed a crucial question: What happened if the environment was characterized, not by gradual change, but periodic discontinuities? What about rapid changes in temperature, or dramatic shifts in the availability of food? Under these conditions, a reliance on gradual change was a one-way ticket to extinction. Instead of slow change, discontinuities required a different version of Darwinian theory—that of punctuated equilibria in which

long periods of gradual change were interrupted periodically by massive discontinuities. What then? Under these conditions, survival or selection goes to those species with the characteristics needed to exploit the new environment. Evolution progresses through long periods of incremental change punctuated by brief periods of revolutionary or discontinuous change.

So it seems to be with organizations. An entire subfield of research on organizations has demonstrated many similarities between populations of insects and animals and populations of organizations. This field, known as "organizational ecology," has successfully applied models of population ecology to the study of sets of organizations in areas as diverse as wineries, newspapers, automobiles, biotech companies, and restaurants.[4] The results confirm that populations of organizations are subject to ecological pressures in which they evolve through periods of incremental adaptation punctuated by discontinuities. Variations in organizational strategy and form are more or less suitable for different environmental conditions. Those organizations and managers who are most able to adapt to a given market or competitive environment will prosper. Over time, the fittest survive—until there is a major discontinuity. At that point, managers of firms are faced with the challenge of reconstituting their organizations to adjust to the new environment. Managers who try to adapt to discontinuities through incremental adjustment are unlikely to succeed. The processes of variation, selection, and retention that winnow the fittest of animal populations seem to apply to organizations as well.

To understand how this dynamic affects organizations, we need to consider two fundamental ideas; how organizations grow and evolve, and how discontinuities affect this process. Armed with this understanding, we can then show how managers can cope with evolutionary and revolutionary change.

Organizational Growth and Evolution.

There is a pattern that describes organizational growth. All organizations evolve following the familiar S-curve shown in Figure 43.1. For instance, consider the history of Apple Computer and how it grew. In its inception, Apple was not so much an organization as a small group of people trying to design, produce, and sell a new product, the personal computer. With success came the beginnings of a formal organization, assigned roles and responsibilities, some rudimentary systems for accounting and payroll, and a culture based on the shared expectations among employees about innovation, commitment, and speed. Success at this stage was seen in terms of congruence among the strategy, structure, people, and culture. Those who fit the Apple values and subscribed to the cultural norms stayed. Those who found the Jobs and Wozniak vision too cultish left. This early structure was aligned with the strategy and the critical tasks needed to implement it. Success flowed not only from having a new product with desirable features, but also from the ability of the organization to design, manufacture, market, and distribute the new PC. The systems in place tracked those outcomes and processes that were important for the implementation of a single product strategy. Congruence among the elements of the organization is a key to high performance across industries.

As the firm continued its successful growth, several inexorable changes occurred. First, it got larger. As this occurred, more structure and systems were added. Although this trend toward professionalization was resisted by Jobs (who referred to professional managers as "bozos"), the new structures and procedures were required for efficiency and control. Without them, chaos would have reigned. As Apple got older, new norms were developed about what was important and acceptable and

FIGURE 43.1
Punctuated Equilibrium and Organizational Evolution

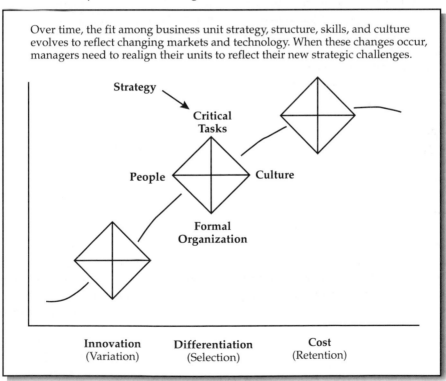

Over time, the fit among business unit strategy, structure, skills, and culture evolves to reflect changing markets and technology. When these changes occur, managers need to realign their units to reflect their new strategic challenges.

Strategy

Critical Tasks

People — Culture

Formal Organization

Innovation (Variation) Differentiation (Selection) Cost (Retention)

what would not be tolerated. The culture changed to reflect the new challenges. Success at Apple and at other firms is based on learning what works and what doesn't.

Inevitably, even Apple's strategy had to change. What used to be a single-product firm (selling the Apple PC and then its successor, the Apple II) now sold a broader range of products in increasingly competitive markets. Instead of a focused strategy, the emphasis shifted to a market-wide emphasis. Not only was Apple selling to personal computer users, but also to the educational and industrial markets. This strategic shift required further adjustment to the structure, people, culture, and critical tasks. What worked in a smaller, more focused firm was no longer adequate for the larger, more differentiated Apple. Success at this phase of evolution required management's ability to realign the organization to ensure congruence with the strategy. The well-publicized ouster of Steve Jobs by Apple's board of directors reflected the board's judgment that John Sculley had the skills necessary to lead a larger, more diversified company. Jobs's approach was fine for a smaller, more focused firm but inappropriate for the challenges Apple faced in the mid-1980s.

Over an even longer period of success, there are inevitably more changes—sometimes driven by technology, sometimes by competition, customers, or regulation, sometimes by new strategies and ways of competing. As the product class matures, the basis of competition shifts. While in the early stages of a product class, competition is based on product variation, in the later stages competition shifts to features, efficiency, and cost. In the evolution of Apple, this can be seen as the IBM PC and the clones emerged. The Windows operating system loosened the grip Apple had maintained on the easy-to-use graphical interface and triggered a battle between three incompatible operating systems—the Mac, IBM's OS/2, and Microsoft Windows. Once Windows became the industry standard in operating systems, the basis of competition shifted to cost, quality, and efficiency. Faced with these realities, Apple managers once

again had to re-balance the congruence among strategy, structure, people, and culture. Success comes from being able to out do the competition in this new environment. So the board of directors replaced Sculley as CEO in 1994 with Michael Spindler, who was seen as having the operational skills needed to run the company in a mature market. Spindler's task was to emphasize the efficiencies and lower margins required in today's markets and reshape Apple to compete in this new market. With Apple's performance stagnant, its board chose a turnaround expert, Gil Amelio, to finish what Spindler could not do.

Notice how Apple evolved over a 20-year period. Incremental or evolutionary change was punctuated by discontinuous or revolutionary change as the firm moved through the three stages of growth in the product class; innovation, differentiation, and maturity. Each of these stages required different competencies, strategies, structures, cultures, and leadership skills. These changes are what drives performance. But while absolutely necessary for short-term success, incremental change is not sufficient for long-term success. It is not by chance that Steve Jobs was successful at Apple until the market became more differentiated and demanded the skills of John Sculley. Nor is it surprising that, as the industry consolidated and competition emphasized costs, operations-oriented managers such as Michael Spindler and, in turn, Gil Amelio were selected to reorient Apple.

To succeed over the long haul, firms have to periodically reorient themselves by adopting new strategies and structures that are necessary to accommodate changing environmental conditions. These shifts often occur through discontinuous changes—simultaneous shifts in strategy, structures, skills, and culture. If an environment is stable and changes only gradually, as is the case in industries such as cement, it is possible for an organization to evolve slowly through continuous incremental change. But, many managers have learned (to their stockholders' chagrin) that slow evolutionary change in a fast-changing world is, as it was for the dinosaurs, a path to the boneyard.

Technology Cycles. Although organizational growth by itself can lead to a periodic need for discontinuous change, there is another more fundamental process occurring that results in punctuated change. This is a pervasive phenomenon that occurs across industries and is not widely appreciated by managers. Yet it is critical to understanding when and why revolutionary change is necessary: This is the dynamic of product, service, and process innovation, dominant designs, and substitution events which together make up technology cycles. Figure 43.2 shows the general outline of this process.[5]

In any product or service class (e.g., microprocessors, automobiles, baby diapers, cash management accounts) there is a common pattern of competition that describes the development of the class over time. As shown in Figure 43.2, technology cycles begin with a proliferation of innovation in products or services as the new product or service gains acceptance.

Think, for example, of the introduction of VCRs. Initially, only a few customers bought them. Over time, as demand increased, there was increasing competition between Beta and VHS. At some point, a design emerged that became the standard preferred by customers (i.e., VHS). Once this occurred, the basis of competition shifted to price and features, not basic product or service design. The emergence of this *dominant design* transforms competition in the product class.[6] Once it is clear that a dominant design has emerged, the basis of competition shifts to process innovation, driving down costs, and adding features. Instead of competing through product or service innovation, successful strategies now emphasize compatibility with the standard and productivity improvement. This competition continues until there is a major new product, service, or process substitution event and the technology cycle kicks off again as the basis of competition shifts back again to product or service variation (e.g., CDs replacing audio tapes). As technology cycles evolve, bases of competition shift within the

FIGURE 43.2
Two Invisible Forces: Technology Cycles and Evolution

Adapted from J. Utterback, *Mastering the Dynamics of Innovation* (Boston, MA: Harvard Business School Press, 1994).

market. As organizations change their strategies, they must also realign their organizations to accomplish the new strategic objectives. This usually requires a revolutionary change.

A short illustration from the development of the automobile will help show how dramatic these changes can be for organizations. At the turn of the century, bicycles and horse-driven carriages were threatened by the "horseless carriage," soon to be called the automobile. Early in this new product class there was substantial competition among alternative technologies. For instance, there were several competing alternative energy sources—steam, battery, and internal combustion engines. There were also different steering mechanisms and arrangements for passenger compartments. In a fairly short period of time, however, there emerged a consensus that certain features were to be standard—that is, a dominant design emerged. This consisted of an internal combustion engine, steering wheel on the left (in the U.S.), brake pedal on the right, and clutch on the left (this dominant design was epitomized in the Ford Model T). Once this standard emerged, the basis of competition shifted from variations in what an automobile looked like and how it was powered to features and cost. The new competitive arena emphasized lower prices and differentiated market segments, not product variation. The imperative for managers was to change their strategies and organizations to compete in this market. Those that were unable to manage this transition failed. Similar patterns can be seen in almost all product classes (e.g., computers, telephones, fast foods, retail stores).

With a little imagination, it is easy to feel what the managerial challenges are in this environment. Holding aside the pressures of growth and success, managers must continually readjust their strategies and realign their organizations to reflect the underlying dynamics of technological change in their markets. These changes are not driven by fad or fashion but reflect the imperatives of fundamental change in the technology. This dynamic is a powerful cause of punctuated equilibria and can demand revolutionary rather than incremental change. This pattern occurs across industries as diverse as computers and cement, the only issue is the frequency with which these cycles repeat themselves. Faced with a discontinuity, the option of incremental change is not likely to be viable. The danger is that, facing a discontinuous change, firms that have been successful may suffer from life-threatening inertia—inertia that results from the very congruence that made the firm successful in the first place.

THE SUCCESS SYNDROME: CONGRUENCE AS A MANAGERIAL TRAP

Managers, as architects of their organizations, are responsible for designing their units in ways that best fit their strategic challenges. Internal congruence among strategy, structure, culture, and people drives short-term performance.[7] Between 1915 and 1960, General Radio had a strategy of high-quality, high-priced electronic equipment with a loose functional structure, strong internal promotion practices, and engineering dominance in decision making. All these things worked together to provide a highly congruent system and, in turn, a highly successful organization. However, the strategy and organizational congruence that made General Radio a success for 50 years became, in the face of major competitive and technological change, a recipe for failure in the 1960s. It was only after a revolutionary change that included a new strategy and simultaneous shifts in structure, people, and culture that the new company, renamed GenRad, was able to compete again against the likes of Hewlett-Packard and Textronix.[8]

Successful companies learn what works well and incorporate this into their operations. This is what organizational learning is about: using feedback from the market to continually refine the organization to get better and better at accomplishing its mission. A lack of congruence (or internal inconsistency in strategy, structure, culture, and people) is usually associated with a firm's current performance problems. Further, since the fit between strategy, structure, people, and processes is never perfect, achieving congruence is an ongoing process requiring continuous improvement and incremental change. With evolutionary change, managers are able to incrementally alter their organizations. Given that these changes are comparatively small, the incongruence injected by the change is controllable. The process of making incremental changes is well known and the uncertainty created for people affected by such changes is within tolerable limits. The overall system adapts, but it is not transformed.

When done effectively, evolutionary change of this sort is a crucial part of short-term success. But there is a dark side to this success. As we described with Apple, success resulted in the company becoming larger and older. Older, larger firms develop structural and cultural inertia—the organizational equivalent of high cholesterol. Figure 43.3 shows the paradox of success. As companies grow, they develop structures and systems to handle the increased complexity of the work. These structures and systems are interlinked so that proposed changes become more difficult, more costly, and require more time to implement, especially if they are more than small, incremental modifications. This results in *structural inertia*—a resistance to change rooted in the size, complexity, and interdependence in the organization's structures, systems, procedures, and processes.

Quite different and significantly more pervasive than structural inertia is the *cultural inertia* that comes from age and success. As organizations get older, part of their learning is embedded in the shared expectations about how things are to be done. These are sometimes seen in the informal norms, values, social networks and in myths, stories, and heroes that have evolved over time. The more successful an organization has been, the more institutionalized or ingrained these norms, values, and lessons become. The more institutionalized these norms, values, and stories are, the greater the cultural inertia—the greater the organizational complacency and arrogance. In relatively stable environments, the firm's culture is a critical component of its success. Culture is an effective way of controlling and coordinating people without elaborate and rigid formal control systems. Yet, when confronted with discontinuous change, the very culture that fostered

FIGURE 43.3
The Success Syndrome

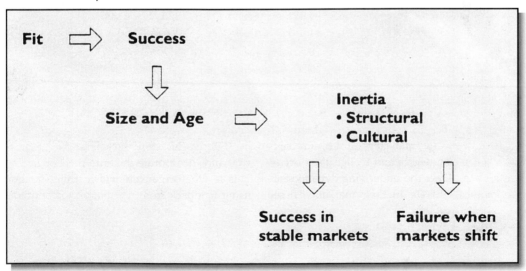

success can quickly become a significant barrier to change. When Lou Gerstner took over as CEO at IBM, he recognized that simply crafting a new strategy was not the solution to IBM's predicament. In his view, "Fixing the culture is the most critical—and the most difficult—part of a corporate transformation."[9] Cultural inertia, because it is so ephemeral and difficult to attack directly, is a key reason managers often fail to successfully introduce revolutionary change—even when they know that it is needed.

THE PARADOX OF CULTURE

The paradox of culture in helping or hindering companies as they compete can be seen in many ways. Consider, for example, the list of companies shown in Table 43.3. These are firms about which there have recently been stories in the business press and in which the culture of the firm was seen as a part of the organization's

success or failure. What is notable about this list is its diversity. The importance of organizational culture transcends country, industry, and firm size. Whether they are electronics giant Samsung, a Hong Kong bank, U.S. conglomerate Allied Signal, a high-tech firm such as Applied Materials or a low-tech company such as Nordstrom, or car manufacturers Nissan, Rover, or General Motors, culture appears to be a critical factor in the performance of the company. The language used in describing the importance of culture is often similar. Yukata Kume, President of Nissan, observed: "The most challenging task I faced when I became president five years ago was to reform the corporate culture . . . I decided that the major reason for our suffering or business predicament lay within Nissan itself."[10] Jack Welch at GE commented on the future demands on organizations: "In the nineties the heroes, the

TABLE 43.3
Firms Recently Mentioned in the Business Press: Culture
as a Factor in Success or Difficulty

Hewlett-Packard	British Airways	Federal Express
Oki Electric	Kodak	Sears
Johnson & Johnson	Allied Signal	Deutsche Bank
General Electric	Home Depot	Pepsico
Silicon Graphics	McKinsey	Philips
Motorola	Royal Dutch/Shell	Bausch & Lomb
Levi Strauss	Southwest Airlines	Applied Materials
Microsoft	PPG	General Motors
Samsung	Nike	Wal-Mart
Siemens	Saturn	Boeing
Nordstrom	IBM	Nissan
Procter & Gamble	Tenneco	Rover
Coca-Cola	Broken Hill Proprietary	Ford
Lucky-Goldstar	Goldman, Sachs	NUMMI
SBC Warburg	Westinghouse	United Airlines
Apple	Bear Stearns	British Petroleum
Swiss Bank Corp	Rubbermaid	Unilever
Nokia	Matsushita	Salomon
Intel	Chrysler	Rubbermaid
Aetna	Medtronics	Kao

winners, will be entire companies that have developed cultures that instead of fearing the pace of change, relish it."[11]

While news articles about successes and failures are not proof of anything, they offer an interesting window on the concerns of practicing managers and savvy journalists. Whether the issue is can Nike successfully export its "Just do it" culture to help drive global growth, or can Nokia, a Finnish maker of mobile phones, shed its stodgy culture in time to compete in the fast-moving telecommunications market, the managerial challenges are similar: How can managers diagnose and actively shape organizational cultures to both execute today's strategies and create the capabilities to innovate for tomorrow's competitive demands? To help focus and frame the crucial issue of managing culture, let's reflect on a few examples in which organizational culture helped firms succeed or was a significant part of their problem in adapting to new circumstances.

Here's the Good News

First, consider the remarkable transformation of British Airways. In 1981, British Airways lost almost $1 billion. Their customers often referred to the airline's initials "BA" as standing for "Bloody Awful." Ask any frequent flyer for his or her experiences on BA during this period and horror stories will emerge. Even the employees were embarrassed. One employee acknowledged that "I remember going to parties in the late 1970s, and if you wanted to have a civilized conversation, you didn't actually say that you worked for British Airways, because it got you talking about people's last travel experience, which was usually an unpleasant one."[12] When the announcement was made by the British government that the firm was to be privatized, the *Financial Times* newspaper sniffed that it might be that some investors would buy the stock, but only because "every market has a few masochists."

A scant five years later, however, BA's profits were the highest in the industry, 94 percent of its employees bought stock in 1987 when the firm went public, and passengers were making statements like the following: "I can't tell you how my memory of British Airways as a company and the experience I had 10 years ago contrasts with today. The improvement in service is truly remarkable." What accounts for this turnaround? The answer is largely to be found in the cultural revolution engineered by top management, Lord King, and Sir Colin Marshall.

After deciding that they were in the service business rather than the transportation business, British Airways put virtually its entire 37,000 person work force through a two-day culture change program entitled "Putting People First." Almost all of the 1400 managers went through a five-day version entitled "Managing People First" (MPF). On the surface this program is not conceptually unique. What separates MPF from most management training sessions is its magnitude, the consistency with which it was applied, and the support of top management. Colin Marshall, the Chief Executive Officer, has called it the "single most important program now in operation" at BA and has addressed almost all of the 64 MPF classes.[13]

The emphasis on the culture change effort at BA was on instilling the new culture, establishing an evaluation scheme that measured not only what managers did but how they did it, and a compensation program with bonuses up to 20 percent based on how managers behave. Managers at BA appreciate that any airline can load passengers on a plane and fly them across the Atlantic. BA understands that they are in the service business and any competitive advantage has to be in the service they offer customers. As Bob Nelson, head of the program noted, "The issue with customer service is that you can train monkeys to smile and make eye-contact, but what the hell do you do when you get a nonstandard requirement?"[14]

With essentially the same work force, flying largely the same routes, and using the same technology, British Airways has become one of the world's leading airlines. Its competitive advantage is not in strategy or technology but in a culture shared throughout the organization that provides a level of service that competitors have found difficult to imitate. The lesson that we need to explore is how senior managers were successful in managing the culture to provide competitive advantage. What was it that they did that their competitors have been unable to do?

Similar success stories abound. Consider a phenomenon in the retail clothing industry, Nordstrom. While firms like Federated, Macy's, and Carter-Hawley-Hale have wrestled with bankruptcy, Nordstrom has grown from 36 stores and 9,000 employees in 1983 to 76 stores and over 35,000 employees by 1995, with average sales per square foot double the industry average. What accounts for Nordstrom's competitive advantage? A close reading of the strategy literature will quickly suggest that it is not the usual factors such as barriers to entry, power over suppliers and customers, or lack of industry rivalry. The retail industry is quite competitive and buyers and suppliers move easily from one firm to another. It isn't location, merchandise, appearance of the stores, or even the piano in the lobby. Each of these is easily imitable. Rather, as anyone who has shopped Nordstrom knows, it is the remarkable service that Nordstrom provides that differentiates it from its competitors. To deliver this service, Nordstrom relies not on the extensive formal controls manifest in policies, procedures, and close supervision, but rather on its culture, which is characterized by a set of norms and values that provide for a *social* control system. This social control system is used to coordinate activities in the face of the need for change and allows Nordstrom to meet the non-standard requirements that are the true test of service.

Here's the Bad News

Until now we have told happy stories, ones in which managers have successfully used organizational culture to provide competitive advantage. But there are equally unhappy stories to tell as well; ones in which the culture of the firm is sometimes linked to failure. And, as suggested earlier, the paradox is often that it is the culture associated with the earlier success of the firm that becomes a part of its downfall. Think briefly about two icons of American business success and the difficulties they currently face: IBM and Sears. (While we use IBM and Sears, the phenomenon is world-wide.)

Between 1990 and 1993, IBM lost a total of $14 billion, with an $8.1 billion loss in 1993 alone. How could this happen? Certainly the computer business is a complex one. IBM was and is a very large firm, which complicates the decision-making process. Nevertheless, numerous presumably smart people were employed specifically to anticipate changes and ensure that the firm was prepared to meet them. How, then, can we account for this failure, a failure that has cost almost 200,000 people their jobs and shareholders a loss of billions of dollars? It would be wrong to underestimate the complex difficulties in managing a firm of IBM's size. Certainly the answer must include aspects of strategy, organizational design, technology, and people.

However, perhaps the most important part of the answer to this question, and certainly a part of any solution, is in the culture of IBM; a culture characterized by an inward focus, extensive procedures for resolving issues through consensus and "push back," an arrogance bred by previous success, and a sense of entitlement that guaranteed jobs without a reciprocal *quid pro quo* by some employees. This culture—masquerading under the old IBM basic beliefs in excellence, customer satisfaction, and respect for the individual—was manifest in norms that led to a preoccupation with internal procedures rather than understanding the reality of the changing market. In his letter to the shareholders in the 1993 Annual Report, CEO Lou Gerstner states, "We have been too bureaucratic and too preoccupied with our own view of the world." He sees as one of his toughest and most critical tasks to change this entrenched and patriarchical culture into one characterized by a sense of urgency. Without this shift, he believes

IBM will continue to squander its talent and technology.

While occurring in a very different industrial context, a similar drama is playing out at Sears, the great American retailer. Again, the picture is a complicated one and it would be wrong to oversimplify it. The broad outlines of the problem are, however, easily visible. Until 1991, Sears was the largest retailer in the U.S. with over 800 stores and 500,000 employees, including over 6,000 at headquarters in the Sears Tower in Chicago. For decades it was the family department store for America, a place where one could buy everything from clothes to tools to kitchen appliances. However, by the mid-1980s, trouble had begun to surface. Market share had fallen 15 percent from its high in the 70s, the stock price had dropped by 40 percent since Edward Brennan had become CEO in 1985, and chronic high costs hindered Sears from matching the prices of competitors such as Wal-Mart, Kmart, Circuit City, the Home Depot, and other low-cost specialty stores.[15]

Under Brennan's leadership, Sears made a number of strategic changes in attempts to halt the slide. Yet the execution of the strategy was dismal. Observers and analysts attributed the failure to Brennan's inability to revamp the old Sears culture that, as one respected analyst noted, was a "culture is rooted in a long tradition of dominating the retailing industry . . . But this success bred in Sears executives an arrogance and an internal focus that was almost xenophobic." Another observed that "the main problem with Sears is that its managers and executives are 'Sears-ized'—so indoctrinated in the lore of past glories and so entrenched in an overwhelming bureaucracy that they cannot change easily."[16] The old Sears culture, like the old IBM culture, was a product of their success: proud, inward-looking, and resistant to change.

The lesson is a simple one: organizational culture is a key to both short-term success *and*, unless managed correctly, long-term failure. Culture can provide competitive advantage, but as we have seen, it can also create obstacles to the innovation and change necessary to be successful. In the face of significant changes in technology, regulation, or competition, great managers understand this dynamic and effectively manage *both* the short-term demands for increasing congruence and bolstering today's culture *and* the periodic need to transform their organization and re-create their unit's culture. These organizational transformations involve fundamental shifts in the firm's structure and systems as well as in its culture and competencies. Where change in structure and systems is relatively simple, change in culture is not. The issue of actively managing organization cultures that can handle both incremental and discontinuous change is perhaps the most demanding aspect in the management of strategic innovation and change.

AMBIDEXTROUS ORGANIZATIONS: MASTERING EVOLUTIONARY AND REVOLUTIONARY CHANGE

The dilemma confronting managers and organizations is clear. In the short run, they must constantly increase the fit or alignment of strategy, structure, and culture. This is the world of evolutionary change. But this is not enough for sustained success. In the long run, managers may be required to destroy the very alignment that has made their organizations successful. For managers, this means operating part of the time in a world characterized by periods of relatively stability and incremental innovation, and part of the time in a world characterized by revolutionary change. These contrasting managerial demands require that managers periodically destroy what has been created in order to reconstruct a new organization better suited for the next wave of competition or technology.[17]

Ambidextrous organizations are needed if the success paradox is to be overcome. The ability to simultaneously pursue both incremental and discontinuous innovation and change results from hosting multiple contradictory structures, processes, and cultures within the same firm. There are good examples of companies and managers who have succeeded in balancing these tensions. To illustrate more concretely how firms can do this, consider three successful ambidextrous organizations, Hewlett-Packard, Johnson & Johnson, and ABB (Asea Brown Boveri). Each of these has been able to compete in mature market segments through incremental innovation and in emerging markets and technologies through discontinuous innovation. Each has been successful at winning by engaging in both evolutionary and revolutionary change.

At one level they are very different companies. HP competes in markets like instruments, computers, and networks. J&J is in consumer products, pharmaceuticals, and professional medical products ranging from sutures to endoscopic surgical equipment. ABB sells power plants, electrical transmission equipment, transportation systems, and environmental controls. Yet each of them has been able to be periodically renew itself and to produce streams of innovation. HP has gone from an instrument company to a minicomputer firm to a personal computer and network company. J&J has moved from consumer products to pharmaceuticals. ABB transformed itself from a slow heavy engineering company based primarily in Sweden and Switzerland to an aggressive global competitor with major investments in Eastern Europe and the Far East. In spite of their differences, each has been ambidextrous in similar ways.

Organizational Architectures

Although the combined size of these three companies represents over 350,000 employees, each has found a common way to remain small by emphasizing autonomous groups. For instance, J&J has over 165 separate operating companies that scramble relentlessly for new products and markets. ABB relies on over 5,000 profit centers with an average of 50 people in each. These centers operate like small businesses. HP has over 50 separate divisions and a policy of splitting divisions whenever a unit gets larger than a thousand or so people. The logic in these

organizations is to keep units small and autonomous so that employees feel a sense of ownership and are responsible for their own results. This encourages a culture of autonomy and risk taking that could not exist in a large, centralized organization. In the words of Ralph Larsen, CEO of J&J, this approach "provides a sense of ownership and responsibility for a business you simply cannot get any other way."[18]

But the reliance on small, autonomous units is not gained at the expense of firm size or speed in execution. These companies also retain the benefits of size, especially in marketing and manufacturing. ABB continually reevaluates where it locates its worldwide manufacturing sites. J&J uses its brand name and marketing might to leverage new products and technologies. HP uses its relationships with retailers developed from its printer business to market and distribute its new personal computer line. But these firms accomplish this without the top-heavy staffs found at other firms. Barnevik reduced ABB's hierarchy to four levels and a headquarters staff of 150 and purposely keeps the structure fluid. At J&J headquarters, there are roughly a thousand people, but no strategic planning is done by corporate. The role of the center is to set the vision and review the performance of the 165 operating companies. At HP, the former CEO, John Young, recognized in the early 1990s that the more centralized structure that HP had adopted in the 1980s to coordinate their minicomputer business had resulted in a suffocating bureaucracy that was no longer appropriate. He wiped it out, flattening the hierarchy and dramatically reducing the role of the center.

In these companies, size is used to leverage economies of scale and scope, not to become a checker and controller that slows the organization down. The focus is on keeping decisions as close to the customer or the technology as possible. The role of headquarters is to facilitate operations and make them go faster and better. Staff have only the expertise that the field wants and needs. Reward systems are designed to be appropriate to the nature of the business unit and emphasize results and risk taking. Barnevik characterizes this as his 7-3 formula: better to make decisions quickly and be right seven out of ten times than waste time trying to find a perfect solution. At J&J this is expressed as a tolerance for certain types of failure: a tolerance that extends to congratulating managers who take informed risks, even if they fail. There is a delicate balance among size, autonomy, teamwork, and speed which these ambidextrous organizations are able to engineer. An important part of the solution is massive decentralization of decision making, but with consistency attained through individual accountability, information sharing, and strong financial control. But why doesn't this result in fragmentation and a loss of synergy? The answer is found in the use of social control.

Multiple Cultures

A second commonality across these firms is their reliance on strong social controls.[19] They are simultaneously tight and loose. They are tight in that the corporate culture in each is broadly shared and emphasizes norms critical for innovation such as openness, autonomy, initiative, and risk taking. The culture is loose in that the manner in which these common values are expressed varies according to the type of innovation required. At HP, managers value the openness and consensus needed to develop new technologies. Yet, when implementation is critical, managers recognize that this consensus can be fatal. One senior manager in charge of bringing out a new work station prominently posted a sign saying, "This is not a democracy." At J&J, the emphasis on autonomy allows managers to routinely go against the wishes of senior management, sometimes with big successes and sometimes with failures. Yet, in the changing hospital supply sector of their business, managers recognized that the cherished J&J autonomy was stopping these companies from coordinating the service demanded by their hospital customers. So, in this part of J&J, a decision was made to take away some

of the autonomy and centralize services. CEO Larsen refers to this as J&J companies having common standards but unique personalities.

A common overall culture is the glue that holds these companies together. The key in these firms is a reliance on a strong, widely shared corporate culture to promote integration across the company and to encourage identification and sharing of information and resources—something that would never occur without shared values. The culture also provides consistency and promotes trust and predictability. Whether it is the Credo at J&J, the HP Way, or ABB's Policy Bible, these norms and values provide the glue that keeps these organizations together. Yet, at the same time, individual units entertain widely varying subcultures appropriate to their particular businesses. For example, although the HP Way is visible in all HP units worldwide, there are distinct differences between the new video server unit and an old line instrument division. What constitutes risk taking at a mature division is different than the risk taking emphasized at a unit struggling with a brand new technology. At J&J, the Credo's emphasis on customers and employees can be seen as easily in the Philippines as in corporate headquarters in New Brunswick, New Jersey. But the operating culture in the Tylenol division is distinctly more conservative than the culture in a new medical products company.

This tight–loose aspect of the culture is crucial for ambidextrous organizations. It is supported by a common vision and by supportive leaders who both encourage the culture and know enough to allow appropriate variations to occur across business units. These companies promote both local autonomy and risk taking and ensure local responsibility and accountability through strong, consistent financial control systems. Managers aren't second-guessed by headquarters. Strategy flows from the bottom up. Thus, at HP the $7 billion printer business emerged not because of strategic foresight and planning at HP's headquarters, but rather due to the entrepreneurial flair of a small group of managers who had the freedom to pursue what was believed to be a small market. The same approach allows J&J and ABB to enter small niche markets or develop unproven technologies without the burdens of a centralized bureaucratic control system. On the other hand, in return for the autonomy they are granted, there are strong expectations of performance. Managers who don't deliver are replaced.

Ambidextrous Managers

Managing units that pursue widely different strategies and that have varied structures and cultures is a juggling act not all managers are comfortable with. At ABB, this role is described as "preaching and persuading." At HP, managers are low-key, modest, team players who have learned how to manage this tension over their long tenures with the company. At HP, they also lead by persuasion. "As CEO my job is to encourage people to work together, to experiment, to try things, but I can't order them to do it," says Lew Platt.[20] Larsen at J&J echoes this theme, emphasizing the need for lower level managers to come up with solutions and encouraging reasonable failures. Larsen claims that the role is one of a symphony conductor rather than a general.

One of the explanations for this special ability is the relatively long tenure managers have in these organizations and the continual reinforcement of the social control system. Often, these leaders are low-keyed but embody the culture and act as visible symbols of it. As a group the senior team continually reinforces the core values of autonomy, teamwork, initiative, accountability, and innovation. They ensure that the organization avoids becoming arrogant and remains willing to learn from its competitors. Observers of all three of these companies have commented on their modesty or humility in constantly striving to renew themselves. Rather than becoming complacent, these organizations are guided by leaders who venerate the past but are willing to change continuously to meet the future.

The bottom-line is that ambidextrous organizations learn by the same mechanism that sometimes kills successful firms: variation, selection, and retention. They promote variation through strong efforts to decentralize, to eliminate bureaucracy, to encourage individual autonomy and accountability, and to experiment and take risks. This promotes wide variations in products, technologies, and markets. It is what allows the managers of an old HP instrument division to push their technology and establish a new division dedicated to video servers. These firms also select "winners" in markets and technologies by staying close to their customers, by being quick to respond to market signals, and by having clear mechanisms to "kill" products and projects. This selection process allowed the development of computer printers at HP to move from a venture that was begun without formal approval to the point where it now accounts for almost 40% of HP's profits. Finally, technologies, products, markets, and even senior managers are retained by the market, not by a remote, inwardly focused central staff many hierarchical levels removed from real customers. The corporate vision provides the compass by which senior managers can make decisions about which of the many alternative businesses and technologies to invest in, but the market is the ultimate arbiter of the winners and losers. Just as success or failure in the marketplace is Darwinian, so too is the method by which ambidextrous organizations learn. They have figured out how to harness this power within their companies and organize and manage accordingly.

SUMMARY

Managers must be prepared to cannibalize their own business at times of industry transitions. While this is easy in concept, these organizational transitions are quite difficult in practice. Success brings with it inertia and dynamic conservatism. Four hundred years ago, Niccolo Machiavelli noted, "There is no more delicate matter to take in hand, nor more dangerous to conduct, nor more doubtful in its success, than to be a leader in the introduction of changes. For he who innovates will have for enemies all those who are well off under the old order of things, and only lukewarm supporters in those who might be better off under the new."[21]

While there are clear benefits to proactive change, only a small minority of farsighted firms initiate discontinuous change before a performance decline. Part of this stems from the risks of proactive change. One reason for RCA's failure to compete in the solid-state market or for SSIH's inability to compete in quartz movements came from the divisive internal disputes over the risks of sacrificing a certain revenue stream from vacuum tubes and mechanical watches for the uncertain profits from transistors and quartz watches. However, great managers are willing to take this step. Andy Grove of Intel puts it succinctly, "There is at least one point in the history of any company when you have to change dramatically to rise to the next performance level. Miss the moment and you start to decline."[22]

NOTES

1. A. Cooper and C. Smith, "How Established Firms Respond to Threatening Technologies," *Academy of Management Executive*, 16/2 (1992): 92–120.

2. R. Foster, *Innovation: The Attacker's Advantage* (New York, NY: Summit Books, 1986), p. 134.

3. B. Virany, M. Tushman, and E. Romanelli, "Executive Succession and Organization Outcomes in Turbulent Environments," *Organization Science*, 3 (1992): 72–92; E. Romanelli and M. Tushman, "Organization Transformation as Punctuated Equilibrium," *Academy of Management Journal*, 37 (1994): 1141–1166; M. Tushman and L. Rosenkopf, "On the Organizational Determinants of Technological Change: Towards a Sociology of Technological Evolution," in B. Staw and L. Cummings, eds., *Research in Organization Behavior*, Vol. 14 (Greenwich, CT: JAI Press, 1992); D. Miller, "The Architecture of Simplicity," *Academy of Management Review*, 18 (1993): 116–138; A. Meyer, G. Brooks, and J. Goes, "Environmental Jolts and Industry Revolutions," *Strategic Management Journal*, 6 (1990): 48–76.

4. There is an extensive literature studying organizations using models from population ecology. A number of excellent reviews of this approach are available in M. Hannan and G. Carroll, *Dynamics of Organizational Populations* (New York, NY: Oxford University Press, 1992); G. Carroll and M. Hannan, eds., *Organizations in Industry: Strategy, Structure & Selection* (New York, NY: Oxford University Press, 1995); and J. Baum and J. Singh, eds., *Evolutionary Dynamics of Organizations* (New York, NY: Oxford University Press, 1994).

5. M. Tushman and L. Rosenkopf, "On the Organizational Determinants of Technological Change: Towards a Sociology of Technological Evolution," in B. Staw and L. Cummings, *Research in Organization Behavior*, Vol. 14 (Greenwich, CT: JAI Press, 1992); M. Tushman and P. Anderson, "Technological Discontinuities and Organization Environments," *Administrative Science Quarterly*, 31 (1986): 439–465; W. Abernathy and K. Clark, "Innovation: Maping the Winds of Creative Destruction," *Research Policy*, 1985, pp. 3–22; J. Wade, "Dynamics of Organizational Communities and Technological Bandwagons," *Strategic Management Journal*, 16 (1995): 111–133; J. Baum and H. Korn, "Dominant Designs and Population Dynamics in Telecommunications Services," *Social Science Research*, 24 (1995): 97–135.

6. For a more complete treatment of this subject, see J. Utterback, *Mastering the Dynamics of Innovation* (Boston, MA: Harvard Business School Press, 1994). See also R. Burgelman & A. Grove, "Strategic Dissonance," *California Management Review*, 38/2 (Winter 1996): 8–28.

7. D. Nadler and M. Tushman, *Competing by Design* (New York, NY: Oxford University Press, in press); D. Nadler and M. Tushman, "Beyond Charismatic Leaders: Leadership and Organization

Change," *California Management Review*, (Winter 1990): 77–90.

8. See M. Tushman, W. Newman, and E. Romanelli, "Convergence and Upheaval: Managing the Unsteady Pace of Organizational Evolution," *California Management Review*, 29/1 (Fall 1986): 29–44.

9. L. Hays, "Gerstner Is Struggling as He Tries to Change Ingrained IBM Culture," *Wall Street Journal*, May 13, 1994.

10. J. Kotter & N. Rothbard, "Cultural Change at Nissan Motors," *Harvard Business School Case*, #9-491-079, July 28, 1993.

11. "Today's Leaders Look to Tomorrow," *Fortune*, March 26, 1990, p. 31.

12. J. Leahey, "Changing the Culture at British Airways," *Harvard Business School Case*, #9-491-009, 1990.

13. L. Bruce, "British Airways Jolts Staff with a Cultural Revolution," *International Management*, March 7, 1987, pp. 36–38.

14. Ibid.

15. See, for example, D. Katz, *The Big Store: Inside the Crisis and Revolution at Sears* (New York, NY: Viking, 1987); S. Caminiti, "Sears' Need: More Speed," *Fortune*, July 15, 1991, pp. 88–90.

16. S. Strom, "Further Prescriptions for the Convalescent Sears," *New York Times*, October 10, 1992.

17. D. Hurst, *Crisis and Renewal* (Boston, MA: Harvard Business School Press, 1995); R. Burgelman, "Intraorganizational Ecology of Strategy Making and Organizational Adaptation," *Organizational Science*, 2/3 (1991): 239–262; K. Eisenhardt and B. Tabrizi, "Acceleration Adaptive Processes," *Administrative Science Quarterly*, 40/1 (1995): 84–110; J. Morone, *Winning in High Tech Markets* (Boston, MA: Harvard Business School Press, 1993); M. Iansiti and K. Clark, "Integration and Dynamic Capability," *Industry and Corporation Change*, 3/3 (1994): 557–606; D. Leonard-Barton, *Wellsprings of Knowledge* (Boston, MA: Harvard Business School Press, 1995).

18. J. Weber, "A Big Company that Works," *BusinessWeek*, May 4, 1992, p. 125.

19. See C. O'Reilly, "Corporations, Culture, and Commitment: Motivation and Social Control in Organizations," *California Management Review*, 31/4 (Summer 1989): 9–25; or C. O'Reilly and J. Chatman, "Culture as Social Control: Corporations, Cults, and Commitment," in B. Staw and L. Cummings, eds., *Research in Organizational Behavior*, Vol. 18 (Greenwich, CT: JAI Press, 1996).

20. A. Deutschman, "How H-P Continues to Grow and Grow," *Fortune*, May 2, 1994, p. 100.

21. N. Machiavelli, *The Prince*, translated by L. P. S. de Alvarez (Dallas, TX: University of Dallas Press, 1974).

22. S. Sherman, "Andy Grove: How Intel Makes Spending Pay Off," *Fortune*, February 22, 1993, p. 58.